So Just and Glorious a Cause is a highly detailed narrative of Wellington's first campaign in the Peninsula. Using memoirs, letters, and previously unpublished primary sources, it covers events from Junot's invasion in late 1807 to the Portuguese revolts in the summer of 1808, and then the sailing of the British expedition and the battles of Roliça and Vimeiro, through to the controversial Convention of Cintra and the liberation of Portugal from the French.

In 1807, with most of Europe under his control, Napoleon looked towards the Iberian Peninsula, hoping to complete his hegemony and extend his reach to South America. He sent one of his most loyal generals, Jean-Andoche Junot, with 25,000 men, to conquer Portugal. The Portuguese had long been caught in the middle between Britain and France. Faced with an invasion he had little hope of preventing, the Prince Regent fled to Brazil, assisted by a Royal Navy squadron, and let his country be occupied.

In the summer of 1808, with the rebellion of the Spanish and Portuguese people spreading across the Peninsula, Britain sent an expedition to liberate Portugal under Sir Arthur Wellesley, the future Duke of Wellington. Still a relatively junior and unknown commander, Wellesley fought an aggressive and successful campaign. He defeated the French first at Roliça and then at Vimeiro but was prevented from sealing his victory by the arrival of more senior officers. The French negotiated generous terms in the Convention of Cintra and were evacuated back to France, ending their occupation of Portugal.

So Just and Glorious a Cause makes extensive use of primary sources from all levels of the French, Portuguese and British forces involved, many of them previously unpublished. The terrible forced marches of the French troops as they crossed the border into Portugal, the frenzied diplomatic efforts in Lisbon, the subsequent brutal occupation, and the Royal Navy blockade are all examined, as well as Vice Admiral Cotton's efforts to fan the flames of revolt in Portugal and offer support for the uprisings. The French, Portuguese and British forces are analysed in detail, as are the logistical challenges of Wellesley's campaign. The narratives of the first skirmish at Óbidos and then the battles of Roliça and Vimeiro are constructed from first-hand accounts from both sides, and many misconceptions about each action are addressed. Finally, numerous myths surrounding the controversial Convention of Cintra are tackled, including Wellesley's part in the negotiations.

Robert Griffith is a military historian and an editor at Helion & Co, working on the From Reason to Revolution series. He has previously written *Riflemen: The History of the 5th Battalion, 60th (Royal American) Regiment 1797-1818* and *At the Point of the Bayonet: The Peninsular War Battles of Arroyomolinos and Almaraz*, both published by Helion.

So Just and Glorious a Cause

Britain and the Liberation of Portugal –
Roliça and Vimeiro, 1808

Robert Griffith

Helion & Company

Helion & Company Limited
Unit 8 Amherst Business Centre
Budbrooke Road
Warwick
CV34 5WE
England
Tel. 01926 499619
Email: info@helion.co.uk
Website: www.helion.co.uk
X (formerly Twitter): @Helionbooks
Facebook: @HelionBooks
Visit our blog at http://blog.helion.co.uk/

Published by Helion & Company 2024
Designed and typeset by Mach 3 Solutions (www.mach3solutions.co.uk)
Cover designed by Paul Hewitt, Battlefield Design (www.battlefield-design.co.uk)

ISBN 978-1-804514-39-9

British Library Cataloguing-in-Publication Data.
A catalogue record for this book is available from the British Library.

For details of other military history titles published by Helion & Company Limited, contact the above address, or visit our website: http://www.helion.co.uk

We always welcome receiving book proposals from prospective authors.

Contents

Preface

It would be hyperbole to call Wellesley's campaign in Portugal in 1808 a turning point in Britain's two-decade-long war against France, but it was a significant waypoint on the long journey to Waterloo. The campaign was the future Duke of Wellington's first independent command in Europe and the start of Britain's almost six-year-long involvement in the Peninsular War. Napoleon's hubris led him to think that Spain and Portugal would fall under his yoke as easily as many of the Italian and German states, but the tenacity of the Iberian people and the constant drain on the Empire's resources that resulted from their long and bitter fight for independence would be a factor in the Emperor's eventual downfall. However, none of the participants in the events of 1807 and 1808 could guess what the future held. But Castlereagh and Canning, the two ministers driving British foreign policy, were quick to grasp the opportunity that Napoleon's ill-judged intervention in the Iberian Peninsula presented, and to see its potential for altering the balance of events on the continent.

Britain's war against France had, to some extent, reached a stalemate. Britannia, in the form of the Royal Navy, ruled the waves, and Marianne, in the form of the Grande Armée, dominated Europe. France could not invade Britain, and the British Army could not tip the balance on the continent. But when representatives of both Portugal and Spain appealed for aid in fighting the occupations of their countries, the British government quickly responded by sending not only money, which was the weapon they typically wielded with allies on the continent, but also troops. The campaign of 1808 was a chance for the British Army to shrug off the South American disasters of 1806 and 1807 and win victories more honourable than those they had achieved against the Danes. The British Army had undergone more than a decade of reform since its last major foray into mainland Europe, and the campaign would show that many of those reforms had resulted in a more capable force but also that there was more work to be done. The British government and press lauded the victories of Roliça and Vimeiro, but Wellesley's troops were fighting a numerically and, in many ways, qualitatively inferior foe. The following campaign against the full might of France ended in an ignominious retreat at Corunna in early 1809. That same year, many of the same troops were involved in the disastrous Walcheren expedition. Both these setbacks illustrate that Britain's war machine was still not the finely honed tool it would become by the end of the Peninsular War. Wellesley and the troops who landed in Portugal still had much to learn: the problems they had to contend with, and their mistakes, illustrate the weaknesses of the British Army's organisation, equipment and training at the time.

Of course, this book is not the first to be written on the Vimeiro campaign. It is covered in the multi-volume histories of the Peninsular War written in the nineteenth and early twentieth centuries. Napier's, Oman's, and Fortescue's writing still colours our perceptions of the campaign, and their many unfounded opinions and biases, and some mistakes, are often repeated by subsequent historians. I have been led astray myself. In my first work of military history, *Riflemen*, I relied heavily on Oman and Fortescue, but now, after delving more deeply into the primary sources, I realise I unknowingly perpetuated a significant error in their narratives of Vimeiro. Doubtless, subsequent historians will uncover new sources and challenge my interpretations, but that is as it should be.

Michael Glover's 1970 *Britannia Sickens* is a more recent study of the campaign, but it concentrates on the strategy and politics of the campaign and only really covers the British point of view. René Chatrand's *Vimeiro 1808* is very good but limited by the brevity of its format. David Buttery's *Wellington Against Junot* provides much better coverage of the other nations involved but does not provide the depth of detail and primary sources that have become more accessible since it was written. Also worthy of attention is Robert Southey's often-overlooked *History of the Peninsular War*, one of the first works on the subject: the early volumes provide good coverage of the Portuguese side of the conflict. Martin Robson's *Britain, Portugal and South America in the Napoleonic Wars* provides an excellent study of Anglo-Portuguese relations in the period and the background to the campaign. For a French perspective, I recommend Natalia Griffon de Pleineville's *La Première Invasion du Portugal par l'Armée Napoléonienne (1807-1808)*.

What I hope to have contributed to the historiography of the campaign is a greater level of detail on the British response and the subsequent campaign. This detail has been made possible by the plethora of sources now available online, translation software enabling me to access French, Portuguese, and German texts, as well as many hours in the archives. I have also tried not to present the campaign as Wellesley versus Junot but include a broader cast of characters, such as Lord Strangford, admirals Smith and Cotton, brigade commanders like Robert Anstruther, regimental officers, and the rank and file. I am not claiming to have come up with a radical new analysis of the campaign, but, by delving deeper into the details, I have discovered devils that shed some new light on the subject.

Acknowledgements

This book would not have been written without the support and encouragement of my editor, colleague and friend, Dr Andrew Bamford. He suggested the topic to me, pointing out that Wellesley's first campaign needed an in-depth modern study, and has been generous with his time and advice through the several years it has taken me to write the book now in your hands. As commissioning and series editor for Helion's *From Reason to Revolution* series for eight years, Andrew has made an enormous contribution to the military history of the long eighteenth century through his support for his authors like me and his ability to see which holes in the historiography needed filling.

I also want to thank Rory Muir for his encouragement and advice. His interest in the project has spurred me to dig deeper and look further. Similarly, I am very grateful to Alexander Mikaberidze and Charles Esdaile for their interest and support. I would also like to thank the excellent online community of Napoleonic historians for sharing sources, helping to decipher difficult handwriting, and pointing me in new directions. Thank you, Gareth Glover, Mark Thompson, Charles Mackay, Moisés Gaudêncio, Garry Wills, Tom Holmberg, Steve Brown, Robert Pocock, Ian Soulsby, Antonio Grajal de Blas, Rory Butcher, Eamonn O'Keeffe, Jacqueline Reiter and Nichols Blake. I would also like to thank the staff of all the archives and museums I have visited. Without you, history would remain unwritten. Extracts from Brigadier General Robert Anstruther's journal are published courtesy of the University of St Andrews Libraries and Museums, with the permission of Toby Anstruther.

A quick note on sources: unless otherwise cited, the biographies and career information for the many British Army officers mentioned in the text has been drawn from the *Printed Annual Army Lists* (held at The National Archives and available for download), *The Royal Military Calendar*, and Challis's *Peninsula Roll Call*. Details of these can be found in the bibliography. If any reader wants to delve deeper into any of the sources cited, then almost all of the books in the bibliography published before 1900 or so can be found online, for free, at Google Books, Archive.org, Hathitrust.org, or sites such as the French or Portuguese national libraries.

Lastly, an apology. In my previous two books, *Riflemen* and *At the Point of the Bayonet*, I managed to name not only the officer casualties mentioned in official dispatches but also the names of almost all the British other ranks killed in action. Unfortunately, the number of casualties in the Vimeiro campaign meant I could not allocate the research hours or the space in the book to record every name this time. Hopefully, the stories in these pages will be sufficient to honour not only their sacrifices but also those of the French and Portuguese.

1

Crisis

France had declared war on Britain in 1793, and, barring the 14-month-long Peace of Amiens, the conflict had now dragged on for 14 years. Many in Britain were becoming weary of war. The Ministry of All the Talents had attempted to make peace, but negotiations had failed.[1] A series of coalitions had been defeated, first by the armies of Revolutionary France and then by Napoleon and his empire. The Fourth Coalition was not faring well. The Prussian army had been beaten at Jena–Auerstedt in October 1806. The Russian army had been defeated at Eylau in February 1807 and would be again at Friedland in June. By July, Tsar Alexander and Napoleon would sign a treaty of alliance at Tilsit.

The Duke of Portland had formed a new government in March 1807. He was far from the ideal wartime prime minister. Historian Rory Muir describes him as 'ill, lethargic and incapable of acting decisively or giving the real leadership his young ministers needed.'[2] It was the team of younger ministers that would drive the strategy for the war. The two key players would be the Foreign Secretary, George Canning, and the Secretary of State for War and the Colonies, Robert Stewart, Viscount Castlereagh.

The Royal Navy had prevailed against the combined French and Spanish fleets at Trafalgar in October 1805, but the threat from the French navy was still present. Blockading the French coast, protecting trade routes, and securing widely dispersed colonies required considerable numbers of ships, men and cash. The Royal Navy's 107 ships of the line far outnumbered the 43 of the French, but only a portion could be kept on blockade duty in the Channel, and the rest were spread from India to the West Indies. Once the ships of France's allies, or potential allies, were factored in, the numbers could theoretically just tip in Napoleon's favour with a total of 109.[3] For the British, preventing Napoleon from adding to his naval forces by alliance or conquest remained a key objective.

While the French had no hope of defeating Britain at sea without help, Britain's army was too small to make an appreciable contribution to the war on mainland Europe. The regular army had grown fourfold from the start of the war, from 40,000 in 1793 to 166,000 in 1806, with another

---

1   R. Muir, *Britain and the Defeat of Napoleon 1807-1815* (New Haven: Yale, 1996), p.9.
2   Muir, *Britain*, p.5.
3   C.W. Vane (ed.), *Correspondence, Despatches, and other Papers of Viscount Castlereagh* (London: Shoberl, 1851), vol.VIII, pp.107–109. Memorandum respecting the State of the Naval and Military Forces of Great Britain, with reference to Operations defensive and offensive, December 1807.

75,000 militia.[4] However, with troops committed to colonial garrisons and home defence, only a small portion of the army was available for offensive operations.[5]

Historian John Elting called the British Army's campaigns prior to the Peninsular War 'a series of disasters, hasty scuttles, and pratfalls.'[6] Whilst perhaps not entirely fair, that assessment is not too far off the mark. The initial campaign in the Low Countries had been a failure, but primarily not one of the British Army's making. Further forays to the Netherlands, Italy, and Germany had achieved very little. Victories such as the Battle of Maida in 1806 were some solace, and the successful campaign to remove the French from Egypt in 1801 had been a high point. However, the return to Alexandria in 1807 was another disaster, and more bad news would soon come from South America.

The problem was not with the quality of the British troops, or even the generals, but rather a combination of identifying opportunities that were either geographically insulated from the bulk of French forces or that involved fighting alongside a reliable and numerically stronger ally, plus the limitations of having a small number of available troops and then having to transport them by sea. These factors often led to questionable choices for the destination of the few men that Britain could spare, but there was often political and diplomatic pressure to do something rather than nothing. However, Britain's main contribution to the land war was the subsidies paid to its allies.

Economic Warfare

With France and Britain unable to defeat each other on land or sea, the economic theatre became an important battleground. Each had the aim of denying the other the means to fight. From the start of the war, the profits from sugar, cocoa, coffee, cotton and rum, boosted as they were by slavery, meant that capturing the French colonies in the Caribbean was part of British strategy. As Henry Dundas, Secretary of State for War, said in 1799, 'our principal effort should be to deprive our enemies of their Colonial possessions. By doing so we weaken their power while at the same time we augment those commercial resources which are the bases of our maritime strength.'[7] This was mostly achieved by 1807, denying France raw materials and revenue.

With Prussia's defeat, Germany's trading centres entered Napoleon's sphere of influence. In Berlin, in November 1806, he issued a decree that forbade any trade with Britain by countries under his control. The decree was also sent to allies such as Spain, Naples and Holland. Napoleon aimed to strike at the British financial system's bedrock, severely limiting its ability to subsidise continental allies and fund its armed forces. What became known as the Continental System was an intensification of the trade policies that all powers undertook at the time. Trade was seen as a zero-sum game; for one country to benefit, another had to suffer. Blockades, embargoes, and tariffs were common.[8]

---

4   The National Archives (TNA): WO 1/903: Return of the Effective Men in the British Army 1793–1806.
5   Muir, *Britain*, p.15.
6   J.R. Elting, *Swords Around a Throne: Napoleon's Grande Armée* (London: Weidenfield & Nicolson, 1989), p.507.
7   H. Dundas to R. Wellesley 31 October 1799, in A. Mikaberidze, *The Napoleonic Wars, A Global History* (Oxford: Oxford University Press, 2020), p.xiv.
8   Mikaberidze, *Napoleonic Wars*, pp.228–229.

However, the Continental System was never fully implemented. Smuggling, already an important industry for most coastal nations, became rife, and many French allies and client states were reluctant to impose the restrictions. Even Napoleon bent his own rules when it suited the needs of France. For the system to work, any gaps needed to be plugged, so putting diplomatic and, if needed, military pressure on the few neutral states that remained until they conformed became a crucial part of French foreign policy. Napoleon also began to see any reluctance to implement the system as an affront to his hegemony over the continent and as an excuse to force those few countries still struggling to maintain neutrality to pick a side. His side.

Despite the patchiness of its implementation, the Continental System did impact British trade. The rising costs of raw materials and reduced export markets caused an economic slump, making it all the more imperative that Britain find markets elsewhere.[9] From late 1807, Britain retaliated with Orders in Council, which forced all neutral vessels to acquire a licence to trade with French-controlled ports from the Elbe to Brest. This led Napoleon to tighten the Continental System further and issue two new decrees from Milan that extended the controls.[10]

South America

In 1803, Spain and France signed a treaty which allowed Spain to remain neutral in return for payments to France.[11] The wealth of Spain's South American empire would be used to bolster France's coffers. The raw materials, gold and silver, and markets of South America had long been of interest to Britain, and some illicit trade was already taking place. However, there was little desire in Britain for new colonies.[12] The American War of Independence had demonstrated the problems they could cause. British policy on South America was tinged with caution lest a revolution in the colonies took undesirable turns, but also with the fear that, if nothing were done, the region would fall under French control.[13] In September 1806, Napoleon made tentative plans to invade Portugal while sending an expedition to Brazil to secure Portugal's main colony.[14]

At the same time, in Britain, a proposal was made to take key strategic points on the South American continent and hope that the rest gradually came into the British sphere. If the colonists did rebel against Spain, then Britain could support them.[15] Two days later, dispatches reached London from Commodore Sir Home Riggs Popham and Major General William Carr Beresford, informing the government that Buenos Aires had been captured.[16] No such expedition had been officially authorised. Popham and Beresford had been part of the force sent to capture the Dutch colony at the Cape of Good Hope. Once this had been achieved, Popham persuaded the force commander to let him take some troops across the Atlantic to capture Buenos Aires.

9   M. Robson, *Britain, Portugal and South America in the Napoleonic Wars* (London: Tauris, 2011), p.14.
10   Mikaberidze, *Napoleonic Wars,* p.231.
11   Mikaberidze, *Napoleonic Wars*, p.182.
12   Robson, *South America*, p.81.
13   Vane (ed.), *Correspondence*, vol.VII, pp.285, 288.
14   Robson, *South America*, p.87.
15   M. Robson, 'Sir Arthur Wellesley as a "special advisor": politics and strategic planning 1806-8', in C. Woolgar (ed.), *Wellington Studies V* (Southampton: University of Southampton, 2013), p.40.
16   *The Gazette*, 13 September 1806.

Popham's jaunt may not have been authorised, but literal wagonloads of captured silver parading through the streets of London made the benefits of trade with South America obvious.[17] British merchants had long sought access to South American markets and now lobbied the government for further action. Reinforcements were sent under Lieutenant General John Whitelocke, but, by the time they arrived, the Spanish colonists had already defeated the original force. Whitelocke was defeated at Buenos Aires and then surrendered, returning home to disgrace and a court martial.[18]

The situation in Europe offered few opportunities for intervention, so, despite the disasters, various schemes in South America continued to be considered. A key unofficial advisor to Castlereagh for the various expeditions contemplated was fellow Irishman and friend, Major General Sir Arthur Wellesley. Wellesley had made a name for himself in India and, as an MP and as Chief Secretary for Ireland, he was a member of the government. Wellesley produced detailed plans for the various schemes, including operations against what are now Mexico and Venezuela.[19] The then Prime Minister, Lord Grenville, wrote of Wellesley in 1806: 'I have so very high an opinion of his talents and military knowledge, and particularly of his powers of exciting spirit and confidence in his troops … that I am very desirous of his being employed there if the scale of our operations be large enough for him.'[20]

In early 1808, South American revolutionary Francisco de Miranda persuaded the government to support fresh attempts by the colonists to gain independence. Wellesley met with Miranda and amended his earlier plans for the attack on Mexico. The government approved the plan, which was further amended to include an attack on Caracas.[21] However, Wellesley doubted the wisdom and practicality of the venture.[22] Nevertheless, preparations continued.

Copenhagen

The signing of the treaties at Tilsit broke up the Fourth Coalition and fundamentally changed the situation in Europe. Britain had simply run out of significant allies. Article five of the treaty between France and Russia stated that the two powers would demand 'Copenhagen, Stockholm and Lisbon to close their ports to the British, force them to recall their ambassadors and to declare war on Britain.'[23] The aim was for the continental blockade to stretch from the Baltic to the Mediterranean.

As well as quickly learning of the treaties, British agents soon began to report rumours of neutral Denmark being pressured to close its ports to British trade. A series of mistaken, misleading, and misinterpreted reports led the British government to suspect that the French might invade or force the Danes to hand their still-significant fleet over to them.[24] The Baltic was an essential source

---

17   *Morning Herald*, 22 September 1806.
18   Muir, *Britain*, p.7
19   R. Muir, *Wellington: The Path to Victory 1769-1814* (New Haven: Yale, 2015), pp.185–187.
20   Robson, 'Wellesley as special advisor', p.45.
21   Muir, *Wellington*, p.230.
22   2nd Duke of Wellington (ed.), *Supplementary Despatches, Correspondence and Memoranda of Field Marshal Arthur Duke of Wellington* (London: Murray, 1860), vol.VI, p.62.
23   P. Hicks, 'Napoleon, Tilsit, Copenhagen, and Portugal', *Napoleonica, La Revue,* <https://www.cairn.info/revue-napoleonica-la-revue-2008-2-page-87.htm#no25>, accessed 31 March 2022.
24   Mikaberidze, *Napoleonic Wars*, p.338.

of naval stores for Britain, and the Danish fleet could quickly deny access. The Danes wanted to remain neutral, but they faced increasing pressure from the French and British.[25]

In July, the British resolved to send a sizeable force to seize the fleet before it fell into Napoleon's hands. The danger of France getting its hands on the ships was not all imaginary. Later that month, Napoleon ordered his Foreign Minister Talleyrand to tell the Danish Crown Prince, 'he should choose either to make war on England, or to make it on me'.[26]

As historian John Fortescue puts it: 'It was Denmark's misfortune to lie between hammer and anvil.'[27] Britain had already hammered the Danes once for similar reasons in 1801. On that occasion, the Royal Navy had attacked the Danish fleet, but, since then, Copenhagen's defences had been improved so that could not be repeated. The British fleet arrived in early August, and the city was besieged after a series of small actions. The Danish commander was summoned to surrender, with the British promising to leave once the fleet was secured and that it would be returned at the war's end. The offer was refused. British batteries opened fire and began to set large parts of the city ablaze. The Danes were forced to capitulate and the fleet was handed over.[28] The brief campaign did not garner any honour for Britain and was widely condemned, with even King George calling it 'a very immoral act.'[29] For other countries that found themselves between hammer and anvil, Copenhagen would be a powerful example of the consequences of choosing one side or the other, or perhaps of not picking a side quickly enough.

Portugal

With his northern flank secure, Napoleon cast his eyes southward. He had long seen Spain for what it was, a reluctant ally, and something needed to be done about that, but it was Portugal that he turned his attention to first. On 19 July, the day after the British decided to act against Denmark, he wrote to Talleyrand from Dresden:

> … you will inform the Minister of Portugal that the ports of Portugal must be closed to England by the 1st of September; failing this, I will declare war on Portugal … the ministers of Spain and France will withdraw from Lisbon, and the two powers will declare war on Portugal; an army of 20,000 Frenchmen will go to Bayonne on the 1st of September, to join the Spanish army and conquer Portugal.[30]

Ten days later, Napoleon issued orders for the army to assemble at Bayonne, near the Spanish border, and requested officers be found who were familiar with Portugal.[31]

In 1386, England and Portugal had agreed an alliance at Windsor. The relationship had started as that of two equal powers and had helped Portugal remain independent as the four kingdoms

25   G. Glover, *The Two Battles of Copenhagen 1801 and 1807* (Barnsley: Pen & Sword, 2018), pp.102–106.
26   H. Plon, & J. Dumaine (eds), *Correspondance de Napoléon 1er* (Paris: Imprimeur de l'Empereur, 1865), vol.15, 12962, p.459.
27   J.W. Fortescue, *A History of the British Army* (London: Macmillan & Co, 1906), vol.VI, p.62.
28   Fortescue, *British Army*, vol.VI, pp.63–73.
29   George III to Canning, 26 August 1807, quoted in Glover, *Two Battles*, p.167.
30   Plon & Dumaine (eds), *Correspondance*, vol.15, 12928, p.433.
31   Plon & Dumaine (eds), *Correspondance*, vol.15, 12947, pp.448–449.

of Spain united. However, as Britain pros-
pered, Portugal declined, and the alliance
became more one-sided. British wool had
been traded for Portuguese wine since
the Middle Ages, and there were sizeable
British mercantile communities in both
Oporto and Lisbon. Much of the wealth of
Brazil and other colonies flowed onwards
to London.[32] Within the Portuguese court,
many saw rapprochement with France
as a way of tempering Britain's commercial dominance over Portugal. Others
supported maintaining close ties with
Britain to help retain the Portuguese colonial empire, which could quickly become a
target in any conflict.

Prince João. (Anne S.K. Brown Military Collection)

With Queen Maria suffering severe clin-
ical depression after the deaths of both her
husband and eldest son, her second son,
Prince João, ruled as regent. His advisors
or his wife, Carlota Joaquina, daughter of
Carlos IV, the King of Spain, easily influenced him. Portugal had been in decline
for many years; revenues from Brazilian
gold were falling, much of the capital had
to be rebuilt after the devastating earthquake of 1755, and many institutions, including the army,
resisted desperately needed reforms.[33] But Portugal still had a sizeable fleet, and Britain feared
these warships falling into the hands of the French. As well as its fleet, two other factors made the
subjugation of Portugal attractive to Napoleon. Firstly, Lisbon's harbour was large and well-placed
for interdicting Atlantic trade and launching expeditions to South America. Secondly, diverting
some of the Spanish army into Portugal would weaken Spain. Napoleon had already arranged for a
substantial force of Spanish troops to be placed in northern Europe to achieve the same end.

Portugal had faced almost constant threats from Spain and France since the 1790s. Initially,
Portugal fought alongside Spain against France in the War of the Pyrenees. Defeated, Spain
became an ally of France. Portugal was left isolated, with the country's finances put under strain
by the costs of the war.[34] Britain sent a force of 5,000 men to help secure Portugal from either its
neighbour or France. The troops were mostly foreign infantry, with some British regiments and
cavalry. They arrived in 1797 and, though slowly reduced in number, stayed until August 1802.[35]

32   C. Willis, 'Wellington and Portuguese reservations about the Old Alliance', in C. Woolgar (ed.), *Wellington
     Studies II* (Southampton: University of Southampton, 1999), pp.124–125.
33   H. Livermore, 'Portugal on the Eve of the Peninsular War' in P. Griffith (ed.), *Modern Studies of the War in
     Spain and Portugal, 1808-1814* (London: Greenhill, 1999), p.386.
34   Livermore, 'Portugal', p.386.
35   Fortescue, *British Army*, vol.IV, pt.II, pp.601–605, 806.

The very brief War of the Oranges in 1801 saw Spain and France invade Portugal and capture some territory, including the town of Olivença. British troops moved towards the border but did not get involved in the fighting. In the Treaty of Badajoz, Portugal agreed to close its ports to British shipping, but peace between Britain and France in 1802 saw trade return to normal. In 1803, after the resumption of war, Britain sent Lieutenant Colonel James Stewart to judge the state of the Portuguese army and the nation's defence. His report was damming; regiments were understrength, the men were either too old or too young, and the magazines were insufficient. Stewart concluded that Portugal could not be defended. Britain became reluctant to help if Portugal would not help itself. Jean Lannes, the future *maréchal*, was briefly the French ambassador in Lisbon and aggressively demanded Portugal side with France. João dismissed some ministers who supported close ties with Britain and declared neutrality. In 1804, Napoleon again demanded that Portugal close its ports to Britain and began to make plans for an invasion. He sent his aide de camp, Jean-Andoche Junot, as the new ambassador to try and persuade rather than bully João to acquiesce. However, Trafalgar dissuaded Spain from further entanglements, and Napoleon had more pressing problems with the Austrians and Russians. In 1806, invasion was again threatened, but, again, it came to nought. The problem for France was that it relied on Brazilian cotton and other commodities. If Portugal closed its ports or were invaded, then a Royal Navy blockade would have consequences for the French economy. Britain did send a fleet and troops to help dissuade any French action, but they were not allowed to land by the Portuguese. Within the court and the government, some elements thought Portugal's best hope was to accept French hegemony while others wanted to remain neutral and continue to trade with Britain. Policy and debate swung between the two camps.[36]

After receiving Napoleon's letter from Dresden, Talleyrand summoned the Portuguese ambassador and relayed an ultimatum – Portugal's ports must be closed to Britain, British goods and citizens seized, diplomatic ties with London severed, and the Portuguese fleet put at France's disposal.[37]

João had no option but to accede to some of the demands. He agreed to close the ports but told Talleyrand that his honour would not allow him to seize British property or imprison its subjects. It was not enough, partly because the Portuguese fleet was squarely in Napoleon's sights.[38] Along with French and Spanish ships blockaded in Cadiz and other ports since Trafalgar, the Portuguese vessels would give Napoleon a powerful force poised to cross the Atlantic or sail northwards to the Channel.

On 8 September, Napoleon wrote first to Carlos IV and then to Prince João. He asked the Spanish monarch for his support and ended his note with, 'it is necessary, above all, to wrest Portugal from the influence of England and to force the latter power to desire and ask for peace.'[39] His letter to João was both an appeal and a veiled threat:

> Your Royal Highness is led by events to choose between the continent and the [British].
> Let him attach himself closely to the general interest, and I guarantee in his person, in his
> family, the preservation of his power. But if, against my hopes, Your Royal Highness were

---

36   Livermore, 'Portugal', pp.390–394; Mikaberidze, *Napoleonic Wars*, pp.245–246.
37   Livermore, 'Portugal', p.394.
38   Mikaberidze, *Napoleonic Wars*, p.246.
39   Plon & Dumaine (eds), *Correspondance*, vol.16, 13131, p.18.

to put his trust in my enemies, I would only regret a decision which would detach him from me and which would postpone the decision of his important interests to the chances of events.[40]

Napoleon pointed out that every other nation had fallen in line with the Continental System and that full compliance was Portugal's only option.

News of the threats to Portugal began to reach London in early August 1807, during the early stages of the Copenhagen operation. Dispatches arrived at the Foreign Office from the British minister in Lisbon, Lord Strangford. His opinion was that Spain would be easily convinced to support any French action in Portugal and that João would have to comply with at least some of Napoleon's demands. Strangford was lobbying the Portuguese government for a pledge that the property and liberty of British subjects in Portugal would be respected, and he informed London that the Regent and his ministers were willing to resist Bonaparte on this point.[41]

The Portuguese hoped for a moderate British response to anything they were forced to do to appease Napoleon, promising future trade benefits in return. Strangford also told Canning that 'any attempt on the part of England to save Portugal by military succours would be utterly unavailing.' The Portuguese army had improved in recent years, but 'its discipline and spirit are yet far from respectable.' However, Strangford was optimistic that Napoleon would not immediately carry out his threat as Spain was not ready to take control of Portugal and pointed out that previous ultimatums passed. He also wrote, naively perhaps, that 'amongst all the wild ambition of Bonaparte's character, there exists a sort of occasional respect for general opinion which may perhaps deter him from the atrocious and unwarrantable pursuit of forcing this inoffensive country into war.'[42]

Canning began to fear that the British would have to mount another operation similar to Copenhagen, with the same end in mind – denying a fleet to the French. Some initial measures were taken to ensure a British squadron and an expeditionary force became available soon. On 7 September, the Portuguese ambassador in London, Domingos António de Sousa Coutinho, was told by Canning that Britain had to concentrate on self-preservation. If Portugal was forced to side with France, then Britain might have to go to war with Portugal. However, Canning did offer to help the Portuguese government and court to relocate to Brazil, and also later wrote to Sousa that if Portugal was forced to close its ports, then Britain would understand, but he also stated that he felt such a move would not be enough for Napoleon.[43] In a memorandum on the subject, Castlereagh argued that the move to Brazil was 'indispensably necessary for our salvation', as it could provide a base from which Britain could prise the Spanish colonies away from Madrid and out of the clutches of Napoleon.[44]

At the end of August 1807, Strangford's contacts asked him if Britain would help defend Portugal. He replied that they could not commit to defending a country that seemed unwilling to defend itself, but that Britain would assist the Regent in relocating to Brazil.[45] Orders had been given to the Lisbon arsenal to prepare and refit the fleet for the voyage to Brazil. António de Araújo, minister for foreign affairs, war and the kingdom, told Strangford that the Regent would not sail in a British

40   Plon & Dumaine (eds), *Correspondance*, vol.16, 13243, p.83.
41   TNA: FO 63/55: Strangford to Canning, 21 August 1807.
42   TNA: FO 63/55: Strangford to Canning, 21 August 1807.
43   Robson, *Portugal and South America*, pp.115–118.
44   Vane (ed.), *Correspondence*, vol.VI, pp.357–358, undated.
45   TNA: FO 63/55: Strangford to Canning, 29 August 1807.

ship but that the presence of a squadron off the Tagus to support an evacuation would be helpful. He also said that if French troops did cross into Portugal, then the Regent would declare war on France.[46]

On 11 September, news reached London of Whitelocke's defeat at Buenos Aires. This shook faith in Britain's army both abroad and at home. When the news reached Lisbon, Strangford reported that the views of the Prince and his councillors were 'much affected by the lately arrived accounts of the reverse which His Majesty's arms have suffered in Spanish South America.'[47] Then, on the 16th, London received the news of the victory at Copenhagen. Neither the defeat nor the victory did anything to improve Britain's reputation on the continent. João was still resisting French demands. Strangford told Canning that the Regent thought that his relocation to Brazil would eventually lead Spain to lose its colonies there and significantly strengthen British trade with the region, so Napoleon would lose far more than he gained if he invaded.[48] It was an opinion that would turn out to be prescient.

Reports continued to reach both London and Lisbon of a French army at Bayonne. In late August, Strangford had informed Canning, 'The prefect of Bayonne has received an Imperial order … requiring him to prepare cantonments and provisions for 21,000 troops to be stationed in that district, under the command of General Junot; who … left Paris on the 17th Inst.'[49]

On 8 September, Strangford, writing from his sickbed with a severe fever, was able to send London a comprehensive and largely accurate list of the troops who were to be gathered at Bayonne, down to the regiments and battalions involved, their strengths, and their arrival dates. The force listed totalled 23,611 men.[50] There were also reports of Spanish troops at San Roque, near Gibraltar, being told to hold themselves in readiness. With the hope of getting them to stay there, Strangford spread a rumour that British forces from Sicily and Egypt were getting ready to land in southern Spain. The rumour apparently reached Godoy, the Spanish prime minister, who Strangford reported thought himself to have 'an important and authentic secret'.[51] He also told Canning that the Spanish 'dread the admission of French troops into the Peninsula', and wanted to persuade Napoleon to be satisfied with the half-measures Portugal was prepared to take.[52] Strangford continued to press João to go to Brazil before it was too late and put himself and the fleet out of reach of the French.

On 25 September, Strangford met the Regent and again pressed him to sail for Brazil, using 'every argument in my power to induce His Royal Highness to consent to the only measure which now affords him a chance of continuing to exist as an independent sovereign.'[53] Strangford was convinced that the Regent knew it was a step he would have to take eventually and that he would have Britain's support when he did. Strangford also pointed out to João that if he became a vassal of France, Britain would have to act forcefully against Portugal. João stated that his religion and duty meant he could not abandon his people until the last moment. He would try everything to retain Portugal's independence and was aware of the advantage his going to Brazil would bring to Britain, gaining the trade they had lost with Europe. He argued that if the British wanted to

---

46   TNA: FO 63/55: Strangford to Canning, 29 August 1807, second letter.
47   TNA: FO 63/55: Strangford to Canning, 3 October 1807, fourth letter.
48   TNA: FO 63/55: Strangford to Canning, 8 September 1807.
49   TNA: FO 63/55: Strangford to Canning, 29 August 1808, third letter.
50   TNA: FO 63/55: Corps qui formeront le Camp à Bayonne.
51   TNA: FO 63/55: Strangford to Canning, 8 September 1807, second letter.
52   TNA: FO 63/55: Strangford to Canning, 8 September 1807, third letter.
53   TNA: FO 63/55: Strangford to Canning, 26 September 1807.

increase commerce with South America, then they should do it at a cost to their enemies and not their friends. He also warned that if he had to close the ports to British shipping, Britain should understand he was only doing whatever he had to in order to save Portugal. There would be no evacuation until everything else had been tried.

Despite his best efforts, Strangford had to report to Canning, the day after his audience, that the Regent had decided to close the ports and that this would be done once a Portuguese squadron was back from the North African coast. A frigate had sailed with a recall order.[54] However, this concession did not prevent the Spanish and French ambassadors from leaving Lisbon on 30 September. In early October, the optimism in Strangford's dispatches to Canning began to fade, and he reported signs that the Portuguese were improving the defences of the Tagus against any possible British action. Strangford had another audience with João on 16 October, in which the Prince responded to the threat of Britain taking or destroying his fleet. The Regent had received information that a British force was on its way to seize his fleet. No such expedition had sailed, but one was being planned. The Regent was convinced that George III would not resort to attacking an ally, as Napoleon would, 'whose only offence was her weakness, and whom while apparently yielding to the imperious demands of her too powerful enemies, endeavours to give every proof of regard for Great Britain.' Portugal would resist the seizure of the fleet and, like Denmark, had done nothing to offend Britain.[55]

While the Regent and his advisors continued to try to save their country, Napoleon had already made his decision. War was inevitable, no matter what concessions João made. On 17 October, Napoleon ordered his troops to cross the border into Spain and, on the 20th, declared war on Portugal.

On the 22nd, Canning and Sousa signed a secret convention in London. The convention allowed Britain to occupy Madeira if France and Portugal went to war, offered British help for an evacuation to Brazil, and committed the Portuguese to not letting their navy fall into any French hands.[56] João is often portrayed as a weak and vacillating ruler, but whether it was by dithering, luck, or good judgment, it was surprising that Portugal had managed to go so long without picking a side, or having one picked for them.

Talleyrand and the Spanish representative, Eugenio Izquierdo, met and decided the details of Portugal's fate. The Treaty of Fontainebleau, signed on 27 October, divided Portugal into three. The northern provinces and Oporto were to be given to the King of Etruria, a small kingdom created, and then recently dissolved, by Napoleon in northern Italy. The French would retain the central and richest provinces around Lisbon until a general peace, their long-term fate to be decided then. Godoy would be given the southern provinces as his own principality. Portuguese colonies would be divided between Spain and France.[57] On the same day the treaty was signed, Rear Admiral Sir William Sidney Smith was given command of a squadron. Three days later, with the French army already crossing Spain, he received his secret instructions to assist with the evacuation to Brazil.[58]

---

54   TNA: FO 63/55: Strangford to Canning 26 September 1807, second letter.
55   TNA: FO 63/55: Strangford to Canning 20 October 1807.
56   Robson, *South America*, pp.128–131.
57   Hicks, 'Napoleon, Tilsit, Copenhagen, and Portugal'.
58   TNA: ADM 2/1365: Sir Sidney Smith - Instructions for his guidance, 30 Oct 1807.

2

Invasion

The Tempest

Général de division Jean Andoche Junot was born on 24 September 1771 in Bussy-le-Grand, in Côte d'Or. His father hoped he would become a lawyer or a priest – his middle name came from Saint Andochius of Autun, on whose feast day he was born.[1] He went on to study law but did not have the patience for it. He served part-time in the Garde Nationale from 1789, and then in 1791, after a year working as a clerk, his father secured him a place in the 2e bataillon des volontaires de la Côte d'Or. In June 1792, Junot's battalion distinguished itself at La Grisoëlle, where he took a sabre wound to the head. Soon after, he was elected *sergent* and earned himself the nickname 'The Tempest' from his comrades for his fiery nature.[2]

Junot first came to Napoleon's attention during the siege of Toulon in 1793. The stories have perhaps grown in the retelling, but it is claimed that Junot was eating with his comrades when a British shell crashed into their tent, hitting one of them. While the shell's fuse burnt down, Junot grabbed a glass of wine and proposed a toast; 'This is in memory of those of us who are going to perish.' They all remained motionless until the shell exploded, killing one of them, and they then toasted again, 'To the memory of a brave man.'[3] Bonaparte heard of Junot's reputation and employed him as a courier.[4] Learning that he was literate, he made him his military secretary. Once, when Bonaparte was dictating to him, a shell exploded nearby and covered them both in debris. Junot said, 'Exactly, I needed sand to blot my paper.'[5]

When Bonaparte was promoted to *général de brigade,* he got Junot promoted to *sous-lieutenant* and took him as his aide de camp. By 1795, he was a *capitaine* in the 1er Régiment de Hussards and then, later the same year, a *chef d'escadron* in the 3e Dragons. Blond and handsome Junot made a dashing cavalryman, even catching the eye of Pauline, Bonaparte's sister, for a time. In 1796, Bonaparte named Junot his premier aide de camp, and in May, he took captured enemy colours

---

1   C.H. Mackay, *The Tempest: The Life and Career of Jean-Andoche Junot, 1771–1813* (Florida State University: PhD thesis, 1995), p.7.
2   S. Dubief, 'Le General Junot en Egypte', Napoleon.org, <https://www.napoleon.org/histoire-des-2-empires/articles/le-General-junot-en-egypte/>, accessed 5 May 2022.
3   P. Thiébault, *Mémoires du General Baron Thiébault* (Paris: Plon, 1895), vol.IV, p.117.
4   Mackay, *Tempest*, p.15.
5   N. Griffon de Pleineville, *La Première Invasion du Portugal par l'Armée Napoléonienne (1807-1808)* (Paris: Economica, 2017), p.17.

to the directory and was promoted to *chef de brigade*. At the Battle of Lonato, Junot led a brigade, charged into the enemy and got cut off. Surrounded, he killed six Austrians and captured an enemy commander. However, he received several severe sabre cuts to his head and body, which put him out of action until the following year.[6]

Junot, by Bertie Greatheed. (From *An Englishman in Paris*)

Junot accompanied Bonaparte to Egypt and, in 1799, he was promoted to *général de brigade*. Bonaparte's order of the day on 21 April 1799 began: 'The General-in-chief, wishing to give a particular mark of satisfaction to the three hundred brave soldiers commanded by General Junot who in the battle of Nazareth repulsed three thousand cavalry, took five colours, and covered the battlefield with enemy corpses.'[7] Junot maintained control of Cario during a serious revolt, but when Bonaparte deserted his army to return to France, Junot was far from Cairo and left behind. He followed in October on a merchantman.[8] HMS *Theseus* captured the ship, and Junot was taken to Jaffa, where he met Commodore Sir Sidney Smith. He was eventually exchanged in 1800.[9] In October of that year, he married Laure Adélaïde Constance Permon; she was 15, and he was 30. The couple soon became infamous for high living and extravagant spending.

In 1801, he was promoted to *général de division* and commanded the Paris garrison until 1803. English artist Bertie Greatheed met Junot several times during the Peace of Amiens. Greatheed comments on his devotion to Bonaparte, reporting that Junot said, 'Mahomet had his Omar, why should not Bonaparte has [*sic*] his Junot?'[10] Greatheed also mentions the fact that Junot had had two severe head wounds, one from an Austrian sabre and one from a pistol ball, the latter of which led his comrades to think him dead and prepare to bury him, and which left a deep hole in the crown of his head.[11] Following another meeting, where Junot told several war stories, Greatheed wrote:

6   N.D. Jensen 'General Jean Andoche Junot', Frenchempire.net, <https://www.frenchempire.net/biographies/junot/>, accessed 5 May 2022.

7   Dubief, 'Junot en Egypte'.

8   Mackay, *Tempest*, p.64.

9   Dubief, 'Junot en Egypte'.

10   J.P.T. Bury and J.C. Barry (eds), *An Englishman in Paris: 1803* (London: Bles, 1953), p.44. Translations of French in original inserted.

11   Bury and Barry (eds), *Englishman*, pp.45, 78.

Would I had the whole conversation of the day on paper. It would present a picture the most perfect I can conceive of a thorough soldier with all his open rough virtues, and honourable murders on his head. A man kind hearted, even tender I believe, till on the command of another man he thinks it his duty to banish every feeling of humanity from his soul, and become more terrible than the tigre of Sumatra. In war he would have no quarter, in seiges [sic] no capitulation; he would turn out old man, woman and child to their fate, he would disobey all orders to surrender from his General and hang all those of the garrison who should propose it, he would have a battle on every breach, and then die amid the ruins of the place.[12]

Junot was appointed to various other commands, but when Napoleon created the first *maréchaux* Junot's name was not among them. Napoleon recognised Junot's weaknesses: he lacked the patience, self-discipline and meticulousness to excel in command. Without Napoleon's patronage, he would probably have risen no higher than command of a cavalry brigade.[13]

In 1805, Junot was appointed ambassador to Lisbon. He got on well with Prince João and impressed him with his smart hussar uniform, but when he heard that the Grande Armée was on the march again he left without permission to serve as Napoleon's aide de camp. In January 1806, he was made Governor-General of Parma and Piacenza, where a revolt had broken out. Junot executed rebels and burned villages, but was not as harsh as Napoleon wanted and put effort into improving the region's government.[14] His next post was military governor of Paris.

It is possible that Napoleon selected Junot for the Portugal command to reward his friend, long deprived of an active corps command, or even perhaps because he wanted him out of Paris due to Junot's affair with his sister Caroline, wife of *maréchal* Murat. Junot was also beginning to display erratic and violent behaviour, which some attributed to his head wounds, leading to reprimands from the Emperor. Whatever the reason for his appointment to the Corps d'Observation de la Gironde, as historian Alphonse Grasset puts it, Junot 'had enough energy to lead an army, even an untrained one, and enough devotion to the person of the Emperor to carry out his instructions blindly.'[15] Napoleon did not expect Junot to come up against any significant opposition, and of course, after his brief stint as ambassador, Junot was familiar with the country and Prince João. Maximilien Foy, who would serve under Junot in Portugal, later made this assessment of Junot:

Junot was born with a talent for observation. In every question his piercing glance saw instantaneously where the difficulty lay. All the good that a sudden inspiration could produce might be expected from him; but nothing of that for which a methodical and continuous system of conduct is required. All his valuable qualities were stifled by a fiery temper, habits of dissipation, and such obstinate aversion to labour, that it palsied the exertions of those to whom he delegated some portions of his power.[16]

In his memoirs, Junot's chief of staff, *général de brigade* Paul Thiébault, characterises Junot's appointment as an error on the part of the Emperor and a punishment for Junot. It was, he claims,

12   Bury and Barry (eds), *Englishman*, p.75.
13   Mackay, *Tempest*, pp.34–36.
14   Mackay, *Tempest*, pp.101–106.
15   A. Grasset, *La Guerre d'Espagne 1807-1813* (Paris: Berger-Leverault, 1914), vol.1, pp.78–79.
16   M. Foy, *Junot's Invasion of Portugal* (Felling: Worley, 2000), p.81.

a facet of the increasingly toxic court jealousies and rivalries between Napoleon's top generals and ministers. Thiébault argues that Junot was intensely disliked by *général de division* Savary, a rising star, and mentions the affair with Caroline. Thiébault wrote, 'Intoxicated with his master's favour, Junot had persuaded himself that it could have no end, and that his greatness and his fortune would have no more limits than his hopes.'[17]

Junot joined his corps in September of 1807 and, according to Thiébault, soon afterwards advised a gathering of the senior officers of the importance of the mission and what might await them in Portugal. He then reminded them of his accomplishments and bravery, finishing by informing them, 'And yet, gentlemen, it is not these feelings, it is not these titles which decided Napoleon to place me at your head. No. You are under my orders because I am better than you.'[18] *Adjutant major* Viennet, who met Junot at one of the camps the corps was drawn from, described him as: 'A rough, surly man, dissatisfied with everything, cursing, swearing at everyone and at everything. I have seen in my life many characters of various natures, but I have never seen one more sullen than this imperial favourite, infatuated with his power and mocking the laws which his master held most dear.'[19] Napoleon had promised Junot a dukedom and his *maréchal*'s baton if he did well in Portugal. He would get one but not the other.

The Army of Observation

The order creating the Corps d'Observation de la Gironde and appointing Junot its commander was issued by Napoleon on 2 August. The corps would be based around Bayonne, near the border of France and Spain. The men would be drawn from three *camps volant* (flying camps) at Pontivy in Brittany, Saint-Lo in Normandy, and Napoléon in the Vendée (which has since reverted to its former name of La Roche-sur-Yon).

The *camps volants* had been created to act as mobile reserves to guard the coast against Royal Navy raids and be ready to quell any fresh insurrections in the Vendée. However, most of the units in them were little more than cadres or depots, and the men were primarily convalescents or raw recruits. Conscription was becoming increasingly unpopular, but, with his seemingly never-ending campaigns demanding more and more men, Napoleon was forced to call up the 1808 class of conscripts a year early. However, he did have to promise the Senate that they would be placed in training camps and not sent on campaign until 1 January 1808. This meant that the camps in western France received many of these conscripts during 1807. So, whilst the camps appeared to hold enough men to form a corps on paper, most were only partly trained. This included the men of the cavalry and artillery, who required more instruction than the infantry.[20] Depots at Toulon and whichever other barrels could be scraped were scoured for any men available. The units from the Pontivy, Saint-Lo and Napoléon camps would form the 1er, 2e and 3e divisions, respectively.[21]

With limited time and men available, most regiments set out on the long march to Bayonne woefully understrength. The cavalry could not gather enough horses, and the artillery was short of guns. In his history of the Peninsular War, Foy, a *colonel* with Junot's artillery at the time, was

---

17   Thiébault, *Mémoires*, vol.IV, p.120.
18   Thiébault, *Mémoires*, vol.IV, p.130.
19   Griffon de Pleineville, *Première Invasion*, p.17.
20   Grasset, *Guerre d'Espagne*, vol.1, pp.72–76.
21   Grasset, *Guerre d'Espagne*, vol.1, pp.78–79.

not complimentary about the corps' quality. He points out that two of the infantry regiments, the 70e and 86e, had not participated in the recent campaigns, and so contained a high proportion of older soldiers. However, many of the other infantry units were third battalions made up of recent conscripts and significantly understrength, and there were also Swiss, Piedmontese and Hanoverian regiments. The cavalry, too, were fourth squadrons of raw recruits cobbled together in provisional regiments. In total, the corps fielded just over 25,000 men.[22]

On 10 October, Junot sent Napoleon a lengthy report on the state of his corps. After remarking on his lack of staff officers, he commented on the divisions, saying that the 1er was the 'most complete', that the 2e lacked officers and was not as well trained as the 1er, whilst the 3e was 'considerably weaker than the first two; the strength of most of its battalions are so small that I do not believe that it would be possible for your majesty to let them exist, as they are, since they are composed almost entirely of officers and sub-officers…' As for the cavalry, he wrote, 'The turnout of this division is quite good; its training is almost nil. I hope they will work.' He ended his report with, 'Loaded with the heavy burden of a command-in-chief, I will often need direction; but I am sure that I will not stray from the right road, if your majesty deigns to preserve for me the least part of the kindness with which he has always showered me.'[23]

A Particular Service

As soon as the convention between Britain and Portugal was signed, preparations were made to send a Royal Navy squadron to support, and perhaps compel, the embarkation of João and the Portuguese government for Brazil and to stop his fleet from falling into French hands. Rear Admiral Sir William Sidney Smith received his commission to command a squadron for a 'particular service'[24] on 27 October and on the 30th received his instructions. When Smith arrived off the Tagus, he was to contact Lord Strangford and conform himself to such 'intuitions and recommendations as his Lordship may from time to time transmit to you'. Smith was to assist in the fitting out of the Portuguese fleet, if required, and to accompany the Regent to Brazil if he chose to leave. Smith had to ensure as much of the fleet sailed as possible and to secure or destroy any vessels that remained, with the agreement of the Portuguese. He was also told to protect British subjects but only to enter the Tagus on the express wishes of Strangford.[25]

Smith had a high public profile, diplomatic experience, and knowledge of unconventional operations. Born in 1764 in London to a moderately prosperous military and naval family, he always went by his middle name. He joined the navy at the age of 13 and took part in several major actions during the American War of Independence. He rose to command the sloop *Fury* (16) in 1782 and then the frigate *Alcmene* (28) in 1783, but his ship was soon paid off following the peace, and he remained unemployed for several years and travelled on the continent.[26]

In 1790, Smith entered the service of Gustav III of Sweden, commanded a light squadron, and fought gallantly against the Russians in the Baltic. Gustav knighted him for his service. He travelled

22   Foy, *Invasion*, pp.5–9.
23   C. Sepulveda, *Historia Organica e Politica do Exercito Português* (Coimbra: Imprensa da Universidade, 1917), vol.XII, pp.95–98.
24   E. Howard, *Memoirs of Admiral Sir Sidney Smith* (London: Bentley, 1839), vol.II, p82.
25   TNA: ADM 2/1365: Wellesley-Pole to Smith, 30 October 1807.
26   T. Pocock, *A Thirst for Glory, the Life of Admiral Sir Sidney Smith* (London: Aurum, 1996), pp.1–12.

again between 1791 and 1792 and came into contact with various other heads of state. In 1793, he was in Turkey when war broke out with France. Eager to get into the fight, he purchased a ship at Smyrna and manned it with 40 British seamen who were also stranded because of a blockade by two French frigates. He evaded them and reached Toulon, where a British and Royalist force was besieged. When the port was abandoned, he was tasked with burning the French fleet. In 1794, he was given command of the *Diamond* (38), took part in several small actions, and led a squadron of frigates on the French coast. In 1796, he was attempting to cut out a privateer when he was captured. Due to his burning of the French fleet at Toulon and the various clandestine operations he had supported on the coast, the French did not treat him as an ordinary prisoner of war but incarcerated him in the Temple prison in Paris. He remained there for two years before escaping with the support of Royalist spies.

After he returned to Britain, he commanded the *Tigre* (74) and sailed for the eastern Mediterranean, taking charge of the squadron watching Alexandria and the French army in Egypt. He was instrumental in defending the city of Acre during the siege, forestalling Bonaparte's plans for further eastward expansion. Without official sanction, he negotiated the Treaty of El Arish between the Ottomans and the French, which would have seen the French repatriated with their arms had the British government not baulked at the idea. Smith then supported Lieutenant General Sir Ralph Abercromby's operations to drive the French from Egypt, which resulted in them being repatriated under similar terms. He returned to London, circulated in high society and was rumoured to be having an affair with Princess Caroline, wife of the Prince of Wales. When war broke out again in 1803, he was given a squadron in the Channel Fleet, but blockade duty did not suit him. He was always carrying out small raids, often incurring his superior's wrath for not simply obeying his orders. He was promoted to rear admiral in 1805 and helped to plan a raid on the invasion fleet at Boulogne using experimental craft, which proved unsuccessful. In 1806, he was back in the Mediterranean, capturing Capri, defending Sicily, and fighting the Turks. When he received his orders for Lisbon, he had been back in Britain for several months. His health was poor, and he was 'almost crippled by a hurt suffered on his knee in Egypt.'[27] Smith was undoubtedly a talented officer, but he was also vain and thirsty for fame. His superior in the Mediterranean, Vice Admiral Lord Collingwood, wrote of him, 'the man's head is full of strange vapours and … he annoys me more than the French or Spanish fleet.'[28]

At Lisbon, Smith would work with Percy Clinton Sydney Smythe, sixth Viscount Strangford. Strangford was born to an Irish family in London in 1780, so he was 27 to Smith's 43. Strangford was educated at Harrow and graduated from Trinity College, Dublin, in 1800. He was an accomplished poet and part of London's literary circles. He succeeded to his title in 1801 and a year later began his diplomatic career as secretary to the legation in Lisbon. In 1804 he became chargé d'affaires, and in 1806 was named minister plenipotentiary ad interim while Lord Fitzgerald, the previous minister, was absent.[29] Strangford has been much maligned by historians and contemporaries, mainly based on his youth and inexperience. However, he knew the Portuguese court and government well, was well-liked by Lisbon society, and socialised with the literary set and the British community.[30] Laure Junot, who met Strangford during her husband's brief tenure as ambassador, described him as 'an agreeable and well-bred man'.[31]

---

27   Raleigh, 'Naval Transactions on the Coast of Portugal', *The Naval Chronicle*, vol.XXI, Jan-Jun 1809, p.378.
28   Pocock, *Thirst*, p.195.
29   D. Murphy, 'Smythe, Percy Clinton Sydney', Dictionary of Irish Biography, <https://www.dib.ie/biography/smythe-percy-clinton-sydney-a8181>, accessed May 2022.
30   Robson, *South America*, pp.44-45.
31   L. Junot, *Memoirs of Madame Junot* (Paris: The Napoleon Society, 1895), vol. IV, p.63.

Sir William Sidney Smith at the siege of Acre. (Public Domain)

Someone who worked alongside Strangford during Lord Rosslyn's 1806 mission to Lisbon was Lord Brougham, and he did not think much of him at all. In a letter to Rosslyn, Brougham wrote:

> My temper has been tried perpetually by his infinite childishness in doing business, and indeed in doing every thing else; and really, however unpleasant to say so, there is a defect about him which I can still less pardon than his want of sense – I mean his total want of that first-rate quality which gives a man's words the right to be believed ... I only lament that the consequences of his character here are a total want of respect, either from common society or from those he has to do business with. I don't wish to judge harshly, but I can scarcely wonder at this, from what I know and see of him. Certainly he is not the man to change a ministry here. Pray discourage him from writing loose letters to you, for his silliness makes him brag of it everywhere, and so, I suppose, do his blackguard companions...[32]

Either Strangford's superiors at the Foreign Office did not share Brougham's opinion or Strangford had enough influential friends to get the job anyway, but he was promoted to be the British minister. He certainly seems to have had the support of some in the Portuguese government, with Araújo writing in a report for the Prince Regent, 'I have the pleasure of adding that Strangford is well in our favour ... It would be highly convenient to send word England to maintain this minister here for, should they send Lord Fitzgerald, it would be terrible.'[33] On the face of it then, at a moment of acute crisis, Britain's interests in Portugal rested upon the unsteady shoulders of a maverick admiral and a diplomat still wet behind the ears.

Canning wrote to Strangford on 22 October, informing him of the convention and giving him instructions for a series of possible scenarios. If Portugal shut its ports against Britain but did nothing else, then Strangford was to stay in Lisbon. If the Portuguese went further and remaining in Lisbon became impossible, then Strangford was to request a ship from the British fleet off Cadiz to take him, the consul James Gambier, and the embassy archives to Britain. If the Regent sailed to Brazil and asked Strangford to accompany him, he was to do so. Canning was pleased that the Regent was willing to go to Brazil rather than capitulate to Napoleon but regretted that he would not go sooner. He thought there was still a danger that if the Portuguese yielded enough to France for the crisis to blow over, the country could revert to apathy and inaction, and if Napoleon bullied Portugal into submission, he would do the same elsewhere.[34]

Strangford's dispatches remained optimistic that the Portuguese would keep to the terms of the convention. Canning, however, began to have doubts. During this crucial time, Castlereagh was unwell, so Canning was driving policy, with Lord Hawkesbury taking up Castlereagh's duties. Before Smith had even sailed, Canning was lobbying Hawkesbury to increase the size of the squadron so that it was strong enough to destroy the Portuguese fleet if it was in danger of falling into Napoleon's hands and to gather a force of 5,000–6,000 troops to be sent to the Tagus. Canning amended Smith's instructions to include him sending a strongly worded note to the Portuguese on his arrival, outlining their commitments in the convention, and if the Regent did not intend

32   Brougham to Rosslyn, 11 October 1806, in H. Brougham, *The Life and Times of Henry Lord Brougham* (New York: Harper Bros., 1871), vol.I, p.257.
33   K. Light, *The Saving of an Empire* (Ely: Melrose, 2009), p.14.
34   TNA: FO 63/56: Canning to Strangford, 22 October 1807, two letters.

to embark for Brazil, then to ensure the Portuguese fleet was destroyed, and to blockade the port until that was done.[35]

Canning also wrote to Strangford noting the preparations being made to defend the Tagus that the young diplomat had told him about in his last dispatch, stating that 'it seems hardly to be doubted that the Portuguese Government entertain a notion of carrying their compliance with the demands of France farther than the mere shutting of their ports against this country'. Canning was adamant that the idea of a nominal war between Britain and Portugal was absurd, and that Britain would react forcibly to any declaration. The Portuguese had to comply with the convention. He also made sure that Strangford was clear that the most important articles of the convention were the ones that dealt with the securing of the Portuguese fleet and that he should employ 'every means, whether of persuasion or menace, to procure their instant execution.'[36] The fleet must sail for Brazil, with or without any of the Royal family, as soon as Smith arrived, and not a single ship should end up in French hands.[37]

On 9 November, Smith raised his flag on HMS *London* at Plymouth. He was hoping to proceed to sea, but the wind was not favourable.[38] Most of the squadron was anchored in Cawsand Bay, but the *Hibernia* was in Torbay after having sheltered from a gale. The Admiralty sent Smith additional orders that, should Strangford be absent from Lisbon, he was 'to dispatch to Lieutenant General Sir John Moore at Gibraltar with the utmost expedition any instructions or information His Lordship may have left for the Lieutenant General.'[39] He was also instructed to cooperate with Moore if he joined the squadron at the mouth of the Tagus. In mid-September Moore, who was in command of British troops on Sicily, had received orders to sail to Gibraltar. He had left at the end of October with 7,258 rank and file, but his exact whereabouts were not known in London.[40]

Smith's squadron sailed at 11:00 a.m. on 11 November.[41] It packed a considerable punch with a first-rate, a second-rate and four third-rates, and would have been manned by about 4,000 officers, sailors and marines.

Table 1. Rear Admiral Sir Sidney Smith's squadron, November 1807

Vessel	Guns	Captain
Hibernia	110	Charles Schomberg
London	98	Thomas Western
Marlborough	74	Graham Moore
Elizabeth	74	Henry Curzon
Monarch	74	Richard Lee
Bedford	74	James Walker
Solebay	32	Andrew Sproule
Viper	4	Lt William Sidney Smith Towning

Source: TNA: ADM 50/50: 9 November entry. Additional details from Winfield, *British Warships in the Age of Sail 1793-1817*, Kindle Edition.

---

35   TNA: FO 63/56: Canning to Smith, 6 November 1807.
36   Canning to Strangford, 7 November 1807, quoted in Robson, *South America*, p.141
37   TNA: FO 63/56: Canning to Strangford, 7 November 1807.
38   TNA: ADM 1/19: Smith to Wellesley-Pole, 9 November 1808.
39   TNA: ADM 2/1365: Wellesley-Pole to Smith, 7 October 1807.
40   Maurice (ed.), *Diary of Sir John Moore*, vol.II, p.195.
41   T. O'Neil, *A Concise and Accurate Account of the Proceedings of the Squadron under the Command of Rear Admiral Sir Sydney Smith in Effecting the Escape of the Royal Family of Portugal to the Brazils* (London, privately published, 1810), p.4.

Into Spain

On 12 October, Napoleon wrote to Henri Clarke, his Minister of War, to order Junot to march to Portugal and 'that there is not a moment to lose in order to forestall the English.'[42] Additional staff, artillery, and troops were being sent to Junot's command and regiments of the 3e Division had been told to send every soldier available to bolster their numbers. He also informed Junot that a second corps of observation of 30,000 men was going to form at Bayonne and asked that Junot send him details of the terrain and towns as he passed through Spain.[43] He had plans for further action in the Peninsula.

The order reached Junot on the 17th, and the army began their march a day later. The plan was for the corps to travel via Valladolid, Salamanca and Ciudad Rodrigo before entering Portugal. Napoleon wanted Spain to contribute 10,000 men to Junot's corps and to send two additional divisions of 6,000 men each to Oporto and the southern bank of the Tagus.[44]

The instructions issued for the march by Junot's chief of staff, *général de brigade* Paul Thiébault, on 17 October detailed everything from rendering military honours to Spanish officers to arrangements for preventing stragglers to specifying halts of five minutes per hour and two breaks of an hour each day. Thiébault was an experienced officer who had worked steadily up the ranks and published a manual for staff officers in 1800.[45] His order concluded with an appeal for the troops to be worthy of 'marching under our triumphant eagles'.[46]

However, Junot knew that his army was marching too soon. Upon receipt of Clarke's order to march, he replied with his concerns about the ability of the Spanish to subsist his men and that his corps was not yet ready, writing: 'I fear that many things are missing, and the haste with which we are leaving will not allow us to remedy them; but I only know how to obey, and the order … will be punctually executed'.[47] Junot hurriedly wrote to the Spanish to inform them that the corps would soon cross the border and to remind them of their commitment to supply provisions. The Bayonne arsenal was scoured for the ammunition, caissons, howitzers, and carriages needed to complete the artillery, but there were still insufficient horses to pull them, and so much had to be left behind.[48]

To reduce the logistical issues, the corps marched in 16 columns: four for each infantry division and four for the cavalry. The first column of the 1er Division had already marched from Bayonne on 16 October to get closer to the border. The next column marched on the 17th and so on until the last column of the cavalry was to leave on the 31st. The first column entered Spain on 18 October. The route for the columns was to take them through Burgos, Valladolid and Salamanca. The first column was to arrive in Salamanca on 11 November and the last on the 26th.[49] Some of the planned stages were as few as nine miles, and some just over 20, but most were in the mid-teens.

---

42   Plon & Dumaine (eds), *Correspondance*, vol.16, 13238, p.80.
43   Plon & Dumaine (eds), *Correspondance*, vol.16, 13267, pp.98–99.
44   Plon & Dumaine (eds), *Correspondance*, vol.16, 13257, pp.90–91.
45   J.L. Sigler, *General Paul Thiébault His Life and His Legacy* (Florida State University: PhD Thesis, 2006), pp.2, 165–168.
46   Grasset, *Guerre d'Espagne*, vol.1, pp.439–443.
47   Grasset, *Guerre d'Espagne*, vol.1, p.109.
48   Grasset, *Guerre d'Espagne*, vol.1, pp.110–111.
49   Grasset, *Guerre d'Espagne*, vol.1, p.438.

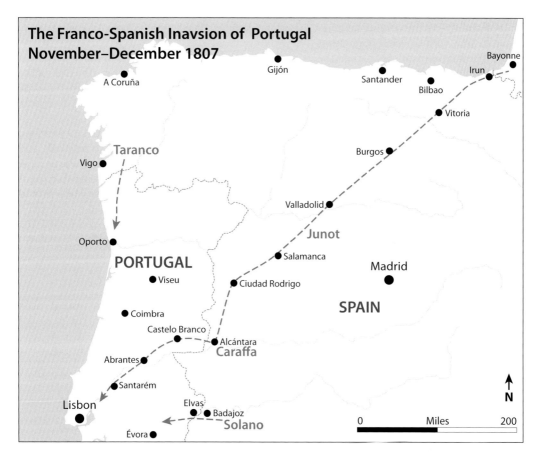

The Franco-Spanish Inavsion of Portugal
November–December 1807

Junot tried to remedy as many of the insufficiencies in his corps as possible. He ordered each regiment to establish a temporary depot at Bayonne to gather up those left behind in the hospitals and any reinforcements that arrived into provisional companies that would then follow the main army as escorts to subsequent convoys of supplies and matériel.[50] Just as the 2e Division was due to march, its commander became ill and had to be replaced by Louis-Henri Loison. The 1er Division was commanded by Henri-François Delaborde, the 3e by Jean Pierre Travot and the cavalry division by François-Etienne Kellermann (the son of the *maréchal*). All the divisional commanders were very experienced officers, more so than perhaps even Junot.

As the 70e Ligne in the first column crossed the Bidasoa and entered Spain, they exchanged salutes with Spanish troops. In his history of the war, Foy paints a rosy picture of the reception given to the French by the Spanish, listing the towns that put on lavish receptions.[51] However, the quarters for the troops were often crowded and quickly became unsanitary, and the provisions were

50   Grasset, *Guerre d'Espagne*, vol.1, pp.117–118.
51   Foy, *Invasion*, p.19.

of poor quality. As the columns entered the poorer regions after Salamanca, significant tensions began to arise with the local population.

The incessant rain quickly turned the roads to mud, and the poor fodder led to the replacement of the artillery horses with oxen or mules, both of which slowed the rate of march. The trail of the corps was soon marked by dozens of men left behind in hospitals who could walk no further. The strategic consumption was worsened by recruiters from the Spanish army encouraging desertion, especially amongst the foreign corps.[52]

Napoleon still thought of Junot's mission as diplomatic rather than military. On 29 October, Clarke had written to Junot that he was to stress to the Portuguese that he came to negotiate and the operation 'will have succeeded if … you succeed in making yourself master of the Portuguese fleet'.[53] On the 31st, Napoleon complained that the corps was marching too slowly and that Junot should have marched in three columns rather than 16. Worried that the British would beat him to Lisbon, Napoleon dictated a new route and schedule. Junot received these orders on 6 November. He was told to ensure the 1er Division was at Salamanca by the 10th and Alcántara by the 20th. The army would then march for Abrantes, which looked like a four-day, 25-league march to Napoleon. It would then be another 50 leagues to Lisbon, and he expected Junot to be there by 1 December.[54]

Table 2. Corps d'Observation de la Gironde, 1 November 1807

	Commander	Battalions/ Squadrons	Regiment	Location	Present		Depot		Joining		Hospital		Total
					Officers	Troops	Officers	Troops	Officers	Troops	Officers	Troops	
Corps	*gén. de div.* Junot												
Chief of Staff	*gén. de brig.* Thiébault		État-major général		20								
Deputy Chief of Staff	*adj. comm.* Bagnéris												
1er Division	*gén. de div.* Delaborde		État-major	Villodrigo	4						1		
1er Brigade	*gén. de brig.* Avril		État-major	Celada	2								
	chef de bat. Recouvreur	3e	15e Ligne	Burgos	25	937		5		25	3	42	**1,037**
	colonel Rouyer	1er & 2e	70e Ligne	Villodrigo	63	2,299	1	28		30		62	**2,483**
	chef de bat. Felber	1er	4e Suisse	Celada	39	1,145	1	21		17	2	78	**1,303**
2e Brigade	*gén. de brig.* Brenier		État-major	Burgos	3								
	colonel de la Chatre	2e	47e Ligne	Celada	32	1,166	1			12		61	**1,272**
	colonel Lacroix	1er & 2e	86e Ligne	Burgos	59	2,191	1	34		40	1	157	**2,483**
				Div. Total	227	7,738	4	88	0	124	6	400	**8,578**
2e Division	*gén. de div.* Loison (Absent)		État-major		2								
1er Brigade	*gén. de brig.* Charlot		État-major	Monasterio	3								
1er Rég. Prov.	*major* Meslier	3e	2e Légère	Monasterio	9	987	1	17		8		141	**1,163**
		3e	4e Légère		14	703		9		7		137	**870**

52 P. Thiébault, *Relation de l'Expédition du Portugal faite en 1807 et 1808* (Paris: Magimel, Anselin & Pochard, 1817) p.11.

53 Grasset, *Guerre d'Espagne*, vol.1, p.99.

54 Plon & Dumaine (eds), *Correspondance*, vol.16, 13314, pp.128–130.

	Commander	Battalions/ Squadrons	Regiment	Location	Present Officers	Present Troops	Depot Officers	Depot Troops	Joining Officers	Joining Troops	Hospital Officers	Hospital Troops	Total
2e Rég. Prov.	*major* Petit	3e	12e Légère	Bribiesca	14	870		4	1	7		106	1,002
		3e	15e Légère		21	1,011	1	18		16		109	1,155
2e Brigade	*gén. de brig.* Thomieres (Abs)												
3e Rég. Prov.	*major* Bertrand	3e	32e Ligne	Pancorbo	14	939	1	27		11		129	1,121
		3e	58e Ligne		21	976	1	17		29		153	1,197
	colonel Segeesser	2e	2e Suisse	Miranda	36	1,033	1	55		31	1	83	1,240
				Div. Total	134	6,519	5	147	1	109	1	858	7,748
3e Division	*gén. de div.* Travot		État-major	Vitoria	4								
1er Brigade	*gén. de brig.* Graindorge (Abs)												
1er Rég. Prov.	*major* Durlong	3e	31e Légère	Vitoria	16	506				1		78	601
		3e	32e Légère		28	1,060	1	10		13		49	1,161
	colonel Miquel	3e & 4e	26e Ligne		28	445	1	31				113	618
	colonel Maransin	1er & 2e	Legion du Midi		27	839	1	21		4		10	902
2e Brigade	*gén. de brig.* Fuzier		État-major	Zumarraga	1								
	chef de bat. Creste	3e & 4e	66e Ligne	Mondragon	38	897	1	25			1	147	1,109
	chef de bat. Petavy	3e & 4e	82e Ligne	Zumarraga	34	726	1	31	1			23	816
	colonel Striffler		Légion Hanovrienne	Mondragon	17	766	1	24				25	833
				Div. Total	193	5,239	6	142	2	17	1	445	6,040
Division de Cavalrie	*gén. de div.* Kellerman			Astigarraga	2								
1er Brigade	*gén. de brig.* Margaron		État-major	Saint-Jean-de-Luz	1								
1er Rég. Prov.	*major* Weiss	4e	26e Chasseurs à cheval	Tolosa	7	214						20	241
2e Rég. Prov.	*major* Contant	4e	1er Dragons	Astigarraga	6	273				1		18	298
		4e	3e Dragons		6	267				2		22	297
2e Brigade	*gén. de brig.* Maurin (Abs)												
3e Rég. Prov.	*major* Theron	4e	4e Dragons	Irun	6	254				2		6	268
		4e	5e Dragons		5	244				2		23	274
4e Rég. Prov.	*major* Leclerc	4e	9e Dragons	Saint-Jean-de-Luz	7	284						13	304
		4e	15e Dragons		4	278						15	297
	chef de esc. Thomas		Gendarmerie impériale		1	39							40
				Div. Total	45	1,853			0	7	0	117	2,019
		Companies											
Artillerie	*colonel* Douence			Tolosa	8	1							
		4e	1er Regiment à Pied		2	50						7	59
		8e, 10e & 12e	3e Regiment à Pied		6	183				24		12	225
		15e & 16e	6e Regiment à Pied		5	182						20	207

	Commander	Battalions/Squadrons	Regiment	Location	Present		Depot		Joining		Hospital		Total
					Officers	Troops	Officers	Troops	Officers	Troops	Officers	Troops	
			D'ouvriers			4							
	Enterprise Jullien		Artillery Train (Civilian)		3	280						12	295
				Art. Total	24	700			0	24	0	51	786
Génie	*colonel* Vincent			Tolosa	8								
				Grand Total	651	22,049	15	377	3	281	8	1,871	25,171

Source: Grasset, *La Guerre d'Espagne*, vol.1, État B and Foy, *Invasion*, pp.7–9, for the regimental commanders' names. There were one officer and 16 men on leave, six men facing disciplinary proceedings, nine men had deserted, and nine were escorting prisoners.

The best routes for travelling from Spain to Lisbon led from either Ciudad Rodrigo in the north, going west into Portugal and then south via Coimbra to Lisbon, or from Badajoz south of the Tagus, which was the easiest route but would have put Junot's army on the wrong bank of the river. Looking at a map, the more direct route via Abrantes seemed logical but was fraught with difficulties. Napoleon had in his possession a 40-year-old plan for the invasion of Portugal that *général de division* Charles Dumouriez had originated when still a young officer in the French royal army. Dumouriez's plan called for a quick march into Portugal so the French would arrive at Lisbon before Britain could send troops. Crucially, the plan called for a substantial build-up of supplies before the operation, as Dumouriez considered the region impracticable without considerable logistical support.[55] However, Napoleon was dismissive of such concerns and ended his letter with, 'I do not intend that, under the pretext of lack of food, his march should be delayed for a day: that reason is only good for men who do not want to do anything; 20,000 men can live anywhere, even in the desert.'[56]

Junot objected to the criticism and the new route but obeyed nonetheless. He ordered that rest days be cancelled and that the even-numbered columns perform a double march for a day so that when the army arrived at Salamanca it would be formed in eight columns. From Valladolid, the daily stages were lengthened to around 25 miles. The troops were already exhausted, and the regiments had to be issued money for shoe repairs as many were already barefoot. To comply with the Emperor's order, Junot had to risk the ruin of his army.[57] Charles de Soucy, aide de camp to Kellermann, wrote, 'I am travelling through the ugliest country I have ever seen … we are doubling the stages and we are not allowed to have a break, so that the cavalry, which is already very weak, will be entirely on foot when we arrive in Portugal.'[58]

On the 12th, Napoleon outlined what Junot was to do at Lisbon: occupy the ports, seize the fleet and have the French flag flown on all government buildings. French naval officers and a battalion of naval gunners were to board the Portuguese fleet, along with 200 infantrymen on each ship. The

---

55   Grasset, *Guerre d'Espagne*, vol.1, pp.102–106.
56   Plon & Dumaine (eds), *Correspondance*, vol.16, 13327, p.139.
57   Grasset, *Guerre d'Espagne*, vol.1, pp.132–133.
58   Griffon de Pleineville, *Invasion*, p.30.

Portuguese crews were to be kept on board, and the ships readied for sea. As soon the fleet and forts were secure, the Portuguese army was to be disarmed, and the ablest men transferred to French service. The Prince Regent would be informed that he was going to France. British property would be seized and would help pay for the occupation. British subjects would be arrested. Napoleon also warned Junot to set an example for the army and avoid plundering himself. He should also watch Thiébault, who had previously been accused of looting.[59]

With the weather getting worse and the marches getting longer, the condition of the corps was quickly deteriorating. *Capitaine* Jaques Louis Hulot, leading the 1er Division's artillery, wrote in his memoir:

> The snow was melting and very cold: I still feel pain when I remember that the bumps made one of the corporals fall under the wheels, he had been lying sick and half-frozen on a car. At San-Espiritu, a miserable village halfway up the mountain, I had the good fortune to find a small amount of barley and straw; there was nothing for the men, but we were consoled by seeing our horses regain some of their legs. At last, at ten o'clock in the evening, we thought we were saved at the entrance to the suburb of Ciudad-Rodrigo … Alas! … everything was full of men and devoid of food and fodder. In vain, I deployed all the energy of my age and need, I could obtain nothing, neither from the Spaniards nor from the French, so I ordered my skirmishers and soldiers of the train to seek … means of sustenance for the troop and the teams, as well as requisition oxen. The few remaining oxen in the vicinity were fought over and snatched from each other; each corps wanted them for their baggage. One of my best sergeants was wounded by a stiletto in the course of this painful mission. We had just made twenty-two leagues without food … on a very bad road and in snowy weather; the men were weakening, the horses were falling from fatigue and starvation, the dilapidated equipment needed repairs, and it was necessary to leave the next morning and follow the division![60]

From Ciudad Rodrigo to Alcántara, the roads faded to mere trails over the barren and rocky ground. The caissons carrying the infantry's ammunition were slowly abandoned as they became mired in the mud or broken. There was very little to eat and barely any shelter for the troops. The rain and snow turned the streams at the bottom of each valley into freezing torrents. In his history of the campaign, Thiébault wrote: 'This army, which had marched with such regularity from Bayonne to Salamanca, fell near Rodrigo into real disorder … The plunder became general, the massacre reciprocal, the situation of the army appalling.'[61]

Capitaine Louis Begos, *adjutant major* of the second battalion of the 2e Régiment Suisse, recalled crossing swollen torrents in deep ravines where the water came up to the men's waists and marching through an almost impenetrable forest:

> This forest presented yet another kind of danger: it was traversed by troops of brigands, who had their hands full with all our stragglers. During the 24 hours that we remained in this abominable place, we suffered every imaginable misery. At every moment we found

59   Plon & Dumaine (eds), *Correspondance*, vol.16, 13351, pp.156–158.
60   J.L. Hulot, *Souvenirs Militaires du Baron Hulot* (Paris: Spectateur Militaire, 1886), p.196.
61   Thiébault, *l'Expédition*, p.22.

unfortunate French soldiers mutilated, with their throats slit; some of them buried alive, after having been completely stripped of their hair. These savage murders, so cowardly, infuriated our men, who could only see the time and the moment to take revenge for such atrocities.[62]

Begos' battalion emerged from the forest and reached a village on the Spanish side of the border with Portugal, with only half their men with the main body.

The Spanish division, commanded by *Teniente General* Juan Caraffa, that was to march with Junot gathered at Alcántara and consisted of eight infantry battalions, four cavalry squadrons, a company of horse artillery, and two companies of sappers and miners.[63] The government's original plan had been to gather Caraffa's force of 17,000 at Ciudad Rodrigo, with another 8,000 under *Teniente General* Marqués Solano mustering at Badajoz and a third force of 6,500 commanded by *Teniente General* Francisco Taranco gathering on Portugal's northern border at Tui.[64] The Spanish had stripped the garrisons of the whole country to furnish enough men to fulfil their Fontainebleau commitments.

The abrupt change in invasion route into Portugal meant that Caraffa had to reverse direction and march to Alcántara with whatever troops he could gather. The lead elements of the Spanish arrived on the 16th after forced marches similar to those suffered by the French and in a similar state. They quickly consumed the food in the town. The area was too impoverished to supply so many troops, and the roads were so bad that carts of supplies could not easily get there.[65] Junot arrived soon after Caraffa, and, together, they managed to gather enough food to supply half a ration of bread, an ox, and two goats per battalion.[66] The meagre provisions were clearly inadequate for an already exhausted army that had yet to face the worst of its march to Lisbon. After marching through constant rain, most of the corps' ammunition had been ruined. Lead and powder were scavenged from the local population. The problem of paper for cartridges was solved by ransacking the archives and library of the Knights of Alcántara, a military religious order, destroying countless ancient manuscripts and books. In two days, 150,000 cartridges were made and distributed to the troops.[67]

Junot's corps was already near breaking point, but, with so little food in the area and the Emperor's orders not to rest until they reached Lisbon, he had little choice but to order the army to continue without waiting for his men to rest and regroup.

Temerity and Indecision

On 20 October, Strangford told Canning that the decree excluding British shipping from Portuguese ports had been written and would be issued on the 30th. HMS *Raven* (16), detached from the squadron off Cadiz, had been stationed off the bar to warn British ships of the impending

---

62   L. Bégos, *Souvenirs des Campagnes du Lieutenant-Colonel Louis Bégos* (Lausanne: Delafontaine, 1859), pp.28–29.
63   Foy, *Invasion*, p.18.
64   Grasset, *Guerre d'Espagne*, vol.1, p.144.
65   Grasset, *Guerre d'Espagne*, vol.1, pp.135–136.
66   Grasset, *Guerre d'Espagne*, vol.1, p.146.
67   Grasset, *Guerre d'Espagne*, vol.1, p.147.

closure. The atmosphere in Lisbon was becoming tense, with handbills circulating calling for the people to rise against a prince who was planning to abandon them and widespread fear that the city would suffer the same fate as Copenhagen.[68] Araújo had sent a note to Strangford a few days previously explaining that Portugal had no choice but to give in to French demands and close the ports to avoid an invasion it could not defeat. He also said that Portugal could not send the fleet to Brazil immediately as it would leave the Tagus undefended. Preparations for embarkation would continue, but the Prince would not abandon his people until the last possible moment.[69] On the 27th, Strangford sent Canning a copy of the edict closing the ports but opined it would not mollify Napoleon and that the Portuguese had been foolish to do it without an assurance that it would.[70] Attempts by Strangford to get the Regent's heir, the Prince of Beira, to be sent to Brazil failed. João was convinced that Britain would not take hostile action against Portugal, but preparations for defending the Tagus continued.[71]

While Strangford concentrated on pressurising the Portuguese court and government, James Gambier – consul general, a former major in the Life Guards, and nephew to the similarly named admiral who commanded at Copenhagen – concentrated on protecting the interests of the British community. On 17 October, a convoy of 64 vessels he had organised sailed from Lisbon with most British residents on board, escorted by HMS *Lively* (38). A similar convoy of 46 vessels sailed from Oporto.[72]

At the beginning of November, the Portuguese ambassador returned from Paris, insisting that Napoleon would destroy the Portuguese monarchy if his demands went unmet. The Regent held a council of state, which agreed unanimously that there was no sign that Napoleon would accept anything less than his original demands and that Portugal should accede to them while attempting to offend Britain as little as possible. However, preparations for embarkation continued in case appeasement did not work; valuables were gathered and placed on board the ships. Strangford told Canning that despite the Prince's 'temerity and indecision' and optimism that he had conceded enough, the evacuation would only occur once French troops entered Portugal.[73]

On 6 November, Strangford reported to Canning that Portuguese batteries had fired upon HMS *Raven*, and, in response, two British privateers captured two Brazil ships. Gambier and Strangford advised all remaining Britons to leave as soon as possible. However, their departure was soon being forced upon them. Araújo told Strangford that while the British representatives were in Lisbon, it would give France and Spain reason to think that a secret arrangement was in place between Britain and Portugal. Strangford replied that he did not feel obliged to help Portugal give in to France by leaving voluntarily. Three days later, on 9 November, orders were given for the seizure of British property and the prevention of any Briton leaving Portugal. Strangford demanded that the *Raven* be allowed into the Tagus to take him and Gambier aboard. The next day, they got their passports and permission for the *Raven* to enter the port, but the weather had forced the sloop out to sea. Despite everything, Strangford was still optimistic that the secret convention would be implemented and the Prince would seek British protection and leave Lisbon.[74]

---

68 TNA: FO 63/56: Strangford to Canning, 20 October 1807.
69 TNA: FO 63/56: Araújo to Strangford, 17 October 1807.
70 TNA: FO 63/56: Strangford to Canning, 27 October 1807. Edict closing ports, 20 October 1807
71 TNA: FO 63/56: Strangford to Canning, 28 October 1807.
72 Robson, *South America*, p.147.
73 TNA: FO 63/56: Strangford to Canning, 2 November 1807.
74 TNA: FO 63/56: Strangford to Canning, 6, 9 & 10 November 1807.

The Russian Squadron

The threat posed to British interests by a French occupation of Lisbon was about to be greatly increased. Russian *Vitse-admiral* Dmitry Nikolaevich Senyavin had been operating in the Mediterranean since late 1805. His squadron had fought the French at Cattaro and Ragusa in 1806, and then clashed with the Ottomans at Lemnos and blockaded the Dardanelles. At one point he also proposed a joint operation with a Royal Navy squadron under Vice Admiral Sir John Duckworth.[75] However, following the agreement between Napoleon and Tsar Alexander at Tilsit, Senyavin had been ordered to the Baltic. He sailed from Corfu in late October and entered the Atlantic. There his ships were caught in a severe westerly gale.[76] Between 8 and 12 November, nine ships of the line and two frigates of the squadron were forced to take shelter in the Tagus.[77]

Prince João welcomed the Russian ships, even though their numbers exceeded the limit of warships of other nations that were allowed into Lisbon's harbour. A limit that had been set to maintain Portugal's neutrality. What João, Senyavin, and Smith in the approaching British squadron, did not know was that Alexander had declared war on Britain on 26 October. The addition of that many ships to the already powerful Portuguese fleet had the potential to be a serious threat to Britain and complicated the strategic situation. For the moment though, Senyavin set about repairing his damaged ships and establishing cordial relations with the authorities.

Table 3. *Vitse-admiral* Senyavin's squadron

Ship	Guns	
Tverdoi	80	Vice Admiral Senavien/Captain Maleef
Silnoi	80	Captain Maligin (acting)
Raphael	80	Captain Bourtchensky (acting)
Mostuoi	74	Captain Crowe
Elene	74	Captain Bouitchensky
Jaroslaw	74	
Selaphael	74	Captain Rojnoff
Ratvisan	64	Rear Admiral Greig Captain Artishiff
Skoroi	80	Captain Skeltin
Venus	44	
Kilduine	32	
Ships expected from Gibraltar		
Seid el Badar	80	Captain Bailie (Turkish prize)
St Peter	74	Commodore Baratnisky
Orel	80	Captain Bouitchensky
Mosco	74	Captain Etssen
Leochy	36	(Frigate)
Spitzbergen	20	(Sloop)

Source: TNA: ADM 1/19, List of the Russian Squadron now at Anchor in the River Tagus from a most authentic source, 17 November 1807. All spellings as per the original.

---

75   Mikaberidze, *Napoleonic Wars*, pp.401–402.
76   D.D. Horward, 'Portugal and the Anglo-Russian Naval Crisis (1808)', *Naval War College Review*, vol.34, no.3 (May–June 1981), p.48.
77   TNA: ADM 1/19: Smith to Wellesey-Pole, 18 November 1807.

Senyavin was born in 1763 to a noble family near Kaluga, southeast of Moscow. He became a naval cadet in 1778 and visited Portugal as a midshipman in 1780. He took up his first command in 1786 and fought in the Turks, 1788–1791. He was back in the Mediterranean in 1798–1799 and then returned to Russia to become commandant of the port of Kherson. He was then promoted to *kontr-admiral* and given the command of the port of Reval (now Tallinn), before being promoted again and given the command of the Mediterranean squadron.[78] Vice Admiral Collingwood had a far better opinion of Senyavin than he did of Smith: 'Admiral Sinavin and I were great friends: he seemed to like me, and I had a kind of regard for him, because he professed to hate the French.'[79] There were strong links between the British and Russian navies at the time as many Royal Navy officers chose to enter Russian service rather than remain on half-pay. Indeed, Senyavin's squadron contained several British officers, and his second in command, *kontr-admiral* Alexei Samuelovich Greig, was the son of a Scottish officer.

Lord Strangford immediately informed Canning of the arrival of the first Russian ships on 10 November.[80] On the 17th he told London that the frigate *Venus* was to sail to Gibraltar, where some of the squadron had briefly stopped, with orders for more vessels to join Senyavin in Lisbon. The *Venus* did not return, and the other six Russian ships expected did not enter the Tagus. Strangford also sent Canning copies of letters from Senyavin to the Russian minister in Lisbon. The Russians planned to winter at Lisbon as many of the ships were in a poor state and needed repairs and provisions. Strangford, wrongly, believed that the arrival of the Russian squadron was no mere accident and that it was part of a plot hatched by the French. He added that, 'Some late dispatches from the Portuguese minister at Petersbourg to M. d'Arujo, having fallen into my hands, I thought it my duty to make myself master of their contents, and being in possession of many of the cyphers belonging to their cabinet I succeeded in making them out.' Portugal had asked Russia for support in persuading Napoleon not to invade, and Alexander had agreed to do what he could. Strangford warned Canning that many of the deciphered dispatches indicated 'ill-will' on the part of Russia towards Britain.[81]

When Napoleon learned of the Russian squadron's arrival in Lisbon he was certainly eager to take advantage of its presence and wrote to Alexander on 7 December:

> Admiral Siniavin's squadron has arrived in Lisbon; fortunately my troops should be there by now. It would be good for Your Majesty to give authority to Count Tolstoy [the Russian ambassador in Paris] over this squadron and the troops, so that, when the opportunity to employ them arrives, we can do so without waiting for new directions from St Petersburg.[82]

---

78   A. Mikaberidze, *The Russian Officer Corps in the Revolutionary and Napoleonic Wars* (New York: Savas Beatie, 2005), p.356.

79   G.L. Newnham Collingwood, *A Selection from the Public and Private Correspondence of Vice Admiral Lord Collingwood* (London: Ridgway, 1828), p.279.

80   TNA: FO 63/56: Strangford to Canning, 10 November 1807.

81   TNA: FO 63/56: Strangford to Canning, 17 November 1807.

82   Plon & Dumaine (eds), *Correspondance*, vol.16, 13383, p.187.

Across the Border

On 17 November, Junot issued a proclamation to the Portuguese people:

> Inhabitants of the kingdom of Portugal, a French army is about to enter your country; it comes to emancipate you from English dominion, and makes forced marches that it may save your beautiful city of Lisbon from the fate of Copenhagen. This time the hopes of the perfidious English government will be deceived … Your Prince declares war against England; we make therefore common cause. Peaceable inhabitants of the country, fear nothing! My army is as well disciplined as it is brave. I will answer on my honour for its good conduct. Let it find the welcome which is due to the soldiers of the Great Napoleon; let it find, as it has a right to expect, the provisions which are needful.[83]

However, following that gracious opening, Junot went on to say that if any Portuguese who were not soldiers took up arms against the French, they would be shot. The same fate awaited anyone urging others to take up arms: their towns or villages would be fined and hostages taken, and the first place that resisted would be burnt to the ground.

The next day, the voltigeurs of the 70e Ligne occupied the village of Segura, just across the border. On the 19th, the rest of the advance guard crossed into Portugal, commanded by *général de brigade* Antoine Maurin. It consisted of the two battalions of the 70e Ligne and, from the Spanish army, the Húsares de María Luisa and two companies of sappers from the Regimiento Real de Zapadores y Miradores.[84] They marched to Rosmaninhal, due west across the border, and then to Castelo Branco. On the 20th, the rest of the 1er Division followed, with the other divisions taking slightly different routes while much of the artillery lagged behind.[85]

Junot had no accurate map of the Portuguese side of the border and could not find a local guide.[86] The area they were about to march through was wilder and even more barren than the Sierra de Gata. The route crossed five significant tributaries of the Tagus and many smaller rivers and streams, all cutting through the mountains in deep ravines. Each fast-flowing, freezing-cold river would have to be forded at the height of the rainy season. Such conditions were difficult enough for infantry, but it was even more challenging for *capitaine* Hulot and his artillery. The sides of the river valleys were so steep and the paths so narrow that steps had to be cut into the rocks for the horses, and the guns lowered to the bottom with ropes.[87]

Capitaine Bleuler of the 4e Régiment Suisse noted in his diary that his unit had to wade through rivers '10 to 20 times a day'.[88] As the troops progressed deeper into Portugal, discipline began to falter as they were pushed beyond their limits. The columns plundered the few homes they encountered. Junot was forced to chastise Maurin: 'Everywhere I have received complaints against your column; they complain particularly that we have … taken a lot of cattle. I do not like this way of

---

83   R. Southey, *History of the Peninsular War* (London: Murray, 1828) vol.1, pp.100–101.
84   Foy, *Invasion*, p.27.
85   Grasset, *Guerre d'Espagne*, vol.1, pp.150–151.
86   Sepulveda, *Historia*, vol.XII, p.108.
87   Hulot, *Souvenirs*, pp.210–211.
88   A. Maag, *Geschichte der Schweizertruppen im Kriege Napoleons I in Spanien und Portugal* (1807-1814) (Biel: Kuhn, 1892), vol.1, pp.107–108.

French troops on the march to Lisbon. (From *The Life of Napoleon Bonaparte*, by William Milligan Sloane)

waging war.'[89] He also berated him that the sappers had done nothing to improve the roads for the subsequent columns and that no provisions had been gathered together in depots. The lack of provisions was hardly Maurin's fault as there were simply none to be had. *Maréchal des logis chef* Jean-Auguste Oyon of the 4e Dragons recalled crossing into Portugal and the extremities that the troops had to resort to:

> The manners of the inhabitants are more and more revolting; we only communicate with them by mistreating them; they yield only to force what they owed to humanity and to the orders of their government; their conduct towards us has made us wicked and demanding; we no longer ask; we take with brutality; discipline is lost; it will not be able to return until we have resumed ordinary life.[90]

At Sobreira Formosa, Junot was so exhausted that Thiébault had to help him to his bed, where he stayed while Delaborde and Thiébault attempted to rally and reorganise the column.[91] The situation was even worse in the 2e and 3e Divisions, made up of raw recruits unseasoned to campaigning.

89 Grasset, *Guerre d'Espagne*, vol.1, p.152.
90 J.A. Oyon, *Campagnes et Souvenirs de Maréchal de Logis Jean-Auguste Oyon* (Wagram Press, Kindle Edition), Kindle Location 1696.
91 Thiébault, *Mémoires*, vol.IV, p.141.

When the troops arrived at Castelo Branco on 21 November, the town's bakeries were put to work baking bread for the troops, but they had to be guarded to prevent theft. Not enough bread could be baked or food found, so widespread looting broke out. Junot had to have two soldiers caught pillaging shot, which almost caused a mutiny.[92]

For the cavalry, the march to Abrantes pushed the men and the horses beyond their limits, as Jean-Auguste Oyon recalled:

> Here our sufferings redouble; killings are on the rise; hunger and fatigue greatly increase our losses; we are exhausted! In the depths, always torrents to cross; infantry and cavalry leave their men and horses there; the artillery can no longer follow, it has lost its entire train; we are constantly climbing steep mountains, by paths which only goats frequent … When a horse stumbles, it rolls with its rider into abysses from which they can never come out.[93]

Junot arrived at Rosmaninhal on 21 November and, after what he had seen on the march, ordered his deputy chief of staff, *adjutant commandant* François Bagnéris, to return to Zarza la Mayor to ensure rations were gathered for the stragglers.

Louis Begos, *adjutant major* of the second battalion of the 2e Régiment Suisse in the 2e Division, and escorting the artillery, recalled how much worse the march got after Castelo Branco. Some days, they managed to march only seven or eight miles. There was too little food and forage, and the villages were deserted. One day, they managed to gather 'two goats for every three hundred men and twenty-five chestnuts a day for each man, with a quarter of a pound of bread and a pint of wine.'[94] As the Swiss were marching through territory already picked clean by other troops, Begos had to lead foraging expeditions further from the route of march, one of which yielded an ox, six sheep and some bread from a village that was only grateful that the troops did not take everything. They found plenty of beehives and berries in the woods, but honey and fruit could not sustain the troops for long. At another village, they had to resort to firing warning musket shots to convince a crowd of angry Portuguese to sell them a sufficient quantity of sheep, pigs, chickens, flour and bread for the battalion.[95]

Thiébault provides distances for each stage of the appalling route from Alcántara to Abrantes:

Alcántara to Rosmaninhal	32 miles
Rosmaninhal to Castelo Branco	37 miles
Castelo Branco to Sobreira	37 miles
Sobreira to Cortisada	16 miles
Cortisada to São Domingos	16 miles
São Domingos to Abrantes	13 miles[96]

The French staggered into Abrantes on 24 November and finally managed to get some provisions. Junot wrote to Napoleon from the town on the 25th:

---

92   Grasset, *Guerre d'Espagne*, vol.1, p.154.
93   Oyon, *Campagnes*, Kindle Location 1704.
94   Begos, *Souvenirs*, pp.33–34.
95   Begos, *Souvenirs*, pp.35–36.
96   Thiébault, *l'Expédition*, p.49. Thiébault uses lieues de Poste, which have been converted to miles (2.664 miles per lieue) and rounded.

After excessively difficult marches in a region with no resources and through dreadful paths, crossed at every step by torrents, and without having received a ration of bread from Alcantara, my first two divisions finally arrived this morning in Abrantes; but leaving behind them about 1,200 men … the troops are so fatigued, that it is not possible for them to go further without rest and I have decided to give them a stay here. This town has fewer resources than I thought it would have; nevertheless I will be able to give them meat, vegetables, wine and a little bread, which will help them to recover their strength.[97]

Junot admitted that he had lost 'a few men through fatigue, and a few others, stragglers and looters, will have been murdered by the inhabitants', perhaps understating his losses. He was also highly critical of the Spanish troops; 'it is impossible to see anything more badly conducted, more badly disciplined, and of less value. General Caraffa, who commands the Division, is a brave man, but the individual officers are worthless and do not do their duty'.[98] Thiébault estimated that Caraffa's division lost 1,700–1,800 men to starvation, fatigue, drowning, or falls in the final stages of the march.[99] Junot also squarely blamed the Spanish for not providing enough rations for his troops from Salamanca onwards.

Oyon of the 4e Dragons recalled the relief of reaching Abrantes:

Here the scene changes completely: two days ago we were still in the rains and hurricanes, suffocating in the ravines or rushing from the top of the mountains, surrounded by frightful abysses, in the middle of an arid and wild nature. Today we walk on level ground, our paths have become passable; the weather is calm, the sky cloudless, the air soft and pure: I would even say sweet. We leave the snow behind us; we will no longer feel the cold or the frost.[100]

The Language of Menace

Smith's squadron sighted the Spanish coast on 14 November and then sailed south toward Portugal, approaching Oporto on the 15th and Lisbon the day after. Unfortunately, with a strong westerly wind blowing into the Tagus, Smith's large ships-of-the-line could not get close to the shore, and several had their yards and masts damaged by the gales.[101] Portuguese fishermen told Smith that the port was closed to the British.[102]

On 17 November, Smith managed to get a fishing boat to take his secretary, a former artist named Richard Speare, into Lisbon:

I immediately sent my secretary with a letter to Lord Strangford notifying my arrival off the port, the object of my coming and my readiness to cooperate with his Lordship in conformity to my instructions, giving my secretary orders to land, and go directly up to

97   Sepulveda, *Historia*, vol.XII, p.108.
98   Sepulveda, *Historia*, vol.XII, p.109.
99   Thiébault, *Mémoires*, vol.IV, p.139.
100   Oyon, *Campagnes*, Kindle Location 1903.
101   Light, *Empire*, pp.49–51.
102   O'Neil, *Account*, p.5

his Lordship's residence with my letter without asking, or waiting to be asked questions on the way which he effected without interruption in very blowing weather on the morning of yesterday (the 17th). His arrival proved to be very opportune as in the course of that night (the 17th) His Majesty's Minister … received a letter from the Portuguese Minister M. d'Araujo urging his immediate departure 'by land or sea' … In consequence … his Lordship decided to come to His Majesty's Squadron and he is now safely on board the London as also the archives of the delegation, having quitted the Tagus in a fishing boat and reached the Active privateer brig stationed outside of the bar by Mr. Gambier for the purpose of warning British vessels or any other contingency.

Consul James Gambier had stayed in Lisbon to try and secure the release of some British subjects. After relaying reports that France and Spain had declared war on Portugal 'about the 24th of October' and that Junot had reached Salamanca, Smith told the Admiralty of the Russian squadron's arrival, which he said had 'the known intention of wintering in that port', and that he was, 'naturally anxious for precise instructions how to act towards the Russian ships, it being considered not unlikely that they may combine with the Portuguese navy and cooperate with it in endeavouring to oppose His Majesty's forces in their efforts to attain the objects for which they were sent hither.'[103]

On 20 November, Smith transferred his flag along with his baggage and Strangford to the *Hibernia*, which had recently arrived, as had the 80-gun *Foudroyant*. On the same day, Strangford suggested to Smith that, given the seizure of British property and detention of British subjects, the squadron began a blockade of the Tagus.[104] Strangford thought the Regent's concessions would almost certainly not prevent France and Spain from invading and that the Portuguese should be told that if any enemy troops did enter the country, then the blockade would be extended from just war matériel to the food imports that Lisbon depended upon. This would cause immediate hardship, but Strangford hoped that João 'will doubtless consider that as the Protection of Great Britain has not been lightly offered so ought it not to be rashly rejected for ever.'[105] Strangford wrote to Canning on the same day, informing him of the decision to institute a blockade and hoping he had not overstepped his authority.[106] Unbeknownst to him, he was only pre-empting orders already on their way from London.

One of the King's Messengers, Charles Sylvester, was on board the *Confiance* (22) with dispatches from Canning and the Admiralty and a copy of the secret convention of 22 October. The sloop was sailing ahead of two more 74s, *Plantagenet* and *Conqueror*, and approached the bar of the Tagus on the 21st. The Portuguese batteries opened fire, and the *Confiance*'s captain, Commander James Yeo, moved out of range to pursue two vessels, one of which turned out to be a brig with British subjects and Gambier on board.[107]

Sunday, 22 November, was a busy day for Smith. His admiral's journal records receiving two letters from Strangford, the first announcing the necessity of a blockade and the second that 'the time is arrived for measures of hostility against Portugal'. His journal also notes the receipt of 'Most Secret orders from their Lordships grounded on the shutting of the Ports of Portugal', dated

---

103   TNA: ADM 1/19: Smith to Wellesley-Pole, 18 November 1807.
104   TNA: ADM 1/19: Strangford to Smith, 20 November 1807.
105   TNA: ADM 1/19: Strangford to Smith, 20 November 1807.
106   TNA: FO 63/56: Strangford to Canning, 20 November 1807.
107   TNA: ADM 51/1966: *Confiance* log, 21 November 1807.

12 November. He also received orders to take the newly arrived ships under his command. His out-letters included one to the newly appointed agent for prisoners of war, John Bell, directing him to 'require the release of British subjects detained', especially the women and children. He also informed all consuls in Lisbon of the blockade, told Araújo of it, and relayed a request from Strangford for a meeting with the Prince.[108]

Smith's reply to his orders from the Admiralty, dated 22 November, opened with him stating that he was: 'proceeding in concert with Lord Viscount Strangford'. Once the westerly wind abated, a flag of truce would go in, and the blockade would be rendered more closely. Smith also requested more frigates as the tides and wind made getting near the bar hazardous for his larger ships. He then said: 'I am decidedly of opinion that the Portuguese fleet is quite out of reach of any attack to be made by a fleet *alone* however superior in number and efficiency.' The fleet would be vulnerable to crossfire from the forts which lined the river and could not anchor out of cannon shot. A combined sea and land operation was the only option. The army could secure forts and let the fleet sail out again with the captured Portuguese ships. He was basing this option, he said, on his visit some years earlier and information from Gambier, 'who appears to have been very observing and indefatigable in the collection of it'. He then outlined, in detail, why the prevailing winds and the coast made enforcing a blockade very difficult and that there was little hope of maintaining one during the winter without considerable risk to the ships. This meant, in his opinion:

> … devoting an adequate land force immediately, to the object in question and thus to finish the affair at once. The presence of a British Army equal in numbers to the French but superior in discipline and prowess, drawing its resources from a navigable river would certainly more than counterbalance the present paramount influence of Bonaparte and enable to British Plenipotentiary to resume that which he had had hitherto. Fear in one party and corruption in another seem to have urged and forced the councils of the Prince Regent (most unwillingly on his part) to his present fatal line of Policy.[109]

The dispatch ended with, 'Lord Strangford keeps the door of negotiation open by offering to land for the sake of another conference which however we intend shall not admit of a general truce to paralyse our efforts and operations, or any thing short of the objects specified in our instructions.'

Strangford's reply to Canning, dated 24 November, expressed his relief about getting orders to implement a blockade when he was already on the verge of doing so. Setúbal had been included in the blockade, on Strangford's authority, and ships had begun to be intercepted. He told Canning that the blockade had put Lisbon into a state of 'great alarm and distress.' Strangford concurred with Smith's opinion that troops would be needed before any attempt was made to force the Tagus. He thought a force of 9,000–10,000 would be sufficient, as long as the Russians remained neutral, and so had 'recommended to Sir Sidney Smith to send without delay for the forces under the command of Genl. Moore, to be united to them which are to be sent from England'. He also told Canning that Smith was concerned about the safety of transports on the Portuguese coast, so he planned to use whichever body of troops arrived first to seize a favourable port or anchorage, possibly Peniche, until joined by the other body. HMS *Redwing* (16) had come from Cadiz in response to Strangford's request for a ship to take him from Lisbon and brought the news that, as of the 18th, Moore had

---

108 TNA: ADM 50/50: 22 November 1807.
109 TNA: ADM 1/19: Smith to Wellesley Pole, 22 November 1807.

not yet arrived at Gibraltar. He then wrote, 'The Redwing is to return immediately to her station charged with my dispatches to Genl. Moore.'[110] The *Redwing* then spent several days patrolling 10–30 miles off the Rock of Lisbon, presumably in the hope of intercepting Moore on his way to Britain.[111]

The weather continued to be so bad that it was not until the 26th that Smith could close with the *Trafalgar* privateer to give them the dispatches to take back to Britain. He could not spare any of his smaller naval vessels. By that date, however, he could add in a postscript that *Confiance* had sailed into the Tagus under a flag of truce on the 24th with his note for Araújo and notification of the blockade and had briefly been fired upon by mistake.[112]

Smith's letter to Araújo, dated the 22nd, informing him of the blockade was a mix of regret and threat. He said the lack of Portuguese preparations to conform to the secret convention meant he had no choice but to blockade the port. The only way it could be lifted was by the surrender of the Portuguese fleet, which would then be returned after the war. He then continued:

> I am desirous from due respect to his Royal Highness's feelings and situation to avoid the language of menace, indeed while that of France as well as its conduct is of the most menacing description tending to nothing less than the subjugation of the European Territory of the ancient Royal House of Braganza, it is scarcely necessary to say that the British Fleet and Army destined as it is to counteract the views and operations of our enemies when and wheresoever to be found cannot have been assembled for the mere purpose of demonstration or simple blockade and I trust it will be admitted and believed that my government requires and expects something more from such a force and my humble but earnest endeavours than mere passive service … I will however still hope that the recent example of Copenhagen will operate on the reasonable and dispassionate part of the Prince Regent's council and prevent Lisbon becoming the theatre of similar scenes of horror with the additional evils of famine insurrection and the presence of a foreign permanent garrison.[113]

Smith obviously did not try that hard to 'avoid the language of menace', and the Portuguese government must have been in no doubt that they were between the hammer of the Royal Navy and the anvil of the French army. The letter ended with the offer of Lord Strangford landing under a flag of truce to talk face-to-face with João. The squadron immediately began to enforce the blockade, boarding neutral or friendly vessels to warn them off (including some late arrivals from the Russian squadron) and taking Portuguese ships as prizes.[114]

Smith and Strangford knew the preparations the Portuguese were making to defend Lisbon, not against the French but from the Royal Navy. The British consul, James Gambier, had written a lengthy memorandum on 20 October regarding the distribution of the Portuguese forces around Lisbon, a copy of which was sent to Sir John Moore. Gambier details the three corps, each of 6,000 men, which were to garrison Lisbon, the forts on the Tagus, and the surrounding coast. He then stated: 'The force thus distributed is evidently intended to defend any attack which may be made

110 TNA: FO 63/56: Strangford to Canning, 24 November 1807.
111 TNA: ADM 51/1715: *Redwing* log, 24–30 November 1807.
112 TNA: ADM 51/1966: *Confiance* log, 24-26 November 1807.
113 TNA: ADM 1/19 Smith to Araújo, 22 November 1807.
114 Light, *Empire*, p.63.

from the sea and not for the purpose of opposing the advance of the French or Spanish troops on the Frontiers.'[115] As confirmation, Gambier also reported that Gomes Freire de Andrade, a general commanding one of the three corps, had asked Araújo specifically if the object was to defend the port or the country and had been told it was the port. Gambier wrote another memorandum on 29 October with the latest troop movements and said three 'corps of observation' would be formed to watch the Spanish border.[116] It was, of course, far too little and far too late.

The Approach to Lisbon

While most of Junot's corps enjoyed a brief rest at Abrantes, at Tomar, just 20 miles away, there was a Portuguese army regiment (the Regimento de Infantaria n.º 18, 2º Porto, according to Junot), which given the state of the French, may have proved a serious threat, but Junot sent a letter demanding the commander provide rations for the French and the *coronel*, lacking any instructions from Lisbon, acquiesced.[117]

Junot also sent a friendly letter to Araújo, complaining that supplies had not been organised for his corps and pointing out that his men had not yet fired a shot and it would be a shame if they were forced to do so.[118] The brigades that slowly arrived in Abrantes over the next few days were in no fit state to fight anyone. They were emaciated, covered in mud, and ravaged by fevers. Their uniforms were in tatters, they were shod with goat skins or rags, and their baggage had been abandoned in the mountains. Junot created depots and hospitals in Castelo Branco and Abrantes to gather provisions and cater for the many sick. The French also went door-to-door in Abrantes, confiscating shoes for the troops. They seized 4,000 pairs and requisitioned another 10,000 new pairs.[119]

Junot could not afford to wait for his men to fully recover if he was going to meet Napoleon's schedule for his arrival in Lisbon. The advanced guard was reinforced with Spanish dragoons and the grenadiers and voltigeurs of the 1er and 2e Divisions, formed into four battalions. They marched at noon on the 26th, followed by the first two divisions the day after, the 3e after a rest day, and then the cavalry after that. The guns and baggage would travel on the Tagus by barge. Caraffa's Spanish division marched to Tomar, Leiria and then Oporto. The 70e Ligne and Spanish sappers had already been sent on to Punhete (now Constância) to protect the construction of a bridge over the Zezere river. Junot hoped to cross on the evening of the 26th, but he was told by *colonel* Charles Vincent, his chief engineer, that the river had risen 11 feet in less than an hour and swept half the bridge away.[120]

The first troops attempted to cross the Zezere in boats the next morning but were swept down to the Tagus by the current. Junot and Thiébault's boat made it across but was overturned several feet from the bank. The rest of the troops had to wait until the river went down. An envoy from the Portuguese government, Oliveira de Barreto, greeted the French general with a reply to his letter. Junot was assured of Portugal's friendship, and it was only requested that Lisbon be allowed to

115 TNA: ADM 1/19: Distribution of the Portuguese Military Force, 20 October 1807. The rear of the document states explicitly that a copy was sent to Moore, but does not say how.
116 TNA: ADM 1/19: Memorandum of the Portuguese Military Force, 29 October 1807.
117 Sepulveda, *Historia*, vol.XII, p.109.
118 Grasset, *Guerre d'Espagne*, vol.1, p.166.
119 Thiébault, *l'Expédition*, p.53.
120 Grasset, *Guerre d'Espagne*, vol.1, p.169.

defend itself against the British. Barreto also let slip that everything was ready for Prince João and the government to sail for Brazil.[121] Barreto's news was confirmed by François-Antonie Hermann, the French consul-general, who had also travelled from Lisbon to meet the French troops. Junot sent both men back to Lisbon; Barreto with a letter for João and Hermann with instructions to try and delay João's departure.[122] Junot would have to get to Lisbon quickly to prevent João and the Portuguese fleet from slipping through his fingers.

The Embarkation

Prince João's decision to embark had been taken on 24 November at a state council meeting, as soon as the Portuguese government learned of Junot's arrival at Abrantes.[123] The meeting also lifted the closure of the ports to British shipping and established a council of regency to rule Portugal when João left. On the 26th, João issued a proclamation to inform his people of his decision:

> Having sought by all possible means to preserve the neutrality … I see that troops of the Emperor of the French and the King of Italy, whom I had united with on the Continent, marching through the interior of my Kingdom, persuading me not to be troubled any longer; and that they are on their way to this Capital: And wanting to avoid the disastrous consequences that could follow from a defence, which would be more harmful than useful, serving only to shed blood to the detriment of humanity, and capable of further igniting the discord of troops that have passed through this kingdom, with the promise of not committing the slightest hostility; knowing full well that they are directed particularly against my Royal Person, and that my loyal subjects will be less disturbed if I leave this kingdom: I have resolved, for the benefit of my subjects, to travel with the Queen, my lady and mother, and with the whole Royal Family to the Americas, and to establish myself in the city of Rio de Janeiro until a general peace.[124]

Araújo had written to Strangford on the 25th that the Prince would meet with him, that the royal family would sail to Brazil, and that the French had arrived at Abrantes. The *Confiance* left Lisbon on the 26th with the replies and arrived back with the squadron on the morning of the 27th. Yeo hove to near the *Hibernia* and sent a boat across to the flagship and awaited orders while the various letters were digested.

With permission granted and much to discuss with the Portuguese government, Strangford sailed back to Lisbon in the *Confiance* early in the afternoon of the same day. Smith's nephew, Lieutenant Charles Thurlow Smith, went as well as signal officer. Struggling against wind and tide, the sloop had to anchor just inside the bar at the entrance to the Tagus, which meant that Strangford had to make his way overland into Lisbon and only arrived in the early evening of the 28th.[125] Once in the city, Strangford found the embarkation already well underway:

121 Grasset, *Guerre d'Espagne*, vol.1, p.170.
122 Sigler, *Thiébault*, p.185.
123 Light, *Empire*, p.205.
124 Sepulveda, *Historia*, vol.XVII, p.108.
125 TNA: ADM 51/1966: *Confiance* log, 27–28 November 1807.

Lisbon was in a state of sullen discontent, too dreadful to be described. Bodies of armed and unknown persons were seen roaming the streets, in utter silence, without any lawful or obvious purpose in view; and every thing seemed to indicate that the departure of the Prince, if not instantly effected, would be delayed by popular tumults, until rendered impracticable by the actual arrival of the French.[126]

Strangford went to Araújo's house but found it barricaded and was told he was already on one of the ships. Eventually, he found him on the *Medusa* and had a long conversation with him. Araújo gave him more detail on the discussions in the council of state and the decision to leave. However, as Strangford told Canning, the minister also said that:

… the decree had not yet been promulgated, since HRH still entrained a hope that matters might be accommodated.
This observation made me tremble for the success of the project, which appeared to me to be in danger of failure, if delayed for a single moment.
I took therefore the immediate resolution of consulting, not the precise tenor of the last instructions, but the known wishes of His Majesty's Government, and I instantly wrote a letter to the Prince Regent, offering him in the name of His Majesty, protection, assistance and friendship; forgiveness of those acts of hostility, to which he had been unwillingly compelled, and promises of succour and support for the future, but naming as the price of those advantages his departure for the Brazils in the space of two hours from the receipt of my letter.[127]

Strangford sent word to Smith that the articles of the secret convention were being executed so he could revert to the original purpose of his squadron and come nearer to the Tagus but not pass the forts. He also told him that the French were just nine leagues (27 miles) from Lisbon.[128] Strangford then resolved to see the Prince as soon as he could:

I saw that not a moment was to be lost, and that my duty was to destroy in HRH's mind all hopes of accommodating matters with the invaders of his country, to terrify him with dark and gloomy descriptions of the state of the capital which I had just left, and then dazzle him suddenly with the brilliant prospects before him, to direct all his fears to a French Army and all his hopes to an English fleet…[129]

Meanwhile, Smith was so impatient for news that he sent a Spanish lugger that had been taken as a prize into the Tagus. It took a letter to Strangford to send word via Smith's nephew, who could use any mast to relay a signal, and new orders for Yeo of the *Confiance*. To Strangford, he wrote:

I need not tell you how impatient I am to have a word or sign from you. The weather is settling which will I hope, allow me to come nearer in; pray hasten pilots to the ships; I

126 TNA: FO 63/56: Strangford to Canning, 2 December 1807.
127 TNA: FO 63/56: Strangford to Canning, 2 December 1807.
128 TNA: ADM 1/19: Strangford to Smith, 28 November 1807.
129 TNA: FO 63/56: Strangford to Canning, 2 December 1807.

have authorised Captain Yeo, in case his flag of truce is no longer required for its original use, to haul it down & act against the French; to immediately occupy the batteries within his reach that are tenable. He is at any rate to gain possession of Bugio…[130]

Smith also sent a note to Araújo, which he left unsealed so Strangford could read it, telling the diplomat that 'it was calculated for wavering politicians'. Smith still feared that the Prince might give in to Junot. The letter included unrealistic schemes such as the Prince declaring a levée en masse and trying to defend Lisbon, the moment for which had long since passed. Smith also added, 'This state of suspense is unbearable.'[131] Strangford quickly replied to Smith, saying that whilst the Portuguese would not give up the forts, orders had been given to treat the British ships as friendly, and the powder had been removed from the batteries. He also asked Smith to sail closer to the mouth of the Tagus.

Strangford returned to the *Confiance* at 8:00 a.m. on the 29th, but it is unclear when he met with Prince João on the *Principe Real*. The log of the *Confiance* records his return, the sending of an officer in a fishing boat to Smith, weighing anchor at 9:30 a.m., the sailing of the Portuguese ships, and even the flogging of two men with 18 lashes each for neglect of duty, but not when Strangford left again.[132] In two letters to Canning, he stated that he crossed the bar at the mouth of the Tagus with the Prince, but he does not say how or when he went on board.[133] A copy of an extract from a letter from Lieutenant Charles Thurlow Smith to his father stated that 'At 8 in the morning we came away again. Lord Strangford found the Prince on board ship. I followed him out in the boat.'[134] Strangford later wrote of his meeting with the prince:

> I had, a long and a most confidential interview with His Royal Highness. I found Him, as I expected, under considerable apprehensions as to the nature of His situation with regard to His Majesty [King George III]; but 'fully determined' (I use his own words) 'to throw Himself on His Majesty's forgiveness, and, at all events, to prefer the noble enmity of England to the false and insidious friendship of France.' His resolution to depart was irrevocably taken. It required no confirmation from me.[135]

However, Araújo had already refused permission to occupy the forts because he feared subsequent retribution by the French. The Prince had refused permission also, as it was expected that Smith would only get Strangford's letter once the fleet had already weighed, so there was no need for the British squadron to enter the Tagus and, hence, no need for them to occupy the forts.[136] Strangford warned Smith against any action to occupy the forts or doing anything else that could complicate matters:

> It is utterly inexpedient to throw any unnecessary difficulties in the way of H.R.H.'s depar-
> ture, or to raise any questions that may be avoided, for I am convinced that so great is the

130   The British Library (BL): Add Mss 46837: Smith to Strangford, 28 December 1807.
131   BL: Add Ms 46837: Smith to Strangford, 28 November 1807.
132   Light, *Empire*, pp.69-70.
133   TNA: FO 63/56: Strangford to Canning, 29 & 30 November/2 December 1807.
134   BL: Add Ms 46837: Smith to father, 7 December 1807.
135   P. Strangford, *Observations on Some Passages in Lieut-Col Napier's History of the Peninsular War* (London: Murray, 1828), p.22.
136   Light, *Empire*, p.69; TNA: FO 63/56: Strangford to Smith, 28 November 1807.

The Embarkation of the Portuguese Royal Family. (Biblioteca Nacional de Portugal)

discontent of the People, and so strong the consequent alarm of H.R.H. that all depends on the support and encouragement which H.R.H. may receive from us, and of which I have given him the most frank and unequivocal assurance.[137]

The embarkation had begun on the morning of 27 November at Belem. The wide dockside between the convent and the river was filled with carts, baggage and anxious crowds. Prince João arrived in his carriage from the Adjuda palace before the troops who were meant to see him safely onto a boat arrived. He had to gently force himself through the throng to reach the steps leading to the water's edge. Historian Robert Southey later wrote: 'He was pale and trembling, and his face was bathed in tears. The multitude forgot for a moment their own condition in commiseration for his; they wept also, and followed him, as the boat pushed off, with their blessings.'[138]

More of the royal family then arrived from the palace at Queluz, including the Queen, who had not been seen in public for 16 years. The family members were split up between the various ships in case any disaster should befall the fleet.

The scenes on the dock became chaotic as more and more of the aristocrats, officials, and wealthier inhabitants tried to get berths on the ships. Families became separated, with some members left behind and others only finding out their missing relatives had been embarked once

137 TNA: ADM 1/19: Strangford to Smith, 28 November 1807.
138 Southey, *History*, vol.I, p.110.

the fleet arrived in Brazil.[139] Space was limited. Many took far too much baggage; Araújo took 37 cases of papers, books and possessions with him.[140] The envoy from Junot, Hermann, with Barreto, arrived on the evening of the 27th with placatory messages, but the embarkation continued, and orders were given to spike the guns in the forts along the river.

A strong westerly wind prevented the fleet from sailing until the 29th. The fleet commander was *Vice-almirante* Manuel da Cunha Souto Maior, and it consisted of eight ships-of-the-line, four frigates, three brigs and a schooner of the Portuguese navy,[141] plus around 20–30 merchantmen. Estimates put the number of people embarked at up to 15,000, and the fleet carried the contents of the treasury and the whole apparatus of the Portuguese state.[142] The leading ships sailed close to the Russian squadron to gauge their reaction. They did nothing, so the rest of the fleet sailed past them out into the Atlantic and toward the waiting Royal Navy squadron.

HMS *Plantagenet* spotted some of the fleet manoeuvring in the Tagus on the morning of the 28th, signalling 'strange sail in sight' to the *Hibernia*. The *Hibernia* closed with the *Foudroyant* on the 29th and spotted the fleet leaving the Tagus at 9:00 a.m.[143] As a precaution, Smith had his ships beat to quarters and clear for action. However, the *Confiance* signalled that the Prince was on board the fleet, and soon after, Smith received Strangford's letter that he had written the night before. Smith's journal records '50 sail in sight' by that time.[144]

Strangford had sailed out of the Tagus on the *Principe Real* with João.[145] He briefly returned to the *Hibernia* to consult with Smith, and then they went aboard the Portuguese flagship to meet with the Prince. Smith proposed that his squadron fire a salute in honour of the Prince Regent, which João agreed to but had to say that it would not be returned by the ship he was on as his mother, the Queen, was on board and she was not in the best of health. The 21-gun salute was duly commenced by the British squadron at 4:30 p.m. and returned by the Portuguese half an hour later.[146] Smith was concerned about the state of the Portuguese ships and, while aboard the *Principe Real,* had spoken with *Vice-almirante* Souto, later reporting to the Admiralty:

> I took the Admiral apart and asked him what it was as to efficiency for self defence or for the long voyage; he frankly and at once said 'in no state for either' and indeed to the eye it appeared but too evident that preparations had not been made, probably from the counteracting influence of the Party in Power who wished to deter the Prince from embarking and to render not impossible for him to proceed. They have multitudes of helpless men women and children refugees and heaps of baggage (as at the evacuation of Toulon) on board, very few seamen, neither water or provisions for a voyage of any length…[147]

Smith offered to supply what water and provisions he could spare from the squadron. During his interview with the Prince, Smith also made a request:

139 Southey, *History*, vol.I, p.112.
140 Light, *Empire*, p.37.
141 TNA: ADM 1/19: List of the Portuguese Fleet that sailed out of the Tagus on the 29th of November.
142 Robson, *South America*, p.168.
143 TNA: ADM 50/50: 28 and 29 November.
144 TNA: ADM 50/50: 29 November.
145 O'Neil, *Account*, p.16.
146 TNA: ADM 50/50: 29 November.
147 TNA: ADM 1/19: Smith to Wellesley-Pole, 1 December 1807, '5, Secret'.

I proceeded to request that the fort of Bugio at the mouth of the Tagus should be given to me in deposit as a security for the free exit of the remaining ships, to this His Royal Highness objected on the ground of it being unfair on his part towards the Russians with whom he was at peace, and who had been received on the ground of hospitality. His Royal Highness refused with great delicacy and feeling but was quite fixed in his determination on this head…[148]

However, the Prince continued to say that Smith could ask the Council of Regency he had left in charge of the country. Strangford suspected that the Prince did not want to issue the order for the fort to be surrendered because he feared it would not be obeyed. The garrison at the São Julião da Barra fortress had already refused to spike their guns and throw their powder into the Tagus.[149]

Forte de Sao Lourenço do Bugio was a small round tower on a sandbank in the mouth of the Tagus, built in the sixteenth century. It commanded the entrance to the Tagus, and its possession would have enabled Smith to enforce the blockade more easily. He could not claim the fort under the convention with Portugal as his entry into the Tagus had not been necessary to ensure the departure of the Prince. Despite the Prince's refusal, and probably thinking that any negotiation with the council of regency would be unsuccessful once the French took over the city, Smith decided to take the fort anyway, later writing: 'I therefore detached the marines of the London, Hibernia and Marlborough to obtain possession by force or otherwise during the momentary interregnum or cessation of all authority.'[150] In other words, he decided that there was a brief window between the Prince leaving and the Council of Regency taking over in which he was free to embrace his maverick tendencies and do as he wished.

Smith put his plan into action. The frigate *Solebay* received 91 marines from the *London,* the *Confiance* 62 from the *Hibernia,* and 78 marines from the *Marlborough* were ordered to the sloop *Redwing.*[151] Lieutenant Thomas O'Neil was amongst the Royal Marines from the *London* transferred to the *Solebay* and later wrote: 'At seven in the morning of the 30th, the frigate was close in with the fort: it blew a tremendous gale; with a heavy sea, that rendered it impossible for us to disembark. At eight we saw the French flag flying on every fort'.[152]

Entry into Lisbon

On 28 October, Junot and the vanguard marched 12 miles beyond the Zezere before nightfall and then on to Santarém 24 miles further by noon the next day through torrential rain. The troops were allowed to eat and rest for an hour and then marched another 15 miles to Cartaxo. On the 29th, they marched nearly 40 miles and, at 10:00 p.m., entered Saccavém on the edge of Lisbon. Waiting for the French was *Tenente General* Martino de Souza e Albuquerque with a delegation from the Council of Regency that João had left in charge of the country. They told Junot that João and the fleet had sailed to Brazil. It was not news to the French; various merchants and notables had already come from the city to pay homage to the country's new rulers. While João absenting himself in many ways could make the transition of power easier, the fleet was Junot's prime objective, and he

148 TNA: ADM 1/19: Smith to Wellesley-Pole, 1 December 1807, '5, Secret'.
149 TNA: FO 63/56: Strangford to Canning, 2 December 1807.
150 TNA: ADM 1/19: Smith to Wellesley-Pole, 1 December 1807, '5, Secret'.
151 Light, *Empire*, p.77.
152 O'Neil, *Account*, pp.25–26.

knew that Napoleon would be disappointed. Junot wrote another proclamation and sent it and the Regency delegation to the city with instructions to maintain calm and order.[153]

With elements of the British fleet still off the mouth of the Tagus and a power vacuum in the city, Junot decided to march into Lisbon early on the morning of 30 November. The 70e and most of the rest of the vanguard were too exhausted to continue, so he gathered the regiment of grenadier companies, barely 1,500 men, and sent orders back for the divisions to march as soon as they could.

At 8:00 a.m., the ragged column, headed by Junot and his staff, entered the city to the sound of the grenadiers' drums. As Foy wrote:

> They had at last made their entrance, those formidable warriors before whom Europe was dumb and whose looks the Prince Regent had not dared encounter. A people of lively imagination had expected to see heroes of a superior species, colossuses, demigods. The French were nothing but men. A forced march of eighteen days, famine, torrents, inundated valleys, and beating rain, had debilitated their bodies, and destroyed their clothing. They had hardly strength enough left to keep the step to the sound of the drum.[154]

Their muskets were rusty, their cartridges damp, and their artillery was far behind them. Any show of resistance by the Portuguese would probably have stopped them, as historian Robert Southey puts it: 'The very women of Lisbon might have knocked them on the head.'[155] However, most of those with the will and means to command such resistance had already sailed for Brazil. Thiébault wrote in his memoirs:

> Then, at intervals of one or two days, the shreds of the army's corps followed in an ever more miserable state, the soldiers appearing as living corpses. Elite companies of one hundred and forty men did not have fifteen, and eagles [regiments] arrived with two hundred men instead of two thousand five hundred. All day long, and not counting those who went down the Tagus in boats prepared at Abrantes and Santarem, soldiers arrived carried by peasants and transported on donkeys, without weapons, without clothes, without shoes, and almost moribund; several expired at the gates on arrival.[156]

Junot was met and then escorted by troopers from the Lisbon Guarda Real da Polícia. With the troopers was Comte Jean-Victor Novion, an emigré who had fled France in 1792, commander of the Lisbon police. Novion had managed to keep order in the city following the fleet's departure, and as the ragged French columns marched into Lisbon, he made sure there was little protest.[157]

The French quickly took possession of the forts, and the troops were garrisoned in seven monasteries and convents around the city.[158] Junot hurried through Lisbon to Belem and, at the Forte de Bom Sucesso, found that not all the guns had been spiked and fired on the few remaining ships in the river, preventing them from leaving. He sent troops to garrison Forte de São Julião and

153 Grasset, *Guerre d'Espagne*, vol.1, p.172.
154 Foy, *Invasion*, p.55.
155 Southey, *History*, vol.1. p.115.
156 Thiébault, *Mémoires*, vol.IV, p.146.
157 Sigler, *Thiébault*, pp.186–187.
158 Anon., *Memoria Histórica da Invasão dos Francezes em Portugal no ano de 1807* (Rio de Janeiro: Impressão Regia, 1808), pp.7–8.

marched back to the city. It was raining heavily, but the streets were lined with sullen crowds, and the balconies and windows of the houses were full of anxious faces.[159]

Thiébault and his staff immediately got to work gathering rations for the arriving troops, finding accommodation for the officers and ensuring the barracks were up to French standards, creating hospitals for the thousands of sick, and requisitioning another 25,000 pairs of shoes.[160] Junot wrote to the Emperor to tell him that he had captured Lisbon but failed to seize the Portuguese fleet or to prevent João from leaving. After detailing the difficulties of the march and all the steps he took to try and get to Lisbon before the Prince left, he wrote: 'Sire, you must realise how sorry I was to see the aim of all sorts of toils and privations slip away so close to me; but on the other hand, is it not a benefit to have the Prince so promptly removed from the possession of Portugal?'[161] He argued that the wealth of those who had sailed could now be seized. He also claimed that the population greeted him with relief, glad they had not suffered the same fate as Copenhagen.[162]

Between Bayonne and Lisbon, 1,700 French soldiers died of fatigue, famine, or drowning.[163] The 1er Division, having more seasoned troops, suffered fewer losses than the others but still could only muster 1,500 men when it entered Lisbon. However, one of the voltigeur companies of the 70e did manage to lose only a single man on the whole march. Some regiments were down to just one-tenth of their effective strength. However, most of the men would slowly rejoin their units over the coming weeks. Brenier's brigade left Bayonne with 3,600 men and arrived in Lisbon with just 300, but when all the stragglers and sick rejoined only 27 were still missing.[164]

The Spanish division commanded by *Teniente General* Marqués Solano entered Portugal from Badajoz on 2 December. It marched along the left bank of the Tagus to occupy the southern provinces. *Teniente General* Don Francisco Taranco, marching from Galicia, reached Oporto on 13 December. Neither force experienced any opposition from Portuguese forces. However, the governor of Valença, on the northern border, did close his gates to the Spanish until he had confirmation that Lisbon was in French hands and Prince João had abandoned the country.[165]

Whilst the Portuguese army, desperate for reform and riven with superannuated officers, would have been no match for the corps that left Bayonne, they might have been able to give the corps that arrived at Lisbon a good fight. However, if they had managed to defend their country, Napoleon would have only sent more troops and possibly a more able commander. The Portuguese realised that once Napoleon's patience had worn out with their attempts to appease both the French and the British, subjugation of some form was inevitable. As historian Charles Oman puts it:

> There is certainly no example in history of a kingdom conquered in so few days and with such small trouble as was Portugal in 1807. That a nation of three million souls, which in earlier days had repeatedly defended itself with success against numbers far greater than those now employed against it, should yield without firing a single shot was astonishing. It is a testimony not only to the timidity of the Portuguese Government, but to the numbing power of Napoleon's name.[166]

---

159 Southey, *History*, vol.1. p.116.
160 Thiébault, *l'Expédition*, pp.73–74.
161 Sepulveda, *Historia*, vol.XI, p.115.
162 Sepulveda, *Historia*, vol.XII, p.113.
163 Foy, *Invasion*, p.57.
164 Thiébault, *l'Expédition*, pp.77–78.
165 C. Oman, *A History of the Peninsular War* (Oxford: Clarendon Press, 1902), vol.1, p.31.
166 Oman, *History*, vol.1, p.26.

To the Brazils

As the Portuguese fleet sailed out of the Tagus, the favourable easterly wind changed to a gale from the west, which, according to one eyewitness, 'obliged all the ships to carry a press of canvass, and claw off a lee shore with split sails.'[167] Some Royal Navy ships, including the *Hibernia*, suffered damage to their masts, yards and rigging.[168] With many of the Portuguese ships in a poor state of repair and heavily overcrowded, the storm, which lasted several days, must have been a frightening experience for those fleeing to Brazil. Smith and his squadron did their best to maintain contact and support the Portuguese ships, and they eventually managed to collect almost all of them back together.

Strangford's dispatch to Canning, written on the 29th on the *Hibernia*, began:

> I have the honour of announcing to you that the Prince-Regent of Portugal has effected the wise and magnanimous purpose of retiring from a kingdom which he could no longer retain, except as the vassal of France; and that his royal highness and family, accompanied by most of his ships of war and by a multitude of his faithful subjects and adherents, have this day departed from Lisbon, and are now on their way to the Brazils, under the escort of a British fleet.
>
> This grand and memorable event is not to be attributed, only, to the sudden alarm excited by the appearance of a French army within the frontiers of Portugal. It has been the genuine result of the system of persevering confidence and moderation adopted by his majesty towards that country; for the ultimate success of which I had, in a manner, rendered myself responsible; and which, in obedience to your instructions, I had uniformly continued to support, even under appearances of the most discouraging nature.[169]

Smith's first dispatch to the Admiralty after the sailing, headed '22 Leagues West of the Tagus 1 December 1807',[170] blames the closing of the ports to Britain and other hostile actions on the 'Portuguese government being so much influenced by a misplaced terror of the French arms' and that the Prince Regent was coerced by 'the abject timidity or the base corruption of some members of His Royal Highnesses Council.' He then goes on to say that given the importance of preventing the Tagus from becoming a French naval base 'by the simple change of colours on board the Portuguese fleet' and the risk that a union of the French and Spanish fleets would then pose to Ireland and the rest of the British Empire, he felt justified in implementing a strict blockade. Smith also comments that he assented to Strangford going back to Lisbon on the 27th because Smith had 'the fullest reliance that his knowledge of the national and individual characters of those he had to deal with, together with his promptitude, perspicuity, energy and firmness' would be able to induce the Prince to sail for Brazil. He then continued: 'I have now, sir, the heartfelt satisfaction of announcing to you that my hopes and expectations from this hazardous step which Lord Strangford handsomely volunteered under very unpromising circumstances considering the

---

167 Raleigh, 'Naval Transactions', p.381.
168 Light, *Empire*, p.82.
169 TNA: FO 63/56: Strangford to Canning, 29 November 1807.
170 TNA: ADM 1/19: Smith to Wellesley-Pole, 1 December 1807, marked 4.

vicinity of the French army and the state of the elements, were realised to the utmost extent.' After describing the sailing of the fleet and the exchange of salutes, Smith ends his dispatch with:

> Impressing every beholder except the French Army on the hills with the most lively emotions of gratitude to providence that there yet existed a Power in the world able as well as willing to protect the oppressed; inclined to pardon the misguided; and capable by its fostering care to found new empires and alliances; from the wreck of the old ones destroyed by the ephemeral power of the day; on the lasting basis of mutual interest.

On the same day, the 1st, Smith ordered the *Elizabeth* and the *Plantagenet* back to the Tagus to re-establish the blockade. On the 6th, he reported to the Admiralty that he had managed to gather the whole Portuguese fleet, except for one brig, after the storm and that the weather was such that repairs and the redistribution of passengers could occur. *Vice-almirante* Souto reported that all ships except the *Principe de Brazil* could get to Rio de Janeiro and that ship would sail for Britain. Smith then stated that he had ordered Captain Graham Moore (brother of Sir John) of the *Marlborough*, whom he appointed commodore, to escort the convoy to Brazil with the *Monarch*, *London* and *Bedford* and to remain there to help protect the colony from the Spanish. The frigate *Solebay* would follow, as would other smaller ships whenever they became available.[171]

The *Foudroyant* sailed for Madeira with the Portuguese *Medusa*, which needed provisioning.[172] Commodore Moore and the rest of the Portuguese fleet sailed on to Brazil while Smith returned with the *Hibernia*, *Conqueror* and *Redwing* to continue the blockade of Lisbon. The *Confiance* parted company from them on 7 December and sailed for Britain with Strangford and dispatches on board.

Both Strangford and Smith received praise for their parts in the successful evacuation of the Portuguese royal family and, more importantly, in preventing the Portuguese fleet from being taken by the French. William Wellesley-Pole, secretary to the Admiralty, wrote to Smith that the Lords of the Admiralty professed their 'high approbation of your judicious and able conduct in the management of the service entrusted to your charge.'[173] Canning wrote that 'Strangford has been eminently instrumental in this business.'[174]

However, there were some debates about where the credit should be placed. With Strangford being awarded the Order of the Bath for his part but Smith receiving no such honour, there were some complaints from Smith's supporters in the navy that his part had not been adequately acknowledged. The opposition-supporting newspapers questioned if the government could claim credit for something precipitated by the French invasion more than any other factor. *The Times* argued that Napoleon forced the decision on the Prince Regent and 'ministers are neither to be censured, nor indeed greatly praised, for an act, in the execution of which they could have but a small share.'[175]

The debate over credit came to the fore again in 1828 following the publication of William Napier's *History of the War in the Peninsula and in the South of France,* in which he wrote:

---

171 TNA: ADM 1/19: Smith to Wellesley-Pole, 6 December 1807.
172 Light, *Empire*, pp.84–85.
173 Robson, *South America*, p.251.
174 Robson, *South America*, p.251.
175 Robson, *South America*, p.250.

Lord Strangford … whose previous efforts to make the royal family emigrate had entirely failed, was then on board the squadron with the intention of returning to England; but Sir Sidney threatened to bombard Lisbon if the prince regent hesitated any longer, and thus urged on both sides, he embarked with his whole court, and sailed for the Brazils on the 29th of November, a few hours before Junot arrived.

Lord Strangford's despatch relating this event, although dated the 29th of November on board the Hibernia was written on the 19th December in London, and so worded as to create a notion that his exertions during the 27th and 28th caused the emigration. This was quite contrary to the fact; for the prince regent, yielding to the united pressure of the admiral's menaces and the annunciation in the Moniteur, embarked on the 27th, before Lord Strangford reached Lisbon, and actually sailed without having had even an interview with that nobleman, who consequently had no opportunity to advance or retard the event in question. Nevertheless, Lord Strangford received the red riband and Sir Sidney Smith was neglected.[176]

Napier was a Whig and harboured some antipathy towards the Tory administration of Lord Portland, especially as he felt that Canning and Castlereagh had treated Sir John Moore, whom Napier greatly admired, quite shoddily. Also, Strangford and Napier's brother, Lieutenant General Sir Charles Napier, were on opposite sides of the then-burning international topic: Greek Independence.[177] Napier's suggestion that it was the threat of a Copenhagen-style bombardment that was more persuasive than Strangford's diplomacy does not take account of the fact that such an operation would have been impractical without possession of the Tagus forts, and the Portuguese must have been aware that without British troops the threat to their fleet, while it remained in the Tagus, was minimal.

Strangford felt bound to answer the imputations in Napier's book and published *Observations on Some Passages in Lieut-Col Napier's History of the Peninsular War*. In the 36-page pamphlet, Strangford stated that while his original dispatches were written in Lisbon, he had, at Canning's request, edited and collated them on his arrival in London to remove references to individuals still in Lisbon, plans for taking the forts, and other operational details, and to form the various dispatches into one for publication. He also pointed out that João had decided to embark on 24 November, before Smith's threatening note had been delivered and before his own final meeting with the Prince Regent, and that the French invasion forced the decision to embark.[178]

Napier replied with his own pamphlet, *Reply to Lord Strangford's 'Observations' on Some Passages in Lieut-Col Napier's History of the Peninsular War*, in which he conceded some of Strangford's points but maintained that Smith's threat to bombard Lisbon was more important than Strangford's long relationship and negotiations with the Portuguese in prompting the Prince Regent to embark once the French had crossed the border.[179]

---

176 W. Napier, *History of the War in the Peninsula & in the South of France* (London: Warne, 1886), vol.I, p.90.
177 Robson, *South America*, pp.252–235.
178 Strangford, *Observations*, passim.
179 W. Napier, *A Reply to Lord Strangford's 'Observations' on Some Passages in Lieut-Col Napier's History of the Peninsular War* (London: Murray, 1828).

Strangford then replied to Napier's reply with another pamphlet, *Further Observations on Some Passages in Lieut-Col Napier's History of the Peninsular War*, in which he refuted Napier's defence.[180] Perhaps the only one to profit from this tiff was the publisher John Murray, who published all the pamphlets. Napier's two main points – that Strangford's dispatch was somehow concocted in London to give him credit that he was not due, and that Smith's threats caused the embarkation – are at odds with the extant papers and dispatches in The National Archives and the timeline of events. The removal of much of the context from Strangford's published dispatch does, perhaps inevitably, increase the focus on his own actions. Still, it would be a rare government that did not try to claim more credit for something it was only partially responsible for.

João was never going to abandon Portugal until there was no other option and French troops were approaching Lisbon. To have embarked precipitately would have probably been as likely to lose him his throne as staying in Lisbon. Canning and Sousa's convention laid the groundwork for the embarkation. Strangford's good relationship with the Prince Regent and his constant reassurances of British support were the carrot to Smith's stick, but the promise of Royal Navy support to the Portuguese fleet once it sailed was probably far more important than the slightly hollow threat of hostile action.

In Strangford's correspondence to Canning, there is a definite tone of youthful enthusiasm and exuberance, sometimes bordering on naïveté perhaps, but, from the start, he was consistent in his view that the Prince would, when the point of crisis came, embark. Furthermore, according to his dispatches at least, he was unrelenting in lobbying the Portuguese and representing British policy. He was also not afraid to make decisions beyond his instructions when circumstances required. That the threat the Portuguese felt from Napoleon, who had, after all, conquered most of Europe, was greater than that from their ancient ally Britain, who had recently twice failed to conquer a Spanish colony, explains Prince João's policy of French appeasement more than any alleged failure of diplomacy on Strangford's part.

Whilst Strangford was the target of Napier's ire, Smith was the target of John Fortescue's criticism in the sixth volume of his *History of the British Army*. Fortescue claimed that the arrival of Sir John Moore's 8,000 men, who were travelling from Sicily, could have fundamentally altered the events in Portugal and that Smith should have been communicating with Moore. He stated: 'Considering the circumstances, the neglect of Sidney Smith in this instance appears almost criminal, for the entire issue at Lisbon might well have turned upon the arrival of Moore's battalions; and, knowing the man as we do, we shall probably not be wrong in ascribing his conduct to his incorrigible jealousy and selfishness.'[181]

However, there are several issues with this argument. Firstly, no one knew precisely where Moore's convoy was, but Smith had learned from the *Redwing* that Moore had not yet appeared at Gibraltar. Orders had been sent to Gibraltar for Moore to cooperate with Smith and Strangford, but he did not arrive in Gibraltar until 1 December, after the embarkation had taken place.[182] Secondly, as has been shown, there is evidence that Smith gave his dispatches for Moore to Commander Thomas Ussher of the *Redwing* which was patrolling off the Portuguese coast. Lastly, in his dispatch of 1 December, after the embarkation, Smith wrote that the reason that he had decided not to send for

180   P. Strangford, *Further Observations on Some Passages in Lieut-Col Napier's History of the Peninsular War* (London: Murray, 1828).
181   Fortescue, *British Army*, vol.VI, p.103.
182   J.F. Maurice, *The Diary of Sir John Moore* (London: Arnold, 1904), vol.II, p.196.

'Boney stark mad or more ships colonies & commerce', by Cruikshank. A frustrated Napoleon kicks Talleyrand into the Tagus while Smith taunts the Emperor from a boat. (Anne S.K. Brown Military Collection)

Moore at that point was that, with the prevailing strong westerly winds, there was nowhere the transports could shelter and 'that transports could not easily keep off a lee shore.'[183] He also said that with the Portuguese fleet gone, there was no reason to risk the transports without having an immediate operation for Moore's force to undertake. Saying that Moore's force could have substantially altered the course of events relies on such a long chain of counterfactuals as to be meaningless. Successive British assessments had concluded there was no point in offering the Portuguese military assistance if they were unwilling or unable to defend themselves.

As the Prince Regent sailed across the Atlantic, his capital was in French hands and French and Spanish troops would soon occupy the rest of the country. Whilst almost all the Portuguese navy had sailed, there remained a powerful Russian squadron that could still be a significant menace to British shipping in the Atlantic. The blockade would have to be maintained over the winter, and plans would be made to try and neutralise the threat.

183   TNA: ADM 1/19: Smith to Wellesley-Pole, 1 December 1807, 5 Secret.

3

Occupation

On the afternoon of 30 November, Junot met with a delegation of the Council of Regency and settled into the Palácio de Quintela, which he took for his headquarters and residence. Writing to Napoleon, Junot quickly reassured him that the city was calm and the shops were open. To make up for not capturing the entire Portuguese fleet, he also told him three ships of the line and two frigates that had been left behind because they were not seaworthy could be repaired. With many of the country's administrators gone, the French found it difficult to gather information on the state of the nation. Still, Junot outlined ambitious plans for reorganising and taking control of government institutions or creating them anew. He suggested France take direct control of Portugal and that Napoleon appoint a member of his family as ruler. He closed with:

> For me, Sire, if I have not entirely fulfilled the intentions of your majesty, I can at least assure him that I have done all that it was possible to do; my army will return to me this justice. I have no other ambition than to learn from your majesty that you are satisfied with my zeal, and that you do not deign to attribute to me events, which in no way depend on me.[1]

The main body of 1er Division arrived on the 1st – just 1,500 men of an original 9,000 – and further troops arrived over the subsequent days, including the cavalry on the 6th, reduced to just 1,000 men riding ruined horses. Stragglers would continue to arrive for weeks afterwards. As the divisions arrived, they were distributed into Cascais (just beyond the mouth of the Tagus), Peniche (a fortress 60 miles up the coast), Torres Vedras (in the hills to the north) and around Lisbon itself. The army's medical staff warned Junot that up to a third of the men would soon be on the sick list as they were so debilitated that they would be vulnerable to fevers and disease; dysentery and scabies were quickly rife. With many of the soldiers' uniforms in tatters, Junot had to source new clothing locally, some of which was produced from cloth seized from British merchants.[2] By 15 December, Junot could report to Clarke, the minister of war, that of the 25,000 men he had left Bayonne with, he now could field barely 16,000. Some 4,500 were in hospitals, and a further 4,000 had been left

---

1 Junot to Napoleon, 30 November 1807, in Sepulveda, *Historia*, vol.XII, pp.116–117.
2 Grasset, *Guerre d'Espagne*, vol.1, pp.181–184, 192.

at various points on the march. As well as securing Lisbon, Junot had to guard the coast against British landings and secure his communications back to Spain. He did not have enough men.[3]

With the contents of the Portuguese treasury on their way to Brazil, Junot had no money to feed his army or govern the country, so on 3 December, he instituted an emergency tax to raise two million crusados. The effects of a poor harvest and the blockade had already put the Portuguese economy under strain. The flight of much of the country's wealth did further damage. With many of the administrators and merchants also having left, the ability of the country to recover was compromised.[4]

Two factors complicated Junot's administrative challenges. The first was that he was not in charge of the whole country. Under the Treaty of Fontainebleau, the French and Spanish had split the country. *Teniente General* Don Francisco Taranco occupied the province of Entre-Douro-e-Minho in the northwest, while *Teniente General* Marqués Solano occupied Alentejo and the Algarve to the south. This left Junot with Beira and Estremadura in the centre of the country and Trás-os-Montes in the northeast, although there was some debate over this area with the Spanish.[5] The Spanish thus held most of the productive agricultural regions whereas Lisbon's wealth was based on trade, which was stymied by the blockade. The second complication was the Council of Regency that Prince João had left in charge of the country and with whom Junot had to try to work to ensure the cooperation of the existing structures of the state.

On 6 December, Junot wrote to Napoleon again, informing him that *capitaine de vaisseau* Jean-Jacques Magendie had arrived to take charge of the Portuguese navy. Magendie was an experienced officer who had commanded the *Bucentaure* at Trafalgar. He would eventually get back into service two ships of the line, three frigates and seven smaller vessels left in various states in the Tagus.[6]

Colonel Vincent thoroughly inspected the fortifications and barracks in and around Lisbon. His report began: 'Urgent work is needed to improve and repair the fortifications and to maintain and clean the military buildings.'[7] He recommended many improvements to the various forts. He concluded that 'one can advance without exaggeration that the present state of the defence of the most important point of the port is almost nil.'[8]

In a second letter to Napoleon, also written on 6 December, Junot went into great detail about his administrative and financial challenges and ended the letter with: 'Forgive me, Sire, if I occupy your majesty with so many details; it is because we have no administrator here capable of deciding any of these questions, and the fear of doing wrong gives me the boldness to ask directly for your majesty's orders.'[9] Junot was clearly out of his depth.

Contrary Winds

In the early hours of 2 December, Lieutenant Colonel Sir Robert Wilson arrived back in London after a diplomatic mission to the continent. He had raced from St Petersburg with news that Russia

---

3   Grasset, *Guerre d'Espagne*, vol.1, pp.181–184, 192.
4   Grasset, *Guerre d'Espagne*, vol.1, pp.188–189.
5   Grasset, *Guerre d'Espagne*, vol.1, p.190.
6   Thiébault, *l'Expédition*, p.86.
7   Sepulveda, *Historia*, vol.X, p.106.
8   Sepulveda, *Historia*, vol.X, p.112.
9   Junot to Napoleon, 6 December 1807 (2), in Sepulveda, *Historia*, vol.XII, p.129.

Vice Admiral Sir Charles Cotton. (© Crown Copyright, UK Government Art Collection)

had declared war on Britain, beating a Russian messenger to London. The Russian squadron in the Tagus turned from being a quandary to a threat. The Duke of Portland, the prime minister, wrote to Canning the same day on the subject, 'is it not a question, and one that will not admit a moment's delay, whether it should not be taken possession of?'[10] The cabinet considered increasing the blockading squadron's size and seizing Senyavin's ships. It was decided to augment the Lisbon station and Lord Mulgrave, First Lord of the Admiralty, appointed a more senior officer to take command – Vice Admiral Sir Charles Cotton.

Cotton, a friend of Mulgrave, had had a long, if not particularly distinguished, career. Born in 1753, the third son of a landed Cambridgeshire family, he entered the navy as a midshipman at the relatively late age of 19 in 1772. However, his career progressed quickly due to the patronage of the Earl of Sandwich, the First Lord of the Admiralty – a friend of his father. He saw action several times during the American War of Independence and, within seven years, was captain of the *Boyne* (68) and fought at the Battle of Martinique before being given the *Alarm* (32). On half-pay during the peace, he was given command of the *Majestic* (74) in 1793 and, at the Glorious First of June, took the French *Sans Pareil* (80). In January 1795, with his two older brothers having died, he succeeded to his father's baronetcy. In 1797, he was promoted to rear admiral and continued to serve in the Channel on blockade duty and, for a short time, in the Mediterranean, rising to vice admiral in 1802.[11] In the opinion of *The Naval Chronicle*: 'He was a gallant, persevering, humane, and excellent commander; a good man, a ready friend, and inviolably attached to his King and Country.'[12]

---

10   Portland to Canning, 2 December 1807 in Robson, *South America*, p.160.
11   Paul C. Krajeski, *In the Shadow of Nelson* (Westport: Greenwood Press, 2000), chapters 1–4.
12   Anon., 'The Late Admiral Sir Charles Cotton, Bart.', *The Naval Chronicle*, vol.27, January–June 1812, p.213.

The naval reinforcements that Cotton would take with him to the Tagus included the *Minotaur* (74), *Antelope* (50), *Nymphe* (36), *Nautilus* (18) and *Millbrook* (12) – which would give the squadron some much-needed smaller vessels.[13] However, with the Tagus being so well protected by forts, any operation against the Russian squadron would also need considerable numbers of troops. Fortunately, Major General Brent Spencer had, on 1 December, been given command of just over 8,000 troops gathering at Portsmouth and due to sail for Sicily.[14] On 4 December, Castlereagh, now back at his post after his illness, ordered Spencer to proceed to Sicily but added, 'it is intended that in your passage to Sicily you should in the first instance proceed off the Tagus, where it is not improbable you may be employed for a time upon another service…'[15] He also wrote to Lieutenant General Sir John Moore to inform him that Spencer would touch at Lisbon and that he had instructions to place himself under Moore's command if Moore was actually there. He also told Moore that 'from the recent conduct of the Court of Russia, in renouncing all connections with His Majesty, the capture of the Russian Fleet in the Tagus is to be considered as one of the principal objects to which you are to direct your exertions.'[16] Unfortunately, Moore sailed from Gibraltar on 15 December for Britain, arriving in Portsmouth on the 30th, so may never have received those orders.

Spencer was also an experienced and capable officer. He was born in Ireland in 1760 and joined the 15th Foot as an ensign in 1778, quickly seeing action in the West Indies. He was promoted to lieutenant a year later and taken prisoner when the garrison on St Kitts was forced to surrender. By 1783 he was a captain and he then moved to the 13th Foot to get his majority, again serving in the West Indies and distinguishing himself at the capture of Port-au-Prince in 1794. He was promoted to lieutenant colonel in the short-lived 115th Foot before exchanging into the 40th in 1795 and was then sent to the Caribbean for the third time. He led his regiment against the Caribs on St Vincent, and on St Domingo in 1797, he was given a brigade. By the following year, he had nearly 8,000 troops under his command and operated against Toussaint L'Ouverture until the island's evacuation. He was made an aide de camp to the king in 1798 and led the 40th in the expedition to the Helder in 1799, winning praise from Sir Ralph Abercromby and the Duke of York. He again won praise from Abercromby during the 1801 Egyptian campaign and was several times mentioned in *The Gazette* for his coolness under fire, zeal, and ability. He then had several staff jobs in Britain, was promoted to major general in 1805, and became a favourite of George III who made him an equerry. He spent much of his time at court but was then given command of a brigade for the Copenhagen expedition. He had only been back in Britain for a couple of months when he was given the command of the reinforcements for Sicily.[17] From around 1800, Spencer had also been involved in a long but discreet romantic relationship with Princess Augusta, the sixth child of the King, which may have led to a secret marriage.[18]

Cotton received additional orders on 9 December. The Russian squadron had become 'an object of the greatest importance', and he was told to cooperate with Spencer to capture it.[19] Cotton's orders illustrate that 10 days after the Portuguese fleet had sailed for Brazil, the British government

---

13   Robson, *South America*, p.180.
14   National Library of Scotland (NLS): Adv Ms 46.3.6: General Order, London, 1st December 1807.
15   TNA: WO 1/226: Castlereagh to Spencer, 4 December 1807.
16   TNA: WO 1/226: Castlereagh to Moore, 4 December 1807.
17   E.M. Lloyd, 'Sir Brent Spencer', *Oxford Dictionary of National Biography* (ODNB), <https://doi.org/10.1093/ref:odnb/26116>, accessed January 2021.
18   D.M. Stuart, *The Daughters of George III* (Stroud: Fonthill, 2016), pp.110–120.
19   TNA: ADM 2/1365: Admiralty to Cotton, 9 December 1807.

was still ignorant of the events in Portugal. The admiral's orders also stated that should an attack on the ships in the Tagus not be practicable, he should continue the blockade and asked him not to delay Spencer's voyage to Sicily for too long.

Historian Robert Sutcliffe used the preparations for Spencer's convoy as one of the case studies in *British Expeditionary Warfare and the Defeat of Napoleon* that illustrate the challenges Britain faced when sending large numbers of troops abroad, especially at short notice. Transports were cargo vessels hired by the government from their owners on three- or six-month contracts. The process was overseen by the Transport Board of the Admiralty, which had agents in each major port. While the government kept some ships on contract to cover eventualities, it would have been uneconomic to keep the large numbers required for major expeditions ready at all times. When the government requested the board provide ships for a particular service, as Castlereagh did in November 1807 for Spencer's troops, the board and its agents would have to assess what ships were to hand, if they matched the requirements for the particular service, and then approach ship brokers to hire what was needed. The ship owners would have to judge if the government contract would be more or less profitable than carrying commercial cargo. Adam Smith's invisible hand of supply and demand would govern the price that the board had to pay to get the ships it needed when it needed them.[20]

Many ships were available that matched Castlereagh's criteria. They had been used for the South American and Danish expeditions and operations in the Mediterranean, but they required significant repairs and refitting. This was the first cause of the delay in Spencer's expedition sailing as there were insufficient dry docks or the necessary skilled labour. The Victualling Board was charged with providing provisions for the transports, and the sudden demand put strains on the local supply chains at the ports. This was another cause of delay, especially as orders to replenish several Royal Navy ships took precedence. Another problem was where to put the thousands of soldiers arriving at the ports to embark. The local barracks quickly filled up, and army commanders often preferred the troops to be embarked immediately to stop them from deserting; this added to pressure to get the ships ready to receive them. The transport agent at Portsmouth, Captain Charles Patton, was finding it increasingly challenging to fulfil all the various demands on his time and had to get Captain John Halstead and three lieutenants to assist him. Bedding needed to be ordered or washed, ships coming in from previous services needed to be fumigated, and unusually low tides prevented some ships from coming out of dry-dock and even grounded some victualling craft. Patton hired in some more vessels and eventually solved the myriad of problems to get the troops embarked. However, the final delay of a week was due to the transports being not fully provisioned and watered in time. In total, it took six weeks from notification to the expedition sailing.[21]

In his memoir, Ensign John Patterson of the 50th Foot referred to the vessel he embarked upon as 'an old tub, battered and knocked about by many a gale, and in her look and trim was by no means inviting.'[22] If a ship owner took a transport out of service for repair, then that ship was not making them any money, so many delayed maintenance and repairs as long as they could, meaning that many transports were in a poor state.[23]

20 R. Sutcliffe, *British Expeditionary Warfare and the Defeat of Napoleon, 1793–1815* (Woodbridge: Boydell, 2016), pp.45–49.
21 Sutcliffe, *Expeditionary*, pp.106–111.
22 J. Patterson, *The Adventures of Captain John Patterson* (London: T & W Boone, 1837), pp.9–10, 13–14.
23 R. Knight, *Convoys* (New Haven: Yale University Press, 2022), p.146.

On 17 December, Edward Cooke, undersecretary at the War Office, wrote to Spencer that, as the wind was favourable, the convoy should sail as soon as possible and to confer with Cotton to see if those vessels not ready could sail later, warning that: 'If you remain, a change may detain you for several weeks.'[24] On the 18th, Spencer wrote, 'If the wind continues fair we expect to sail at daylight tomorrow morning.'[25] The next day, Castlereagh sent Spencer Smith's dispatches, including the news that the Portuguese fleet had sailed, but told him that he should still sail with Cotton to Lisbon to assess if anything could be done to capture the Russian squadron.[26]

The embarkation return that was completed on 18 December listed a total of over 8,500 officers, men, women and children.[27] The force included British and King's German Legion infantry and brigades of Royal Artillery and KGL artillery, with drivers. It was, however, a force designed to replace and reinforce troops garrisoning Sicily and not for offensive action in Portugal. There was no cavalry, but, more importantly for any action against the Tagus forts, there was no siege train, no engineer officers, and no engineering supplies. The only way Spencer could have taken the forts was by a costly coup de main.

On the 19th, Cotton informed the Admiralty from the *Minotaur* at Spithead that the transports would be fully provisioned that day and ready to sail early the next morning. By 5:30 p.m. on the 20th, the convoy of 65 vessels, plus the escorts, was past The Needles and out into the Channel.[28] Being all too familiar with the weather around the coast of Britain, Cotton had set four different rendezvous in case a storm separated the convoy:

1.   In case of separation and a westerly gale being the length of the Start to repair to *Torbay*
2.   In case of separation and being the length of the Lizard to repair to *Falmouth*
3.   In case of separation and being far advanced in the Bay of Biscay to repair 12 Leagues S.W. *of Cape Finistere*
4.   Secret. – Off the Rock of Lisbon[29]

The sailing of the expedition had been delayed by the administrative complexities of hiring, gathering, and provisioning transports, but its progress to its destination would now be down to another factor that often limited Britain's ability to send troops overseas quickly: the weather.

The convoy sailed with an easterly wind and, by the 24th, had reached a position approximately 120 miles west of Brest, approaching the notorious Bay of Biscay. However, the wind then changed to coming from the southwest and continued to blow from that direction, 'At times excessively hard'. On the 25th, the *Millbrook*'s bowsprit and foremast were carried away, and on the 28th the winds had developed into a strong gale, with heavy rain, which separated the convoy. On the 29th, only 32 vessels were still in company with Cotton's *Minotaur*; the rest, including the *Nymphe* and *Nautilus*, were out of sight. The *Minotaur* was taking on water and had to keep two pumps going, so, with the strong wind continuing to come from the southwest, Cotton decided to head

24   TNA: WO 1/226 Cooke to Spencer, 17 December 1807.
25   TNA: WO 1/226 Spencer to Hawkesbury, 18 December 1807.
26   TNA: WO 1/226 Castlereagh to Spencer, 19 December 1807.
27   TNA: WO 1/226: Embarkation return, 18 December 1807.
28   TNA: ADM 1/339: Cotton to Wellesley-Pole, 19 & 20 December 1807.
29   TNA: ADM 1/339: Rendezvous, 18 December 1807.

for Falmouth. The battered remnants of the convoy still with Cotton arrived there on the 31st; the rest headed for the more southerly rendezvous.[30]

The storm also came close to being very costly for Spencer's troops. George Weale, from Hatton near Warwick, had briefly been a midshipman until he was invalided out of the navy. He then enlisted in the Loyal Nottingham Foresters before transferring quickly to the 29th Foot. He was on board the 50-gun HMS *Antelope,* acting as clerk to Spencer's adjutant general, Lieutenant Colonel George James Bruere Tucker. Weale later wrote of the voyage:

> In this gale, a brig, having on board 200 detachments, for the regiments in the Mediterranean Islands, sprang a leak, and fired guns of distress; the Antelope bore down to her, but could lend her no assistance, the sea running mountains high, and the night coming on, until the next morning, when the wind was a little abated; the whole of the crew was saved, but with the loss of everything except their lives … It is out of the power of language to describe the sensation of horror every one must have felt, to be within the hearing of the heart-piercing shrieks of so many fellow-creatures, ready to be swallowed up by the pitiless deep without being able to afford them the smallest relief, but He who can calm the raging of the sea, saved them; the vessel got what is called water logged, and as soon as the men were got out, she was sent to the bottom, by the Primrose Schooner firing some shot through her hull.[31]

Lieutenant Henry Grove, a Royal Navy officer and a transport agent on the *London* transport, reported to Cotton that, on the 29th, the *London* was in company with the *Nymphe* and *Nautilus* and about 30 other transports, but on the night of the 1st they observed a vessel making a distress signal. At daylight, they recognised it as the *Thomas,* which had lost its foremast and bowsprit, but the seas were too rough to render assistance. At that time, 20 vessels were still in sight, and they were about 180 miles southwest of Brest. Not seeing any escorts, and with the *London* labouring in the heavy seas, they headed to Falmouth followed by about eight other vessels.[32]

Irishman Captain Harry Ross-Lewin of the 32nd Foot, a seasoned soldier who had served in the West Indies and at Copenhagen, wrote of the storm:

> … it blew a perfect hurricane, the most vivid lightning flashing round us, the sea running mast-high, breaking over the ship in every direction, and at length pooping us, and bursting in the cabin windows. One would absolutely have thought that we should have been blown out of the water. We saw at different times ships with signals of distress flying, driving under bare poles.[33]

In his memoir, he went on to recount that the water came through the cabin windows 'with such force as to wash one of our officers from his seat, and carry him under the companion-ladder, (where he remained for some time paddling in the water, with a fur cap that he wore pulled over

30   TNA: ADM 1/339: Cotton to Wellesley-Pole, 31 December 1807; ADM 50/54: 29 December 1807.
31   G. Weale, *An Interesting Memoir of George Weale* (Leamington: private publication, 1838), p.19.
32   TNA: ADM 1/339: Grove to Cotton, 5 January 1808.
33   Harry Ross-Lewin, *The Life of a Soldier: A Narrative of Twenty-Seven Years' Service in Various Parts of the World* (London: Bentley, 1834) vol.I, p.170.

his eyes, and fancying that he and the ship were going to the bottom)'.[34] All the officers' possessions and provisions were washed from one side of the cabin to the other as it pitched and rolled. Once the storm passed, they were approached by a French privateer, but it veered off once they saw the troops lining the sides of the ship.

Many transports did manage to cross the Bay of Biscay and make their way down the Iberian coast; 25 made it to Gibraltar by 23 January.[35] Neither Cotton nor Spencer mentioned any of the transports being sunk by the storm in their correspondence.

On 1 January, Cotton told the Admiralty that, along with the *Minotaur* and *Antelope*, there were 17 transports at Falmouth carrying parts of most of the regiments that had embarked.[36] Spencer wrote to the War Office that he was at Falmouth with some of the transports, which were being re-provisioned and watered, and that he did not know where the rest of them were but hoped that at least some had reached the rendezvous off Cape Finisterre or the Tagus. Spencer included a return of the transports at Falmouth which listed 14 and three victuallers, carrying 2,347 officers and men, 128 women and 68 children. The return of vessels at that time unaccounted for was far longer, with 38 transports, four victuallers and three ordnance transports carrying 5,321 officers and men, 287 women and 169 children.[37]

Over the next few days, Cotton reported the arrival at Falmouth of further transports, sightings of others in the Channel, and news of some that had taken shelter in other ports, such as Plymouth and Portsmouth. On 6 January, Castlereagh ordered Spencer to remain at Falmouth until further orders and told him that the transports that had sought shelter at Portsmouth and Plymouth had been ordered to join him.[38] On the 9th, Cotton received orders to proceed to sea with the *Minotaur* as soon as possible.[39]

Incalculable Evils

On 13 December, riots broke out in Lisbon following the ceremonial lowering of the Portuguese flag and its replacement by the tricolour of France. Parties of French soldiers were surrounded and pelted with stones. Some of the French opened fire, inflaming the rioters still more. As night fell, the disorder spread to engulf most of Lisbon. Junot spent the evening at dinner and then the opera, trying to maintain an aura of calm authority. By dawn on the 14th, battalions of French troops and artillery were deployed on the streets to quell the riot, and, after more deaths on both sides, peace was finally restored.[40]

On the 14th, Junot published a series of measures that he said were designed to ensure the security of the honest inhabitants of the city. These included a ban on all assemblies, and a military tribunal would try anyone caught in a mob. They would be put to death if they had taken up arms

---

34   Ross-Lewin, *Life*, vol.I, p.171.
35   A. Aspinall (ed.), *The Later Correspondence of George III* (Cambridge: Cambridge University Press, 1970), vol.V, 3615, p.13.
36   TNA: ADM 1/339: Cotton to Wellesley-Pole, 1 January 1808.
37   TNA: WO 1/226: Spencer to unnamed (probably Cooke), 1 January 1808.
38   TNA: WO 1/226: Castlereagh to Spencer, 6 January 1808.
39   TNA: ADM 1/339: Cotton to Wellesley-Pole, 10 January 1808.
40   Anon., *Memoria*, pp.28–35.

or been one of the leaders.[41] On 16 December, Junot wrote to Napoleon and blamed the riots on English spies.[42] When Napoleon received the news of the insurrection from Junot, he scolded him for being too lenient, said that he should have 60 people shot, and warned him that he would be driven from Lisbon by the English if he did not take a firmer hand.[43]

On 23 December, before news of the revolt reached him, Napoleon issued a decree of 12 articles. The first four articles stated that an extraordinary contribution of 100 million francs would be imposed on Portugal and that all royal property was to be seized, as was the property of all who sailed to Brazil. Articles five to nine dealt with Junot's corps, which was to be renamed the Armée de Portugal. The last three articles ordered the finance ministry to send officials to Portugal to help run the customs, tax and postal systems and told the Minister of Police to send someone to lead the police in Lisbon.[44] Napoleon did not think that the occupation was secure or that Junot was doing all that he should:

> I find that the path you are following is not good, because it is not farsighted. Like men who have no experience of conquest, you lull yourselves into vain illusions: all the people before you are your enemy. You will have, as soon as the sea is tenable, Englishmen on your coasts and intrigues in your provinces. Then all the means that you will have left to the Portuguese will turn against you; for at last the Portuguese nation is brave.[45]

One obvious focus for dissent was the Portuguese army. A decree had been issued on 4 December prohibiting the general population from using firearms, even for hunting; a second followed later, forcing the militia to disarm, and then another seizing all guns. However, despite their inaction during the invasion, the regular army had the most potential to resist the occupation. On 12 November, Napoleon told Junot: 'You will get rid of the most outstanding men, and who could give you anxiety, by ordering them to serve in Paris. You may even assemble from the Portuguese army a corps of 5 to 6,000 men, officers and soldiers, by directing them in columns of 1,000 men over France, and declaring that I take them into my service.'[46] Then, on 20 December, he advised, 'Do not lose a moment in destroying the Portuguese army. What is easy in the first month becomes very difficult later on.'[47]

A return of the Portuguese army for October 1807 gave a total strength of 23,381.[48] On 22 December, Junot ordered all soldiers with more than eight years and less than six months of service to be discharged.[49] The implementation of this reorganisation of the army was hampered by the division in authority between the Spanish- and French-occupied provinces. But by late February, the 24 Portuguese regiments had been merged into five line regiments and one of light infantry.[50] This reduction enabled the forced retirement of the least capable or elderly officers. The artillery

41   TNA: ADM 1/339: Proclamation, Junot 14 December 1807.
42   Sepulveda, *Historia*, vol.XII, p.131, Junot to Napoleon, 16 December 1807. There seems to be no foundation for his suspicions.
43   L. Lecestre, *Lettres inédites de Napoléon 1er (An VIII — 1815)* (Paris: Librairie Plon, 1897), vol.I, p.136.
44   Plon & Dumaine (eds), *Correspondance*, vol.16, 13409, pp.210–211.
45   Plon & Dumaine (eds), *Correspondance*, vol.16, 13416, pp.214–215.
46   Plon & Dumaine (eds), *Correspondance*, vol.16, 13429, p.227.
47   Plon & Dumaine (eds), *Correspondance*, vol.16, 13406, p.204.
48   Grasset, *Guerre d'Espagne*, vol.1, p.446.
49   TNA: ADM 1/339: Proclamation, 22 December 1807.
50   Grasset, *Guerre d'Espagne*, vol.1, p.200.

was also reorganised into a single regiment, and the cavalry, which had long since lost most of its horses to the French units in desperate need of remounts, was formed into two regiments. The whole was placed under the command of the Marquis d'Alorna, a Portuguese nobleman who was eventually made a *général de division* in the French army.

Over 10,000 men began their journey into France and imperial service in March. Junot retained one infantry and one cavalry regiment, plus the artillery. Vast numbers of the men deserted on the way through Portugal and Spain. The residue was quickly renamed the Légion Portugaise and sent to depots in France. They underwent a series of reorganisations and saw service in various campaigns, with their numbers later being replenished with Prussian and Spanish prisoners of war. The Légion marched into Russia with the rest of the Grande Armée, but most did not return. Only 800 men mustered at their depot in 1813, and the remnants were converted to pioneers.[51]

On 1 February, Junot, who was having difficulty extending his rule beyond Lisbon, abolished the Council of Regency and, in contravention of the Treaty of Fontainebleau, claimed authority over the whole of Portugal. On the same day, as Junot announced the change in administration, *général de division* Loison at Mafra issued a statement that Jacinto Correia had been found guilty of a 'great crime' and sentenced to death. The statement ended with: 'Portuguese, your gratitude is due to his excellency [Junot] who watches over your safety, and be careful to guard yourselves against those who by availing themselves of your credulity may lead you into excesses the incalculable evils of which would fall on yourselves.'[52] The great but unpublicised crime that Correia had committed was the killing with a scythe of two French soldiers who had accosted him. He was executed by firing squad on 25 January.

Isolated outbreaks of resistance continued to fester. Some of the locals insulted a hundred sick French soldiers from the 58e Ligne on their way to the thermal baths at Caldas da Rainha to be cured of the itch. Grenadiers were sent to enforce French control of the town and drunkenly brawled with some Portuguese soldiers. No one on either side was killed, but a few men were wounded. Loison was sent to the scene to quell the unrest. Twenty men were arrested and nine were executed.[53] Junot told Napoleon, 'This terrible example will teach the Portuguese people what they must fear to dare to insult French soldiers.'[54]

Madeira

The Portuguese island of Madeira, 600 miles southwest of Lisbon, lay across the Atlantic trade routes and was an important watering and victualling stop. Britain had occupied the island in 1801 to prevent it from falling into French hands. As early as September, Strangford had begun a letter to Canning with 'I have ventured to take a step of which I trust that you will approve, although in so doing, I have in some degree pledged the faith of His Majesty's government,' surely a phrase that no Foreign Secretary can want to hear from one of their diplomats.[55] He went on to say that, from previous arrangements, he had judged that a temporary occupation of Madeira might be likely, so he had asked the Portuguese that the garrison not be reinforced and that no orders contrary to

---

51   G. Dempsey, *Napoleon's Mercenaries* (London: Greenhill, 2002), pp.199–206.
52   TNA: ADM 1/339: No. 17, Loison's statement.
53   Anon., *Memoria*, p.52.
54   Sepulveda, *Historia*, vol.XII, p.168, Junot to Napoleon, 14 February 1808.
55   TNA: FO 63/55: Strangford to Canning, 21 September 1807.

British interests be dispatched to the governor. In return, he had promised that no British expeditions would be sent there or to other Portuguese territories without first informing the Portuguese. He explained to Canning that the Regent was still annoyed about how he was told of the last occupation after the fact, and thought it best to avoid a repeat. The occupation of the island was made part of the secret convention, but, as with the embarkation for Brazil, there was some prevarication and delay in the agreement being enacted.

Both a portion of the troops with Sir John Moore and those with Spencer were considered for the operation, but by mid-November, Castlereagh, Canning, and Hawkesbury had decided to send Major General William Carr Beresford with 3,658 troops from the 1/3rd, 11th, 1/25th and 1/63rd Foot and two artillery companies. They were to sail under the protection of Rear Admiral Samuel Hood with four ships of the line and four frigates.[56]

Canning and Sousa put into place arrangements to inform the governor of the island of the British approach and to allow the appearance that the island had surrendered to a superior force rather than by pre-arrangement. HMS *Comus* (22), sailing ahead, found that news of the embarkation to Brazil had reached the island and that no attack was expected. On the morning of Christmas Eve, 1807, Beresford and Hood approached Funchal, the capital, to find the defensive batteries unmanned. A boat was sent with two of Beresford's staff carrying a summons to the governor to surrender within 30 minutes. The governor acquiesced, and Beresford began to land his troops. By nightfall, the forts were in British hands, and the island became a crown colony until it was handed back to the Portuguese during the summer of 1808.[57]

Blockade Duty

Cotton arrived off the Portuguese coast on 14 January 1808 with the *Minotaur*, *Talbot* and *Cheerful*. He sent the *Cheerful* to Oporto with orders for the ships on blockade duty there and then continued south to meet up with Smith the next day. The *Nymphe* and *Nautilus* had arrived at the Rock of Lisbon rendezvous with 22 transports three days previously (but had been driven off by weather). Cotton wrote orders for them to continue to Gibraltar when they returned. He also sent the *Solebay* frigate to Brazil and the *Elizabeth* to the Azores 'on account of the number of sick she had on board', presumably to aquire fresh fruit, meat and vegetables. This left Cotton with the *Hibernia*, *Alfred*, *Agamemnon*, *Defence*, *Ganges*, *Foudroyant*, *Conquerer*, *Plantagenet*, *Ruby*, *Minotaur* and *Talbot* off the Tagus, with the *Raven* and the *Cheerful* at Oporto.[58]

On the 16th, Cotton ordered Smith to transfer his flag to the *Minotaur* while transferring his own to the larger *Hibernia*.[59] Smith thought the ship, which needed repair and was taking on water, was unsuitable for an officer of his rank. After a gale further damaged the *Minotaur*, he shifted his flag to the *Foudroyant*, with Cotton's agreement. The *Minotaur* did not sail for repairs in Britain until mid-March. Smith sailed in the *Foudroyant* with the *Agamemnon* in late February to take command of the Brazil station.

56   D. Gregory, 'British Occupations of Madeira During the Wars against Napoleon', *Journal of the Society for Army Historical Research*, vol.66, No. 266 (Summer 1988), p.86.
57   M. De La Poer Beresford, *Marshal William Carr Beresford* (Newbridge: Irish Academic Press, 2019), p.26.
58   TNA: ADM 1/339: Cotton to Wellesley-Pole, 16 January 1808.
59   TNA: ADM 50/50: 16 January 1808.

Cotton's primary task was to continue the blockade of the Tagus, but there was also a French squadron that had escaped from Rochefort on the 17th to worry about. As well as bottling up the Russian squadron and any Portuguese ships that the French managed to get ready for sea, the hope was that the blockade would cause food shortages in Lisbon, which would put pressure on Junot to withdraw and even perhaps make *Vitse-admiral* Senyavin ready to negotiate some kind of surrender of his ships.[60]

On 18 January, Cotton wrote to Senyavin that he had in his care dispatches for him and the Russian consul from the Russian minister in London but that he was 'apprehensive that they may be intercepted if I trust them to any other conveyance than a Russian officer in your confidence.' Cotton closed the letter by saying that he was: 'Lamenting most sincerely that the correspondence between two nations like ours, which have been so long in amity with each other, and whose mutual interest it certainly was to continue so, should for a moment be subject to any difficulty.'[61] It was easy enough for Cotton to write the letter, but it was much harder to deliver it to an enemy-held port. A few days later, he had to tell the Admiralty he had found no direct way to communicate with the Senyavin.[62] Cotton's solution was to order Captain Charles Ekin of the *Defence* to send the crew of a Spanish lugger his ship had taken off Setúbal into the Tagus under a flag of truce and hand the letter to the Portuguese or Spanish officer receiving the flag of truce, or to one of the more intelligent prisoners in the hope that it 'may probably reach its destination.'[63] On 1 February, he informed the Admiralty that he had sent a second copy of the letter 'by a conveyance most likely to ensure its delivery.'[64]

Cotton's fears about the security of his communications with Senyavin were well-founded. On 4 February, Junot wrote to Napoleon that he had intercepted the letters sent with the Spanish prisoners and included translations of them with his dispatch.[65] In early January, Junot had taken measures to try and prevent any communication with the Royal Navy. All the fishing boats were registered and numbered, with the crew having to present their papers when challenged by the guard boats. The boats all had to be within the bar at sunset, and infractions would lead to the seizure of the boat or corporal punishment for repeat offenders. However, crowds would still gather on the heights overlooking the mouth of the Tagus to look longingly at the blockading squadron until Junot also banned these gatherings.[66]

However, these measures were not entirely successful. Cotton informed the Admiralty that a boat had come from the shore on 27 January carrying John Carpenter and William Ford, two British merchants who had stayed behind in Lisbon to collect debts owed to them. On the 23rd, the house where they and several other Britons resided had been surrounded by French soldiers. Five were seized and sent to prison. All their property was confiscated, and heavy fines were imposed with further ones for their release. Presumably, Carpenter and Ford escaped the net or had paid for their release. The Russian fleet gave them sanctuary for several days. They reported that Russian officers 'are by no means on terms of friendship with the French' and that Senyavin had only once

60   Robson, *South America*, pp.181–182.
61   TNA: ADM 1/339: Cotton to Senyavin, 18 January 1808.
62   TNA: ADM 1/339: Cotton to Wellesley-Pole, 25 January 1808.
63   TNA: ADM 1/339: Cotton to Wellesley-Pole, 25 January 1808.
64   TNA: ADM 1/339: Cotton to Wellesley-Pole, 1 February 1808.
65   Sepulveda, *Historia*, vol.XII, p.154, Junot to Napoleon, 4 February 1808.
66   Southey, *History*, vol.1, pp.139–140.

The Rock of Lisbon, by Charles Hamilton Smith. (Yale Center for British Art, Paul Mellon Collection)

been ashore to meet with Junot.[67] They also told Cotton that the Portuguese were extremely dissatisfied; business was at a standstill, the wheat in store would only last until the middle of March, and farmers had wine in their vats they could not sell now the British trade had ceased. On 2 February, nine more refugees arrived with the squadron, including Edward Colvil of the Portuguese artillery college and three artillery cadets.[68]

On 8 February, Cotton informed the Admiralty that:

> A flag of truce was yesterday sent out of the Tagus, from which two Russian officers, and a French officer, came onboard the Hibernia – by one of the former (having taken means to separate them) I understand the Russians to be extremely dissatisfied with their situation, subject as they are to the immediate controul [*sic*] of the French, who have possession of all the old batteries on the banks of the Tagus and are daily erecting new ones; – the result of a long conversation with Mons. Le Conseiller de Cour Politica, the Russian officer above alluded to, sent to me as perfectly possessing Admiral Seniavin's confidence, was, that

---

67   TNA: ADM 1/339: Intelligence gained from Carpenter and Ford.
68   TNA: ADM 1/339: Cotton to Wellesley-Pole, 2 February 1808.

however disposed the Russian officers might be to quit the Tagus the thing was not practicable, closely watched as they are by the French; – that they are however ready to put in
force any measure directed by their Emperor, of whom they speak in terms of the highest
admiration, and state without reserve, their opinion as to his being ill advised to the steps
recently taken by him causing the present rupture with England.[69]

Cotton had previously lamented his lack of small ships (and that the ones he had were mostly
detached) that made imposing a blockade on a lee shore with only line-of-battle-ships almost
impossible, but the Admiralty did send him reinforcements; the *Hercule* (74), *Lively* (38) and *Rapid*
(12). The first carried Cotton's new second in command, Rear Admiral William Albany Otway,
and orders for Smith to go to Brazil. The *Lively* managed to get close enough to the Tagus to
enable Captain George McKinley to report on 6 February that he could see eight large Russian
ships and a frigate in a line from Belém to Cacilhas point, a line-of-battle-ship flying a French
broad pennant near the arsenal, and several ships under repair.[70] On the 8th, with better weather,
McKinley observed further details of the enemy ships in the river, including gunboats and other
smaller vessels, also stating that 'I observed them exercising a regiment dressed in blue with white
pantaloons and drilling their squads in the field at the back of Fort St Julian.'[71]

It was also McKinley that Cotton chose to sail to the Burlings (Berlengas), a group of small rocky
islands six miles off Peniche, one of which had a small fort. Occupying them would help control
shipping coming down the Portuguese coast, and Cotton had been given orders to take possession
of them before he left Britain. On 15 February, McKinley wrote to Cotton that:

> I proceeded with His Majesty's ship under my command accompanied by the Viper
> schooner to the Burlings and on my approaching them on the 12th instant, I observed on
> the large Island a guard of soldiers in the fort, on which I sent a flag of truce desiring them
> to surrender, which they refused; I sent another pointing out the necessity of them so
> doing, but not complying they hoisted Portuguese colours and fired, which was returned
> by His Majesty's Ship under my command, when they struck their colours.[72]

Cotton sent the *Rapid* with marines from the *Hibernia* to take over the garrison. Another reason
Cotton was eager to take the islands was to see if there was a good water source there, but McKinley
reported that the only water source was a dripping rock in a cave that could only fill a butt per day.
He also said that the fort was strong and defensible, and 'I do not think it a safe anchorage for any
of His Majesty's Ships; and the Island within itself produces nothing.'[73] Later in the month, he sent
Cotton a chart drawn by the *Lively*'s master and informed him that he had erected a signal post 'on
the same principle as on the English coast' and enclosed a list of the signals to be made by passing
or approaching ships.[74]

With no friendly harbour nearby, Cotton faced significant logistical problems keeping his
ships provisioned and watered. Gibraltar was the nearest port where his ships could be repaired

69   TNA: ADM 1/339: Cotton to Wellesley-Pole, 8 February 1808.
70   TNA: ADM 1/339: A state of the enemy observed lying in the Tagus, 6 February 1808.
71   TNA: ADM 1/339: McKinley to Cotton, 9 February 1808.
72   TNA: ADM 1/339: McKinley to Cotton, 15 February 1808.
73   TNA: ADM 1/339: McKinley to Cotton, 15 February 1808 (second letter).
74   TNA: ADM 1/339: McKinley to Cotton, 26 February 1808.

or re-victual, but visiting there would take a ship off station for several days. Ships also watered on islands off Baiona, near the Spanish port of Vigo, and some even went as far as the Azores or Madeira for supplies. The *Hindoostan* storeship did arrive at the beginning of February but had limited victuals on board. Ships sent to the Azores, Madeira or Vigo would be off station for as much as a fortnight, and the squadron was, by 7 February, critically short of water.[75] On 27 January Cotton had sent a list of all the supplies needed by each vessel in his squadron and the totals included: 479,236 pounds of bread, 30,161 gallons of wine, 15,080 gallons of spirits, 34,223 pieces of beef, 68,447 pieces of pork, 2,131 bushels of pease, 1,598 bushels of oatmeal, 102,620 pounds of flour, 8,555 pounds of suet, 17,109 pounds of raisins, 25,670 pounds of butter, 51,331 pounds of cheese, 25,670 pounds of sugar, 4,250 gallons of vinegar, and 1,650 tons of water.[76]

On the night of 13–14 February, the *Confiance* was back and off the Tagus. Recently-promoted Captain James Yeo heard rumours from Lisbon, probably via fishermen, that the Russian squadron was about to sail. He sent Masters Mates Trist and Largue in the cutter and jolly boat to row guard at the mouth of the river. They quickly spotted a French gunboat at anchor near Fort São Pedro, and they 'instantly boarded in a most gallant manner, and, after an ineffectual resistance on the part of the Enemy, captured her.' The gunboat, *Le Cannonier No.1*, was commanded by *ensign de vaisseau* Gandolphe and had one 24-pounder and two brass 6-pounders, with a crew of 50. Yeo reported to Cotton that:

> Great praise is due to Mr. Trist and his small Party for the Intrepidity they displayed, when it is considered our boats had only 16 men in all, opposed to such superior force, under heavy batteries, and were hailed and fired at, long before they reached her; I therefore beg leave to recommend Mr. Trist, having passed for lieutenant near twelve months; Mr. Trist speaks of Mr. Largue in terms of warm approbation, as also of Mr. Taylor, the carpenter, and all the seamen and marines of the Party. I am happy to add, it was accomplished without any loss on our side, the enemy had three killed and nine wounded.[77]

Ironically, Gandolphe's orders included instructions to 'take a position that will secure him against any surprise on the part of the English cruisers on the outside of the bar.'[78] *Confiance* took the *Le Cannonier* in tow and later recovered any useful stores before breaking the gunboat up. Yeo landed the French prisoners at Lisbon under a flag of truce to the applause of Portuguese onlookers. Cotton appointed Robert Trist a lieutenant in the *Alfred*.

New Orders

While Cotton was beginning to carry out his orders off the Tagus, Spencer and most of his troops were still aboard the transports on the south coast of Britain after being scattered by the gale. Over the next few weeks, transports continued to arrive at Falmouth, including ones that had taken shelter at other ports. However, on 16 January, Castlereagh sent new orders. With the French

---

75   Raleigh, 'Naval Transactions', pp.385–386.
76   TNA: ADM 1/339: Demand for provisions, 27 January 1808.
77   TNA: ADM 1/339: Yeo to Cotton, 14 February 1808.
78   Raleigh, 'Naval Transactions', p.393.

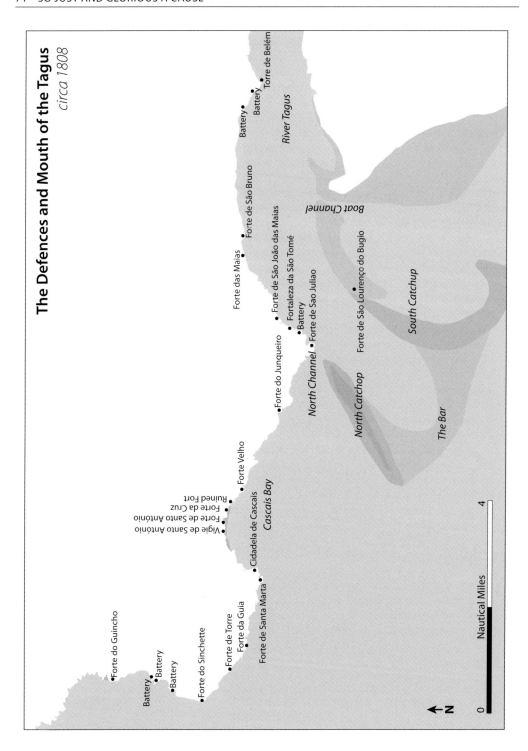

The Defences and Mouth of the Tagus
circa 1808

army entering Spain in large numbers, it was feared that they could besiege Gibraltar and occupy Ceuta, a Spanish enclave on the African coast across the straits from Gibraltar. Castlereagh had been warned of the danger by Sir Arthur Paget, the British ambassador in Constantinople, who told him that French possession of the enclave would mean 'the entrance into the Mediterranean will be difficult beyond all calculation, and to get out of it will be nearly impracticable, except with strong leading winds.'[79]

Paget also warned that any operation against Ceuta should not be launched from Gibraltar as the preparations would be observed. Nevertheless, Spencer was ordered to sail to Gibraltar, consult with the acting Commander-in-Chief and Governor, Lieutenant General Sir Hew Dalrymple, and the naval commander there, and take possession of Ceuta if the operation appeared feasible. Castlereagh was also of the opinion that since the scattering of the transports had so reduced his force, there probably was little he could do at Lisbon but that he was to stop there and consult with Cotton on the way to Gibraltar. A 'confidential officer', Major Samuel Browne, would accompany Spencer to brief Dalrymple.[80] Browne, of the York Light Infantry Volunteers, was assistant secretary and aide de camp to the Duke of York at Horse Guards. He was promoted to lieutenant colonel and appointed deputy quartermaster general on Spencer's staff the day of Castlereagh's letter.

On 23 January, Castlereagh ordered Spencer to proceed to sea. The number of rank and file with Spencer at Falmouth had now risen to just under 4,000, with 39 transports, ordnance ships and victuallers.[81] Brigadier General Miles Nightingall joined the expedition on 6 February. Another gale delayed sailings, and it was not until 21 February that Spencer could write to Castlereagh from HMS *Antelope*, 'I have the honor to acquaint your Lordship that the convoy is now getting under weigh...'[82] It had been 65 days since the troops had originally finished embarking in December. Being an island protected Britain from invasion, but the fickleness of the wind put severe limits on the speed of response to any strategic developments overseas until the age of steam.

The convoy arrived off the Tagus on the 26th. Spencer immediately had a conference with Cotton. The two agreed that the strength of French and Spanish forces in Portugal meant that any attempt on the forts by Spencer's troops was impracticable.[83] Without an occupation of the forts, the Royal Navy squadron would be at the mercy of the nearly 400 guns of the forts, plus the 750 of the Russian squadron itself.[84]

Le Duc

In some ways, the early spring of 1808 in Portugal was the calm before the storm. While Junot struggled to get a grip on the country, Napoleon's eye was already wandering toward its larger neighbour. On 4 March, he wrote another long and critical letter to Junot, mostly complaining that he had not yet sent all the Portuguese troops out of the country. Napoleon wrote: 'If you reread the letters I have written to you since your entry into Portugal, you will see that you have done nothing of what I wanted. You answer me with beautiful words, but you do not do what I want. It

---

79   Vane (ed.), *Correspondence*, pp.361–362, Paget to Castlereagh, 27 December 1807.
80   TNA: WO 1/226: Castlereagh to Spencer, 16 January 1808.
81   TNA: WO 1/226: Castlereagh to Spencer, 23 January 1808 and Spencer to Castlereagh, 24 January.
82   TNA: WO 1/226: Spencer to Castlereagh, 21 February 1808.
83   TNA: WO 1/226: Spencer to Castlereagh, 29 February 1808.
84   Krajeski, *Shadow*, p.65.

is annoying for me to see my plans thwarted in this way.'[85] He also told Junot, again, that he did not want troops to be cantoned in Lisbon itself, where they could be overwhelmed by a mob.

Junot's response to Napoleon on the issue of troops in Lisbon illustrates how Napoleon's orders from afar took little account of realities on the ground. He told the Emperor that he had only the 15e Ligne in the citadel, an elite battalion at his headquarters, and the 70e and 86e with most of the cavalry in the rest of the city. He did promise to move some of the troops to a camp but pointed out that the scarcity of wood meant that huts could not be built and that in the rainy season troops in tents would be prone to disease, and likewise, in the summer, they could not stand the heat. Having the troops in barracks or cantonments was best for their health, and also, the extent and topography of Lisbon meant that any unrest could be quickly quelled by troops stationed in the city.[86]

Napoleon requested that Junot place a division at Almeida in case the Spanish division in Galicia marched towards Valladolid, which was on the main route from France. Given that Junot only had three infantry divisions, this would have been a significant and unrealistic re-distribution of his forces. Napoleon also warned Junot, 'It is possible that I myself will soon be going to Spain.'[87] After receiving Junot's letter of 23rd February detailing the withdrawal of Solano's Spanish division from southern Portugal, Napoleon insisted that Junot send a strong division to Elvas and the Spanish border if he had not already done so. The Emperor was beginning to make plans for Spain with little regard for the security of Portugal.[88]

Junot received these orders at the end of March. While there was probably no immediate danger of a British counter-invasion until the weather improved, *général de brigade* Paul Thiébault, Junot's chief of staff, began to plan for one. With the danger of Lisbon erupting in revolt if the French tried to make a stand there, Thiébault sent a staff officer with some engineering experience, *lieutenant* Alexis Vallier, to complete a survey eight leagues around Lisbon. His report came back with the suggestion of fortifying the peninsula around Setúbal, on the left bank of the Tagus. This would allow Forte Bugio, which guarded the entrance to the Tagus, to be supported. The coast was rugged enough that no landing could be attempted on the peninsula itself, and the terrain lent itself to defence and, as long as communication was maintained with Elvas, the army could hold out long enough for relief to come from Spain. Unfortunately, as Thiébault wrote in his memoirs, Junot was not the man to put such a detailed and systematic plan into action.[89]

The withdrawal of Solano's division in the south caused considerable problems for Junot because he had far more territory to occupy with his French troops. At the same time, Napoleon was demanding that two-thirds of his forces be placed near the Spanish border. Far from having surplus troops ready to assist the French forces in Spain, Junot was asking Paris for reinforcements:

> The Spaniards being no longer in Portugal, the army is too weak as it is, being obliged to be divided; it should be increased by a quarter … The occupation of Elvas, Alentejo and the Algarve employs about 5,000 men, but this is not enough, for at least 4,000 men must be available in Setúbal, and the left bank of the Tagus requires at least 9,000 men; the provinces of Minho, Tras os Montes and Beyra, at least 5,000. The garrison of Lisbon, and

---

85   Plon & Dumaine (eds), *Correspondance*, vol.16, 13620, p.388.
86   Sepulveda, *Historia*, vol.XII, p.183, Junot to Napoleon, 17 March 1808.
87   Plon & Dumaine (eds), *Correspondance*, vol.16, 13626, pp.393–394.
88   Plon & Dumaine (eds), *Correspondance*, vol.16, 13627, p.395.
89   Thiébault, *Mémoires*, vol.IV, p.171.

the forts of the coast, require at least 10,000 men, which makes the total of my army, and I shall have nothing available.[90]

Junot estimated that he needed about 12,000 more men.[91] He warned Napoleon that:

… far from being able to remove a single man from the points where they are now employed, both for the guarding of the coasts and of the forts, it would be necessary on the contrary to be able to increase them; the Algarve is not sufficiently defended, and if the enemy, from whatever side entered it, established the theatre of a war there … it would be very difficult for us to end it, because there is no communication in the interior.[92]

Perhaps in the spirit of trying a little carrot instead of the sticks of the stinging rebukes that he had been sending to Junot, Napoleon granted him the title of Duc d'Abrantes. The town of Abrantes was chosen for Junot's title to commemorate the difficult march into Portugal.

Events took a slightly bizarre twist in April when a chicken produced an egg on which the letters V D S R P were visible on the shell. The letters were interpreted to mean 'Vive Dom Sebastião Rei de Portugal' – Long live Dom Sebastião King of Portugal.[93] Sebastião was a sixteenth-century king who disappeared fighting the Moors during the Battle of Alcácer Quibir. Like the English King Arthur, he was supposed to return when Portugal faced its darkest hour and lead the nation to glory. People flocked to see the egg, which was paraded around the city on a silver platter until Junot took possession of it. Another miraculous egg later appeared inscribed with 'Morran os Franceses' – death to the French. Junot demonstrated that such an effect could be achieved using acids and presented several eggs emblazoned with 'Vive l'Empereur'. This dampened the ardour of the egg's believers.[94]

Great Tumults

The coming of spring improved the weather for the Royal Navy squadron blockading the Tagus. However, the perils of the sea were never to be taken lightly and on 25 March, the schooner *Millbrook* was wrecked, 'having been driven from her Anchors, on the Burling Island.'[95] Her crew were saved, but it was still a blow for Cotton, depriving him of one of his few vessels able to operate close inshore. The arrival of eight victuallers from Plymouth in early March solved many of the squadron's supply problems. Later in the month, four transports arrived carrying water, and they were to remain dedicated to the squadron to help keep it supplied.[96]

On 28 March, a small vessel flying Portuguese colours sailed out of the Tagus. On board was Miguel Setaro, a former contractor who had supplied the Royal Navy and British Army with provisions and was now providing the same services to the French army. Acting without any official

90   Sepulveda, *Historia*, vol.XII, p.181, Junot to Napoleon, 17 March 1808.
91   Sepulveda, *Historia*, vol.XII, p.174, Junot to Napoleon, 8 March 1808.
92   Sepulveda, *Historia*, vol.XII, pp.185–186, Junot to Napoleon, 29 March 1808.
93   Southey, *History*, vol.I, pp.173.
94   Oman, *History*, vol.I, pp.214–215.
95   TNA: ADM 1/339: Cotton to Wellesley-Pole, 8 April 1808.
96   C.D. Hall, *Wellington's Navy* (London: Chatham, 2004), p.22.

sanction, Setaro requested permission to import flour to support the Portuguese population. He stated that the French had secured adequate supplies, but only two or three weeks' worth remained for the locals. In his report to the Admiralty, Cotton stated, 'to such request I, of course, (agreeable to the tenor of my instructions) gave a decided negative.'[97] A month later, Cotton reported that Setaro must have been mistaken about the amount of food in Lisbon as no news of distress had reached the squadron.[98]

Setaro told Cotton that many respectable merchants wished to travel to Brazil. Fifteen vessels, carrying both cargo and passengers, were prepared to sail. Cotton agreed that they could, but the vessels needed to be searched. The admiral also gleaned from Setaro that around 15,000 French troops were in or near Lisbon and that the Spanish garrison at Setúbal had been ordered back to Spain, but that order had then been countermanded. In his report of the conversation, Cotton then stated:

> By the post of last Friday positive accounts are said to have been received from Spain as follows. Viz. that on the 16th instant, the populace understanding a French Army to be approaching Spain and believing the Prince of Peace [Godoy] to be the principal insti-gator thereof surrounded his house, broke into the same and demanded his person, which not immediately finding everything of value or consequence was broken and destroyed; that after some time he was discovered in the act of endeavouring to escape over the roof and was secured, but by the interference of the magistracy under the King's authority, his person was recovered and protected.[99]

Cotton continued to outline more details of the unrest and how King Carlos had been obliged to strip Godoy of his honours and positions. Cotton also told the Admiralty that: 'Murat with a numerous French Army was said not to be far from the capital, and altho' the populace were roused to enthusiasm to resist its entry, yet they wanted a leader.'[100] In early April, Captain Conway Shipley of the *Nymphe* heard reports of King Carlos abdicating.[101]

Napoleon was increasingly seeing Spain as a weak ally. The previous October, Carlos' heir, Prince Fernando, had plotted against his parents and requested Napoleon's protection, but the scheme had been discovered. The court was riven by division, and the state desperately needed reform. In the wake of the Fernando affair, Napoleon ordered the 25,000 men of the 2e Corps d'Observation de la Gironde to cross the border into Spain while more troops gathered in southern France. By early 1808, Napoleon had 50,000 troops on the soil of a supposed ally, and he began to see the best solution to his Spanish problem as bringing the country more directly under his control. Probably to provoke a crisis, Napoleon demanded Spanish territory and a permanent alliance in return for Spain getting all of Portugal. Carlos, seeing the way that the wind was blowing, prepared to flee to South America. Napoleon gave the command of the troops in Spain to *maréchal* Joachim Murat, and the French began to occupy Spanish fortresses. Fernando tried to pre-empt any French takeover by staging a coup of his own. His supporters fanned the flames of frustration and fear of the population, and a large crowd gathered at the palace at Aranjuez. Fighting broke out, with

97   TNA: ADM 1/339: Cotton to Wellesley-Pole, 29 March 1808.
98   TNA: ADM 1/339: Cotton to Wellesley-Pole, 27 April 1808.
99   TNA: ADM 1/339: Cotton to Wellesley-Pole, 29 March 1808.
100 TNA: ADM 1/339: Cotton to Wellesley-Pole, 29 March 1808.
101 TNA: ADM 1/339: Cotton to Wellesley-Pole, 7 April 1808.

some of the guards on Fernando's side. The King and Queen were forced to abdicate. Both Carlos and Fernando appealed to Napoleon for support, and the Emperor invited them to Bayonne.[102]

When Cotton's report of the meeting with Setaro reached London, Castlereagh sensed an opening. He instructed the Admiralty to order Cotton to offer terms to the authorities in Lisbon for the lifting of the blockade. The terms were to be that the Russian squadron was to be surrendered to the British but returned six months after a peace between Russia and the allies, that the Russian officers and crew be returned to Russia without any conditions, and that the Portuguese ships in the ports and enemy merchantmen were also to be surrendered. Neutral vessels were to be allowed to sail subject to inspection and other conditions. If the terms were met, the blockade would be relaxed, and provisions allowed in. If all conditions were met apart from the surrender of the Russian ships, then Cotton was authorised to allow provisions in but then to maintain a blockade to prevent the Russians from sailing.[103]

Portuguese refugees fleeing from Lisbon and other ports and seeking shelter on the ships of the Royal Navy were becoming an increasing problem for the squadron. On 7 April, Cotton reported to the Admiralty that HMS *Comus* had picked up 175 refugees. He had already sent 173 to Britain on the *Hindoostan* transport on the 5th. Thirty-five more had been taken aboard ships of the squadron since then. The new arrivals were put on the *Caledonia* transport, which had just arrived with water and, under the care of a master's mate, ordered to Plymouth. Cotton had to send them back to Britain to preserve rations and water, 'and make room for other Refugees, of which there is reason to expect many hundreds – urged I believe to emigrate from the great dislike they have toward their French oppressors, and dread of approaching want – the stores of grain being greatly reduced.'[104] Cotton requested that transports be sent to take the refugees directly to Brazil. The number of refugees was such that Cotton had to appeal to the Admiralty, 'that the whole of the captains serving under my command have, on behalf of themselves and the officers, represented to me the great inconvenience and expense they are put to by entertaining Portuguese refugee officers, and the better sort of people that fly to the British fleet for protection…' and that they desired some form of compensation for their expenses 'unavoidably incurred in support of Our National Character for Humanity.'[105] The flow of refugees to Cotton's ships was reduced by a decree that Junot issued on 5 April.[106] The articles of the decree ordered the officers commanding the batteries and forts to fire upon any approaching British boats, even if they were flying a flag of truce, on pain of court-martial. Anyone attempting to board Royal Navy ships would be convicted by a military tribunal to at least six months in prison or even death, depending on the circumstances. Anyone facilitating escapes to the squadron would similarly be treated as a spy or an 'unlawful seducer' and sentenced to death, as would anyone inciting French or Portuguese troops to desert. Rewards were offered to anyone supplying information on those attempting to escape or helping them. Anyone emigrating would forfeit their property.

Cotton received the order to open negotiations on 27 April. While he promised the Admiralty that he would do what he could, he doubted his ability to open communication due to Junot's

102 C. Esdaile, *The Peninsular War* (London: Allen Lane, 2002) pp.29–35.
103 Anon., *Papers presented to Parliament in 1809* (London: Strahan, 1809), pp.232–241, Castlereagh to Admiralty and Wellesley-Pole to Cotton, 16 April 1808.
104 TNA: ADM 1/339: Cotton to Wellesley-Pole, 7 April 1808.
105 TNA: ADM 1/339: Cotton to Wellesley-Pole, 18 April 1808.
106 TNA: ADM 1/339: Decree of 5 April 1808.

decrees banning contact with the squadron.[107] However, in accordance with his new orders, Cotton wrote and had translated into Portuguese a proclamation, the wording of which closely followed the suggestions from London.[108] To distribute the proclamation, Cotton planned to have fishing boats boarded off the coast from Setúbal to Oporto. It would then be read to the crews, and they would be given copies. Cotton hoped that some copies would then manage to get to those in authority, and, in the meantime, he would write a draft convention.[109]

The operations of the squadron continued as normal. Early on the morning of 23 April, the boats of the frigate HMS *Nymphe* (36) and the sloop *Blossom* (18) attempted to cut-out the French sloop *La Gavotte* (20), formerly the Portuguese *Gaivota Real*, commanded by *lieutenant de vaisseau* Leblond-Plassan which had a crew of 150 and was lying at anchor just above Belém. After some initial attempts were aborted, eight boats carrying 150 men left the two Royal Navy vessels in two divisions led by Captain Shipley of the *Nymphe* and Commander George Pigot of the *Blossom*. William James included a detailed account of the action in his *Naval History of Great Britain*:

> The British boats entered the Tagus in the order prescribed, and, ascending with the tide, got near enough, by the time it became slack water, to see the vessels in the harbour. Wishing to have a good tide to carry out his prize, Captain Shipley waited until he saw the vessels swing with the ebb. Unfortunately for the success of the enterprise, there was a fresh in the river, and the tide in consequence, when the ebb had fairly made, ran at the rate of seven knots an hour. Notwithstanding this unexpected difficulty, the boats got tolerably close to the enemy's vessel before they were discovered. Upon being hailed by the Garotta [*sic*] (the French captain saying in good English, 'My good fellows, you had better keep off, you will all be killed if you come on board'), who lay within pistol-shot of the guns of Belem castle, and had for her additional protection a floating battery carrying long 24-pounders, the boats of the two divisions cast themselves off and severally made towards her.
>
> The gig soon darted out of eight of the other boats, and at about 2 h. 30 m. A.M., on the 23rd, boarded the French brig on the larboard bow. Captain Shipley, having sprung into the Garotta's fore-rigging, was in the act of cutting away the boarding-netting, when he received a musket-ball in his forehead and fell dead into the water. The next in command of the gig was Mr. Charles Shipley, the late captain's brother, but not attached to the Nymphe, nor even, we have heard, belonging to the naval profession. His fraternal affection overcoming every other consideration, Mr. Shipley ordered the gig's crew to shove off from the enemy's vessel, and endeavour to pick up their captain.[110]

With the tide preventing the other boats from closing on the *La Gavotte*, the attack was abandoned. One seaman was killed, and a midshipman and Royal Marine corporal were wounded. Shipley's body was washed up on shore. Cotton ended his account of the action to the Admiralty with 'I feel extreme regret at the painful necessity of thus recording the Death of Captain Shipley

---

107 TNA: ADM 1/339: Cotton to Wellesley-Pole, 27 April 1808.
108 TNA: ADM 1/339: Cotton, proclamation.
109 TNA: ADM 1/339: Cotton to Wellesley-Pole, 28 April 1808.
110 W. James, *The Naval History of Great Britain from the Declaration of War by France in 1793 to the Accession of George IV* (London: Bentley, 1859), vol.IV, pp.327–329.

who was a most excellent, brave, and highly meritorious officer.'[111] George Pigot was promoted to replace Shipley as captain of the *Nymphe*.

Junot celebrated the defence of the sloop in an order of the day on 24 April, including a little Gallic exaggeration of the British casualties:

> On this occasion, the enemy lost at least forty men. The officer commanding the expedition was killed by M. Leblond-Plassan; his hat and pistol were left in the possession of the commandant of the marine. We lost only one man, who formed one of the detachment of the Hanoverian legion on board *La Gavotte*.[112]

On 1 May, Commander Matthew Smith of the sloop *Nautilus* cruising off Oporto wrote to Cotton: 'In Spain matters are in great confusion, the French troops save a few, have retired from Madrid into camp, owing to the discontent of the populace still, as they are, the Spaniards have no hope but to yield to Napoleon.' Smith continued to say that King Carlos had travelled to Bayonne to meet Napoleon, that Fernando would also be a hostage and that Napoleon's brother, Lucien, would be placed on the Spanish throne. He also wrote that '... every account mentions the great tumults at Madrid, but that the French are in such force on the North of the Pyrenees they will carry the point.'[113] Events in the Iberian Peninsula were about to take a most dramatic, and for Napoleon unwelcome, turn.

Dos de Mayo

Maréchal Murat had been placed in command of the French troops in Spain on 20 February, and, in early March, his forces began to take control of the fortresses in the north. He was ordered to send troops south to Madrid and ensure that Godoy, King Carlos IV and the rest of the royal family were sent north to meet with Napoleon. Obfuscation and lies were used to thinly veil French intentions. Fernando's followers thought that Napoleon intended to give the throne to the prince but recognised that any direct conflict with the French would probably lead to the end of the dynasty. The revolt at Aranjuez was orchestrated to force the replacement of Carlos with Fernando, who would then appeal to Napoleon for protection. Spain was riven with division and simmering discontent from many different causes, many linked to reforms that either went too far or not far enough for portions of the population. Many looked to the French as a means to the change they desired. Following the abdication of Carlos, King Fernando VII rode into Madrid to widespread approbation, but Murat had by then occupied the city and did not recognise the new ruler. Napoleon summoned all the parties to Bayonne, where he told both Carlos and Fernando to renounce the throne, which they did at the beginning of May. But by then, violence had already spread through Spain, and Madrid was in open revolt.[114]

The uprising of 2 May began when a crowd gathered at Aranjuez on rumours that the last members of the royal family were being sent to France. A mob surrounded two carriages outside

111 TNA: ADM 1/339: Cotton to Wellesley-Pole, 23 April 1808.
112 M. Foy, *History of the War in the Peninsula under Napoleon* (London: Treuttel, 1827), vol.II, pp.563–564.
113 TNA: ADM 1/339: Smith to Cotton, 1 May 1808.
114 Esdaile, *Peninsular War*, pp.32–36.

'Death of Velarde on May 2, 1808', by Manuel Castellano. (Museo de Historia de Madrid, CC BY-SA 4.0)

the palace, and Murat, whose headquarters were close, ordered them cleared. Shots were fired, and 10 Spaniards were killed. The crowd scattered, but far from fleeing for their homes, they gathered any weapons they could find and began to attack the French. With most French troops garrisoned outside the city, as Napoleon had repeatedly told Junot to do at Lisbon, few troops were caught in the initial violence but columns soon entered the city. Despite some heroic resistance by Spanish troops, most of the crowds were outgunned and quickly killed, wounded or dispersed. By the afternoon, the casualties were in the hundreds, and the city was quiet. As night fell, the executions began.[115]

---

115 Esdaile, *Peninsular War*, pp.38–39.

4

Revolt

A Conjunct Operation

Major General Brent Spencer and his troops had been kicking their heels at Gibraltar for two months. On 18 March, he had written to Castlereagh to let him know that the proposed attack on the Spanish enclave of Ceuta on the African coast was impossible. He sent the four battalions of the KGL and the recruits for the regiments in Sicily to that island and requested the immediate return of the detachments of the 29th, 32nd, 50th, and 82nd Foot, plus his staff and medical personnel, which had managed to cross the Channel on their first attempt and had subsequently been sent on into the Mediterranean.

News of the Spanish uprisings quickly reached Gibraltar. The acting governor, Lieutenant General Sir Hew Dalrymple, wrote to Spencer on 12 May explaining that he had proposed to *Teniente General* Francisco Javier Castaños, the local Spanish commander, that in the event of open conflict between France and Spain, the royal family should sail to Spanish territories in South America from Cadiz, and also that Spanish batteries should allow the Royal Navy to take the French squadron at Cadiz, which had been there since the Battle of Trafalgar. He wrote, 'As this plan did not seem sufficiently digested, and depended on previous arrangements, which would probably create delay and consequently failure, I have strongly urged the seizure of the French Fleet as the first act of hostility against France' and that such an action would 'stamp a character of vigour upon the Spanish councils.' He advised Spencer to embark, even without a clear plan of cooperation from the Spanish, as it was important that Britain take maximum advantage of the developing situation and concluded, 'I foresee no concurrence of circumstances which in the present situation of Spain can justify any other than a conjunct operation between the troops and the Ships of War.'[1]

By 14 May, Spencer was writing to Castlereagh from the 16-gun sloop *Minorca* in Gibraltar Bay of his 'intention in concurrence with Sir Hew Dalrymple, of employing the Troops under my command, to take advantage of any circumstance in the present unsettled state of affairs in Spain that might promise a favourable result to the British Interest.'[2] Following conversations with Sir Hew and the naval commander Rear Admiral John Child Purvis, Spencer and his remaining troops had embarked and were about to sail for Cadiz to cooperate with Purvis 'in any enterprize

---

1   BL: Add MS 49489: Dalrymple to Spencer, 12 May 1808.
2   TNA: WO 1/226: Spencer to Castlereagh, 14 May 1808.

or measure that may be likely in our opinion to benefit the Public Service.' And that it was 'not the intention to incur any imprudent risk or to undertake any thing that does not promise speedy and probable success.'[3] The officers at Gibraltar were acting on their own initiative.[4]

The embarkation return of Spencer's force shows a total of 3,107 officers and men. However, the 32nd and 82nd Foot only had roughly half their men present, and the 29th and 50th had approximately two-thirds,[5] the remainder being in Sicily.

By 29 May, Spencer was off Cadiz and writing to Castlereagh from HMS *Atlas* (74):

> Every account received from Spain for some time previous to my departure from Gibraltar agreed in representing that the eyes of the Spanish Nation were opened and beginning to view, in true light, the intentions of the French rulers in regards to Spain; that the false and perfidious pretexts under which a French Army had been introduced into the country, and the persons of the King and Royal Family attacked were unmasked; and that a consequent spirit of indignation and animosity was universally excited, promising a firm and general resistance to the treachery and unjustifiable aggressions of the French.[6]

Purvis and Spencer had hoped that the presence of British troops with the Royal Naval squadron that had already been blockading Cadiz would imbue confidence in the locals to rise against the French, and they would then accept Britain's assistance in taking the French ships that were sheltering in the port. Ensign Charles Leslie of the 29th recalled the arrival of the convoy at Cadiz on 18 May:

> From our position we could clearly see every ship of the enemy's fleet, because, from their lying in the upper harbour, there was only the low, narrow strip of land which unites Cadiz to the mainland between us and them. The combined fleet consisted of five or six French ships of the line, with some frigates, under the command of Admiral Rossilly, six Spanish sail of the line, and some frigates.
>
> Being anchored pretty much inshore, many of the inhabitants came off to welcome us, shouting, 'Viva, viva, los Ingleses!' and expressing most earnest wishes to unite with England in driving the French from their town and country.[7]

Purvis and Spencer wrote to Spanish officers and published some proclamations but only felt able to offer general sympathy and support rather than any specific action. The senior Spanish army officer at Cadiz was *Teniente General* Marqués Solano – who had recently returned from Portugal. Purvis and Spencer wrote to him that Britain was in 'no way hostile to the Spanish Nation. On the contrary they again anxiously proffer their co-operation and are ready to afford any means your Excellency shall point out as necessary to forward those views which may be likely to benefit the British and Spanish Nations.'[8] They urged Solano to make a quick decision, but Spencer had to

---

3   TNA: WO 1/226: Spencer to Castlereagh, 14 May 1808.
4   TNA: WO 6/185: Castlereagh to Spencer, 17 May 1808.
5   TNA: WO 1/226: Embarkation Return, Gibraltar 13 May 1808.
6   TNA: WO 1/226: Spencer to Castlereagh, 29 May 1808.
7   Leslie, C., *Military Journal of Colonel Leslie, K.H, of Balquhain* (Aberdeen: Aberdeen University Press, 1887), p.19.
8   BL: Add MS 49489: Spencer and Purvis to Solano, undated.

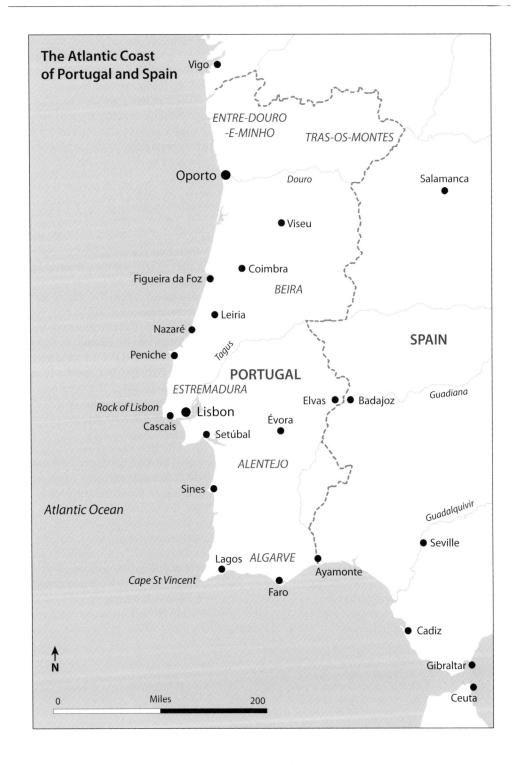

The Atlantic Coast
of Portugal and Spain

Vigo

ENTRE-DOURO
-E-MINHO

TRAS-OS-MONTES

Oporto

Douro

Salamanca

Viseu

Coimbra

Figueira da Foz

BEIRA

Leiria

Nazaré

SPAIN

Tagus

Peniche

PORTUGAL

ESTREMADURA

Elvas Badajoz

Guadiana

Rock of Lisbon

Lisbon

Évora

Cascais

Setúbal

ALENTEJO

Sines

Atlantic Ocean

Guadalquivir

Seville

Lagos

ALGARVE

Cape St Vincent

Ayamonte

Faro

Cadiz

N

Gibraltar

Ceuta

0   Miles   200

report to Castlereagh that the governor had 'not felt himself bold enough to oppose the views of the French.'[9] In a private letter to Lieutenant Colonel James Willoughby Gordon, military secretary to the Duke of York, Spencer wrote that Solano had marched from Portugal on the road to Madrid intending to oppose the French but met with one of Murat's staff officers and then turned for Cadiz where he assumed command. Spencer told Gordon, 'whilst the Government of the Province remains rested in the Marquis's hands there is little or no probability that the friendly disposition in our favor and the utmost hatred and dislike of the people against the French would be excited. We understand the Marquis has lost much of his former popularity by the conduct he has pursued.'[10] Solano's lack of action was to cost him dearly.

The Loss of the *Rapid*

On 16 May, Cotton reported to the Admiralty that Junot's efforts to reduce the flow of refugees to his squadron had largely succeeded and that very few had joined over the previous three weeks.[11] However, the blockade continued to bite, and Junot, possibly after hearing of the unrest in Spain, had responded to the offer of a maritime capitulation.

On the 18th, Miguel Setaro returned to the *Hibernia,* but this time on behalf of Junot. He told Cotton that a copy of his proclamation had been sent to Napoleon at Bayonne and that an answer was expected shortly. In the meantime, Junot asked that possible terms be returned with Setaro. Cotton responded that officers of rank should negotiate such things and that Junot should send someone out under a flag of truce. Setaro gave Cotton detailed reports of events in Madrid and said that if the revolt was successful, something similar could occur in Portugal, but Junot's confiscation of all arms might limit the ability of the people to rise up. He then hinted 'that a transport or two loaded with arms might be highly beneficial.'[12] However, Cotton passed on his doubts about Setaro's sincerity to his superiors. When Napoleon received a copy of Cotton's proclamation, his response to Junot was dismissive:

> I suppose you did not respond to it in any way. It is just a way of intriguing the country and finding out what is going on. As for the maritime surrender, I do not know what Admiral Cotton means. A capitulation is a dishonourable act in military terms. It can only be responded to with cannon fire.[13]

On the same day that Cotton met with Setaro, one of the squadron's vessels was lost in action. HM Sloop *Primrose* (16), Commander James Mein, and HM Gun-Brig *Rapid* (12), Lieutenant Henry Baugh, were sailing off Cape St Vincent when they spotted two feluccas to windward, coming around the cape. Mein hoisted the signal to give chase, but the two vessels eluded them and anchored in Sagres Bay under the protection of a shore battery. Mein did not give up easily, though, as he suspected the feluccas were Spanish, even though they were flying Portuguese colours. He ordered the *Rapid* to take the lead, as she had the shallower draft and a Portuguese pilot on board.

---

9   TNA: WO 1/226: Spencer to Castlereagh, 29 May 1808.
10   BL: Add MS 49489: Spencer to Gordon, 29 May 1808.
11   TNA: ADM 1/339: Cotton to Wellesley-Pole, 16 May 1808.
12   TNA: ADM 1/339: Cotton to Wellesley-Pole, 18 May 1808.
13   Plon & Dumaine (eds), *Correspondance*, vol.17, 13968, p.188, Napoleon to Junot, 23 May 1808.

The sloop and the brig sailed into the bay to cut out the feluccas. While the boats were being lowered, a shot from the battery hit the bow of the *Rapid* below the waterline, stoving in some of the planking.[14] Lieutenant Baugh's report stated:

> The vessel filled so fast with water that although both pumps were immediately set to work I had only time to hail the Primrose Sloop, Captain Mein, and request the assistance of his carpenter, who found any attempt to repair the Rapid's damages impossible, and a few minutes after myself and crew had quitted her she sunk, only being able to save a very few articles.[15]

After the crew of the *Rapid* had all been rescued, Mein still did not give up on taking the feluccas. During the night, he sent boats to take them, but with the wind freshening, they returned at daylight after failing to reach them. He then tried again:

> Upon reconnoitring the bay on the 19th I perceived one of the vessels still remaining, and seeing two Gibraltar Privateers to leeward, I worked to windward of the battery during the day:– At 7 PM having the three cutters manned and armed in tow I bore up and after the shot from the batteries had passed over us I ordered the boats off, to row in shore as close as their oars would allow them, I then made sail close in and engaged the batteries and in less than half an hour, they were completely silenced; the boats performed this service according to my orders under the direction of Lieutenant Lawrence first of this sloop, but unfortunately the vessel had made her escape.[16]

Nothing to Fear from the English

On 17 May, Junot wrote to Napoleon, 'In spite of the latest events in Spain, and the insinuations which the malevolent sought to spread in the Portuguese population, in spite of public misery and the shortage of food, which made us fear famine every day, the people of Lisbon, and Portugal as a whole, have maintained themselves in the most perfect peace.'[17] The next day, he sent Setaro to Cotton seeking terms for the proposed maritime capitulation. In his letter to the Emperor, he said that the people of Portugal wanted Napoleon to nominate a new king to take over the country, but, as events were quickly to show, this was far from the case.

Despite the unrest in Spain, Napoleon still sought to add South America to his sphere of influence. Murat in Madrid had sent orders to Junot for a small squadron of ships to be prepared to sail whenever Cotton's squadron was blown off station. Junot told Napoleon that he would arm six gunboats and get them ready to sail to Veracruz and the Spanish colonies, with dispatches for the viceroy there and a cargo of muskets. However, he had to admit he did not have enough sailors to man them. Napoleon had also asked for as much information as possible, including maps and charts, on Brazil and its defences.[18] He wrote to Murat with a long list of instructions relating to South America, including appointing new governors for the colonies and sending ships, men and

---

14   TNA: ADM 1/339: Mein to Cotton, 25 May 1808.
15   TNA: ADM 1/339: Baugh to Cotton, 25 May 1808.
16   TNA: ADM 1/339: Mein to Cotton, 25 May 1808.
17   Sepulveda, *Historia*, vol.XII, p.190, Junot to Napoleon, 17 May 1808.
18   Sepulveda, *Historia*, vol.XII, pp.203–204, Junot to Napoleon, 17 May 1808.

arms.[19] Tsar Alexander had placed the Russian squadron in the Tagus under the orders of Napoleon. The Emperor wrote to *Vitse-admiral* Senyavin, asking him for detailed returns and reports on the status of the ships. He was also pressing Junot to complete the repairs and refits to the ships the Portuguese had left behind and asking them to be victualled for six months.[20] At the end of May, he asked Junot if Lisbon harbour could accommodate 50 warships and 100 transports.[21]

However, while looking across the Atlantic may have been absurdly optimistic, the situation in Spain made Napoleon order Junot to move some troops to the border. On 11 May, he told Junot to send *général de division* Loison with 400 cavalry, 16 guns and 3,200 infantry to Almeida to co-operate with *maréchal* Bessières at Burgos and to be ready to act against Ciudad Rodrigo, Salamanca or Valladolid.[22] Two days later, he also ordered him to send 2,400 infantry and 400 cavalry with four guns to Elvas to be ready to act against Badajoz or further into Spain. He also stressed that all troops sent to the border should be French, ruling out Junot using any of the Swiss, German or Italian troops in his corps. Surprisingly, Napoleon told Junot that he could replace the troops in their existing posts with men of Carafa's Spanish division.[23]

With Solano's division withdrawn from the south and the remnants of Taranco's division sent to Galicia, it was only Carafa's Spanish troops that remained in Portugal, with 4,000 in Oporto and the rest in detachments dispersed around Lisbon, Mafra, Santarém, Setúbal, and Sesimbra. As soon as news of the insurrections in Madrid reached Badajoz, *Teniente* Moretti of the Guardias Valonas (Walloon Guards) was sent to sound out Caraffa about his returning to Spain. With his troops so spread out, he felt he could not risk antagonising the French. His soldiers were not always as reticent, and tensions rose between French and Spanish troops. Many deserted and headed for the border. The Regimiento de Línea Murcia marched en masse in defiance of their commander. French troops were sent to stop them, but the Spanish overcame them, inflicting casualties, and marched on. Not surprisingly, Junot then began to confine the Spanish troops or separate them into smaller detachments under the control of larger bodies of French.[24]

Junot did his best to comply with Napoleon's orders to send troops to the border, but the shortage of food made any troop movements difficult, and the lack of transport made sending food with the troops impossible.[25] However, he told Napoleon that the detachments would seriously weaken his army and that he had insufficient troops in Oporto, Coimbra and the Algarve.[26] He was proved correct as these would be the first regions to rebel against the French occupation. On 30 May, Junot told Napoleon that he had fewer than 12,000 infantry left and needed 5,000 in Lisbon, 4,000 in the forts on the Tagus, and 3,000 in Setúbal and on the left bank of the Tagus. He also needed to defend Peniche and did not know how he could gather 6,000 men in a mobile force to counter any British invasion without inviting insurrections in the areas denuded of troops. He also did not have enough guns, artillerymen, or suitable horses.[27]

19   Plon & Dumaine (eds), *Correspondance*, vol.17, 13998, pp.212–213, Napoleon to Murat, 26 May 1808.
20   Plon & Dumaine (eds), *Correspondance*, vol.17, 13840, p.83, Napoleon to Senyavin, 10 May 1808. 13842, Napoleon to Junot, 10 May 1808, pp.84–85.
21   Plon & Dumaine (eds), *Correspondance*, vol.17, 14023, p.234, Napoleon to Junot, 29 May 1808.
22   Plon & Dumaine (eds), *Correspondance*, vol.17, 13861, p.100, Napoleon to Junot, 11 May 1808.
23   Plon & Dumaine (eds), *Correspondance*, vol.17, 13880, p.118, Napoleon to Junot, 13 May 1808.
24   Southey, *History*, vol.II, pp.35–37.
25   Sepulveda, *Historia*, vol.XII, p.199, Junot to Napoleon, 24 May 1808.
26   Sepulveda, *Historia*, vol.XII, p.205, Junot to Napoleon, 27 May 1808.
27   Sepulveda, *Historia*, vol.XII, p.209, Junot to Napoleon, 30 May 1808.

Napoleon tried to calm Junot's fears of any landings by the British. On the 18th he wrote:

> I have ordered General Solano to return to Cadiz. 8,000 Spaniards are enough for you,
> 4,000 in Porto and 4,000 on the left of the Tagus; they will do you the service of guarding
> the coast, and you will be master of everything. Sweden, Sicily and the thousand and one
> points which the English are obliged to guard or occupy, and the events in Spain, give
> reason to believe that they will not attempt anything in Portugal.[28]

However, the British government were closely watching events in the Iberian Peninsula and would
soon be drawing up their plans to intervene.

For the Rescue of the World

On 21 May 1808, the British newspapers began to carry accounts of the Dos de Mayo uprising. The
initial reports were taken from Dutch newspapers, copying *Le Moniteur Universel*. *The Sun*, relying
on the French accounts, related how Murat had to rescue members of the Spanish royal family
from a mob and then roused the garrison:

> A firing took place from two ranks, and in a short time the multitude were dispersed.
> General Grouchy was ordered to disperse the crowds in the street of Alcala [Calle de
> Alcalá] – thirty pieces of cannon with grape shot, and a charge of cavalry, cleared all the
> streets. Yet the insurgents, though they fled from the streets into the houses, fired from
> them upon French soldiers – Generals Guillot and Daubin broke open the doors, and all
> who were found with arms in their hands were put to death. – General Damesnel made
> two charges with cavalry in the square, and had two horses killed under him. The insur-
> gents made for the arsenal to seize the arms and cannon – they broke in, but Gen. Lefaen
> arrived in time to save the arms. All who were found in the arsenal were put to death.[29]

A week later, reports from Spanish sources had reached London, and the papers were beginning
to report wider disturbances across the country. The *Public Ledger and Daily Advertiser* thought
the French would 'find it extremely difficult indeed to subdue that general spirit of independence
which appear to manifest itself throughout Spain.'[30]

Spanish fever broke out in earnest following the arrival of a delegation from the northern province of Asturias. The Vizconde de Matarrosa and Andrés Ángel de la Vega Infanzón, two young
Spanish noblemen, had rowed out into the Bay of Biscay from Gijon and boarded the *Stag*, a privateer from Jersey. They offered the captain 500 guineas to take them to Britain, and they arrived in
London on 8 June after landing at Falmouth, seeking British aid.[31] The proclamation they carried
declared that since the king had been forced to cede powers to Napoleon, the Junta of the Asturias
had taken supreme powers until the monarchy was restored and that the Junta had 'in consequence,

---

28   Plon & Dumaine (eds), *Correspondance*, vol.17, 13931, p.161, Napoleon to Junot, 18 May 1808.
29   *The Sun*, 21 May 1808.
30   *Public Ledger and Daily Advertiser*, 28 May 1808.
31   G. Daly, *The British Soldier in the Peninsular War* (Basingstoke: Palgrave Macmillian, 2013), p.20.

resolved to oppose with arms, and has solemnly declared war against, the French.'[32] After meeting with them, Canning wrote to King George that afternoon, passing on their request for assistance and saying that the neighbouring provinces of Leon and Galicia were also in revolt against French rule. The King sent an immediate reply:

> His Majesty cannot but feel willing to afford every support to those loyal subjects of the Spanish monarchy who are desirous of opposing unjust usurpation, but he conceives that nothing should be done hastily, and that it will be advisable to wait for further advices from Sir Hew Dalrymple and Admiral Purvis, while every preparation may be made to give effect to the decision which may ultimately be taken.[33]

The following day, the opposition-leaning *Morning Chronicle* fully supported giving the Spanish people assistance:

> Spain is no longer our enemy when she ceases to act under the controul [*sic*] of France. By Assisting Spain against France, we should be fighting our own battles; we should be opposing a mound to the overwhelming tide of conquest before it reaches our shores; we should be proclaiming to the subject states of Europe, that no peoples disposed in earnest to combat for their liberties will be allowed to struggle unaided…[34]

Such sentiments soon spread to parliament. In a debate on affairs in Spain on 15 June, opposition Whig MP Richard Brinsley Sheridan said:

> Sir, I may be wrong; I am far from wishing ministers to embark in any rash and romantic enterprise in favour of Spain; but, sir, if the enthusiasm and animation, which now exists in a part of Spain, should spread over the whole of that country, I am convinced that since the first burst of the French revolution, there never existed so happy an opportunity for Great Britain to strike a bold stroke for the rescue of the world.[35]

In his reply, Canning stated that 'there exists the strongest disposition on the part of the British government to afford every practicable aid in a contest so magnanimous.' Supporting a popular war of liberation against foreign rule was also attractive to the Whig opposition, and the cause offered a rare and fleeting moment of consensus in British politics.[36]

Ministers were already making plans to intervene, with Castlereagh having written to the King on 1 June seeking approval for a force for service off the coast of Spain, but with South America as a possible alternative destination.[37] However, the situation was still far from clear. Whereas Portugal and Britain were traditional allies, Spain and Britain were traditional enemies, having been at war

---

32   Vane (ed.), *Correspondence*, vol.VI, p.363, Asturias Proclamation.
33   Aspinall (ed.), *Later Correspondence*, vol.V, p.82, 3669, George III to Canning, 8 June 1808.
34   *Morning Chronicle*, 9 June 1808.
35   'Affairs of Spain'. Hansard, <https://hansard.parliament.uk/Commons/1808-06-15/debates/f43c66f5-6765-485b-970a-a6c2b380d208/AffairsOfSpain>, accessed March 2022.
36   J. Bew, *Castlereagh* (London: Quercus, 2011), p.228.
37   Aspinall (ed.), *Later Correspondence*, vol.V, p.82, 3667, Castlereagh to George III, 1 June 1808.

'The Spanish-bull-fight, – or-the Corsican-matador in danger', by James Gillray. The heads of European states look on as the Spanish bull breaks the chain of French occupation and attacks Napoleon while urinating on their imposed king, Joseph. (Anne S.K. Brown Military Collection)

for almost 40 of the previous 100 years. Spain was a colonial and commercial rival, and British policy had for many years been concerned with limiting or reducing its empire.

The government was still concerned about the fate of the Spanish colonies in South America and Napoleon's designs upon them. Castlereagh wrote to the Duke of Manchester, governor of Jamaica, on 4 June with news of events in Spain and then stated that the government wanted to prevent the colonies from falling into French hands.[38] He asked Manchester to pass on the news to Cuba's governor and even offer troops to help defend the island. It was hoped the colonies would declare temporary independence from the rule of Madrid until the monarchy was restored under British protection.

One of the government's key sources of information on the situation in Spain was Sir Hew Dalrymple at Gibraltar. As early as April, a Gibraltarian merchant named Viali, who knew Castaños well, introduced Dalrymple to a confidential agent of the Spanish general who then acted as a conduit between the two. Dalrymple later wrote: 'The communications from Algeciras to this gentleman were frequently by letter, under feigned names and figurative expressions; but on

---

38   Vane (ed.), *Correspondence*, vol.VI, p.365, Castlereagh to Manchester, 4 June 1808.

more important occasions, by meetings, in the Spanish lines, between Mr. Viali and the Secretary of General Castaños, or some other confidential person employed by that General.'[39] Soon after the revolt in Madrid, on 8 May, Viali met with Castaños' secretary. British support for taking the French fleet at Cadiz, securing Ceuta, and occupying Minorca were all discussed. Dalrymple was cautious not to promise more than he was authorised to do so and fed all the information back to London. Eventually, one of Dalrymple's staff, Captain Samuel Ford Whittingham (13th Light Dragoons), was attached to Castaños' headquarters.[40] A Spanish speaker, Whittingham had previously been sent to Spain on a secret mission for Prime Minister William Pitt.[41]

The situation in Spain was still in flux, with rumours and plans that came to nothing abounding. With events moving so quickly and communication so slow, the government's instructions to the officers in the region could only be very vague. Rear Admiral Purvis off Cadiz was told 'to act as circumstance shall point out in support of the efforts of the Spanish nation.'[42] Castlereagh wrote to Dalrymple in early July that 'I am to convey to you His Majesty's approbation of the line of conduct which you have so judiciously pursued…' and then continued to urge him to 'neglect no means in your power for encouraging the spirit and assisting the efforts of the Spanish nation…' In the same letter, he stated:

> It must be evident, that if this noble spirit that has burst forth, and which seems to be universal thro' the provinces of Spain, can be maintained for any considerable time that the most beneficial results may take place not only to Spain itself but to Europe & the world; if on the contrary the effort shall turn out to be merely momentary, & shall languish, or cease upon conflict or ill success, not only the servitude of Spain, but that of Europe may be for a long period irrevocably fixed.[43]

Dalrymple was left in no doubt that the support of the Spanish patriots was a priority for the government.

The government was eager to do what it could to support the Spanish. On June 16, Canning ordered that Spanish prisoners of war in Britain be released. Colonel Sir Thomas Dyer, Major Joshua Roche, and Captain Robert William Patrick (all Spanish speakers) were sent to Gijon to ensure the safe disembarkation of the arms the government was sending to the Junta of Asturias and also to gain information on the strength of both the Spanish and French forces in the area.[44]

On 26 June, Lord Mulgrave, First Lord of the Admiralty, reported to the King that Captain William Tremlett of HMS *Alcemene* had just arrived with two deputies from Galicia. Canning informed the King later that: 'The accounts which these gentlemen bring of the state of affairs in Spain are highly satisfactory, as shewing that the spirit of resistance to France has pervaded a greater portion of the Kingdoms and Provinces of Spain than any former reports had described.'[45]

---

39   H. Dalrymple, *Memoir written by General Sir Hew Dalrymple of his Proceedings as Connected with the Affairs of Spain, and the Commencement of the Peninsular War* (London: Boone, 1830), p.13.
40   Dalrymple, *Memoir*, p.15.
41   R. H. Vetch, revised by Charles Esdaile, 'Whittingham, Sir Samuel Ford', ODNB, <https://doi.org/10.1093/ref:odnb/29328>, accessed July 2022.
42   TNA: WO 6/185: Castlereagh to Purvis, 28 June 1808.
43   TNA: WO 6/185: Castlereagh to Dalrymple, 6 July 1808.
44   Vane (ed.), *Correspondence*, vol.VI, p.371, Castlereagh to Dyer, 19 June 1808.
45   Aspinall (ed.), *Later Correspondence*, vol.V, pp.89–90, 3676, Mulgrave to George III, 3677, Canning to George III, 26 June 1808.

A significant military intervention in support of the Spanish patriots was the kind of strategic opportunity to materially affect the course of the war on the continent that the government had been looking for. A chance to act on the European stage rather than on the periphery in the West Indies or South America. As historian Christopher Hall wrote: 'In a purely military sense it is hard to conceive of any area in Europe that was better suited for Britain to maintain a protracted land campaign against the Napoleonic Empire than the Iberian Peninsula.'[46] The Peninsula had 1,500 miles of coastline, with most of the major population centres on or near the sea, which would both ensure that any British force could be maintained and supported by the Royal Navy and also that the French would have to be dispersed and have to rely on the poor internal road system with long lines of communication back to France. A hostile population would make those lines of communication vulnerable to disruption.[47]

The force that Castlereagh wrote to the King about on 1 June was the one that had been gathering in Cork for a possible operation in South or Central America, for which Lieutenant General Sir Arthur Wellesley had assisted in the planning and was destined to command. On 30 June, Castlereagh sent instructions to Wellesley that the occupation of Spain and Portugal: 'has determined His Majesty to direct a corps of his troops … to be prepared for service and to be employed under your orders in counteracting the designs of the enemy, and in affording to the Spanish and Portuguese nations every possible aid in throwing off the yoke of France.' However, as the deputies from Asturias:

> … do not desire the employment of any corps of His Majesty's troops in the quarter of Spain from whence they are immediately delegated, but have rather pressed; as calculated to operate a favourable diversion in the favour; the importance of directing the efforts of the British troops to the expulsion of the enemy from Portugal, that the insurrection against the French may thereby become general throughout that Kingdom as well as Spain, it is therefore deemed expedient that your attention should be immediately directed to that quarter.[48]

Wellesley's instructions gave him considerable latitude to act as circumstances dictated and to land on the coast of Spain if a landing in Portugal was deemed impractical or if the Spanish decided that they did want British troops. He was also told that an additional 10,000 troops were being prepared, and it was hoped that these would be ready to sail in three weeks. Castlereagh closed with, 'The entire and absolute evacuation of all the Peninsula by the troops of France being, after what has lately passed, the only security for Spanish independence, and the only basis upon which the Spanish nation should be prevailed upon to treat, or to lay down their arms.'[49]

---

46   Hall, *Wellington's Navy*, p.3.
47   Hall, *Wellington's Navy*, pp.3–4.
48   TNA: WO 6/185: Castlereagh to Wellesley, 30 June 1808.
49   TNA: WO 6/185: Castlereagh to Wellesley, 30 June 1808.

'The noble Spaniards. Or Britannia assisting the course of freedom all over the world, whither friend or foe!', by Cruikshank. (Anne S.K. Brown Military Collection)

A Most Material and Satisfactory Change

On 6 June, Spencer wrote to Castlereagh, 'A most material and satisfactory change has taken place in the affairs of the Spanish Dominions.'[50] On 30 May, with the situation looking unpromising and no sign of cooperation from Solano and the authorities in Cadiz, Spencer had contemplated a return to Gibraltar to water and provision the transports and await further orders. However, *Contra almirante* Enrique MacDonell, a Spanish officer of Irish descent, and Don Pedro Cruiz, a judge of the Royal Court, arrived with the Royal Navy squadron under a flag of truce to take up Purvis and Spencer's offer of British assistance. They informed the British that a supreme junta had been formed in Seville, and Solano had been killed by a mob frustrated at his reluctance to act against the French.[51]

The Spanish delegation returned to the squadron on 31 May and invited the British officers to a conference in Cadiz. Purvis and Spencer were initially reluctant to send anyone ashore until the question of the French fleet had been settled, but eventually, they acquiesced in case a refusal was taken as a lack of confidence in the new regime. Captain Sir John Gore of the *Revenge* and Lieutenant Colonel Sir George Smith were sent ashore.

---

50   TNA: WO 1/226: Spencer to Castlereagh, 6 June 1808.
51   'La trágica muerte del General Solano', *Instituto Nacional Sanmartiniano*, <https://sanmartiniano.cultura.gob. ar/noticia/general-solano/>, accessed August 2022.

After a long negotiation, they returned to the squadron with the junta's proposal for an agreement between themselves and Britain. The first article proposed that the peace of 1783, following the American War of Independence, be restored 'in all its points'. The second stated that as France was the common enemy, they hoped Britain would assist them 'with all necessary means in their power.' The third dealt with sending news of the uprising to the American colonies. The fourth hoped that Spanish vessels would no longer be interfered with by Royal Navy ships. The final article stated that the French squadron would be dealt with as soon as an agreement was reached.[52]

Considering the importance and implications of the Spanish proposal, Purvis and Spencer convened a council of war to consider their response. After some deliberation with their officers, Spencer and Purvis submitted their answer. As far as the first article was concerned, they felt they did not have the necessary powers but would convey any Spanish envoys to Britain so a definitive peace could be made. They also thought that they could not abandon their instructions entirely, so they could only agree to a limited armistice, which would include all Spanish ships being free to sail without hindrance (but with naval and military stores still subject to some limitations), as long as Cadiz was opened to British shipping. Any Spanish envoys to the Americas would be conveyed there, and, lastly, they reiterated the importance of quickly dealing with the French squadron before any further cooperation could be contemplated.[53] The Spanish troops in Cadiz were preparing to take the batteries covering the French fleet, and Purvis was asked to anchor his ships across the harbour and to be ready to assist if needed. British troops would not be required.

Spencer told Castlereagh that 200,000 Spanish were under arms in the various provinces, but they desperately needed 50,000–60,000 stands of arms, ammunition, and some cannon. He went on to say: 'The system of warfare intended to be adopted is to act generally on the defensive as much as circumstances will allow, confining their offensive operations to cutting off supplies from the French and intercepting the small detachments and divisions they may detach.' This plan of operations had been strongly recommended to the Spanish generals by Smith as the most likely to succeed. Spencer wrote: 'It has been hinted to me that a British land force advanced to Seville and acting with the Spanish troops would prove of the utmost advantage to their cause … but it is my determination not to venture into the interior.'[54] Castlereagh later replied that the government fully approved of the negotiations Spencer and Purvis had opened with the Spanish.[55]

On 10 June, Spencer again updated Castlereagh on events and informed him that the Spanish had asked him to march his force to Jerez, 20 miles inland from Cadiz, but that he had refused, 'As my corps is but small & totally unequipped for any interior movements' and because it would be contrary to his instructions which limited him to operating near the coast. However, he had intelligence that a French force of around 5,000 men under the command of *général de brigade* Jean-Jaques Avril was marching to Tavira, just across the Portuguese border. Part of the force was advancing along the coast in small vessels and planned to land in the rear of the Spanish. Spencer told Castlereagh, 'I propose preceding tomorrow against this Corps and shall land my force should any favourable opportunity offer of attacking them at no great distance from the sea.'[56] The transports carrying the detachments that had sailed to Sicily were in sight, as were those carrying the

52   TNA: WO 1/226: Spanish proposal.
53   TNA: WO 1/226: British answer.
54   TNA: WO 1/226: Spencer to Castlereagh, 6 June 1808, private. A stand of arms was usually a musket, a bayonet, and a cartridge box.
55   TNA: WO 1/226: Castlereagh to Spencer, 6 July 1808.
56   TNA: WO 1/226: Spencer to Castlereagh, 10 June 1808.

6th Foot from Gibraltar. Once everything was ready, the British troops would sail for Ayamonte, just on the Spanish side of the border.

Table 4. Spencer's troops, 19 June 1808

Corps	Cols	Lt. Cols	Majs	Capts	Subs	Staff	Sgts	Drms	Rank & File		Total
									Fit	Sick	
Royal Artillery		1		5	6	1	4	4	243	2	266
RA Drivers									13	1	14
Royal Engineers				1	1				2		4
Royal Staff Corps				1	2		2	1	43	2	51
1/6th Foot		1	2	10	25	5	52	22	946		1,063
29th Foot		1	2	8	19	6	40	17	789	17	899
1/32nd Foot		1	2	9	28	6	48	19	862	12	987
1/50th Foot		1	2	8	16	6	49	22	930	18	1,052
1/82nd Foot		1	2	9	22	6	46	16	881	48	1,031
Total	**0**	**6**	**10**	**51**	**119**	**30**	**241**	**101**	**4,709**	**100**	**5,367**

Source: BL: Add MS 49489: State of the corps under the command of Major General Spencer, off Ayamonte, 19 June 1808.

Despite the change of regime in Cadiz, the French squadron in the harbour had continued to refuse any terms, so on 9 June, operations against them began. Spanish batteries and mortar boats opened fire at 3:00 p.m. The French returned fire, and the duel lasted until nightfall. Ensign John Patterson of the 50th Foot witnessed the exchange of fire:

> The enemy was resolved to maintain his quarters as long as he could fire a shot, and therefore returned the salute, with all the heavy metal he could bring to bear against the works, sending in a broadside, with such tremendous effect as to rattle the tiled roofs about their ears and other wise deface the beauty of their buildings.
>
> Lying so far in the offing, we could see nothing but a thick cloud of smoke, rising above the calm surface of the bay; the exhibition going forward behind this curtain, was completely hidden from our view. The cannonade however, was audible enough, and its music sadly tantalized our seamen in the fleet, who burned to lend a hand in an affair which was so much to their taste.[57]

The Spanish renewed the bombardment on the morning of the 10th, and at 2:00 p.m., the French hoisted a flag of truce. However, their proposed terms were unacceptable, and the bombardment was recommenced. After further negotiations, the French finally surrendered on the 14th.

Brigadier General Nightingall arrived with the 29th and 32nd Foot off Ayamonte on 12 June but could gain no intelligence of any French movements but did hear that the Portuguese were rising everywhere against their occupiers.[58] Spencer arrived on the 14th and eventually heard that the French troops moving along the coast had learned both of Solano's death and the arrival of

---

57   Patterson, *Adventures*, pp.26–27.
58   BL: Add MS 49502: Nightingall to Gordon, 14 June 1808.

British troops. Avril aborted his advance and instead moved inland, leaving small detachments along the Algarve coast, including 200–300 men at Villa Real, just the other side of the Guadiana River to Ayamonte. Spencer did contemplate ejecting the French from Villa Real, but they had a secure line of retreat to forts along the coast, which could not be taken without landing guns, and he thought that they might reoccupy the town and punish the inhabitants once the British left. A Spanish force that had left the garrisons in Portugal was also heading for Ayamonte, and Captain Boyles of the *Windsor Castle*, the ship carrying Spencer, landed 200 stands of arms for them, all he could spare.[59] In return, the Spanish governor offered fresh fruit and vegetables to the British ships. Spencer allowed each transport to send a boat ashore. Lieutenant Charles Leslie of the 29th was lucky enough to be one of the first to go ashore:

> But not being aware that the mouth of the Guadiana consisted of several branches, and that the enemy was in immediate possession of the Portuguese branch, we entered the main channel. On passing a battery which commanded the entrance, we were challenged, but taking no notice we pushed on and soon entered a branch on the Spanish side, by which we reached Ayamonte. I then learned the escape I had just made of being taken prisoner, as the battery we had passed was occupied by the enemy. The other boats had entered by a channel in the Spanish territory. We being the first English who had landed in Spain since the breaking out of the patriotic cause, were received with the most enthusiastic demonstrations of joy by the inhabitants.[60]

On 17 June, Dalrymple at Gibraltar wrote to Spencer that he had received a letter from Cotton 'requesting the co-operation of your corps; with the assistance of which, if it amounts to 5 or 6000 men, he does not seem to doubt of being able to take possession of the whole of the maritime means now collected in that river.'[61] Spencer wrote to Castlereagh that he would comply, subject to the agreement of Collingwood, who had arrived off Cadiz. Collingwood agreed and Spencer began to sail along the Algarve coast in the *Scout* (16), leaving the troops behind under the command of Nightingall and taking Lieutenant Colonels Bathurst and Tucker with him. On 21 June, Spencer was off Lagos and informed Castlereagh that, 'at Faro they have already risen, have taken or destroyed a detachment of about 200 men, have seized the arms and ammunition of the province which the French had collected in a depôt, and also about 40,000 dollars in gold which the French General had amassed.'[62]

Popular Commotions

On 31 May, off Lisbon, a boat approached HMS *Blossom* (18). On board was a boy, presumably British, whom a Mr Wilson had found starving on the streets of the city and sent to the squadron for his protection. Commander George Pigot sent a letter back to Wilson asking if he could supply

---

59 TNA: WO 1/226: Spencer to Castlereagh, 17 June 1808.
60 Leslie, *Military Journal*, p.25.
61 Dalrymple, *Memoir*, p.263, Dalrymple to Spencer, 17 June 1808.
62 TNA: WO 1/226: Spencer to Castlereagh, 21 June 1808.

any intelligence on the situation in the city.[63] Wilson, a merchant who had remained in Lisbon, sent back a hastily written reply:

> First then as positive, this day I saw seventeen ammunition wagons under escort set off for Cadiz, four thousand troops, (particularly infantry) set off tomorrow and on Thursday to follow them.
>
> There now remains sick and well about four thousand in the Forts and environs of Lisbon. This from one of the overseers of the Bread-baking. The number of Spanish troops supposed three thousand (much scattered) they are most arrogantly treated sometimes, nay, principally without cartridges …
>
> The General Junot and staff they are fortifying the castle of St. George (a citadel in the centre of the city) as they seem dreading a popular commotion.[64]

The ammunition wagons and troops marching for Cadiz may have been Avril's force that Spencer had helped dissuade from entering Spain by his arrival at Ayamonte.

Wilson went on to state that letters from Spain were being delayed and censored and that French accounts of the uprisings were full of falsehoods, but that accurate reports were reaching Lisbon: 'In fact such is the distress, such is the anger of the populace that every hour threatens an Insurrection.' He then detailed the state of the Russian and French ships in the harbour and mentioned that the Russians despised the French and would probably not intervene if the British attacked Lisbon. The situation of the population was becoming dire: 'Every day bread grows scarcer, the want of employment among the lower classes misery most miserable.' Wilson then wrote that 5–10,000 troops landing below Forte de Sao Juliao could march on the city, and the population would rise in support. Pigot passed Wilson's information up the chain of command, leading Cotton to ask Dalrymple to send Spencer back to the Tagus.

Wilson made his own escape and was on board the *Hibernia*, being interviewed by Cotton, by 9 June. Cotton told the Admiralty, 'He appears an intelligent man and confirms in the most positive manner the heads of the information contained in his said letter.' Cotton repeated Wilson's assertion that only around 3,000–4,000 French troops and 5,000–6,000 Spanish were in the Lisbon area. The Spanish troops were mainly without officers and lacked much of their equipment and discipline. There had even been skirmishes between the French and Spanish.[65] Cotton's acceptance of Wilson's figures has attracted some criticism from historians.[66] However, with Napoleon's repeated demands for Junot to send troops to the border fortresses and the dispatch of Avril towards Cadiz, it is entirely possible that, for a short time, French troop numbers in and around Lisbon did drop considerably.

Indeed, Wilson's figures were soon confirmed by a Spanish officer, Don Sebastian Solis, who came aboard the *Hibernia* two days later. He had been sent by the junta at Seville to urge the Spanish troops to revolt against the French, assist the Portuguese, or march into Spain. Solis met with *Teniente General* Caraffa but could not persuade him to act. Cotton told the Admiralty on the 12th:

---

63   TNA: ADM 1/339: Percy to Cotton, 2 June 1808.
64   TNA: ADM 1/339: Wilson to Pigot, 31 May 1808.
65   TNA: ADM 1/339: Cotton to Wellesley-Pole, 9 June 1808.
66   See Robson, *South America*, p.218 and Krajeski, *Shadow*, p.81.

From every account I have been able to procure there is not more than 4000 French Troops in Lisbon, from whom the Spaniards are completely separated, and against whom the Populace are highly incensed; so that I feel it a duty, to state to their Lordship's my opinion that five or six thousand British Troops, might effect a Landing, gain possession of the Forts on the Banks of the Tagus, and by cooperating with His Majesty's Fleet give to our possession the whole of the Maritime Means now collected in the Tagus.[67]

There was probably a very narrow window of opportunity when a force of around 5,000 men, landed near Lisbon, could have sparked a revolt, and had a chance at taking the forts. Still, it would have been a hazardous operation and, if it had failed to succeed quickly, may have ended in disaster. The French may have stood firm in the forts, or Junot might have been able to divert men back to Lisbon; the weather may even have turned, meaning the troops could not be supported or re-embarked; or the locals may have been hesitant to actually rise up when faced with the decision.

Events were, in any case, moving far more quickly than the speed of sailing ships back and forth to Britain or even down to Gibraltar and Cadiz. On the same day that Wilson had arrived aboard the *Hibernia*, Cotton also met with Commander George Creyke of the *Eclipse* from Oporto. Creyke reported that on the evening of the 6th, the Spanish troops had taken the few French in Oporto prisoner and marched for Spain the following day. The Portuguese flag had been raised over the forts, and the *Eclipse* had fired a salute, which was then returned. A delegation rowed out and told Creyke that the Prince Regent's government had been restored in Oporto.[68]

The French governor of Oporto was *général de division* François Jean Baptiste Quesnel. He had a small staff and an escort of a troop of dragoons, but there were no other French forces in the city. Following orders from the junta of Galicia, the local Spanish commander, Don Domingo Bellesta, arrested Quesnel and his men and then placed guards around the city to prevent anyone from leaving. Bellesta and his men marched for Spain the next morning, taking their prisoners with them. Before he left, though, he gathered the city's senior officials and urged them to raise the Portuguese flag and form a junta.

Quesnel and the other officers gave their parole and were led through the city to hoots and jeers from the crowds of Portuguese. The Spaniards marched them to La Coruña, where they were held until the French took the town in January 1809 and liberated them. Englishwoman Harriot Slessor, the widow of a general who had been in Portuguese service, had stayed in Oporto when almost all of the rest of the British community had left. She recorded the reaction of the people of Oporto to their new-found freedom in her diary:

> The first impulse of the people was to assemble in immense crowds, and as the news spread like wildfire the country people flocked in from all the villages round. Every hour brings us fresh intelligence of what is passing. Porto is at this minute a scene of wild disorder, the people running about the streets wild with joy at the idea the French are gone. The bells ring without ceasing, and the cry unanimous is '*Viva Portugal, Viva Englaterra, e Viva Espana*'.[69]

---

67   TNA: ADM 1/339: Cotton to Wellesley-Polc, 12 June 1808.
68   TNA: ADM 1/339: Cotton to Wellesley-Pole, 9 June 1808.
69   A. Hayter, *The Backbone, Diaries of a Military Family in the Napoleonic Wars* (Durham: Pentland Press, 1993) p.158.

Oporto, by Henri l'Eveêque, 1817. (Biblioteca Nacional de Portugal)

However, after the celebrations died down, the junta that took control proved hesitant, and the new military commandant, *Brigadeiro* Luis de Oliveira da Costa, was considered sympathetic to the French. Costa even tried to arrest *Major* Raimundo Pinheiro, commander of the fort of Foy do Douro, for raising the Portuguese flag and contacting the Royal Navy.[70]

However uncertain the rising was at Oporto, news of it soon spread and inspired smaller towns and villages in the region to declare against the French. Cotton lost no time in acting to help ferment a similar rising in Lisbon. After he met with Creyke, he issued a proclamation relaying the news and promising support for a similar rising in the city.[71]

Sebastian Solis had warned Caraffa to be on his guard and not to let his troops be disarmed – which he suspected would happen once Junot got news of the events in Oporto. Cotton had to report though that, 'The caution was however neglected and a 3 o'clock this morning the whole of the Spanish Troops at Lisbon being summoned to one of the squares which was planted round with artillery, suffered themselves to be disarmed and sent on board some unserviceable ships in the Tagus.'[72] Solis did not call Caraffa a traitor but told Cotton he was a weak and unworthy commander. Cotton sent the *Eclipse* back to Oporto on the 11th with a proclamation to be

---

70 M. Amaral, *The Portuguese Army and the Commencement of the Peninsular War* (Lisbon: Tribuna, 2007), p.8.
71 TNA: ADM 1/339: Proclamation, 9 June 1808.
72 TNA: ADM 1/339: Cotton to Wellesley-Pole, 11 June 1808.

distributed via fishermen to the scattered Spanish garrisons on the way that told them of the rebellion of Spanish troops and Junot's reaction.[73]

The flow of information to Cotton increased in mid-June, with the fishing boats and others trading fruit and bread freely with the squadron. The Portuguese harvest had begun, and the food shortages were ending. Cotton told the Admiralty that reports in the French-run *Gazeta de Lisboa* 'betray symptoms of much alarm'. He also relayed some unwelcome news: 'An American Gentleman who this day came on board the Hibernia, stated that the French General Junot, is concentrating his forces at Lisbon where they now amount to 10,000 Men.'[74] The window of opportunity for a coup de main on the Tagus forts had firmly closed.

Miguel Setaro, who had previously tried getting Cotton to relax the blockade, wrote to Cotton on 16 and 20 June. His letter of the 16th reported that a battalion had been sent to Oporto from Torres Vedras and also that *général de division* Loison was marching there from Almeida with as many men as could be spared, but he thought that, if the Portuguese rebels held the passage of the Duoro, they might be prevented from entering the city. He added, 'My private opinion is that General Junot will think better of it and will concentrate all his troops in Lisbon and in its neighbourhood, in order to oppose any attack from the British or to put himself in a situation to obtain an honourable capitulation.' The French were stockpiling supplies at Peniche, but their main fear was being cut off from the French forces in Spain. He added, '*I am sure* they have nothing to fear from the inhabitants of Portugal, in their *present situation* before a Landing of Troops takes place and they can be supplied with Arms and Provisions.'[75] On the 20th, Setaro confirmed that the battalion from Torres Vedras had been recalled, and an aide de camp of Loison's had returned from Almeida, possibly after having delivered orders countermanding his general's march from the border.[76]

In his covering letter to the Admiralty, sent with Setaro's letters, Cotton wrote, 'The manner he now comes forward together with the allusion to Junot's intention of putting himself in a situation to obtain an honorable capitulation – induces me to hope things are approaching to a crisis in Lisbon.'[77]

On 24 June, the *Scout* arrived with Cotton's squadron. Spencer, Tucker and Bathurst went on board the *Hibernia* for a conference. The recent concentration of French forces around Lisbon was critical to their discussion. Three deserters from the Légion Hanovrienne had come on board the *Hibernia* on the 22nd, and they were subjected to a 'minute examination' by Cotton and the army officers.[78] Spencer considered the deserters intelligent men, and the information they gave was highly detailed. No hint is provided in the surviving papers of the rank or role of the deserters or how they came to have the information that they revealed to Spencer and Cotton.

---

73   TNA: ADM 1/339: Proclamation, 11 June 1808.
74   TNA: ADM 1/340: Cotton to Wellesley-Pole, 18 June 1808.
75   TNA: ADM 1/340: Setaro to Cotton, 16 June 1808. Emphasis in the original.
76   TNA: ADM 1/340: Setaro to Cotton, 20 June 1808.
77   TNA: ADM 1/340: Cotton to Wellesley-Pole, 20 June 1808.
78   TNA: ADM 1/340: Cotton to Wellesley Pole, 24 June 1808.

Table 5. French Troops in Portugal according to the Hanoverian deserters

In Lisbon and the Neighbourhood				
French Infantry		Total		
15th Regt	Two Battalions	800		
66th Regt	One Battalion	800		
70th Regt	Four Battalions	3,000		
82nd Regt	Two Battalions	800		
86th Regt	Three Battalions	2,000		7,400
French Cavalry				
3rd/9th Regts	Chasseurs a Cheval			2,000
Foreign Infantry				
Hanoverian Legion	One Battalion	800		
Swiss	One Battalion	800		1,600
In St Ubes and the forts on the Southern side of the Tagus				
31st Regt	Chasseurs mostly	One Battalion		800
32nd Regt	Italian mostly	One Battalion		800
Troops marched to the Eastern Frontiers of Portugal				
86th Regt	One Battalion	700		
26th Regt	Two Battalions	1,000		1,700
Foreign Infantry				
Legion du Midi		800		
Swiss	Three Battalions	2,400		3,200
In some part of Portugal unknown to the Deserters				
47th Regt	Four Battalions			3,000
		Total		20,500

Source: TNA: WO 1/226: French Force in Portugal as Stated by Three Hanoverian Deserters, 22 June 1808.

In addition to the units, numbers and locations, the deserters also reported that three regiments of Spanish infantry and one of cavalry had been disarmed and were prisoners on board ships, including some of the Russian fleet. They added that 150 Russians from each ship had been landed and were doing duty in Lisbon, and that Junot had very little artillery in Portugal and was strengthening the citadel in Lisbon. There are many errors in the Hanoverians' information: the numbers of the battalions for some regiments are wrong; the cavalry at Lisbon were dragoons and not chasseurs, and the strength given for them is that of all Junot's cavalry; and Russian sailors had not been landed to do duty ashore. While the individual unit strengths are also inaccurate, the total force strength was far closer to reality than previous intelligence given to the British. However, it was still an underestimate by several thousand. The intelligence that Cotton had received that there were now around 10,000 French near Lisbon was confirmed, though.

Spencer reported to Castlereagh that although the Portuguese people were 'in a ripe state to throw off the French yoke', the concentration of forces around Lisbon meant that they were 'fully capable of resisting a much larger force than could possibly be landed by Sir Charles Cotton and myself.'[79] Spencer believed that a siege train would be needed to tackle the Tagus forts. Cotton's report to the Admiralty concurred with Spencer's to the War Office:

---

79   TNA: WO 1/226: Spencer to Castlereagh, 24 June 1808.

… the French General seems to have concentrated his force there to such numbers as would render success in landing so small a body of men extremely doubtful. The Major General therefore, holding in view the vast importance the troops under his command may be of in Spain, and considering the support of that country the primary object of His Majesty's Government thought it best (in which opinion I concurred) to rejoin his forces…[80]

Council of War

In Lisbon, Junot was becoming increasingly worried and isolated. On 1 June, he informed Napoleon of an uprising at Badajoz and the desertion of more Spanish troops. He had ordered *général de division* Kellermann's column marching to Cadiz to divert to Elvas and intervene at Badajoz. Junot had also ordered troops to pursue the Spanish deserters. He admitted to Napoleon that he felt 'embarrassed in such a critical moment, having been obliged to send the only available troops that I have, and if something were to happen in Lisbon Portugal would be on fire, in an instant'.[81] He also said he regretted sending Loison to Almeida and that he had started to send multiple duplicates of his dispatches to Paris in case they got intercepted. Junot's letter to Napoleon a week later reads like someone trying to stop a wildfire on a neighbour's property from spreading to their own with only a garden hose. He had had to send more troops to Elvas and other points on the Spanish border to try and maintain his communications with Murat. He sent Spanish troops to occupy forts in the Algarve, even though they were of doubtful loyalty; he had no others to spare. He was also worried about the 3,500 Spanish troops in Oporto but had no French troops to send to keep them in check and commented that Quesnel was 'a wise and firm man, but what can he do alone against all?'[82] Napoleon's letter to Junot, dated 3 June, still mainly concentrated on plans to ready ships to cross to South America.[83]

On the morning of 9 June, Junot received news of the Spanish revolt at Oporto and the arrest of Quesnel and his staff. He quickly decided to stop the rot from spreading and ordered the disarming of the remaining Spanish troops in Portugal. Caraffa was summoned to headquarters and arrested before he had any hint of anything happening. Some Spanish regiments were ordered to march and then surrounded; others were taken in their barracks. Some regiments heard what was happening and managed to escape towards Spain. However, the vast majority were disarmed quickly and successfully.[84]

With Badajoz and Ciudad Rodrigo firmly in the hands of the Spanish patriots, Junot called off movements in their direction, deciding there was nothing he could do to help the French in Spain. Instead, he sent *général de division* Loison from Almeida to Oporto with the 1er Régiment provisoire légère and six guns to regain control of the city. A battalion of 12e Légère would march from Torres Vedras to support him. *Général de brigade* Charlot would remain at Almeida with the 4e Suisse and 32e Ligne. The 5e Régiment provisoire dragons would move from Almeida to Elvas.

---

80   TNA: ADM 1/340: Cotton to Wellesley Pole, 24 June 1808.
81   Sepulveda, *Historia*, vol.XII, p.210, Junot to Napoleon, 1 June 1808.
82   Sepulveda, *Historia*, vol.XII, p.218, Junot to Napoleon, 7 June 1808. This is the last letter from Junot's letter book, apparently recovered from the battlefield of Vimeiro.
83   Plon & Dumaine (eds), *Correspondance*, vol.17, 14053, p.263, Napoleon to Junot, 3 June 1808.
84   Thiébault, *l'Expédition*, pp.115–118.

In the south, *général de brigade* Avril was to occupy Estremoz and Évora with a battalion of the 86e Ligne and the 4e Régiment provisoire dragons, with the other battalion of the 86e detached to Elvas. *Colonel* Maransin and the Légion du Midi were to occupy Mértola and Alcoutim on the Guadiana, and he was also to take a battalion of the 26e Ligne under his orders to defend the course of the Guadiana and the coast from Faro to Villa-Real – a stretch of coast 30 miles long.[85] The French forces were now spread extremely thinly.

On 16 June, the festival of Corpo de Deus was held in Lisbon. This was the city's largest and most important procession of the year. Junot had been warned not to let the festival take place in case it became the catalyst for unrest, but he did not want to appear uncertain of the population's loyalties and let it go ahead. He did, however, take the precaution of placing 12 cannon in the Rossio square and ordering the entire garrison under arms. The procession was to start and finish at the church of São Domingos near the Rossio. As soon as it began, the crowd became unruly, which quickly spiralled into widespread rioting. Some French troops fired on the crowds, and others fled. The initial cause of the unrest is unclear, and it was possibly caused by unfounded rumours of a British landing or even the hue and cry of the capture of a thief. Had the violence been planned, or had there been someone to lead it, then it could have been the start of something more serious. As it was, Junot went to the church and forced the priests to rejoin the procession and lead it on its regular route; calm was eventually restored.[86] Even though the disorder in Lisbon was short-lived, Thiébault claims that the festival in other parts of the country marked the start of a general uprising against the French.[87]

News of the uprisings in Spain and other parts of Portugal and rumours of a British army off the coast were discussed in the cafés and bars, in the streets and behind closed doors. Anti-French pamphlets were printed and circulated, and Junot's edicts and proclamations were defaced or torn down. Those who had supported the regime began to have second thoughts.[88] Random acts of violence against French troops increased, and lines of communication to France, which had run through Spain, were effectively cut.

On 26 June, Junot called a council of war of the available generals and department heads to consider his options. The consensus of the council was that the only option was to concentrate troops in and around Lisbon. Garrisons would only be left at the fortresses of Almeida, Elvas and Peniche. Setúbal on the left bank of the Tagus would be held as long as possible. Troops would guard a series of lines north of Lisbon, the outermost from Leiria, through Ourém, to Tomar – the next being between Santarém, Rio Maior, Óbidos and Peniche. Finally, the closest to Lisbon was from Sintra to Sacavém. Provisions would be gathered, and hard-tack biscuits baked. The forts and batteries on the Tagus would be prepared and guns inspected. The sick would be concentrated in hospitals that could be defended and that were near the sea. The ships holding the Spanish were to be kept as far from the city as possible. Lisbon was to be held 'until the last extremity', and if it had to be abandoned, then the troops would march to Elvas to link up with French forces in Spain.[89] Thiébault maintained that the council displayed the unanimity of the French commanders and staff, later writing: 'This conference thus produced the triple good of clarifying our position, of

85   Thiébault, *l'Expédition*, pp.119–120.
86   J.M.F. dos Santos, *Lisboa e a Invasão de Junot: população, periódicos e panfletos* (1807-1808) (MA Dissertation: Universidade Nova de Lisboa, 2014), pp.82–83.
87   Thiébault, *l'Expédition*, p.124.
88   Dos Santos, *Lisboa*, pp.84–86.
89   Thiébault, *l'Expédition*, pp.128–129.

compensating for the insufficiency of our means; as much as they could be, finally, of increasing our strength by the effect of a complete and reciprocal confidence.'[90]

On 26 June, Junot issued another proclamation in which he berated the Portuguese for their ingratitude towards the French, especially Napoleon, saying that they were better off under French rule and outlining his efforts to improve the country. The proclamation ended with: 'All cities and towns where arms have been taken up against my army, and whose inhabitants shall have fired at my troops will be given up to plunder, totally destroyed and its inhabitants put to the sword. Every individual caught with arms will be shot immediately.'[91]

So Just and Glorious a Cause

In Oporto, Costa continued to be reluctant to defy the French and unrest simmered, fuelled by Raimundo Pinheiro who was hiding nearby and advocating for a full rebellion. On 18 June, a rumour circulated that a French force was approaching. The Portuguese flag was raised again, the arsenal opened to any who wanted to arm themselves to defend the city, and four cannon were made ready. Pinheiro marched into the city with an armed party of Spaniards and declared that more were on their way. This galvanised the population further. Men, women, priests, and friars dragged guns up to the heights of Villa Nova. Church bells were rung, muskets were fired into the air, and drums were beaten. Costa and other perceived French sympathisers were imprisoned.[92]

On the 19th, a crowd assembled before the Bishop of Oporto's palace. Bishop Antonio de Sao Jose e Castro stepped out onto the balcony, blessed the crowd, and then led them to the cathedral to ask for God's blessing for their endeavours. A provisional government was formed, with two representatives each from the clergy, the magistrates, the military and the citizens, with the Bishop at its head. The junta immediately declared that the rule of the Prince Regent was re-established, sought military aid from surrounding areas, and began to re-form the regular and militia regiments. The mood in Oporto continued to be febrile, with rumours abounding and French sympathisers or suspected spies attacked. Other towns throughout the provinces of Trás-os-Montes and Entre-Douro-e-Minho declared for the Prince Regent, and the movement began to spread south into Beira.

On the day the junta took power, HMS *Talbot* (18), off the mouth of the Duoro, noticed the Portuguese colours flying from the fort and exchanged salutes. Commander Alexander Jones was invited ashore and met with the Bishop. Jones returned the next day, the 20th, with Commander Creyke of the *Eclipse*. It was agreed that Creyke would provide a party of seamen to man the guns of a merchantman to cover the pontoon bridge across the river, over which the French would have to come if they were going to retake the city.[93] The Bishop also gave Creyke a letter for Cotton, appealing for arms and assistance.

Despite all the rumours and misinformation, the threat from the French was real. *Général de division* Loison had received his orders from Junot on 16 June and marched towards Oporto the next day. This happened to be the same day that Junot wrote new orders for him to abandon

---

90   Thiébault, *l'Expédition*, p.130.
91   TNA: ADM 1/340: Proclamation of the Duke of Abrantes 26 June 1808.
92   Southey, *History*, vol.II, pp.63-65.
93   Hayter (ed.), *The Backbone*, p.167.

Almeida and return to Lisbon as quickly as possible, but, by the 20th, he had marched 70 miles to Lamego. He crossed the Duoro on the 21st and headed for Amarante. He halted for the night at Mesão Frio, where he heard that awaiting the French in the steep, vine-clad hills of the Serra do Marão were a mix of former Portuguese regulars and insurgents, perhaps numbering in their thousands. He was then told that the baggage, still on the riverbank near the ferry, was being attacked. Loison went back with two companies of light infantry to drive off the attackers: during a brief but fierce action, Loison was slightly wounded.[94]

Loison had a very well-earned reputation for brutality. Southey describes him as 'one of those men after Buonaparte's own heart, who, being equally devoid of honour and humanity, carried on war in the worst spirit of the worst ages, plundering and massacring without shame and without remorse.'[95] He had his left arm amputated after a hunting accident in 1806, and the Portuguese gave him the nickname Maneta, which means one-handed. The phrase 'ir para o Maneta' – go to Maneta – entered the Portuguese vernacular as a warning, 'be careful or you will be sent to Maneta', much as the bogeyman is used to frighten British or American children.

On the morning of the 21st, the French cleared the surrounding heights, and then Loison let his troops plunder the nearby villages. Later that day, he marched his men up into the hills to the pass of Os Padroes da Teixieria, but, seeing the number of the Portuguese now barring his way and the strength of their position, he decided to withdraw back across the Duoro to Almeida, pursued for a time by the Portuguese who, though poorly armed, outnumbered him considerably.[96] The Portuguese followed Loison as he marched to Lamego and took the road south. At Castro Daire on 25 June, the Portuguese engaged the rear of the French column and inflicted around 300 casualties, taking two howitzers and much of the baggage.[97] By forcing Loison to abandon his advance on Oporto, the mix of pike-armed locals, militia, and former regulars protected what was to become the centre of the resistance to the French and provided a significant boost to Portuguese morale.[98]

An armed patrol was sent south from Oporto towards Coimbra to discover the size of the French garrison there. Gathering peasants and former Ordenança (local militia) on the way, the force grew. Learning that the French garrison was only 100 men, they marched into the city. A patrol of two French and two Portuguese cavalry challenged them on a bridge. Shots were exchanged, and three of the horsemen were killed or wounded. The fourth, who was Portuguese, quickly declared his loyalty to his country and joined the rebels. The remainder of the garrison fired a few shots and laid down their arms. A junta was quickly formed, and Coimbra was added to the areas under rebel control.[99]

Cotton was receiving regular updates on events in northern Portugal from Creyke off Oporto. Creyke's letters of 24 and 25 June arrived with Cotton on 3 July with a Portuguese schooner carrying 49 French or French sympathisers sent by the Bishop of Oporto to the squadron for their safety.[100] Creyke informed Cotton that the government in Oporto had 'assumed a settled form' and that 3,000 British troops would help to ensure the city's security and enable the Portuguese forces

---

94 Elio da Cruz, 'Padrões da Teixeira', <http://padroesteixeira.blogspot.com/2006/05/padres-da-teixeira.html>, accessed September 2022.
95 Southey, *History*, vol.II, p.84.
96 A. Halliday, *The Present State of Portugal and the Portuguese Army* (Edinburgh: Clarke, 1812), pp.126–127.
97 Amaral, *Portuguese Army*, p.10.
98 Amaral, *Portuguese Army*, p.10.
99 Southey, *History*, vol.II, pp.75-78.
100 TNA: ADM 1/340: List of prisoners, 7 July 1808.

to march south. Plenty of volunteers joined regiments at Oporto, but Creyke wrote that there were not enough muskets. Cotton sent 200 stands of arms, which were all he could immediately spare.[101]

On 7 July, the Bishop wrote to the Portuguese minister in London, Domingos António de Sousa Coutinho, asking him to request aid directly from King George and the British government. On the Bishop's shopping list were arms, accoutrements, cloth for uniforms, gunpowder, provisions, cash and 'a body of six thousand men at the least, including cavalry.'[102]

The junta in Oporto asked *Marechal de campo* Bernardim Freire de Andrade to serve as military governor, and he arrived in the city on 28 June. He was soon joined by his cousin, *Brigadeiro* Miguel Pereira Forjaz, who would serve as his chief of staff. There were few trained soldiers, arms were very scarce, and there was little in the way of supplies or money, but nonetheless, the junta ordered that eight of the line regiments and four of light infantry be re-established as well as several militia, ordenença and volunteer units.[103]

Coimbra was, and is, home to one of the world's oldest universities, and students and faculty played a key role in the revolt there. On 25 June, two students of mathematics, *Sargento* Bernardo António Zagalo (of 1º Regimento de artilharia) and *Sargento* António Inácio Caiola (11º Regimento de infantaria), were ordered to lead 40 volunteers south from the city to Figueira da Foz, a small port at the mouth of the Mondego river.[104] The French had a small garrison there in Forte de Santa Catarina. The small band of volunteers grew to over 3,000 as men joined them from the villages they marched through, but few of them were armed with anything more than farm implements. They arrived early in the morning of the 26th, and the French immediately retreated into the fort while the town's population joined the rebels.[105]

The inhabitants of Figueira must have sent word to the British garrison on the Berlengas Islands 60 miles to the south, as 2nd Lieutenant George Huskisson of the Royal Marines, commanding there, sent a small boat a similar distance south to the British squadron off the Tagus. It arrived on the morning of 4 July with a letter addressed to Cotton dated 27 June:

> In this town of Figueira, there are more than three thousand people, armed to take Fort St. Catarina at the mouth of the river Mondego, of which some Frenchmen are in possession. We have neither discipline or arms to intercept any succour which may come from Peniche; therefore we earnestly beg of Your Excellency to send us all the succour of men, arms and ammunition possible.[106]

Zagalo and the students had been ordered back to the north. Events moved quickly, though, and another letter from Figueira arrived with Cotton very soon after the first:

> On the 26th June I received an order from my Governor in arms at Coimbra to attack the Fortress of St. Catarina at the mouth of the bar of Figueira, which was garrisoned by a body of Frenchmen commanded by a Lieutenant of Engineers and a Sub Lieutenant of Artillery:– Forty armed students were sent to help me, which united to

101 TNA: ADM 1/340: Cotton to Wellesley-Pole, 3 July 1808.
102 Anon., *Papers*, pp.895–896.
103 F. De La Fuente, *Dom Miguel Pereira Forjaz* (Lisbon: Tribuna, 2011), pp.48–49.
104 Amaral, *Portuguese Army*, p.11.
105 Southey, *History*, vol.II, pp.81–82.
106 TNA: ADM 1/340: Felles to Cotton, 27 June 1808.

Forte de Santa Catarina in Figueira da Foz, now a restaurant. (Author's photo)

forty soldiers, the only ones that could carry arms. I sent to the neighbouring people to form a body; after this I summoned the commander of the said fort to surrender. He answered he would not, unless he might march with his men and baggage to join his General at Peniche; this I denied, and on the following night I picked out the best men, and put them in such order, that at the first signal they might attack the said fort in all directions. On the 27th between 10 and 11 o'clock after giving my orders I went myself towards the fort to speak to the commander to see if I could persuade him to surrender and spare the effusion of blood, but it was not possible to convince him. I then made a signal to my people to attack the fort which they did with such ardor, that in less than a quarter of an hour I had the pleasure to see myself the master of it; and took prisoners seventy-eight Frenchmen, a Lieutenant of Engineers and Sub Lieutenant of Artillery, both Portuguese.[107]

This account of the capture of the fort differs significantly from the one that historian José Accursio das Neves put in his *Historia Geral Invasão dos Franceses em Portugal*, one of the earliest Portuguese histories of the war, and which Robert Southey repeated in his *History of the Peninsular War*. Neves wrote that the fort's commander was *Tenente* Cibráo, a Portuguese engineer, who was afraid to surrender the fort because his family were in French-held Peniche but likewise did little to ensure its defence. In Neves' account, far from the rebels storming the fort, Cibráo did eventually capitulate on the condition that the garrison would be allowed to cross the river and march to Peniche, with arms but without ammunition. When they came out of the fort, they were searched, and some were found to be carrying cartridges. With the terms broken, the garrison were made

---

107   TNA: ADM 1/340: Suare to Cotton, undated.

prisoners, with the students having to protect them against the anger of the locals before they were marched to Coimbra.[108]

Cotton saw an opportunity to do more than support the Portuguese with arms or urge them to rise up with proclamations. Writing to the Admiralty on the same day he received the letters, he stated:

> From the repeated requests made to me by the loyal inhabitants of all parts of the Kingdom of Portugal for aid and assistance: and Figueira being most advantageously situated – easy of access – only 18 leagues from Oporto, with nothing I understand to interrupt the direct communication between those places – together with its requiring but a small garrison to occupy or retain; – I have thought it my duty in order to manifest a disposition rendering something more than promise in support of a cause so extremely interesting, to detach a party of 200 Royal Marines in His Majesty's Ship Alfred, to garrison the forts at that place; – and I entertain the most sanguine hope that however trifling their numbers, the effect may be highly beneficial from the spirit that the presence of British soldiers must at this moment create …[109]

Cotton's orders to Captain John Bligh of the *Alfred* began by detailing from which ships the 200 Royal Marines would be drawn. A first-rate ship of the line, such as *Hibernia*, would typically have a Royal Marine complement of a captain, three subalterns, four sergeants, four corporals, two drummers, and 156 marines. A third-rate, like the 74s in Cotton's squadron, would usually have a captain, two subalterns, three sergeants, two corporals, two drummers, and 115 marines.[110] The numbers detailed to go ashore at Figueira were perfectly sustainable and would not compromise their role onboard their ships.

Royal Marine officers were often men who did not have the means to afford an army commission but otherwise came from similar backgrounds to their comrades in the army. The marines themselves were recruited in much the same way and from the same strata of society as soldiers. Their main duties were to provide sentinels for the captain's cabin and other sensitive locations. They were drilled every day but did not have the space to practice the column and line formations used by the army. However, their role as sharpshooters during action at sea did mean they had significantly more live-firing practice than soldiers. They typically fired around 16 rounds per month.[111] However, the ever-increasing manpower demands of the war did lead to the same type of qualitative issues that the army occasionally suffered from. On 5 June, Captain Henry Curzon of HMS *Elizabeth* (74) wrote to Cotton to complain about the marines onboard, saying, 'Almost the whole party is composed of raw recruits, and the greater part of the worst character and description'. He said that they were not physically fit enough for their duties, were not reliable sentinels, and were affecting the discipline of the ship. He wanted them all replaced. At Curzon's request, a survey had been made of the marines in March and had found them wanting.[112] Cotton had forwarded the report to the Admiralty and did the same with Curzon's letter. On 7 August, at the

---

108 J.A. Neves, *Historia Geral Invasão dos Franceses em Portugal* (Lisbon: Ferreira, 1810), vol.3, pp.226–233; Southey, *History*, vol.II, pp.81–82.
109 TNA: ADM 1/340: Cotton to Wellesley-Pole, 4 July 1808.
110 N. Blake, *Steering to Glory: A Day in the Life of a Ship of the Line* (London, Chatham, 2005), p.198.
111 Blake, *Glory*, pp.89–90, 169.
112 TNA: ADM 1/339: Curzon to Cotton, 5 June 1808.

Admiralty's request, he sent another survey, which found eight men unfit for service and stated that 'The detachment appears to have been neglected. Extremely dirty and of an un-soldierlike appearance and defective in its arrangements.'[113] Cotton asked for the unfit men to be replaced.

Captain George Lewis of the *Hibernia* was selected to command the detachment. He had joined the Royal Marines in 1793, served on several ships and ashore at various Royal Marine head-quarters, plus periods of recruiting service at Worcester and Stroud. He was on HMS *Caesar* at the Battle of Cape Ortegal, just after Trafalgar, when the *Caesar*, as part of Captain Sir Richard Strachan's squadron, helped capture four French ships of the line. Lewis would go on to serve in Holland in 1813 and at Bladensburg, Baltimore and Washington during the War of 1812, rising to lieutenant general shortly before his death in 1854.[114]

John Bligh was the son of a Royal Navy captain, nephew of an admiral, and distantly related to William Bligh of *Bounty* infamy. He had joined the navy aged 11 in 1782 as a captain's servant. He was promoted steadily, fighting in many actions, and was given his first command in 1797 – the *Alfred* was his eighth. At Copenhagen in 1807, he had superintended the landing of the troops and stores, so was a good choice to go to Figueira.[115] Bligh's orders from Cotton continued:

> You are carefully to reconnoitre the said place, and deeming it proper, cause the officers and 200 Royal Marines above mentioned to be landed … either to garrison the forts or be employed on other service likely to leave the inhabitants at liberty to act on the defen-sive or offensive as occasion may require, but on no account are the Marines to proceed into the interior of the country by which any risk may be run to prevent their retreat and re-embarking, in the event of adverse circumstances rendering such a measure necessary, and which you are to provide and bear particularly in view.[116]

Bligh was to raise the Portuguese flag after he landed and invite any loyal Portuguese subjects to rally around it. He was to furnish arms and ammunition (Cotton supplied him 500 stands of arms) and every assistance to the population to shake off French rule, but Cotton cautioned him not to make any promises beyond what his force could accomplish and to keep in regular communication with the squadron. Cotton also supplied a proclamation that Bligh was to have translated, printed and distributed. In it, Cotton urged the Portuguese 'to take up arms in so just and glorious a cause!' and closed with: 'Seven months experience must have convinced you of the effect of French friend-ship: It is now to British Faith and Assistance; aided by your own Energy and Efforts, that you will I trust be indebted for the restoration of your Prince; and the independence of your country!'[117]

Bligh reported back to Cotton on 9 July:

> [The Marines] now occupy a hill above the town on the north side of the river, where they can with ease maintain their position against treble their forces and in the event of any adverse circumstances rendering their retreat necessary, it can be effected with safety, from a fort at the entrance of the port, nearly within gun-shot of where the ship lays …

---

113 TNA: ADM 1/340: Survey of Elizabeth's marines, 6 August 1808.
114 TNA: ADM 196/58/2: George Lewis.
115 Anon., 'Memoir of Rear Admiral Bligh, C.B.', *United Service Journal*, part 1, 1831, pp.343–345.
116 TNA: ADM 1/340: Cotton to Bligh, 4 July 1808.
117 TNA: ADM 1/340: Proclamation, 4 July 1808.

Coimbra is a strong place situated on the high road to Lisbon, and where they are collecting their force from all parts of the country to advance to Lisbon;– they have hitherto been delayed for want of arms and ammunition, and I have in consequence of the application, sent them 40 barrels of powder and 300 stand of arms, and trust with this aid, that they will soon commence their march. The instant I can get affairs a little settled here it is my intention to ride over, when I hope to be able to send you a more circumstantial account.[118]

Bligh and Lewis had also offered the locals that the Royal Marines could train 200 of their volunteers.[119] Bligh wrote to Cotton again the next day that, 'An express has arrived from Coimbra' with news that the French under *général de brigade* Margaron had taken Tomar and Leiria on the 6th and that the junta in Coimbra expected that that town and Figueira would be next. Bligh wrote, 'The panic is such, notwithstanding their numbers, as to leave me no option. I have therefore made arrangements secretly, to embark the Marines, the instant circumstances render it necessary.' Bligh had ordered Commander Thomas Dench of the *Nautilus* to assist in covering the embarkation.[120] Cotton told Bligh that if Figueira was attacked to withdraw as late as possible and offer shelter to as many as he could on the ships. If forced to re-embark, Bligh was to take the marines to Oporto and land them there to occupy a fort, or whatever the government there desired.[121]

Margaron's march northwards from Lisbon with around 4,500 troops was designed to check the spread of the insurrection towards the capital and get word of Loison, who had not been heard from for some time.[122] Rebels from Coimbra had helped to liberate Condeixa, Pombal, Leiria and some of the small forts on the coast. On the morning of 5 July, Margaron approached Leiria. The villagers gathered what arms they could. The French commander sent a prisoner into the town to ask them to lay down their arms. They refused, and the French stormed into the village, quickly overwhelming the defenders and then massacred the inhabitants, killing around 600 indiscriminately.[123] Margaron marched on to Tomar, which did not resist in order to avoid the same fate.

On 5 July, Cotton received a delegation of two officers from Lagos in the Algarve requesting aid and a request from Nazaré, near Peniche. On 7 July, Leiria asked for British assistance. The frequency that requests were being received prompted Cotton to provide the Admiralty with lists of which towns had requested assistance and which arms and ammunition had been sent.

Table 6. Arms, accoutrements and ammunition given to the Portuguese

Date	Place	Supplies
3 July	Oporto	200 stand of arms and accoutrements.
4 July	Figueria	500 stand of arms and accoutrements, 8,200 cartridges, 1,000 flints, accompanied by 220 Royal Marines.
5 July	Nazareth	60 stand of arms and accoutrements, 3,000 cartridges, 160 flints.
5 July	Lagos	100 stand of arms and accoutrements, 3,000 cartridges, 200 flints.
7 July	Leiria	50 stand of arms and accoutrements, 3,200 cartridges, 160 flints, 15 barrels of powder.

Source: TNA: ADM 1/340: List of Stores, Arms, Accoutrements and Ammunition Supplied to the Portuguese Government.

118 TNA: ADM 1/340: Bligh to Cotton, 9 July 1808.
119 Krajeski, *Shadow*, p.85.
120 TNA: ADM 1/340: Bligh to Cotton, 10 July 1808.
121 TNA: ADM 1/340: Cotton to Bligh, 13 July 1808.
122 Mackay, *Tempest*, p246.
123 Southey, *History*, vol.II, pp.126–127.

Cotton's replies to requests for aid were always prompt, eloquent, and finely crafted to assure and encourage the rebels. His letter to the people of Sines is typical and worth quoting at length:

> The undersigned Admiral, commanding the British fleet off the Tagus, has received with much pleasure the thanks of the loyal inhabitants of Sines, of St Jago, and the surrounding towns and villages. Whom he has the happiness to assure, that a British Army is now on its way to assist Portugal in the present Glorious Struggle for all that is dear to men; for the preservation of their holy religion; for the restoration of their lawful prince; the protection of their wives and children; and the independence, nay very existence, of their country.
>
> It is not to be told to the true and loyal Portuguese, now roused into action, that these objects are worth every sacrifice, of ease, comfort, rest and even life. The spirit of patriotism will *create* soldiers; and let it be remembered, the oppressors of Portugal are but men, and few in number; they cannot stand against a justly indignant and exasperated population.
>
> Although every assistance Great Britain can yield to her ancient ally in so virtuous, just and honourable cause; will be afforded; yet *all* must depend upon the energy and efforts of the native inhabitants of Portugal, 'tis for them to evince the spirit of their forefathers, and prove that the youth of Lusitania, once the most enterprising and flourishing of nations, still retain their native valour, and *Roused by Oppression* resolutely determine to fight, under favour of God; for their holy religion; their parents, wives and children; for the restoration of their prince and salvation of their country. Throughout the northern part of Portugal, the universal cry is 'Conquer or Die' and the only badge of honour worn is inscribed 'Liberty and Vengeance'.[124]

As July progressed, Cotton began to hear of the additional forces being prepared back in Britain to assist the rebels in Portugal. On 8 July, HMS *Hyperion* passed through the fleet, and Cotton informed the Admiralty that 'from such ship Mr Adair; destined to the Mediterranean upon a secret mission, came onboard the Hibernia to inform me that Major General the Right Honourable Sir Arthur Wellesley K.B. might be shortly expected upon this coast with an army of 9000 men.' Robert Adair, diplomat and MP, was on his way to negotiate a treaty with the Ottomans at Constantinople.[125] Cotton wrote that he had sent the *Lively* to cruise north of Oporto to meet the troop convoy and tell Wellesley the present state of Portugal. He also sent the *Hercule* to cruise six leagues to windward of the Berlengas in case the *Lively* missed them. He informed the Admiralty that the best place to land would be Figueira.[126]

On 10 July, Cotton received dispatches from the vessels off Oporto and Viana. He was told that the arrival of a Colonel Browne at Oporto had 'inspired considerable confidence' but told the Admiralty 'that officer has not yet imparted to me the object of his mission.'[127] On the 13th, the *Plover* (18) arrived from Plymouth, having sailed on the 4th, carrying dispatches from Castlereagh confirming that Wellesley had been ordered to Portugal and a letter to Spencer with discretionary orders to join his force, should the situation in Spain allow it. Castlereagh directed that Cotton

124 TNA: ADM 1/340: Cotton to people of Sines, 14 July 1808.
125 W. P. Courtney, revised by H. C. G. Matthew, 'Sir Robert Adair', ODNB, <https://doi.org/10.1093/ref:odnb/84>, accessed October 2022.
126 TNA: ADM 1/340: Cotton to Wellesley-Pole, 9 July 1808.
127 TNA: ADM 1/340: Cotton to Wellesley-Pole, 10 July 1808.

send Spencer information on events in Portugal so that he could judge where his force could be best employed. Also aboard the *Plover* were Lieutenant Colonel Trant and Captain Préval, from whom Cotton received the details of their and Lieutenant Colonel Browne's mission.[128]

Castlereagh had written Browne's orders on 21 June:

> As it is proposed to send a force immediately off the Tagus, and as it is desirable to obtain the most accurate information of the present state of the enemy's force at Lisbon, and the means of resistance they can oppose to an attack upon that place, His Majesty has been pleased to direct that you should proceed forthwith in a ship of war that is ordered to take you on board and convoy you to Oporto, from which place, by the most recent intelligence, the French have been expelled.
>
> Upon your arrival, your endeavours will be directed to obtain the most precise information of the enemy's force in Portugal, and the positions which it at present occupies, and you will also take measures for establishing channels of communication with the interior of the country, by which intelligence may be secretly conveyed from the coast to the fleet off Lisbon. Having made these arrangements, and having obtained such information as you are enabled personally to collect, you will proceed without delay off the Tagus, and report to Sir Arthur Wellesley the result.[129]

Samuel Browne had started his career in the army with the New Romney Fencible Cavalry, one of the many units raised to defend against a possible French invasion. He then purchased a cornet's commission in the 6th (Inniskilling) Dragoons in March 1798.[130] By May 1800, he had risen to captain and, the following year, served as an assistant quartermaster general in Abercromby's Egyptian expedition. He was briefly based in Malta before being sent to Lord Cornwallis and the peace negotiations at Amiens. In 1803, he became Deputy Inspector General of the Recruiting Service, and then in 1806, he was appointed assistant secretary and aide de camp to the Duke of York.[131] In 1807, he was made a major in the York Light Infantry Volunteers. He was promoted to lieutenant colonel just before joining Spencer at Falmouth in January, after which he must have returned to Britain from Gibraltar. Lieutenant Colonel Gordon, the Duke of York's secretary, suggested to the Duke that Browne take 18-year-old Ensign Henry Wyndham of the 1st Foot Guards, who could speak Portuguese, to assist him.[132] Wyndham would much later win fame by helping to close the gates of Hougoumont during the Battle of Waterloo.

Also sent with Browne was Nicholas Trant, often referred to erroneously as 'a British officer in the Portuguese service'.[133] Whilst he would be so later, in the spring of 1808, he was still very much in the British service but had had an unusual career. Born in Ireland in 1769, he had, like many Catholics, opted to serve in the Brigade Irlandaise of the French army – in his case, as a *lieutenant* in the Régiment de Walsh-Serrant.[134] After the outbreak of the revolution, he left France

---

128 TNA: ADM 1/340: Cotton to Wellesley-Pole, 13 July 1808.
129 TNA: WO 72/29: Castlereagh to Browne, 21 June 1808.
130 *The London Gazette*, 17 March 1798.
131 Anon., *The Royal Military Calendar or Army Service and Commission Book* (London: Egerton, 1820), vol.IV, pp.186–187.
132 BL: Add Ms 49502: Wyndham to Gordon, 22 July 1808. Wyndham mentions translating proclamations.
133 Oman, *History*, vol.I, p.234.
134 J. Roussel, *État militaire de France, pour l'année 1788* (Paris: Onfroy, 1788), p.286.

and, in 1792, served as a volunteer on the staff of the Duke of Brunswick, then continued to serve in the Low Countries. He was given a cornet's commission in the 1st Dragoon Guards, without purchase, in May 1794. He quickly moved to the 84th Foot as a lieutenant and served with his new regiment at Flushing and then the Cape of Good Hope. He then moved to a regiment of the Irish Brigade, which was sent to Portugal and was at Minorca when it was captured. He helped to oversee the conversion of one of the Spanish foreign regiments into the Minorca Regiment, gaining his majority in the new unit in 1799. In 1801, he saw action with his regiment in Egypt. By the signing of the Peace of Amiens, he was a lieutenant colonel but sold his commission in May 1802. Perhaps he had little interest in peacetime soldiering. However, by December 1803, he was back in the army as an ensign in the Royal Staff Corps.[135] In 1808, he was still only a lieutenant. He volunteered for the role of cooperating with the Portuguese army but suggested to the Duke of York that he be given the local rank of lieutenant colonel as it would improve his standing with the Portuguese.[136] Sir Arthur Wellesley later referred to Trant as 'a very good officer, but a drunken dog as ever lived.'[137]

Born in Saint Domingue in 1758, Captain François Préval was a *lieutenant* in the Corps du Génie of the French army before the revolution.[138] He must have left France as an émigré as the *List of the Officers of His Majesty's Foreign Corps* of 1797 has a Captain Francis Galien de Preval serving as an engineer with Lowenstein's Fusiliers (one of the many foreign corps in British service), with his commission dated 27 July 1796.[139] When that regiment and many other foreign corps were merged into the 60th Foot and lost their artillery and engineers, he seems to have briefly entered Portuguese service. He is listed in the *Almanach Para o Anno de 1800* as *Sargento Mor* (major) Francisco Paulo Galien de Preval of the Corpo Real de Engenheiros, but was 'absent from the kingdom with permission'.[140] At some stage, he must have re-entered British service as in an 1814 *Gazette* entry for a brevet promotion from major to lieutenant colonel, he is listed as 'F.P. Preval, late of the Royal Foreign Engineers'.[141] In a letter to Wellesley, Castlereagh refers to him as an 'officer of Engineers acquainted with the defences of the Tagus', presumably, that knowledge dated from his time in Portuguese service.[142] Préval was ordered by Cotton to remain on the *Hibernia* to await the arrival of Wellesley, and whilst he did so, he collected what up-to-date information on the Tagus forts he could.[143]

With Browne already in Oporto, Cotton was able to reassure Bligh at Figueira that:

> Colonel Trant has joined me this instant, from England, and proceeds without delay in the Plover to advise you of the best means to be adopted at the present moment; he will

---

135 E.M. Lloyd (revised by Gordon L. Teffeteller), 'Nicholas Trant', ODNB, <https://doi.org/10.1093/ref:odnb/27664>, accessed June 2022; De La Poer Berresford, *Beresford*, endnote 22 p.275; *The London Gazette*, 11 November 1794; Anon., 'Major-General Sir Nicholas Trant, K.C.T.S.', *The United Service Journal*, part 1, 1840, pp.99–100.

136 BL: Add MS 49502: Trant to Gordon, 16 July 1808.

137 P. Henry, *Notes of Conversations with the Duke of Wellington 1831-1851* (London: Muray, 1889), p.40.

138 Anon., *Bulletin des Lois du Royaume de France* (Paris: La Imprimerie Royale, 1820), vol.9, p.926; J. Roussel, *État militaire de France, pour l'année 1788* (Paris: Onfroy, 1788), p.cdxxvii.

139 TNA: WO 65/168: List of the Officers of His Majesty's Foreign Corps.

140 Anon., *Almanach Para o Anno de 1800* (Lisbon: Galhardo, 1800), p.164.

141 *The London Gazette*, 9 July 1814, p.1392.

142 TNA: WO 6/185: Castlereagh to Wellesley, 30 June 1808.

143 TNA: WO 55/977: Préval to Morse, 'end of July'.

acquaint you of the hourly expectation I have to see Sir Arthur Wellesley with 10,000 men, and whom, Major General Spencer, with the troops under his command, is directed to join.[144]

By that point, Bligh had told Cotton that Figueira had been made more secure by roads being cut up and made impassable for artillery and cavalry. The province had been declared in danger, and every able man was told to appear in arms. A letter from Coimbra had arrived at the town saying Margaron had been joined by Loison and requesting more British troops, but, if they could not be spared, then they asked for a British officer to inspect the works performed for defence and suggest improvements. Bligh also stated that the 2nd Oporto regiment (600 strong) had arrived at Coimbra and that 4,000 Spanish troops were expected from Almeida, which should have made Coimbra safe. However, he feared that Figueira could be the French target as it was the only place that troops could be landed; 60 transports could enter the river at once, and there was a safe anchorage outside the bar. At Bligh's request, Cotton sent 100 extra marines and said one or two officers could go to Coimbra.[145] Loison had marched from Almeida towards Lisbon as ordered, punishing harshly any town or village that showed any sign of resistance. Once Junot had received word from him, he was ordered to join with Margaron and *général de brigade* Thomières from Peniche and march towards Coimbra to crush the rebellion there. Thomières had already marched up the coast to retake, sack and loot Nazaré. However, as the combined force passed Leiria, they were recalled to Lisbon.

Browne's first report from Oporto to Wellesley is dated 9 July but takes the form of a journal of his activities past that date. He had arrived in the *Peacock* (16) on the 7th and met with Captain Edward Galway of the *Antelope*. Galway took him to meet the Bishop, and Browne told him that his mission 'could not fail to forward the undertaking of the people and that I was desirous of obtaining the best information of the enemy's force in Portugal, and the positions which it at present occupies.'[146] On the morning of the 9th, he met with Freire and Forjaz. The Portuguese officers passed on all the information they had. They estimated the French force as 14–15,000, with 5,000 at Almeida and the rest around Lisbon. As it turned out, this was an underestimate by around 10,000. Browne was then told of Loison's and Delaborde's movements and that the patriots did not think Oporto was threatened. He was then given a detailed breakdown of the Portuguese regular and militia forces, totalling just under 26,000 men, many of whom were unarmed.

The Portuguese also gave Browne copies of two letters intercepted from Junot. In one to Loison, dated 7 June, Junot worried that he has not heard from him since he departed from Lisbon but urged him to hasten on to Ciudad Rodrigo and to do all he can to stop the insurrection at Badajoz from spreading. Loison was also, ironically, urged to protect French couriers. The second letter Loison was to send on to *maréchal* Murat in Madrid if he could. Junot informed Murat that he was doing what he could about Badajoz but that guarding the Spanish troops and the continued harassment by Cotton's squadron was overstretching the small number of troops he had, and he appealed for Murat's support.[147]

British resident of Oporto, Hariot Slessor, mentioned Browne in her diary:

144 TNA: ADM 1/340: Cotton to Bligh, 13 July 1808.
145 TNA: ADM 1/340: Cotton to Wellesley-Pole, 14 July 1808.
146 TNA: WO 1/237: Browne to Wellesley, 9 July.
147 TNA: WO 1/237: Junot to Loison and Junot to Murat, 7 June 1808.

Colonel Browne is sent by the Duke of York, to be informed of the real state of Portugal. It seems when they left England, it was a doubt if we were or not still under French government, and they were very well pleased at finding our port again open to the English. With other officers they were presented to the Bishop, who seemed most gratified with this visit. The next day they all dined with the Bishop, and it was settled that next day, the 10th of July, that the Bishop, with Colonel Browne etc, should ride out into the country and point out the proper situations most eligible to annoy the enemy in case of a visit. As appointed, a very numerous assemblage of persons met early in the morning on the 10th at the Palace, to accompany the Bishop. The party made a formidable appearance, the Bishop at their head, between officers, clergy, and gentry.[148]

The party were out most of the day inspecting the defences on the left bank of the Duoro that covered the likely approach of the French. Browne reported that: 'The utmost zeal was apparent in every person; the peasants were working cheerfully upon the defences; the troops are encamped at all the commanding points, which are strengthened by ditches, palisades, and abattis, and artillery appears to be judiciously placed.'[149] The Bishop and his commanders did not seem to be that concerned about an attack on Oporto but were worried that there were large numbers of French troops in motion and no clear information on their intent. Browne gave them advice on the defences. The Bishop was grateful for everything that Browne and Cotton were doing but equally was eager for more help, including British engineers and artillery officers.

Browne sailed south in the *Peacock* to update Cotton and then returned to Oporto to help organise the Portuguese forces. On 21 July, he wrote again to Wellesley, informing him that, 'after leaving the Tagus, I had opportunities to observe the coast to the northward, and from the heavy surf which falls constantly upon it, even in light winds, there is scarcely a point between the Tagus and Mondego, which can be depended upon for the disembarkation of troops, except Peniche, which is occupied by the enemy.' He then mentioned that he had stopped in Mondego Bay on the 18th so the *Peacock* could disembark the 100 Royal Marine reinforcements Cotton had sent. Browne found the Royal Marines:

> … posted at the entrance of the small town of Figueira, situated on the north side of the river, which is a bar harbour, but safe anchorage within, of very easy access for transports, and well suited for the disembarkation of troops. The river being fordable, about six miles above the town, an armed launch from the Alfred is stationed to cover the pass.[150]

Captain Bligh relayed to Browne all the intelligence that he had: Loison's force was not yet satisfactorily accounted for; 15,000 rations had been requisitioned at Pombal; Loison had burned Nazaré and committed great excesses at Leiria; Delaborde had marched north from Lisbon on the 2nd but was still only at Leiria; French advance posts were only 15 miles from Figueira. With only the marines, a Portuguese militia regiment, and the armed population at Figueira, Browne did not see how the town could resist a serious attack by the French. He even doubted that Coimbra could be held as 'although there is very good will in the people, their exertions are so short-lived, and with

148 Hayter, *Backbone*, pp.175–176.
149 TNA: WO 1/237: Browne to Wellesley, 9 July.
150 TNA: WO 1/237: Browne to Wellesley, 14 July.

so little combination, that I do not see, any hope of their being able to resist the advance of the enemy, even, to Oporto, if that place is really the object of General La Borde.' It was not clear to him if Delaborde's objective was to gain provisions, advance on Oporto, or interrupt communication between the rebel-held areas and Lisbon. Browne stated that Trant had left to go to Coimbra 'to ascertain the real state of the country.'[151]

Trant's report from Figueira, dated 17 July, the day he arrived there, was addressed to Brigadier General Charles Stewart, Castlereagh's half-brother and military undersecretary at the War Office, although copies may also have been sent to Browne. He wrote that since a landing was likely in the area, 'I am aware that my services will be more effectively employed with the Patriots, in endeavouring to influence an active and concerted cooperation with the Lieutenant General's [Wellesley's] movements.' He sent a return of the forces he had been told were at Coimbra: 950 regular infantry and 320 cavalry; 1,664 militia' six 4-pounders and three 2-pounders with 75 artillerymen. More regular infantry was expected imminently, and there were many thousands of unarmed peasants who would also fight. Trant thought the patriots might march to attack the French if the enemy advanced from Leira and Tomar, where an estimated 4,000 French troops were under Margaron. Trant stated that a 'partial affair took place there some days back in which, as might be expected the patriots were compelled to fall back.' The widespread view was that the longer French resistance continued, the more likely there would be a general uprising. Trant ended his report by saying he would set out for Coimbra the next day and remain there until he received further orders from Wellesley.[152]

Browne's report to Stewart was written on the 22nd. He reported that he was established in Oporto and 'fully in the confidence of the Bishop and his military council.' He was in daily communication with Trant in Coimbra and hoped 'to be able to lay before Sir Arthur much useful information on his arrival.' The regulars and militia at Coimbra had risen to 5,000 men, but only two-thirds were armed, but the Bishop had asked him to send a courier to Trant to urge him 'to restrain the dangerous imprudence of the Patriots' as the French facing them under Delaborde and Loison could not be less than 8,000. Browne had also been lobbying the junta and had 'urged, with success, the necessity of providing depots of provisions for a large army, to be in readiness to be conveyed from hence by water to the point which may be fixed on by Sir Arthur Wellesley'.[153]

Pillage and Flames

The situation in the country's southern half was no better for Junot and the French than in the northern provinces. With the Spanish troops gone, the French spread far too thinly, and Spencer's force sailing along the coast, many towns and villages had already declared for the Prince Regent. *Général de brigade* Avril was tasked with securing Évora and Estremoz on the main road to Elvas – the only viable route of retreat into Spain. *Général de brigade* Antoine Maurin commanded in the Algarve but was ill, so the command fell to *colonel* Jean Pierre Maransin of the Légion du Midi. Maransin had orders to defend the Guadiana and the coast from Faro to the Spanish border. In mid-June, rebels from Olhão, led by a Portuguese *coronel*, seized arms from a fort near Faro and

---

151   TNA: WO 1/237: Browne to Wellesley, 14 July.
152   TNA: WO 1/237: Trant to Stewart, 17 July 1808.
153   TNA: WO 1/237: Browne to Stewart, 22 July 1808.

opened communication with the Royal Navy. The 200-strong French garrison in Faro itself asked for reinforcements. Eighty men set sail from Tavira in three vessels but were intercepted and forced to surrender by Portuguese fishermen, but 200 reinforcements did arrive from Villa Real. The French marched on Olhão but were ambushed and withdrew. After some hesitation, the people of Faro rose against the occupiers, stopped the French from re-entering the town, and took the French arsenal and military chest. Maurin, in his sick bed, was taken prisoner along with 70 other French officers and other ranks who were then sent to the Royal Navy off the coast. The visible presence of British ships off the coast gave confidence to the rebels. A junta was appointed, and the insurrection soon spread throughout the Algarve.[154] Maransin, with his force of only 1,200 men, was cut off from Lisbon and in danger of becoming surrounded. He ordered a retreat to Mértola inland, and the insurgents harassed the French as they marched.

Towns in the neighbouring province of Alentejo had also begun to rebel. On 19 June, the town of Vila Viçosa rose up and attacked the company of the 86e Ligne stationed there. The French took some casualties but managed to rally in an old fort. The rebels tried to storm the fort twice, but the French held out despite taking fire from rooftops and a bell tower that overlooked their positions. Avril marched from Estremoz with three more companies of the 86e, dragoons and artillery. They forced their way into the town at the point of the bayonet, and over 200 rebels were killed. The town was sacked, and the ringleaders were executed.[155]

A few days later, Maransin sent a detachment of 100 infantry and 30 dragoons to Beja to raise provisions, but they were refused and forced out of the town. On 25 June, Maransin marched on Beja with 950 troops to punish the inhabitants. Heavily outnumbered, the French scaled the town walls with ladders whilst pioneers battered down the gates with axes. The rebel resistance was spirited and lasted several hours, but with few of them armed, the outcome was inevitable. The French took 80 casualties. Around 1,200 rebels were killed in the fighting, and more were later put to death. The town was looted and burnt.[156]

Following the council of war at the end of June, orders were sent to the outlying forces to withdraw to Lisbon, except for garrisons at Elvas, Almeida and Peniche. Many of the messengers were intercepted or could not find a safe route; it took a week for Loison to get his orders. Kellermann left 1,400 men at Elvas and then marched for Lisbon, picking up Avril and Maransin as he went. The vacuum left by the French withdrawal allowed the rebellion to spread unchecked, but the rebels had few arms, lacked leadership and organisation, and so could do little to press their advantage. The French now had a force of around 24,000 in and around Lisbon, which the rebels had no hope of challenging in battle. However, Junot needed to secure his lines of communication to Elvas, if only to receive news from Spain. Constant and disturbing rumours of the spread of the insurgency replaced solid information. It was difficult enough for the French commanders to know the actual state and locations of their own forces, let alone the constantly growing numbers of rebels and the ever-lurking British off the coast. On 24 July, Junot ordered Loison to leave the capital with 7,000 men and march towards the border fortress, quelling the uprising as he progressed through Alentejo.[157]

154 Southey, *History*, vol.II, pp.88-94; Oman, *History*, vol.I, p.212.
155 Southey, *History*, vol.II, pp.96-104; Thiébault, *l'Expédition*, pp.132–133.
156 Thiébault, *l'Expédition*, pp.135–136.
157 Thiébault, *l'Expédition*, p.157; Oman, *History*, vol.I, pp.215–218.

The Battle of Evora

Loison's force consisted of the 2e Régiment provisoire d'infanterie légère (made up of the 3rd battalions of the 12e and 15e Légère), the Légion Hanovrienne, the 3rd battalion of the 58e Ligne, a battalion and a half of the 86e Ligne, and the 4e and 5e Régiments provisoires de dragons. These were organised into two brigades under Solignac and Margaron. In addition, *colonel* Saint Clair commanded two battalions of grenadiers and *colonel* d'Aboville was in charge of eight artillery pieces.[158]

Loison's advance guard, made up of the 12e Légére, brushed aside 1,500 Portuguese, mainly consisting of the Voluntários de Estremoz, at Montemor-o-Novo on the 28th, killing 50 and taking 100 peasants prisoner, who Loison disarmed and released.[159] At 11:30 a.m. on the 29th, Loison approached the city of Évora. The junta had placed *Tenente General* Francisco de Paula Leite de Sousa in charge of their forces, which amounted to around 600 infantry, predominantly militia and volunteer troops, with 120 cavalry. Many were poorly armed with whatever weapons had been hidden from the French, and the cavalry horses were gathered from the city and ridden by farm workers and labourers with little or no training.[160] The Spanish garrison at Badajoz had sent a similar number of infantry, led by *Coronel* Moretti, the Húsares de María Luisa (who had been part of Junot's initial invasion force), and seven guns. The allies perhaps fielded between 1,700 and 3,000 men, but, with the improvised nature of many of their units, exact strengths are uncertain.[161]

The Voluntários de Estremoz fell back on the city, and as the French dragoons moved forward, they began to take fire from Portuguese skirmishers. Unwisely, perhaps, the allies had opted to form outside of the city. The walls behind were lined with the inhabitants, including many clergy, armed with whatever they could find.

Loison went forward with Solignac and Margaron to assess the allied position. Their right occupied high ground in front of the city, their centre followed the ridge, and the citadel backed their left. What little cavalry they had were placed behind the guns, and skirmishers were placed in front of the line infantry. The allied guns consisted of a howitzer and three cannon on the right near a windmill above the Lisbon road, two howitzers and two cannon in the centre, and four cannon on the left above the road to Estremoz. The Portuguese were on the right of the allied line, and the Spanish on the left. Solignac was ordered to attack the enemy left and Margaron the centre and right. The grenadiers were placed between the brigades as a reserve.[162] The French dragoons were positioned on the flanks to prevent troops fleeing on the roads to Estremoz or Beja.

The French overwhelmingly outnumbered the allies, and Loison quickly advanced toward them. The allied guns and infantry kept up a brisk fire as the French approached but soon began to retreat, leaving behind many casualties and seven of their guns. The Spanish cavalry fled before contact with the dragoons, and their infantry also soon broke. Leite left the field and headed for Olivenza, but most of his infantry sought shelter in the city.[163]

---

158   Griffon de Pleineville, *Invasion*, p.142.
159   Thiébault, *l'Expédition*, p.158.
160   Anon., *Mappa Historico-militar-politico e Moral da Cidade de Evora ou Exacta Narraçaõ do Terrivel Assalto que á Mesma Cidade deo o General Loison com Hum Excercito de Nove Mil Homens em o Fatal dia 29 de Julho de 1808* (Lisbon: Galhardo, 1814), vol.I, p.32.
161   Oman, *History*, vol.I, p.218.
162   Thiébault, *l'Expédition*, pp.159–160; Anon., *Mappa*, vol.I, p.44.
163   Oman, *History*, vol.I, p.218.

The French surrounded the city and prepared to attack, while the remains of the Spanish and Portuguese regiments reinforced the ramparts, bastions, and towers of the city's defences. Solignac was ordered to attack the city from the citadel to the gates leading to Elvas, Estremoz and Arraiolos. Margaron was to act on the side facing Beja, Montemor-o-Novo, and around the aqueduct. Solignac's and Margaron's troops, carrying ladders, managed to quickly escalade the town walls in several places.

The light infantry of Solignac's brigade climbed the walls with ladders or by using bayonets as pitons; some even entered via the old sewers or posterns. The inhabitants threw whatever they could at the French, including bricks and stones. Loison brought up cannon to clear the barricades at the gates, which were then dismantled by hand. Troops rushed in, spreading through the town, and putting the inhabitants to the sword. Margaron led troops into the main square, where a fierce battle took place, with the allies firing from the surrounding rooftops and towers down onto the French troops.

Some Spanish troops fled towards Estremoz, but Solignac, with a battalion of infantry, pursued them, killed around 300, and took many prisoners. The 4e Régiment provisoire de dragons then charged and killed 150 more. Difficult terrain slowed the dragoons down and gave the Spanish hussars time to escape.[164]

Loison wrote in his dispatch: 'I can only praise the bravery of the soldiers: they marched with intrepidity; but I have never seen such pillaging and cruelty.'[165] However, *lieutenant* Dainville partly blamed Loison for the pillaging after the battle:

> The massacres and the other scourges of war which had lasted all night were still going on, and were causing the new victims to utter groans which, coming out of the partly destroyed houses, indicated that the thousands of corpses scattered about and obstructing the passageway did not form the entire population of this unfortunate town which had had to suffer. I wandered with a feeling of painful curiosity through the districts where I had once liked to walk; everywhere the same horrors had been committed, everywhere one met only the dead and the dying; I could not help feeling an unpleasant resentment against General-in-Chief Loison, who was to make an example of the surrounding provinces ready to rise up against us, but who, I think, should not have prolonged his stay beyond the first moment when it would have been impossible for him to stop the fury of the soldiers.[166]

Between 3,000 and 4,000 Portuguese were killed or wounded, and 2,000 were taken prisoner, whereas the French suffered 90 killed and around 200 wounded.[167] Loison imposed a new council to govern in the name of the Emperor, but which lasted less than a fortnight. Estremoz submitted to him rather than experiencing the same punishment as Évora. Loison entered Elvas and then marched for Portalegre and then Abrantes. Loison wrote that at Evora, 'The youngest soldiers earned the title of old soldiers.'[168] For many of the conscripts who had marched from France, it would have been their first experience of a major battle. They had also had six more months of drill

---

164 V. de Saint-Just, *Historique du 5e Régiment de Dragons* (Paris: Hachette, 1891), pp.247–248.
165 Griffon de Pleineville, *Invasion*, p.147.
166 Griffon de Pleineville, *Invasion*, p.148.
167 Griffon de Pleineville, *Invasion*, p.149.
168 Thiébault, *l'Expédition*, p.160.

and training and were perhaps not the raw recruits they once had been. The Portuguese rebels' spirit and bravery cannot be denied, but they were poorly armed and formed into improvised units without the best officers, NCOs and troops who had already marched off to France to serve the Emperor. It remained to be seen how well Junot's men would fare against Wellesley's and Spencer's British troops.

Dogs and Englishmen

After consulting with Cotton, Spencer rejoined the convoy off the coast of the Algarve on 25 June. He reported to Castlereagh that the 'Portuguese flag is flying along the whole extent of this coast on all the forts and batteries.'[169] The convoy checked in at Ayamonte to ensure all was quiet on the Spanish/Portuguese border and then continued to Cadiz. When they arrived on the 27th, many transports were getting short of water. On 28 June, Spencer issued a general order allowing field and staff officers to visit Cadiz during the day and wrote that he hoped other officers would soon be able to visit the city.[170]

Spencer was conscious that many of his troops had been on the transports for far too long. So, when the governor of Cadiz, Tomás de Morla y Pacheco, offered barracks for 2,000 men at the port of Santa Maria across the bay from Cadiz, he accepted. Nightingall's brigade of the 29th and 32nd Foot was duly landed early on 3 July. Morla had said that if any reverse befell the main Spanish force in Andalusia under Castaños, they would ask for Spencer's assistance and request the British squadron's aid in defending Cadiz. Spencer told Castlereagh that until he received further orders, he would keep a portion of his force ashore to refresh the troops but would not advance inland. He also relayed various rumours of Spanish successes against the French, but all were unconfirmed.[171]

For many of the officers and soldiers of Spencer's force, Santa Maria was their first experience of the Iberian Peninsula. Lieutenant Charles Leslie of the 29th recorded his first impressions in his memoir. He noted the warm welcome that the British received from many of the Spaniards but commented that the higher classes were more reserved and even resentful of British assistance. The Spanish patriots had taken to wearing a red cockade with the cypher of King Fernando on it and Spanish ladies embroidered some and gave them to British officers, who had been ordered to wear them above their black ones. Santa Maria was a fashionable summer retreat for the wealthier section of Cadiz and the officers were invited to many dances and other social events.[172]

The weather was brutally hot, with Captain George Landmann recording 92°F (33°C) in his room and 104°F (40°C) outside in the shade.[173] Nightingall wrote that he had 'severely felt' the heat and that it had 'brought on some of my old Bengal complaints.'[174] Captain Harry Ross-Lewin of the 32nd Foot also wrote of the heat in his memoir: 'We had excellent quarters, but the heat was excessive; yet our people walked about at all times of the day, as if they were in their own country, to the surprise of the Spaniards, who said that none but Englishmen and dogs would expose themselves

169   TNA: WO 1/226: Spencer to Castlereagh, 25 June 1808.
170   NLS: Adv.MS.46.3.6: General order, 28 June 1808.
171   TNA: WO 1/226: Spencer to Castlereagh, 3 July 1808.
172   Leslie, *Military Journal*, pp.28–30.
173   Royal Engineers Museum (REM): 4201-305: Landmann to Holloway, 10 July 1808.
174   BL: Add Ms 49502: Nightingall to Gordon, 18 July 1808.

to such a sun.'[175] Spencer ordered the 50th foot to land on the 15th and the 82nd on the 16th, with the 32nd returning to their ships to make room in the barracks.[176]

Requests from the Spanish for aid were not long in coming. Spencer had to advance Morla 40,000 dollars to pay the Spanish sailors in the fleet at Cadiz as they were about to be discharged due to a lack of funds to pay them. He had also received a request from Castaños to advance to Jerez, 10 miles from Santa Maria, in case the Spanish general needed support.[177] Spencer decided to take the 29th and 32nd, a combined light infantry battalion comprising all the light companies except the 6th Foot's, and some artillery. However, he did feel uneasy about the move. He told Castlereagh, 'I naturally experience considerable uneasiness, being now two months without a line from His Majesty's Ministers and I am confident your Lordship will pardon me, if I express the anxiety I feel, either to have fuller instructions; or the presence of a superior officer.'[178] However, Spencer could not find any horses or mules to pull his guns or carts for the baggage and did not feel that he could risk moving his troops without them having artillery support.[179]

Unfortunately, a lack of horses was not the only problem facing Spencer's artillery. In addition to the artillery originally embarked in Britain, a detachment from the artillery at Gibraltar had been added to the expedition in May. In June, the senior Royal Artillery officer, Lieutenant Colonel George Ramsay, had reported to Royal Artillery headquarters at Woolwich that except for the actual guns, the brigade was 'in the most incomplete state' and he feared that they would be of 'little use to the army'. They had only been able to find harnesses for five of the six guns taken from Gibraltar, and those had been in store for nine years so Ramsay thought that they would be rotten. No wagons or tumbrils for ammunition had been loaded onto the transports, and they had only two or three small tumbril carts.[180] Ramsay landed the car brigade – the transport section supporting the gunners – at Santa Maria on 15 July, and it was found to be in 'a very confused state'. Half the company had been embarked for Sicily while the other half was sent with Spencer. Shafts and wheels for the guns sent to Sicily had been embarked with Spencer and vice versa, with the result that Ramsay did not have enough wheels for his wagons.[181]

On 15 July, HMS *Hyperion* arrived with diplomat Robert Adair onboard, who had already delivered news of Sir Arthur Wellesley's imminent sailing to Cotton. Adair briefed Spencer on what the government knew of the insurrection in other parts of Spain, and he also delivered new orders for Spencer from Castlereagh, dated 28 June. The orders told Spencer that Wellesley would sail from Cork with 9,000 men and would 'act together' with Spencer's force 'in support of the efforts of the Spanish nation'. If Spencer was at Gibraltar, he was to return to Cadiz and await Wellesley there, acting as he saw fit in the meantime 'in aid of the common cause'. Spencer was also told to send Wellesley 'such information as you may receive, and such opinions as you may be enabled to form as to the practicability of his corps being advantageously employed in that quarter.'[182] At that stage, the government intended that Wellesley's force would be employed in Spain. Portugal was not mentioned as a destination.

175 Ross-Lewin, *Life*, vol.I, p.198.
176 NLS: Adv.MS.46.3.6: General orders, 13 and 15 July 1808.
177 BL: Add Mss 49484: Whittingham to Dalrymple, 2 July 1808.
178 TNA: WO 1/226: Spencer to Castlereagh, 13 July 1808.
179 TNA: WO 1/226: Spencer to Collingwood, 7 July 1808.
180 TNA: WO 55/1193: Ramsay to Macleod, 8 June 1808.
181 TNA: WO 55/1193: Ramsay to Macleod, 21 July 1808.
182 TNA: WO 6/185: Castlereagh to Spencer, 28 June 1808.

Spencer was still in Santa Maria and had not gone to Jerez due to the transport issues. He immediately wrote Wellesley a dispatch with up-to-date information on what was happening in Spain, although he did regret that he could not provide more 'authentic intelligence'. He suggested to Wellesley that Cadiz was 'the first place, from whence you will chuse your line of conduct' and pointed out it was close to the seat of the new Spanish government and that Wellesley's presence would encourage the Spanish. However, he warned him of the problems of procuring local transport. He still intended to go to Jerez if he could solve the transport problems but wrote that it was so close to Santa Maria that if Wellesley decided to make an attempt on Lisbon, then he could reembark within 48 hours. If Barcelona became the favoured target, he assumed Wellesley would stop at Cadiz on the way.[183]

Dalrymple also received a copy of Castlereagh's orders placing Spencer under Wellesley's command. The letters from Dalrymple to Spencer often display disapproval of the latter's actions, including elements of his decision to land his troops.[184] Dalrymple's son, Captain Adolphus John Dalrymple, who was one of his father's ADCs, wrote to his mother on 23 July that:

> Gen'l Spencer has chosen to take a line of conduct entirely his own to every part of which my father has seen cause to object, & he has thought it necessary in one of the instances to let that be seen; this said Gen'l is supposed to be a favourite at the Horse Guards & they may though be disposed to take his part, if they do *that openly*, my father seems to have resolved not to stay in this command…[185]

Of course, Spencer was not under Dalrymple's command and was entitled to choose his own line of conduct within the scope of his orders from London. The antipathy seems to have been mutual as, later in the year, an officer close to Spencer commented that Spencer would resign rather than serve under Dalrymple as he hated him.[186]

Two days after writing Spencer's orders, Castlereagh changed them, ordering him to join Wellesley off the Tagus unless he was engaged in any operation that, in his judgement, should not be abandoned.[187] These orders had travelled in the *Plover* with Trant and had been received by Cotton on 13 July, who then sent them on to Cadiz. It is unclear when Spencer received this second set of orders as he does not list them as having been received in his reply to Castlereagh of the 18th, but on 20 July, he issued an order for the troops to re-embark from Santa Maria.[188] On the 22nd, he wrote to Castlereagh that the news of *général de division* Dupont's defeat at the Battle of Bailén (16–19 July) by Castaños had removed any anxiety he had at leaving and that the Spanish commanders felt that they no longer required his support.[189] By 2 August, the convoy was off the Tagus, and Spencer proceeded in the *Nautilus* sloop to meet Wellesley.[190]

While Spencer's force had seen no combat in the more than six months since they had left Britain, their presence off the coasts of Portugal and Spain had concerned the French and bolstered

183   TNA: WO 1/226: Spencer to Wellesley, 18 July 1808.
184   BL: Add Mss 49484: Dalrymple to Spencer, 5 July 1808.
185   National Army Museum (NAM): 1994-03-129-69: A. Dalrymple to Lady Dalrymple, 23 July 1808.
186   BL: Add. MS 49503: Cooke to Gordon, 6 September 1808.
187   TNA: WO 1/226: Castlereagh to Spencer, 30 June 1808.
188   NLS: Adv.MS.46.3.6: General order, 20 July 1808.
189   TNA: WO 1/226: Spencer to Castlereagh, 22 July 1808.
190   TNA: WO 1/226: Spencer to Castlereagh, 2 August 1808.

both the Portuguese and Spanish patriots. The three weeks or so that the regiments had spent being rotated from the transports to Santa Maria had given them time to acclimatise to the climate and conduct some training during the cooler hours of the day. They would prove to be a valuable addition to the expedition preparing to embark from Cork. Wellesley would arrive off the coast of Portugal with most of the country already liberated by the Portuguese themselves. Lieutenant Colonels Browne and Trant would be able to provide him with plentiful intelligence and information on the strength of the Portuguese forces. Cotton, who had been so active in supporting the patriots, would also be able to provide further information and had ensured the most logical location to land troops, Figueira da Foz, was secured by the Royal Marines. Junot's communications with France had been severed by the Spanish revolt, and he had, apart from a few garrisons in fortresses, been forced to concentrate his forces in Lisbon. However, the poorly armed and barely re-formed Portuguese army was not in a state to defeat the French in the field. That was the task that would fall to the British Army.

5

Embarkation

On 14 June, Lieutenant General Sir Arthur Wellesley was ordered by the Duke of York, Commander-in-Chief, to take command of the force gathering at Cork and Spencer's troops, then at Gibraltar.[1] Wellesley was a younger son of an Anglo-Irish aristocratic family, born in 1769; like many younger sons, he had opted for a career in the army. After briefly attending Eton and being educated by private tutors, Wellesley attended the French Royal Academy of Equitation in Angers. When he was 17, his family purchased him an ensign's commission in the 73rd Foot. He then transferred to the newly formed 76th to gain a step up to lieutenant. He later exchanged to the 12th Light Dragoons and then purchased a captaincy in the 58th Foot. Through family connections, he was made an aide de camp to the Lord Lieutenant of Ireland, the Marquess of Buckingham, but also spent enough time with his regiments to become a competent officer.[2] After moving between more regiments and a promotion to major, he purchased a lieutenant colonelcy in the 33rd Foot and became their commanding officer at only 24.

His first campaign was under the Duke of York in the low countries in 1794, where he was one of the youngest and least experienced commanding officers. Historian Huw Davies claims that 'It was in the Low Countries that Wellesley gained an appreciation of rigorous command, vigorous discipline, good relations with allied armies and population alike, and the importance of reliable logistics and intelligence, precisely because, on all these counts, the British Army had failed.'[3] Some more recent assessments of the Flanders campaign point to more structural issues as the root of the army's problems. However, the point remains that there were plenty of learning opportunities for a young and up-and-coming officer.[4] Wellesley's biographer, Rory Muir, says of his first campaign, 'he learnt that war was a serious business which should be undertaken in a thoroughly professional spirit or not at all. Having discovered what defeat was like, he gained a fierce determination not to experience it again.'[5]

Wellesley then took the 33rd to India, where, helped by the patronage of his brother Richard, who was governor general, he flourished and gained further experience. However, he perhaps learnt as much from his failures in India as his successes. A night attack by the 33rd on Sultanpet Tope in 1799 ended

---

1   TNA: WO 72/29: York to Wellesley, 14 June 1808.
2   Muir, *Wellington*, p.20.
3   H. Davies, *Wellington's Wars, the Making of a Military Genius* (New Haven: Yale University Press, 2012), p.9.
4   See R.N.W. Thomas, *No Want of Courage: The British Army in Flanders, 1793–1795* (Warwick: Helion, 2022) for a detailed examination of the Duke of York's army.
5   Muir, *Wellington*, p.37.

in confusion and a hurried withdrawal.[6] The vast distances involved in campaigning in India meant that logistics were vital to success, but during the advance into Mysore in 1799 the army outstripped its supplies; while there were many factors, the failure of Wellesley's arrangements was one.[7]

Wellesley developed a 'Light and Quick' approach to warfare in the following years. Based on short but decisive campaigns and dependent on good intelligence, logistics and mobility, combined with aggressive decision-making. His first independent campaign, against Dhoondiah Wagh (1800), went well. However, against the Marathas in 1803 he did not adapt his tactics or strategy for a very different enemy with well-trained infantry and plenty of artillery and, according to Davies, underestimated his enemy and discounted intelligence that did not fit his preconceived opinions.[8] At Assaye, the Marathas did not break in the face of disciplined British and sepoy troops, and Wellesley's men took very heavy casualties due to his miscalculations. Wellesley learnt his lesson, and his next battle at Argaum was a significant tactical success.[9] Davies writes that in the Deccan campaign of 1803, Wellesley was 'manifestly incompetent in the organisation of this intelligence collection; and arrogant to the point of imbecility in the analysis of that intelligence and in his interpretation of the nature of his enemy.' Despite these failings, the campaign still ended in victory, but Wellesley did not make the mistake of thinking the successful outcome meant that there was nothing he could learn from the campaign. He recognised his errors and sought to learn from them.[10] Davies ascribes one of Wellesley's greatest foibles as 'his constant attempts to apportion blame elsewhere' and gives the example of him blaming local Indian leaders for losing a fortress that Wellesley could have easily garrisoned himself. He also blamed allies who did not live up to his preconceptions rather than realising that his expectations may have been at fault.[11] There would be occasions in the coming campaign in Portugal where Wellesley's tendency to evade blame came to the fore again.

Rory Muir is more positive about Wellesley's time in India:

> Eight years in India had given Arthur Wellesley an extraordinary range of experience. As a soldier, he had not merely seen action, but learnt to command an army on campaign and in battle. He had shown boldness, daring and courage, but also meticulous planning and preparation, and great care for the welfare and discipline of his troops. ... He had demonstrated the intelligence and breadth of vision to devise a plan of campaign that was sufficiently flexible to allow for myriad uncertainties, but which still helped shape events to his own advantage. ... He had, as all generals must have, the necessary ruthlessness to send men forward and watch them die to achieve his objectives. He had the quick eye and bold spirit to seize a fleeting opportunity and throw his army into a sudden attack; the cool head to adjust his plans in the midst of battle in the face of an unexpected setback; and the character and personality to inspire men to follow him, loyally and with confidence, into the cannon's mouth. A good general – and Wellesley was already a very-good general – needed all these abilities, and they were not things that could be tested except amid the heat and dust of battle.[12]

---

6   Davies, *Wars*, p.2.
7   Davies, *Wars*, p.15.
8   Davies, *Wars*, pp.20, 38, 52.
9   Davies, *Wars*, p.73.
10   Davies, *Wars*, pp.61, 68.
11   Davies, *Wars*, pp.27–28.
12   Muir, *Wellington*, p.163.

In 1805, Wellesley returned from India with a knighthood, a considerable fortune, and some acclaim from his victories. However, his brother Richard's term had been controversial and much of his time was spent helping the family and their allies defend him. He became an MP in 1806 and then a member of the government in 1807 as Chief Secretary for Ireland, effectively the minister with responsibility for Ireland, subordinate to the Lord Lieutenant. However, he was still keener on a military career than a political one. He commanded the Reserve in the Copenhagen expedition, handling his troops well at Kjøge.[13]

Without a general staff, British ministers relied on a more informal network of generals they trusted and knew to put the flesh on the bones of any strategic plan. With his close ties to the government and personal relationship with Castlereagh, Wellesley was a general that the Ministry of All the Talents and the Portland administration often turned to for military counsel. The quality and thoroughness of the advice he had given, especially regarding the various South American plans, was a significant factor in his being given command of the expedition.[14]

In 1806, the then Prime Minister, William Grenville, wrote of Wellesley, 'I have so very high an opinion of his talents and military knowledge, and particularly of his powers of exciting spirit and confidence in his troops, which I have heard so very strongly stated by indifferent persons, that I am very desirous of his being employed there if the scale of our operations be large enough for him.'[15] Another Prime Minister, William Pitt, also thought highly of him:

> Sir Arthur Wellesley is unlike all other military men with whom I have conversed. He never makes a difficulty or hides his ignorance in vague generalities. If I put a question to him, he answers it distinctly; if I want an explanation, he gives it clearly; if I desire an opinion, I get from him one supported by reasons which are always sound. He is a very remarkable man.[16]

While Wellesley may have had many political connections, historian George Jaycock argues that he 'only had limited connections among leading soldiers and military cliques of the day.'[17] He was not one of the primarily Scottish officers who had led brigades or regiments under Abercromby in Egypt in 1801. He was not one of the 'scientifics', those officers who were beginning to study the theory and practice of war more methodically, and he was not a graduate of the new Royal Military College at High Wycombe. Also, since one of his close political allies and patrons was the Duke of Richmond, who had fought a duel with the Duke of York, he was not a favourite at Horse Guards either. While patronage and favour were part and parcel of how Georgian society worked, they could nevertheless cause some resentment. Wellesley's career in India had benefitted from his being the brother of the governor general, but some of those who perceived themselves as having been passed over for the commands that Wellesley was given harboured resentment; hints

---

13   Davies, *Wars*, p.87.
14   C. Esdaile and R. Muir, 'Strategic Planning in a Time of Small Government: The Wars Against Revolutionary and Napoleonic France, 1793-1815, in C. Woolgar (ed.), *Wellington Studies I* (Southampton: University of Southampton, 1996), p.26.
15   Grenville to Windham, 23 September 1806, quoted in Robson, 'Special Advisor', p.45.
16   Quoted in M. Glover, *Britannia Sickens, Sir Arthur Wellesley and the Convention of Cintra* (London: Leo Cooper, 1970), p.36.
17   G.E. Jaycock, *Wellington's Command: A Reappraisal of His Generalship in the Peninsula and at Waterloo* (Barnsley: Pen & Sword, 2019), p.25.

of nepotism may have taken some of the shine off the reputation he earned in India in the eyes of other officers. For example, he was given the governorship of Seringapatam over the head of Major General David Baird, who was more senior. Wellesley being given command of the Maratha campaign was also controversial, and Lieutenant General James Stuart, who was far more senior, threatened to resign. In 1803, Baird opted to return to Britain rather than continue to be overlooked in favour of Wellesley.[18]

Wellesley undoubtedly owed his command of the expedition preparing to sail from Cork to his close connection to the government. He was fourth from the bottom of the list of lieutenant generals, having only been promoted to that rank in April 1808, along with 30 other major generals. However, the government also placed their trust in him because of his evident competence and the quality of the advice he had previously given them.

At the end of a covering letter to the Duke of York's list of staff officers for the expedition, Lieutenant Colonel James Willoughby Gordon, the Duke's military secretary, wrote to Wellesley: 'God bless you, take care of yourself; you have brought golden opinions from all sorts of people, and cannot fail to be eminently useful to your country.'[19] But not everyone thought that Wellesley was the best man for the job. Colonel William Clinton, the quartermaster general in Ireland, wrote in his diary on 3 July:

> Much mischief may be done to the cause by the landing of a corps under such a man as Sir. A Wellesley, who, though, I believe is a very gallant man, has not hitherto shewn judgement in his military career in any instance and who, I fear, would not advert to the grand requisite of the strictest discipline being maintained by any troops of ours who should set foot on the Spanish shore.[20]

While still in London, Wellesley reportedly dined with Irish MP John Croker on 14 June. After dinner, Wellesley, apparently 'lapsed into a kind of reverie', and Croker asked him what he was thinking:

> Why, to say the truth, I am thinking of the French that I am going to fight. I have not seen them since the campaign in Flanders, when they were capital soldiers, and a dozen years of victory under Buonaparte must have made them better still. They have besides, it seems, a new system of strategy, which has out-manoeuvred and overwhelmed all the armies of Europe. 'Tis enough to make one thoughtful; but no matter: my die is cast, they may overwhelm me, but I don't think they will out-manoeuvre me. First, because I am not afraid of them, as everybody else seems to be; and secondly, because if what I hear of their system of manoeuvres be true, I think it a false one as against steady troops. I suspect all the continental armies were more than half beaten before the battle was begun. I, at least, will not be frightened beforehand.[21]

---

18   Jaycock, *Command*, pp.45–46.
19   Special Collections, Hartley Library, University of Southampton (UoS): WP 1/206: Gordon to Wellesley, 15 June 1808.
20   Quoted in Muir, *Wellington*, p.235.
21   L.J. Jennings (ed.), *The Croker Papers* (London: Murray, 1885), vol.I, p.13.

This conversation is often quoted in Wellington biographies and histories of the Peninsular War and interpreted to mean that Wellesley was talking about defeating attacking French columns with defending British infantry in line.[22] However, that is not explicit in what is reported. In his online commentary to his biography of Wellesley, Rory Muir raises the possibility that the conversation, while plausible, actually took place later and should not be relied upon.[23] An experienced general like Wellesley would not have thought defeating an adversary could be reduced to a single tactical system or situation. It would also have been uncharacteristic and illogical of Wellesley to have been planning to conduct his campaign in Portugal by fighting defensively when it was his army that had to dislodge the French.

Wellesley dined with the Spanish deputies from Asturias at Canning's house on 15 June and then left London the next day, the 16th.[24] He was in Dublin by 27 June for the baptism of his two infant sons (Arthur, 17 months, and Charles, seven months) and received Castlereagh's final instructions on 4 July. He arrived in Cork on the 6th, and on the 8th, the newspapers reported, 'Sir Arthur Wellesley and the General Officers of the Expedition and of the garrison with their respective suites, were elegantly entertained at Mansion house, Cork.'[25]

Uncertainty and Indecision

Any decision to send troops abroad involved many parts of the government. The Prime Minister, Foreign Secretary and Secretary of War might shape the policy, but the Master General of Ordnance had to provide the artillery and ammunition, the Chancellor of the Exchequer had to supply provisions and members of the Commissariat, the First Lord of the Admiralty the escort, and the Transport Board the vessels. The Home Secretary had to say if the current state of the country meant that troops could be spared from home service, the Commander-in-Chief had to recommend the regiments that were fit for service and appoint the staff and general officers, and finally, the Secretary at War had to issue movement orders to get the troops to march to the ports.[26]

Castlereagh wrote to the Duke of York, the Commander-in-Chief at the beginning of June asking him to increase the corps awaiting embarkation at Cork from 5,000 to 8,000 infantry and to appoint a staff adequate for a force of 12,000 men, which accounted for additional troops joining them at Gibraltar. He also requested that a dismounted cavalry regiment be held in readiness for immediate embarkation.[27] On the 10th, he wrote Lord Chatham, the Master General of the Ordnance, asking him to supply ordnance and stores for two brigades of light 6-pounders and one brigade of 9-pounders, together with entrenching tools for 8,000 men and engineers stores 'according to a requirement furnished by Sir A. Wellesley.' Chatham was also requested to hold two 10-inch and four 5½ inch mortars in readiness. On 14 June, Castlereagh asked that 30,000 stand of arms, 30,000 pikes, four million musket cartridges and 100,000 musket flints be immediately embarked on ships allocated for that purpose.[28]

22   For example, C. Oman, *Wellington's Army* 1809-1814 (London: Arnold, 1913), pp.78–79.
23   Muir, 'Commentary for Volume 1, Chapter 14', *Life of Wellington*, <https://lifeofwellington.co.uk/commentary/chapter-fourteen-dublin-and-westminster-october-1807-july-1808/>, accessed 1 June 2022.
24   Muir, 'Commentary for Volume 1, Chapter 14'.
25   *Saunder's Newsletter*, 12 July 1808.
26   Esdaile and Muir, 'Strategic Planning', p.21.
27   TNA: WO 1/418: Castlereagh to York, 3 & 7 June 1808.
28   TNA: WO 1/418: Castlereagh to Chatham, 10 June 1808.

One burning question for the British government was whether the Spanish insurrection would last. Writing to Dalrymple at Gibraltar on 6 July, Castlereagh wrote:

> It must be evident, that if this noble spirit that has burst forth, and which seems to be universal thro' the provinces of Spain, can be maintained for any considerable time that the most beneficial results may take place not only to Spain itself but to Europe & the world; if on the contrary the effort shall turn out to be merely momentary, & shall languish, or cease upon conflict or ill success, not only the servitude of Spain, but that of Europe may be for a long period irrevocably fixed.[29]

The news from Spain was causing the government to delay deciding upon a destination for any expedition. Reports received from southern Spain had not yet indicated much inclination on the part of the Andalusians to rise up against French occupation. In contrast, the government did have plenty of evidence of revolts in the northern provinces. Castlereagh wrote to Wellesley on 21 June that the cabinet wanted more news from the north of Spain before deciding where to send the expedition, that they were 'Unwilling you should get too far to the Southward whilst the spirit of exertion appears to reside more to the northward.'[30] With not all regiments or equipment yet gathered at Cork, the indecision would not delay the expedition sailing.

The troops waiting to sail on the transports speculated about their destination. Spain was very much favoured. As an aide de camp to Major General Ferguson, Captain William Warre (23rd Light Dragoons) would have been better informed than many but told his mother on 27 June:

> It is very uncertain when we shall sail. We are waiting for the Donegal 74, Capt. Malcolm, and Crocodile frigate, and for some transports, with Artillery and Cavalry, and some empty ones to thin those now here, which are very much crowded, though hitherto quite healthy. The additional room allowed looks like a longer voyage than we expected, though Cavalry and our taking horses seems to contradict this idea. I am rather for going to Spain. It is a noble service assisting a nation fighting for its independence ... At all events, our assisting to the utmost of our power the mother country will greatly facilitate our establishing the independence of America, whither I hope will be our ultimate destination.[31]

Captain William Gomm (9th Foot), wrote to his wife from the barracks in Mallow on 1 June:

> General Brownrigg [Quartermaster General] has written to us to say that as soon as the transports arrive at Cork, we are to sail in company with the 40th and 91st Regiments, now on board at that port, in the first instance for Gibraltar ... The General further says that upon our arrival at Gibraltar we may expect to be immediately employed upon active service; and some of us are romantic enough to flatter ourselves that the coast of Spain is ultimately our point of destination. The country is stated to be in a sad state of disorder, but unless we are confident of being received à bras ouverts [with open arms], such an attempt I should think would not be made.[32]

---

29   TNA: WO 6/185: Castlereagh to Dalrymple, 6 July 1808.
30   TNA: WO 1/228: Castlereagh to Wellesley, 21 June 1808.
31   E. Warre (ed.), *Letters from the Peninsula 1808-1812* (London: Murray, 1909), p.15.
32   F.C. Carr-Gomm (ed.), *Letters and Journals of Field-Marshal Sir William Maynard Gomm* (London: Murray, 1881), p.96.

When a second delegation arrived in London, this time from Galicia, its members informed the government of the widespread uprisings in their province and the substantial number of troops they had put into the field. They also said that provinces in the east and south were in revolt. The expedition would need a safe deep-water port to operate from, which meant Ferrol, Vigo, or Cadiz if the force were to land in Spain. The Galician deputies ruled out Ferrol and Vigo, saying that they did not want the direct support of British troops, echoing what those from Asturias had already said, and with Spencer having tried at Cadiz, the only remaining options on the Peninsula were Lisbon or Gibraltar.[33] The cabinet, at last, decided on a destination for Wellesley's expedition: Portugal.

The Corsican Tiger at Bay! by Thomas Rowlandson, published 8 July 1808. Patriotic greyhounds attack Napoleon while John Bull fires from the white cliffs of Dover. Austria and Russia contemplate breaking with the French, and even the Dutch wait their turn. During the summer of 1808 the papers and print shops were full of such predictions of trouble ahead for Napoleon after his rash actions in Spain. (Metropolitan Museum of Art, The Elisha Whittelsey Collection)

While the main convoy was to rendezvous of Cape Finisterre, Wellesley was ordered to sail ahead in a frigate to Corunna to learn first-hand the state of the insurrection in Spain and judge how best to undertake operations in Portugal and to evaluate if he needed Spencer's troops as well

---

33   Glover, *Sickens*, p.40.

as his own. If further reinforcements were needed, the convoy would shelter in a port such as Vigo until more troops could be sent.

Castlereagh told Wellesley that Lieutenant Colonel Browne and Captain Préval had both been dispatched to Portugal. Wellesley was to assure the Spanish and Portuguese people that the force was there only to help them and that as the situation was changing rapidly, he was to use his best judgment on exactly where and how to deploy his troops.[34]

The situation was indeed changing rapidly. The receipt, later on the 30th, of Cotton's letter of 12 June, in which he relayed intelligence that at that time there were not more than 4,000 French troops in Lisbon, made Castlereagh write additional instructions the same day. Wellesley was not to go to Corunna but instead send a confidential officer. Castlereagh wrote: 'You will of course feel it of the most pressing importance that your Armament should proceed off the Tagus, *not separating yourself from it*, with the least possible delay.'[35] Wellesley was also informed that artillery that had been destined for a different service and which included six 10-inch mortars, had been ordered to sail for the Tagus and that two additional battalions – the 1/36th and 2/14th – that were near Cork had been added to the expedition, but if they were not embarked in time, he was to sail without them. The 2/14th at Fermoy was quickly replaced by the 1/45th, which had recently moved from Middleton to Cork. The 20th Light Dragoons had left Portsmouth, as had an additional 3,000 tons of transports. To help arm the Portuguese or Spanish patriots, the 30,000 stands of arms and pikes had also been sent to be used at Wellesley's discretion.

As fresh intelligence arrived from Cotton and Dalrymple on the state of the insurrections in Portugal and Spain and the strength of the French forces, the government felt the need to add to the size of the expedition, hence Castlereagh's comments about the 10,000 men who would follow Wellesley to the Peninsula. This larger force needed a more senior commander. The King had always been concerned about entrusting such an important expedition to a young and junior general such as Wellesley. The increase in troop numbers was the perfect excuse to appoint someone else. The officer selected was another member of the government, the Master General of the Ordnance, Lord Chatham. In a private letter dated 30 June, the same day as he wrote Wellesley's orders, Castlereagh told him, 'Lord Chatham will command the 10,000 men preparing here. If the whole works well, when we get the Baltic Force back, we shall have a respectable Army. I trust however you will have settled matters at Lisbon long before we shall have anything ready to follow you.'[36] As Chatham was considerably more senior to Wellesley in the *Army List*, Wellesley would have been aware that he would likely be superseded in command soon after arriving in Portugal. However, Chatham ended up declining the command. Speaking to Colonel Anstruther on 18 July, Chatham said he had 'declined going mainly because he apprehended the whole business would be done by Wellesley before he could possibly get there.'[37] However, Chatham's biographer, Dr Jaqueline Reiter, suspects the reason may well have been the very poor health of his wife.[38] Leaving aside who was to be appointed, it is clear that Wellesley knew before he sailed that he would not have long to achieve something before a more senior officer would take over.

---

34 TNA: WO 6/185: Castlereagh to Wellesley, 30 June 1808.
35 TNA: WO 6/185: Castlereagh to Wellesley, 30 June 1808, second letter.
36 UoS: WP 1/205: Castlereagh to Wellesley, 30 June 1808.
37 St Andrew's University Library, Special Collections (StAUL): msdep121/8/2/3/4/4: Field diary of General Robert Anstruther on campaign in Portugal, p.4.
38 J. Reiter, *The Late Lord, The Life of John Pitt 2nd Earl of Chatham* (Barnsley: Pen & Sword, 2017), p.99.

Troops Destined for Continental Service

Wellesley's second in command was to have been Major General Alexander Mackenzie, but when Spencer's troops were added to the force he was removed from the expedition as he was senior to Spencer. So, organising the gathering force in Cork was left to Major General Rowland Hill, who had been in command at nearby Fermoy, as the senior officer present.[39] On 23 June, Wellesley wrote to Hill from Dublin Castle: 'I rejoice extremely at the prospect I have before me of serving again with you, and I hope that we shall have more to do than we had on the last occasion on which we were together. I propose to leave town for Cork as soon as I shall receive my instructions from London.' Wellesley and Hill had served together in a rapidly abandoned expedition to Hannover at the end of 1806. The lengthy letter continues to outline many of the arrangements, including a temporary brigade structure:

> There remains nothing now but to brigade the troops, which may be a convenience for the present, and give us the assistance of the General Officers in the different arrangements which may be necessary on board the transports. But what we shall do now can only be temporary, as the whole corps must necessarily be new modelled when we join General Spencer. The Veteran battalion must be put out of the question, as that corps must go into the garrison of Gibraltar.
>
> The corps might be brigaded as follows: the 95th and the 5th batt. of the 60th; the 5th, 9th, and 38th; the 40th, 71st, and 91st. You will alter this arrangement, if the corps belonging to your brigade are not put together, and you will put such (if all the corps of your brigade are not embarked for this service) corps as you please with the 9th. Let General Fane then command the Light brigade; General Craufurd the Highlanders; and General Ferguson, who belongs to Spencer's corps, that brigade which has been, and will hereafter be yours. The Veteran battalion to report to General Fane, until it shall be otherwise disposed of.[40]

An expedition the size of the one gathering at Cork needed a substantial number of staff officers, chosen by the Commander-in-Chief, not the commander of the expedition, but by 1 July many of the officers appointed had, like Wellesley himself, not yet arrived, nor even been officially notified that they had an appointment on the staff. Some positions would be filled by officers with Spencer, including Lieutenant Colonel Tucker (50th Foot) as deputy adjutant general, Lieutenant Colonel Bathurst (60th Foot) as deputy quartermaster general, Major Rainey (82nd Foot) as assistant deputy quartermaster general, and Reverend M. Matthews as chaplain.[41] The senior officer in each department would take charge until Spencer's troops joined with Wellesley's.

A vital part of any army going on campaign was the staff of the Commissariat and the Paymaster, both of which came under the purview of the Treasury. On 13 June, Charles Stewart, military undersecretary at the War Office, wrote to George Harrison, assistant secretary at the Treasury, to request that the Lords Commissioners of the Treasury order 'a proper proportion' should proceed with the 8,000 men embarking at Cork, and suggested either sending a deputy commissary general

---

39   Muir, 'Commentary for Volume 1, Chapter 14'; E. Sidney, *The Life of Lord Hill* (London: John Murray, 1845), p.74.
40   BL: Add MS 35059: Wellesley to Hill, 23 June 1808.
41   TNA: WO 72/29: York to Wellesley, 14 June 1808.

or allowing the commissary currently attached to Spencer's corps to take the role. Stewart also asked that the Paymaster General appoint a paymaster for the expedition.[42] Five assistant commissaries, eight clerks, six storekeepers and 12 bakers were gathered at Portsmouth, and the Transport Board asked to provide them passage to Cork.[43]

The regulations for embarking troops were contained in the *General Order for Troops Destined for Continental Service,* which outlined what could be taken on campaign and what should be done before embarkation.[44] The opening paragraph stated that 'On Orders being received for Embarkation, all heavy and superfluous Baggage, all Sick Men, and those unequal to active Service, all Sick and Lame Horses are to be left at the Barracks from which the respective Corps march, under the care of a Subaltern Officer, and a proportion of Non-Commission Officers from each.' The returns for the battalions earmarked for the expedition in June and July 1808 do record men either 'given' – usually men transferred to the second battalion of the regiment or a veteran battalion – and 'discharged', either recommended or not recommended. For most regiments preparing to embark at Cork, the numbers in each category are small, less than 10, but the 1/91st transferred 52 men in June. Likewise, there are inflows to the battalions marked in the 'joined' – recruited – and 'received' – transferred, usually from second battalions – columns. Again, the numbers are generally small, but in May, the 1/38th had received 50 men and the 1/71st 325, which would have meant a third of their strength were new to the battalion.[45] The return of the troops at Cork under the command of Wellesley dated 1 July is displayed in Table 7. As can be seen, there are substantial inflows and outflows of troops.

As well as official discharges and transfers, 50 soldiers chose to desert during June, with the 4th Royal Veterans having 13 men who decided that another foreign posting was too much for them. The veterans were destined for Gibraltar where they could free up a line battalion. Officers who did not want to go abroad could resign their commissions or exchange into another regiment. Ensign Thomas Hodson of 1/9th absconded from his battalion as it was waiting to embark on 16 June. He had sent in his resignation but had not yet received confirmation of its acceptance. He is later marked as resigned in the *Army List*.[46] In a list of absent officers, eight are marked absent without leave, which usually meant that their leave had expired and they had not yet returned to the regiment, or that, in an age of slow communications, an application for extension had not reached its destination. Other officers were absent as they were assigned to staff roles with other corps, such as Ensign William Morgenthal of the 5/60th, who was on Moore's staff, or Lieutenant Vale Flemming of the 9th, who was recruiting at Birmingham. The 1/9th also had nine officers, including their paymaster and surgeon, absent because they were prisoners of war.[47] Major Gabriel Davy, commanding the 5/60th Rifles, was so concerned about the number of officers absent from the battalion that he wrote to the military secretary to the Duke of York, colonel-in-chief of the 60th Foot, informing him that there were 'two captains, three lieutenants, and one ensign, employed upon the staff and recruiting service; and that eight lieutenants are wanting to complete

---

42   TNA: WO 1/418: Stewart to Harrison, 13 June 1808.
43   TNA: WO 6/156: Pipon to Commissioners of Transport, 16 June 1808.
44   TNA: WO 123/129: General Order for Troops Destined for Continental Service, 15 June 1807. A new version was issued 12 July 1808, the day the expedition sailed.
45   TNA: WO 17/1079: Monthly Return of Infantry in Ireland, May, June & July 1808.
46   TNA: WO 65/58: 1808 Army List.
47   TNA: WO 17/2464: List of absent officers. In 1805, a transport carrying part of the regiment was wrecked on the French coast, and 262 other ranks and nine officers were taken prisoner.

Table 7. Troops at the Cove of Cork, 1 July

Regiments	Commanding Officer	Officers Present					Staff					NCOs Present		Rank and File						Wanting to Complete			Alterations Since Last Return					
		Lt Cols	Majs	Capts	Lts	Ens	Paymst.	Adjts	QMs	Surgs	Ass. Surgs	Sgts	Drms	Present, Fit	Sick, Quarters	Sick, Hosp.	On Command	Recruiting	Furlough	Sgts	Drms	R&F	Joined	Received	Given	Discharged	Dead	Deserted
Royal Artillery	Lt Col. Robe	1	1	4	4						2	5	4	221	5													
RA Drivers	Lt Col. Robe				2							6	2	164	1													
Royal Engineers	Capt. P. Patton			1	1																							
1/5th Foot	Lt Col. J. MacKenzie	1	2	9	17	8	1	1	1	1	2	53	21	951	15	37		3					7	10	6	3	1	3
1/9th Foot	Lt Col. J. Stuart	1	2	9	17	5	1	1	1	1	2	51	21	916	7	2			1	2	1	30		101	121		1	4
1/38th Foot	Lt Col. Grenville	1	2	9	19	7	1	1	1	1	2	54	22	921	34	32			1			12	1	21	24	18		9
1/40th Foot	Lt Col. J. Kemmis	1	2	9	23	6	1	1	1	1	2	50	18	871	44	72	6				1	7	1	98			3	6
5/60th Foot	Maj. W.G. Davy		2	7	11	7	1	1	1	1	2	52	21	931		13	1	1	2	2	1	53			9	11	1	2
1/71st Foot	Lt Col. D. Pack	1	1	8	21	5	1	1	1	1	2	52	22	813	72	62	5		2			46					1	3
1/91st Foot	Lt Col. J. Robinson	1	2	8	21	3		1	1	1	2	52	20	888	22	21	1	5	4			59	268					9
4 cos 2/95th Foot	Maj. R. Travers		1	4	9	4					1	20	8	396		3												1
4th Royal Veteran Bn.	Lt Col. Daly	1		6	10	4		1		1	1	47	20	749		26	254		19			152		6	21	5	1	13
		8	15	74	155	49	6	7	7	8	18	442	179	7,821	200	268	267	9	29	4	3	359	277	236	181	37	8	50

Source: TNA: WO 17/2464: Return of Troops at stationed at the Cove of Cork, 1 July 1808.

the battalion to its proper establishment.' He also stated 'that of the subalterns doing duty with this regiment at least four (from youth and inexperience in the profession) are unfit to be trusted with the command of detachments' and he asked that the Duke urgently appoint more officers.[48] The battalion's sergeant major, Matthew Fürst, was promoted to ensign to fill one of the vacancies.[49]

The *General Order for Troops Destined for Continental Service* was also very keen on minimising baggage:

> The incumbrance of Baggage to Troops engaged in active operations is a most serious evil. On the contrary, an Army without this impediment, is ever prepared for Enterprize, ready to avail itself of every favourable circumstance, and defeat and foil it's [*sic*] enemy, as much by the promptitude and celerity of it's movements as by it's Valor in the Field of Battle.

Limits were set for what officers and other ranks could take with them. The officers' baggage was limited to one trunk, one portmanteau, a pair of canteens and 'bedding of the lightest, and most portable kind'. The total weight of baggage allowed depended on the officer's rank, with commanding officers being allowed two and a half hundredweight (127 kg) but subalterns only one hundredweight (51 kg). Sergeants, drummers and the rank and file had a prescribed list of articles that they were allowed to take in addition to their arms and accoutrements:

> For each Soldier,
> 3 Shirts,
> 1 Black Stock,
> 3 Pair Worsted or Yarn, Ancle Socks,
> 2 Pair Strong Shoes, shod with Nails or Plates, at the Toes and Heels, round at the Toe, and made to come up high round the Ancle,
> 1 Piece of Pipe Clay,
> 2 Combs,
> 1 Piece of Soap,
> 1 Small Sponge,
> 1 Pair of Shoe Brushes,
> 1 Blacking Ball,
> 1 Cloths Brush,
> 1 Pair loose coarse Canvas Trousers, to be worn on Marches, at Night, and on Duties of Fatigue,
> 1 Worsted Cap,
> 1 Great Coat.

Soldiers were also to have two good flints, their arms in good order, and the battalions' armourer sergeants had to have the necessary knowledge and tools. Once an order to embark had been received, officers' servants were to parade with the unit once per day and practice with their

48   Davy to military secretary, 7 June 1808, quoted in G. Rigaud, *Celer et Audax* (Oxford: Hall & Stacy, 1879), p.27
49   R. Griffith, *Riflemen: The History of the 5th Battalion, 60th (Royal American) Regiment, 1797-1818* (Warwick: Helion, 2019), p.128.

muskets. The *General Order* also stated that 'Regiments must be frequently Paraded, and Exercised in Marching Order. The Infantry must be accustomed to Firing with Blank Cartridges, when so Accoutred, that they may feel less encumbered, in the presence of the Enemy, when they must necessarily carry their Packs, Canteens, and Haversacks.' The cavalry was to practice packing forage and to be exercised while carrying it, and the infantry should undertake route marches in full kit of several miles to get used to their loads. Camp equipage, including haversacks and canteens, arrived on two transports from Portsmouth at the end of June and were issued by the quartermaster general's department to the individual regimental stores.[50]

The tone of the *General Order* often implies that many of the day-to-day tasks an army had to conduct on campaign were not regularly practised at other times. For example, 'It is most particularly enjoined to Officers Commanding Divisions and Brigades, to take every opportunity of instructing and practicing the Troops under their Orders, in the Duties of Posting Advanced Guards and Picquets, in forming Flanking Parties, and Patroles, and in planting Videts and Sentries...' If circumstances permitted, the artillery, cavalry, and infantry should be exercised together, and light artillery, cavalry, and infantry 'should be practically instructed in the performance of the Duties and Exercises to which these Corps are peculiarly adapted.' However, it is not clear if the troops ordered to embark at Cork had any opportunity to exercise together, certainly not with the artillery and cavalry coming from England. The map on the next page gives the location of the battalions as of 1 June.[51] Any co-located battalions would have probably taken part in field days together, but the eventual brigade structure of the expedition did not keep all such units together.

The British Army's successful campaign in Egypt in 1801 had been built upon training in Menorca and then rehearsing amphibious landings on the Turkish coast. The commander, Lieutenant General Sir Ralph Abercromby, had the time to mould his troops into a cohesive force.[52] His regimental and brigade commanders had the time to get to know one another and their commander. This was not to be the case for Wellesley and his men. Some of the regiments barracked in the same towns may well have performed field days together earlier in the year, but there is no evidence that the expedition as a whole, including the staff and brigade commanders, had any time to form themselves into a cohesive force, especially as Wellesley did not arrive long before the expedition sailed and a significant portion of the troops were with Spencer.

The *General Order* also limited the number of women that could be embarked: 'Women, only in proportion of six to every hundred Men, will be permitted to embark. They should be carefully selected, as being of good Character, and having the Inclination and Ability to render themselves useful: it is very desirable, that those who have Children should be left at home.' Whilst the number of women was strictly adhered to, if for no other reason than the Transport Board would refuse to transport more than six per 100, the selection criteria seem to have been wholly ignored according to the evidence of contemporary letters and memoirs. The favoured method appears to have been some form of drawing lots. Any attempt by a commanding officer to select the wives based on character or potential utility might have led to severe dissension in the ranks. In contrast, the soldiers

50   Wellington (ed.), *Supplementary Despatches*, vol.VI, p.87.
51   TNA: WO 17/1079: Return of infantry in Ireland, 1 June 1808.
52   P. Macksey, 'Abercromby in Egypt: The Regeneration of the Army', in A. Guy (ed.), *The Road to Waterloo* (London: Sutton, 1990), p.103.

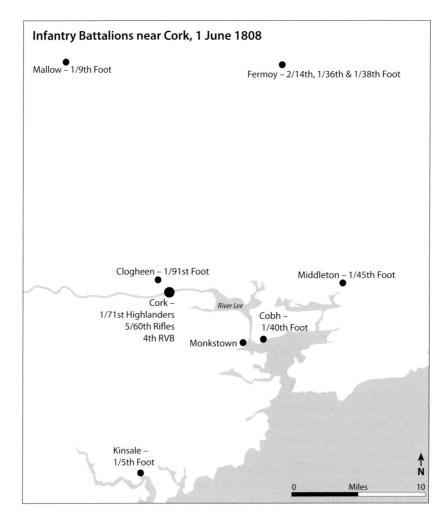

and their wives would have accepted a more random and fair procedure. A total of 817 women and 666 children sailed with the expedition.[53]

The number of wives and children left behind is not recorded. The government did allow the women to claim subsistence of up to 2d per mile, claimed in a complex scheme from the overseers of parish relief in the parishes she passed through, to get to her home parish. However, it was not until 1812 that the legislation was amended to allow for payment for crossings between Ireland and Britain.[54] The women left behind could often claim some allowances from regimental funds

---

53   Details of the convoy given to Cotton on 26 July by Lieutenant Gerrard Fleetwood, quoted in Krajeski, *Shadow*, p.96.
54   D. Clammer, *Ladies, Wives and Women British Army Wives in the Revolutionary and Napoleonic Wars 1793–1815* (Warwick: Helion, 2022), pp.33–34.

or charity. William Warre informed his mother: 'We had a gay ball here on Friday [24 June], in a storehouse fitted up with flags, for the relief of the distressed soldiers' wives. We had a good many people, and collected about £50 free of expenses little enough among so many objects.'[55] The distressed wives were not the only beneficiaries of the officer's charity; there was also an assembly for the relief of the prisoners taken on a Dutch frigate, the *Gelderland* (32), captured by HMS *Virginie* (38) off the coast of Ireland in May.[56]

With no concern for operational security, the Irish and British newspapers published a running commentary on which regiments were gathering at Cork and where the expedition was bound. However, not all the information was accurate. On 14 June, the *Dublin Evening Post* reported, 'A large body of troops, not less than 10,000 destined for Spain, have been assembled, and a considerable part of them embarked. Sir Arthur Wellesley will have chief command, with some of the ablest General Officers under him.' The paper then provided a list of the regiments assigned to the expedition, including details such as 100 men of the 2/9th Foot marching into Dover to join the first battalion in Ireland. The expected destination for the expedition was Gibraltar, and then a point in Spain would be chosen.[57] On the 18th, the same paper was reporting that the expedition was 'preparing with the utmost activity' and noted the arrival of more transports and regiments at Cork, including details like the fact that the 2/14th Foot and Wexford Militia would be replacing the 5/60th and 1/71st as the regiments based at Cork.[58] On 22 June, the *Hibernian Journal* noted, 'From the General change of quarters among the regiments in the Southern District, the great road from Dublin to Cork has at present every appearance of being peculiarly a military road.'[59] Just after the expedition sailed, the *Dublin Evening Post* also noted the effect of so many troops embarking:

> In consequence of the reduction of the troops in this garrison by the late embarkation, the duty has fallen so heavily upon the Rosscommon and Wexford Militia Regiments, which remain in barrack, that the Yeomanry Corps of this city [Cork] have very handsomely volunteered their services to take guards occasionally to lighten it. This spirited and considerate offer has been received with proper acknowledgements; and on Sunday next the city duty will be committed to the Yeomanry, for that day only.[60]

The 1/36th and 1/45th Foot were the last infantry battalions added to the expedition, and both were significantly weaker than the battalions that had been assigned from the start, with each having less than 600 effectives.[61] The 2/14th had a similar strength and were initially added to the battalions to go by Castlereagh but were replaced by the 1/45th. This was perhaps because second battalions were supposed to be stationed within the United Kingdom to recruit and train men for their first battalions. The 1/14th had been posted to India in 1807 and would remain in the east

55   Warre (ed.), *Letters*, pp.15–16.
56   Lincolnshire Archives (LA): MG/4/5/15/10: Algernon Langton to Mrs Massingbird, 8 July 1808. 'Capture of the Gelderland, 19th May 1808', <https://threedecks.org/index.php?display_type=show_battle&id=716>, accessed June 2022.
57   *Dublin Evening Post*, 14 June 1808.
58   *Dublin Evening Post*, 18 June 1808.
59   *Hibernian Journal*, 22 June 1808.
60   *Dublin Evening Post*, 13 July 1808.
61   TNA: WO 17/1079: Return of infantry in Ireland, 1 June 1808.

for the rest of the war, so, if the 2/14th was sent on campaign, the first battalion would struggle to replace losses due to disease. The 1/45th had been part of the second invasion of Spain's Rio de la Plata colony and had been slowly rebuilding its strength since arriving in Ireland.[62]

For the 5/60th Rifles, the expedition was their first campaign since 1799, and Major Davy wrote a long regimental order outlining what he expected from his riflemen:

> As there is every reason to imagine that the battalion will shortly be honoured with an opportunity of distinguishing itself in the field, the Commanding Officer feels it his duty to recall the attention of the younger part of the officers to the absolute necessity of making themselves acquainted with the several duties of the outposts, that they may be enabled to lead and instruct the men entrusted to their care. He also expects they will seriously consider that any neglect on their part before the enemy may cause the most fatal consequences, (from the particular service allotted to the battalion) not only to themselves, but to the whole army.
>
> He doubts not their own good sense will point out to them the necessity of impressing upon their minds that vigilance and activity are the first duties required from an officer on an outpost, and hopes they will not lose the opportunity of profiting by the advice which may be given to them by such of their brother officers who have had the advantage of acquiring experience upon actual service.
>
> The men are to understand that by the maintenance of order and discipline we can alone look forward to a successful opposition to the designs of an enemy; they must on every occasion conform with alacrity to the orders of their officers, and as great fatigue is often connected with the duties of light troops, they must cheerfully submit, and bear like men the hardships attending a soldier's life. He feels convinced of their bravery, and is satisfied that they will never yield in that respect to any troops in his Majesty's service.
>
> The true 'Rifleman' will never fire without being sure of his man, he should if possible make use of forced balls, and only load with cartridges in case of necessity, as when a brisk fire is to be kept up. And he will recollect that a few well-directed shots, that tell, will occasion greater confusion than thousands fired at random and without effect, which will only make the enemy despise our fire, and inspire him with confidence in proportion as he finds us deficient in skill and enterprise.
>
> It is particularly recommended to the men, and will be strictly enforced, to behave with humanity to the people in an enemy's country, and not to plunder or destroy their houses, or attempt their lives, without the most urgent necessity, or an order to that effect. Interest and humanity both require the maintenance of a strict discipline, as the only way to conciliate the minds of the people, and to make them our friends. A contrary conduct, besides all other disadvantages attending, will certainly reflect strongly on the credit of the Corps.
>
> It is the duty of every officer carefully to provide for the wants of his men. This, he may be assured, will give him their confidence and esteem, and on some particular occasion the maxim may be adopted that, 'necessity knows no laws;' but it must never be forgotten, that the 'laws' are again in force the moment that necessity ceases, and the officers will recollect that the wants of their men are not to be provided for by allowing individuals to plunder or maraud.

---

62   S. Brown, *Wellington's Redjackets* (Barnsley: Frontline, 2015), pp.21–22.

The officers should endeavour to learn the capacities and characters of their men that they may employ them to the best advantage; this may be easily done by conversing with them, and hearing their opinion and sentiments on different subjects.

The Commanding Officer will feel sincere pleasure in recommending and rewarding all such non-commissioned officers and men as may distinguish themselves by their good conduct in the field; but if, on the contrary, any man should be guilty of cowardice, desertion, or any other such infamous crime as may reflect on the credit of the Corps, he will show no mercy to such an offender, but use every exertion to bring him to the punishment he deserves.[63]

An anonymous soldier of the 1/71st Highlanders wrote of the long weeks waiting for the expedition to sail:

… we lay snug in the Cove of Cork for about five weeks; during the whole of which time, the deck of the vessel that I was in, was a continual scene of uproar and jovial mirth. Every afternoon the piper played his best reel-tunes, to which the men danced in high glee; liquor was also very plentifully handed about. This was chiefly owing to the settlement of a long arrear of pay due to the soldiers, who had arrived from America.[64]

Officers had more freedom to entertain themselves. Captain Jonathan Leach of the 95th Rifles wrote in his memoir: 'During the four or five weeks which we remained in the Cove of Cork, waiting for the arrival of Sir A. Wellesley from England, we amused ourselves with boating parties to Glanmyre, and other places of considerable beauty on the river, and in frequent trips to the city.'[65] For Captain William Warre, the campaign would take him back to a country he knew well. His father, James Warre, was a partner in the family wine business based in Oporto. While waiting to sail, he wrote to his father:

We are exceedingly anxious to get away, after six weeks' delay. The Army are in the highest spirits; indeed the cause we are engaged in is the noblest a soldier could wish, and to support the liberties and independence of a country so lately our enemy. To forget all animosity and cordially join against the common enemy of Europe, the would-be Tyrant of the world, is worthy of the British name; and a soldier's heart must be cold indeed that would not warm with enthusiasm in such a cause. I am not one of the most sanguine; you know my opinion of armed mobs, though in this, from the accounts we have received, there is an appearance of system and order that promises well. May God assist the Right. It may be the crisis of the Tyrant's power. If he fails now, it may open the eyes of Europe.[66]

63 Rigaud, *Celer et Audax*, p.19
64 Anon., *Vicissitudes in the Life of a Scottish Soldier* (London: Colburn, 1827), pp.2–3. This work was probably based on the story of a real soldier, but was ghost-written and semi-fictionalised by George Gleig, who had a hand in many 'memoirs'. See M. Greig, *Dead Men Telling Tales* (Oxford: Oxford University Press, 2021), p.157.
65 J. Leach, *Rough Sketches of the Life of an Old Soldier* (London: Longman, 1831), p.41.
66 E. Warre, (ed.), *Letters*, p.6. The letter is dated 8 June but given some other details, such as the arrival of Wellesley and the 36th and 45th Foot, this must be an error and 8 July is more likely. The manuscript letter in the National Army Museum also has the 8 June date (NAM: 1997-04-067)

Many of the troops embarked at Cobh (Cove) wrote letters home. Second Captain William Granville Eliot of the Royal Artillery wrote to his wife on 7 July to say that their destination was still secret, but everyone expected they would rendezvous at Gibraltar. He, like many others on board the ships, had children, including Howard, born at the end of January. He ended his letter with: 'God bless you and the darlings. I never see a little one but I think of you all, and can never pass one without giving it a halfpenny.' Sadly, his young son died 10 days later.[67] For some, the risks of the campaign they were embarking upon were on their minds. Captain Henry Mellish (87th Foot), another aide de camp to Major General Ferguson, told his sister, 'Remember my dear girl that to attain the honors of my profession we must require the dangers of it. I think we shall have not only a pleasant but an active & honorable service & that we shall meet again & talk of dangers past with increased pleasure in proportion to their magnitude.'[68] Mellish's last letter to his sister before the convoy sailed, dated 5 July, is full of hope for the coming campaign:

> I fear, as I have been silent some time, you must have began to think we had sailed. We have had a most weary sojourning here instead, but our prospects begin to brighten. Sir Arthur Wellesley will be here tomorrow & Captain Malcolm (our Commodore) has received his definitive orders to sail with what ships are ready. We may perhaps be detained a day or two, as some of the transports masts are bad, but that will be the utmost. We shall cut a very respectable appearance a seventy four, two frigates & about seventy sail of transports. Spain seems certainly to be our destination. Indeed the accounts from that country hold out a very fair prospect of doing something brilliant, if we get there directly. We have one great advantage in disembarking in a country friendly to us, we shall not have our force weekend in effecting a landing. We have some of the finest troops with us that ever were seen & several well informed officers on the staff that may be of great service in organising the Spaniards.[69]

Deputy assistant quartermaster general Captain Algernon Langton (61st Foot) wrote to his sister on 8 July:

> I have been so busily employed since I wrote my last letter to my mother, that I have scarcely had a quiet half hour, and I am now writing amidst the confusion of an office; which is the only sitting room I have; and of course where every body is following a different pursuit, and making a different noise …
>
> We are still uncertain as to our movements; though Sir Arthur Wellesley being arrived there appears to be nothing to detain us; & Captain Malcolm, who convoys us, and takes out Sir Arthur in the Donegal, has received his final instructions, and has given theirs to the masters of the transports – which is commonly considered as the prelude to sailing. Campbell, two other Wycombites [graduates of the Royal Military College] & I, go out in a store ship; which is a kind of thing we prefer to all others, because we shall have it all to ourselves, & be our own masters.

---

67   National Army Museum (NAM): 1959-03-127: Correspondence of William Granville Eliot, Royal Artillery 1805-1809, Eliot to wife, 7 July 1808..

68   Nottingham University, Manuscripts and Special Collections (NU): Me4C2/1/6: Henry Mellish to Ann Mellish, 22 May 1808.

69   NU: Me4C2/1/9: Henry Mellish to Ann Mellish, 5 July 1808.

You will I dare say see accounts in the papers of the troops being in high spirits:– which is a kind of cant they always make use of;– but certainly most applicable in the present instances: for never was an occasion so likely to inspire people. The prospect is the most glorious possible; & I do trust that no jealousy on the part of the Spaniards, nor any other case, will prevent our landing in Spain:– from whence we shall all, of course, return grandees, and Knights of the Golden Fleece etc [A Spanish order of chivalry].[70]

The South American Effect

Although the debate within the government about where to send Wellesley and his men may have been centred on the choice between Spain and Portugal, the option of South America was still on the table almost until the expedition sailed. The persistence of the government's plans to send an expedition to South America in the face of two previous embarrassing failures was caused both by a certain degree of economic necessity and continued and valid fears of Napoleon's ambitions in the area. The fact that the force at Cork was originally intended to go to either South or Central America, and that such a destination remained an option, had a significant impact on the make-up and equipment of the expedition.

One way that the South American option affected the expedition was in the selection of the regiments. In a memorandum on the state of the army dated 1 February 1808, 10,000 men of the 30,000 of the disposable force had 'been selected with a view to more distant operations'.[71] In another memorandum, undated but clearly written in early 1808, Castlereagh stated that the British troops selected for an attack on Caracas would have to be 'selected from those corps that have been seasoned to a tropical climate'. He then listed Spencer's corps at Gibraltar and two battalions of the 60th (but not the 5/60th) as possible sources for these troops. In another document where he listed the regiments at Cork, Gibraltar and elsewhere Castlereagh proposed a force to go to Monte Video and another to Caracas or Mexico which included the 5/60th but none of the other battalions at Cork.[72] Sending troops used to a tropical climate was thought, probably correctly, to reduce deaths from disease as the soldiers who had survived previous postings had some resistance to the prevalent fevers. The 5/60th had been based in Surinam on the northern coast of South America from 1799 to 1802. This seasoning to the climate may well have influenced the selection of the battalions, especially in the case of the 5/60th as the 60th (Royal American) Regiment of Foot was, as the title suggests, meant to operate in the Americas. Of the nine line battalions embarked at Cork six had been involved with one of the two unsuccessful expeditions to the Rio del Plata and had only returned in December 1807.

On 1 June Castlereagh submitted a plan to the King for the expedition to Spain, but that plan still contained an option for the force to continue to South America if no opportunity for action presented itself on the Iberian Peninsula. The same day Wellesley submitted a memorandum on the force required for South America, which began:

70   LA: MG/4/5/15/10: Algernon Langton to Mrs Massingbird, 8 July 1808.
71   Vane (ed.), *Correspondence*, vol.VIII, p.161.
72   Vane (ed.), *Correspondence*, vol.VII, pp.385–389.

According to the plan of operations at present in contemplation, a corps, consisting of about 8000 men, are to proceed from Cork to join General Spencer's corps of about 5000 off the coast of Spain; and in case affairs in that quarter should not hold out a prospect of a successful result, it is proposed either to send all the troops to the West Indies, with a view to the operations to be carried on in the Spanish colonies in the Gulf of Mexico, or to divide the corps, and to send 8000, reinforced by a regiment of cavalry, to the River de la Plata, and 5000, reinforced by two regiments of cavalry, to the West Indies, who will there receive reinforcements which will enable them to carry on the proposed operations against the Caraccas at the appointed season.

The object of this memorandum is to point out the extent of the equipments, &c., which ought to be provided for each of these corps, the periods at which the equipment for each ought to be prepared and to sail from England, and the mode in which it is proposed to make the detachments, as far as regards divisions of stores, &c.[73]

As well as troops from Cork and from Spencer's corps, more were to be drawn from the garrison at Halifax, Nova Scotia. The memorandum then went on to list in detail the artillery, ammunition, and engineers' stores required for each of the proposed operations. Wellesley's memorandum covered stores from the Board of Ordnance and provisions but did not mention any men or equipment from the Commissariat. An additional memorandum dated 6 June covered the naval forces that would have to support each of the proposed operations.[74] A third memorandum, undated, which recommended attacking Caracas as the most viable option, included a list of troops to be used:[75]

Regiments	Rank & File
Four regiments (General Spencer's corps) at Gibraltar	3,673
One regiment at Madeira	1,000
From England three regiments	3,000
Two regiments of dragoons	1,200
Black pioneers	300
From England artillery	300
Drivers belonging to the commissariat	200
	12,673

Wellesley provided the War Office with a series of orders for the Victualling Board, for Spencer, and for Beresford at Madeira. In his orders for the Transport Board, he wrote that transports for 3,000 infantry should be held in readiness on 20 June at either Falmouth or Cork, and that transport for 1,200 cavalrymen and 600 horses would also be required, which implies that half of the cavalry would be dismounted until horses were sourced locally. He again provided a detailed list of stores and artillery required from the Board of Ordnance.[76] In his final memorandum on the subject, Wellesley urged the government to act in support of the Spanish patriots:

73   Wellington (ed.), *Supplementary Despatches*, vol.VI, p.68.
74   Wellington (ed.), *Supplementary Despatches*, vol.VI, p.73.
75   Wellington (ed.), *Supplementary Despatches*, vol.VI, p.75.
76   Wellington (ed.), *Supplementary Despatches*, vol.VI, pp.77–79.

That which I recommend is to send to Gibraltar all the disposable force that can immediately be spared from England, there to join General Spencer's corps, to be prepared to act as circumstances would point out. Arms and ammunition in large quantities ought to be sent with this corps, and its commander to be instructed to encourage the insurrection to the utmost of his power. If it should be found impracticable to make any impression upon the French authority in Spain by the means of the insurrection, he should be then instructed to encourage the principal people of the kingdom to emigrate to America, under the engagement of establishing there an independent government. As the troops are not at present wanted in England, and the transports are already in the service, no inconvenience can result from this measure; and if it should be found that nothing can be done in Spain, the same troops might proceed upon the service in contemplation in the Spanish colonies in America.[77]

Even though the focus had clearly shifted towards action in Spain, any troops sent there could be ordered to continue across the Atlantic to the Americas. So, well into June, the make-up, equipment and transport for the expedition had to take this possibility into account. Even when Wellesley's instructions had been finalised at the end of June, Castlereagh had not entirely abandoned the possibility of the expedition ending up in South America, writing in a private letter:

I have thought it upon the whole better for the present to withhold any instructions about S. America for obvious reasons, I shall keep however the arrangements as settled in view, and if hopes should be dashed in Europe, which God forbid, I trust you will have the means of securing powerful support from Old Spain in that then only remaining effort for Spanish independence.[78]

For Want of Horses

The most significant South American effect was probably in the allocation of horses to the expedition. The government was always reluctant to transport too many horses abroad because of the cost. Horses were typically allocated eight tons of shipping each, four times as much as a man, so the typical transport cost was £8–10 per month per horse, as opposed to £2 per man per month. The average horse transport could carry around 35 horses. In addition to the space and carefully constructed horse stalls, each horse also needed 10 pounds of hay, eight pounds of oats, some bran, and six gallons of water daily. Because of the cost, the Transport Board typically only held transports for 1,000 horses in readiness, and many transports were already supporting Moore in the Baltic and Spencer at Gibraltar. Horse transports were also often smaller vessels so they could get over bars into rivers for easier off-loading, and the most popular type of vessels were the colliers used to transport coal from the northeast to London. Taking too many of these colliers out of service could raise the price of coal in the capital, and it took time to clean the colliers of coal dust and construct the stalls. All these factors meant that there were never enough horse ships.[79]

77   Wellington (ed.), *Supplementary Despatches*, vol.VI, p.80.
78   UoS: WP 1/205: Castlereagh to Wellesley, 30 June 1808.
79   Sutcliffe, *Expeditionary*, pp.168–169, 171, 190-191.

Transporting horses by sea was difficult and often detrimental to the horses' health. The horses were arranged in two rows, with their heads facing towards a central trough. They were prevented from lying down by securing their heads to small posts, their chest and haunches were padded with sheepskin to prevent chafing, and the hold had to be well-ventilated.[80] John Shipp of the 11th Light Dragoons, one of the first veterinary surgeons to be assigned to a cavalry regiment, lost five horses after five days of rough seas that turned a short journey across the North Sea into a 10-day voyage. The following passage from Shipp's biography on the five deaths is worth quoting at length to illustrate the problems involved:

> [Troop Farrier Martin] had the previous experience of caring for horses at sea that Shipp lacked; he never left them, examining every one almost every hour for swelling of the body or other hints of digestive troubles. If the evacuations were less than the fodder consumed, the rectum was back-raked and clysters [enemas] of warm sea water thrown in. Blankets soaked in hot sea-water constantly applied to the belly and back proved very helpful in emptying the bowels.
>
> Shipp soon realised that overcrowded digestive organs were the source of most sickness among horses at sea. The motion of the ship affected the brain which reacted on the stomach and intestines. Some horses, too, had difficulty in passing urine.
>
> The first pair died from what Martin called the sleepy staggers, and what Shipp suspected was a maritime apoplexy. At first drowsy, they began to show signs of stomach upset, followed by a swelling more or less of the whole body. Slung to prevent them falling down, although the pressure of the slings on the belly naturally hindered evacuation, John bled them, taking away four pints since the brain was affected, but a couple of hours later they collapsed and died.
>
> Seasickness claimed the next victim, or so it might be called since it tried to vomit. But this is something a horse cannot do, and it became so violent that as there was no hope of a cure, it was separated from its companions, with the greatest difficulty owing to the rolling of the ship and the near-terror of the other horses. Panic always hovered, bat-like, in that gloomy stinking timber-walled cave. Once free, Martin killed it with his axe. John understood now why the farriers carried one. If shot, the heavy pistol ball might have passed through the horse's head and killed one of the sweating privates nearby.
>
> The remaining pair simply died so suddenly no relief was possible; John decided cases of maritime apoplexy. Considerable commotion was caused when the sailors got the hatch cover off and slung the carcases into the sea.[81]

Ten years later, Shipp was with the 23rd Light Dragoons and on a three-week voyage to Portugal in which the regiment lost 11 horses. When they landed, many were so weak that they could not be ridden, and it took two weeks to get them back into condition.[82]

In his 1 June memorandum on proposed operations in the Peninsula and the Americas, Wellesley wrote: 'I recommend that horses may be sent for the ordnance required [to Cork], and

---

80   J. Mollo, *The Prince's Dolls* (London: Leo Cooper, 1997), p.42.
81   E.G. Gray, *The Trumpet of Glory* (London: Hale, 1985), p.39.
82   Gray, *Trumpet*, p.65.

if not wanted in Spain they will be returned to England.'[83] So, it was not envisaged that artillery horses be transported across the Atlantic, but Wellesley did think them necessary for operations in Spain. As well as horses to pull the artillery, the cavalry would obviously need theirs. The 20th Light Dragoons sailed from Portsmouth with their horses, but since there were 384 cavalrymen and only 238 horses, not all would be mounted when they landed.[84] The lack of horse transports may have been the cause for the shortfall.

The staff and some infantry officers also required horses to fulfil their duties. According to the *General Order for Troops Destined for Continental Service*, lieutenant generals were allowed six horses, major generals four, brigadier generals and colonels on the staff three, brigade majors two, aide de camps two, deputy adjutant generals and deputy quartermaster generals three, their assistants two, infantry commanding officers two, and field officers and adjutants one.[85] A total of 34 horses were embarked for 24 staff officers, significantly less than the theoretical maximum the *General Order* allowed for, and, according to the returns, no horses were embarked for the regimental officers.[86] In his letter to Hill on 23 June, Wellesley had written:

> I understand there is a vessel at Cork to carry thirty six horses for the Officers, besides those intended for the Commissariat horses; and I shall be obliged to you if you will desire that spare room may be kept for my horses, and those of my Aides de Camp, which will arrive at Cork in a day or two. To carry horses to Spain, however is like carrying coals to Newcastle.[87]

The final sentence was omitted from the published version of the letter, possibly due to the subsequent controversy about the number of horses that went with the expedition.[88] Wellesley may have been referring to horses suitable for the staff rather than the type of horses that the expedition needed, which were draft horses for the artillery.

The guns and artillerymen were embarked at Portsmouth, with the cavalry, and at Plymouth.[89] Transports for artillery horses were ordered as early as 9 June: 'Cavalry ships for 300 Horses for the Artillery be forthwith ordered from the Downs to Cork'.[90] However, no artillery horses were supplied by the Board of Ordnance for the expedition. According to Lord Chatham, the Master General of the Ordnance, Wellesley's force had 'been long destined for [a] remote service [South America]', and the 'equipment was judged necessary for this object.'[91] The commander of an expedition usually made his needs known to the Ordnance in a face-to-face meeting.

---

83   Wellington (ed.), *Supplementary Despatches*, vol.VI, p.70.

84   TNA: WO 72/29: Return of officers, Non-Commissioned Officers and Men embarked and sailed for Portugal, Transport Office, 16 November 1808.

85   TNA: WO 123/129: General Order for Troops Destined for Continental Service, 15 June 1807.

86   TNA: WO 72/29: Return of officers, Non-Commissioned Officers and Men embarked and sailed for Portugal, Transport Office, 16 November 1808.

87   BL: Add MS 35059: Wellesley to Hill, 23 June 1808.

88   J. Gurwood (ed.), *The Dispatches of Field Marshall the Duke of Wellington* (London: John Murray, 1837–1839), vol.IV, p.14; J. Reiter, "'As Far as the Ordnance Department is Concerned': Sir Arthur Wellesley, Lord Chatham and the Politics of Military Decision-Making, 1808-1809', *Journal of the Society for Army Historical Research*, vol.101, no.402, Autumn 2022, pp.178–179.

89   Anon., *Proceedings*, p.127.

90   TNA: WO 1/418: Castlereagh to Commissioners of Transport, 9 June 1808

91   Draft memorandum by Chatham, dated 23 January 1809, quoted in Reiter, 'Ordnance Department', p.179.

However, with Wellesley mostly still in Ireland he was not available for much of the time, and the Ordnance was a cumbersome and slow-moving bureaucracy that may not have been able to adapt to the rapidly changing situation quickly enough.[92] This sluggishness was exacerbated by a cabinet that could not decide exactly where the expedition was going and what resources it would need.

The way the Royal Artillery was organised separated horses from men and guns. The gunners belonged to Royal Artillery battalions, split into companies, but a foot artillery company did not include any guns, drivers, horses, caissons, limbers, or carts. The Corps of Royal Artillery Drivers provided the men and horses for the gun carriages and carts. When artillery was needed for an expedition guns, carriages and carts were allocated from stores along with enough men and horses from the gunners and drivers to make up a brigade, the tactical unit of foot artillery. Foot artillery was drawn by horses from place to place, but most of the men marched on foot. Each cannon or howitzer would require four or six horses, depending on the gun's weight. Ammunition tumbrils and forge carts also needed two to four horses each. The number of drivers and horses required for foot artillery brigades serving abroad is detailed in Table 8.

Table 8. Drivers and horses needed per Royal Artillery gun

	Officers	NCOs	Drivers	Riding horses	Draught horses
12-pdr	1	5	74	13	123
9-pdr	1	5	74	13	123
Heavy 6-pdr	1	4	53	12	84
Light 6-pdr	1	3	44	11	70

Source: C.E. Franklin, *British Napoleonic Field Artillery* (Stroud: Spellmount, 2012), p.140.

The artillery embarked for the expedition consisted of one brigade of 9-pounders and two of light 6-pounders.[93] This implies that 35 riding horses and 263 draught horses were required. Given the rapidly changing situation, could the Ordnance have provided sufficient horses to Wellesley at Cork in late June or early July? A return of the Corps of Royal Artillery Drivers in Ireland, dated 20 June, states that there were 17 riding and 176 draft horses in Cork, with a further six riding and 57 draft horses each in nearby Fermoy and Bandon. The total number of horses for the whole of Ireland was 1,843.[94] So, the Ordnance did have the horses required, where they were needed.

As the expedition gathered and began to embark in mid-June, Wellesley sought to address the lack of horses for the artillery and the lack of any provision to transport supplies once the expedition had landed. Using his position as Chief Secretary for Ireland, he sought to get two troops of the Corps of Waggoners, part of the Irish Commissariat, allocated to the expedition. Wellesley initially asked for 300 commissariat drivers as they would do the job better than soldiers, which was often who commanders had to resort to using. A return of the two troops of the Corps of Waggoners states that they consisted of two captain-lieutenants (Robert Taggert and George Lennon), four lieutenants, 20 sergeant conductors, eight smiths and farriers, two harness-makers,

92   Reiter, 'Ordnance Department', p.179.
93   TNA: WO 1/228: Return of Ordnance and Ammunition for Field Ordnance Embarked on the Transports, Cove 9 July 1808.
94   TNA: WO 17/2769: Distribution of the Corps of Royal Artillery Drivers in Ireland, 20 June 1808.

one wheel-maker, 181 privates and 300 horses.[95] The horses would be assigned to the artillery once landed, and the drivers would be used to drive whatever carts and draft animals could be sourced locally in Portugal. The Commissariat's carts would be left behind due to a lack of space on the transports. The whole business exasperated Wellesley and forced him to write to Castlereagh:

> I declare that I do not understand the principles on which our military establishments are formed, if, when large corps of troops are sent out to perform important and difficult services, they are not to have with them those means of equipment which they require and which the establishment can afford, such as horses to draw artillery and drivers attached to the Commissariat, when these means are not wanted at home; and, what is more, considering that the number of horses and drivers in England, all of whom the public could command in case of emergency, never can be wanted excepting for foreign service.[96]

There were various administrative hurdles to overcome for the officers and other ranks of the Corps of Waggoners to serve overseas. The commissions and pay of the officers, and that of the other ranks of the two troops, had to be brought up to the same level as those belonging to the Royal Wagon Train in Britain, and the other ranks had to volunteer for foreign service.[97] On 2 July, Castlereagh told Wellesley, 'You will make the best arrangements in your power for carrying with you such part of the Corps of Drivers as you find necessary & I shall take care that what you settle upon this point shall be carried into execution.'[98] On 3 July, Wellesley wrote to Hill:

> I have received my instructions, and I understand that the cavalry and some ships to receive the 36th and 45th regiments sailed from the Downs and Portsmouth on the 30th. I shall be at Cork on Wednesday [the 6th], and I hope that we shall sail immediately afterwards. The horses of the Commissariat will be at Cork on Tuesday and Wednesday, and I shall be obliged to you if you will arrange with General Floyd respecting the early embarkation.
>   I would have taken horses of the Artillery if I could have got them; but, alas I could not, and have therefore those which will probably only do our work till we shall get others.[99]

In total, 238 horses for the cavalry, 306 for the artillery, and 34 for the staff were embarked.[100] The last Irish Commissariat horses arrived from Dublin, over 160 miles from Cobh, on 9 July.[101]
    Speaking in Parliament after the campaign, Wellesley stated:

---

95 Wellington (ed.), *Supplementary Despatches*, vol.VI, pp.83–86; 'Strength Of Two Troops Of The Irish Commissariat Corps...', in Anon., *Parliamentary Reports: Accounts &c* (London: House of Commons, undated), vol.IX, pp.20–21.

96 Wellesley to Castlereagh, 29 June 1808, in Wellington (ed.), *Supplementary Despatches*, vol.VI, p.87.

97 Wellington (ed.), *Supplementary Despatches*, vol.VI, pp.83–87.

98 TNA: WO 1/228: Castlereagh to Wellesley, 2 July 1808.

99 Wellesley to Hill, 3 July 1808, in Sidney, *Hill*, pp.76–77.

100 TNA: WO 72/29: Return of officers, Non-Commissioned Officers and Men embarked and sailed for Portugal, Transport Office, 16 November 1808.

101 BL: Add MS 49485: Henry Torrens to James Willoughby Gordon, 9 July 1808.

… there might, no doubt, be other reasons for the choice made of horses for the commissariat and the artillery. It was obvious, however, that with the operations in the Tagus in view, such an ample equipment was not necessary, as would be required for those which he afterwards undertook. He must also state, that when he embarked at Cork he was to proceed to the coast of Spain, without any certainty whether he should be allowed to land at all, or if he should, where he might land; and it was therefore considered that the horses must suffer considerably from being kept a long time on board, and consequently those of an inferior description were chosen, which, under all the circumstances, might be best fitted for a service of this nature.[102]

Writing to Wellesley just after the expedition sailed, Castlereagh justified the lack of horses and transports: 'The great delay and expense that would attend embarking and sending from hence all those means which would be requisite to render the army completely moveable immediately on its landing, has determined His Majesty's government to trust in a great measure to the resources of the country for their supplies.'[103] Lord Chatham wrote that Wellesley had 'chose[n] to take the Commissariat horses from Cork, thinking them adequate for the service, rather than to make a requisition for artillery horses from hence.'[104]

The question of the artillery horses was mentioned at the inquiry into the Convention of Cintra after the campaign. Wellesley then stated:

… the expedition which sailed from Cork under my command was originally destined to go to the coast of Spain, to be prepared to act as circumstances might require; and as it was very uncertain that the troops would ever land in Spain, and it was thought that the horses of the artillery would suffer and might be lost to the service by being kept so long in the transports, as it was probable we might be on the coast of Spain unemployed, it was expedient to equip the ordnance sent on the expedition with horses taken from the Irish Commissariat. These are generally horses cast from the cavalry, or bought at low prices, such as twelve or thirteen pounds each; and although not bad horses, they are not so good and efficient as those belonging to the artillery.[105]

Unhappy with the implied criticism of the Ordnance in other testimony at the inquiry, Chatham wrote to the King to defend his department and stated:

It was distinctly understood (and the signification of your Majesty's pleasure as well as Sir Arthur Wellesley's requisition shew it) that no horses were to accompany the expedition, but an ample detachment of gunner drivers was thought essential, and they accordingly embarked with the companies of artillery. When Sir Arthur Wellesley's destination was suddenly changed, and he received orders thro' the Secretary of State to proceed

---

102 'Convention of Cintra', Hansard, <https://api.parliament.uk/historic-hansard/commons/1809/feb/21/convention-of-cintra>, accessed October 2021.
103 Castlereagh to Wellesley, 15 July 1808, in Gurwood (ed.), *Wellington's Dispatches*, vol.IV, p.29.
104 Draft memorandum by Chatham, dated 23 January 1809, quoted in Reiter, 'Ordnance Department', p.179.
105 Anon. (ed.), *Copy of The Proceedings upon the Inquiry Relative to The Armistice and Convention, &c Made and Concluded in Portugal, in August 1808, between The Commanders of the British and French Armies* (London: House of Commons, 1809), p.31.

immediately, with the force assembled at Cork, to the coast of Portugal, he, having his gunner drivers with him, thought it better to take the commissariat horses from Ireland, thinking them adequate to ye service, rather than to make a requisition for artillery horses from hence, which were in perfect readiness, and stationed to ye westward; and when I suggested afterwards whether it might not be expedient to send them, I was given to understand that the state of the transport tonnage would not permit it.[106]

So, on the one hand, Wellesley, at one point, said that he asked for artillery horses but was denied, while, at another, he implied that they were never planned to be taken. On the other hand, Chatham says that he offered horses, but Wellesley refused them. No letters directly requesting or denying artillery horses for the expedition have yet come to light. The surviving correspondence suggests that due to the original South American destination of the expedition, artillery horses were not considered until it was too late to source them. However, with artillery horses present in Cork and its environs, it is remarkable that a better solution than the Irish Commissariat horses could not have been found. Whatever the reasons or the rationale for the number of horses embarked, the lack of mobility, transport, and mounted cavalry would significantly impact the course of the coming campaign. On 19 August, after the first major action, Wellesley wrote: 'I think Lord Chatham will repent that he did not allow me to have Artillery Horses. Those we have are very fair, & very good of their kind. But marching as we do every day we ought to have the best horses the Army could afford, instead of the worst & likewise a regt. of Mounted Cavalry.'[107]

A Fair Wind

As news reached London in early June of the Spanish risings and it became evident that an expedition might be sent to support the patriots, the War Office requested that the Commissioners of Transports assemble all available transports for both infantry and cavalry at the Downs anchorage off the coast of Kent, and to make ready any coppered victuallers and store ships in the Thames. To increase the number of vessels available, the price of the coppered ships was increased from 19s to 25s per ton.[108] Transports varied from as little as 100 tons to over 400, with most being between 220 and 400 tons, meaning that a full-strength battalion of 1,000 men would need between five and 10 vessels.[109] On 9 June, Castlereagh wrote to the Commissioners that the King had approved increasing the size of the force at Cork to 8,000 men, with two brigades of artillery and a detachment of cavalry. He requested that horse ships for 300 horses be sent to Cork for the use of the artillery and the same sent to Portsmouth for the 20th Light Dragoons.[110]

As the transports arrived, the troops embarked at Monkstown or Cobh at the mouth of the river Lee, around 10 miles downstream of Cork. As there was a considerable interval between some

106 Aspinal (ed.), *Correspondence*, vol.V, p182.
107 Wellesley to Wellesley-Pole, 19 August 1808, in C. Webster, 'Some Letters of the Duke of Wellington to his Brother William Wellesley-Pole', *Camden Miscellany*, vol.XVIII (1948), p.5.
108 TNA: WO 6/156: Stewart to Commissioners of Transport, 6 & 8 June 1808. Coppered vessels had copper plating on their hulls which limited marine growth and increased their speed.
109 Sutcliffe, *Expeditionary*, p.51.
110 TNA: WO 1/418: Castlereagh to Commissioners of Transport, 9 June 1808

of the regiments embarking and the expedition sailing, Wellesley became concerned about the welfare of the troops and wrote to Hill on 25 June:

> I have now to request that you will make arrangements with the agent of transports, that the soldiers embarked may have fresh provisions and vegetables every day; and that the stock of provisions in the transports may be kept up to the original quantity which each is capable of containing.
>
> I also think it very desirable that the soldiers should have permission to go ashore as they may wish, under such regulations as you may think proper; and that the regiments should be sent ashore and exercised in their turns.[111]

Wellesley also wrote to Charles Stewart at the War Office that the transports were too crowded and some troops should be disembarked and barracked within a day's march of Cork.[112] Hill replied to Wellesley on 27 June, agreeing that 1½ tons of shipping per man in the hot weather was not enough, and the transports were overcrowded. He added that he had arranged that two regiments would be landed in the mornings and two in the afternoons to exercise the troops.[113] The summer weather was hot; temperatures peaked in July at over 30°C.[114] Castlereagh responded quickly, and an additional 3,000 tons of transports were ordered to sail to Cork from the Downs.[115]

The Royal Navy escort for the expedition was led by HMS *Donegal* (74), commanded by Captain Pulteney Malcolm, an old friend of Wellesley's. Malcolm may have transported him part of the way to India in 1796, and his brother, John, had known Wellesley well in India. Malcolm was an experienced captain who had joined the navy in 1778 and had commanded the *Donegal* since 1805. He had won praise for his actions during the storm that followed the Battle of Trafalgar when he assisted Nelson's battle-damaged fleet.[116] The frigates *Resistance* (38) and *Crocodile* (22), commanded by Captains Charles Adams and George Cadogan, completed the escort. Cadogan was brother to one of Wellesley's sisters-in-law. The *Donegal* had come directly from blockade duty off the French coast and needed to take on supplies and water. On 11 July, Wellesley went on board to consult with Malcolm and make plans for landing the troops in Portugal.[117]

The transport agent in charge of the convoy was Lieutenant Gerrard Fleetwood. Wellesley was impressed with him as he later wrote to Lord Mulgrave, the First Lord of the Admiralty, praising Fleetwood: 'He is the most active, intelligent, and zealous of all the Officers that I have seen in that line of the naval profession, and he really deserves promotion.' On the same day, he wrote to the Commissioners of the Transport Board. 'I cannot say too much in praise of his zeal, intelligence, and activity; and I have great pleasure in adding, that his conduct has given equal satisfaction to Captain Malcolm, of the Donegal, to whom the conduct of the naval part of the service

---

111   Wellesley to Hill, 25 June 1808, in Gurwood (ed.), *Wellington's Dispatches*, vol.IV, p.15.
112   Wellesley to Stewart, 25 June 1808, in Gurwood (ed.), *Wellington's Dispatches*, vol.IV, pp.15–16.
113   UoS: WP 1/205: Hill to Wellesley, 27 June 1808.
114   S. Murden, 'The Heatwave of July 1808', *All Things Georgian*, <https://georgianera.wordpress.com/2018/07/17/the-heatwave-of-1808/>, accessed December 2022.
115   TNA: WO 1/418: Stewart to Wellesley, 29 June 1808.
116   See P. Martinovich, *The Sea is My Element* (Warwick, Helion, 2021).
117   Martinovich, *Element*, p.114.

was intrusted.'[118] Sadly, Wellesley's entreaties fell on deaf ears, and Fleetwood died in 1811, still a lieutenant.

On 7 July, Wellesley wrote to Castlereagh:

> I arrived here last night, and I find that the 20th Dragoons and the 3,000 tons of shipping for the infantry have not yet arrived. The Irish Commissariat horses for the draught of the artillery are not yet all arrived, and will not be on board till Saturday. I propose to wait till that day for the Dragoons and the additional tonnage, and, if they should not then have arrived, I shall sail with what is ready, and let the rest follow.[119]

Wellesley also told Castlereagh that four transports were in Cork that had not been included in the lists of vessels supplied to him by the Transport Board and that these extra ships had enabled him to embark more of the troops, but that if the additional 3,000 tons did not arrive to ease the overcrowding, he would have to leave either the 36th or the Royal Veteran Battalion behind to follow later. There was also one transport loaded with pikes, one with entrenching tools, two with arms, one with flour and three with oats that had not yet arrived.[120]

Table 9. Troops Embarked at Cork

Regiment	Date Embarked	Field Off.	Capts	Lts	Staff	Sgts	Drms	R&F
Royal Artillery		2	4	4	2	11	6	391
Royal Engineers			1	1				
1/5th Foot	18 June	2	8	24	6	52	21	990
1/9th Foot	17 June	3	7	18	5	51	21	933
1/36th Foot	9 July	2	8	28	4	49	22	591
1/38th Foot	16 June	3	8	27	6	52	22	957
1/40th Foot	16 June	3	9	27	5	54	20	926
1/45th Foot	6 July	3	8	17	6	38	22	500
5/60th Foot	15 June	2	7	18	6	52	21	936
1/71st	17 June	2	8	27	5	52	22	891
1/91st	16 June	1	9	22	5	46	20	917
2/95th (4 Coys)	9 May & 8 June	1	4	13	2	20	8	400
4th Royal Veteran Battn.	17 June	1	6	14	4	40	20	737
Total		25	87	240	56	517	225	9,169
Grand Total								10,319

Source: TNA: WO 17/2464: Troops embarked from Cork under the command of Lt Gen. Sir Arthur Wellesley.

---

118 Wellesley to Mulgrave, 26 August 1808, and Wellesley to Commissioners of the Transport Board, 26 August 1808, in Gurwood (ed.), *Wellington's Dispatches*, vol.IV, pp.124–125.
119 Wellesley to Castlereagh, 7 July 1808, in Vane (ed.), *Correspondence*, vol.VI, p.383.
120 Wellesley to Castlereagh, 7 July 1808, in Vane (ed.), *Correspondence*, vol.VI, p.384.

The four troops of 20th Light Dragoons, 349 rank and file, were embarked at Portsmouth on 27 June and arrived on 7 July. The 1/36th Foot embarked at Monkstown on the 9th.[121] The last troops to arrive were 170 transfers from the 2/45th for the regiment's first battalion.

On 10 July, Wellesley informed Castlereagh that the commissariat horses for the artillery had arrived the previous day and had been embarked, and that the 20th Light Dragoons and the ships for the 36th and 45th Foot had also finally reached Cobh harbour. However, contrary winds were preventing the expedition from sailing. On the 11th the winds were still contrary, but the ships carrying the arms for the Asturias had arrived. Finally, on 12 July, Wellesley wrote, 'I have the pleasure to inform you that we have been able to get out this morning, with a fair wind; and have every hope of a good passage.' Wellesley would transfer from the *Donegal* that evening to the *Crocodile* and sail ahead to Corunna.[122]

Castlereagh had ordered that he send someone else to Corunna, but Wellesley informed him that:

> Upon a review of your instructions and intentions, and a consideration of the state of affairs in Spain, according to the last accounts, I rather think that I shall, as soon as I have got everything away from Cork, best serve the cause by going myself to Corunna, and joining the fleet off Cape Finisterre or the Tagus. I propose, accordingly, to go on board one of the craft, and I expect to be at the rendezvous before the troops.[123]

Lieutenant Colonel Henry Torrens, Wellesley's military secretary, wrote to Horse Guards that Wellesley preferred to go to Corunna himself rather than send another officer, 'In fact he was at a loss who to send, and did at one time mean to employ me on this service.' He also wrote, 'The troops are quite healthy and a finer armament never sailed from the British Islands!'[124]

On 12 July, Captain Pulteney Malcolm wrote in his log on the *Donegal*:

> Winds southward. Light breezes & cloudy made convoy signal to weigh Master attended and pilot came on board – at 4.45 weighed and made sail out of the harbour. Returned a salute to Carlisle fort. Shortned sail and hove to.
>
> Waited for convoy. During which time punished Thomas Humphrey with 24 lashes for desertion and Joseph Bessiard with 36 for fighting and striking a superior officer.[125]

At 3:00 p.m., the *Donegal* made sail again, and the convoy sailed for the Peninsula. The make-up of the convoy that sailed from Cobh is shown in Table 10; six store ships also sailed from the Downs on the same day. It is worth noting that the tonnage of the transports carrying just over 600 horses was nearly equal to that of those carrying almost 10,000 men.

On the 13th, the *Dublin Evening Post* reported from Cork that 'The Expedition, under the command of Sir Arthur Wellesley, sailed early yesterday morning from this port, with the wind east and the fleet was clear of land by the evening.' The paper said that Lisbon or Cadiz were the

---

121   TNA: WO 17/2464: Return of troops embarked for Portugal and Spain in the year 1808; *Saunder's Newsletter*, 12 July 1808.
122   TNA: WO 1/228: Wellesley to Castlereagh, 10, 11, & 12 July 1808.
123   Wellesley to Castlereagh, 7 July 1808, in Vane (ed.), *Correspondence*, vol.VI, p.383.
124   BL: Add MS 49485: Torrens to Gordon, 9 July 1808.
125   TNA: ADM 51/1880: *Donegal* log, 12 July 1808.

probable destinations, with Cadiz being the more likely and stated: 'No expedition ever sailed which carried with it perhaps so fully and sincerely the public wishes for its success: there never was a more popular service than that for which it is supposed to be intended.'[126]

Table 10. Transports at Cork

Purpose	Number	Tonnage
Troop transport	40	5,565
Horse transport	18	5,065
Victualler	4	1,389
Forage transport	4	859
Camp stores	2	453
Ordnance stores	7	1,926
Total	**75**	**25,257**

Source: TNA: WO 72/29: Extract from the Return of officers, Non-Commissioned Officers and Men embarked and sailed for Portugal, Transport Office, 16 November 1808.

---

126 *Dublin Evening Post*, 13 July 1808.

6

The French

The French the Armée de Portugal that awaited Wellesley and his troops was essentially the same force that had left Bayonne the previous autumn. Comparing Table 2 in Chapter 2 with Table 11 below, which displays the state of the Armée de Portugal as of 1 January 1808, shows a few changes in battalion numbering and a slight increase in numbers, but the brigading and the regiments are largely unchanged.

Table 11. The Armée de Portugal, 1 January 1808

	Commander	Battalions/ Squadrons	Regiment	Strength	
				Men	Horses
	gén. de div. Junot				
Chief of Staff	*gén. de brig.* Thiébault				
Governor of Oporto	*gén. de div.* Quesnel				
Commandant of Cascaés	*gén. de brig.* Solignac				
Commandant of Engineers	*colonel* Vincent				
Commander of Artillery	*gén. de brig.* Taviel				
1er Division	*gén. de div.* Delaborde				
1er Brigade	*gén. de brig.* Avril	3e	15e Ligne	1,033	
		1er & 2e	70e Ligne	2,299	
		1er	4e Suisse	1,190	
2e Brigade	*gén. de brig.* Brenier	2e	47e Ligne	1,210	
		1er & 2e	86e Ligne	2,116	
		7 bat.		**7,848**	
2e Division	*gén. de div.* Loison				
1er Brigade	*gén. de brig.* Charlot	3e	2e Légère	1,255	
		3e	4e Légère	1,196	
		3e	12e Légère	1,302	
		3e	15e Légère	1,314	
2e Brigade	*gén. de brig.* Thomieres	3e	32e Ligne	1,265	
		3e	58e Ligne	1,394	
		2e	2e Suisse	755	
		7 bat.		**8,481**	
3e Division	*gén. de div.* Travot				
1er Brigade	*gén. de brig.* Graindorge	3e	31e Légère	653	
		3e	32e Légère	983	
		3e	26e Ligne	537	

	Commander	Battalions/ Squadrons	Regiment	Strength	
				Men	Horses
		1er	Legion du Midi	797	
2e Brigade	*gén. de brig.* Fuzier	3e & 4e	66e Ligne	1,004	
		3e	82e Ligne	861	
		1er	Légion Hanovrienne	703	
		8 bat.		**5,538**	
Division de Cavalrie	*gén. de div.* Kellerman				
1er Brigade	*gén. de brig.* Margaron				
		4e	26e Chasseurs à cheval	244	145
		4e	1er Dragons	261	153
		4e	3e Dragons	236	153
2e Brigade	*gén. de brig.* Maurin				
		4e	4e Dragons	262	180
		4e	5e Dragons	249	175
		4e	9e Dragons	257	203
		4e	15e Dragons	245	169
		7 squad.		**1,754**	**1,178**
Artillerie & Genie			Companies of 1er, 3e, 6e Regiment à Pied	619	
			Artillery Train (Civilian)	375	313
			8e Batt. Military Equipages	303	280
				1,297	**593**
Total				**24,918**	**1,771**

Source: Foy, *History*, vol.II, p.541.

In his history of the campaign, Junot's chief of staff, Thiébault, included a statement of the army's strength on 15 July:

Infantry	
Light	6,676
Line	12,549
Swiss	2,088
Legions	1,646
Total	22,959

Cavalry	2,193
Artillery	690
Artillery train	373
Labourers	30
Engineers	18
Supply train	292
Grand Total	26,533[1]

---

1   Thiébault, *l'Expédition*, p.238.

Thiébault also stated that the army had received 4,453 replacements from depots and hospitals since leaving France.[2] Even before Junot marched, Napoleon had ordered the Minister of War to form provisional battalions and squadrons made of companies of the understrength units destined for Portugal. These reinforcements were allowed to include conscripts of the 1808 class, and so many were probably raw recruits. His correspondence with Clarke shows considerable irritation with the low strengths of many of the battalions, and he gave repeated orders that the regimental depots provide the missing men.[3] As early as November and December 1807, over 3,793 men gathered near the border to follow their regiments into Portugal. Junot had ordered that each regiment leave a small depot in Bayonne to receive men, gather them into companies, and send them to Portugal as convoy escorts.[4] After the invasion, Thiébault had organised routes both for stragglers from Zarza la Mayor and reinforcements from France. The main route for troops entered Portugal at Elvas and continued through the province of Alentejo to Lisbon. A route was established for couriers through Coimbra and Almeida to Cuidad Rodrigo to France. Patrols of French cavalry and gendarmes secured Junot's communications back to Paris, but this route, and the route for troops, were soon cut by the risings in Spain and Portugal.[5]

Additional troops for the Armée de Portugal continued to be sent from France in 1808, although the bottoms of the barrels were being well and truly scraped. In March, Napoleon ordered that 150 refractory conscripts, those who had resisted the call-up, be sent from the depot at Bayonne to reinforce the 66e Ligne. In April, he told maréchal Berthier to assemble 600 sick and unattached men of the regiments in Portugal at San Sebastian into a marching battalion and send them to Almeida.[6] As late as July, with communications to Portugal cut by the rebellion in Spain, men from Junot's regiments continued to gather in southwest France. On 14 July, Napoleon ordered Clarke to form two marching battalions composed of companies from the Légion du Midi, Légion Hanovrienne, 15e and 31e Légère and 26e, 32e, 58e, 66e and 86e Ligne, and told him that further companies were leaving Paris.[7] They, of course, never reached Portugal, and Junot would have to face Wellesley with the troops he already had.

A French infantry division was typically made up of two or three brigades, each usually consisting of two regiments. In the British Army, a regiment was an administrative organisation rather than a tactical unit, with battalions of the same regiment rarely serving together. In the French army, it was the norm that multiple battalions of the same regiment would serve together. Most regiments had three or four battalions, with the higher numbers generally used as a depot and for home service. The regimental staff, led by the *colonel*, consisted mainly of administrative and supply officers, surgeons, eagle-bearers, musicians, and other support staff. Some regiments had only a single battalion in Portugal, so two battalions from different regiments were grouped into temporary provisional regiments commanded by a *major*. A battalion was commanded by a *chef de bataillon* who was supported by an *adjudant major* and a small staff. When the troops left Bayonne, a French infantry battalion consisted of two elite companies – grenadiers and voltigeurs – and seven fusilier companies. The strength of a battalion was supposed to be 1,100 men, but

---

2   Thiébault, *l'Expédition*, p.239.
3   E. Picard, E., and L. Tuetey (eds), *Unpublished Correspondence of Napoleon I* (New York: Duffield, 1913), vol.I, pp.665-666, 669, 675, 690, 702.
4   Grasset, *Guerre d'Espagne*, vol.I, pp.118, 444.
5   Sigler, *Thiébault*, p.194.
6   Picard & Tuetey (eds), *Unpublished*, vol.II, pp.138, 156.
7   Picard & Tuetey (eds), *Unpublished*, vol.II, pp.337–338.

many of Junot's units were well below that level, especially in the 2e and 3e Divisions. However, on 18 February 1808, Napoleon decreed that all infantry regiments would have five battalions, with four available for operations and the fifth being a depot. The number of companies per battalion was reduced to six: grenadiers, four fusilier companies and the voltigeurs.[8] The decree went on to detail the complex reallocation of officers and re-organisation that would have to take place. This would have been easy for regiments based in France, but for the regiments in Portugal who could not easily give or receive men with their other battalions, it would have been more of a challenge, especially as many of the units were still understrength and lacked experienced men. Foy states that the battalions in Portugal retained their nine-company structure.[9]

An infantry company was commanded by a *capitaine*, with a *lieutenant* and a *sous-lieutenant* below him. The senior NCO was a *sergent-major*. As well as the *sergents* and *caporaux*, each company had a *caporal fourrier* who assisted the *sergent-major* and arranged quarters for the company. Men of both elite companies received extra pay. The grenadiers were selected from the tallest men in the battalion and generally had to have served at least four years. The voltigeurs, the equivalent of a British light company, were usually shorter men but fit and were issued with a shorter pattern musket. The voltigeur company officers and NCOs were issued with a rifled carbine. The standard weapon of the French infantry was the 1777 model musket. It had a calibre of 0.69 inches and a barrel length of just under 45 inches. The dragoon version used by the voltigeurs had a barrel of 42 inches, which was still longer than the 39 inches of the British East India pattern musket. The elite companies could often be detached and formed into composite grenadier or voltigeur battalions.[10] Soldier's wives could also march with the troops with two per battalion given the official role of *blanchisseuses* – laundresses – who also helped with cooking and assisted the surgeon. To provide the troops with life's little luxuries, *cantinières*, usually the wives of NCOs, also accompanied the soldiers on campaign, but the returns do not say how many women accompanied the army to Portugal.

While he was happy to send men from France to reinforce Junot, Napoleon was adamant that the Armée de Portugal was to be paid for and supplied from the resources of the occupied country, stating that 'Nothing should be given to the Army of Portugal from the Treasury of France.'[11] Junot's regiments had to source replacement equipment, uniforms and accoutrements from Portuguese arsenals and merchants. This would necessarily mean that there could have been some variation from uniform and equipment standards set in France. Most French line infantry wore a blue coat with white lapels and red collar, cuffs and piping. Breeches were white. Junot made some accommodation for the hot weather as a British officer observed of the French, 'every man being dressed in long white linen frocks – their shakos, pouches, &c., covered with the same material – and their uniform coats being strapped outside their knapsacks.'[12]

As an army of occupation, opportunities for large-scale manoeuvres would have been limited, but each regiment would have been able to continue to drill and train their men. As early as 18 December 1807, Junot's chief engineer, *colonel* Vincent, prepared a report on an open space in the Campo de Ourique area of Lisbon, which was the only area that was big enough for the encampment and manoeuvring of multiple battalions but even that needed to be expanded to accommodate a

---

8   Plon & Dumaine (eds), *Correspondance*, vol.16, 13574, pp.338–341.
9   Foy, *History*, vol.II, p.541.
10   T.E. Crowdy, *Napoleon's Infantry Handbook* (Barnsley: Pen & Sword, 2015), chapter 4.
11   Picard & Tuetey (eds), *Unpublished*, vol.II, p.184.
12   Leslie, *Journal*, p.52.

full brigade.[13] With the need to garrison various fortresses and towns, most of the regiments would have spent much of the occupation dispersed, which would have limited training opportunities, especially once the unrest began. Many troops would have seen their first combat during the rebellion, although such actions would often not have been the same as facing regular troops.

1er Division

Général de division Henri-François Delaborde was the son of a baker. Born in Dijon in 1764, he had joined the Régiment de Condé before the revolution and was a *caporal* when he left the army in March 1791. However, by October, he joined the 1er bataillon des volontaires de la Côte d'Or and was elected *lieutenant.* Junot was a soldier in the second battalion of the same regiment. At La Grisoëlle, where Junot received his first wound, Delaborde distinguished himself and took over when his commander was killed. By July 1792 was *lieutenant-colonel en chef* of the second battalion and Junot's commander. At Toulon, when Junot was still a *sergent*, Delaborde was a *général de brigade* and was promoted to *général de division* in December 1793. He still held the same rank 15 years later and for the rest of his career, which stretched beyond Waterloo. He participated in the War of the Pyrenees and then in campaigns in southern Germany, where he continued to perform well and win praise. He was continually employed during the early years of the

Général de division Henri-François Delaborde. (Bibliothèque Nationale de France)

Empire until he was given command of the best of the divisions ordered to Portugal.[14]

Avril's Brigade
Born in Vienna in 1752, *général de brigade* Jean-Jacques Avril began his military career as a *sous-lieutenant* of colonial militia on the l'Ile-de-France (Mauritius) in 1775. He rose to *capitaine* and command of a company of men of colour. In 1793, he travelled to France and joined the 15e Chasseurs à Cheval, keeping the same rank. He distinguished himself during the brutal

13   Sepulveda, *Historia*, vol.X, pp.116–118.
14   G. Six, *Dictionnaire Biographique des Généraux et Amiraux de la Révolution et de l'Empire: 1792-1814* (Paris: Librarie Historique et Nobiliaire, 1934), vol.I, pp.312–314.

counterinsurgency in the Vendée and was a *général de brigade* by 1795. He gained further experience pacifying rebels in Normandy and Genoa before being assigned first to the defence of the coast around Brest and then the Portuguese invasion. In August 1808, Junot made him commandant of Lisbon castle.[15]

The 3/15e Ligne was one of the many third battalions pressed into service for the invasion of Portugal. Historian Alphonse Grasset looked at the records of the regiments in the Armée de Portugal and gave an analysis of the age and experience of each of them. He found that two-thirds of the 3/15e were veterans aged 27–30, with several NCOs in their early 40s. The remaining third were mostly conscripts from 1805 with two years' service, plus a few from the classes of 1807 and less from 1808.[16] The 3/15e was commanded by *chef de bataillon* Jean-Pierre Recouvreur.

The two battalions of the 70e Ligne were probably the best unit in the Armée de Portugal, at least according to Grasset's analysis. Three-quarters of the soldiers were veterans aged 30–32, with many NCOs in their early 40s. The remaining quarter were almost all conscripts of 1806, with only a few from 1807 or 1808.[17] *Colonel* Jean-Victor Rouyer commanded the 70e. Many of the men may have served for 10 years or more, but the regiment had not seen combat since Marengo in 1800, although a company serving as marines had been at Trafalgar.

There was a long history of Swiss troops serving in the French army. The regiments that served during the Empire had been formed in 1803 as part of an agreement where, in return for military protection, Switzerland would provide 16,000 troops. Four infantry regiments and four companies of artillery were formed. Each regiment consisted of a headquarters, three field battalions and a depot battalion. The battalions were made up of eight fusilier companies, plus grenadiers and voltigeurs. The reorganisation of February 1808 was not applied to the Swiss regiments until 1811. The Swiss troops wore brick-red coats and white breeches and, from a distance, looked confusingly similar to British troops. The coats of the 4e Suisse had sky-blue facings.[18] Recruited from cantons across Switzerland in October 1806, the 1/4e Suisse had an average age of between 25 and 30, with some under 20 and some over 30. Grasset could not confirm if any had campaigned before and characterised their dedication to the Empire as 'problematic.'[19] *Chef de bataillon* Béat Felber commanded the 1/4e, but half of the second battalion accompanied them to Portugal, led by *capitaine* Salomon Bleuler, one of the regiment's *adjudant majors*.[20] The 1/4e had spent much of its time in Portugal based at Almeida but was also part of Loison's various marches to quell the rebellion.

By the summer, they formed the garrison at Peniche and remained there apart from the two elite companies which, under the command of Bleuler, would be some of the first troops to engage the British.

Brenier's Brigade

Général de brigade Antoine-François Brenier de Montmorand was born in 1767 and entered the service of Spain as a cadet in 1781. He returned to France five years later to join the Compagnie des gendarmes ordinaires du roi, part of the king's guard, and then from 1787 to 1791, was an aide de camp to two different generals. In 1793, he was appointed *chef de bataillon* of the 6e bataillon

15 Six, *Dictionnaire*, vol.I, pp.35–36.
16 Grasset, *Guerre d'Espagne*, vol.I, p.434
17 Grasset, *Guerre d'Espagne*, vol.I, p.434
18 S. Ede-Borrett, *Swiss Regiments in the Service of France* 1798-1815 (Warwick: Helion, 2019), pp.38, 53–54.
19 Grasset, *Guerre d'Espagne*, vol.I, p.434
20 Dempsey, *Mercenaries*, p.289.

des Côtes Maritimes de l'Ouest and was then provisionally promoted to *chef de brigade* by repre-sentatives of the people. He went on to serve with the 14e and then the 63e Ligne and took part in the Italian campaigns of 1796–1798, in Holland in 1798, and then back to Italy in 1799, where he was wounded at Verona and bayoneted at the crossing of the Adda. He was promoted to *général de brigade* towards the end of that year and then held various other commands and appointments before being assigned to Delaborde's division.[21]

The men of the 2/47e Ligne were old soldiers who had participated in several campaigns but not the recent ones in Prussia and Poland. The average age was 30; only one-fifth of the battalion were conscripts from 1806 or 1807, with a few from 1808. With these proportions, the conscripts could be well mentored by the veterans. The regiment had last fought in Italy in 1799. The battalion was under the command of *colonel* Pierre-Denis de la Chârte, who had enlisted in the army before the revolution and then fought throughout the Revolutionary Wars, rising through the ranks.

Half of the men of the 1e and 2e battalions of the 86e de Ligne had an average age of 30–32, with some over 40. Another quarter were conscripts of the 1806 class, with the rest made up of conscripts of 1807, plus some from 1808. Again, in Grasset's opinion, this meant that the veterans could train the conscripts well.[22] The 86e were commanded by *colonel* Mathieu Lacroix, who had entered the army in 1781 and had fought in many battles. His regiment, though, did not have a long list of battle honours to its name; it had seen some campaigning in the Vendée and at Stockach, but in 1803, the 1e and 2e battalions were sent to Saint-Domingue and decimated by disease. The regiment was then re-formed back in France.

2e Division

Général de division Louis-Henri Loison was born in 1771 and enlisted in a colonial battalion in 1787 but soon deserted. He returned six months later and bought himself out of his enlistment. When France was threatened after the revolution in 1791, he volunteered again and became a *sous-lieutenant* in the 29e Régiment d'Infanterie. The following year he became a *capitaine* in a regiment of hussars, and a year after that, he was appointed *adjutant général chef de brigade* by the representatives of the people. However, he was soon involved in a controversy which presaged his reputation for brutality in Portugal. As historian Charles Mullié wrote in his *Biographie des Célébrités Militaires*:

> The speed of his promotion had been earned by true military talents and brilliant valour which sometimes went as far as recklessness. It has been claimed, however, that he had neither disinterestedness, nor humanity, nor elevation in character. His brothers-in-arms even went so far as to admit that he was greedy for fame. We would be tempted to believe that this judgement is nothing less than severe, if we did not recall the accusation which weighed on him at the time of the capture and devastation of the abbey of Orval, on the borders of the Grand Duchy of Luxembourg. In the case of the latter, it is not surprising that he was accused of having committed odious acts of violence, and was about to be judged by a court that was prepared to deal with him severely, when a commissioner of

---

21   Six, *Dictionnaire*, vol.I, pp.157–158.
22   Grasset, *Guerre d'Espagne*, vol.I, p.434

the Convention managed to save him from the peril that threatened him, and had him reinstated in his duties.[23]

Loison was promoted to *général de brigade* in 1795 and then served under Bonaparte in Paris on 13 Vendémiaire when the young Corsican prevented a Royalist coup. Loison then sat as the president of the war council, responsible for judging the leaders of the insurrection. In 1799, he saw action in Switzerland and was wounded at Altdorf and distinguished himself at several other actions to the extent that Masséna promoted him to *général de division*. He then served in Italy in 1800, further cementing his reputation. During the Ulm campaign in 1805, he served under Ney at the Battle of Elchingen and was crucial in securing the victory. After fighting dozens of battles, he lost his arm after being wounded in a hunting accident in 1806.

Général de division Louis-Henri Loison. (Public Domain)

During that year and the next, he campaigned in Germany before being given the command of one of Junot's divisions.[24] Grasset characterises the men of the 2e Division as follows:

> The battalions which compose this division are the 3rd battalions of regiments of the Grande Armée, to which they serve as depots. They were considerably depleted of veterans by the drafts which the battles of Jena, Eylau and Friedland required. Conscripts are found in greater numbers, the veterans are men sent back from the Grande Armée because of infirmities, illnesses or wounds. The registers of these battalions are often very badly kept.[25]

Charlot's Brigade

Général de brigade Hugues Charlot had perhaps the longest service of any of the generals of the campaign. He was born in 1757 and, in 1776, enlisted in the Régiment de Foix. In 1782, he took part in suppressing the Genevan revolution and was then honourably discharged. However, in 1790 he was a *capitaine* in the 3e bataillon de volontaires de l'Isère. By summer of 1793, he was a

23   Charles Mullié, *Biographie des célébrités militaires des armées de terre et de mer de 1789 à 1850* (Paris: Poignavant, 1851), vol.II, p.237.
24   Six, *Dictionnaire*, vol.II, pp.128–130.
25   Grasset, *Guerre d'Espagne*, vol.I, p.435.

chef de bataillon in the 118e Demi-brigade. At Toulon, he served with the French headquarters and helped to capture the British commander. Charlot then served in Italy from 1794–1798, during which time he fought at many major battles, was wounded by a bullet to the left thigh at the Battle of Brenta and was promoted to *chef de brigade*. On his return to France, he was promoted to *général de brigade* in 1803 and employed at various camps on the west coast before being given command of his brigade for the campaign in Portugal.[26]

Like many European armies, the French had been far ahead of the British Army in having light infantry regiments as part of its order of battle. In 1808 there were 31 régiments d'infanterie légère in the French army, numbered 1er to 32e (the 30e had been disbanded). Instead of having grenadier, voltigeur and fusilier companies like the line infantry, they had carabinier, voltigeur and chasseur companies. However, the specialist skirmisher role of the light infantry regiments had begun to diminish, especially after the 1804 introduction of voltigeur companies into line regiments. They were seen as more elite regiments than standard line units and were perhaps more likely to be part of advance or rear guards, but most of the skirmishing was carried out by the voltigeur companies.[27] All the light infantry battalions were grouped into provisional regiments. *Major* Meslier commanded the 2e and 4e, and *major* Jean-Martin Petit the 12e and 15e.[28]

According to the available records, Grasset states that five-sixths of the 3/2e Légère were conscripts from 1806 or 1807, with one-sixth being older soldiers aged 27–30. However, the documents he examined only went as far as April 1807, when the battalion had a strength of around 300 men. When the battalion marched into Spain, it was over 1,100 strong, and so Grasset claims that the extra 800 men were 1808 conscripts, making three-quarters of the battalion raw recruits that Napoleon had promised would not serve abroad when he called up the class early. The registers of the 3/4e Légère that Grasset examined contained only 56 men, most of them conscripts of 1806 and 1807. When the battalion left Paris in April 1807, it had just over 100 men. By the time it left Saint-Lô for Bayonne, it was 878 strong, which implies around 775 1808 conscripts had joined it. Grasset states: 'This battalion was therefore a battalion of young men, most of whom, having arrived in June 1807, had only four months' service in October.'[29]

The records of the 3/12e Légère were also poorly kept, but Grasset concludes that, like the other battalions of the brigade, the vast majority of the men were 1808 conscripts, with only a small proportion from 1806 or 1807.[30] According to the regimental history, a provisional company of two officers and 209 men arrived at Torres Vedras, where the battalion was quartered, from France at the end of December 1807. In early 1808, additional reinforcements brought its strength up further. In early July, the 3e battalion became the 4e as a new 3e was formed in France from the 1er and 2e battalions. The 4/12e took part in the brutal suppression of the insurgency at Leira under the command of *général de brigade* Margaron. The elite companies were left there while the rest of the battalion returned to Lisbon and were then part of *général de division* Loison's force that fought at Evora.[31] The various columns that operated against the insurgency seemed to take little account of existing brigade or divisional structures, and the troops were gathered ad hoc.

---

26 Six, *Dictionnaire*, vol.I, p.224.
27 See T. Crowdy, *French Light Infantry 1784–1815* (Warwick: Helion, 2021), chapter 3.
28 Thiébault, *l'Expédition*, p.360.
29 Grasset, *Guerre d'Espagne*, vol.I, p.435.
30 Grasset, *Guerre d'Espagne*, vol.I, p.435.
31 C.J.E. Malaguti, *Historique du 87e Régiment d'Infanterie de Ligne* (Saint-Quentin: Moureau, 1892), pp.340–345. The 12e Légère later became the 87e Ligne.

The 3/15e Légère were the most experienced battalion in the brigade, with only half its strength made up of conscripts from 1806, 1807 and 1808. Of the remaining half, two-thirds came from the conscripts of 1804 and 1805, with the rest from 1801–1803 with an average age of 25.[32] Once in Portugal, the 3/15e occupied Torres Védras, except for its carabiniers, who remained in Lisbon as part of the elite regiments which had become an army reserve. The battalion changed its number to the 4e following changes to the regiment in June 1808 and participated in the escalade of the town walls at Evora.[33]

Thomières' Brigade

Born in 1771, Jean-Guillaume-Barthélemy Thomières's career was similar to many of his colleagues. He also started in a volunteer battalion, in his case, the 5e bataillon de volontaires de l'Hérault, in which he was elected *capitaine*. He soon became an aide de camp. He served with various generals throughout the 1790s, including in the Italian campaigns. He also occasionally served as a staff officer in the same period. By 1797, he was one of Victor's aides de camp and was promoted *chef de batallion* but continued to serve his general. After postings to the camp at Boulogne and the headquarters of the Grandé Armée, he became aide de camp to *maréchal* Lannes and then *adjudant-commandant* on his staff. He was promoted to *général de brigade* in July 1807, so his brigade under Junot was his first active command.[34]

Tambour-major, 15e Léger, 1809, by Pierre Albert Leroux.
(Anne S.K. Brown Military Collection)

The battalions of the 32e and 58e Ligne formed another provisional regiment commanded by *major* Bertrand. Two-thirds of the men of the 3/32e were conscripts from mostly 1806 or 1807, with some from 1808 – the other third comprised men from 23 to 33 years old. Veterans were rare, as

32   Grasset, *Guerre d'Espagne*, vol.I, p.435.
33   V. Belhomme, *Historique de 90e Régiment d'Infanterie de Ligne, ex-15e Légère* (Paris: Tanera, 1875), pp.70–71.
34   Six, *Dictionnaire*, vol.II, p.498.

they were all in Germany or hospitals.[35] The battalion suffered severely on the march into Portugal. As late as February 1808, when it was garrisoning the fortress at Péniche, a return showed 19 officers and 950 men present under arms, 544 in hospitals, 60 detached, and 100 reinforcements on their way from Paris. By the summer, the battalion was part of the Almeida garrison, with a large detachment occupying Abrantes.[36] Grasset found the records of the 3/58e to be missing and so found it impossible to draw any conclusions about its composition.[37]

The 2e Suisse was formed in October 1806, and their red coats had royal blue facings. *Chef de bataillon* Octave de Laharpe commanded the battalion, and *colonel en second* Joseph de Segesser was also present.[38] Grasset also found the records of the 2/2e Suisse to be scant and could only conclude that the average age was probably 18–23 and that for most of the men, Portugal was their first campaign.[39] Junot was quite dismissive of the battalion; 'the 2nd Swiss behave as a mass of Brigands ... Their officers have no talent and are without character.'[40] *Capitaine* Louis Begos, *adjudant major* of the 2/2e, described the initial formation of the battalion at Avignon as problematic because most of the soldiers were conscripts and the officers were inexperienced.[41] The battalion was initially stationed at Abrantes but, after three months, was ordered to garrison the border fortress of Elvas.

3e Division

Général de division Jean Pierre Travot, born in 1767, had enlisted in the Régiment d'Enghien in 1786 and became a *caporal* before he was discharged in 1789. He rejoined the ranks after the revolution and was elected *lieutenant-colonel en second* of the 2e bataillon du Jura in October 1791. Most of his time was spent on the coasts of France and fighting the rebels in the Vendée. In 1796, he captured the rebel leader Charette and was promoted to *général de brigade* and appointed commander of the Vendée department. He stayed there until 1802 and then commanded a department in Italy before being promoted to *général de division* in 1805 and taking command of a division in Nantes. He was posted to the Vendée again in 1807 before being appointed to command the 3e Division.[42]

The majority of the 3e Division were not French but Italian. Or rather, they may have been born Italian, but France had since annexed their countries or regions, and Napoleon and the French government now considered them to be French and liable for conscription.

Graindorge's Brigade

Général de brigade Jean François Graindorge had seen considerably more action than his divisional commander and had the scars to prove it. Born in 1771 he became a *lieutenant* in the 1er bataillon de volontaires de l'Orne in 1791. He was shot in his right thigh at La Grisoëlle in June 1792, where

35   Grasset, *Guerre d'Espagne*, vol.I, p.435.
36   G.L.E. Piéron, *Histoire d'un régiment, la 32e Demi-Brigade* (Paris: Vasseur, 1890), p.160.
37   Grasset, *Guerre d'Espagne*, vol.I, p.435.
38   Dempsey, *Mercenaries*, pp.280–281.
39   Grasset, *Guerre d'Espagne*, vol.I, p.436.
40   Mackay, *Tempest*, p.180.
41   Bégos, *Souvenirs*, p.25.
42   Six, *Dictionnaire*, vol.II, p.509.

Junot received his first wound and was shot in the head in September. A year later, he was shot in the body at Hondschoote, after which he was promoted to *capitaine*. At Charleroi in 1794, he took three sabre cuts to his head and one to his left arm. In September 1795, he took a ball to his left knee at the crossing of the Rhine. In 1796 and 1797, he saw further action around the Rhine but avoided being wounded and received a battlefield promotion to *chef de bataillon*. He went to Switzerland in 1799 and fought at Zürich and the crossing of Limmat. He was promoted to *chef de brigade* by Massena. In 1805, he was promoted to *général de brigade*, commanding a brigade in Lannes' V Corps. In November, he fought at Dürenstein, where he was captured. Released in 1806, Graindorge returned to his brigade, saw action at Saalfeld, was wounded again at Jena, and served at Pultusk. In February 1807, Graindorge fought at three more battles and was then assigned to his brigade in the 3e Division.[43]

The 31e and 32e Légère were formed into another provisional regiment commanded by *major* Durlong. The 31e had been formed in 1801 from the 1er Piémontaise demi-brigade légère. The men of 3/31e were mainly 20–27 years old, with some aged 28–30, and were all Italian.[44] The 32e Légère had been raised in 1805 after France annexed the Ligurian Republic in northwest Italy and instituted conscription there. The records of the 3/32e Légère had not been kept up to date, and Grasset could not come up with even an average age for its men.[45]

The veterans of the 26e Ligne were all in the West Indies, so the third battalion was made up of conscripts of 1806–1808 with an average age of 20–23 years old.[46] Curiously, some former members of this regiment and the 66e Ligne were part of Wellesley's expedition sailing towards Portugal. In September 1806, a convoy of five French frigates and two corvettes taking reinforcements to the 26e, 66e and 82e in the West Indies was intercepted by a Royal Navy squadron, and four frigates were captured. Many of the conscripts of the 26e and 66e came from the Rhineland and Belgium, respectively, regions that had only recently been annexed by France and who had little loyalty to the Empire. When the captured frigates arrived in Britain, many men volunteered to serve in the British Army rather than become prisoners of war. The 5/60th Rifles recruited 100 of the German and Flemish speakers, many of whom would go on to serve throughout the Peninsular campaign and beyond.[47] In Portugal, the 3/26e, commanded by *colonel* Miquel, was posted for a time in the Algarve.

The Légion du Midi was formed after France annexed Piedmont in northwest Italy. The unit was called a legion as it was intended to include light infantry, artillery, and line infantry. However, recruitment was lower than anticipated, and only the line infantry was formed with the same nine-company structure as French regiments. The first and second battalions were decimated by disease in the West Indies, and the third and fourth battalions were renumbered accordingly. The quality of the recruits continued to be low, and in early 1806, Napoleon ordered the replacement of the senior officers to try and improve the unit. By the time the first battalion marched to Bayonne in 1807, Napoleon had given up on the Légion and planned to let it wither away until it could be disbanded. The second battalion followed the first to Bayonne, but the combined strength of both battalions was only 839 when they marched into Spain. This had dropped to 797 by January and was included in the return of that month as a single

43   Six, *Dictionnaire*, vol.I, p.518.
44   Grasset, *Guerre d'Espagne*, vol.I, p.436.
45   Grasset, *Guerre d'Espagne*, vol.I, p.436.
46   Grasset, *Guerre d'Espagne*, vol.I, p.436.
47   Griffith, *Riflemen*, pp.120–123.

battalion. The Légion was led in Portugal by *colonel* Jean Pierre Maransin, a volunteer of 1792, who often commanded in the Algarve when *général de brigade* Maruin was ill. The legion saw action at Beja during the insurrection, when *chef de batallion* Crampigny was killed and three officers wounded, one of whom, *capitaine* Dubois, later died of his wounds. The Légion was then stationed at Forte de São Julião da Barra, but the grenadier company may have been included in the grenadier regiments that were formed to act as a reserve for the army, one of which was commanded by Maransin. The Légion wore a dark brown coat with iron grey or scarlet cuffs or collars, depending on the battalion.[48] Grasset found no useful details of the men's age or experience in the Légion's registers but noted that the men were almost all volunteers from Turin with very few conscripts.[49]

Fuzier's Brigade

Born in 1757, *général de brigade* Louis Fuzier was another of the generals who started his career in the Royal army, in his case with the Régiment de Bourbon in 1776. By the time of the revolution, he was a *sergent-major*. His regiment became the 56e Demi-brigade in 1791, and he quickly rose to *capitaine*. In 1792–1794, he served in the defence of Lille, at the sieges of Antwerp and Maestricht, the Battle of Neerwinden, Dunkirk, and Maubeuge. Appointed *chef de bataillon* and then *général de brigade* in the spring of 1794, he was wounded at Trazegnies by a canister shot that shattered his right arm and injured him in the thigh. In 1796, he was ordered to suppress an uprising in Saint-Pol but was accused of being anti-republican and suspended, although he was later reinstated. He then fought against the British and Russians in the Netherlands in 1799. After campaigning in Germany in 1800, he was appointed to the command of the Charente-Inférieure department in 1801 and then served in the Vendée from 1805 until his appointment in the 3e Division.[50]

Like the 26e, the veterans of the 66e were in the West Indies. The third and fourth battalions in Portugal contained conscripts from 1804 to 1806 but also large numbers from 1808. The average age was 20–25, and the men were mostly experiencing their first campaign as the battalions had previously been on coastal defence duty.[51] *Chef de bataillon* Cresté commanded the battalions.

The 3/82e was another unit whose records Grasset found to be sorely lacking. He estimated that the battalion was probably composed mainly of conscripts from 1805–1807, with around 100 from 1808.[52] However, the regimental history of the 82e states that in August 1807, 772 conscripts of the 1808 class joined the 3e and 4e battalions before marching to Portugal under the command of *chef de bataillon* Pétavy. In January 1808, Junot received orders to merge the two battalions into one, which became the 3e and was then reorganised into the six-company structure. The supernumerary officers were sent back to the depot in France. In March, two columns of reinforcements arrived from France, totalling over 400 men. The 3/82e was also part of Margaron's column that marched from Lisbon to stop the insurgents at Leira and Tomar. By the end of July, they were back in the Lisbon garrison.[53]

---

48 Dempsey, *Mercenaries*, pp.147–154.
49 Grasset, *Guerre d'Espagne*, vol.I, p.436.
50 Six, *Dictionnaire*, vol.I, p.477.
51 Grasset, *Guerre d'Espagne*, vol.I, p.436.
52 Grasset, *Guerre d'Espagne*, vol.I, p.436.
53 P. Arvers, *Historique du 82e Régiment D'Infanterie de Ligne* (Paris: Lahure, 1876), pp.98–100.

After the French occupied Hannover in 1803 and disbanded its army, Napoleon hoped to recruit some of the unemployed soldiers. The Légion Hanovrienne was raised as a light infantry battalion and three cavalry squadrons. Only the infantry marched to Portugal, the Légion's first campaign. The battalion was composed of four companies of chasseurs and one elite company of carabiniers. Enlistment was voluntary, but recruits eventually came from various German states. The infantry wore a red coat with blue collar, cuffs, and lapels, with white pantaloons and waistcoats – very similar to British infantry.[54] According to Grasset, three-quarters of the Légion were between 19 and 27 years old, with the remaining quarter being 28–37.[55] He states that there was no indication that they had campaigned before, but, given their age and the fact that the Légion was partially recruited from prisoners of war, they likely had, but not for France. Grasset also noted their high desertion rate and believed they were not troops who could be counted on. *Colonel* Louis-Cyriac Striffler commanded the legion. Striffler came from the Alsace and was a *lieutenant* in a volunteer battalion in 1792, rising to *chef de bataillon* by 1795. He had been the Légion's infantry commander since its formation.

The Cavalry

Général de division François-Etienne Kellermann was the son of *maréchal* Kellermann of Valmy fame. Born in 1770 he joined the Régiment Colonel Général des hussards as a *sous-lieutenant* aged 15. In 1791, he went to the United States with the French ambassador, where he learned English. He returned to France in 1793, became an aide de camp to his father, and took part in the siege of Lyon, after which he and his father were arrested. The two Kellermanns managed to justify their actions to the revolutionary authorities and were released. The younger Kellermann then enlisted as a volunteer in the 1er Hussards and, in 1794, once again became one of his father's aides. In 1795 he was appointed an *adjudant général* and *chef de brigade* in the Armée d'Italie. He served in numerous actions including Lodi, the siege of Milan, and Rivoli, and was wounded by several sabre cuts at the passage of the Tagliamento. In March 1797, he was honoured by Bonaparte with the task of taking the captured enemy colours to Paris. He was promoted to *général de brigade,* then returned to Italy to become commander of Macdonald's advance guard. In 1800, at Marengo, he timed the charge of his brigade perfectly to secure the victory. Promoted to *général de division* for his services, he led a cavalry division at Austerlitz and was wounded. In 1806, he was appointed commander of the cavalry of the Armée de Réserve under his father, and then in 1807 given the command of Junot's cavalry.[56]

Kellermann's cavalry, comprised of the fourth squadrons of their regiments, was organised into four provisional regiments. The first comprised just the 26e Chasseurs à Cheval and was commanded by *major* Weiss. The second contained the men of the 1er and 3e Dragons and was led by *major* Contant of the 3e. The third and fourth regiments were made up of the 4e and 5e, and 9e and 15e, commanded by *majors* Théron (4e) and Leclerc (9e), respectively.[57]

A French cavalry regiment usually had four squadrons, each comprising two companies. The first three squadrons were the ones that were supposed to go on campaign, while the fourth acted as the depot to train recruits. However, the lack of available units in 1807 meant that Junot's cavalry

54   Dempsey, *Mercenaries*, pp.164–165.
55   Grasset, *Guerre d'Espagne*, vol.I, p.436.
56   Six, *Dictionnaire*, vol.II, pp.2–4.
57   R. Burnham, *Charging Against Wellington: Napoleon's Cavalry in the Peninsula 1807-1814* (Barnsley: Frontline, 2011), pp.2–3, 324.

was all made up of fourth squadrons and contained mostly inexperienced recent conscripts still being trained. Training took longer for cavalry than for infantry because recruits had to acquire the skills of horsemanship as well as combat. Each cavalry squadron had an establishment of around 250 men. Regiments were commanded by a *colonel*, with a *major* often in charge of the depot. A *chef d'escadron* commanded each squadron, a *capitaine* each company. The numbers of junior officers and staff were roughly equivalent to the infantry, with the addition of veterinarians and blacksmiths to look after the horses.[58] The cavalry had lost a significant portion of its horses in the march into Portugal, with only around 1,000 making it to Lisbon.[59] Junot requisitioned those of the Portuguese cavalry regiments to get them back up to strength, but 600 of the cavalry were still unmounted as of 1 January.

Margaron's Brigade

Général de brigade Pierre Margaron joined the Légion des Ardennes in 1792 and rose quickly to *lieutenant-colonel* and then *chef de brigade* in 1793. He was briefly suspended before being reinstated and then sent to the Armée du Nord, where he served on the staff. In 1796, Margaron served with the Armies of the Sambre and Meuse, and then in 1798, he moved to the Armée d'Italie as *chef de brigade* of the 1er Cavalerie. He was wounded at Novi and had his right leg broken at Fossano. He later led the light cavalry brigade under Michaud at the passage of the Adige in January 1801. In 1803, he was promoted to *général de brigade* and in 1805 he commanded a light cavalry brigade in Soult's IV Corps. At Austerlitz, he was wounded by two musket shots. After some leave in 1806, he fought at Jena, Nossentin, Biezun, and Mohrungen before being assigned to Junot's cavalry in the summer of 1807.[60]

The 4/26e Chasseurs had previously been in the service of the King of Sardinia and the men were all Italians.[61] Nicolas Tiole of the 26e also mentions that there were many subjects of the King of Sardinia – whose kingdom covered both the island of Sardinia and Piedmont in north-west Italy – in the 2e and 31e Légère and the 1er Dragons.[62] With the records of the 1er, 3e and 4e Dragons incomplete, Grasset found it impossible to draw too many conclusions from their registers but estimated their average age at 20–25 years old.[63] The regimental history of the 3e Dragons mentions the 4e Escadron having 'the best of the recruits of 1807.'[64]

Maurin's Brigade

Born in 1771, *général de brigade* Antoine Maurin was a trooper of the 6e Chasseurs à cheval in 1792. At the Battle of Roër, he was one of the first to swim across the river to attack the enemy's entrenchments. He was made a *sous-lieutenant* in the 20e Chasseurs à cheval in 1794 and distinguished himself at Kreutznach and Limbourg, where he was promoted on the battlefield. He received several sabre cuts at Burgwindsheim. During this time, he also began to serve on Bernadotte's staff and went with him to Italy, was promoted to *capitaine* and became one of his aides de camp. He

---

58   Burnham, *Charging Against Wellington*, pp.228–231.
59   Mackay, *Tempest*, p.180.
60   Six, *Dictionnaire*, vol.II, pp.154-155.
61   Grasset, *Guerre d'Espagne*, vol.I, p.437.
62   Jean Barada, 'Notes sur L'Expédition de Portugal 1807-1808,' *Carnet de la Sabretache*, No. 263 Jan-Feb 1920, p.202.
63   Grasset, *Guerre d'Espagne*, vol.I, p.436.
64   A. De Bonnières de Wierre, *Historique du 3e Régiment de dragons: 1649-1892* (Nantes: Bourgeois, 1892), p.75.

3e Dragon, possibly by Weiland. (Anne S.K. Brown Military Collection)

quickly rose to *chef d'escadron* and *adjudant général*. He remained with his general in the Armée du Rhin and Armée de l'Ouest. In 1802, he was promoted to *chef de brigade* of the 24e Chasseurs à cheval, serving in Italy and with the Grandé Armée in 1805. He was then appointed *général de brigade* and given his brigade in Junot's cavalry in 1807. He commanded the advanced guard on the march into Portugal and then commanded in the Algarve. He was ill when he was captured by rebels in June 1808 and handed over to the Royal Navy as a prisoner of war.[65]

Grasset found little information in the records of the brigade's units. Half of the 4/5e Dragons were conscripts from 1807 and a quarter from 1806, with the remainder including men from 22 to 32 years old.[66] Two-thirds of the men of the 4/9e Dragons were conscripts of 1807, with the last third being a mix of conscripts from 1804–1806, with some from 1808 and a dozen veterans of 30 or over.[67] Half of the 4/15e Dragons were conscripts of 1807. The other half included conscripts of 1805 and 1806, with the men ranging from 22 to 27 years old. More than two-thirds of the men were 20 years old.[68]

Conclusion

Many of the rank and file in the Armée de Portugal were young and inexperienced, but their generals had been forged in the wars of the revolution and Napoleon's many campaigns. Many had been in their ranks for over a decade. Other senior officers of the Armée de Portugal, such as the commander of the artillery *général de brigade* Albert-Louis-Valentin Taviel, the Junot's chief of staff *général de brigade* Paul Thiébault, *colonel* Charles Vincent, the chief engineer, and the various other staff officers, all had careers that stretched back to the early days of the revolution or beyond. Many had gained high rank early and had fought in many more campaigns than their British equivalents. However, in the British system once an officer was a colonel, they continued to be automatically promoted by seniority as they worked their way up the *Army List*. This was not the case in the French army. Officers who quickly rose to command brigades or even divisions during the Revolutionary Wars often failed to progress further for some time, even if they had more ability and experience than favoured officers such as Junot. One British officer dining with Junot and his staff after the campaign noted:

> Junot's second aid-de-camp, near whom I was seated at dinner, surprized me much by the light and disrespectful manner with which he spoke of the military talents of his General, who, he said, was a *bon officier de cavalerie, mais rien d'autre* [good cavalry officer, but nothing else]. I was equally amazed at finding that this man, as well as most of the officers who composed Junot's staff, and those of the other French Generals, were men of a certain age, much past the flower of youth.[69]

---

65   Six, *Dictionnaire*, vol.II, p.174.
66   Grasset, *Guerre d'Espagne*, vol.I, p.436.
67   Grasset, *Guerre d'Espagne*, vol.I, p.436.
68   Grasset, *Guerre d'Espagne*, vol.I, p.437.
69   A. Neale, *Letters from Portugal and Spain* (London: Phillips, 1809), p.60.

7

Landing

The convoy from Cork did not suffer any of the storms that had beset Spencer's expedition the previous December. The log of the *Donegal* records 'light airs' or 'light breezes' for the first few days, but the direction of the wind was variable and often against them, so their progress was slow. It turned 'squally with heavy rain' on 19 July, and then the wind remained 'fresh breezes' or 'moderate' until they reached the rendezvous at Cape Finisterre.[1]

Private James Hale recalled the voyage fondly in his memoir: 'The whole of this voyage proved very pleasant, having fine weather and such an easy sea; and to see such a quantity of fish alongside the ship, as there were sometimes, made it appear still more pleasant: some appeared to our view to be five or six feet in length.'[2] On 18 July, Hill updated Castlereagh on the convoy's progress, which at that point was just over 200 miles south of Cork and a similar distance west of Brest: 'In the absence of Lieutenant-General Sir Arthur Wellesley, it affords me particular satisfaction to inform your Lordship by the La Gloria, that none of the transports that sailed with the armament from Cove on the 12th of this month are missing, and that the troops are perfectly healthy.'[3]

Sir Arthur Wellesley had sped ahead of the main convoy the day after leaving Cork in HMS *Crocodile* heading for Corunna, the main port of the Spanish province of Galicia. The *Crocodile* entered the harbour on 20 July, and Wellesley was greeted warmly. He had several conferences with the Junta that had taken control of the province. He learnt that the revolt had spread to most of the country and about the victory at Bailén, but also that the Spanish had been recently defeated at Medina de Rioseco on 14 July 1808. Over 20,000 Spanish had been routed by around 12,000 French north of Valladolid. Despite this, the Junta of Galicia told Wellesley firmly that they did not want the assistance of British troops but only needed arms, ammunition, and money. The British government was already sending aid. A few hours after the *Crocodile* sailed into Corunna, diplomat Charles Stuart had arrived with £200,000 from Britain to help the Spanish fight the French. Two transports, the *Union* and the *Patty*, originally intended to sail with Wellesley's convoy and carrying cannon, ammunition, gunpowder, and swords, had recently arrived at nearby Gijon. The Junta told Wellesley that his expedition should help liberate Portugal, as that would secure a communication route between the Spanish armies in the north and those in the south.[4]

---

1   TNA: ADM 51/1180: *Donegal* log.
2   J. Hale, *Journal of James Hale, late Sergeant in the Ninth Regiment of Foot* (Cirencester: Watkins, 1826), p.14. The 'fish' were probably dolphins.
3   Sidney, *Hill*, pp.77–78. *La Gloria* was presumably a merchant ship the convoy had closed with.
4   TNA: WO 1/415: Wellesley's narrative, pp.52–53.

Wellesley told Castlereagh that the situation in Spain was still unclear as communications between the provinces were difficult, but he did see the northern provinces as being key as they could cut French lines of communication back to France, and he thought that the Junta in Asturias should be persuaded to accept British troops to help.[5] Wellesley also gained more information about the situation in Portugal from the Spanish:

> In respect to my own operations, I find that Junot has collected it is supposed 12,000 men at Lisbon; and the French still hold Almeida, and other points in Portugal, with 3000 more. The three northern provinces of Portugal are in a state of insurrection, and there is a Portuguese army at Oporto, to join which 2000 Spanish troops have marched from Galicia, and they will arrive there about the 24th or 25th. From the intelligence which I have received here I can form no opinion whether I shall be joined by General Spencer or not. Mr. Stuart heard from the Brilliant on his passage that General Spencer had left Cadiz, after the Spaniards had got possession of the French fleet, and had gone to Aya Monte, at the mouth of the Guadiana, to stop the progress of a French corps which was coming by that route from Portugal into Andalusia. They had heard nothing here of this movement; but they had heard a report that 5000 British troops had been in General Castaños' army and had behaved remarkably well, but on what occasion, and what troops, they did not know.[6]

While the information from Portugal that Wellesley relayed was broadly correct, the tale of Spencer's men serving with Castaños was not. The letter to Castlereagh then continued:

> I understand that there is a Spanish corps of 20,000 men in Estremadura, at Almarez, on the Tagus, which corps will impede the communication between Junot and the army at Madrid; and it may be reasonably expected that the number of French now in Portugal will be the number which we shall have to contend with.
>
>   The Junta express great anxiety respecting my operations in Portugal, and have strongly recommended me not to attempt to land at Lisbon, or in the neighbourhood of the French army. They urge as an objection to this measure, that I shall thereby entirely lose the advantage of the co-operation of the Spanish and Portuguese forces at Oporto, who will not be able to approach Lisbon till they have heard that I have disembarked; and they recommend that I should disembark at Vigo or Oporto, and bring the allies with me to Lisbon. It is impossible for me to decide upon this or any other measure till I shall know more of the situation of affairs. I should have no doubt of success, even without General Spencer's assistance, or that of the allies, if I were once ashore; but to effect a landing in front of an enemy is always difficult, and I shall be inclined to land at a distance from Lisbon.[7]

Still uncertain exactly where he would land his troops, Wellesley sailed south, briefly rendezvousing with the convoy off Cape Finisterre and then continuing to Oporto, where he arrived on the 24th.

5   TNA: WO 1/228: Wellesley to Castlereagh, 21 July 1808.
6   TNA: WO 1/228: Wellesley to Castlereagh, 21 July 1808.
7   TNA: WO 1/228: Wellesley to Castlereagh, 21 July 1808.

The convoy arrived the day after.[8] Again, he was welcomed warmly and met with the Bishop, military commanders, and Lieutenant Colonel Browne. Wellesley was informed that 5,000 Portuguese militia and regular troops were at Coimbra, and over 12,000, mostly poorly armed peasants, were in Oporto; the 2,000 Spaniards from Galicia had not arrived yet. The resolve of the Portuguese to eject the French from their country had not lessened. However, the defeats suffered by the Spanish worried them, and they still lacked money, trained soldiers, and arms for the eager volunteers.[9]

The Bishop of Oporto and the Portuguese commanders said their troops would collaborate with Wellesley's expedition once it landed, while further forces would defend Oporto and blockade Almeida. Wellesley asked the Bishop for 150 horses for the 20th Light Dragoons, 500 mules and some carts to help alleviate the lack of transport with the expedition. The Bishop promised they would be at Coimbra when the expedition disembarked.[10] Wellesley and his aides spent the night at the home of the absent British consul. While at Oporto, he also met with James Walsh, Harriot Slessor's son-in-law, and arranged a contract to supply beef cattle to the expedition.[11] Browne told Wellesley that Trant and 6,000 Portuguese troops were armed and ready to cooperate with the British at Coimbra.[12] Browne and Walsh later left Oporto on 1 August to travel down to Figueira after helping to secure horses, mules, and provisions for the expedition. Wellesley's military secretary, Torrens, said of Browne that he 'had every possible information collected with regard to the state of the country' and then wrote:

By letters which have been intercepted from Junot, it appears that he considers his situation to be extremely critical and is very pressing on the subject of reinforcements: and it is supposed here that the French Army under Marshal Bessieres has no other object but that of relieving him. It is reported by letters received from the frontier this morning that the French had turned the flank of the Spanish Army, was pushing into this Kingdom and had arrived on this side of Benevente! If they succeed in getting down here before we are in possession of Lisbon and the *army is in it*, our hands will be full enough![13]

Again, much of the information that Torrens reported was wrong. The French in Spain had their own hands full, and no reinforcements were coming for Junot. At Oporto, Captain McKinley of the *Lively* gave Wellesley a letter, dated 17 days previously, from Cotton, which updated the general on all that the Royal Navy had been doing to support the patriots in Portugal and that:

General Junot has I learn concentrated his force in and near Lisbon to the amount of 11,000 effective men, and has been busily employed securing the citadel of Saint George in the centre of Lisbon; and throwing up works and creating fortification round that City, inland as well as on the sea coast, to strengthen all the points by which an opposing Army may be supposed to approach.[14]

8   TNA: ADM 51/1880: *Donegal* log. Most sources, including Wellesley, state that the *Crocodile* met with the convoy on the 22nd but the log of the *Donegal* says it was the 23rd.
9   TNA: WO 1/228: Wellesley to Castlereagh, 26 July 1808.
10   TNA: WO 1/228: Wellesley to Castlereagh, 26 July 1808.
11   Hayter (ed.), *The Backbone*, pp.182–183.
12   TNA: WO 1/237: Browne to Stewart, 27 July 1808.
13   BL: Add MS 49485: Torrens to Gordon, 25 July 1808.
14   TNA: WO 1/228: Cotton to Wellesley, 9 July 1808.

Cotton also told Wellesley of the 300 Royal Marines at Figueira da Foz, recommended it as a possible disembarkation point, and suggested that Wellesley sail down to the Tagus for a face-to-face meeting.

The convoy's arrival at Oporto was especially poignant for Captain William Warre. He wrote to his father on 25 July while off the city:

> I have just heard a Frigate is going to England, and the boat is waiting to take my letter, so I have only time to say we are all well. I think we are to land at Lisbon and attack Junot. This is my idea, but nothing is known. To express my feelings at seeing the spot of my birth, the place in which I spent some of the happiest days of my life, would be impossible, or how tantalised at not being able to communicate. Should we land, you shall hear further and by first opportunity. At present they are calling for my letter.[15]

There was no time for anyone else to land at Oporto besides Wellesley, as Captain Malcolm was waiting for the general to return before sailing. The vessel bound for Britain was the brig *Peacock*. As it was delayed, Warre had a chance to add a postscript to his letter: '... we are making all sail for Figueira, where we are to land to-morrow morning in order, I understand, to cut off a French Corps marching to Lisbon to Junot's assistance, and then to march to Lisbon and try his mettle.'[16]

With the convoy still at anchor off Oporto, Wellesley briefly went aboard the *Donegal* and gave Malcolm orders for the convoy to sail to Mondego Bay as Cotton's letter had suggested. He then sailed for the Tagus in the *Crocodile*. He found Cotton on the *Hibernia* anchored in Cascais Bay on the afternoon of 26 July.[17] The main topics of their meeting were the impossibility of any attack directly on the Tagus and where to land the troops. Figueira was by far the best choice and was soon agreed upon. A landing close to Lisbon – for example, in the small bays around the Rock of Lisbon – would be too close to French troops, running the risk of an opposed landing, and also too far from those of the Portuguese who would not then be able to assist the British. With Peniche held by the French, landing there was also out of the question.

After receiving intelligence from Cotton, Browne, Spencer, and the Portuguese, Wellesley estimated that the Junot had between 16,000 and 18,000 men and that a disposable force of around 14,000 was available for the defence of Lisbon.[18] He told Gordon at Horse Guards the French had 15,000 men.[19] He discounted the idea that they numbered more than 20,000, a figure based on the information from the three Hanoverian deserters interrogated by Cotton and Spencer and which actually underestimated French strength by over 4,000 men. In September of the previous year, Lord Strangford had told the government that the troops gathering at Bayonne to invade Portugal totalled more than 23,000.[20] That information, which included a breakdown of the force, does not seem to have been passed on to Wellesley. Browne had written to Wellesley on 9 July and estimated the French force at between 14,000 and 15,000 but may or may not have revised that estimate when they met face-to-face.[21] William Warre told his father that he

15   Warre, *Letters*, p.19.
16   Warre, *Letters*, p.20.
17   TNA: ADM 50/57: Entry for 26 July.
18   TNA: WO 1/415: Wellesley's narrative, p.57.
19   Wellesley to Gordon, 21 July 1808, in Wellington (ed.), *Supplementary Despatches*, vol.IV, p.90.
20   TNA: FO 63/55: Corps qui formeront le Camp à Bayonne.
21   TNA: WO 1/237: Browne to Wellesley, 9 July 1808.

had heard that the French around Lisbon now numbered around 12,000.[22] On 16 August, the *Morning Chronicle* published a letter from Oporto that stated that the original invasion force was 20,000 and estimated that Junot had 17,000 men around Lisbon, of which he could probably field around half.[23]

There was obviously some debate and uncertainty about the French strength, but Wellesley's estimate of the disposable force around Lisbon would prove to be reasonably close to the mark, even if he underestimated the total number of French troops in Portugal. It is curious why Wellesley discounted the intelligence of the Hanoverian deserters. They provided detailed information (see Table 5), and two experienced officers, Cotton and Spencer, debriefed them. The information is so detailed that the question could be raised about how three foreign soldiers serving France had come by it, but the men were obviously convincing.

Based on what he had learnt of the French numbers, it seemed necessary to Wellesley that Spencer's force join his. He had last received news of Spencer on 26 July when he met HMS *Plantagenet* while sailing to his meeting with Cotton. Captain Henry Cooke (Coldstream Guards) was onboard with Spencer's dispatches, saying that he intended to stay in Andalusia for the moment, but that information was out of date and Spencer was already on his way north. Not knowing this, Wellesley wrote to Spencer to ask him to join him unless he was actively engaged in operations.[24] In a letter to his friend and ally, the Duke of Richmond, Wellesley betrayed some irritation with Spencer:

> Spencer has sent me a paper of information stating that the French force in Portugal amounts to 20,000 men; and although he knows I have only 10,000, and that he was not employed on any service to the south, he had determined to remain on shore at Xerez near Cadiz: but I have ordered him to join me, and I expect him in a day or two; and as I don't believe the French have so many as 20,000 men, I shall commence my operations as soon as he with his 5,000, or a reinforcement expected from England of 5,000 men, shall join me.[25]

Cotton was keen on a secondary landing south of Lisbon, but Wellesley thought splitting his forces would be risky and preferred to land all his troops, including Spencer's, at Figueira. However, he did see the advantages of a diversion as he approached Lisbon and told Cotton that he would send the 4th Royal Veteran Battalion to the Tagus, where, with the marines of the squadron, it could make some kind of demonstration to divert Junot's attention.[26] He told Cotton that the 4th Veterans were 'a good corps, but the soldiers being old, and disabled by wounds and otherwise for active service, cannot march. I have therefore sent them to the fleet off the Tagus, in order that the enemy may be induced to believe that we intend to make an attack in that quarter.'[27] Cotton sent word to Bligh at Figueira to re-embark the marines once the troops had begun to land.[28]

---

22   Warre, *Letters*, p.21.
23   *The Morning Chronicle*, 16 August 1808.
24   TNA: WO 1/228: Wellesley to Castlereagh 1 August 1808; Wellesley to Spencer, 26 July 1808.
25   Wellington (ed.), *Supplementary Dispatches*, vol.VI, p.95.
26   Gurwood (ed.), *Wellington's Dispatches*, vol.IV, pp.61–62.
27   Wellington (ed.), *Supplementary Dispatches*, vol.VI, p.103.
28   TNA: ADM 50/57: Entry 26 July 1808.

While Wellesley was with Cotton, the convoy was sailing south and arrived at Mondego Bay early on the morning of 26 July and anchored off Figueira.[29] Second Captain William Granville Eliot, Royal Artillery, wrote to his wife, Harriet, on the 27th; 'The country appears beautiful and just that kind of climate you have so much wished to live in. The hills are completely covered with vineyards and the white houses, and distant mountains form the most beautiful landscape you can imagine.'[30]

As Bad an Anchorage

On 24 July, Captain Pulteney Malcolm issued his orders for how the fleet was to anchor. Each regiment's transports were to anchor around the transport carrying the unit's headquarters:

> 5th Foot – *Norfolk*
> 9th Foot – *Defence*
> 36th Foot – *Mestaer*
> 38th Foot – *Atlas*
> 40th Foot – *Indefatigable*
> 45th Foot – *Whitby*
> 60th Rifles – *Malabar*
> 71st Foot – *Lord Mulgrave*
> 91st Foot – *Fortuna*
> 95th Rifles – *Amity*
> 20th Light Dragoons, and all horse ships – *General Eliot*
> Artillery, Engineers and Camp equipage – *Donegal*
> Armed Victualers and Veteran Battalion outside the *Donegal*.[31]

While Mondego Bay may have been the best available anchorage, it was not a good one. A bar had formed where the Mondego flowed into the sea, and, due to the Atlantic swell, there was usually considerable surf there. Malcolm later said that there were only four or five days during the whole time he was in the bay that the bar could be passed in standard boats without danger. The landing of the troops would rely on local craft, including larger boats and coastal schooners. Some of the convoy could sail into the more sheltered waters of the river, if their draft was not more than 11 feet, but only 20–25 could be accommodated at once.[32]

Captain Howard Elphinstone, senior Royal Engineer with Wellesley, wrote to his corps' headquarters:

> The bay we are now riding in is as bad an anchorage as it is possible to conceive, entirely open to the Atlantic and foul wind. The bar at the entrance of the river is extremely dangerous and only to be past in very fair weather or the most high water. Capt. Patten

---

29 TNA: ADM 51/1880: *Donegal* log.
30 NAM: 1959-03-127: Eliot to Harriet Eliot, 27 July 1808.
31 *The Dublin Evening Post*, 23 August 1808.
32 Anon. (ed.), *Proceedings*, pp.35–36.

and Mr Wells were upset in the surf a few evenings ago and they near drowned. However they are now quite well as are the rest of the officers.[33]

However, Elphinstone struck a lighter note in a letter to his wife:

> I went on shore yesterday after dinner to stretch my legs. The people seem quite rejoiced at our arrival. Junot has but a small force in Lisbon such as I think will surrender upon our appearance. The distance we have to march is about 70 miles. I believe I have a horse and mule already secured for me, so it will be an entertaining excursion. Who knows but we may eat our Christmas dinner together in Lisbon…[34]

On 29 July, Wellesley wrote his orders for the disembarkation of the troops. The horse ships and the ordnance transports would enter the river. The infantry would be loaded onto boats from the transports in the roads and then cross the bar, enter the river and be landed on the south bank. The memorandum then continued:

1st. The haversacks and canteens now in the regimental stores are to be given out to the men.

2d. Tin camp kettles are to be issued from the Quarter Master General's stores to the regiments.

3d. The Commissary must issue to each of the Paymasters of regiments, on account of the Paymaster General, the sum of £1000 for each of the regiments, and in that proportion for the artillery, dragoons, and 95th companies, which he will receive from the Donegal. A month's pay may also be issued on the same account to the Officers of the Staff.

4th. General Hill will inform the Officer commanding the 20th light dragoons that he is to receive a sufficient number of horses to mount all his men; that he will therefore be prepared to land the horse appointments of the men who have at present no horses.

5th. The following arrangement to be made respecting baggage. The men to land, each with one shirt and one pair of shoes, besides those on them, combs, razor, and a brush, which are to be packed up in their great coats. The knapsacks to be left in the transports, and the baggage of the Officers, excepting such light articles as are necessary for them. A careful serjeant to be left in the head quarter ship of each regiment, and a careful private man in each of the other ships, in charge of the baggage; and each Officer who shall leave any baggage in a transport must take care to have his name marked on each package, and each numbered, and give a list of what he leaves to the soldier in charge of the baggage, in order that he may get what he may require.

6th. The men will land with three days' bread and two days' meat, cooked.

7th. The Commanding Officer of artillery is to land the three brigades of artillery, each with half the usual proportion of ammunition, the forge cart, &c. He will also land 500,000 rounds of musket ammunition for the use of the troops, for which carriage will be provided.

33   TNA: WO 55/977: Elphinstone to Morse, 31 July 1808.
34   REM: 4201-274: Elphinstone to Frances Elphinstone, 27 July 1808.

8th. Each soldier will have with him three good flints.

9th. Besides the bread above directed to be landed with the soldiers, three days' bread to be packed up in bags, containing 100 lbs. each, on board each of the transports, for the number of soldiers who shall be disembarked from it.

10th. Mr. Commissary Pipon to be directed to attach a Commissary, and the necessary number of clerks, &c., to each brigade, to the cavalry and to the artillery. He will hereafter receive directions to take charge of the bread above directed to be prepared, and to make his arrangements for victualling the troops.

11th. Three days' oats to be landed with each of the horses.

12th. The horses of the Irish Commissariat to be handed over, when landed, to the Commanding Officer of the artillery, who will allot the drivers to take charge of them; and then the Officers and drivers belonging to the Irish Commissariat to place themselves under the orders of Mr. Pipon.

13th. The Officers commanding companies will make an arrangement for purchasing mules for the carriage of camp equipage, for which they have received an allowance in the embarkation money.[35]

The mouth of the Mondego river. Modern breakwaters and industrial development have radically altered the coastline since 1808. The Royal Marines occupied the hills behind the town. (Author's photo)

Wellesley rejoined the transports at anchor off Figueira on 30 July. On the 31st, he issued a general order to the troops that not only covered further administrative and organisational issues but how the troops were to behave, it began:

> The troops are to understand that Portugal is a country friendly to His Majesty, that it is essentially necessary to their own success that the most strict obedience should be preserved, that properties and persons should be respected, and that no injury should be done which it is possible to avoid. The Lieutenant-General declares his determination to punish in the most exemplary manner all who may be convicted of acts of outrage and of plunder against the persons or property of any of the people of the country.

---

35   Gurwood (ed.), *Wellington's Dispatches*, vol.IV, pp.48–50.

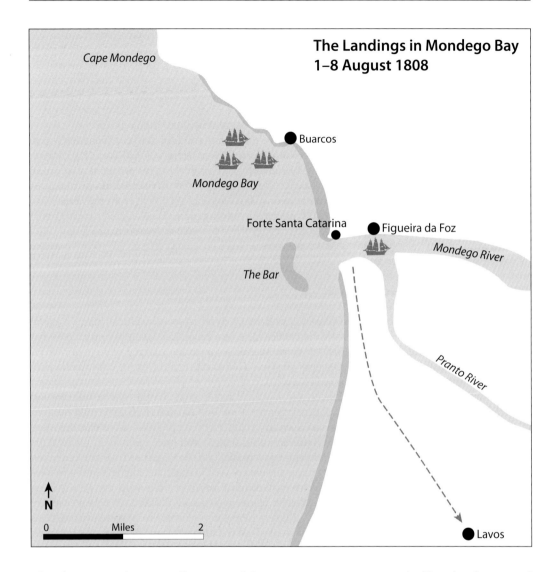

**The Landings in Mondego Bay
1–8 August 1808**

Cape Mondego

Buarcos

Mondego Bay

Forte Santa Catarina

Figueira da Foz

Mondego River

The Bar

Pranto River

N

0 Miles 2

Lavos

Churches were to be especially respected. Rations were set at one pound of bread or biscuit and one pound of either salted or fresh meat. If the soldiers had fresh meat, they were not entitled to any spirits. If they had to have salted meat, they were allowed a quarter of a pint of spirits or a pint of wine. The women were to have a half ration and the children a quarter, but no wine or spirits would be issued for either. Men were entitled to three pounds of firewood in camp. The order went on to outline the paperwork that would accompany the issuing of rations or requisitions by the commissariat with the phrase 'in *triplicate*', with the emphasis, being used frequently. Wellesley also stated that:

The officers and soldiers are to understand that they are to pay for everything they require from the country, excepting provisions, forage, wood, and carriages allowed by the public. For these articles when required, and not issued by the Commissary, they will make requisitions in the country, and give receipts; but they are to make these requisitions only by order of a General or other officer commanding a brigade or detachment.[36]

Wellesley was determined to keep the goodwill of the Portuguese population.

It would be their first time organising such a large disembarkation for some of Wellesley's staff. Deputy Assistant Quartermaster General Captain James Dawes Douglas (45th Foot) later wrote: 'On the 31st of that month received an order to commence disembarking the Army next morning … It was suggested by some of the party that I should wait upon Sir Arthur Wellesley, state our inexperience and request more detailed instructions.' But Douglas got a boat from the *Donegal* to take him ashore and, with a naval lieutenant, selected a landing place. He sketched it, was almost drowned crossing the bar of the Mondego, and then returned to make his report to Wellesley.[37] The landing would begin on 1 August.

This Most Complicated Arrangement

When he returned to the convoy, Wellesley found that Captain Lord Burghersh (3rd Dragoon Guards) had arrived from Britain with dispatches. The one from Castlereagh confirmed what Wellesley had feared since before he had left Cork: the force was to be enlarged and a more senior commander appointed. Lieutenant General Sir Hew Dalrymple would be in command, with Lieutenant General Sir Harry Burrard as his second.

Once Castlereagh had received Spencer and Cotton's intelligence, based on the information from the three Hanoverian deserters and other sources, that the French in Portugal could number 20,000, the plans that had already been in motion to add to the expedition were enacted. Two brigades would embark at Harwich and Ramsgate imminently, and once Lieutenant General Sir John Moore's transports had been refreshed and re-victualled, he too would sail. Moore had taken 10,000 men to Sweden, Britain's only remaining ally except for Portugal, to help defend the Swedes from France and Russia. Arriving in May, he soon found himself at odds with the erratic King Gustavus IV Adolphus, who wanted to use British troops to regain Finland from Russia, capture Zealand from Denmark, or invade Norway. These schemes ran counter to Moore's instructions from the government, and so he declined, which angered the king. The row between the two men escalated, and the king forbade Moore to leave Stockholm. Moore had to escape surreptitiously back to his troops, still on board the transports off Göteburg. The expedition then sailed back to Britain at the start of July.

Wellesley's and Spencer's troops totalled 13,913. Another 3,163 were coming from Ramsgate and 1,672 from Harwich. Moore's British and King's German Legion troops added a further 10,864 men. The 18th Light Dragoons, 640 men, had also been ordered to embark, which, with a final contribution of an infantry battalion from Madeira under Beresford, made a grand total of 30,562

---

36   Wellington (ed.), *Supplementary Despatches*, vol.IV, pp.91–94.
37   Brown, *Redjackets*, p.27.

troops.[38] This command was too large for a very junior lieutenant general, and a more senior commander was required. With Lord Chatham declining the command, the government had to find someone else quickly. Moore and his second in command, Lieutenant General the Honourable John Hope, were both senior to Wellesley but still not senior enough for such a large command. After the expedition to Sweden and issues with his behaviour in Sicily before that, Moore did not have the government's confidence. So, with Dalrymple already in theatre at Gibraltar and thoroughly acquainted with events in southern Spain, he was a very logical choice.

Castlereagh wrote to Dalrymple: 'I am to acquaint you that His Majesty having highly approved of the zeal and judgement which has marked the whole of your conduct under the late important events which have taken place in Spain, has been graciously pleased to intrust to you for the present the chief command of his forces to be employed in Portugal and Spain.'[39]

Hew Whitefoord Dalrymple was born in December 1750 and was 57 years old. His father died when he was three, and his mother remarried. He was commissioned an ensign in the 31st Foot, his stepfather's regiment, in 1763 and he became a lieutenant three years later. He was employed on recruiting service in Edinburgh while he attended university there. In 1768, he obtained a captaincy in the 1st Foot and went with them to Minorca. He also attended manoeuvres in Germany to 'make myself acquainted with the military system of Austria and Prussia.'[40] He gained his majority by raising a quota of men for the 77th Foot in 1777 and commanded the regiment as it formed. His stepfather's connections and patronage then obtained him a knighthood in 1779. He missed serving in the American War, married an heiress, and became a captain and lieutenant colonel in the 1st Foot Guards by purchase.[41] By the outbreak of war in 1793, he was a colonel. He soon saw active service for the first time in Flanders with the Guards grenadier battalion, fighting at Famars, the siege of Valenciennes, and the battles before Dunkirk. He found his first experience of war horrifying. He was promoted to major general in 1794 and took a series of commands within Britain and the Channel Islands. He was promoted to lieutenant general in 1801 and appointed lieutenant governor of Gibraltar in 1806.[42] Historian Michael Glover, in his history of the campaign and subsequent convention, *Britannia Sickens*, points out that whilst Dalrymple's army career may have spanned 45 years, only one of those had been on active service. However, he was already on the spot, and the alternative commanders were similarly inexperienced with less local knowledge.[43] While Dalrymple's actions at Gibraltar since the start of the uprisings in Spain had won the government's and the King's approval, not all of Dalrymple's activities to date had met with their approbation. On 26 June, Charles Stewart at the War Office had to write to him to ask for an explanation as to how reports of his communications with Castaños had appeared in the British papers.[44]

Glover claims that Canning did not want command falling on Moore if anything happened to Dalrymple. In his book, he analyses the potential pool of choices for the second in command, given that they had to be senior to Moore but junior to Dalrymple. There were 74 officers in the

---

38   TNA: WO 1/228: Statement of troops, annexed to Castlereagh's letter on 15 July.
39   TNA: WO 6/185: Castlereagh to Dalrymple, 15 July 1808.
40   NAM: 1994-03-129-83: Dalrymple, statement of service.
41   Officers in the Guards had dual ranks; one in the regiment and a more senior one in the army.
42   S. Wood, 'Dalrymple, Sir Hew Whitefoord, first baronet', *ODNB*, <https://doi.org/10.1093/ref:odnb/7049>, accessed October 2022.
43   Glover, *Sickens*, p.60.
44   TNA: WO 1/418: Stewart to Dalrymple, 26 June 1808.

Army List between the two men; 12 were ineligible as they were Royal Marine or ordnance officers, two more were foreign, two were senior government ministers (Richmond was Lord Lieutenant of Ireland and Chatham had already turned down Dalrymple's job), three were in the colonies, another was on his way back from the West Indies and another in Vienna, and eight were serving too far from London to be readily available. These factors weeded out 29, and 14 were even older than Dalrymple. Of the 31 left, only one had seen active service recently, John Hely-Hutchinson, who was a Whig. Four others had been on half-pay since their regiments were disbanded after the American War. Sir Harry Burrard was in London, well-liked by York and friendly with Moore.[45]

Burrard was born in 1755 and entered the Royal Military Academy, Woolwich, as a cadet in 1768. He joined the Royal Artillery in 1772 but transferred to the 60th Foot in 1776, became a captain and served in America during the War of Independence. He became an MP through the interest of his family in 1780. He exchanged into the 1st Foot Guards as a captain-lieutenant and lieutenant colonel in 1789. He too, served with the Guards in Flanders in 1794/1795 and was promoted to colonel. In 1798, he was a major general and second in command of an expedition to destroy the locks of the Ostend–Bruges Canal. The mission was successful, but poor weather prevented the troops from being re-embarked, and they were captured. Burrard was exchanged six months later. In 1799, he commanded a brigade in the Helder expedition. In 1805, he was promoted to lieutenant general and was second in command to Lord Cathcart for the expedition to Copenhagen in 1807, gaining a baronetcy for his services.[46]

On 15 July, Castlereagh wrote to Wellesley that he had decided to increase the force 'to provide effectually for an attack upon the Tagus' and secondly, 'To have such an additional force disposable beyond what may be indispensably necessary for such an operation, as may admit of a detachment being made to the southward, and there with a view to secure Cadiz if it should be threatened by the French Force under General Dupont.'[47] Castlereagh did not know that Dupont had already been defeated, but the plan was for the force to be split into two, with Dalrymple commanding the whole. Dalrymple had already assured the junta in Andalusia that 10,000 British troops would be available to cooperate with the Spanish in the south. However, an attack on the Tagus was still to be the priority and the exact division of the 30,000 troops between Portugal and Andalusia, and when it occurred, would be decided by Dalrymple as circumstances dictated. If Cadiz was threatened, its defence was to be seen as another priority. In a private letter written the same day, Castlereagh told Wellesley:

> I have made every effort to keep in your hands the greatest number of men, and for the longest time that circumstances would permit. I shall rejoice if it shall have fallen to your lot to place the Tagus in our hands: if not, I have no fear that you will find many opportunities of doing yourself honour and your country service.
>
> Sir Hew Dalrymple will put you in possession of the steps I have deemed it my public duty to take, to secure to the service the most extensive and beneficial exercise of your exertions.[48]

---

45   Glover, *Sickens*, pp.64–65.
46   A.W. Massie, 'Burrard, Sir Harry, first baronet', *ODNB*, <https://doi.org/10.1093/ref:odnb/4098>, accessed October 2022.
47   TNA: WO 6/185: Castlereagh to Wellesley, 15 July 1808.
48   Vane (ed.), *Correspondence*, vol.VI, p.385.

It was Castlereagh's intention that Dalrymple's command was to be supervisory. On 14 July, he had written to the King:

> With respect to the arrangement of the command, upon conference with his Royal Highness the Commander-in-Chief, it is humbly submitted to your Majesty, as it is probable that the force may act in two separate corps, whether the superintending command might not be advantageously continued in Lt.-Genl. Sir Hew Dalrymple, who might be directed to leave the garrison of Gibraltar in charge of M. Genl. Drummond and to repair himself either to Lisbon or Cadiz as the service might require, taking upon himself the command of the whole force, and distributing it according as circumstances should point out, as most for the advantage of the common cause.
>
> The favorable opinion your Majesty has been pleased to express of the Lt. General's judgment and conduct under the trying circumstances in which he has latterly been placed-the knowledge he must possess of the views and characters of those who are now at the head of affairs in Spain, and the degree in which he appears to have conciliated and to possess their confidence are considerations which have induced your Majesty's confidential servants to be of opinion that upon the whole your Majesty's views cannot be more advantageously promoted under present circumstances than by continuing the command in Sir H. Dalrymple, with Lt. Genl. Sir H. Burrard second in command. The station these officers hold in your Majesty's service will admit of the most active and distinguished young officers being brought forward under them, which will give your Majesty the benefit of their enterprize and ability without departing from that attention to standing in the service which your Majesty was pleased to signify your commands should be attended to in any arrangement that was to be submitted for your Majesty's approbation.[49]

Of course, the distinguished young officer that Castlereagh was most concerned about was Wellesley, but the government envisaged one corps under him and one under Moore acting semi-independently; one in Portugal and one in southern Spain. The King replied that he was 'satisfied that Sir Hew Dalrymple, from his experience & knowledge of the Spaniards, will prove well calculated for the general direction of affairs, while he cannot have a more zealous and more steady second in command than Sir Harry Burrard.'[50]

Historians have hotly debated the choice of Dalrymple and Burrard. Rather unkindly, Michael Glover sums Burrard up as 'an amiable old buffer who could command a brigade provided that he was not expected to do anything too complicated. Everyone who knew him liked him but no one had a very high opinion of his mental equipment.'[51] Charles Oman hints at the closeness of Burrard to the Duke of York as the reason for his appointment but supports the logic of Dalrymple getting the command.[52] William Napier is typically more opinionated about the supersession of both Moore and Wellesley: 'Thus two men, comparatively unknown and unused to the command of armies, superseded the only generals in the British service whose talents and experience were indisputable.' He then said that 'envy, treachery, and base cunning' lay behind the decision.[53]

---

49   Aspinall (ed.), *Later Correspondence*, vol.V, pp.103–104.
50   Aspinall (ed.), *Later Correspondence*, vol.V, p.105.
51   Glover, *Sickens*, p.66.
52   Oman, *History*, vol. I, p.226.
53   Napier, *History*, vol.I, p.115.

Charles Esdaile claims that Dalrymple 'had greater first-hand knowledge of the Peninsula than anyone else in the British army' and that Burrard 'brought some useful qualities with him, even if it was only a talent for smoothing ruffled feathers.'[54]

The Duke of Cumberland firmly believed that his brother, the Duke of York, should have been given the command but claimed that the government was scared of the reaction they would get from the newspapers. Cumberland's second choice was General Lord Moira, who had served in the American War and in the Low Countries in the 1790s, but, in common with many senior officers, he had seen little recent active service.[55] Whoever was appointed also had to be acceptable to the King and the government and be available immediately, which ruled out experienced or talented officers serving aboard.

Sir John Moore, although senior to Wellesley, was still relatively junior. He was also not a favourite with the government. Moore noted in his diary that the cabinet had not liked how he had expressed himself in his dispatches from Sicily. He thought he had the support of Castlereagh and York but believed he had two or three enemies in the cabinet (one of whom was probably Canning).[56]

Moore's convoy from Sweden anchored in the Downs on Friday, 15 July, and the senior naval officer received orders to reprovision the ships immediately. Moore was ordered to London and arrived on Saturday evening. On Sunday, he saw Gordon, York's secretary, and learned his force was going to Spain or Portugal. Moore wrote in his diary:

> I understood from Gordon and from others that there had been much intriguing about the command. Ministers had done everything in their power to give it to Sir Arthur Wellesley; but he was so young a lieutenant-general that the Duke had objected to it, and, afraid of disgusting the army and the nation by such an appointment, they had given it up. Disappointed in their favourite object, they were determined it should not be given to me, and, to prevent the possibility of its falling to me, Sir Harry Burrard was named as second...[57]

Moore met with Castlereagh on Monday afternoon. The main topic of conversation was Sweden, and any role for Moore in the Peninsula was not mentioned. Castlereagh stated that some in the cabinet thought elements of the Swedish expedition had not been handled as well as they might, but, according to Moore, the conversation was polite. Moore's next visit was to the Duke of York, who seemed embarrassed that Castlereagh had said nothing about a command in the Peninsula. Late that night, Moore received a note that Castlereagh wanted to see him again at 3:00 p.m. the next day and to be prepared to leave London. At that meeting, Castlereagh told Moore of the situation in the Peninsula and that Dalrymple and Burrard were being placed over Wellesley. According to Moore:

> It was thus by inference only that I was to understand that I was to proceed on this service as a lieutenant-general under Sir Hew Dalrymple and Sir H. Burrard. This I thought a most extraordinary manner of behaving to me. I naturally expected when, returning from

54   Esdaile, *Peninsular*, p.96.
55   Aspinall (ed.), *Later Correspondence*, vol.V, p.111n.
56   Maurice (ed.), *Diary*, vol.II, pp.201–202.
57   Maurice (ed.), *Diary*, pp.239–240.

a command-in-chief, that if it was thought necessary to send me on with the troops I had thus commanded, in a far inferior station, that something by way of explanation or excuse would have been said to me, but it was evident from Lord Castlereagh's manner that he was ashamed of himself, and he never could bring himself to say plainly the station I was to hold.[58]

Moore then went on to say:

When, therefore, he seemed to have finished all he had to say, which was nearly what I have stated, I said to him: 'My Lord, the chaise is at my door, and upon leaving your Lordship's I shall set out for Portsmouth to join the troops with whom I perceive it is intended I should proceed as lieutenant-general. It may perhaps be my lot never to see you again. I, therefore, think it right to express to you my feeling of the unhandsome treatment I have received from you.' He said he was not sensible of the treatment to which I alluded. I therefore recapitulated all that had passed since my arrival in the Downs. 'Had I been an ensign it would hardly have been possible to treat me with less ceremony. It is only by inference at this moment that I know I am to be employed, for your Lordship has never told me in plain terms that I was appointed to serve with the army under Sir Hew Dalrymple as a lieutenant-general, and, coming from a chief command, if it was intended to employ me in an inferior station I was to expect that something would be said to me.'[59]

Moore then continued, at length, in a similar vein. Castlereagh said that he was 'not sensible' of giving Moore any reason to complain, and Moore then left abruptly. Castlereagh felt obliged to lay Moore's claims of ill-treatment before the King in a delicately worded letter that fell short of recommending that the King remove Moore from the command, but not by far. The King replied:

The King regrets very much that any unpleasant circumstances should have occurred between Lord Castlereagh and Sir John Moore, but as the latter has given an assurance that what has passed will not diminish his zeal in any service in which he may be employed, his Majesty cannot but approve the determination to which his Ministers have come not to suffer what is represented in Lord Castlereagh's letter to affect the military arrangements which had already been made.[60]

On 22 July, when Moore was at Portsmouth, Castlereagh wrote to him:

I think it right that you should not leave England without hearing from me that I have communicated to the King's Ministers (as I felt it my duty, and conceived it to be your purpose that I should do) the complaint which you made to me in our last interview, of 'unhandsome and unworthy treatment' received by you on the part of the King's Government, and on mine, in the mode of carrying their measures into effect.

58   Maurice (ed.), *Diary*, p.242.
59   Maurice (ed.), *Diary*, p.242.
60   Aspinall (ed.), *Later Correspondence*, vol.V, p.109.

At the same time, that this complaint is felt by them, as it is by me, to be unfounded, I have to assure you that had not the arrangements of the army been so far advanced as that they could not be undone without considerable detriment to his Majesty's service, there would have been every disposition on their part humbly to have advised his Majesty to relieve you from a situation in which you appeared to consider yourself to have been placed without a due attention to your feeling as an officer.[61]

Moore took this, not perhaps without cause, to be an effort to get him to write a terse reply which would give the government an excuse to recall him. However, Moore restrained himself, wrote a polite response, and sailed. Esdaile characterises Moore as 'Opinionated, vain and highly strung' and 'much given to intrigue and complaint', some of which is perhaps borne out by the above exchanges.[62] However, Wellesley respected Moore and had recommended him to Castlereagh in April.[63]

Castlereagh went to some pains to ensure Wellesley had a chance to distinguish himself in Portugal. In his letter informing Wellesley of Dalrymple's appointment, he said that Wellesley should continue to carry out his original instructions 'with every expedition that circumstances will permit without awaiting the arrival of the Lieut. General.'[64] He also sent a second private letter to Dalrymple, which he opened by again congratulating him on his new command and the way he had performed his duties in Gibraltar since the revolts in Spain had begun, but then continued:

Permit me to recommend to your particular confidence Lieutenant General Sir Arthur Wellesley. His high reputation in the service, as an officer would, in itself, dispose you, I am persuaded, to select him for any service that required great prudence & temper combined with much military experience.

The degree, however, to which he had been for a length of time past in the closest habits of communication with His Majesty's ministers, with respect to the affairs of Spain, having been destined to command any operation that circumstances might render necessary for counteracting the views of France against the Spanish Dominions in South America, will, I am sure, point him out to you as an officer of whom it is desirable on all occasions to make the most prominent use that the rules of the service will permit.[65]

In his memoir, Dalrymple wrote of this letter and his orders:

Under all the circumstances of the case, I think it can scarcely be wondered at, that I received these communications with, at least, as much surprise as satisfaction. This ebb and flow of approbation and confidence was not satisfactory; and something seemed to lurk under this most complicated arrangement, which bore, I thought, a most unpromising aspect. But I was at a distance from Government; had no means of stating difficulties, or of receiving explanations or advice; and could, therefore, only hasten, as far as circumstances would allow, to obey His Majesty's commands, by repairing to Portugal,

61   Maurice (ed.), *Diary*, p.251.
62   Esdaile, *Peninsular*, p.95.
63   Vane (ed.), *Correspondence*, vol.VI, pp.230–231.
64   TNA: WO 1/228: Castlereagh to Wellesley, 15 July 1808.
65   TNA: WO 6/185: Castlereagh to Dalrymple, 15 July 1808, private & confidential.

there to assume, 'for the present,' the command of an army already in the field, and actually engaged in active operations against the enemy.[66]

Dalrymple's displeasure at the wording of Castlereagh's letter seems to have lasted some time. In September, Brigadier General Anstruther noted in his journal that Dalrymple had shown him 'a very private letter desiring that Wellesley might be employed and trusted as much as possible. Sir H very indignant at this.'[67]

Wellesley's secretary, Henry Torrens, who had not known Wellesley long, wrote of the coming change of command: 'I shall be sorry for this on so many accounts; but it is naturally to be expected as he is so young a Lieut. Gen. I must say that I never met a man more completely au fait in all the details of command than Sir Arthur Wellesley.'[68] In a private letter to Castlereagh, Wellesley wrote:

[Wellesley-]Pole and Burghersh have apprised me of the arrangements for the future command of this army; and the former has informed me of your kindness towards me, of which I have experienced so many instances, that I can never doubt it in any case. All that I can say upon that subject is, that whether I am to command the army or not, or am to quit it, I shall do my best to insure its success; and you may depend upon it that I shall not hurry the operations, or commence them one moment sooner than they ought to be commenced, in order that I may acquire the credit of the success.[69]

Wellesley was a little franker in his letter to Richmond, placing the blame for his supersession on Spencer's report of the French numbers in Portugal:

He sent this same account to England, where they took the alarm, and ordered out 5,000 men and Moore's corps of 10,000 men, with several general officers, senior to me, and Sir Hew Dalrymple to command the whole army. I hope that I shall have beat Junot before any of them shall arrive, and then they [the government] will do as they please with me.[70]

The news that Wellesley also found waiting for him when he returned to the convoy that Dupont had been defeated at Bailén convinced him that Spencer would have no reason to remain at Cadiz and would soon join him. He was also informed that the reinforcements under Brigadier Generals Anstruther and Acland had been due to sail from Harwich and the Downs on the 19th and could be expected any day. Wellesley also learned that Loison had been sent to quell the rising in the Alentejo, and so, as he later stated 'I therefore considered that I might commence the disembarkation of the Troops without risk of their being attacked by superior numbers before one or both the Reinforcements should arrive.'[71] Landing his troops before reinforcements arrived would also give the Portuguese renewed confidence and more time for his men to acclimatise and for the army to get organised. It would also increase the chances of him being able to advance and bring the French to battle before Dalrymple or Burrard turned up.

66 Dalrymple, *Memoir*, p.52.
67 StAUL: msdep121/8/2/3/4/4: Anstruther's journal, p.51.
68 BL: Add MS 49485: Torrens to Gordon, 1 August 1808.
69 Gurwood (ed.), *Wellington's Dispatches*, vol.IV, p.55.
70 Wellington (ed.), *Supplementary Despatches*, vol.VI, p.95.
71 TNA: WO 1/415: Wellesley's narrative.

Landing

On 1 August, Malcolm wrote in his log that in the morning, the *Donegal* 'sent all the boats to disembark the troops, stores &c.'.[72] There were two landing places, one at Figueira across the bar in the Mondego and the other on the beach at Buarcos, a village just north of Figueiras.[73] Troops landing at Buarcos had to be ferried across the river to the southern bank.

Looking north towards Buarcos from the breakwater at the mouth of the Mondego. Even on a fine day in April, there were warnings advising against swimming because of the surf and currents. (Author's photo)

Waiting to disembark on the transports anchored in the bay was uncomfortable for the troops. With nothing between Portugal and America, the Atlantic swell can be very high when it reaches the coast. Nazaré, 50 miles down the coast, is now famous for its record-breaking surfing. Captain Jonathan Leach (95th Rifles) recalled, 'The long and heavy swell made the yards of the ship at times almost touch the water, as she rolled from side to side, which caused some awful breakages amongst our wine-glasses and crockery-ware.'[74] Captain Fletcher Wilkie (38th Foot) wrote the swell caused the ships 'to roll so heavily, that it was a matter of great difficulty either to get on board or to leave them. I have been on board a light transport in a heavy gale of wind, but the rolling was

---

72 TNA: ADM 51/1880: Entry for 1 August 1808.
73 'Tim Weatherside', Letter to the Editor, *The Naval Chronicle*, vol.20, p.304.
74 Leach, *Sketches*, p.41.

not to my recollection near so heavy as that the ships were undergoing in Mondego Bay in a perfect calm.'[75] Henry Torrens wrote:

> It is impossible to describe anything more tremendous than the surf along this coast: it would be absolutely impracticable to land here in the face of an enemy; a country cannot have a better defence. Our debarkation commenced this morning; we could only get one brigade on shore the whole day – nor will it be completed until the day after tomorrow.[76]

The transports themselves did not have enough crew to man boats, so either Royal Navy or local boats rowed the troops ashore. The assistance of the local fishermen, familiar with the conditions, became vital to the disembarkation.

The regiments landed on the first day were the 1/36th and 1/45th Foot and the 5/60th and 2/95th Rifles. Ensign Roderick Murchison of the 36th Foot, 16 years old and a graduate of the Royal Military College, in a letter written soon afterwards, told his uncle that he had 'disembarked on the south side of the river Mondego, under General Fane, exactly opposite the town of Figuiera. The troops passed the bar of the river chiefly in small schooners which trade along the coast, and also in Portuguese boats.'[77] Writing of the same event 46 years later, he was more expansive and perhaps more creative:

> Early on the 1st of August, the 36th, forming part of the first brigade, disembarked with the 60th Rifles and other regiments under General Fane. Fortunately it was a fine calm hot day, with little or no surf on the sterile and uninhabited shore, with its wide beach and hillocks of blown sand. The inhabitants of Figuiera, on the opposite bank of the river, stood under their variously-coloured umbrellas, and my boat being to the extreme left, I could scan the motley group, in which monks and women predominated. Just as I was gazing around, and as our boat touched the sand, the Commodore's barge rapidly passed with our bright eyed little General. Perhaps I am the only person now (1854) living, who saw the future Wellington place for the first time his foot on Lusitania, followed by his aide-de camp, Fitzroy Somerset, afterwards Lord Raglan. He certainly was not twenty paces from me, and the cheerful confident expression of his countenance at that moment has ever remained impressed on my mind.[78]

Wellesley had already stepped ashore at Oporto. Leach recalled the reception the troops received:

> Whilst we were drawing up our men near the landing-place, and waiting for further orders, we were beset with a host of padres, friars, and monks, of all ages, each carrying a huge umbrella of the most gaudy colour imaginable; intended, no doubt, to protect their complexions, which vied with those of chimney sweeps. These gentry welcomed us with vivas, and protested that, with our assistance, every Frenchman in Portugal should speedily be annihilated. Our visitors were not confined to the male sex; for some olive

---

75   Fletcher Wilkie, 'Recollections from the Peninsula', *United Service Journal*, November 1843, p.422.
76   BL: Add MS 49485: Torrens to Gordon, 1 August 1808.
77   A. Geikie, *Life of Sir Roderick I. Murchison* (London: Murray, 1875), vol.I, p.27.
78   Geikie, *Life*, vol.I, p.25.

beauties, with sparkling eyes and jet black hair, were induced to take a peep at us; and, before we parted, some of the more favoured of us were presented with flowers and fruit from the hands of these damsels.[79]

Once ashore, the troops marched south through ankle-deep hot sand to the village of Lavos, a distance of about four miles. With the sweltering temperatures and the fact that the men had been onboard the transports for weeks, the march proved taxing for many. Murchison described the march in a letter:

> The brigade being formed was then marched in open columns along the coast, chiefly through very heavy sands, about two leagues, and encamped near the village of Lavaos, where Sir Arthur established head-quarters for the night. As by his orders two shirts and two pair of stockings and a great-coat were to compose the whole of the baggage of officers and soldiers, and that not such a thing as a donkey or any other animal was procurable, our whole kit, including three days' provisions, was on our backs, which, with a brace of pistols and the 36th regimental colours, loaded me absolutely to the utmost of my strength. Even our old Colonel was compelled to tramp through the sands this day, which he did with the greatest alacrity.[80]

Private John Macfarlane of the 71st Highlanders commented: 'The sun was very hot, the sand was deep, the water we had with us was warm, and we could not drink it.'[81] Another of the Highlanders claims four of the 71st died of thirst on the march.[82]

On the 1st, while the landings were beginning, Wellesley wrote to Castlereagh from the *Donegal*:

> The information of the state of the enemy's force in Portugal, communicated to me by General Spencer, (which, however exaggerated the accounts he had received may be, deserve attention,) & the expectation held out by your Lordship, that a reinforcement would arrive here at an early period, have necessarily induced me to delay the commencement of the operations of the troops under my command till the arrival of the corps from England or of General Spencer.

In a private letter to Castlereagh on the same day, he was more explicit in discounting Spencer's estimate of the French strength, writing: 'I have reason to believe General Spencer's account of the French force in Portugal is exaggerated.'[83] In his dispatch, he continued to outline his plans:

> I shall consider the possession of the harbour & city of Lisbon as the immediate object of our operations, which must be attained by that of the forts by which the entrance of the Tagus is guarded. It is probable that it will be necessary to attack two of these forts,

---

79   Leach, *Sketches*, p.42.
80   Geikie, *Life*, vol.I, p.27.
81   E. Robson, 'Peninsular Private', *Journal of the Society for Army Historical Research*, vol.32, no.129 (Spring,1954), p.5.
82   Anon. *Journal of a Soldier of the Seventy-First* (Edinburgh: Tait, 1819), pp.52–53.
83   Gurwood (ed.), *Wellington's Dispatches*, vol.IV, p.55.

Cascaes and St. Julian, with heavy ordnance; & it is obvious that the enemy will not allow us to undertake those operations till he will have been driven from the field.

The positions which he would take for the defence of these posts must be all turned from the heights to the northward of Lisbon, and, indeed, unless prevented by our possession of these heights, the enemy would have it in his power to renew the contest in different positions, until he should be driven into Lisbon or retire. The last will be rendered difficult, if not impossible, excepting in boats across the Tagus, by the adoption of the line of attack by the heights to the northward, which I also prefer, as being more likely to bring the contest to the issue of a battle in the field.[84]

As the landing was proving difficult because of the surf, he expected that he would not have finished disembarking his troops before Spencer or reinforcements from Britain arrived. He would start his march towards Lisbon once either came.

Torrens wrote to Gordon on the same day, the 1st, and said that the available intelligence put the French strength at 15–18,000 near Lisbon, but that accounts varied too much to be certain, 'But although a regular return we have seen of their army makes at Lisbon 18,500 men, it is generally believed that they do not much exceed 15,000.' Where this 'regular return' had come from and why it was discounted, he does not say. Torrens continued:

We have no organised force of the Portuguese that any dependence can be placed upon except about 5000 men to whom Sir Arthur has issued arms: Thus our success cannot be calculated upon against a strong army established in the country, without a reinforcement or a junction with Gen. Spencer's Corps.[85]

The remaining regiments from Cork continued to land on 2 August. Private James Hale (9th Foot) recalled in his memoir:

We remained on board until the 2d of August, and soon after sun rise, that morning, a signal was made to disembark: therefore, as soon as we were supplied with three day's provision, which was done without delay, we proceeded towards the shore. When the Portuguese understood that we were their protectors, they came flocking down on the beach in droves; and there being no convenience for landing, without getting into the water, the Portuguese men came running into the water, above their knees, to carry us out of the boats; and what made it still more pleasing to us, the young women came flocking around us, with their aprons full of fruit; some with oranges, some with grapes, and some with figs, &c. crying, 'Veavo, Veavo, Englees' that is, 'Long live the English.' It being so warm in that country, at that time of the year, the men had not much trouble in taking off their clothes to carry us out of the boats.[86]

Quartermaster Sergeant William Gavin of the 71st Highlanders was sent ashore by Lieutenant Colonel Pack to purchase mules for the regiment. He was rowed to the shore in a Portuguese boat:

---

84   TNA: WO 1/228: Wellesley to Castlereagh, 1 August 1808.
85   BL: Add MS 49485: Torrens to Gordon, 1 August 1808.
86   Hale, *Journal*, pp.14–15.

The surf is so great in this bay that the natives can with difficulty weather it. Wave succeeded wave, mountains high, and when it approaches the boat the crew abandon their oars and threw themselves flat in the bottom of the boat, invoking the Blessed Virgin and all the saints in the calendar. After a complete ducking and a terrible fright we got on shore, but found all horses and mules taken off by the French army.[87]

If the landings were frightening for the men they would also have been for the horses, but most seem to have landed in the river's calmer waters. On 30 July, Lieutenant Colonel William Robe, commanding the expedition's artillery, wrote that 'the Horse ships are ordered into the harbour preparatory to Disembarkation'.[88] Sergeant Norbertus Landsheit of the 20th Light Dragoons, a German from Krefeld, describes landing:

We were directed to stand upright in the boats, with bridle in hand, and prepared, in case of any accident, to spring into the saddle; a judicious precaution, which proved in two or three instances eminently useful. One punt capsized upon the surf, but no lives were lost, because the horses sometimes swimming, sometimes wading, carried their riders ashore.[89]

One Royal Navy officer, on his return to Britain, wrote a letter to the Editor of *The Naval Chronicle* about the landings:

On my return from a long cruise, I went, as is my custom, to a grog-shop, and asked for a file of papers, to see what the black and white gentlemen had said of our late exertions; and in the Gazette letter, September 3, as they call it, I read that 'the difficulties of landing the provisions of the army were in great part done away by the zeal, activity, and intelligence of Captain Malcolm, of his majesty's ship Donegal.' I do not pretend to be quite exact as to the printed words, but nearly so: and your readers may refer to them. Now, Mr. Editor, I'll tell you what the noble captain of the Donegal did; for I am certain, from the modesty of his character, it will never otherwise be made known. Captain Malcolm was senior at Figueras, in a small squadron, consisting of his own ship, Donegal, Resistance, Captain Adams, and Crocodile, Captain Cadogan. I need not tell you, Mr. Editor, that Captain Malcolm had charge of full 75 sail of transports, which had sailed with troops from Cork, under Sir Arthur Wellesley; God bless him! Well, on making the Portuguese coast, the ships came to anchor in Mondego bay; and on the fifth day began landing. Sir Arthur had in the mean time gone off Lisbon to Sir Charles Cotton for intelligence. There were two landing places, one at Buarcos, and the other at Figueras. Captain Malcolm, finding a heavy surf breaking both on Figueras bar and the beach at Buarcos, immediately set the example to his men of jumping from the boat into the sea, and carrying the men and their canteens, &c. to the shore. Their officers and men immediately followed so noble

---

87   G. Glover, (ed.), *The Napoleonic Archive: Volume 1: British Line Infantry Memoirs* (Godmanchester: Trotman, 2021), p.159.

88   TNA: WO 55/1193: Robe to Macleod, 30 July 1808.

89   G. Gleig, *The Hussar* (London: Henry Colburn, 1837), vol.I, p.248. It should be noted that Landsheit's was one of several 'memoirs' that Gleig published, and even his own account of his service in the 85th is now seen as partially fictionalised.

The landing of the British Army at Mondego Bay, 1808, by Henri L'Eveque. (Anne S.K. Brown Military Collection)

an example; and they all continued on this arduous service for several days and nights. Frequently owing to the surf from the N.W. swell, they were unable to return to their ships, and remained during the night in their wet clothes on the ground.[90]

Many witnesses to the landings at Figueira and Buarcos say no lives were lost, including Murchison and Leach. Warre wrote that 'the whole army landed without any loss but a horse or two'.[91] However, some memoirists do say there were some casualties amongst the troops. Hale says in his memoir that a boat of the 45th Foot was overturned crossing the bar, and several soldiers and seamen were drowned.[92] Landsheit also mentions that there were some casualties, but not many.[93] The writer of the letter to *The Naval Chronicle* says, 'I should think that at the three landing places boats were stove which must have cost our government nearly 2,000l. Many sailors' lives were also lost, owing to the surf…' but he is talking also of the two landings that came later.[94] Malcolm estimated that 20 boats were lost during the landings further south near Vimeiro and that six or seven men of the Royal Artillery and King's German Legion were drowned, but he mentions no losses at Mondego Bay.[95] On the 3rd, Malcolm noted in his log, 'at 4 sent all the boats to assist disembarking the last brigade & the commander in chief left the ship.'[96] Wellesley travelled to Lavos to set up his headquarters and wait for Spencer or other reinforcements.

---

90   Letter to the Editor, p.304.
91   Warre, *Letters*, p.22.
92   Hale, *Journal*, p.15.
93   Gleig, *Hussar*, p.248.
94   Letter to the Editor, p.305.
95   Anon. (ed.), *Proceedings*, p.36.
96   TNA: ADM 51/1880: Entry for 3 August 1808.

Every Exertion in My Power

Spencer arrived off the Tagus on 2 August and briefly met with Cotton before proceeding to Figueira in the *Nautilus* sloop, leaving the transports under the charge of *Bulwark* and *Lively*.[97] He arrived at Mondego Bay on the 4th while the artillery and stores from Cork were still being landed. The transports arrived over the subsequent days, and all the troops were landed by the 8th.[98] After the return of the gunners and guns from Gibraltar, Spencer's force stood at 4,314 rank and file, plus 71 of his original artillerymen and drivers.[99] On 6 August, with the newcomers expected at the Lavos camp, the 71st, 36th, 40th, 91st, and 45th Foot were ordered to move out of their tents so Spencer's men could have them. The regiments that moved out were issued billhooks to cut down trees and bushes to make huts.[100]

Sergeant Joseph Martin of the 29th Foot was one of the men who arrived with Spencer's convoy:

> This was on Saturday, the 6th of August. When our commanding officer went on board the agent ship, for the necessary instructions, he was informed of this [Wellesley's] expedition having landed, and we received orders for landing the next morning at four o'clock, which was attended to with the greatest precision. It was under a thousand disadvantages that we made our landing good. Notwithstanding the enemy was not there to receive us, we had to encounter as formidable a foe a tremendous swell on the water, which endangered our boats; a surf running on the beach, which terrified the best of mariners. One or more of our boats was upset, but providentially no lives were lost. Had it not been for the timely assistance of the Portuguese with their life-boat, some of us must inevitably have perished; but as soon as we landed we commenced our march, in expectation of meeting with the enemy.[101]

Captain Harry Ross-Lewin recalled in his memoir that there was a rock that broke up the waves, and many boats tried to land at that point; he also remembered the assistance of the Portuguese:

> They swam about the boats, diving under the heavier waves, and reappearing in the hollow of the sea, ready to pick up any soldiers whose boats might be swamped. According as the flat boats reached the rock, the Portuguese placed our men across their shoulders, and carried them, their arms, ammunition, and three days' provisions in perfect safety to the shore. No people could have behaved better, and very few would have behaved so well.[102]

Lieutenant Charles Leslie, also of the 29th, wrote in his memoir:

> All was now bustle on board. Animation shone in every countenance. Our anxious hopes of being employed in active service were now about to be realised. Everyone was employed in selecting the few articles requisite for a campaign, and getting their heavy baggage

---

97   TNA: ADM 1/340: Cotton to Pole, 3 August 1808.
98   TNA: ADM 51/1880: Log entries, 4–8 August 1808.
99   Anon., *Proceedings*, p.31.
100 Wellington (ed.), *Supplementary Despatches*, vol.VI, p100.
101 J. Martin, Letter, 22 October 1808, *The Naval Chronicle*, vol.20, p.443.
102 Ross-Lewin, *Life*, vol.I, p.207.

properly secured. This was effected with no small trouble. A tremendous swell caused the ship to roll in the most violent manner, and everything was slipping and flying about. We got into flat boats soon after midday, but the process of disembarkation became a tedious and dangerous operation. Owing to the swell and dreadful surf, only a few boats could approach the beach, where Portuguese fishermen were employed in wading to meet them and conduct them to the shore. During this we had to remain for hours tossing and rolling, about till our time came. Several boats were upset, and one containing a part of our Grenadiers lost arms and everything, and the men narrowly escaped with their lives. It was late when we reached the army encamped on the heights above the small town of Lavos. It was so dark that we had some difficulty in finding our tents; and in regard to food, nothing whatever could be got, so we had to content ourselves with a morsel of ship biscuit and a glass of rum from our haversacks. We then wrapped ourselves in our cloaks, and lay down on the benty [coarse, withered] grass, eagerly seeking repose after our fatigues. Vain hope! The orderly sergeant disturbed our incipient slumbers by warning us that the army was to be under arms at two o'clock in the morning.[103]

Lieutenant George Wood of the 82nd Foot did not even get to rest after a tiring march through the sand from the beach; he was:

… placed on the quarter-guard, stationed on the top of a hill which commanded an extensive view of all approach to the camp. Here was my couch for the night – a great contrast to the snug warn berth I had been used to on my marine excursion: indeed, I now began to wish I had made choice of the Navy for my profession, from its greater apparent advantages.

Unfortunately for the officers of Spencer's corps, the local supply of mules had already been exhausted, so they could not get any animals for their baggage.[104] Wood reflected on the loads that both soldiers and officers had to carry from the bay:

… the men are of course more burdened, but then they are from infancy more inured to hardships and proportionably better able to bear the inclemency of the weather, and the fatigues and privations incident to war, than those who are nursed in the lap of luxury, which, unfortunately for me, had been my lot in the early part of my life; and I had been rendered almost too delicate for this hardy service, by the over-anxiety and care of too fond a mother.[105]

Cotton continued to receive intelligence and forward it both to London and Wellesley. A letter dated 5 August and written by 'A friend to the English – Portuguese Patriot' related the Portuguese defeat at Evora (which was blamed on a traitor wetting the gun powder), *général de division* Loison's subsequent movements, and troops marching northwards from Lisbon.[106] Cotton also passed on

---

103 Leslie, *Journal*, pp.31–32.
104 H. Everard, *History of Thomas Farrington's Regiment, subsequently designated the 29th (Worcestershire) Foot* (Worcester: Littlebury, 1891), p.274.
105 G. Wood, *The Subaltern Officer* (London: Prowett, 1825), pp.48–49.
106 TNA: ADM 1/340: Lisbon, 5 August 1808.

intelligence from a Dr Powell, who came onboard the *Hibernia* on the evening of the 5th and claimed the city was in great confusion and stated:

> The French force detached under General Loison to the Southward of which 1200 cavalry certainly formed a part has been severely handled, and their being able to return to Lisbon, is doubtful – he says, after such detachment there was not more than 7,000 troops remaining in Lisbon, – 3,000 of which have proceeded to the northward to Obeda [Óbidos, possibly], between Leria and the coast, a little to the southward of Peniche.[107]

Cotton stated that Powell, who had been aboard the *Hibernia* before, claimed to be a friend to one of Junot's secretaries, and that his intelligence had previously 'proved tolerably correct'. Sadly, it was not entirely so on this occasion as Loison, far from being severely handled, had been brutally successful at Evora, but his information on French troop numbers seems broadly correct.

With his men disembarked, Spencer took the opportunity of his last dispatch to Castlereagh to praise the exemplary conduct of the troops, especially given how long they were confined to their ships, the good conduct of the officers and his staff, and the excellent discipline of the regiments. He ended his letter with: 'That they will merit the notice of the judicious commander who now commands us, whose discrimination will shortly confirm all I have said of them; nor shall my endeavours be wanting to meet his wishes by every exertion in my power.'[108]

After disembarking their men or cargo, most transports sailed north to shelter at Oporto. The *Donegal* and the *Resistance* remained off Figueira with some transports whose draft would mean they could not cross the bar at Oporto and eight vessels whose stores might be needed.[109] The transports carrying the Royal Veteran Battalion sailed to the Tagus, where, with Royal Marines from the squadron, they could form a diversion as Wellesley approached Lisbon.

A Delightful Vale

Captain Eliot (Royal Artillery) described the camp at Lavos as 'On a heath surrounded by vineyards and Indian corn fields. The grapes altho' very fine, are scarcely ripe in many places.'[110] James Hale wrote, 'we encamped on a sort of a woody common, without tents or blankets; but every man had a watch coat, and there being such a quantity of myrtle bushes on our camp ground, we set to work, and gathered a parcel together, which made us a comfortable bed.'[111] Private Stephen Morley (5th Foot) was much more enthusiastic about the camp but less so about the local wine:

> Encamped in a delightful vale, and as soon as we had piled our arms, and cleaned the appointments, some peasants from the villages came in with bread, aye! and wine too! We thought that a soldier, with his pittance to be enabled to purchase patrician beverage was the ultimatum so long and ardently desired. The bread too! yellow, we naturally thought

---

107 TNA: ADM 1/340: Intelligence.
108 TNA: WO 1/226: Spencer to Castlereagh, 7 August 1808.
109 TNA: ADM 7/41: Cotton to Wellesley-Pole, 14 August 1808.
110 NAM: 1959-03-127: Eliot to Harriet Eliot, 7 August 1808.
111 Hale, *Journal*, p.16.

that eggs were plentiful. The wine however, turned out to be sour weak drink, and the bread was yellow, because made of Indian Corn. No matter! it was very good when new.[112]

While the brigades encamped on the heath, many of the staff were quartered in the village's houses, which quickly became overcrowded, so the latecomers of Spencer's force struggled to find lodgings.[113] William Warre, aide de camp to Major General Ferguson, wrote in a letter to his mother on 8 August:

General Ferguson's staff here occupy an old fellow's house, where we are comfortable enough, from Mrs Wm. Archer of Figueira's attention in sending us out everything we can want. Otherwise I know not what we should have done, as Figueira is 4½ miles off, and not a thing eatable or drinkable (besides the rations) nearer. We are up in the morning at 3 A.M., and, what with visiting the outposts, or line, and guards, 7 or 8 hours a day on horse or mule back, so that we are quite ready to lie down 3 in a small room (for which luxury we are not a little envied), at nine o'clock, and sleep as sound as on the finest down beds in the world, but for turning out now and then in the night, to interpret or some other trifle (from nobody speaking the language but me in the Brigade), which now consists of the 66th [sic], 40th, 71st Highlanders, all tried Regiments on service, and longing to meet these so much vaunted Frenchmen.[114]

The camp slowly grew as the brigades were landed and naturally became an attraction for the locals. Eliot continued, 'The better description of ladies come to the camp attended by their father confessor & servants mounted on mules with a kind of chair for a saddle on their backs they are dressed much in the stile of our great great grandmothers are represented, and are one shade lighter in complexion than the lower order.'[115] Several monks also came to the camp, and, while some visitors spoke French, Eliot had not met anyone who spoke English.

Castlereagh had told Wellesley:

There is every reason to believe, from the ardour of the inhabitants, both of Spain and Portugal, that so soon as a British army can establish itself on any part of the coast, not only numbers will be anxious to be armed and arrayed in support of the common cause but that every species of supply which the country produces for subsisting and equipping an army will be procurable.[116]

This was a very optimistic way to send an army to war, but the merchants of Coimbra sent 50,000 oranges, 5,000 lemons, 50 sheep, 12 calves, 500 fowls, 100 turkeys, and 50 pigs, plus cartloads of melons, peaches, vegetables, beans and 24 boxes of preserved fruits to help feed the army.[117] For

---

112 S. Morley, *Memoirs of a Serjeant of the 5th Regt. of Foot, Containing an Account of his Service in Hanover, South America, and the Peninsula* (Cambridge: Ken Trotman, 1999), p.44.
113 G. Landmann, *Recollections of My Military Life* (London: Hurst & Blackett, 1854), vol.II, pp.84–85. Landmann's memoir seems to have been embellished in parts, but it is still a useful source.
114 Warre, *Letters*, pp.23–24.
115 NAM: 1959-03-127: Eliot to Harriet Eliot, 7 August 1808.
116 TNA: WO 6/185: Castlereagh to Wellesley, 15 July 1808.
117 NAM: 1959-03-127: Eliot to Harriet Eliot, 7 August 1808.

Jonathan Leach, it was the noises made by some of the gifts from Coimbra that left the greatest impression on his memories of Lavos, 'the squeaking of pigs – the bleating of sheep – the various and discordant notes of geese, ducks, fowls, and turkeys – with the diabolical groaning of the carts, the wheels of which are never greased in Portugal, created such a concert of vocal and instrumental music, as no description could do justice to.'[118]

The Latin root of the Portuguese language helped relations between Wellesley's officers and the Portuguese population. One officer who served in the country noted:

> The Portuguese language is far from difficult, especially to one who has been tolerably grounded in the Latin, to which it has a great affinity, preserving many words yet uncorrupted. In conversation with the ecclesiastics of the better orders, the advantages of a classical education will be eminently conspicuous; and with the peasantry, where I have frequently been at a loss for the Portuguese word, I have coined one with a Latin derivation, which has generally answered my purpose.[119]

For the soldiers, many of whom would not have had any education, let alone a classical one, it must have been harder to make themselves understood but they probably got along with hand gestures and the age-old British habit of speaking loudly and slowly. This was the case for some of the officers as well. Harry Ross-Lewin recounted the tale of an officer who became known as 'Jack the interpreter' for his attempt at helping a commissary give some Portuguese muleteers their instructions. He told them, while pointing in the required direction, 'Portuguesios, the commissario – wants the mulos – to-morrowo – presto – la, la.'[120]

On 1 August, Wellesley wrote a memorandum to his Deputy Commissary General, James Pipon, outlining what the army would need to advance towards Lisbon. A supply of four days' worth of bread would have to be kept up at Lavos so the men could have that quantity with them when the order to march was given. The army on mules would carry a further three days' supply. For the 10,000 men, this would require 130 mules carrying 224 pounds each. Wellesley then wanted an additional 10 days' bread, five days' meat, and 10 days' spirits to be carried on carts, sourced locally, to form a depot. This would require 307 carts. The medical department would require another two carts. Another 250 mules would be needed to carry 2,000 rounds of musket ammunition each, and 30 mules would be necessary to carry the entrenching tools (but these were later put onto carts pulled by 12 mules).[121] These requirements would take time to gather from the resources of the region.

Wellesley issued another memorandum to Pipon on the 3rd that covered how the mules were to be organised into divisions, the rations for the muleteers and forage for the mules, the appointing of a muleteer *capataz* for each division of mules, and the provision of 100 mules and 150 carts to be held ready for any reinforcements. Hiring mules, carts, muleteers, and drivers must have been progressing well, as Wellesley also ordered that any above the numbers he specified should be discharged.[122] Lieutenant Colonel Browne's 'regulations and arrangements' for the mules provided by the junta in Oporto had set out much of the system that Wellesley adopted. The 500 mules

---

118 Leach, *Sketches*, p.43.
119 W.G. Eliot, *A Treatise on the Defence of Portugal* (London: Egerton, 1811), pp.116–117.
120 Ross-Lewin, *Life*, vol.I, p.230.
121 Gurwood (ed.), *Wellington's Dispatches*, vol.IV, pp.57–58.
122 Gurwood (ed.), *Wellington's Dispatches*, vol.IV, pp.59–60.

were to be divided into five divisions, with a commissary attached to each to secure supplies for the mules and drivers, pay any expenses, and keep accounts. A farrier with tools was also to be appointed for each division. The British would pay 300 Reales (1s 11¾d) per day for each mule, and for pairs of larger mules for pulling the artillery, the rate was 900 Reales (3s 11½d) per day. Each muleteer in charge of four mules (or two artillery mules) would be paid 240 Reales per day – slightly more than the 1s per day a private soldier earned.[123] The muleteers and bullock drivers would be provided one pound of bread and half a pound of meat per day, with the mules getting 10 pounds of straw, plus a quarter of an 'alquiler' of barley or corn, and a bullock a similar amount of straw or corn.[124] So, while solving many of Wellesley's logistical problems, the locally hired mules and bullocks would also mean many more mouths to feed.

On 4 August, Wellesley thanked Browne for his help procuring mules but then stated that the army still lacked the 150 needed to pull Spencer's artillery and asked, 'Are there no draft mules left in the country?' So, the limit of what could be supplied had possibly been reached. The Bishop of Oporto had provided a chaise and a cart for Wellesley's use.[125]

Whilst Wellesley's memoranda to Pipon may have contained the attention to logistical detail he would become famous for, the execution by Pipon and his staff was lacking: On the 8th, Wellesley wrote to Castlereagh:

> I have had the greatest difficulty in organizing my commissariat for the march, and that department is very incompetent, notwithstanding the arrangements which I made with Huskisson upon the subject. This department deserves your serious attention. The existence of the army depends upon it, and yet the people who manage it are incapable of managing anything out of a counting house.
>
> I shall be obliged to leave Spencer's guns behind for want of means of moving them; and I should have been obliged to leave my own, if it were not for the horses of the Irish Commissariat. Let nobody ever prevail upon you to send a corps to any part of Europe without horses to draw their guns. It is not true that horses lose their condition at sea.[126]

Henry Torrens was damming of Pipon's abilities: 'I am sorry to say that our Commissary General has no kind of arrangement. I really never saw a man more at a loss!'[127] To help Pipon, Wellesley assigned three officers to the commissariat department: Captain Nicolas Hamilton (5th Foot), Lieutenant Francis Nelson (40th Foot), and Cornet Henry Turton (6th Dragoons Guards).[128] Wellesley also wrote to the Bishop of Oporto to request that Mr Fernandez of Figueira, who had proved very useful in helping the army get supplies, accompany the army as it marched as a temporary commissary.[129]

Wellesley's frustration at his lack of transport is evident in a general order written on 8 August:

123 BL: Add Ms 49502: Browne's 'regulations and arrangements', 27 July 1808.
124 Wellington (ed.), *Supplementary Despatches*, vol.VI, p.97.
125 Gurwood (ed.), *Wellington's Dispatches*, vol.IV, pp.62–63.
126 Gurwood (ed.), *Wellington's Dispatches*, vol.IV, pp.72–73.
127 BL: Add MS 49485: Torrens to Gordon, 7 August 1808.
128 Wellington (ed.), *Supplementary Despatches*, vol.VI, p.102.
129 Wellington (ed.), *Supplementary Despatches*, vol.VI, p.104.

The Lieutenant-General is also under the necessity of drawing the attention of the officers of the army to an order twice issued to send to the Commissary's depot all carts and mules detained in camp. He now requests the General officers commanding brigades will send round the lines, and cause all carts, not absolutely hired by individuals, to be sent to the Commissary's depot in charge of a guard. As there are also several of the public mules detained in camp by officers, the Lieutenant-General hopes those who have them will send them back *forthwith*.

The practice of pressing carts and mules is positively forbid.[130]

It was on the same day, the 8th, that Wellesley ordered Captain Taggert to 'land as soon as possible with the detachment of the Irish Commissariat waggons under his command, and march forthwith to the village of Lavos, where he will report himself to the Deputy-Commissary-General.'[131] Presumably, Wellesley had not wanted to add to the numbers of men ashore and needing to be fed until the army was preparing to march and needed the drivers' services. In a letter to Burrard, Wellesley warned him of the lack of transport:

As for mules for carriage, I am afraid you will get none; for I believe my corps has swept the country, very handsomely, of this animal. You must therefore depend for the carriage of your bread upon the carts of the country, drawn by bullocks; each of these will carry about 600 lbs., and will travel in a day about twelve miles; but I do not believe that any power that you could exert over them, particularly when they shall have already made an exertion against the enemy, by the assistance which they have given to me, would induce the owners of the carts to go from their homes a greater distance than to the nearest place where you could get carts to relieve them.[132]

The local transport infrastructure was sufficient to suit the needs of the local people but not to meet the needs of an army of 10,000 men or more. The lack of mules and carts would severely hamper the efforts of the commissaries who accompanied the army, and it would become apparent that the commissaries themselves were not up to the challenges they faced.

The Commissariat came under the jurisdiction of the Treasury, not the War Office or Horse Guards. Its personnel were civilians who were responsible for the purchasing and distribution of food and forage. Previous forays onto the continent had been made in more economically and agriculturally developed areas, such as the Netherlands, that had better transport infrastructure and were closer to Britain. However, in his study of the Flanders campaign of the 1790s, Robin Thomas outlines several problems that the Commissariat encountered even there. The Commissary General at the Treasury was Brook Watson, who had been a commissary in both the Seven Years War and the War of American Independence, but he was sent to the army three weeks after the first troops had landed and struggled to make the necessary contracts with local suppliers. He also found it difficult to find experienced personnel with the required business, language and logistical skills. Supply issues continued in the following years as even in such a fertile area, it proved difficult to source enough provisions to feed a large force, and a lack of coordination between the commander,

---

130 Wellington (ed.), *Supplementary Despatches*, vol.VI, p.105.
131 Wellington (ed.), *Supplementary Despatches*, vol.VI, p.107.
132 TNA: WO 1/228: Wellesley to Burrard, 11 August 1808.

the Duke of York, and Watson often caused temporary shortages. With no army transport organisation, Watson had to rely on locally hired carts, and this proved to be highly problematic and led to the formation of the Corps of Royal Waggoners in 1794. Thomas does argue, however, that the problems the Commissariat faced and largely overcame in Flanders 'had been an undeniable proving-ground in the formation of the British Army's professional commissariat service.'[133] When the logistical chain broke down, it was often because of factors outside of the Commissariat's control. The men who had served under Watson went on to lead the commissariat departments of later campaigns, and one of them, Havilland Le Mesuruier, wrote *The British Commissary,* in which he set out 'the establishment of a plain, practical, and efficient system, founded upon actual experience.'[134]

James Pipon was born in Jersey in 1770. He began his career as a commissary in 1797 at Guildford and then moved to Rye before being assigned to Sir Ralph Abercromby's expedition to the Mediterranean in 1800. When the troops landed in Egypt early the following year, Pipon was placed in charge of the magazine formed at the landing beach. Following the Egyptian campaign, Pipon was posted to Minorca until it was returned to Spain under the Treaty of Amiens. Le Mesuruier, a fellow Channel Islander who had served with Pipon before, was in overall charge of the commissariat in the Mediterranean and wrote of Pipon, 'I wish to add that I am extremely happy to find the departments at Minorca under the management of an officer so well known to me, and in the arrangements of this army I shall take care to continue you in your present situation, being well persuaded of its being properly filled.'[135]

Once he returned to Britain, Pipon filled several posts before being assigned to Cathcart's expedition to Germany as deputy commissary general. The troops landed in North Germany, and Pipon had to face the problems of severe winter weather and a cash shortage, but wagons, draft horses and contractors willing to supply the army were all readily found. Pipon was, however, criticised by Sir Brook Watson, still Commissary General at the Treasury, for his arrangements for how contractors delivered directly to regiments rather than to magazines. However, the senior officers of the expedition supported Pipon's methods. After the expedition was abandoned in January 1806, Pipon spent almost two years in London sorting out the accounts until placed on half-pay in January 1808.[136]

Given his experience, it is curious that Pipon was deemed so far out of his depth in Portugal. Perhaps he had difficulty adapting to the local circumstances. When Pipon later requested a testimonial, Wellesley wrote that he had not been dissatisfied with 'his want of zeal, but his want of experience and ability to conduct the great concerns which he had undertaken.' And 'that the situation which he filled required other qualities which I could not say with truth that he possessed'.[137] The government had undoubtedly not learned the lessons of the Flander's campaign and had again sent an army aboard without adequate transport, which must have hampered Pipon's efforts from the start. The poor local road network and the fact that Portugal was not self-sufficient in food and relied on imports would have been contributing factors. Still, Wellesley's criticism seems to be based on how Pipon responded to these challenges.

---

133 Thomas, *Courage,* p.129.
134 H. Le Mesurier, *The British Commissary* (London: Egerton, 1801), p.3.
135 A.J.N. Young, 'James Pipon of Noirmont in the Commissariat', <https://www.theislandwiki.org/index.php/James_Pipon_of_Noirmont_in_the_Commissariat>, accessed February 2023.
136 Young, 'Pipon'.
137 Wellington (ed.), *Supplementary Despatches,* vol.VI, p.188.

On 8 August, Wellesley wrote a long letter to Sir Harry Burrard, who was expected with Moore's troops from Britain, updating him on the situation in the Peninsula, his reasons for ruling out landings closer to Lisbon, and his immediate plans. His estimates of the French force had not changed; the disposable force around Lison was, he thought, 14,000, of which 3,000 would have to be left in the city and forts. This meant he expected to face 11,000 if Junot marched north to meet him. Wellesley was aware that *général de brigade* Thomières had been sent north from Lisbon to monitor British movements and was at Alcobaça, just over 40 miles from Lavos. He told Burrard he would march to Alcobaça and Óbidos, check on the situation at Peniche, and then proceed to Lisbon via Mafra and the hills to the north of the city. As the troops from Harwich and Ramsgate under Acland were expected to arrive before Burrard, Wellesley had left word for him to sail south and fall in with Captain Bligh on the *Alfred,* who would be in communication with the troops onshore. If Wellesley felt Peniche needed to be captured, then Acland's troops would perform that task, and if not, they would proceed to the Tagus to land in one of the bays around the Rock of Lisbon once Wellesley himself was close enough to the city. However, he did say that had he thought that Acland's troops would have their own commissariat, he would have had them land at Figueira and march to Santarém, a distance of 90 miles, 'from which situation he would have been at hand either to assist my operations or to cut off the retreat of the enemy.' He then wrote, 'If, however, the command of the army remained in my hands, I should certainly land the corps which has been lately under the command of Sir John Moore at Mondego and should move it upon Santarem.'[138] Santarém lay on the Tagus and was 50 miles inland. Such a move would place Moore in an excellent position to cut off Junot's main line of retreat from Lisbon, but Wellesley did not offer an opinion on how Moore was to accomplish the march, even if he did have commissariat staff with him, given that Wellesley was already denuding the surrounding area of mules and carts. Brigadier General Anstruther was to travel some of the same ground in September and offered the opinion that had Moore marched there, 'the subsistence of the Army would have been difficult.'[139] As the army marched south, the *Alfred* and several transports would follow their movements down the coast and resupply the army as needed. The *Alfred*'s 24-pounders could also be landed if the army needed heavier guns. Wellesley gave Bligh a list of where he expected the army to be and when, and requested that he anchor at each point in case either supplies were needed or Wellesley needed to communicate.

Of course, Wellesley could have waited at Figueira for the reinforcements to join him, and then the combined army would have been assured of superiority of numbers over the French. But Wellesley did also feel a time constraint. Part of it was probably an eagerness to accomplish his orders before being superseded, but there was also concern over worsening sea conditions should operations be delayed. As he later stated:

> Adverting therefore to the advanced state of the season, the necessity of communicating with the Sea Coast, and the certainty that that communication would be nearly impracticable after the month of August, and to the still dispersed state of the French Forces in Portugal, I considered it to be important to endeavour to perform those operations to which the army was equal, and for which it was equal, and for which it was fully equipped and prepared, without loss of time.[140]

---

138 TNA: WO 1/228: Wellesley to Burrard, 8 August 1808.
139 StAUL: msdep121/8/2/3/4/4: Anstruther's journal, p.59.
140 TNA: WO 1/415: Wellesley's narrative, p.66.

Wellesley undoubtedly had many, often conflicting, intelligence sources to assess, but another was becoming available. Deserters were coming in from the French and must have had to travel some distance to reach the British camp. Sufficient numbers had arrived that Wellesley placed deputy assistant adjutant general Captain George Ralph Payne Jarvis (36th Foot) in charge of them and to arrange rations for them.[141] There may also have been an attempt at disinformation by the French. On 10 August, Cotton wrote to Wellesley that Dr Powell had returned to the *Hibernia*, this time seeking a passport to visit Wellesley, purportedly on behalf of Junot, to see if the British commander would receive a flag of truce. This was not a sign the French wanted to surrender but merely to talk. Cotton wrote, 'thinking some sinister motive wither to ascertain your numbers, positions or instructions, might influence his request I declined furnishing a passport but stated my opinion, that you would receive a flag of truce if an officer of rank, were sent with the usual formalities.' Dr Powell also told Cotton that Loison had not returned from the south and had suffered 3,000 casualties at Evora, which was false. But did also say that Loison was seeking to 'form a junction with the chief part of the French troops, now advanced 10 leagues to the northwest of Lisbon. Their exact position not known, but in number not more than 7000 men.'[142] This, at least, was closer to being accurate.

While preparations for the advance from Lavos continued, Major General Hill sat as president of a court martial of three men from the 5/60th Rifles at 8:00 a.m. on 8 August. The court sat in Major Arbuthnot's quarters near the headquarters and consisted of six field officers and six captains, with Captain Jarvis acting as deputy judge advocate.[143] Privates George Guentes, Francis Marschefsky and Christoph Lemke were tried for murder.[144] The trial papers have not survived, so it is not known who they murdered, but it seems likely that it was a local Portuguese. A newspaper report in September stated that locals had brought in three deserters from the battalion, and presumably, these were the same three men.[145] Guentes was acquitted, but Marschefsky and Lemke were found guilty and sentenced to hang. However, they were later pardoned by Wellesley 'in consequence of the general good conduct of the Corps to which they belong particularly on the 17 and 21 of August.'[146] Lemke was soon transferred to the 2/60th, but Wellesley ordered Marchefsky to be discharged and sent to serve in the fleet.[147] Commuting the sentences of courts martial was something his orders expressly forbade, as the power was reserved for the King.[148]

As the expedition advanced towards Lisbon, the continued support and goodwill of the local population would be vital for provisions and intelligence, so the troops needed to treat the locals with respect. Wellesley and Cotton had agreed upon a proclamation, written by the admiral, to be issued to the Portuguese people and which Wellesley arranged to be printed in Coimbra:

> The time is arrived to rescue your country, and restore the government of your lawful Prince.
>
> His Britannic Majesty, our most gracious King and master, has, in compliance with the wishes and ardent supplications for succour from all parts of Portugal, sent to your aid a British army, directed to co-operate with his fleet, already on your coast.

---

141 Wellington (ed.), *Supplementary Despatches*, vol.VI, p.98.
142 TNA: ADM 1/340: Cotton to Wellesley, 10 August 1808.
143 Wellington (ed.), *Supplementary Despatches*, vol.VI, p.102.
144 TNA: WO 90/1: Courts Martial Register, f.67.
145 *Saint James' Chronicle*, 8 September 1808.
146 TNA: WO 1/228: Jarvis to Rider, Judge Advocate General's Office, 4 September 1808
147 TNA: WO 12/7073: Muster book, 5/60th.
148 TNA: WO 72/29: York to Wellesley, 14 June 1808.

The English soldiers, who land upon your shore, do so with every sentiment of friendship, faith, and honor.

The glorious struggle in which you are engaged is for all that is dear to man the protection of your wives and children; the restoration of your lawful Prince; the independence, nay, the very existence of your kingdom; and for the preservation of your holy religion. Objects like these can only be obtained by distinguished examples of fortitude and constancy.

The noble struggle against the tyranny and usurpation of France will be jointly maintained by Portugal, Spain, and England; and in contributing to the success of a cause so just and glorious, the views of His Britannic Majesty are the same as those by which you are yourselves animated.[149]

A pressing question for Wellesley was what support he could actually expect from Portuguese troops. Writing to Burrard, he had said of the Portuguese: 'Their troops have been completely dispersed, their Officers had gone off to the Brazils, and their arsenals pillaged, or in the power of the enemy. Their revolt, under the circumstances in which it has taken place, is still more extraordinary than that of the Spanish nation.'[150] Lieutenant Colonel Trant was acting as a liaison between the British and Portuguese armies. Wellesley had sent Trant instructions that 5,000 stands of arms would be landed and, except for 500 that Cotton had promised to the deputies from Sines, would be given to the regular troops commanded by *Marechal de Campo* Freire. But Wellesley wanted to know how many troops he, in fact, had.[151] He did not know for sure that Freire was to cooperate with him and wrote to the Bishop of Oporto to find out but also told Trant to ask Freire not to advance until the British were ready.[152] Wellesley would have been happy to get 5,000 regulars and 2,000 irregulars from the Portuguese and told Trant on 3 August:

> I am decidedly of opinion that it is necessary to watch the enemy's movements from the northward, and upon the Douro, with the remainder of the Portuguese troops that can be collected; for I acknowledge that I give no credit to the truth of the reported second or third Spanish victories at Benavente.
>
> It is very evident from your account that the Portuguese are not accurately informed even of the first action which was fought, not on the 12th, but the 14th of July; and not at Benavente, to which town the Spanish troops retreated, but at Rio Seco.[153]

The Battle of Medina de Rioseco, 14 July 1808, was a Spanish defeat, and Wellesley had learned this at Corunna. Such errors must not have given him much confidence in Portuguese intelligence. Freire's orders from the Bishop in Oporto did tell him to cooperate with Wellesley:

> He determines that the aforesaid Marechal de Campo will combine his Military Operations with the General of the Troops of His Britannic Majesty, already landed in this Kingdom,

---

149   Gurwood (ed.), *Wellington's Dispatches*, vol.IV, pp.58–59.
150   Gurwood (ed.), *Wellington's Dispatches*, vol.IV, p.68.
151   Lambeth Palace Library: MS 3263: f.175 - Memorandum of Trant's Instructions from Sir A Wellesley at Figueira.
152   Gurwood (ed.), *Wellington's Dispatches*, vol.IV, p.56.
153   Gurwood (ed.), *Wellington's Dispatches*, vol.IV, p.60.

cooperating to the same end of restoring the Throne to the Regent Prince of Portugal. If it becomes necessary to grant capitulation to the French Army, it can be negotiated, always in accordance with the aforesaid British General on those articles which purely concern the Enemy Army, according to the Laws of War, always safeguarding the Sovereignty and Magistrates' Rights, which respect the individual nations.[154]

Wellesley asked Trant to arrange a meeting between him and Freire, which was subsequently set for noon on 7 August at Montemor-o-Velho, 15 miles from Lavos. There was already some tension between Wellesley and the Portuguese. On 6 August, he wrote, somewhat tersely, to Trant:

> There is nothing so foolish as to push these half disciplined troops forward; for the certain consequence must be, either their early and precipitate retreat, if the enemy should advance, or their certain destruction. I am determined not to move a man of my army till I am fully prepared to support any detachment I may send forward; and for this reason I object to send any troops to Leyria, in answer to various applications which have been made to me by a Portuguese Commissary, who has applied for protection, being, as he says, employed to collect supplies for the British troops, and which will probably fall into the hands of the enemy, if he should not be supported.
>
>   I have uniformly objected to sending any detachment or any person forward till I should be enabled effectually to protect them; and I should have sent on in ample time to secure everything for the army that it could require, or that Leyria could afford. It is unfortunate, therefore, that this gentleman has been sent forward, particularly if the consequence should be the loss of the supplies which Leyria might otherwise have afforded.[155]

Wellesley and Freire met as planned on the 7th. The British general inspected the Portuguese troops and delivered the arms. Freire wanted to delay the advance slightly to allow more time to gather supplies and then for the British troops to move inland with his forces via Pombal and Santarém, but Wellesley needed to stay close to the coast to maintain his communication and supply lines with the navy and to cover the arrival of the imminently expected reinforcements. He asked that Freire advance by the more coastal route, but the Portuguese commander would only commit to marching as far as Leiria by the 10th.[156] Freire had written to the junta on the 6th regarding his own supply problems:

> And on this subject, I must tell you that the Military Treasury, which is here for the moment, is depleted of money, having already spent what it asked for: the living expenses are still provided by this department, which has sent orders for nothing more than to make approvals; and since this department is not yet set up, it can do nothing.
>
>   The assistant superintendent has not yet appeared here and consequently this department is ineffective, as it is of the utmost importance that there is little transport here, and

154 Order from Junta to Freire, 3 August 1808 in 'Documentos', *Boletim do Arquivo Histórico Militar*, vol.1 (1930), p.165.
155 Gurwood (ed.), *Wellington's Dispatches*, vol.IV, pp.63–64.
156 De La Fuente, *Forjaz*, p.52.

it can barely supply the Requisitions of the English Army. We need at least fifty teams and three hundred pack animals that must be sent as soon as possible.[157]

On the 8th, Freire told Oporto that he had only 60 rounds of ammunition per man and that he still needed more arms despite the 5,000 muskets supplied by the British.[158] In another letter, he reminded the junta 'that the transport of ammunition and supplies, especially biscuit, should be done along the coast, but it is advisable that it is done as soon as possible because they are objects of first necessity and their lack is of the most disastrous consequence.'[159] On the 9th, he stated:

> Yesterday the conference proposed by General Wellesley took place in Montemor-o-Velho, but he arrived so late that I could not get here in time to inform you of the result yesterday; and today I wanted to inform you of the embarrassment in which we find ourselves after learning more about the circumstances. General Wellesley intends to march immediately and in case we could not accompany him, he proceeds alone in the expedition. Your Excellency may well know that in such a case it is necessary to strengthen our means because it is a matter of the honour of the Nation, the Government and each one of us and therefore I agreed that on Friday of this week we would meet him in Leiria, leading the forces that Your Excellency will see in the note that I am sending with this.[160]

With all the troops and ordnance landed, arrangements for the supply of the British force made, and such transport as could be found locally sourced and organised, Wellesley was, at last, nearly ready to move from Lavos. On 8 August, he wrote again to the Duke of Richmond:

> My advanced guard will move to-morrow, and the army on the 10th. The enemy is nearly in the situation in which he was. He has a corps of about 2000 men in my front; and he has sent a corps of 4000 or 5000 men across the Tagus into Alentejo, apparently with an intention to open his communication with Spain and to suppress the commotion in the Portuguese province of Alentejo, and to drive out 2000 or 3000 Spanish troops which had advanced from Spanish Estremadura. He will not succeed in opening a communication with Spain; and if he does not look sharp, I shall be at Lisbon before that detachment can return.[161]

Portugal was Lost to Us

Wellesley's information on French movements was out of date. In his campaign history, Thiébault wrote that as soon as the French learned of Wellesley's arrival, 'there was no longer any doubt that Portugal was lost to us.'[162] Although British troops had long been expected, reports from Thomières caused panic at French headquarters and increased the unrest in the city. A dozen members of

---

157   Freire to Junta, 6 August 1808, in 'Documentos', p.164.
158   Freire to Junta, 8 August 1808, in 'Documentos', p.168.
159   Freire to Junta, 10 August 1808, in 'Documentos', p.173.
160   Freire to Junta, 8 August 1808, in 'Documentos', pp.169.
161   Wellington (ed.), *Supplementary Despatches*, vol.VI, p.105.
162   Thiébault, *l'Expedition*, p.172.

the Lisbon police, the Guarda Real da Polícia, decided to desert to the patriots. The commander of the first company, Elesiário de Carvalho, invited his men to go to the rebels rather than fight their fellow Portuguese. *Sargento* Teixeira persuaded many of the fourth company to rebel, and men from other companies soon joined them. They all met at a prearranged location and formed a squadron of 56 files before riding out of the city. *Chef de la Légion de Police* Novion sent orders for them to be stopped, but *Sargento* Gambôa, in charge of the picket ordered to stop the deserters, instead joined them, and they rode on for Coimbra, arriving on 4 August.[163]

After the Battle of Evora, Loison marched to Elvas with his 7,000 men to raise the blockade there. Once he heard of the landings, Junot urgently sent several messengers with orders for him to return via Abrantes. Loison then marched the 90 miles to that town in five days. The weather was scorching and the French had failed to obtain food or water from the belligerent local population, some of whom misdirected the occupiers to non-existent streams or poisoned wells. Loison lost many men to thirst, and the Portuguese swiftly killed any stragglers.

To slow down the British advance, and give time for Loison to arrive, Delaborde was ordered to march north from Lisbon with five cannon, 150 of the 26e Chasseurs à Cheval, the two battalions of the 70e Ligne, and the 2e Régiment provisoire d'infanterie légère. One brigade of Delaborde's division, the cavalry, and the artillery were assembled for a field day at Campo de Ourique on the 5th and marched on the morning of the 6th. They had reached Rio Major, 70 miles from the British camp at Lavos, by the 9th.[164] Their route had been chosen to counter any attempt by the British and Portuguese to block Loison's return, but when this did not happen, and the British stayed close to the sea, Delaborde marched to Alcobaça to link up with Thomières, who commanded the 2e Légère and 4e Suisse at Peniche and Óbidos. Delaborde arrived there on the 10th. Junot also sent *colonel* Vincent and several of his engineers with Delaborde to reconnoitre the areas where the army might have to fight.

The British and Portuguese troops north of Lisbon were not the only threat to Lisbon. Insurgents from the Alentejo and Algarve were gathering at Alcácer do Sal, 50 miles southeast of Lisbon on the south bank of the Tagus. Kellermann left Lisbon on 11 August with 50 of his cavalry and then collected 800 men of the 31e and 32e Légère from Setúbal and dispersed the rebels at Alcácer do Sal, who were more numerous than formidable.[165]

Junot asked Senyavin to make a demonstration against Cotton's ships blocking the Tagus to distract the British or to send some of his crews to garrison the forts along the river to free up French troops for more active operations, but the Russian refused and said he would only fight if the British tried to force the Tagus. Manning the city's defences required the commitment of the 15e, 26e, 47e and 66e Ligne, plus the Légion du Midi and a depot battalion of 1,200 men drawn from all the regiments.[166]

163 Elesiário de Carvalho, 'Relação da deserção de um Corpo de Cavalaria do Guarda da Polícia de Lisboa, que chegou a esta Cidade no dia 4 do corrente', *Colecção da Minerva Lusitana*, <https://www.arqnet.pt/exercito/minerva19.html>, accessed January 2023.
164 Thiébault, *l'Expedition*, p.175.
165 Foy, *Invasion*, p.147.
166 Foy, *Invasion*, pp.147–148.

8

The British

On 1 August 1808, the Duke of York sent Castlereagh a long memorandum on the state of the British Army. It began:

> It may, I think, be stated, without fear of dispute, that the army of this country is, at the present moment, larger, more efficient, and more disposable, than at any former period of our history. Great and unusual exertions have been made to procure the men, and the circumstances of the war have allowed sufficient time to discipline and form them.[1]

That the army was in such a good state was mainly due to the stewardship of York and Castlereagh. As a later field marshal, Lord Carver, wrote, 'To the Duke of York, in forging the weapon, and to Castlereagh, for keeping the ranks filled, Wellington was to owe much when he assumed command in the Iberian peninsula'.[2] The British Army's first campaign in the Revolutionary War in Flanders had exposed its unpreparedness for war and problems with training, command, and logistics. Historian Richard Glover wrote, 'for the first fifteen years at least of the wars that sprang from the French Revolution, the British Army was the least feared and least respected of all France's principal enemies.'[3] Glover blamed the poor quality of the army on 10 years of neglect in training and discipline since the end of the American War of Independence and poor methods for officer selection.

The Duke of York had led the army in that first campaign in Flanders but had since had over a decade to institute reforms to address some of the issues. He had overseen the founding of the Royal Military College in 1801 to train junior and staff officers. The curriculum for the senior department included languages, mathematics, fortifications, surveying, and many of the regulations and instructions of the army of Frederick the Great. The cadets of the junior department were schooled in many of the same subjects but also riding, fencing, swimming and drill.[4] As of 1808, only small numbers of officers had graduated from the college, but it was a sign of a trend to an increasing professionalisation of the officer corps and the move towards a more scientific approach

---

1 Vane (ed.), *Correspondence*, vol.VIII, p.179. Memorandum concerning the State of the Army, 1 August 1808.
2 Quoted in J. Peaty, 'Architect of Victory: The Reforms of the Duke of York', *Journal of the Society for Army Historical Research*, vol.84, no.340 (Winter 2006), p.342.
3 R. Glover, *Peninsular Preparation: The Reform of the British Army 1795–1809* (Cambridge: Cambridge University Press, 1963), p.2.
4 Glover, *Preparation*, pp.204–206.

to war that was displayed by many of the experienced staff officers of the expedition. A parallel development was the establishment of the Depot of Military Knowledge as part of the quartermaster general's department at Horse Guards. The depot collected information, maps, plans, and books to act as a repository of knowledge that could be called upon when planning operations.[5]

The Duke had also been instrumental in addressing the British Army's lack of light infantry and bringing it into line with continental armies. Following his experiences in Flanders, he oversaw the formation of émigré light infantry units, several rifle-armed. In 1797, when those troops had been decimated by disease in the West Indies, he formed the remaining rifle-armed chasseurs into a new fifth battalion of the 60th Foot. He then followed this with the formation of the Experimental Corps of Riflemen, whose initial purpose was to train riflemen for the line regiments' light companies, but the corps was eventually formed into the 95th Foot. During York's tenure, two separate manuals were written and distributed for light infantry and riflemen, one by the commanding officer of the 5/60th and another by the director general of the Royal Military College, former French general François Jarry. These were distributed to all infantry regiments. In 1803, York ordered Major General Sir John Moore to convert two line battalions to specialist light infantry regiments, the 43rd and 52nd, and to form a light infantry training camp at Shorncliffe.[6]

The Duke of York had also sought to reform officer selection and promotion. He required all officers seeking their first commission to supply a recommendation from a field officer in the hope that this would reduce applications by unsuitable candidates. He ordered that all applications for promotions go through the regular channels of the commanding officer or colonel of the regiment.[7] He also sought to temper the purchasing of promotions by imposing minimum lengths of service in each rank to ensure inexperienced but wealthy officers could not end up in command of regiments, as had happened in Flanders. Purchase was only involved in a minority of promotions, and the biographies of the brigade and battalion commanders in this chapter will show various paths to advancement. Some officers purchased all their promotions, some none, but most fell somewhere in between. The reforms, however, did not stop officers with influential patrons, like Henry Fane, from rising rapidly – and he only purchased one of his promotions. Wellesley, who had greatly benefited from the lax regulation of the purchase system, praised York's reforms and stated in early 1809 that 'the officers are improved in knowledge; that the staff of the army is much better than it was' and then went on to praise York's other reforms, 'everything that relates to the military discipline of the soldiers and the military efficiency of the army has been greatly improved since His Royal Highness was appointed Commander-in-Chief.'[8]

York overhauled the machinery of recruitment for the army, and legal changes, such as enabling limited-term enlistment, had been made by the previous administration, but these had not produced all the increase in numbers required. Castlereagh made further and wider-reaching reforms to the Militia that not only freed up regular units from home defence but also enabled large numbers of Militia who had experienced and liked military service to volunteer for the regulars, for short or long service and with an agreement not to be drafted from their chosen regiment. Many of these men had entered the Militia in 1803, were fully trained and had served for five years.[9] Militia officers were given the incentive of a regular commission if they brought 40 volunteers from their

---

5   Peaty, 'Architect', pp.345–346.
6   Griffith, *Riflemen*, Chapters 1 and 11.
7   Glover, *Preparation*, p.152.
8   Glover, *Preparation*, p.160.
9   Glover, *Preparation*, p.249.

regiments with them. Historian John Fortescue calls Castlereagh's measures 'heroic' and says, 'In the course of 1807 and the first three months of 1808 there had been raised in all forty-five thousand recruits; and, since the casualties of 1807 fell below fifteen thousand, there was a solid gain of thirty thousand men.'[10] Many of the battalions that landed in Portugal had benefitted from these reforms and had received large drafts of militiamen.

Richard Glover attributes the improvement in the British Army between 1795 and 1809 to York: 'he created uniformity where there had been previously been only disorder; this he did by steady and unremitting attention to the training of the troops.'[11] While many of the army's shortcomings had been addressed, some structural issues remained. Training was still an issue as there were very few spaces where large bodies of troops could be exercised together, so while troops could be drilled in companies, battalions and sometimes brigades, there was little opportunity for multiple brigades with cavalry and artillery to learn to work together.[12] Also, the fact that the Army, Ordnance and Commissariat were separate organisations caused significant inefficiencies and problems, as was illustrated by Wellesley's problems with the Commissariat and the artillery horses. These structural issues would not be addressed until well into the Victorian era.

While the Duke of York's reforms had begun to make a difference by 1808, the British Army was still largely untested and inexperienced. In his Preface to the 1810 edition of his *Universal Military Dictionary,* Charles James analyses the state of military science and the merits of how it is applied in the armies of Europe. Of the Royal Navy, he wrote:

> Our present extent of naval power is, in great measure founded on our superior knowledge, on the skill and science of our officers, and of the confidence which practice, experience, and success, must give our seamen; a fleet manned by seamen, and always on the ocean, must have every advantage over the fleet of another nation which goes but seldom to sea, whose decks are crowded with landsmen, and whose officers have yet their duty to learn.[13]

James then immediately contrasted the state of the navy with that of the army: 'If experience gives such advantage in naval affairs, why should it be imagined, that an army, almost of recruits, and commanded by officers who have little knowledge of actual warfare, should be superior to one whose soldiers are veterans, and whose officers have won their blood-stained laurels in many a hard contested field.'[14] He then claimed that a marine-based war of 'descent and alarm' was the only one suited to the means and dispositions of Britons. He contrasted the European nations. where war often flowed across their borders, with Britain:

> The peculiar situation of England renders this danger less imminent than in any other free country; her armies dispersed over nearly the whole face of the habitable globe; her regular troops but little employed in any kind of active service, but desultory war; her militia, which never sees the face of an enemy, and her armed population always at home, and following their civil pursuits.[15]

---

10 Fortescue, *British Army*, vol.VI, p.183.
11 Glover, *Preparation*, p.142.
12 Glover, *Preparation*, p.195.
13 C. James, *An Universal Military Dictionary* (London: Egerton, 1810), p.xx.
14 James, *Dictionary* (1810), pp.xx–xxi.
15 James, *Dictionary* (1810), pp.xlvi.

James was writing after the victories at Roliça and Vimeiro, the evacuation from Corunna, and the disaster at Walcheren. However, James' 1816 edition of his dictionary opens with a long dedication to the Duke of York. He wrote that under York's administration, 'the British army has arrived at a state of discipline and regulation, by which success abroad has been obtained, and tranquility at home secured.'[16] The years between 1810 and 1816 were, of course, marked by a string of Wellington's victories in Portugal, Spain, France and at Waterloo. However, James wrote, 'victories, after all, are little more than the fruits and consummation of those well digested principles by which the arduous science of war is managed, and without which no army can be well conducted, or finally triumphant.'[17]

By 1808, the reforms to the British Army had begun to take effect, and a more scientific approach to war was gaining favour amongst some senior officers. However, what the British Army really needed was the 'practice, experience, and success' that James said gave the navy its confidence. The Peninsular War would deliver those benefits, but the force gathered at Lavos still lacked them.

Brigading

On 7 August, Wellesley issued a general order that integrated Spencer's troops with those that had sailed from Cork into a new brigade structure. Each brigade was assigned a brigade major to assist the brigade commander and an assistant commissary to distribute rations and forage to the brigade.

> *1st Brigade* Major General Rowland Hill
> 1/5th, 1/9th and 1/38th Foot; Brigade Major Fordyce, Assist. Commissary Capt. Hamilton
> *2nd Brigade* Major General Ronald Ferguson
> 1/36th, 1/40th and 1/71st Foot; Brigade Major Talbot, Assist. Commissary Dillon
> *3rd Brigade* Brigadier General Miles Nightingall
> 29th and 1/82nd Foot; Brigade Major Stewart, Assist. Commissary Lt Nelson
> *4th Brigade* Brigadier General Barnard Foord Bowes
> 1/6th and 1/32nd Foot; Brigade Major Butler, Assist. Commissary Cornet Turton
> *5th Brigade* Brigadier General James Caitlin Craufurd
> 1/45th, 1/50th and 1/91st Foot; Brigade Major Blair, Assist. Commissary Aylmer
> *6th (Light) Brigade* Brigadier General Henry Fane
> 5/60th and four companies 2/95th Rifles; Brigade Major McNeil, Assist. Commissary
> Lamont[18]

The brigade numbering was based on the seniority of each brigadier, and this, in turn, fed into their position in the line, with Hill, the senior brigade commander, having the post of honour on the right of the line, Ferguson, being next most senior, on the right, and so on. When the army was formed in line of battle, the order of the brigades would be, from the right: 1st, 3rd, 5th, 4th, 2nd. The 6th, as a body of light infantry, would be positioned to the front, rear or on the flanks as required. This

---

16   C. James, *An Universal Military Dictionary* (London: Egerton, 1816), p.v.
17   James, *Dictionary* (1816), p.v.
18   Wellington (ed.), *Supplementary Despatches*, vol.VI, p.101.

order of the brigades would place the stronger three-battalion brigades on the flanks and in the centre. Spencer's battalions remained together in the brigades he had set on 17 July, apart from the 50th which had been unattached,[19] and Spencer himself became Wellesley's second in command.

Wellesley had previously issued a general order on 3 August brigading the troops he had brought from Cork before Spencer arrived, and several essential elements of that order remained in force. The order specified that the army would be formed in a line two ranks deep. The regulations specified that lines three ranks deep were to be the norm, but did offer the flexibility of forming in two ranks:

> The fundamental order of the infantry, in which they should always form and act, and for which all their various operations and movements are calculated, is in three ranks:-The formation in two ranks is to be regarded as an occasional exception that may be made from it, where an extended and covered front is to be occupied, or where an irregular enemy, who deals only in fire, is to be opposed.[20]

Forming in two ranks extended the length of a battalion's frontage. A third rank, however, did allow men to step forward and fill vacancies in the line caused by casualties, and the third rank could be formed into a reserve behind the first two ranks to act on the flanks or where needed. A two-rank line would have to contract its frontage to fill gaps caused by casualties. The use of two ranks rather than three, however, dated back at least as far as the American War of Independence, so Wellesley was far from the first commander to abandon the three-rank line.

The 3 August general order also specified, 'When the army shall move from its left, the 95th and 5th battalion 60th will lead the column in the ordinary course. When the army shall move from its right, the 95th and 5th battalion 60th must form the advanced guard...'[21] The riflemen from both regiments would act as their role intended, as the army's advance guard. The *Regulations for the Exercise of Riflemen and Light Infantry and Instructions for their Conduct in the Field*, written by the 5/60th's lieutenant colonel, Francis de Rottenburg, specified an arrow-headed formation of detached groups of light infantry acting on the flanks and far in advance, backed up by a reserve, to head a column of march.[22] However, the riflemen were not Wellesley's only light infantry. The order also specified that:

> The Lieutenant-General requests the General officers commanding brigades will, on all occasions of march and formation of the line of their respective brigades, place the light infantry companies belonging to the several regiments under their command in a separate corps under the command of a field-officer. In the ordinary formation on parade, and in route marches, these corps of light infantry will be on the left of the brigade. In formation in front of the enemy they will be in front or in rear, according to circumstances; and in the marches of columns to take up a position, they will be on the reverse flank of the column. The light infantry companies will, however, encamp, and do all duties with the regiments.[23]

---

19   NLS: Adv.MS.46.3.6: General order 17 July 1808.
20   Anon., *Rules and Regulations for the Formations, Field Exercises and Movements of His Majesty's Forces* (London: War Office, 1798), p.77.
21   Wellington (ed.), *Supplementary Despatches*, vol.VI, p.96.
22   F. de Rottenburg, *Regulations for the Exercise of Riflemen and Light Infantry and Instructions for their Conduct in the Field* (London: War Office, 1803), p.26.
23   Wellington (ed.), *Supplementary Despatches*, vol.VI, pp.96–97.

British commanders had formed battalions of grenadier or light companies in previous campaigns, detached from their battalions for the campaign's duration. Wellesley's order gave his brigade commander a force of two or three light infantry companies, commanded by a major or lieutenant colonel, to secure their flanks, occupy prominent positions, and counter the French voltigeurs. However, the companies would still camp with and benefit from the operational support of their battalions. Wellesley would continue using light companies this way throughout the Peninsular campaign and at Waterloo.[24]

The 20th Light Dragoons were not brigaded, and their position in the line and the columns of march would be decided in the orders of the day. A subaltern and 20 dragoons would act as a daily piquet and provide patrols and couriers.[25]

Staff

Wellesley's personal staff was headed by his military secretary, Henry Torrens, whom he did not know before his appointment by the Duke of York. However, Torrens had previously been quartered in Lisbon for six months in 1798 and 1799 and was familiar with the area, so he was a sensible choice.[26] Torrens was a very experienced officer, having served in the West Indies and at the Helder where he was severely wounded. He had commanded the 86th Foot in Egypt, marching across the desert from the Red Sea, and subsequently in India. He had served on the staff in England, as military secretary to Lieutenant General Whitelocke in South America, and then as assistant military secretary to the Duke of York.[27]

Wellesley had four aides de camp, whose duties included carrying orders and relaying messages. A contemporary military dictionary notes, 'This employment is of greater importance than is generally believed: it is, however, often entrusted to young officers of little experience, and of as little capacity.'[28] The position was the gift of the general officers themselves, so it was often used to assist the career of family members or exchange patronage with people of influence. Captain Colin Campbell (75th Highlanders) had been with Wellesley since India. At 16, he had run away to sea but was found by his family in Jamaica. He had briefly been a midshipman in the East India Company navy but then joined a Fencible regiment commanded by his uncle before transferring to the regulars. Wellesley had noted his bravery at Ahmednagar in 1803 and made him his brigade major. Campbell would stay with Wellesley until well after Waterloo.[29] Captain Fitzroy Stanhope (1st Foot Guards) had been with Wellesley at Copenhagen and was a son of General Charles Stanhope, Earl of Harrington, Commander-in-Chief of Ireland. Captain Lord Fitzroy Somerset (4th Garrison Battalion) and Wellesley's 20-year-old nephew, Ensign William Wellesley-Pole (29th Foot), were new to the 'family'. Somerset, the youngest son of the Duke of Beaufort, had been recommended to Wellesley by the Duke of Richmond in a letter: '[General] O'Hara used to say he had rather have

24   See R. Griffith, 'Light Bobs and Jäger: Battalions of Light Companies in the Peninsular War', in R. Griffith (ed.), *Armies and Enemies of Napoleon, 1789–1815* (Warwick: Helion, 2022), pp.175–207, for more information on Wellesley's use of the light companies.
25   Wellington (ed.), *Supplementary Despatches*, vol.VI, p.97.
26   BL: Add MS 49485: Torrens to Gordon, 9 July 1808.
27   J. Philipart (ed.), *The Royal Military Calendar* (London: Egerton, 1820), vol.III, pp.390–391.
28   James, *Dictionary* (1816), p.8.
29   Muir, *Wellington*, p.133.

a wife recommended to him than an aide de camp. Notwithstanding this, I will venture to say that FitzRoy Somerset is an active and intelligent fellow, and is anxious to go on service.'[30] Somerset's appointment was typical of the trading of influence and favours that predominated in British politics and society at the time.

Young William's appointment was more of a familial obligation. He had only been gazetted in June, and Wellesley wrote of him;

> He appears pretty well in health, but he is the most extraordinary person altogether that I have seen. There is a mixture of steadiness & extreme Levity, of sense & folly in his composition such as I have never met with in any other instance…
>
> I have been obliged to speak to him pretty sharply once or twice principally relating to his want of care of himself when he was sick; & now he is as much afraid of me as he is of you, & even more so as my authority in my present situation is greater over him; & the nature of our relative situations, & the constant crowd with which I am surrounded prevents all Intercourse between us. I see clearly that he is heartily tired of his new line of Life; that he is dying to return to England, & that he will make use of any pretext to get away.
>
> I propose to endeavour to get the better of his fears, & to prevail upon him to learn something. He is lamentably ignorant & idle; & yet upon some occasions he does not want for Sense & sharpness, while upon others he betrays the ignorance almost of what is called in Ireland a *Natural.*[31]

William's father, also William, was one of Arthur's elder brothers, Secretary to the Board of Admiralty, and a key political ally and supporter of his brother's interests. Wellesley was repaying that support by taking young William with him. However, the two did not get on well. The immature William seemed to expect special attention and favouritism from his uncle that he did not receive.[32] Young William resigned from the army before the end of the year.

Spencer was not given a brigade but made Wellesley's second in command. He was:

> …not to be put on duty as a General officer. The Lieutenant-General requests that he will give such orders to the troops, from time to time, as he may judge necessary, reporting them to the Lieutenant-General when he finds it convenient; and the Major-General's orders are at all times to be obeyed, although they may be contradictory to those previously issued by the Lieutenant-General.[33]

The duties of a second in command were nebulous at best, and Wellesley later wrote that he was not in favour of the role.[34] Spencer had Captain Keating James Bradford (3rd Foot Guards), a deputy

30   2nd Duke of Wellington (ed.), *Civil Correspondence and Memoranda of Field Marshal Arthur Duke of Wellington* (London: Murray, 1860), Richmond to Wellesley, 11 June 1808, p.453.
31   Webster, 'Some Letters', p.8.
32   D. Roberts, '"Uncle Arthur Wellesley? He's not all that!" – Wicked William goes to War', *Wicked William*, <https://www.wickedwilliam.com/uncle-arthur-wellesley-hes-wicked-william-goes-war/>, accessed February 2023.
33   Wellington (ed.), *Supplementary Despatches*, vol.VI, p.101.
34   Gurwood (ed.), *Wellington's Dispatches*, vol.IX, p.592.

assistant adjutant general who had been part of his staff since sailing from Britain, assigned to him to assist him as well as his aides de camp, Captains Robert Francis Melville Browne and George Preston, both from Spencer's former regiment the 40th Foot.

As well as the two sets of troops to merge, Wellesley and Spencer's staffs had to be integrated. As previously planned by the Duke of York, Spencer's assistant adjutant general, Lieutenant Colonel George James Bruere Tucker (50th Foot), took the role of deputy adjutant general. The step up from assistant to deputy reflected the greater responsibility of the position in a larger force. Adjutant Generals were usually:

> … an officer of distinction, who aids and assists the general in his laborious duty: he forms the several details of duty of the army, with the brigade majors, and keeps an exact state of each brigade and regiment … He every day at head quarters receives orders from the general officer of the day, and distributes them to the majors of brigades, from whom he receives the number of men they are to furnish for the duty of the army, and informs them at any detail which may concern them. On marching days he accompanies the general to the ground of the camp. He makes a daily report of the situation of all the posts placed for the safety of the army, and of any changes made in their posts. In a day of battle the adjutant general sees the infantry drawn up, after which he places himself by the general to receive orders.[35]

As well as administration, the adjutant general's department was responsible for discipline.

Also, as arranged by York, Spencer's Lieutenant Colonel James Bathurst (60th Foot) took the role of deputy quartermaster general. A quartermaster general was:

> … a considerable officer in the army, and should be a man of great judgment and experience, and well skilled in geography; his duty is to mark the marches, and encampments of an army; he should know the country perfectly well, with its rivers, plains, marshes, woods, mountains, defiles, passages, &c. even to the smallest brook. Prior to a march, he receives the orders and route from the commanding general, and appoints a place for the quarter-masters of the army to meet him next morning, with whom he marches to the next camp; where, after having viewed the ground , he marks out to the regimental quarter-masters the space allowed each regiment for their camp: he chuses the head quarters, and appoints the villages for the generals of the army's quarters: he chuses a proper place for the encampment of the train of artillery: he conducts foraging parties, as likewise the troops to cover them against assaults, and has a share in regulating the winter quarters and cantonments.[36]

The quartermaster general's department was also responsible for the supply of equipment but not provisions.

Wellesley had not had a chance to get to know either Bathurst or Tucker well, although he may have met both during the Copenhagen campaign. Tucker, born in Bermuda in 1773, joined the army in 1790. He had served in India, Egypt, the Cape (where he was on Baird's staff), and

---

35 James, *Dictionary* (1816), p.5.
36 James, *Dictionary* (1816), p.697.

Copenhagen.[37] Bathurst was an experienced staff officer. First commissioned in 1794, he had served at the capture of Surinam in 1799, in Egypt in 1801, and on the staff in Britain. In 1804, he went to Hannover on the staff of Cathcart's expedition and then was appointed military commissary to the King's German Legion. He was an observer with the Russian and Prussian armies during the Polish campaigns of 1806–1807 and then served on Cathcart's staff at Stralsund and Copenhagen.[38]

Table 12 below lists the combined staff. In addition to the physicians, the surgeons, the apothecary, and the purveyors (who organised provisions and equipment), the medical department also had the assistance of 16 hospital mates. One final position on the staff was filled when Wellesley appointed Sergeant Major Scates (6th Foot) as deputy provost marshal to enforce military justice.[39]

Table 12. Staff officers, commissaries, and medical department

Department	Appointment	Rank & Name	Regiment	Joined from
	Military Secretary	Lt Col. Henry Torrens	89th Foot	Cork
Adjutant General's Department	Deputy Adjutant General	Lt Col. George James Bruere Tucker	50th Foot	Spencer
	Assistant Adjutant General	Maj. Thomas Arbuthnott	5th West Indian	Cork
	Deputy Assistant Adjutant Generals	Capt. Keating James Bradford	3rd Foot Guards	Spencer
		Captain Henry Frederick Cooke	Coldstream Guards	Spencer
		Capt. John Brown	8th Garrison Bn.	Cork
		Capt. Montagu Wynyard	Coldstream Guards	Cork
		Capt. John Elliot	48th Foot	Cork
		Capt. George R.P. Jarvis	36th Foot	Cork
		Capt. Caesar Colclough	82nd Foot	Spencer
		Lt. Kean Osborne	4th Dragoons	Cork
Quartermaster General's Department	Deputy Quartermaster General	Lt Col. James Bathurst	60th Foot	Spencer
	Assistant Quartermaster General	Maj John Rainey	82nd Foot	Spencer
	Deputy Assistant Quartermaster Generals	Capt. Henry Hardinge	57th Foot	Spencer
		Capt. J.H.L. Maw	23rd Foot	Cork
		Capt. Algernon Langton	61st Foot	Cork
		Capt. John Campbell	10th Foot	Cork
		Capt. William Gomm	9th Foot	Cork
		Capt. James Douglas	45th Foot	Cork

37 Obituary, *The Gentleman's Magazine*, February 1809, p.183.
38 Philipart (ed.), *Calendar*, vol.IV, p.124.
39 Wellington (ed.), *Supplementary Despatches*, vol.VI, p.102.

Department	Appointment	Rank & Name	Regiment	Joined from
Chaplain	Chaplain to the Forces	Revd W. Mathews		Spencer
Commissariat Department	Deputy Commissary General	James Pipon		Cork
	Assistant Commissary Generals	George Damerun		Cork
		William Lamont		Cork
		Edward Dillion		Unknown
		Charles Alymer		Unknown
Paymaster General's Department	Assistant Paymaster General	Matthew Ottley		Spencer
	Deputy Commissary of Accounts	James Ramsay Cooper		Cork
	Asst. Deputy Commissary of Accounts	Thomas Clarke		Cork
Medical Department	Inspector of Hospitals	Dr William Randle Shapter		Spencer
	Deputy Inspector of Hospitals	Alexander Thomson		Cork
	Physicians	Dr William Deane		Spencer
		Dr Thomas Hume		Cork
	Surgeons to the Forces	Thomas Kidd		Spencer
		Thomas Frederick Nicholay		Spencer
		William Richard Morel		Cork
		Eli Crump		Cork
		John Gunning		Cork
		Thomas Ross		Cork
	Apothecary	John Hayne Newton		Spencer
	Purveyor	John Wimbrigde		Spencer
	Deputy Purveyor	Charles Mapother		Spencer

Sources: NLS: Adv.MS.46.3.6: General order, 6 August 1808; TNA: WO 72/29: York to Wellesley, 11 June 1808; WO 17/2464: Return of the General and Staff Officers, 1 July 1808 and Lionel S. Challis's 'Peninsula Roll Call', The Napoleon Series, <https://www.napoleon-series.org/research/biographies/GreatBritain/Challis/c_ChallisIntro.html>, accessed February 2023. Some of the commissaries listed on the 1 July return are not listed by Challis as being present in Portugal in August 1808 and so have been omitted. Dillion and Aylmer appear in the general order of 7 August, but not before that. Spencer lists no commissaries in his returns of staff officers.

1st Brigade (Hill)

Major General Rowland Hill was born on 11 August 1772 at Prees Hall in Shropshire, part of a minor landed family. He was a gentle-natured child, and his father had planned for him to go into the law, but, in 1790, Rowland asked to go into the army. His father consented, quickly obtained an ensigncy in the 38th Foot, and arranged for him to attend a military academy in Strasbourg. Hill rose quickly through the ranks, not by purchase but by raising quotas of recruits and moving regiments. By 1793, he was a captain in the 86th and aide de camp to Brigadier General Lord

Mulgrave during the siege of Toulon. Hill won praise from Mulgrave, saw his first combat, and suffered his first wound. He also met Thomas Graham, who subsequently raised his own regiment, the 90th Foot, and offered Hill a majority if he could raise enough men. He fulfilled his quota, and, when the regiment was augmented to 1,000 men shortly afterwards, Hill was promoted on 13 May 1794 to be the junior lieutenant colonel. He was still only 21 years old. He was promoted to full colonel in 1800 and led the 90th during Abercromby's Egyptian campaign of 1801. On 13 March, the 90th were leading the British advance when they were surprised by French cavalry. The volleys of the 90th drove off the enemy, but Hill was wounded. A musket ball struck the peak of the Tarleton helmet he was wearing, and he was concussed. Following the Peace of Amiens, the 90th and Hill went to Ireland.

Major General Rowland Hill. (Public Domain)

Shortly afterwards, he was promoted to brigadier general on the Irish staff.

Hill performed well in Ireland and was promoted to major general in October 1805. He was placed in charge of the embarkation of 5,000 troops at Cork for an expedition to Hannover. The convoy stopped briefly at Deal, where Hill dined with Wellesley, who also commanded a brigade in the expedition. The force arrived off the German coast in December but achieved little and soon returned. Hill then had various commands in Britain before returning to Ireland in early 1807 and being assigned to Wellesley's expedition. Hill's aide de camp was his younger brother, Captain Thomas Noel Hill (53rd Foot).

The 1/9th had been brigaded under Hill for more than four years, and the other battalions since their return from South America.[40]

1st Battalion, 5th (Northumberland) Regiment of Foot

The 1/5th had been sent to Hannover in 1805 and lost 250 men when a transport was wrecked off the Dutch coast. In 1806, they formed part of the reinforcements for South America and took part in the attack on Buenos Aires, which ended in defeat for Whitelocke's army. Private Stephen Morley, a Londoner who had enlisted in the Army of the Reserve in 1804 and then transferred to the 5th while training at Guernsey, and who had since become the regimental clerk, wrote in his memoir that after their arrival in Ireland at the end of 1807:

> In barracks we had leisure to talk over the scenes in which we had been so painfully engaged. That the country was disappointed, is well known, although no blame, it was

---

40   Wellington (ed.), *Supplementary Despatches*, vol.XIII, pp.308–309.

understood, attached to us. Such of the men as could reflect, were amused at seeing how the virulence of party feeling tinged and discoloured the simple facts. The British Soldier is a dunce in politics! it is a subject he despises. To keep his arms in serviceable condition, as well as his clothing and appointments; to be patient under privations; cool and steady in dangers; brave and daring in action; to be obedient to orders, and to have an honest and cheerful heart form the perfection of his character.[41]

The 1/5th was commanded by Lieutenant Colonel John MacKenzie, who had moved from the 2/5th in the spring of 1808. A Scot from Sutherland, he had purchased a captaincy in the 103rd Foot in 1795, and then bought a majority in the 85th in 1801 before going on half-pay the next year. He moved back to active duty and joined the 5th Foot in 1804. Morley thought him a strict disciplinarian. The battalion was bolstered by volunteers from the Irish militia before receiving orders to march to Cork.

1st Battalion, 9th (East Norfolk) Regiment of Foot
The 1/9th Foot had seen action in the Helder in 1799, then, in 1800, was based in Lisbon and took part in the Ferrol expedition. They also fell foul of bad weather on the way to Hannover, and one of their transports was wrecked near Calais and 262 men taken prisoner.

James Hale was one of the many soldiers who had volunteered from the Militia. He had joined the Royal North Gloucester Militia in 1803 and served with them on the south coast. He wrote in his memoir that he, 'was rather inclined to extend my service, so that I might have the opportunity of seeing some other country; for I was then got quite tired of rambling about England, although the militia service is nothing but a mere pleasure, in general.'[42] Hale was not alone; 170 of his comrades joined him in volunteering for the 9th in August 1807. In total, 359 volunteers came from the North Gloucester, Devon, Lancashire, and Berkshire Militia that summer and, in June 1808, 100 men of the 2/9th marched from Canterbury to Dover to join the 1st battalion at Cork.[43] So, as their strength on 1 July stood at 916 rank and file, half of the battalion would have been relatively recent arrivals. Hale recalled his joining the battalion:

When we got within about three or four miles of Fermoy, we were saluted with three cheers by Lieut. Colonel Stewart, (who was then commanding officer of the regiment), together with the band and many of the old soldiers, who came to welcome us home. There we halted, and formed up into a line, that our colonel might see what sort of a bargain he had got; and after a little conversation with the officer that commanded our party, he walked up and down the ranks with a smiling countenance, accompanied by several other officers that belonged to the regiment.— Our party consisted of about four hundred, all young, men. After a little rest, we marched off again, with drums beating and music playing, until we came to Fermoy barracks, and then we were divided as quick as possible, and sent to our respective companies: and for encouragement, our colonel had ordered a good dinner to be ready for us, which each company had placed on the table, together with a can of good porter, which you may suppose was very acceptable to us after a long days' march.[44]

---

41   Morley, *Memoirs*, p.40.
42   Hale, *Journal*, p.5.
43   R. Cannon, *Historical Record of the Ninth, or the East Norfolk Regiment of Foot* (London: Adjutant General's Office, 1848), pp.43–44. *Dublin Evening Post*, 14 June 1808.
44   Hale, *Journal*, pp.10–11.

Lieutenant Colonel John Stewart (sometimes Stuart) had taken command of the battalion in early 1806 while it was based at Shorncliffe Barracks. Stewart had begun his career in the 72nd in 1790, moved to the 88th as a captain in 1799 and then to the 52nd as a major in 1803, and was promoted to lieutenant colonel the same year.

1st Battalion 38th (1st Staffordshire) Regiment of Foot

During the Revolutionary Wars, the battalion had severed in the West Indies. It had then taken part in the capture of the Cape of Good Hope and was one of the first reinforcements sent to South America, taking part in the taking of Montevideo. Like all the battalions that had served in South America, the 1/38th needed to bring itself up to strength from the regiment's second battalion. One of the men to transfer was Joseph Cooley. Born in Hartshill in Warwickshire in 1789, he was an apprentice in nearby Hinckley but ran away and enlisted in the 2/38th when he was 17. He was a Methodist, but from his account it is clear that he succumbed to the temptations of gambling and other diversions that soldiers filled their time with. His battalion moved from Guernsey to Ireland and then:

> We had not been long in Ireland before there came an order for a draft to join the first battalion of the Regiment it was then laying in another part of Ireland. A parade was ordered and every other file of men was taken but it did not fall to my lot to be one of them but I was of a roving mind and had a great desire to see different scenes and different places. Volunteered to go in another's stead as soon as we got to the first battalion we got the rought [route] for Portugal…[45]

As well as reduced numbers, regiments returning from foreign service often faced administrative problems while paperwork caught up with them. In the 38th's case, one issue they had was that their annual clothing issue had gone astray. The battalion had not yet received the clothing that should have been issued at the end of December 1807, and the troops were still wearing the uniforms they had worn in South America.[46]

The commander of the battalion was Lieutenant Colonel the Honourable Charles Greville, second son of the Earl of Warwick. Born in 1780, he began his military career as a cornet in the Warwickshire Corps of Fencible Cavalry at 15. His father was the regiment's colonel, and he was unsurprisingly very quickly promoted to lieutenant. He joined the regulars when he was 16, purchasing an ensigncy and then a lieutenancy in the 10th Foot in 1796, which had just returned from the West Indies and had plenty of vacancies. The regiment sailed for India in the winter of 1798, and Greville then purchased his captaincy the following year. In 1800, the 10th was part of Baird's expedition from India to the Red Sea coast of Egypt and marched across the desert to join up with the rest of the British forces on the Nile. In July 1802, while the regiment was still in Egypt, Greville went on half-pay, transferring to the 81st to do so. His health possibly had suffered from his time in India and Egypt, and he needed to return to Britain. However, he returned to duty when he purchased a majority in the 38th in 1803 and then his lieutenant colonelcy in 1805.

---

45   NAM: 1979-12-21-1: Manuscript memoirs of an unidentified soldier of 38th (1st Staffordshire) Regiment of Foot, of his career in the Army 1808-1815. Some punctuation has been added. Historian Gareth Glover has identified the author as Cooley: <https://www.waterlooassociation.org.uk/2021/09/17/the-story-of-private-joseph-cooley-38th-foot/>, accessed February 2023.
46   BL: Add Ms 49484: Dalrymple to Gordon, 10 September 1808.

2nd Brigade (Ferguson)

Major General Ronald Craufurd Ferguson was born in 1773 in Scotland and commissioned into the 53rd Foot in 1790. He was soon promoted to lieutenant in an independent company, which was then disbanded. While on half-pay, he attended the Berlin Military Academy for two years, but when war broke out in 1793 he returned to Britain and rejoined the 53rd as a captain. He went with his regiment to Flanders and fought at Valenciennes, Dunkirk, Nieuport and Furnes, where he was wounded. In May 1794, he moved to the 2/84th Foot as a major. He was then promoted to lieutenant colonel in September and commanded the battalion. In 1795, both battalions of the 84th helped capture the Cape of Good Hope from the Dutch, but the 2nd battalion was then disbanded. Ferguson was on half-pay until 1799, when he was briefly appointed to the Minorca Regiment before joining the 31st Foot and being promoted to colonel. In 1800, the 31st was part of an expedition to destroy the forts at Quiberon and Belle Isle. In 1801, he returned to Britain to command a fencible regiment before taking various staff positions. In 1805, he was given the command of a brigade in another expedition to capture the Cape, which had been handed back to the Dutch during the Peace of Amiens. His Highland Brigade performed an opposed landing and then covered the disembarkation of the rest of the army. In the actions that followed, he frequently won the praise of Baird, the expedition commander. However, while at the Cape he contracted a liver disease which forced him to return to Britain. He spent the next two years recovering, but during this time was also elected to Parliament. In April 1808, he was promoted to major general and assigned to Spencer's expedition but did not join them until he arrived in Portugal from Cork with Wellesley.[47]

Major General Ronald Ferguson. (Public Domain)

William Warre described Ferguson as 'not amiable in his manners, but very clever'.[48] Ferguson's other aide de camp, Henry Mellish, wrote of his general:

> I am more and more delighted with the General every day. In every point of view the more I see of him the more worthy of admiration I find him. In short I think myself the luckiest

47   R. Burnham, & R. McGuigan, *Wellington's Brigade Commanders, Peninsula & Waterloo* (Barnsley: Pen & Sword, 2017), pp.116–117.
48   Warre (ed.), *Letters*, p.11.

fellow in the world. He has so pleasant a manner of stating what his wishes are, that one cannot but feel a pleasure in conforming to them. In short we should be very ungrateful did we not, as he seems only to think how to make our situation the most pleasant to us.[49]

There is an account of Ferguson during the campaign, going to see Pipon, the deputy commissary general, after hearing that his men had not been issued rations. Pipon said he would attend the general once he finished his dinner. Ferguson immediately went in, grabbed the tablecloth, and pulled the contents of the table onto the floor.[50] Another anonymous officer wrote of Ferguson:

> A better man, or a more gallant soldier, never drew the breath of life, – his greatest happiness consisted in endeavours to do good to his fellow creatures … and everybody loved him. Certainly he was not a man for a Commissary to trifle with, – six feet two in height, with every limb set firm and fully proportioned, – a fine figure, especially with the claymore belted to his side.[51]

Warre had found himself unsuited to the family wine business and was sent to a private tutor in Bonn to learn languages with a view to joining the army. When war broke out between France and Austria, he and another student unofficially joined the Austrians. They were captured during a skirmish, but the French general saw they were just boys and let them go. Warre was commissioned into the 52nd in 1803, aged 19, and was then promoted to lieutenant in the 98th before quickly purchased a captaincy in the 23rd Light Dragoons. In the summer of 1807, he was sent to the Royal Military College in High Wycombe to prepare for service on the staff.[52]

With his knowledge of Portugal and staff training, Warre seems an eminently sensible choice for an aide de camp, but Ferguson's other appointment seems less reasoned. Major generals were usually allowed a single aide de camp, but the Duke of York allowed Ferguson an extra aide. Captain Henry Mellish was a famous, if not infamous, gambler, duellist, sportsman, racehorse owner and boxing promoter. Born in 1782 in Doncaster, he was the son of a victualling contractor and inherited a fortune aged 21. He had purchased a cornetcy in the very fashionable 10th (Prince of Wales' Own) Light Dragoons in 1803, and then paid for his steps up to lieutenant and captain in 1805 and 1806. Mellish was tall, almost six feet, and broad, with black hair, a pale complexion, and a fashionable long hussar moustache. He owned nearly 40 racehorses but frequently lost huge sums on them. In 1807, he fought a duel with the Honourable Martin Hawke over who had obtained the vote of a particular voter for a Parliamentary candidate they were both supporting. Mellish missed, but Hawke's shot passed along Mellish's stomach and then hit his left arm. The wound still troubled him when he was preparing to sail for Portugal.

In the spring of 1808, Mellish's financial affairs were in crisis, so it may have been convenient for him to leave the country for a while. He told his sister that his appointment was 'in every respect … desirable both for my health, my advancement in my profession, & the arrangement of my affairs.'[53] He also told his sister how his appointment had been secured:

---

49   UoN: Me4C2/1/8: Henry Mellish to Ann Mellish, 29 May 1808.
50   F. Wilkie, 'Military Anecdotes', *United Service Journal*, October 1843, p.243.
51   Anon., 'The United Services', *United Service Journal*, December 1843, p.548.
52   Warre (ed.), *Letters*, p.xx.
53   UoN: Me4C2/1/6: Henry Mellish to Ann Mellish, 22 May 1808.

General Ferguson told me that he had appointed his Aid de Camp but if the Duke of York would allow him to take a supernumerary he would with pleasure take me. I immediately went to the Prince of Wales, who sent for me into his dressing room where the Duke of York was & on my mentioning what I wished, he said he would allow it with pleasure, but that he must put me into another Regiment which is going & which should be done directly.[54]

The conversation with the Prince that Mellish relates must have happened after Ferguson was appointed to join Spencer. Mellish exchanged into the 87th Foot from the 10th Light Dragoons in March 1808, although the 87th was not one of the regiments that would end up in Portugal that year.

Ferguson nearly had to find himself two new aides when Warre and Mellish had an accident on the way to Portsmouth, as Mellish told his sister:

Our service has not commenced very auspiciously, but you need not be alarmed for we are all safe and sound. Captain Warre the General's other aid de camp & myself were proceeding here last night in a hack chaise. Just previous to entering Kingston (the night being very dark) the boy contrived to run us onto the footpath against a post & upset us into the road. The chaise was smashed to pieces, but fortunately neither of us were hurt. I fell unluckily on my wounded arm and bruised it a good deal. It is however doing very well. Warre sprained his thumb & wrist very violently but it is getting better. The General arrived just [in] time enough to pick up his wounded staff & on our arrival at Kingston he produced his medical chest & dressed our wounds with such skill. In short our disaster has been rather productive of entertainment than otherwise.[55]

1st Battalion 36th (Herefordshire) Regiment of Foot
The 36th was, along with the 45th, a last-minute addition to the expedition. The battalion had been in India from 1784 to 1798, at Minorca in 1801, joined the 1805 Hannover expedition, and was then sent with the reinforcements to South America before returning to Ireland. For 16-year-old Ensign Roderick Murchison, a graduate of the Royal Military College at Marlow, the campaign would be his first. Murchison much later became a renowned geologist, and a biography was written about him based on his letters and journals. When he joined the battalion in early 1808, he found the officers, 'for the most part quiet, well-disciplined old soldiers, who knew their work and did it, and who, more over, had seen a good deal of active service on the Continent, in India, and in South America.'[56] The biography also describes the battalion's commanding officer, Colonel Robert Burne:

Cool and daring on the field of battle, he was a severe disciplinarian. His piercing dark brown eye proved quick to detect a careless pig-tail, or a failure of pipe-clay either in gloves or breeches. He had drilled his men to the most perfect precision after the method then in vogue, insomuch that his had become what was called a 'crack regiment' at the camp on the Curragh. But with all this attention to the laborious system of training which

---

54   UoN: Me4C2/1/4: Henry Mellish to Ann Mellish, 18 May 1808.
55   UoN: Me4C2/1/4: Henry Mellish to Ann Mellish, 18 May 1808.
56   Geikie, *Life*, vol.I, p.20.

prevailed in his time, he knew how to unbend after his day's work was past. At the mess-table he would sit habitually from five till ten o'clock, setting an example to all his officers in the potation of port. He could not tolerate a drunken man, and he despised a young fledgling Ensign to whom illimitable draughts of his own favourite beverage proved in any way disastrous. He himself never showed any indication of being in the least degree affected, save that 'his nose was gradually assuming that purple colour and bottle-shape which rendered him so conspicuous in the subsequent Peninsular war.[57]

Robert Burne was born in 1753. He purchased an ensigncy in the 36th Foot in 1773 and then paid for the step up to lieutenant in 1777. In 1783, the regiment was sent to India, and he was soon promoted to captain and given the command of the grenadier company. The 36th saw action during the Third Anglo-Mysore War, during which legend has it that Burne killed the leader of Tipu Sultan's cavalry during the capture of Seringapatam. Burne purchased his majority in 1796, and the regiment arrived back in England in 1799. Shortly after, he was promoted to lieutenant colonel and commanded the regiment. He was absent in 1801 due to ill health but returned in 1802 when the regiment was in Ireland. He then led the regiment during the Hannover expedition, when it was in Wellesley's brigade, and then in South America where he distinguished himself during the attack on Buenos Aires. He was promoted to colonel by brevet in April 1808.[58]

1st Battalion 40th (2nd Somersetshire) Regiment of Foot
The 40th had fought with distinction under Abercromby in Egypt. On its return to Britain, it was stationed on the south coast to defend against a French invasion and even went so far as to practice wading into the sea to attack landing craft.[59] In 1806, the battalion sailed for South America and took part in the storming of Montevideo in early 1807 and then the attack on Buenos Aires. Soon after the 1/40th arrived back in Ireland, it received a draft of 250 men from the second battalion. After being ordered to Cork to embark, Colonel James Kemmis arrived with another 100 men from the 2/40th and took command of the battalion.

Kemmis was born in Ireland in 1751 but began his military career a little later than most when he purchased an ensigncy in the 9th when he was 24. His regiment sailed for Montreal in 1776 to reinforce the British garrisons in North America following the outbreak of the rebellion. Kemmis purchased a lieutenancy in June 1777, and his regiment was part of Burgoyne's army in the Saratoga campaign, which ended with the British surrender. He remained a prisoner of war until he was exchanged in 1781. He purchased a captaincy in 1784 but then went on half-pay until 1790, when he exchanged into the 40th. In 1794, he accompanied the regiment to Flanders and saw action again. In the following year, the 40th went to the West Indies. The regiment returned in 1798, and Kemmis was one of only 81 officers and men not to have succumbed to the endemic diseases that decimated British troops in the region. Unsurprisingly, in 1799, Kemmis was promoted to major without purchase. He was with the 40th in the Helder and then fought in Egypt. He was promoted to lieutenant colonel without purchase in 1804, but when the 1/40th sailed for South America, he was on the staff in Ireland. Like Burne, he was promoted to colonel by brevet in April 1808.[60]

---

57   Geikie, *Life*, vol.I, p.21.
58   McGuigan & Burnham, *Brigade Commanders*, pp.69–70.
59   R.H.R Smythies, *Historical Records of the 40th (2nd Somersetshire) Regiment* (Devonport: Swiss, 1894), p.97.
60   McGuigan & Burnham, *Brigade Commanders*, pp.157–158.

1st Battalion 71st (Highland) Regiment of Foot

The men of the 1/71st had made up the bulk of the troops for the first expedition to Buenos Aires and had to surrender themselves and their colours on the defeat of Beresford's force in August 1806. They remained prisoners until Whitelocke's defeat a year later when they were set free as part of the armistice. Nearly 150 of the men opted to stay in South America. They arrived back in Ireland at the end of 1807 and received a draft of 200 men from the 2/71st to rebuild their numbers. In April 1808, they were presented with new colours by Lieutenant General John Floyd to replace those that had been lost. Floyd, who had served alongside the regiment in India, addressed the battalion:

> You now stand on this parade, in defiance of the allurements held out to base desertion. You are endeared to the army, and to your country. You ensure the esteem of all true soldiers, and all good men.
>
> It has been my good fortune to have witnessed, in a remote part of the world, the early glories of the 71st regiment in the field, and it is with great satisfaction I now meet you again with replenished ranks, arms in your hands and stout hearts in your bosoms. Look forward, officers and soldiers, to the achievement of new honour, and the acquirement of fresh fame. Officers, be the friends and guardians of these brave men committed to your charge. Soldiers, give your confidence to your officers;– they have shared with you the chances of war;– they have bled along with you. Preserve your regiment's reputation in the field, early and gloriously gained, and be, like them, regular in quarters ... May honour and victory ever attend you![61]

Like all the battalions that had been defeated in the two disastrous incursions into South America in 1806 and 1807, the men of the 71st may have felt the need to regain their regimental honour and reputation.

The 71st's commanding officer was Lieutenant Colonel Denis Pack. Born in Ireland in 1774, Pack joined the 14th Light Dragoons as a cornet, without purchase, in 1791. Two years later, he was court martialled, possibly for striking a superior officer, found guilty and suspended. However, when his regiment campaigned in Flanders, he accompanied them as a volunteer and saw action at Nieuport and Boxtel. By 1795, he had purchased a lieutenancy and was part of the Quiberon Bay expedition that occupied the Île d'Yeu. A year later, he purchased a captaincy in the 5th Dragoon Guards and spent three years in Ireland. During the rebellion, he was mentioned in dispatches by General Cornwallis. In August 1798, he purchased a majority in the 4th Dragoon Guards and then in 1800, he purchased a lieutenant colonelcy in the 71st Foot and took command of the regiment in April 1801. He was still only 25 years old and had no previous infantry experience.[62]

In 1806, Pack led the 71st in the recapture of the Cape of Good Hope when his battalion was brigaded under Ferguson, and then he took his men across the Atlantic to Buenos Aires. He became a prisoner of war when the British forces surrendered to the Spanish and colonial troops, but then escaped with Beresford and served with distinction with Whitelocke's reinforcements before again surrendering and then being repatriated with the rest of the British troops at the end of 1807.

61   D. Stewart, *Sketches of the Character, Manners, and Present State of the Highlanders of Scotland* (Edinburgh: Constable, 1825), vol.II, p.152.
62   M. De La Poer Beresford, *Peninsular and Waterloo General, Sir Denis Pack and the War Against Napoleon* (Barnsley: Pen & Sword, 2022), pp.1–6.

3rd Brigade (Nightingall)

Brigadier General Miles Nightingall was born in 1768 and was the illegitimate son of General Charles, Earl Cornwallis. While his father's influence certainly helped his career, he was still a very experienced officer in his own right. He was commissioned in the 52nd Foot when he was 19 and joined them in India, where his father was Governor General and Commander-in-Chief. Nightingall served in the Third Mysore War and was promoted to lieutenant. He was appointed a brigade major and fought at Seringapatam and Pondicherry before returning to Britain in 1794 due to ill health. His family purchased him a captaincy in the 115th Foot in 1795, and his father made him one of his aides de camp and then a brigade major while he commanded the Eastern District. Nightingall then purchased a majority and lieutenant colonelcy in quick succession and commanded the 38th Foot at the capture of Trinidad under Abercromby. He again had to return home due to ill health but was soon back in the West Indies as deputy adjutant general on Santo Domingo, but soon returned to England again. His father was, by this time, Lord Lieutenant of Ireland and made him one of his aides before giving him command of a battalion of light infantry companies under John Moore during the rebellion. He was on the staff of the Helder and Quiberon expeditions and then in England before serving his father as his secretary during the peace negotiations at Amiens. In 1803, he returned to India as quartermaster general to Lake's army during the Second Anglo-Maratha War. He was promoted to colonel, and then when his father returned to India he became his military secretary until his death, after which Nightingall became quartermaster general for India. In September 1807, he returned to Britain and was appointed a brigadier general on Spencer's force bound for the Mediterranean.[63]

29th (Worcestershire) Regiment of Foot
The 29th, a single battalion regiment, had spent five years in Halifax, Nova Scotia, and arrived in Britain in the spring of 1807. The 2/50th Foot shared a barracks with the 29th, and one of their officers, John Patterson, wrote that the 29th, 'Being in preparation for active employment, it was now passing through the usual ordeal of drill and ball practise; and consequently the interminable sounds of drums, and bugles, the monotonous din of the drill Serjeants' 'as you were,' accompanied by the clamour from the Adjutants' stentorian lungs, were continually wringing in our ears.' After noting that the 29th had 'been trained up after the manner of the old school.' Patterson commented on the regiment's band: 'We were enlivened by their excellent band; and their corps of black drummers cut a fierce and remarkable appearance, while hammering away on their brass drums.'[64]

Most regimental bands were made up of men on the regiment's rolls, and many recruited musicians specifically for the band. The officers or the regimental colonel bore the cost of the instruments. The drummers, buglers and fifers that made up part of the establishments of the companies were separate from the bands. The bands entertained the officers, played at parades, balls, and other special occasions, and helped with recruiting. Many regiments had some men of colour in their bands or amongst their drummers, as it was deemed fashionable and made them stand out, but the 29th seems to have been particularly known for it. Eight or 10 drummers were sourced from the West Indies in 1759, and there is some evidence of their presence before that. Some may

63   Burnham & McGuigan, *Brigade Commanders*, pp.207–208.
64   Patterson, *Adventures*, pp.6–7.

have originally been purchased as slaves, but, in 1807, an act of Parliament was passed, freeing any slaves that had been enlisted into the army and treating them as if they had volunteered.[65] Three black drummers – James Kearney, James Patison and George Wise – had enlisted during the battalion's time in Halifax, joining the eight men of colour or so who were already serving. All three had been born in Nova Scotia. Peter Asking was also definitely present in Portugal, as he was later awarded the Military General Service medal with clasps for Roliça and Vimeiro.[66] While musicians may have made up a large portion of the men of colour that landed in Portugal, there would also have very likely been others serving as ordinary soldiers, some of whom would have been recruited when regiments were abroad and some of whom would have been recruited from the small but present black population in Britain and Ireland.[67]

While in Nova Scotia, the battalion had been inspected by Major General John Skerrett, who noted 'the high state of discipline in this excellent corps' and continued, 'The men in general of this valuable Regiment, are well sized and young, and as fit for service in my opinion, as any Regiment in His Majesty's Service.' He also praised the battalion's surgeon: 'I cannot say too much in praise of the regularity, cleanliness and high state of good order in which the Regimental Hospital is kept, and the greatest merit is due to Mr Guthrie the surgeon, for his unremitted attention to his duty.' Of the 638 privates present, 410 were English, 83 Scottish, 133 Irish, and 12 were foreign. Two of the 22 drummers were Irish, and the rest were foreign. Most of the foreigners would have been the black drummers and musicians. The median length of service was six to eight years, and most men were 5'8"–5'6".[68] All battalions were regularly inspected, but, unfortunately, not all the resulting reports survive in the archives.

The commanding officer of the 29th was Lieutenant Colonel the Honourable George Lake, son of the recently deceased General Viscount Lake. George was born in 1780, purchased a cornetcy in the 8th Light Dragoons in 1796, and then moved to the 20th Foot as a lieutenant a year later. He then executed a series of swift regimental exchanges to obtain a captaincy in the 4th Foot in 1799. In 1803, he purchased a majority in the 40th and then his lieutenant colonelcy in the 29th. On the face of it, Lake had enjoyed a varied career, but he had done very little, if any, service with any of the regiments he had been commissioned in. He had served his father as an aide de camp in Ireland from 1797–1798 and then again in India from 1801–1807, as well as being for a time his father's military secretary and a deputy quartermaster general on the staff.[69] Whilst he had been in the thick of the action next to this father in many battles during their time in India, he would have had almost no experience commanding a body of troops in combat or of the day-to-day administration of a regiment. Lake joined his regiment at Cosham near Portsmouth the day before they embarked with Spencer. He invited all the officers to breakfast and supplied the men with a

65   J. D. Ellis, 'Drummers for the Devil? The Black Soldiers of the 29th (Worcestershire) Regiment of Foot, 1759-1843', *Journal of the Society for Army Historical Research*, vol.80, no.323 (Autumn 2002), pp.186–193.
66   'The Black Drummers of the 29th', *The Worcester Regiment*, <http://www.worcestershireregiment.com/wr.php?main=inc/em_drummers>, accessed February 2023.
67   J.D. Ellis, 'The Visual Representation, Role and Origin of Black Soldiers in British Army Regiments During the Early Nineteenth Century', *The Black Presence in Britain*, <https://blackpresence.co.uk/the-visual-representation-role-and-origin-of-black-soldiers-in-british-army-regiments-during-the-early-nineteenth-century/>, accessed February 2023.
68   TNA: WO 27/91: Inspection 29th Foot, 2 April 1807.
69   Clive Willis, 'Colonel George Lake and the Battle of Roliça', *British Historical Society of Portugal Review*, 1996, pp.97–98.

'substantial repast'.[70] The intervening months would have allowed him some time to get to know his regiment, but they also spent many weeks aboard ship where the chance to familiarise himself with his command would have been minimal.

1st Battalion 82nd (Prince of Wales's Volunteers) Regiment of Foot

The 82nd had served in the West Indies, Minorca and the Quiberon Bay expedition during the Revolutionary Wars and then took part in the expedition to Copenhagen in 1807. The battalion was praised for its performance at the siege of the city, and Lieutenant Colonel George Smith was knighted for his services. Just before embarking with Spencer, the battalion received drafts from the second battalion and volunteers from the Irish Militia.

As Smith was still serving as liaison with the Spanish, command of the 1/82nd devolved to Major Henry Samuel Eyre. Eyre was born in 1770 in London. In 1788, he purchased an ensigncy in the 11th Foot and a lieutenancy in the same regiment in 1792 before moving to an independent company in 1793 to get the step to captain. He then exchanged into the 57th the same year. In 1795, he went on half-pay in the 94th, possibly to avoid going to the West Indies with the 57th and remained unemployed until he joined the 12th Battalion of the Reserve in 1803. The Army of the Reserve was a short-lived force raised to counter the French invasion threat after the war resumed in 1803. He was promoted to major and then moved to the 82nd in 1804.

4th Brigade (Bowes)

Colonel Barnard Foord Bowes of the 6th Foot was given his brigade by Wellesley due to his seniority; he had not been appointed a brigadier general on the staff of Gibraltar, where the 6th had been based before joining Spencer. Born in 1769, he was commissioned in the 26th Foot at 12 and stayed with the regiment until he purchased a majority in the 85th in 1796. He then purchased a lieutenant colonelcy in the 6th six months later and commanded them during the 1798 rebellion. He was promoted to colonel in 1805 and briefly succeeded to the command of British troops in Canada before rejoining his regiment.[71]

1st Battalion 6th (1st Warwickshire) Regiment of Foot

The 1/6th was stationed in British North America from 1799 to 1806, mainly in Quebec. The battalion received drafts from the second battalion and then embarked for Gibraltar in April 1807. Just before they left England, they were inspected by Spencer. Of the 930 privates, 668 were English, 11 Scottish, 232 Irish, and 19 foreign. Nearly half of 472 had served one year or less, and 324 men were under 5 foot 5 inches tall.[72] In June 1808, the battalion was removed from the Gibraltar garrison and placed under the orders of Spencer.

With Colonel Bowes commanding the brigade, the commander of the 6th was Major Thomas Carnie. Carnie began his army career in 1780 as an ensign with the recently formed 83rd Foot, and may have been with them on the Channel Islands in 1781 when the French attempted to capture

---

70   Leslie, *Journal*, p.7.
71   Burnham & McGuigan, *Brigade Commanders*, pp.54–55.
72   TNA: WO 27/91: Return of 1/6th Foot, 17 April 1807. The return is present in the archives but the confidential report is not.

the islands. Carnie was advanced to lieutenant that year, and the regiment moved to the garrison at New York and remained there for the rest of the American War. The regiment, like many others, was disbanded at the end of the war, and Carnie went on half-pay. In 1787, he returned to duty with the newly formed 74th Foot but exchanged into the 6th before the 74th left for India. Carnie was promoted to captain-lieutenant in 1794, to captain in 1795, and then to major in 1804. During these years, the battalion fought in the West Indies and Ireland during the rebellion. Given the slow pace of his advancement up the ranks and the fact that none of his promotions seem to have been purchased, he likely did not come from a wealthy background.

1st Battalion 32nd (Cornwall) Regiment of Foot
The 32nd was part of Sir Ralph Abercromby's expedition to the West Indies in 1796, spending a year in Saint Domingue, and were reduced to a mere skeleton. The regiment returned to Britain to recruit and then went to Ireland, where it helped quell the rebellion of 1803. The 1/32nd took part in the Copenhagen expedition in 1807 and then received 99 men from the second battalion before embarking with Spencer at the end of the year.

The battalion's commanding officer was Lieutenant Colonel Samuel Venables Hinde. Hinde joined the army as an ensign in the 25th Foot in 1788 and spent the first four years of his career as part of the Gibraltar garrison. In 1792, he purchased a lieutenancy, and, when war broke out the following year, the 25th were embarked on the fleet as marines. Hinde was present when troops landed at Toulon and during the siege. In 1794, he fought in Corsica, including the attack on the Torra di Mortella (which became the model for the Martello towers built to defend the British and Irish coasts) and the capture of San Fiorenzo. He was promoted to captain in 1795, and the 25th continued to serve as marines in the Mediterranean. In 1797, the steadiness of the 25th detachment under Hinde's command on HMS *St George* helped to suppress a mutiny, and he was praised by Earl St Vincent and subsequently awarded a brevet promotion to major. In 1799, he fought and was wounded in the Helder expedition. In 1800, he was appointed a major in the 32nd, went with them to Ireland, and then in 1804 was promoted to lieutenant colonel, taking command of the 1/32nd in 1805.[73]

5th Brigade (Craufurd)

Brigadier General James Catlin Craufurd was born in 1776 and was the illegitimate son of Lieutenant Colonel James Craufurd, then the governor of Bermuda. He purchased a commission in the 24th Foot in 1791 while living in New York. and then purchased a lieutenancy and captaincy in independent companies – temporary units raised the recruit men. In 1793, he moved to the 30th Foot, which was then serving as marines in the Mediterranean. His next step up was becoming a major of foot by purchase in 1795. This meant he was a major in the army but was not part of any regiment. However, a year later, he was appointed to the 98th, which was renumbered to the 91st. A year later, he purchased a lieutenant colonelcy in the same regiment at 21. The money from his promotions probably came from his uncle, an MP, as his father was a gambler heavily in debt. While at the Cape of Good Hope, Craufurd served as an aide de camp to the governor and in 1805, he was promoted to colonel. He and the 91st served in the short-lived expedition to Hannover

73   Phillipart (ed.), *Calendar*, vol.III, pp.352–354.

before he was posted to Ireland and then assigned to Wellesley's expedition.[74] Patterson of the 50th described Craufurd as 'a tall, fine-looking man, with a fair complexion and sandy hair.'[75]

1st Battalion 45th (Nottinghamshire) Regiment of Foot
The 1/45th spent most of the years between 1786 and 1801 in the West Indies, coming to Britain once to rebuild its numbers before being sent out again and suffering more losses from disease. From 1801 to 1806, they were in Britain and Ireland before being sent to South America. Upon returning, this was another battalion that received volunteers from the Militia; in this case, 167 men from Irish regiments.[76] Some of these men may have been those who arrived just before the expedition sailed.

The commander of the 1/45th was Lieutenant Colonel William Guard. He was born in Devon, and in 1789, when he was 16, he purchased an ensign's commission in the 45th and then a lieutenancy at the end of 1790. In early 1791, he joined the regiment on Grenada and then served in Grey's attack on Martinique. In 1795, he purchased a captaincy, in 1797 a majority, and then, in 1799, a lieutenant colonelcy. He took command of the battalion when it returned to Britain in 1801. He was short and a little overweight but commanded the respect of his officers and men. However, his personal life was not going as well as his army career. Guard had returned from South America to find his wife had had a child with another man while he had been away. He brought a court case against his wife's lover and was awarded £3,000 in damages.[77]

1st Battalion 50th (West Kent) Regiment of Foot
The 50th had spent much of the war in the Mediterranean, including a brief period in Portugal, seeing action in Corsica and Egypt, and then during the short-lived 1803 Irish Rebellion. The 1/50th was part of the 1807 Copenhagen expedition before being allocated to Spencer's reinforcements originally destined for Sicily. Ensign John Patterson was ordered, along with a draft of 150 men from the second battalion, to join the first battalion when it was marching to embark. He noted that:

> The 1st battalion of the 50th, or West Kent regiment, commanded by Lieutenant-Colonel George Townsend Walker, was, at that time above a thousand strong, having been completed by men from the second battalion, on its return from the expedition to Copenhagen. In addition to the old hands, they obtained a full supply of young active fellows, who had volunteered from the English Militia,—the whole, officers as well as privates, were in good health and spirits, elated with the prospect of active service, and looking forward to new adventures as well as to encountering the enemy in the field. But it was not alone by numerical strength or physical power that the 50th was likely to be formidable. There was likewise an 'esprit de corps,' a high tone of feeling among them, producing a moral force not easily to be overcome.[78]

74   Burnham & McGuigan, *Brigade Commanders*, pp.87–88.
75   Patterson, *Adventures*, p.34.
76   Brown, *Redjackets*, p.22.
77   Brown, *Redjackets*, pp.22–23.
78   Patterson, *Adventures*, pp.7–8.

But of course, few memoirists ever criticise their regiments.

The battalion's commander, Lieutenant Colonel George Townsend Walker, was another officer with long service behind him. Neither his original commission nor any of his steps up in rank were purchased: ensign 1782; lieutenant 1783; captain-lieutenant 1789; major 1794; lieutenant colonel 1798. Despite not purchasing any promotion, he still rose from ensign to lieutenant colonel in 16 years. During that time, he served in six regiments before joining the 50th as a lieutenant colonel. He served in India, and Flanders, on the staff in various locations, and was sent on several confidential missions to the continent. In 1797, he served as an aide to the British commander in Portugal, and then, in 1799, he was attached to the Russian army in Holland. It was not until 1802 that he spent any prolonged period with the 50th, but he commanded the battalion through Copenhagen and during Spencer's expedition.[79] Patterson described Walker as,

> …a man endued with extraordinary coolness and intrepidity of mind, knew right well how to go about his work; he also knew the stubborn elements of which his regiment was composed. He was of the middle stature, well proportioned, and of a pale complexion; with a remarkably handsome set of features, animated by keen expressive eyes, that were full of intelligence and fire.[80]

1st Battalion 91st Regiment of Foot
The 91st was raised by the Duke of Argyll in 1794 as a kilted highland regiment and initially numbered the 98th before being renumbered in 1796. However, the regiment's Scottishness waned, and, by 1803, the only item of Scottish dress left was the Highland bonnet.[81] Nor, at least as far as the *Army List* was concerned, did the regiment bear its later title of Argyllshire at this time. However, the regiment likely retained some Scottish character as Wellesley initially brigaded them while at Cork with the 71st (and strangely the English 40th) as a highland brigade. The regiment had seen service at the Cape of Good Hope and Hannover before embarking for Portugal. While initial recruitment in Scotland may have filled the ranks, many highland regiments were diluted with English and Irish recruits who were not so keen on wearing the kilt.

The commander of the 1/91st, Lieutenant Colonel James Robinson, had been appointed an ensign in the 3rd Foot in 1793 and then moved to the newly formed 78th to gain the step up to lieutenant in 1794. He moved again in 1795 to the 15th Foot to get his captaincy. He then stayed with the 15th, purchasing his majority in 1801 and lieutenant colonelcy in 1802. He briefly commanded the 2/15th before the battalion was disbanded later that year and he was placed on half-pay. He remained on half-pay until April 1808, when he was appointed to the 91st and took command of the first battalion. So, despite being a lieutenant colonel for six years, he had minimal experience commanding a battalion.

79   Burnham & McGuigan, *Brigade Commanders*, pp.300–302.
80   J. Patterson, *Camps and Quarters, or Scenes and Impressions, of Military Life* (London: Saunders & Otley, 1840), vol.I, pp.216–217.
81   G.L. Goff, *Historical Records of the 91st Argyllshire Highlanders* (London: Bentley, 1891), p.301.

6th (Light) Brigade (Fane)

As the son of an MP and the grandson of an earl, Brigadier General Henry Fane owed his career to his family's political connections. Born in 1778, he was commissioned as a cornet in the 7th Dragoons in 1792, aged 14, but was quickly promoted to lieutenant in the 55th Foot. Commissions at such a young age were common then, but the officers were not expected to serve until their later teens. In 1793, he moved to the 4th Dragoon Guards as a captain-lieutenant and then captain. Also that year, his cousin, John Fane, Earl of Westmoreland and Lord Lieutenant of Ireland, made him one of his aides de camp. A young Arthur Wesley was also one of the Earl's aides. In 1795, he purchased his majority – the first and only step up he paid for. Two years later, at the age of 18, he was promoted to lieutenant colonel: as the junior lieutenant colonel, he did not command the regiment, but he did serve with it during the 1798 rebellion. He became MP for Lyme

Henry Fane, circa 1835. (Anne S.K. Brown Military Collection)

Regis in 1802, a seat in the gift of the Westmoreland family. At the end of 1804 he moved to the 1st Dragoon Guards, commanded the regiment until 1805, and was then promoted to full colonel and made an aide de camp to the King. He had no infantry command experience before his assignment to Wellesley's expedition.[82] Fane's aide de camp was an officer from his regiment, Lieutenant John Dorset Bringhurst.

5th Battalion 60th (Royal American) Regiment of Foot

The 5/60th were formed at the end of 1797 from two émigré regiments and was the first fully rifle-armed battalion in the British Army. The rifles that they, the 95th, and other units were armed with by 1808 were much more accurate than the smooth-bore muskets the rest of the infantry used, but they were slower to load and more expensive to produce. The 5/60th had not seen action since the 1798 rebellion in Ireland shortly after its formation. As a battalion of the Royal American Regiment, the riflemen had spent many years in the West Indies, Surinam on the northern coast of South America, and Nova Scotia before returning to Britain at the end of 1805. The battalion had last been inspected in May 1807 while it was based at Haslar Barracks in Portsmouth. The inspecting officer was Major General Sir George Prevost, the battalion's colonel-commandant and the local commanding general. How impartial he could have been inspecting his own battalion is open to question. Still, Prevost stated that the battalion was 'well disciplined and correct in the Field Exercise

---

82   Burnham & McGuigan, *Brigade Commanders*, pp.108–109.

& Movements prescribed for a Rifle Corps', that the 'men are skilful in firing at targets from different ranges, in various positions', and concluded that despite having received 300 recruits only six months before the battalion was 'fit for immediate service.' Of the 760 privates present, 306 had served under six months. These men had primarily been recruited from non-French prisoners of war, including those from the frigates captured in 1806 (see Chapter Six), so while they may have only served a short time in the British Army, they may well have served longer in French or other service. A majority of the men, 372, had served for five years or more.[83]

In September 1807, the 5/60th had moved to Ireland and had received a draft of 214 men from the Foreign Depot at Lymington in Hampshire. At the beginning of 1808, Colonel de Rottenburg, who had commanded the battalion for almost 10 years, left the battalion on his appointment to brigadier general, and Major Gabriel Davy took command. He was only 28 years old and had first been commissioned in the 61st Foot, aged 17, after leaving Eton. His father had been a major in the East India Company army. Gabriel had joined the 5/60th as a 22-year-old captain in 1802 but had spent much of his service since as an aide de camp and had spent very little time with the battalion. He rejoined it in March 1808 after purchasing his majority over the heads of 13 more senior captains in February of the previous year.[84]

A rifleman of the 5/60th. (From *The Annals of the King's Royal Rifle Corps, Appendix dealing with Uniform, Armament & Equipment*)

2nd Battalion 95th Regiment of Foot

The four companies of the 2/95th Rifles had embarked at Dover on 8 June to sail to Cork. The companies were those of Captains Jasper Creagh, Jeremiah Crampton, Hercules Pakenham, and Jonathan Leach.[85] Major Robert Travers was in command, whose majority dated from 1805

---

83   TNA: WO 27/91: Inspection 5/60th, 1 May 1807.
84   Griffith, *Riflemen*, pp.126–127.
85   G.J. Caldwell and R.B.E. Cooper, *Rifle Green in the Peninsula* (Leicester: Bugle Horn, 1998), vol.I, p.16.

A rifleman of the 95th, unknown artist. (Anne S.K. Brown Military Collection)

making him senior to Davy. Travers, an Irishman, had joined the 85th Foot as an ensign in 1793 and was a captain in the 112th by September 1795. During the 1798 rebellion, he commanded a light company in Sir John Moore's brigade; he then transferred to the newly formed Corps of Riflemen and accompanied them to Ferrol in 1800. The corps became the 95th Foot in 1802, and Travers stayed with them. He was with the 1/95th in South America in 1807. Three of his brothers also served in the 95th.

Travers was bald and wore a wig. Private Benjamin Harris of the 95th described Travers as well-liked but a 'tight hand' and commented that soldiers preferred a sterner officer to a slovenly one. He then continued, 'He was never a very good-looking man, being hard-featured and thin; a hatchet-faced man, as we used to say. But he was a regular good 'un, — a real English soldier; and that's better than if he had been the handsomest ladies'-man in the army.'[86]

The 2/95th was inspected on 5 May at Hythe Barracks by the regiment's colonel, Major General Coote Manningham, who had been instrumental in the corps' formation. Manningham noted that:

> This corps have been extremely fortunate in the species of men they have obtained on the late recruiting from the militia, and are particularly well adapted to their sort of service. They possess youth, a proper height, and activity, and are daily becoming more equal to their duty. The officers are a very fine set of young men, and the corps is in every respect

---

86   H. Curling (ed.), *Recollections of Rifleman Harris* (London: Hurst, 1848), pp.64–65.

in high order. The target practice (so essential for a rifle corps) has been closely attended to whenever the weather would permit…

Manningham also noted that further training in brigade field days was taking place. A third of the 928 privates were Irish, three were foreign, 119 had served for only one year, and another 63 for less than that, but over 350 men had served for five years or more. Separate figures for the four companies embarked are unavailable but would have been broadly in keeping with the rest of the battalion.[87] Three of the four companies of the 2/95th in Portugal had been at Copenhagen – Crampton's, Pakenham's and Leach's.[88]

Cavalry

The British Army's cavalry was smaller as a proportion of the total army than most continental armies. In March 1806, the Duke of York had written to William Windham, Secretary for War, on the subject of recruiting:

> The proportion of Cavalry in all Continental armies is never less than 1/6 and in some amounts to 1/4 of their whole force; whereas in the British army it never has been above 1/8, and now if complete at its present Establishment would not exceed 1/10 of the Force required for the Defence of this country.[89]

As of 1808, the cavalry composed 29,702 of the 254,730 regular rank and file. Roughly one-ninth of the army.[90] The four troops of the 20th Light Dragoons amounted to less than five percent, one-twentieth, of Wellesley's original rank and file.[91] To get that number up to one-sixth would have taken over 1,500 men and horses, equating to around 12,000 tons of shipping or about 35 vessels. The proportion of British cavalry to other troops dropped further once Spencer's troops joined. Junot's cavalry made up only a slightly higher proportion of his troops at seven percent, but they outnumbered the light dragoons by more than four to one.[92]

A 'special inspection' of 20th Light Dragoons had been ordered when they were at Chichester in May, probably with a view to them embarking for foreign service. Six troops were present for the inspection – a further four were in Sicily. The confidential report stated, 'The men are young – well made – and healthy – perfectly fit for service', except for one dragoon, Joseph Tanner. The horses were in 'good condition and fit for service' except for five. The equipment was also in generally good condition, but it was noted that some of the sabre blades were stained by seawater. The report concluded, 'The detachment appears to be in a state of fitness, in every respect, for immediate embarkation.' There were 353 privates present and 199 horses, so the six troops lacked 103 men and 251 horses to bring them up to their established strength. Of the privates, 282 were English, eight

87 TNA: WO 27/92: Inspection 2/95th, 5 May 1808.
88 W. Verner, *History And Campaigns Of The Rifle Brigade* (Wagram Press Kindle Edition), vol.I, Kindle Location 2252.
89 York to Windham, 18 March 1806 quoted in R. Glover, *Britain at Bay* (London: Allen & Unwin, 1973), p.224.
90 Burnham and McGuigan, *British Army Trivia*, p.2.
91 Based on the returns in TNA: WO 72/29.
92 See Table 11.

Scottish, 28 Irish, and 35 were, like Sergeant Landsheit, foreign. Only 33 privates were recruits, with 136 having only served one or two years. Only 41 had served for more than five years.[93]

The 20th Light Dragoons had been part of the first expedition to Buenos Aires, where they mainly fought dismounted, and many would begin the campaign in Portugal in the same manner. The 20th sailed with 384 dragoons and only 238 horses.[94] However, the shortage of draft animals meant that 58 of those were allocated to the artillery, leaving only 180 for the dragoons.

Lieutenant Colonel Browne in Oporto had been tasked with procuring 150 horses for the dragoons. On 31 July, he wrote:

> I believe Portugal was never famous for horses and the French having put in requisition all the horses which were fit for the army. I found it wholly impossible to procure a single horse worth forwarding; in this emergency it occurred to me that mares should answer our purpose equally well, in consequence they have all been put in requisition and out of 1,000 I have been able to select 75, which I hope will be approved; they left Oporto for Coimbra this evening.[95]

More mares were being gathered at stations on the way from Coimbra, and he hoped to find another 75.

The 20th also had to provide order-lies for the generals and staff. Wellesley and Spencer were assigned two each. The other generals, the deputy quartermaster general, and the deputy adjutant general all had one each.[96] These requirements would further reduce the number of dragoons available for the light cavalry's prime roles: reconnaissance, patrols and pickets. The terrain north of Lisbon was not ideal for cavalry combat – there were steep hills, rocky valleys, woods, and winding roads – but Wellesley would still need cavalry to probe forward and keep French reconnaissance parties at bay. The four troops would be formed into two squadrons on campaign, each commanded by the senior troop captain. In overall command was Lieutenant Colonel Charles Taylor.

Lieutenant Colonel Charles Taylor. (*The Cavalry Journal*, 1911)

93   TNA: WO 27/92: Inspection 20th Light Dragoons, 6 May 1808.
94   TNA: WO 72/29: Return of officers, Non-Commissioned Officers and Men embarked and sailed for Portugal, Transport Office, 16 November 1808.
95   BL: Add Ms 49502: Browne to Gordon, 31 July 1808.
96   Wellington (ed.), *Supplementary Despatches*, vol.VI, p.99.

Taylor, born 1772 in Reading, was the son of a doctor. He was educated at Westminster and Oxford, earning a BA and an MA. He was commissioned in the 7th Light Dragoons as a cornet in 1794, without purchase, and by the following year, had purchased his captaincy in the regiment. With the 7th, Taylor had seen action in Flanders and Den Helder in 1799. In 1801, as senior captain of the 7th, he was promoted to a vacant majority and then in 1803, he purchased a lieutenant colonelcy in the 20th Light Dragoons and married. He was then posted to Sicily, where a detachment of the 20th were based, and returned from there in the summer of 1807.

Engineers and Artillery

Royal Engineers
The officers of the Royal Engineers who sailed from Cork were Captain Howard Elphinstone, 2nd Captain Peter Patton, and 1st Lieutenants John Williams, Richard Boteler, John Wells and Frederick English. Captain George Landmann, with 1st Lieutenants Edmond Mulcaster and Cavalier Shorthose Mercer, arrived with Spencer. Elphinstone was the senior and became the expedition's Commander Royal Engineers. Writing to his wife on 27 July, he was bullishly optimistic about the coming campaign, 'Junot has but a small force in Lisbon such as I think will surrender upon our appearance… I am only afraid that the opposition will be so trifling that I shall not get a Majority from the French rogue.'[97] The engineers would be vital if a siege of the Lisbon forts and defences had to be undertaken. In the meantime, they would assist in the reconnaissance, surveying, and mapping the terrain and routes towards Lisbon.

On 31 July, Elphinstone wrote to General Robert Morse, Colonel Commandant of the Royal Engineers, complaining that Captain François Préval would not acknowledge himself to be under Elphinstone's command. Although Préval's status in the army is not entirely clear as he does not appear on the army list for 1808, he originally had a captain's commission dating from 1796, making him theoretically the senior. Elphinstone was so annoyed at the situation that he told Morse that he would resign and return to England rather than continue with the chance of Préval undermining him.[98] However, Wellesley, or someone else, must have smoothed things over as Elphinstone continued as the senior engineer. Wellesley had another task in mind for Préval.

When he was in Portugal in 1800, Préval had been in charge of a corps of guides.[99] A corps of guides at the time was usually a small unit of mounted men who would, as the name suggests, act as guides but also be translators and perform other staff duties. The composition of the corps of guides Préval formed for Wellesley is not recorded, but they would probably have been Portuguese or perhaps trustworthy non-French deserters from Junot's army. Préval was neither young nor well and requested to be relieved and sent home in September. When advising Sir Hew Dalrymple that a new commander of the guides should be appointed, Wellesley wrote:

> I cannot make this request without, at the same time, mentioning my sense of Captain Preval's services, not only in his capacity of engineer, but in that of Captain of Guides.

---

97   M.S. Thompson, *Wellington's Engineers* (Barnsley: Pen & Sword, 2015), p.10.
98   TNA: WO 55/977: Elphinstone to Morse, 31 July 1808.
99   UoS: WP 1/205: Anstruther to Wellesley, 28 June 1808. The letter mentions a memorandum from a guide of Preval's about the area around Cadiz.

In Portugal the services of an Officer in the latter capacity are most essential, there being no map of the country, and no person capable of giving information of a topographical nature; and of all those whose services have contributed to the success of the late operations, there is none who in his line stands higher than Captain Preval.[100]

Préval's successor was Captain George Scovell, who later became famous for breaking French codes.[101]

Royal Artillery

Table 13 shows the cannon, howitzers and artillery ammunition embarked at Cork. Table 14 shows the musket and rifle ammunition, flints, and gunpowder. The transports *Union* and *Patty* sailed for Gijon, so their cargo was destined for the Spanish rebels. The *Harford* and the *Britannia* also carried 30,000 stands of arms and 5,000 sets of accoutrements.[102] Spencer's transports were carrying some ammunition and ordnance as well. The two million musket cartridges from Cork would have given the just over 11,000 musket-armed infantry about 180 rounds each, and they usually carried 60 rounds at a time. The 30,000 rifle cartridges would have given the 1,400 riflemen only about 20 rounds each. However, at this stage of the war, riflemen did not use cartridges extensively. Instead, they loaded with separate powder and ball for greater accuracy at the cost of slower loading. The 300,000 rifle balls equate to approximately 200 rounds per rifleman.

The artillery that sailed from Cork consisted of gunners from Captain Henry Geary's and Captain Richard Raynsford's companies, commanded by Lieutenant Colonel William Robe. Spencer's gunners came from Captain Robert Lawson's company, temporarily commanded by Captain William Morrison. Each of the infantry brigades was assigned either two 6-pounders and a 5½ inch howitzer or three 6-pounders under the command of a captain or a lieutenant. The 9-pounders were formed into two half-brigades (one of three 9-pounders and one of two plus a heavy 5½ inch howitzer) under the supervision of Major James Viney.[103]

On 30 July, Robe wrote to Woolwich to complain about the equipment that had been loaded. His letter echoes Lieutenant Colonel George Ramsay's regarding the equipment embarked at Gibraltar and again lays bare the problems caused by the administrative and logistical separation of gunners, guns, drivers and horses:

> It appears to me necessary, that the officer appointed to command artillery on any expedition, should know something more of the nature of the service intended, than I did, although the precise place for it may not be communicated to him, and that he should not be made to take upon trust, that everything necessary for his service will be found on board his ships. Our equipment is not yet arrived at the state of perfection to render such a mode efficient, and if it is practised, the commanding officer of artillery will find as I have, that his brigades will be wanting in articles extremely necessary, and be very short indeed in stores intended for repair, or for keeping them in good order:– He will perhaps find also, as I have, that his intrenching tools, and even platforms, are sent with the Engineers'

---

100 Gurwood (ed.), *Wellington's Dispatches*, vol.IV, p.140.
101 M. Urban, *The Man Who Broke Napoleon's Codes* (London: Faber & Faber, 2001), p.10.
102 TNA: WO 1/228: Return of Ordnance and Ammunition for Field Ordnance Embarked on the Transports, Cove 9 July 1808
103 N. Lipscombe, *Wellington's Guns* (Oxford: Osprey, 2013), p.38.

Table 13. Field ordnance and ammunition embarked at Cove

	Brass Ordnance						Rounds of Ammunition					
Transport	9-Pdrs	Light 6-Pdrs	3-Pdrs	Heavy 5.5 in Howitzers	Light 5.5 in Howitzers	4.4 inch Howitzer	9-Pdr	6-Pdr	3-Pdr	5.5 In Hvy	5.5 In Lt	4.4 in
Kingston	5	5		1	1		2,030	2,955		418	384	
Rachel							2,012	2,045		210	216	
Caldicott Castle		5			1			750			74	
Clarendon								2,500			436	
Harford												
*Union**			12			12			4,800			2,400
*Patty**			10						4,000			
Total	**5**	**10**	**22**	**1**	**2**	**12**	**4,042**	**8,250**	**8,800**	**628**	**1,110**	**2,400**

*For the province of Asturias, sailed for Gijon.
Source: TNA: WO 1/228: Return of Ordnance and Ammunition for Field Ordnance Embarked on the Transports, Cove 9 July 1808.

Table 14. Small arms and ammunition embarked at Cove

	Musket Ball Cartridges			Rifle Cartridges		Powder in Barrels				Other					
Transport	English	French	22/lb	22/lb	30/lb	90lb	45lb	22.5lb	22.5lb Fine, Rifle	Musket Bayonets	Rifle Balls 22/lb	Musket Flints	Swords	Pikes	Lead Pigs (Tons)
Kingston															
Rachel	2,000,000											79,000			
Caldicott Castle															
Clarendon															
Harford				30,000					212		300,000				
*Union**		620,400	490,983		260,410	59	1,013	58		15,800		800,000	5,469	2,000	79
*Patty**						400	200					400,000	4,000		46
Britannia	2,000,000									14,200		50,000		2,000	
Total	**4,000,000**	**620,400**	**490,983**	**30,000**	**260,410**	**459**	**1,213**	**58**	**212**	**30,000**	**300,000**	**1,329,000**	**9,469**	**4,000**	**125**

* For the province of Asturias, sailed for Gijon.
Source: TNA: WO 1/228: Return of Ordnance and Ammunition for Field Ordnance Embarked on the Transports, Cove 9 July 1808.

Department, for a species of service for which he has not a gun, or a mortar, nor a round of ammunition; I do not make this a matter of complaint to you; I complain not of any thing: because I can go no farther than to use to the best of my ability, the means put in to my power, but I confess, it would have been much more satisfactory to me, had I been permitted an opportunity of stating before I embarked what might have been sent with me, for the real benefit of the service – and I don't think it would have occasioned an hour's delay to the embarkation, or have added a shilling of expense to the country, because the essential articles if not supplied must be purchased.

I have so often mentioned horses, that I ought perhaps apologize for again recurring to that subject: and perhaps it may be said, that I have no reason to mention them, having the horses of the Irish Commissariat ordered to be turned over to me on landing; – fortunate indeed, I think myself to have even them: I know not what figure we should have cut without them; – but when you learn, that they are acknowledged to be cast horses of the cavalry, turned over to the Commissariat, you will readily think, we are not likely to make a very capital figure with them; – I have been also fortunate enough to obtain with them, a promise of shoes from that branch sufficient with the One Hundred Setts supplied to me, to shoe them on first going off: future service must be supplied as it can, and I shall not let it go unsupplied.[104]

Robe then continued to say that the clerk of stores with the expedition had been told two vessels were on their way with six 10-inch and four 5½-inch mortars, which would go some way to providing ordnance for a siege, the 'species of service' he mentioned. The clerk had also been told to expect twenty 24-pounders, which were not included in the bills of lading. These heavy cannon would also have been used for sieges, and Robe assumed that they were to be supplied by the Royal Navy but noted that no carriages had been embarked for them, so they could not be transported if they were landed. He wrote to his headquarters again on 7 August, once the artillery brigades embarked at Cork had landed:

The Brigades are formed and ready to move off, and are completed on a reduced scale of camp equipage etc. for the present and will get on, I hope, better than I had reason to expect from the state of some of the horses we received from the Irish Commissariat. The fine weather we had, and the assistance we have experienced in every manner from Sir Arthur Wellesley has begun to bring them about; but I now deem it my duty, which were I to neglect, I should be highly culpable, to point out to you in the strongest manner the impolicy of sending artillery to a foreign country without horses. Even the horses we now have, old blind and casts from the cavalry as they are, we find superior to what we can obtain from the country. The latter are good of their kind, but small and not of sufficient weight for our carriages. Three hundred good horses would have cost the country no more for transport than as many bad ones; and what we shall do for the Brigade now to be landed [Spencer's] remains to be decided. – Sir Arthur has promised us mules or horses (mares), and such as we receive shall have no difficulty from us if they will but get on.[105]

---

104 TNA: WO 55/1193: Robe to Macleod, 30 July 1808.
105 TNA: WO 55/1193: Robe to Macleod, 7 Auagust 1808.

Royal Artillery gunner (left) and Royal Artillery driver (right), 1806, by Charles Lyall.
(Anne S.K. Brown Military Collection)

Robe continued to say that if he had been informed what had been embarked at Cork, he would not have boarded until everything that would be required had been supplied. He gave the example of the 100 sets of horseshoes he thought that he was requesting as extras, but that turned out to be the only ones he had, and had he not been able to source more from the Commissariat some of the horses would have been unshod. He was at pains to write that he was not writing to moan or make difficulties but that he felt it his duty to point out the problems he faced so they could be avoided for future expeditions. He stated, 'My people of all classes exert themselves, and I am determined to get on.' However, the lack of viable siege artillery and the quality of the artillery horses would influence the conduct of the campaign and the decisions made by Wellesley and his successors.

After the bulk of it had been sent back to Gibraltar, Spencer's remaining artillery consisted of four light 6-pounders and two howitzers. The guns were landed at Figueira, but as only 19 Portuguese mares and 86 mules were available to pull them, three guns were sent back, and the other three were taken as far as Leiria, where they were left along with 14 wagons, all under the charge of an NCO and seven gunners. The horses were redistributed to Wellesley's guns.[106]

---

106 T.H. McGuffie, 'British Artillery in the Vimeiro Campaign', *Journal of the Society for Army Historical Research*, vol.23, no.94 (Summer 1945), p.80.

Conclusion

Up to 1808, the British and French armies had experienced very different wars. Contemporary commentator Robert Southey summed up the situation:

> The war had on our part so long been almost exclusively maritime, that the army had suffered something in reality and more in reputation. The French, always fond of war, had become a military people; their military establishment was supposed to be perfect in all its branches, their troops experienced, their officers excellent, their commanders of the highest celebrity: to oppose them we had Generals very few of whom had ever been tried in command, and officers of whom the far greater number, like their men, had never seen an enemy in the field.[107]

While his argument is imperfect, Southey is broadly correct in many of his assertions. The campaigns the British Army had been involved with had primarily been of short duration and usually on the periphery of the conflict, in the West or East Indies or the Mediterranean. While they had been victorious over experienced French troops, for example, in Egypt in 1801 and at Maida in 1806, they had also experienced recent defeats in South America by colonial Spanish forces and local militia.

The French army under Napoleon had repeatedly bested the rest of the continental armies in campaigns that involved much greater numbers of troops and lasted longer. As a whole, the French army was certainly more battle-hardened than the British, but that was not the case with the units that Wellesley now faced in Portugal. With the exception of the 1er Division, the French troops were largely recent conscripts and foreign troops of questionable quality. Many of the British regiments also included men who had recently joined the ranks, but the proportions were generally lower, and there were longer-serving men in most units that had seen at least one campaign. While many French troops had seen action since arriving in Portugal, fighting poorly armed patriots was not the same as fighting disciplined regular infantry. On balance, the British had the advantage in troop quality, but the French did outnumber Wellesley's force.

Southey's comments on the differences between British and French generals are certainly borne out by the general officers on both sides in Portugal. While Wellesley was undoubtedly, even at this stage of his career, a more capable and experienced commander than Junot, his brigade commanders were less experienced than those of the French. Tables 15 and 16 show the different experience levels between the British brigade commanders and the French divisional and brigade commanders. On average, the French generals had served slightly longer, were older, and had much longer service as general officers. Most had previously led large formations in battle, whereas that was only true of Ferguson for the British.

---

107 Southey, *History*, vol.II, p.167.

Table 15. British General Officers

Name	Years in Army	Years as General Officer	Age (approx)
Rowland Hill	18	6	36
Ronald Ferguson	18	4	35
Miles Nightingall	21	0	40
Barnard Foord Bowes	27	0	39
Caitlin Craufurd	17	0	32
Henry Fane	16	0	29
Averages	**20**	**1.6**	**35**

Table 16. French General Officers

Name	Years in Army	Years as General Officer	Age (approx)
Henri-François Delaborde	25	16	44
Louis-Henri Loison	21	13	37
Jean Pierre Travot	22	12	41
François-Etienne Kellermann	23	11	38
Jean-Jacques Avril	33	13	56
Antoine-François Brenier	27	9	41
Hugues Charlot	32	5	51
Jean-Guillaume-Barthélemy Thomières	15	1	37
Jean François Graindorge	17	3	37
Lous Fuzier	32	14	51
Pierre Margaron	16	3	43
Averages	**24**	**9**	**43**

Table 17 lists the level of experience of the British battalion commanders and shows an average length of service of just under 20 years and that they had held their current ranks for about five years. However, there is considerable variation, and there are problems with gauging experience from lengths of service or time in a rank. Many officers had spent substantial parts of their careers as aides de camp, such as Lake, or periods on half-pay like Robinson, who had spent five of his six years as a lieutenant colonel unemployed. As can be seen in the individual biographies, all of the commanding officers had served in at least one campaign during their career, and some as many as four. However, even an officer's presence at a battle does not tell you how they performed there and what they learned from the experience.

A sample of the officers commanding French units in Portugal in Table 18 shows that the average length of service was not that different to their British counterparts, but they had spent more years in command of a battalion or regiment and tended to be older. While many of the British commanders, both at battalion and brigade level, would go on to prove themselves later in the Peninsular War, few had yet done so. The three actions that occurred as Wellesley advanced towards Portugal would provide ample opportunity to judge the relative merits of the commanders and soldiers of both armies.

Table 17. British Commanding Officers

Name	Unit	Years in Army	Years in Current Regimental Rank	Age (approx)
Lt Col. Charles Taylor	20th LD	15	8	36
Lt Col. John MacKenzie	1/5th	20	2	40
Maj. Thomas Carnie	1/6th	28	4	43
Lt Col. John Stewart	1/9th	18	2	32
Lt Col. George Lake	1/29th	13	1	27
Lt Col. Samuel Hinde	1/32nd	20	4	38
Lt Col. Robert Burne	1/36th	35	9	53
Lt Col. Charles Greville	1/38th	12	3	28
Lt Col. James Kemmis	1/40th	33	4	57
Lt Col. William Guard	1/45th	19	9	35
Lt Col. George Walker	1/50th	26	10	44
Maj. William Davy	5/60th	11	1	29
Lt Col. Denis Pack	1/71st	17	8	36
Maj. Henry Eyre	1/82nd	20	4	38
Lt Col. James Robinson	1/91st	13	6	30
Maj. Robert Travers	2/95th	15	3	38
	Averages	**19.7**	**4.9**	**37.8**

Table 18. Sample of French Commanding Officers

Name	Unit	Years in Army	Years CO	Age
Colonel Pierre-Denis de la Chârte	47e Ligne	27	13	45
Colonel Mathieu Lacroix	86e Ligne	27	7	47
Colonel Jean-Victor Rouyer	70e Ligne	19	15	52
Chef de bataillon Jean-Pierre Recouvreur	15e Ligne	Unknown	1	34
Major Jean-Martin Petit	12e/15e Légère	16	7	36
Colonel Guillaume Miquel	26e Ligne	16	9	44
Colonel Jean Pierre Maransin	Légion Midi	16	9	38
Colonel Louis-Cyriac Striffler	Légion Hanovrienne	16	13	36
Averages		**20**	**9**	**42**

9

Advance

On 8 August, Wellesley wrote orders for Fane's Light Brigade to march at 3:00 a.m. the following morning to 'St. Giao'.[1] As well as his riflemen and the attached artillery, Fane was to take 50 men of the 20th Light Dragoons, commanded by a captain. His orders were to take post at St Giao and then:

> In the evening he will be pleased to push forward some dragoons, with a detachment of 200 infantry, as far as may be judged expedient; and should intelligence be received that the enemy are not at Leyria or in the neighbourhood, General Fane will cause the town of Leyria to be occupied by this detachment either to-morrow evening or on Wednesday morning.[2]

If the French were in force at Leiria, the detachment would fall back to St Giao, and Fane would relay any intelligence to Wellesley. Leiria was important because Wellesley had become aware of a Portuguese supply depot there. He hoped to prevent the French from capturing it, and then, under an arrangement with the Portuguese, Wellesley hoped to draw provisions from it.

The 5/60th and 2/95th were ordered to leave their tents behind, packed, ready to be embarked back on the ships, and the men were to carry four days' worth of bread and a day's ration of meat, cooked. An assistant commissary would march with the brigade to supply further provisions and inquire about what resources the army would likely find near Leiria.[3] The brigade gathered during the night and marched out of the camp to the southeast, well before dawn, through a mix of pine forests growing on sandy soil, barren heaths, and the occasional vineyard.

Sometime during the day on 9 August, Wellesley received further intelligence that Delaborde had joined Thomières somewhere near Leiria and that the French now numbered 5–6,000 in that vicinity. Lieutenant Colonel Trant wrote to Freire that day:

> Colonel Luiz Maria admits that according to the reports of the deserters that he himself questioned the French did not pass Rio Maior yesterday or early Sunday. He thus loses too much time if he intends to occupy Lieria, since these rumours of his approach have

---

1   Faden's 1810 map of Spain and Portugal places St Giao about 10 miles from Lavos and 20 miles from Leiria. This is roughly the location of Guia today.
2   Gurwood (ed.), *Wellignton's Dispatches*, vol.IV, p.75.
3   Gurwood (ed.), *Wellignton's Dispatches*, vol.IV, p.75; Wellington (ed.), *Supplementary Despatches*, vol.VI, p.105.

continued for three or four days; but for myself I do not believe at all that he is coming to the North. There are not more than 5,000 men in all of whom he can at present dispose in the open country; and be assured, General, that he is now subscribing to defensive operations, rather than to undertake an invasion of this neighbourhood. The troops which are being sent to Rio Maior are either those which have recently been in Alcobaça or a reinforcement which is being sent from Santarem or Lisbon to the Fortress of Peniche. In any case, as it would be necessary for this day to pass by sending a courier to Lavos, an English detachment could not reach Leiria before morning, without even considering the delay of a day which has been proposed for our Army. The English will be in that city on Friday morning, so it will be necessary either to wait for that arrival; or if you think that there is reason to believe that the enemy is seriously coming to Leiria, a detachment of cavalry should be pushed forward from Lombal to Leiria tonight with orders to go half a league to the other: In the meantime, Colonel Luiz Maria de Souza could take the necessary steps to ensure the supply of food by having it withdrawn to Venda de Galegos, where some of your troops will be gathered tomorrow, or if you prefer 300 infantrymen can advance from Pombal during the night. They could certainly remain in Leiria until either your troops or those of the English come to their aid. For I do not think that the enemy spoken of is more than 1,000 or 1,500 strong.[4]

Wellesley ordered Fane to halt 'at a wood about a mile in front of the advanced post on the high road to Leyria.' He also told Hill to take his and Ferguson's brigades to join Fane and then proceed to St Giao and take up a position just beyond the village. Wellesley then continued to tell Hill:

If you should hear that the enemy are already in possession of Leyria, it is not worth while to drive them out this afternoon; but if you should have reason to believe that they are not in possession of Leyria, I recommend that you should allow 200 of the riflemen and a few dragoons to feel their way into Leyria, as it is very important, if the enemy be not already there that they should not be allowed to get in there this night.

If you should obtain possession with your 200 men, support them with your whole corps, at as early an hour as possible in the morning, and take up your position in front of Leyria, and halt there to-morrow; but if you should find the enemy in possession of Leyria when you arrive at St. Giao, and you should not send on the detachment of the rifle corps, you will halt at St. Giao in the morning, till I shall join you, which will probably be at 5 or 6 o'clock, and you will be prepared to march at that hour.[5]

Attached to the Light Brigade was Captain George Landmann of the Royal Engineers. According to his memoir, the first day's march was interrupted by an alarm caused by a friendly fire incident. A party of 20 dragoons was in advance of the main column. In the fading light of early evening, they thought they had seen an enemy vedette. They had fired and then galloped back to Fane at the head of the column to report. Fane deployed the brigade across the road and then went forward with his staff and the dragoons. Instead of any French, they found a corporal of the 20th Light

---

4   Trant to Freire, 9 August 1808, in 'Documentos', pp.170–171.
5   Gurwood (ed.), *Wellignton's Dispatches*, vol.IV, pp.76–77.

Dragoons who had gone to look over a small bank and then become separated. When he had found his way back to the road, he had been fired upon by mistake before he could answer the challenge. It was 10:00 p.m. before the column marched on and past midnight before they camped after being on the road for 22 hours.[6] There is no record of whether a detachment of Fane's brigade entered Leiria on the evening of the 9th or not, but it is likely.

The 1st, 2nd and Light Brigades camped for the night of the 9th on the road to Leiria and then pressed on to the town on the 10th. The remaining brigades at Lavos, the 3rd, 4th and 5th, were ordered to march on the morning of 10 August. The remaining mounted 20th Light Dragoons were to form half a mile in front of the artillery park by 4:00 a.m. The staff and the 3rd Brigade's artillery were to form behind them. The 29th and 82nd were then to form up on the hill near the artillery park. The 5th and 4th brigades, with their guns in front of each brigade, were to form up near their camp and follow the column as it marched past them. The reserve artillery and depot mules were to follow the infantry, followed by the baggage of the headquarters and general officers, the baggage of each brigade, the medical stores, and finally, the commissariat mules. The dismounted dragoons and a captain's guard of 50 men from the 4th Brigade were to remain at Lavos as protection for the commissariat and the military chest. Any sick incapable of marching with the army were to be placed in the charge of Dr Deane in Lavos, who would then oversee their embarkation on the *Enterprise* hospital ship. The tents of all the brigades were packed up and delivered to the commissariat. With such a shortage of transport, there were not enough carts or mules to take them with the army, so the men would have to build huts or sleep in the open.[7]

Henry Torrens wrote of the march to Leiria: 'The country is extremely difficult for the march of an army – being hilly and sandy; and as we are badly equipped in the means necessary for the draft of the artillery, we have had more difficulties to contend with than I had any idea of.' He then gave an example of a column that travelled only nine miles in nine hours and complained of the lack of mules and the condition of the Irish Commissariat horses.[8]

The march to Leiria was hard on the men, many of whom had been on board transports for weeks. The weather was very hot during the days, but there was sometimes rain during the night and heavy dew in the mornings. One major problem for the troops was the dust, which Landmann described as 'ankle deep and as light as the best calcined magnesia.' It coated the men to the extent that there was no difference in colour between his blue coat and Fane's scarlet. Marching south also meant that the troops had the dazzling Iberian summer sun directly in their faces, which, with the dust, caused their lips to swell and blister.[9] Wellesley and the bulk of his troops camped eight miles from Leiria on the night of 10 August, then moved forward the next day.

Atrocities Which Exceeded Belief

Arriving at Leiria before the French had been important not only to secure the supply depot, for which Portuguese commissaries had long been lobbying, but also to stop Delaborde's and Loison's forces from combining. As Wellesley later stated:

6   Landmann, *Recollections*, vol.II, pp.97–100.
7   Wellington (ed.), *Supplementary Despatches*, vol.VI, pp.104–109.
8   BL: Add MS 49485: Torrens to Gordon, 12 August 1808.
9   Landmann, *Recollections*, vol.II, pp.107, 114–115.

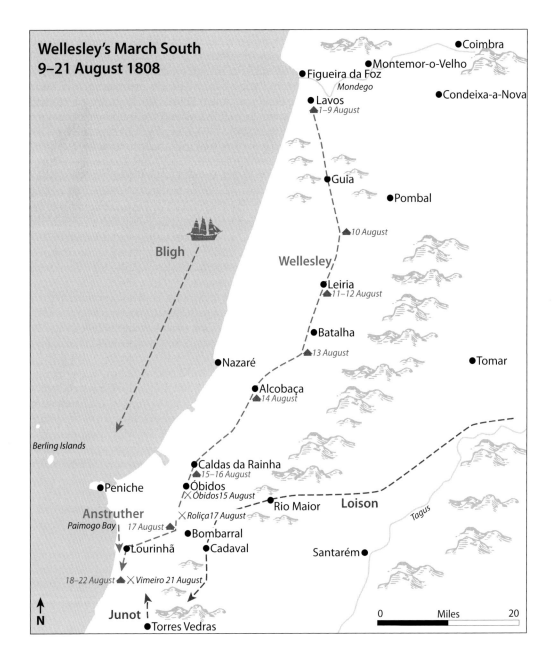

Wellesley's March South
9–21 August 1808

Coimbra
Montemor-o-Velho
Figueira da Foz
Mondego
Condeixa-a-Nova
Lavos
1–9 August

Guia

Pombal

10 August

Bligh

Wellesley

Leiria
11–12 August

Batalha
13 August

Nazaré

Tomar

Alcobaça
14 August

Berling Islands

Caldas da Rainha
15–16 August
Peniche
Óbidos
Óbidos 15 August
Rio Maior
Loison
Tagus

Anstruther
Paimogo Bay *17 August*
Roliça 17 August
Bombarral
Lourinhã
Cadaval
Santarém

18–22 August *Vimeiro 21 August*

N

Junot
Torres Vedras

0   Miles   20

[Leiria] is on the high road from Lisbon to the north of Portugal, to the eastward of which and nearly parallel to the road, there is a chain of high mountains which runs from Leyrya nearly to the Tagus; over which chain there is no good passage for carriages. In consequence of the early arrival therefore of British troops at Leyrya General Loison was obliged to return to the southward before he could effect his junction with General La Borde, who was thus exposed to be attacked when alone…[10]

Wellesley's intelligence led him to believe that Thomières 2,500 men had been joined by Delaborde's 4,000 and were 15 miles away, with an advanced post just three miles distant. Loison was at Tomar, just under 30 miles to the southeast.[11] Delaborde had troops at Batalha on the 11th, just seven miles from Leiria, and was actually at Alcobaça, 20 miles away, himself with the bulk of his men. He had contemplated making a stand at Batalha but thought the position was not a strong one.[12]

Leiria was the first town of any size the British troops had encountered. Captain Fletcher Wilkie (38th Foot) later wrote:

The approach to Leira is pleasing, along an avenue of trees, and the general situation is cheerful and picturesque, to which the position of the Bishop's palace on rising ground gives additional effect. Here we first saw a specimen of the enemy in the shape of four Swiss soldiers in scarlet, who were left behind by mistake in the prison; and here also we saw the French method of picking a lock, by putting the point of the bayonet into the keyhole, and then firing the musket with ball.[13]

The French lock-picking method had been utilised extensively in the town. Many of the houses had been looted and all their furniture smashed; many others had been set on fire. However, the British troops were to learn of worse savagery. Torrens wrote:

Nothing can exceed the Extremities the French have committed in this town. It appears like fable to mention it, and yet it is an absolute fact that they murdered seven Priests in the convent, and absolutely *ravished* all the wives and daughters of the inhabitants: In one instance they tied a Priest in order that he might be present while six men committed this outrage on a young girl his niece!![14]

Leach (95th Rifles) also wrote of the behaviour of the French in the town in his memoirs: 'Here they were guilty of atrocities which exceeded belief. The town bore every mark of recent depredation, plunder, and excess of all kinds. The walls of a convent, into which I went with some other officers, were covered with blood and brains in many places; damning proofs of the scenes which had been recently acted there'.[15] Many of the town's occupants had fled, and the town was nearly empty. The British troops camped amongst olive groves on heights near the town, and Wellesley set up his

---

10   TNA: WO 1/415: Wellesley's narrative, p.68.
11   BL: Add MS 49485: Torrens to Gordon, 12 August 1808.
12   Thiébault, *l'Expédition*, p.177.
13   F. Wilkie, 'Recollections from the Peninsula', *United Service Journal*, November 1843, p.424.
14   BL: Add MS 49485: Torrens to Gordon, 12 August 1808.
15   Leach, *Sketches*, p.44.

headquarters in the bishop's palace. The army halted on the 12th at Leiria, probably to give the men some respite but also to await the arrival of Freire and his Portuguese troops.

Wellesley had time to write a general order to amend some of the arrangements of the army, probably to correct matters he was not entirely satisfied with. For example, he changed how the pickets were to be organised, placing the responsibility with the brigades rather than a single field officer and adjutant each day:

> Each brigade to furnish both an outlying and inlying piquet of a captain and fifty men, with a proportion of officers and non-commissioned officers from each regiment, under the orders of a field officer of the brigade. Care to be taken that the sentries of the outlying piquets of each brigade are double, and communicate with those of the brigades or corps to their right and left whenever circumstances will admit of it. The General officer of the day will visit such of the piquets as he may think necessary, and they will receive their orders from him. All the field officers of piquets will report to him whenever anything particular occurs.[16]

The same general order also stated: 'In column of march the light infantry companies of brigades will move at the head of their respective brigades, and be thrown out to either flank as circumstances may require.' In this position, the light companies could cover the flanks and quickly react to any enemy sighting, or be sent to investigate any feature or village. The order also said that when the troops arrived at the next night's campground, they were to form line of battle and try and ensure the huts were constructed close to that line so that the army could form up quickly in the event of an alarm.[17]

At midnight on 12 August, news came that the French were advancing. The 3rd Brigade was put under arms, and the outposts were reinforced. Two companies of the 29th were sent forward as an advanced picket, but the alarm proved false – caused by a few men of the Guarda Real da Polícia who had deserted to join the rebellion.[18]

Nothing in Common

Marechal de Campo Freire arrived at Leiria on the 12th with 5,500 infantry and 500 cavalry.[19] When Wellesley and Freire had met on 7 August at Montemor-o-Velho, the Portuguese commander had suggested marching towards Santarém, but Wellesley demurred as he needed to stay close to the coast so that he could maintain communications with the fleet. The same disagreement between the allies about how to carry on the campaign soon surfaced again. Both armies were to march towards Lisbon on the morning of 13 August. Orders had been written the previous night, and the time of departure for the Portuguese troops fixed with Freire. However, instead of marching with the British, Freire sent Wellesley a letter via Trant, saying that unless the British commissaries could feed the Portuguese troops, he would take his forces to Santarém via Tomar. Wellesley's

---

16   Wellington (ed.), *Supplementary Despatches*, vol.VI, p.110.
17   Wellington (ed.), *Supplementary Despatches*, vol.VI, p.110.
18   Leslie, *Journal*, pp.35–36.
19   TNA: WO 1/415: Wellesley's narrative, p.66.

reply to Freire was somewhat terse, 'I must beg leave to call to your Excellency's recollection what I have repeatedly told you, that it was not in my power to supply the Portuguese troops with bread'.[20] He reminded Freire that he had already told him at Oporto that he could expect no provisions from the British and at their meeting at Montemor-o-Velho. He also reminded Freire that, at both those meetings, he had requested that the Portuguese supply his army with wine and forage, little of which had been forthcoming. Wellesley had secured the supply depot at Leiria, partly on the understanding that he could draw upon it for his troops, but had then been told by the Portuguese commissary that he only had enough bread to supply Freire's troops. Wellesley continued:

> I am really much concerned that your Excellency's troops should suffer any distress; but you must be aware that the arrangements for providing for them have not fallen upon me; and that I have not required a greater proportion of the resources of the country (particularly not bread) than is necessary for those of His Majesty; and I trust that your Excellency will see the propriety of adopting some arrangement which will provide effectually for the subsistence of the army which you will march to Lisbon; at the same time, that you will allow His Majesty's troops to enjoy such of the resources of the country as I have above mentioned, which they require.[21]

Wellesley later said that he had 'urged the Portuguese General in the most earnest terms to cooperate with me in the deliverance of his Country from the French, if he had any regard to his own honor or to the honor of his country, or his Prince'.[22] From the Portuguese perspective, Freire needed to protect the considerable portion of the country that had already been liberated from French occupation, and he had orders from the Junta in Oporto to that effect. The sacking of towns, such as Evora, that had been re-occupied by the French led to a very understandable fear of Loison's force, which was still on the flank of the allies, and what atrocities they might commit if they advanced into the liberated areas. The Corpo Académico regiment had already been ordered back to Coimbra on 10 August to act as a reserve and protect the city. Given the record of previous British military operations, Freire had understandable doubts that the British troops could defeat the French, and he felt that Wellesley was, in the European theatre at least, an untried commander.[23] Wellesley's reply to Trant on the 13th was even more direct than his letter to Freire:

> I have just received your letter of this date, and I am concerned to find that the arrangements to enable the Portuguese army to take the field, in co-operation with the British troops, have been so much neglected as to render that measure impracticable. I have written to General Freire this day upon the subject of his supplies, upon which I have nothing further to say.
>
> As to his plan of operations, I do not see what purpose it is to answer, in view to the result of the campaign; and I certainly can never give my sanction to anything which appears so useless, and so crudely digested, so far as even to promise to communicate with or aid the person who is carrying it into execution.

20 Gurwood (ed.), *Wellington's Dispatches*, vol.IV, p.86.
21 Gurwood (ed.), *Wellington's Dispatches*, vol.IV, p.87.
22 TNA: WO 1/415: Wellesley's narrative, p.70.
23 De La Fuente, *Forjaz*, p.52.

I have one proposition to make to General Freire, that is, that he should send me his cavalry and his light infantry, and a corps of 1000 regular infantry, to be employed as I choose, and I engage to give these men their bread; and for meat, wine, and forage, they shall fare as well as our troops. If he will accept of this proposition, let the troops join me to-morrow at Alcobaça. If he does not, I beg that he will carry on such operations as he may think proper.

I shall execute the orders which I have received from my government, without the assistance of the Portuguese government; and General Freire will have to justify himself with the existing government of Portugal, with his Prince, and with the world, for having omitted to stand forward upon this interesting occasion, and for having refused to send me the assistance which it is in his power to give.[24]

Wellesley told Trant that if Freire continued to refuse to conform to his plans, he was to return to the British camp. On the 14th, Wellesley wrote to Trant again in even stronger terms:

It is obvious, that whether I am too weak to contend with General Junot, or sufficiently strong for him, there is nothing in common between the Portuguese troops and me. My object is to obtain possession of Lisbon, and to that I must adhere, whatever may be the consequence, till I shall have attained it, as being the first and greatest step towards dispossessing the French of Portugal. They may fight an action with me and retire, or they may retire without fighting, or, what I hope is least probable, they may defeat me.

In the last hypothesis, I have no assistance from General Freire; and in the first two, which I hope are the most probable, I must give my attention to obtaining possession of Lisbon and the Tagus, and leave General Junot to retreat where he pleases, and to do what he pleases.[25]

He continued to say that if Junot was defeated by the British or withdrew from Lisbon and let them take the city, the French would attack the Portuguese, who, under Friere's plan, could be in the path of the French retreat. Given the French superiority in cavalry, Wellesley thought it very likely that if defeated by the British in battle, the French force would still be intact enough to destroy Freire's command. He then questioned the reasoning behind Freire's plan:

Let us now examine why this plan is adopted? The General says it is necessary in order to subsist his troops: I say it is not! He could find some subsistence everywhere, and good arrangements would bring plenty. In this very town [Alcobaça] I got this day as much bread as would have subsisted the whole Portuguese army; and I am convinced from what I see of the country next the sea coast, through which I shall march, that it is the richest in Portugal.

I declare, that I think the plan of operations proposed is so defective and dangerous, that I would recommend to the General, if he will not accompany me, rather to remain at Leyria, or march here and he can be supplied at either place and to wait in security the event of a contest which must take place in a few days.[26]

24   Gurwood (ed.), *Wellington's Dispatches*, vol.IV, pp.87–88.
25   Gurwood (ed.), *Wellington's Dispatches*, vol.IV, p.89.
26   Gurwood (ed.), *Wellington's Dispatches*, vol.IV, p.90.

Trant did his best to persuade Freire in a covering letter added to Wellesley's on the matter of supplying bread:

> I am sending you a translated copy of a letter addressed to me by the General today, which I received on the way; I can add nothing assuredly to the strength of the arguments he uses to engage your cooperation, or at least the abandonment of your plan of campaign. But in the same friendly manner, which I have always wanted to use in my representations on this subject, I can only recommend you, and for the last time, as it will not be time to cooperate in three days time, to come and join us, as the only step which can save you from the accusation of having avoided the support of the Portuguese troops for the object of their national independence.
>
> It is not your personal character, General, that will be in question. Your reputation is established and I have informed General Sir Arthur Wellesley of the proposal you have made to command the detachment of your troops attached to our army; but it is your political conduct that is in question, and for me, who has nothing more to say to you officially in this respect, I can only offer you the advice of a man who, by his stay at your Headquarters, feels an interest in everything that concerns you. I advise you to do your part and to join us and in two marches you will arrive.[27]

In a letter to Castlereagh on the 16th, Wellesley suggested that Freire's real motivation for not wanting to place himself under Wellesley's command and to march his troops with the British was that he feared they were too weak to defeat Junot.[28] Wellesley also admitted to Castlereagh:

> Having found the resources of the country more ample than I expected, I should certainly have undertaken to feed his army according to his desire; as I consider it of importance, on political rather than on military grounds, that the Portuguese troops should accompany our march; only that I have found the British Commissariat to be so ill composed as to be incapable of distributing even to the British troops the ample supplies which have been procured for them; and I did not wish to burden them with the additional charge of providing and distributing supplies to the Portuguese army.[29]

So, the British could have fed all the Portuguese troops if only Pipon and his commissaries had been up to the task. In a private letter to Castlereagh on the same day, Wellesley wrote of the Portuguese troops: 'The fact is, they are afraid of the French.'[30]

On the 13th, Trant presented Wellesley's proposal to feed a portion of the Portuguese troops to a council of Freire and his commanders. The council decided:

> That the proposal to unite part of the troops required to the English army should be settled, because once the difficulties of subsistence had been removed, it was convenient that the Portuguese should have a part in the end of the task of such importance, and which they had

27 Trant to Freire, 14 August 1808, in 'Documentos', p.179.
28 Gurwood (ed.), *Wellington's Dispatches*, vol.IV, p.93.
29 Gurwood (ed.), *Wellington's Dispatches*, vol.IV, pp.93–94.
30 Gurwood (ed.), *Wellington's Dispatches*, vol.IV, p.95.

started without external help, but it was in no way convenient to give away all the cavalry and leave the army without any, nor could the Portuguese army be engaged in blindly following the operations of the British auxiliary troops, exposing all our resources both of subsistence and of troops to the fate of a general action, leaving open on our left a wide field for their incursions, and even to more consequent projects, such as the possession of Coimbra, and even after overcoming this first obstacle to advance the enemy on Porto, the centre of our union, resources and government, because there was the dual purpose, not only to go to Lisbon, but at the same time to prevent any act of desperation with which the common enemy would try in the last resort to get rid of the critical situation in which it finds itself, penetrating to Beira Alta to seek new subsidies for itself, and to reduce our forces; This is a matter that should not only be considered militarily, but also politically, bearing in mind the circumstances in which the inhabitants of these provinces find themselves, and their way of thinking. And finally, it seemed convenient to achieve the proposed objectives, that our independent army, supposing that in correlation with the English, would work to the right of the enemy, putting itself in a position to attack him in concert with the troops of Beira Baixa, in Abrantes, if he was still there, or on the side of Santarém, and even attacking him there seriously, having strengthened the army with everything that, and without loss of time, could be gathered to it, and that our position, to be at hand to perform the indicated ends, should be taken in Ourem, because it is a dominant place, and brings together those essential qualities that can make our forces count, without forcing us to great manoeuvres, for which our troops, without the necessary military practice, cannot be considered suitable.[31]

The Portuguese would provide Wellesley with 1,000 line infantry, 400 light infantry and 250 cavalry. Wellesley deemed these troops 'desirable on political, rather than on military grounds', in that he did not expect much from them but thought it politic that he have some Portuguese troops with him.[32] Trant was given the command of these troops, although there does not seem to be any extant evidence if this was a condition imposed by Wellesley or an idea of Freire's. Trant did later thank Freire for entrusting him with the brigade.[33] However, several letters in the 1930 Boletim do Arquivo Histórico Militar mention Coronel Gaspar de Souza e Quevedo Pizarro's presence with the Portuguese troops that joined Wellesley. So, he may have been the senior Portuguese officer.

Freire retained some of his cavalry for the protection of his force. He wrote to Wellesley on the 15th, again reiterating that he had to defend the provinces that had already been freed from the French by the rebellion, stating that:

This is not an ordinary war, in which it matters less whether the enemy advances in one province or another: now desolation and death will everywhere accompany their arrival and the first. It is my duty, if I can, to prevent such calamities from spreading to the provinces of this kingdom, whose army I command. In these circumstances, far from lending myself to your request to march with the few troops I have left, having already deployed yesterday the contingent you demanded, I shall try to reinforce myself as much as possible in order to prevent the danger that the provinces may face, and to collaborate with your

31   Sepulveda, *Historia*, vol.XI, p.145.
32   Gurwood (ed.), *Wellington's Dispatches*, vol.IV, p.101.
33   Trant to Freire, 1 September 1808, in 'Documentos', pp.164

troops to extinguish the common enemy, which was our first and only objective, or I shall sacrifice myself, if necessary, to prevent this fatal consequence, which seems to threaten us imminently, and which would undoubtedly result in a counter-revolution in the country, in the most disastrous sense.[34]

Freire also updated the Junta on the situation:

> You will see from the enclosed copies what has happened since then and to what extent I have been compromised for lack of instructions, since they do not expressly tell me whether I should, like the English, take care first of all to occupy Lisbon, even at the risk of devastating the provinces which caused the Revolution, and all the endeavours that are ongoing, and which should expect us to do this service, or whether this should be our aim. I confess to Your Excellency that I have spent bitter hours, seeing my reputation compromised even falsely, since I will not give anyone any explanations, nor make anything appear that might give the appearance of less unhappiness between us and the English. But God will help those who, like me, seek only to get things right, without any other passion or partiality.[35]

Perhaps in an effort to ease relations with Wellesley, Freire sent *Commendador* Joaquim Paes do Amaral e Menezes to update the British general on his plans.[36]

As Wellesley was now sure that Loison had marched southwest from Tomar to Torres Novas rather than west towards Leiria, and so was still 30 miles away, he suggested that Freire remain at Leiria for a day or two to solve his supply issues. It was only when Freire received word that the Regimento de Infantaria n.º 24 and some ordenença had bested the French garrison at Abrantes and that the French had withdrawn beyond Rio Maior that he was willing to advance and unite the remainder of his army with the British. The military governor of Beira, *Coronel* Francisco da Silveira, moved from Castello Branco with 3,000 men to cover Abrantes and Santarém to secure the Portuguese interior.[37] As Freire now felt that the interior provinces were secure, he enthusiastically committed to marching his army to join Wellesley's, writing:

> The English ... give us all the help we can need. Their Squadrons protect the coasts of this Kingdom; their armies come to take an active part in this glorious war; and their convoys come to bring an abundance to our ports, and the ammunition we need so much; they disembark, and want to march immediately on the capital to free our compatriots from the captivity that oppresses them and to eliminate once and for all our oppressors. It is therefore necessary that the Portuguese Army does not fail to take part in this glorious expedition and that we march without delay to complete this glorious enterprise.[38]

Unfortunately, by the time the main Portuguese force arrived, the campaign's outcome had already been decided.

---

34   Freire to Wellesley, 15 August 1808, in 'Documentos', p.184.
35   Freire to Junta, 15 August 1808, in 'Documentos', p.185.
36   Freire to Wellesley, 16 August 1808, in 'Documentos', p.191.
37   De La Fuente, *Forjaz*, p.53.
38   Sepulveda, *Historia*, vol.XI, p.149.

Alcobaça

The British troops marched from Leiria at 4:00 a.m. on 13 August, but this time in two columns. The right column would comprise most of the 20th Light Dragoons, the staff, the Light, 1st, 3rd, and 5th Brigades, the artillery park, and the commissariat depot. This column would march along the main road to Lisbon. The left column would consist of 50 of the 20th Light Dragoons and 50 Portuguese cavalry, the 2nd and 4th Brigades, plus the rest of Trant's Portuguese troops, and would march on more minor roads via Batalha.[39] Spencer took a patrol forward and spotted some French cavalry, but they retreated immediately.

The army arrived at 'Calvario' later on the 13th. Staff officer Captain Montagu Wynyard recorded in his journal that the terrain near the village was 'extremely strong and difficult'.[40] 'Calvario' was probably modern Calvaria de Cima a small village around 10 miles south-southwest from Leiria. The army camped just to the south, near a fork in the road, with one route leading to Lisbon and the other to Alcobaça. With some of the riflemen and dragoons, Wellesley pressed forward to reconnoitre as he had received word that the French were near. According to one British officer, 'A Portuguese, supposed to be a spy, was brought before the General. His guilt was so evident that Sir Arthur threatened to hang him the next morning unless he gave a true account of all he knew respecting the French position.'[41] The man revealed that Delaborde was at Alcobaça, positioned on the hills and at the remains of an old Moorish castle.

The army marched early the following day, and this time, the right column would be made up of 50 dragoons, the 1st Brigade and the commissariat. The left column would be made up of the balance of the army, with the 50th Foot being ordered to remain on the campground until 7:30 a.m. and then follow the rest of the left column, presumably as a rear guard.[42] The route took the British troops away from the main road to Lisbon and nearer to the coast, towards Alcobaça and the French and through some narrow passes. Wellesley expected some opposition from the French. The advance guard of the riflemen of the Light Brigade, with some of the dragoons, felt their way forward. Wellesley sometimes ranged ahead with a small party of riflemen and dragoons. Portuguese villagers told of 2,000 Frenchmen a short distance ahead. The baggage and the women were sent to the rear. The column then pushed on and marched past some recently vacated huts belonging to French pickets.[43]

The British troops arrived in Alcobaça without incident, and 'with colours flying and bands playing' to the shouts and cheers of the town's inhabitants.[44] The last French had left the town not long before. Charles Leslie (29th Foot) recalled:

> We dashed after them, and pushed them through Alcobaço in such haste that they left the bullocks which they had killed, but had not had time to serve out to the troops, and also some waggon-loads of stores. As we hurriedly passed through the streets of the town, the inhabitants hailed us with the greatest demonstrations of joy, calling out, 'Viva! viva!' and

---

39   NLS: Adv.Ms.46.3.6: General order 12 August 1808; Wellington (ed.), *Supplementary Despatches*, vol.VI, p.111.
40   M. Wynyard, 'From Vimeiro to Corunna', *Royal United Services Institution Journal*, vol.114, no.656, p.35
41   Neale, *Letters*, p.46.
42   Wellington (ed.), *Supplementary Despatches*, vol.VI, p.111.
43   Wynyard, 'Vimeiro to Corunna', p.35; Leslie, *Journal*, p.36.
44   Neale, *Letters*, p.47.

the ladies strewed flowers upon us from the balconies. We were halted at a short distance beyond the town, and from our position we could trace the retreat of the enemy for a considerable distance by the clouds of dust which they raised.[45]

French soldiers had broken open the wine stores, and some soldiers of the 71st Highlanders found a French soldier, with all his accoutrements, drowned in a large cask.[46] The large monastery Alcobaça was famous for had also been looted of its lavish gold and silver decoration before the French pulled back. The abbot invited the officers of the British army to dinner. Most of the troops were billeted in and around the town, but Fane's Light Brigade camped a little to the south to cover the approach to the town.

While at Alcobaça, some Portuguese came to tell Wellesley that a foraging party of French were in the nearby small fishing port of Nazaré, 10 miles to the west. He sent the light company of the 9th Foot and a troop of the 20th Light Dragoons to pursue the French. James Hale was one of the soldiers of the light company:

… when we came within about a mile of the town, we saw a great smoke ascending: we were then ordered to load, expecting to have something to do very soon. However, when we came there, we found the enemy had evacuated the town, and destroyed it nearly all, by fire; and to the great misfortune of the poor inhabitants, what provisions they could not take away, they destroyed, the wine in particular, for they even beat the barrels to pieces: so all that the inhabitants could accommodate us with, was fruit out of the fields, which they brought to us in abundance.[47]

The British troops stayed the night, and in the morning, the locals shared some wine that the French had missed. As Hale recalled, 'they all sat down with us, and we enjoyed ourselves with fruit and wine as long as we thought proper: and as we did not understand their language, nor they ours, we drank health to each other by motions.'

Once Nazaré was secure, Wellesley sent word to Bligh on the *Alfred*, who was off the port with the transports, that he was sending 120 carts to the coast and hoped that they would be able to return the next day with bread and oats. He also told Bligh, 'The dragoons and their horses will go in the morning, at daylight, for their saddles, &c., and I shall order them to return in the evening.'[48] This implies that some Portuguese remounts had arrived, and the dismounted dragoons went to the transports to pick up their saddles and other equipment. He also sent Bligh three French commissaries captured by Portuguese dragoons at Tomar. Wellesley then wrote:

The enemy have retired to Obidos, about twenty miles from hence; and I propose to follow them in the morning, leaving the articles which you will land for me to follow. If they should quit Obidos, I shall occupy that place to-morrow; and on the next day I shall reconnoitre Peniche. If the enemy should stay at Obidos, I shall either attack them or turn them on the next day; that is, Tuesday. I should think that they will stay, as I imagine that Loison

45   Leslie, *Journal*, p.36.
46   Anon., *Journal of a Soldier*, p.53.
47   Hale, *Journal*, p.17.
48   Gurwood (ed.), *Wellington's Dispatches*, vol.IV, p.90.

has joined the detachment which was here with about 5000 men. They had 3000 or 4000 here [Alcobaça].[49]

The right column of the army, consisting of the 1st and 3rd Brigades with 20 dragoons, was to march at 4:00 a.m. on the 15th for Caldas da Rainha. The left column would march at 4:30 a.m. and consist of the Light and 5th Brigades, the cavalry, the 4th and 2nd Brigades, the artillery park, the spare ammunition, the medical depot, and the commissariat depot. Trant and the Portuguese troops had arrived at the camp late in the evening, so they would not march until 8:00 a.m.[50] An anonymous officer recorded in his journal:

> We quitted Alcobaza [*sic*] on the 15th, proceeding on our march to Caldas; and every step we took confirmed us in our opinion, that the day could not pass without an action. The enemy had made their retreat from Alcobaza in so precipitate a manner, that they had left undisturbed a bridge over a ravine, which we had to pass; had we found this bridge in any way damaged, our progress would have been greatly impeded. They also left behind them two waggons, which were loaded with stores and surgical instruments. Baron Tripp, who was sent forwards to reconnoitre, followed the enemy almost into Caldas; and Sir Arthur, feeling his way with the light troops, entered it without opposition.[51]

According to Ensign Murchison, about halfway between Alcobaça and Caldas 'the French appeared in sight. Their army was drawn up in close column and was ready for action. They however continued their retreat'.[52]

Caldas was a famous spa town, and one officer looked forward to partaking in the waters at the end of the day's march:

> The following day the march was continued to Las Caldas; the day was exceedingly hot, and the road dusty, which made us anticipate with pleasure the delights of a warm bath. The springs, from whence the place derives its name, furnish a pretty steady supply of warm water, strongly impregnated with sulphur, which is conveyed into one large bath of an oblong form; the bottom is of clear white sand; the water is about two and a half feet in depth, and has a slightly greenish tinge similar to that of the sea, but is perfectly transparent, and only smells in a trifling degree of the mineral with which it is so strongly impregnated. We enjoyed the luxury of warm water without any inconvenience from this cause, but the next day, when on the march, and under the influence of a hot sun, the sulphur came out strong, and the odour could scarcely have been greater that attached to 'the gentleman in black' when 'he left his brimstone bed at break of day, to see how his farm on earth was going on.'[53]

---

49   Gurwood (ed.), *Wellington's Dispatches*, vol.IV, pp.90-91.
50   NLS: Adv.Ms.46.3.6: General order 14 August 1808.
51   Neale, *Letters*, p.48. The 'Baron Tripp' mentioned is probably Captain Ernst Otto Tripp (5th Garrison Battalion): Challis's *Peninsula Roll Call* has him on the staff of the expedition.
52   Murchison to his uncle, 23 August 1808, in Geikie, *Life*, vol.I, p.29.
53   Wilkie, 'Recollections from the Peninsula', p.424.

However, Charles Leslie was perhaps a little over-enthusiastic in his bathing: 'I entered the bath suddenly, and without due precaution, and the water was so warm that it made my pores bleed.'[54]

Not all the British troops could enjoy the pleasures of the spa, though. As Caldas was only four miles from the walled medieval town of Óbidos, Wellesley sent four companies of riflemen on ahead to see if the French still occupied it. They did. The first clash between British and French troops in the Peninsula was about to occur.

---

54   Leslie, *Journal*, p.37.

10

The Portuguese

Wellesley was frustrated by his interactions with Freire and disdainful of the possible contribution of Portuguese troops after the meeting at Leiria on the 12th. Although the Portuguese had managed to liberate the majority of their country themselves before British troops arrived, and could defeat isolated French troops, Evora had shown that they could not beat them in a pitched battle. The rebel forces lacked a conventional army's discipline, arms, and cohesion.

The Portuguese army had been in a slow decline long before the French marched into their country unopposed. In 1762, one of Frederick the Great's generals, Graf Wilhelm von Schaumburg-Lippe-Bückeburg, was given command of the army and told to modernise it. Training, arms, regulations and even uniforms were reformed or reorganised on the Prussian model, turning the army into one of the best small armies in Europe. However, with the height of its empire and wealth long since gone, the Portuguese state was slowly withering from lack of resources and apathy amongst the ruling class. The army was allowed to decay again through inactivity and inattention. Its flaws were exposed in the fight alongside Spain against Revolutionary France, but the troops who were engaged did fight reasonably well. In 1795, an Austrian general, Christian August, Prinz Waldeck und Pyrmont, was appointed to reform the army again, but his attempts were hampered by entrenched interests in court and the government, and he died in 1798. In 1800, another German general, Karl Alexander von der Goltz, tried again to institute reforms but was also blocked from making meaningful changes. The dire state of the Portuguese army was then exposed during the brief War of the Oranges, which resulted in a quick defeat and the ceding of territory.[1]

Prince João appointed a military commission to propose reforms, which were agreed upon in 1802, but political infighting and resistance meant that it was not until 1806 that they began to be implemented. The country was split into three regions covering the north, centre and south of the country, with 43 militia regiments and 24 ordenença brigades assigned to them. The regular army consisted of 24 regiments of line infantry, 12 of cavalry, and four of artillery. The reforms were wide-ranging but did not have enough time to make a real difference before Junot invaded.

Given the state that Junot's army was in by the time it neared Lisbon, the Portuguese army could probably have stopped the invasion, at least for a time, but Napoleon would have sent reinforcements, and any armed resistance would have been severely punished. When João and the rest of the court, government, and the wealthy fled for Brazil, many army officers went with them. In January 1808, when Junot issued the decree disbanding the Portuguese army, it had a strength

---

1   R. Chatrand, *The Portuguese Army of the Napoleonic Wars* (Oxford: Osprey, 2001), vol.1, p.7.

Portuguese military uniforms, circa 1800, by Jules Ferrario. (Anne S.K. Brown Military Collection)

of 20,285 officers and men.[2] The fittest soldiers and many of the ablest officers marched out of the country with the Légion Portugaise and deprived the country of the men most likely to be able to effectively resist French occupation, which was just what Napoleon intended.

Soldiers are Not Wanting

In June 1808, the junta in Oporto gave the task of rebuilding the Portuguese army to *Marechal de Campo* Bernardim Freire de Andrade and his chief of staff, Miguel Pereira Forjaz. Oporto was still in turmoil following the rising against the French, with factions vying for control. The Bishop had used his popular support to get control of the military commission, formed on 19 June, but had no knowledge of military affairs. On 20 June, the junta ordered the re-establishment of the Regimentos de Infantaria n.º 6, 9, 11, 12, 18, 21, 23, and 25, plus four battalions of caçadores. Militia, ordenença and several volunteer units were recalled, and all retired soldiers were asked to report to duty:[3]

> The provisional council of the government of Oporto invite the veteran soldiers, to whatever regiment of the line they may belong, to unite with the army of this province, that is, to enter into the ranks with the two regiments of the garrison of this city, which are in the course of organization: and to each man, by way of remuneration, are promised a month's pay and a daily allowance of four vinteins, with clothing, &c, The same pay will be allotted to all the soldiers now on service, as well as those who will join the same regiments, as far as circumstance will admit this extraordinary pay. Likewise the militia will have the same advantages.[4]

---

2   Grasset, *Guerre d'Espagne*, vol.I, p.449.
3   Fuente, *Forjaz*, pp.48–49.
4   Anon., *A History of the Campaigns of the British Forces in Spain and Portugal* (London: Goddard, 1812), vol.I, pp.448–449.

There were not enough weapons, equipment, money, experienced officers and NCOs, or even that most essential commodity for any army – men. However, the implementation of Junot's decrees disbanding the military and seizing arms had not been as assiduously implemented by the Spanish forces occupying the north, so a minimum of the military infrastructure had survived. The junta passed decrees requesting money, horses and supplies for the nascent army and placed an extra export tax on wine and olive oil to provide funds. They also raised a loan of two million cruzados to pay the men of the new regiments. Hariot Slessor noted the reaction to the Junta's appeals in her diary:

> Great contributions have been collected in Porto. The regiments that were disbanded are forming again, but have no clothing. This contribution is to help towards fitting the soldiers out. Great donations have been given. The Wine Company have given 4000 pairs of shoes (200 are made in a day) and many thousand shirts, etc, etc. In short whole regiments will be completely clothed. Very large sums have been presented to the Treasury by rich citizens of Porto. On such an occasion there are not even the poorest individuals that have not come forward with their mite. This kind of work puts one in mind of English patriotism.[5]

Freire and Forjaz arrived in Oporto on 28 June and 1 July, respectively. Rebuilding the army was not going to be easy. As one contemporary commentator wrote:

> … as yet there was no force in existence that could be called a Portuguese army; for although many of the regiments disbanded by Junot had been in some measure re-embodied, yet the great mass of the patriotic force was nothing more than an unarmed, disorganized mob. The public treasury had been drained by the enemy, who was still in possession of the capital; and every description of arms had been carefully removed from the provinces; so that it was not in the power of those who took the direction of affairs to organize any respectable force.[6]

As historian Robert Southey put it, 'There were numbers, and courage, and good will, but every thing else was wanting.'[7] The junta quickly requested aid from Cotton and the British government. The Portuguese minister in London, Sousa, asked for three million cruzados, cloth for uniforms for 40,000 infantry and 8,000 cavalry, 3,000 barrels of powder, arms and accoutrements, plus cargos of salt fish and other provisions.[8] On 8 August 300,000 dollars was sent to Portugal on HMS *Decade*. The British had already sent the Portuguese 17,000 pikes and 30,000 muskets in June, and in August, they sent 8,000 heavy cavalry swords, 2,000 muskets, 120 rifles and 64 pistols.[9]

Forjaz had been part of the military commission attempting to reform the Portuguese army before the invasion. The new army was to be organised based on the 1806 reforms that the commission had not been able to implement fully. A line infantry regiment was to be made up of two battalions, each of five companies. Each company was to have an establishment of 162 men so that

---

5   Hayter (ed.), *Backbone*, p.182.
6   Halliday, A., *The Present State of Portugal and the Portuguese Army* (Edinburgh: Clarke, 1812), p.136.
7   Southey, *History*, vol.II, p.165.
8   Bishop of Oporto to De Souza, 7 July 1808, in Anon., *Papers Presented to Parliament*, pp.895–896
9   Anon., *Papers*, pp.897–898.

a regiment would have a total of 1,659. Caçadore battalions were to be of six companies of 138 men each, giving an establishment of 846. Cavalry regiments were to consist of eight companies of 54 men each, giving a total of 453 for the regiment. So, in theory, the regiments that the junta had ordered to be re-established would together have a strength of 20,000 men, but nowhere near that number were raised.[10]

The Bishop of Oporto's proclamation of 20 July setting the establishment of the regiments that were being raised was relayed to London by Brigadier General Friedrich von der Decken of the King's German Legion, who, along with Brigadier General John Sontag, had been sent by Castlereagh to Oporto in August to liaise with the Portuguese and evaluate the strength of their forces.[11] Decken gives the total establishment of the Portuguese army as follows:

Infantry of the line	13,272
Light Infantry	3,384
Cavalry	1,812
Militia	19,200

The army was split into a Corps of Observation to defend Tras os Montes province, Freire's main army in Estremadura, and a reserve. Decken estimated that Freire's force did not exceed 8,000 men. He wrote to Gordon at Horse Guards on 19 August from Oporto with a damming assessment of matters in the rebellion's capital:

> You can hardly form an idea of the confusion which prevails here, with respect to all military arrangements. The people are in the best spirit possible, but without any order, or regularity, in want of every thing. I doubt whether any use can be made of the Portuguese, except in occupying the large and extensive chain of mountains which cover almost all the provinces of Portugal. I do not think that British officers can be employed with success, to organise and command the Portuguese. The Portuguese hate foreigners, they acknowledge no authority and nobody but the monks has any influence, and even the authority of the Bishop of Oporto extends not far. The want of knowledge of the language is another obstacle. Amongst a great number of Portuguese officers; who I have seen, I found only one, who could speak a little French. I have been under the necessity to employ the waiter of the inn as interpreter with the Bishop, his secretary being absent. The Bishop is esteemed by every body is a very respectable man, but he has no knowledge of transacting business and is 70 years of age; he is as much afraid of his own people as of the French, and has desired me very strongly to beg our commanding General to send some British troops here for his protection.[12]

In his letters to Gordon, Trant stated that the various districts' juntas were unwilling to cooperate and guarded their own authority.[13] Decken would be proved wrong in his assertion that the Portuguese would not take well to being led by British officers, as British NCOs and officers would

10   Fuente, *Forjaz*, p.50.
11   TNA: WO 1/213: Decken to Castlereagh, 18 September 1808.
12   BL: Add. MS 49503: Decken to Gordon, 19 August 1808.
13   BL: Add. MS 49502: Trant to Gordon, 18 July 1808.

be employed by William Carr Beresford when he was appointed to rebuild the Portuguese army in 1809.

Despite the chaos and lack of resources, by 6 July 1808, elements of Regimentos de Infantaria n.º 6, 9, 18 and 21, along with Regimento de Cavalaria n.º 6 and some militia, had started to move south to Coimbra to counter any French threat coming towards Oporto.[14] On 5 August, Freire and Forjaz joined the troops in Coimbra. The force that Freire then marched to Leiria consisted of one battalion each of n.º 6 and n.º 18, both battalions of the most complete regiment, n.º 12, with 1,200 men, and both battalions of n.º 21. There were also three battalions of grenadiers drawn from other regiments, the Oporto and Trás-os-Montes caçadore battalions, the Oporto and Moncorvo militia, and 900 cavalry.[15]

The force that Freire then detached to serve with Wellesley is detailed below:

Regimento de Cavalaria n.º 6 (*Capitão* José Pereira da Costa)	104
Regimento de Cavalaria n.º 11 (*Alferes* Nicolau de Abreu Castelo Branco)	50
Regimento de Cavalaria n.º 12 (*Capitão* Francisco Teixeira Lobo)	104
Guarda Real da Polícia	41
Total cavalry	*299*
Regimento de artilharia n.º 4 (*Capitão* Antonio Bazilio de Faria)	210
Regimento de Infantaria n.º 12 (*Major* Francisco Bernardo da Costa)	605
Regimento de Infantaria n.º 21 (*Major* Francisco Gomes da Cunha Rego)	605
Regimento de Infantaria n.º 24 (*Major* Francisco Lopes da Cunha)	304
Batalhão de Caçadores do Porto (*Tenente Coronel* Velho da Cunha)	569
Total infantry	*2,083*[16]

Torrens was scathing in his assessment of the Portuguese troops: 'We should do much better without them. They have no kind of discipline, being almost without officers.'[17] Ensign Murchison observed, 'there were about four squadrons of cavalry, good-looking, well-mounted dragoons, being the garde de police of Lisbon, who had made their escape from thence on hearing of our disembarkation. The Portuguese infantry was in a most wretched state of discipline.'[18] The Lisbon police were virtually the only formed body of armed men to survive Junot's disbandment of the Portuguese forces and so more recently in conventional discipline, but not all the Portuguese cavalry would have come from the police. An extract of a letter from Freire to the Junta outlines some of the problems the Portuguese were facing in building their army anew:

Five hundred cavalrymen from Regiment No. 6 should come soon, ready and heading for this barracks and the necessary officers for a squadron: and in case of any difficulty, Regiment No. 6 should come here and the Regiment No. 9 should go to [Coimbra] in the state it is in. On the 4th a departure of 124 cavalrymen from the Police Guard of the Court

---

14 Amaral, *Portuguese Army*, p.23.
15 Amaral, *Portuguese Army*, p.27.
16 Ferreira Gil, *A Infantaria Portuguesa na Guerra da Peninsula* (Lisboa: Tipografia da Cooperativa Militar, 1912), vol.I, pp.275–276.
17 BL: Add MS 49485: Torrens to Gordon, 12 August 1808.
18 Murchison to his uncle, 23 August 1808, in Geikie, *Life*, vol.I, p.28.

was apprehended in this city, and they escaped with great risk and in an extraordinary way; they are an excellent troop and arrived at the right time. It seems absolutely essential as a reward and as an example to keep their pay and give the lower officers the following ranks: lieutenants to the first two sergeants, and ensigns to the other four. I have done this temporarily while the approval of the Council is not forthcoming. From the cavalry of Antonio José Rodrigues Praça, together with those who have come lately, a corps of three squadrons will be formed to give them a proper form so they can serve more usefully. Temporary officers nominated, but it is necessary that the Junta authorizes this creation, which can be this new regiment that should be created later in Santarem. According to what I have been able to gather the project of the English general is that we march soon but for this it is essential that we approve the proposals of the Line Corps, as well as those of Caçadores and Militia, because without officers we can not count on corps and at this moment there is no remedy but to depart from the ordinary rules.[19]

Sergeant Norbert Landsheit of the 20th Light Dragoons, an experienced cavalry NCO, was also complimentary about the horsemen of the Guarda Real da Polícia:

… from a very early period after our landing, detachments of Portuguese cavalry came in, by fours and fives, to join us; some led on by an officer, others acting, as it seemed, under their own guidance. They were remarkably fine-looking men; well clothed, well armed, and well mounted, and composed, as they informed us, a portion of the Lisbon Police – the most efficient cavalry force in the kingdom. These the General attached to our two squadrons; and so strong was the friendship which soon arose among us, that our officers were never without the company of the Portuguese officers, nor our men separated from their men, either at meals or during the hours of relaxation. On the morning of the 17th [of August], we had about two troops, or one squadron, in the camp; and their appearance was such as to make us well pleased with the addition which they made to our otherwise feeble force.[20]

More of the police joined the light dragoons on 18 August at Lourinhã.

With the ad hoc nature of the Portuguese army at the time, many of the men likely wore various uniforms or even civilian clothes. Since Count Lippe's reforms, the uniform of the Portuguese infantry had been blue, not dissimilar to the colour the French wore, and it seems that at least some of the officers still had their uniforms. According to Captain Fletcher Wilkie (38th Foot), 'The officers and men of [the detachment with the British troops] were directed to wear on the left arm a bit of white linen, or a pocket-handkerchief tied round, to distinguish them from the French.'[21]

After he had handed over dispatches on 30 July, Wellesley sent Lord Burghersh into the Portuguese interior to get more information on the state of the Portuguese army. Burghersh inspected the regiments at Coimbra and then sent a report to Castlereagh:

19   Freire to Junta, 6 August 1808, in 'Documentos', pp.166–167.
20   Gleig, *Hussar*, vol.I, pp.250–251.
21   Wilkie, 'Recollections from the Peninsula', p.429.

It was my opinion that the troops were good & extremely steady & in good order, considering the time they had been embodied. At Viseu they were not so far advanced, the troops were entirely without arms, & yet from the number of soldiers of the former Portuguese army which their battalions contained I was induced to believe that they might shortly be more effective.

Burghersh travelled as far as Almeida and Guarda, meeting Portuguese commanders and urging them to move on Lisbon. He even wrote to the Spanish commander at Badajoz asking that his troops march to Portugal's aid. He also gave Castlereagh his impression of the state of the forces in Portugal in general, the last sentences of which would prove prescient:

The whole of the lower class of people of Portugal have risen against the French but without arms or ammunition, they have no means carrying into effect the vengeance with which they threaten them, in every village thro which I have passed, the peasants are doing military duty, & armed with pikes or a few muskets have in some places offered so active a resistance to the French, as to force them in some places to abandon their operations. If the Government of this country had arms, soldiers are not wanting. Every peasant is anxious to serve in the defence of his country, but I think the persons at the head of affairs in Portugal are not sufficiently aware that it is not against the trifling force of Junot they have to contend, but against the efforts Bounaparte will hereafter make to reestablish his Dominion in their country. Whether his being able to make the attempt is at this moment probable or not, at least it is possible, & this is the only opportunity this government will have to prepare against it.[22]

---

22   TNA: WO 1/213: Burghersh to Castlereagh, 15 August 1808.

11

Óbidos

Shortly after most of the infantry brigades had arrived at Caldas on the afternoon of 15 August, four companies of riflemen were detached by Wellesley to take possession of the nearby small town of Óbidos. The four companies were Captain Thomas Hammes', John Anthony Wolff's, and Michael de Wend's companies of the 5/60th and Captain Hercules Pakenham's company of the 2/95th, all under Major Robert Travers of the 95th.[1] A small detachment of the 20th Light Dragoons accompanied the 400 or so riflemen. Pakenham was one of the younger brothers of Wellesley's wife, Catherine.

Óbidos sits on a rocky hilltop, surrounded by high medieval walls and with a castle at the northern end. The walls encompass an area of around 500 meters from north to south and approximately 200 meters at their widest point. Inside the walls are densely packed houses with narrow streets. In 1808, there would have been few houses outside of the walls. The area immediately surrounding the town is relatively flat, but other hills, outcrops, and high ridges are nearby.

Général de division Delaborde had left Alcobaça on the 12th and fallen back to Óbidos but decided that the ground was not suitable for a defence. He established a position at Roliça and on the heights behind, about four miles southwest of Óbidos. He did not have all of his division with him. *Général de brigade* Brenier commanded both battalions of the 70e Ligne, and *général de brigade* Thomières commanded the 3/2e and 3/4e Légère, plus the grenadier and voltigeur companies of the 4e Suisse. Cavalry from the 4/26e Chasseurs à Cheval completed the force. According to Thiébault, the French advance guard, closest to Óbidos, consisted of two companies of the 2e Légère, two of the 70e Ligne and the two Swiss companies.[2] Foy places the furthest forward picket at a mill on the Rio Arnóia, which runs from the northwest to the southeast, just outside Óbidos.[3] The French would have occupied various positions to cover the approaches to Roliça and Óbidos and would have had pickets placed in front to warn of the British approach. It is likely that the six companies totalled at most just over 700 men, probably less, but outnumbering the 400 riflemen.

Accounts of the following action are few, and many were written years later. Wellesley described the action to Castlereagh the day after the skirmish:

---

1   All the 5/60th's casualties came from Hammes', Wolff's, or de Wend's companies, so it is logical to assume they were the three companies sent forward with Travers. TNA: WO 12/7073: 5/60th Muster book; Griffith, *Riflemen*, pp.151–152.
2   Thiébault, *l'Expédition*, pp.175–178.
3   Foy, *Invasion*, p.152.

Óbidos, as seen from the road leading from Caldas da Rainha. (Author's photo)

Óbidos, as seen from a tower at the southern end of the town. (Author's photo)

Looking towards Caldas da Rainha from the walls of Óbidos near the castle. The course of the tree-lined Rio Arnóia can be seen running through the centre of the photograph. (Author's photo)

The enemy, consisting of a small picquet of infantry and a few cavalry, made a trifling resistance & retired; but they were followed by a detachment of our Riflemen to the distance of three miles from Obidos. The riflemen were there attacked by a superior body of the Enemy, who attempted to cut them off from the main body of the detachment to which they belonged, which had now advanced to their support; larger bodies of the enemy appeared on both the flanks of the detachment; and it was with difficulty that Major General Spencer, who had gone out to Obidos when he heard that the riflemen had advanced in pursuit of the Enemy, was enabled to effect their retreat to that village. They have since remained in possession of it, & the enemy have retired entirely from the neighbourhood.[4]

So, from this description, it appears that the French at Óbidos opened fire and then fell back. Some riflemen chased the picket for three miles before coming up against more troops. Three miles from Óbidos towards the main French position could have taken them as far as the village of Roliça. The balance of the four companies then came to their support. Major General Spencer then oversaw the withdrawal back to Óbidos.

---

4   TNA: WO 1/228: Wellesley to Castlereagh, 16 August 1808.

The British eyewitness accounts of the skirmish at Óbidos come from the 2/95th. No accounts from the 5/60th or 20th Light Dragoons have been uncovered in archives. In his journal, 2nd Lieutenant John Cox of the 2/95th wrote:

> On approaching the place, the enemy opened a fire of musketry from a windmill on a rising ground adjoining the place, and a few shots came from the town; however, rapid advance of the Riflemen drew the French from all points of their posts, but being rather too elevated with this, our first collision with the foe, we dashed along the plain after them like young soldiers, but we were soon brought up by a body of French cavalry advancing from the main force. A retrograde movement was now imperative, in which we lost an officer and a few men.[5]

So, according to Cox, as the riflemen approached, they were fired on both from the town and a windmill nearby. The French fell back, and the riflemen chased them until they encountered the 26e Chasseurs à Cheval.

An account from the French side also mentions a windmill and comes from *capitaine* Salomon Bleuler, *adjutant major* of the 1/4e Régiment Suisse. On the evening of the 15th, Delaborde visited him at one of his outposts. The two men could see smoke from the fires of the British camp between Caldas and Óbidos but debated if the troops there were British or Portuguese. They then had a conversation about the sound of cannon coming that morning from Peniche, which they supposed was the sound of the garrison there celebrating Napoleon's birthday. According to his account, Bleuler said he would like to celebrate the Emperor's birthday by engaging the enemy outposts. He does not say that he heard firing from the outposts at Óbidos. Delaborde agreed to the request, and Bleuler took his grenadiers forward. The general sent some chasseurs à cheval and a company of light infantry after them. As the Swiss grenadiers approached Óbidos, they encountered the riflemen as they were advancing and were fired on from the castle by artillery. None of the British accounts mention artillery. Bleuler and his grenadiers fell back to a windmill. They held there for a while and exchanged shots with the riflemen, having one grenadier killed and several wounded. Delaborde then arrived with the chasseurs, and the French advanced, chasing the riflemen and 'Portuguese dragoons' back to Óbidos, but when they came to the aqueduct to the southeast of the town, they stopped. Bleuler states that 'his curiosity had been satisfied.' The Swiss casualties amounted to three dead and five wounded, but they captured several riflemen, one of whom had fired on Bleuler from 20 paces but missed. Bleuler then acted as a translator for Delaborde when he interrogated the German riflemen of the 5/60th.[6]

It seems that Bleuler is recounting the French response to the riflemen's advance past Óbidos and the retreat of the French outposts. In reconciling these different accounts, it is perhaps important to remember that the riflemen Bleuler encountered may have come from the 60th and not the 95th. Bleuler recalls firing coming from the town's walls, so perhaps some of the 5/60th had been sent to clear it by Travers. It is also worth remembering that windmills were common at the time, and the one Bleuler mentions is not necessarily the same one Cox mentions.

---

5   Verner, *History And Campaigns*, vol.I, Kindle Location 2605.
6   Maag, *Geschichte der Schweizertruppen*, vol.I, pp.459–460. Apart from a couple of short quotations, Maag is retelling Bleuler's account in his own words. The original of Bleuler's diary is held by Zentralbibliothek Zürich.

The most famous first-hand British account of the skirmish is that of Benjamin Harris of the 2/95th. However, since Henry Curling took down his narrative in the 1830s and it was first published by him in 1848, the passage of time and the telling of the story might have altered his recollection:

> It was on the 15th of August, when we first came up with the French, and their skirmishers immediately commenced operations by raining a shower of balls upon us as we advanced, which we returned without delay.
>
> The first man that was hit was Lieutenant Bunbury; he fell pierced through the head with a musket-ball, and died almost immediately. I thought I never heard such a tremendous noise as the firing made on this occasion, and the men on both sides of me, I could occasionally observe, were falling fast. Being overmatched, we retired to a rising ground, or hillock, in our rear, and formed there all round its summit, standing three deep, the front rank kneeling. In this position we remained all night, expecting the whole host upon us every moment. At day-break, however, we received instructions to fall back as quickly as possible upon the main body. Having done so, we now lay down for a few hours' rest, and then again advanced to feel for the enemy.[7]

Harris's account tallies broadly with John Cox's.

Captain George Landmann, the Royal Engineer attached to the Light Brigade, wrote in his memoir, again written much later and with the benefit of much hindsight and artistic licence, that Fane and the rest of the brigade's staff were at dinner when they heard the distant firing. Fane called for his horse and ordered Captain Geary's guns and the rest of his brigade to advance with him immediately. Landmann continues:

> As we advanced the firing increased, and from time to time was kept up with vigour; but before we arrived at Obidos, about four miles from Caldas, the skirmishing had ceased, and we learnt that the enemy had fired from behind an aqueduct at Obidos, on our advanced guard, quite unexpectedly.
>
> … The French did not attempt to defend the town, but contented themselves with forming behind the aqueduct; and, as the cavalry and riflemen advanced to pass under it, in following the high road, they stepped out from behind the piers of the arches, which till then had concealed them, and fired a general volley, which, to the astonishment of the party, neither killed nor maimed a single man, nor even any of the horses.
>
> From this point they retreated slowly, firing on our men as they followed, and Travers went on advancing a couple of miles or more; when, observing that the enemy were receiving considerable reinforcements, he thought it prudent to retire.[8]

Landmann states that Bunbury was shot through the chest rather than the head and that Fane then remained in Óbidos overnight. Landmann's account does not mention Spencer. Landmann also goes on to say that when he went back to the main army, many different and exaggerated reports of the action were circulating already: 'On my laughing at all those particulars, and flatly

---

7   Curling (ed.), *Recollections*, pp.39–40.
8   Landmann, *Recollections*, vol.II, p.125.

The sixteenth-century aqueduct that runs into Óbidos on the east side of the town, which both Bleuler and Landmann mention in their accounts. (Author's photo)

contradicting them, my good friends were greatly surprised; and I found it no easy matter to persuade them that the whole they had heard on that subject was a mass of fabrication; at length, having related the simple facts, they remained astonished at their own credulity.'[9]

Captain Jonathan Leach of the 2/95th, who would have led his company forward with the rest of the brigade after news of the initial clash had reached Fane, remembered in his memoir: 'Our companies, with some of the 60th, occupied during the night, as an advanced post, an extensive knoll near the road by which the enemy had retired. We remained on the *qui vive* until daybreak, when we prepared to extract as much comfort, by way of toilet and breakfast, from our haversacks, as their narrow compass would admit.'[10] This confirms Harris' account of remaining all night on a hill. First Lieutenant William Cox, brother of John, was also amongst the other three companies of the 95th that came up with Fane, and his account agrees with others from his regiment:

> 15 August: … had a smart skirmish with their rear guard. They occupied the town and fired on our advanced guard as they approached it. They were instantly driven from the town and being followed too far by Captain Pakenham's company which formed the advanced guard, it brought on a smart skirmish in which we lost Lieutenant Bunbury killed, a gallant young fellow, Captain Pakenham was slightly wounded. We took a position in front of the town and remained next day…[11]

This account implies that it was Pakenham's company alone that pursued the French.

One of the brigades that had passed through Caldas and encamped in a vineyard towards Óbidos was Nightingall's 3rd Brigade. At around 6:00 p.m., the alarm was sounded as they heard that the outposts had been engaged. The brigade stood to and marched to their support, but having

---

9   Landmann, *Recollections*, vol.II, pp.123–124.
10   Leach, *Sketches*, p.45.
11   G. Glover and R. Burnham, *Riflemen of Wellington's Light Division in the Peninsular War* (Barnsley: Frontline, 2023), p.69.

travelled about two miles, they met Spencer returning, who told them that the French had been driven from Óbidos, and so they marched back to their camp, but they remained accoutred all night.[12]

An anonymous officer, but one likely to have been on the staff, recorded in his journal:

> Having marked out the ground for the main body of the army to take up its position just beyond the town, Sir Arthur left the light infantry, under the command of Generals Spencer and Fane, with orders to continue advancing till they discovered if the enemy had possession of a fortress [Óbidos], which was seen at about two miles distant from the road, on the Lisbon side of Caldas.
>
> Owing to some misapprehension, a party of the ninety-fifth and sixtieth regiments advanced beyond the post they were intended to have occupied. The consequence was, they were attacked by a detachment of the French, much superior in numbers to their own, aided by the enemy's whole rear guard of 1200 men; and we were surprized while at dinner, with the arrival of Captain Elliot, who informed us, that the enemy had attacked our advanced posts with considerable advantage. Before we could get to the scene of action, this skirmish was over; and the next morning, on visiting the lines with the Commander-in-Chief, it appeared that our loss consisted of from twenty to twenty-five men. The French having retreated after this affair, we took up our advanced posts at Obidos.[13]

Again, this seems broadly in tune with other British accounts.

'Brilos'

Many of the accounts of the skirmish at Óbidos in histories of the campaign mention the action commencing at a place called Brilos, which does not appear on any map of Portugal – contemporary or modern. Napier mentions 'the windmill of Brilos' and places it three miles in front (to the north) of Óbidos, and this seems to be the first mention of a windmill in connection with 'Brilos'.[14] However, the earliest mention of Brilos, with no mention of a windmill, appears to be in *The Gazette Extraordinary* of 3 September 1808, where it is clearly a transcription error for 'Obidos', as contained in Wellesley's dispatch of 16 August to Castlereagh already cited from the original in The National Archives and also reproduced in *Wellington's Dispatches*.[15] Subsequent historians have repeated the *Gazette's* error. Two Portuguese historians, João Pedro Tormenta and Pedro Fiéis, attempted to locate the windmill at Brilos and came up with a possible but implausible corruption of Bairro da Luz.[16] However, the simpler explanation of it being a transcription error

12   Leslie, *Journal*, pp.37–38

13   Neale, *Letters*, pp.48–49.

14   Napier, *History*, vol.I, p.125.

15   *The Gazette Extraordinary*, 3 September 1808, <https://www.thegazette.co.uk/London/issue/16177/page/1185>, accessed March 2023.; TNA: WO 1/228: Wellesley to Castlereagh, 16 August 1808; Gurwood (ed.), *Wellington's Dispatches*, vol.IV, p.94.

16   C. Willis, 'The first French invasion of Portugal: two rash colonels', in C. Woolgar, (ed.), *Wellington Studies V* (Southampton: University of Southampton, 2013), p.73.

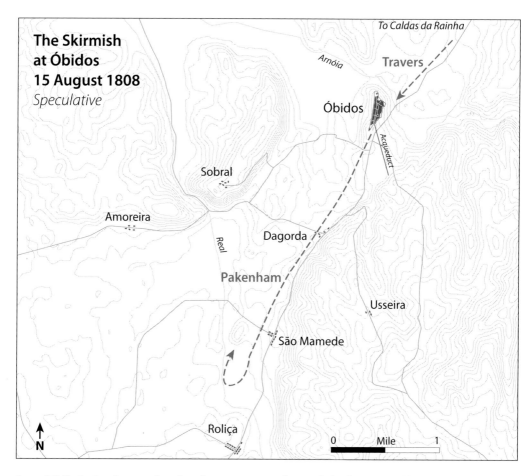

The Skirmish
at Óbidos
15 August 1808
Speculative

To Caldas da Rainha

Arnóia

Travers

Óbidos

Acqueduct

Sobral

Amoreira

Real

Dagorda

Pakenham

Usseira

São Mamede

Roliça

N

0   Mile   1

from Wellesley's often unclear handwriting seems beyond doubt, especially as Gurwood transcribed it correctly in the published dispatches.

Quite Useless

In his dispatch to Castlereagh, Wellesley wrote:

> In this little affair of the advanced posts which was occasioned solely by the eagerness of the troops in pursuit of the enemy, I am concerned to add that Lt. Bunbury, of the 2d batt, 95th, was killed, & the Honorable Captn. Pakenham wounded, but slightly; & we have lost some men, of whose numbers I have not received the returns.[17]

---

17   TNA: WO 1/228: Wellesley to Castlereagh, 16 August 1808.

When he did receive the returns, they revealed that the 5/60th had lost one man killed, five rank and file wounded and 17 rank and file missing. The 2/95th had lost 1st Lieutenant Bunbury killed, Captain Hercules Pakenham wounded, and four rank and file missing.[18] Ralph Bunbury came from Mount William in Tipperary, Ireland and had joined the 34th Foot as an ensign in July 1805 and then moved to the 95th as a 1st Lieutenant in November of the same year, also without purchase.

While Bunbury is often remembered in the history of the Peninsular War as the first officer killed in the Peninsula, the name of the rifleman of the 5/60th who was killed at Óbidos remained obscure until the current author's history of the battalion was published. The man was Private Baptiste Debass, who had joined the battalion in May 1806 and served in Captain Hammes' company. Of the seven men of the 5/60th who entered the general hospital on 15 August, two subsequently died, one on 19 August and one on 12 September. This suggests that some of the wounds suffered at Óbidos were severe.[19]

A history of the 95th, *Rifle Green in the Peninsula*, also lists Privates William Dodd, James Martin and Mathew Maxwell as being killed in action on the 15th and another man wounded but does not cite a source.[20] Verner's *History And Campaigns Of The Rifle Brigade* also says three riflemen were killed, two wounded, and one missing, and cites the muster books but does not name them.[21] It is probable that these extra casualties were included in the original return amongst the missing and were subsequently found to have fallen. So, in total, the skirmish probably claimed the lives of seven riflemen, including Bunbury.

The only French officer casualty recorded was 23-year-old *capitaine* Gottfried von Meiss of the 4e Suisse, who was wounded on his left arm.[22] Total French losses are unclear, but Natalia Griffon de Pleineville puts them at 15.[23]

Wellesley was clearly irritated that the riflemen had allowed themselves to be drawn into chasing the French. Had they stuck to their orders, they would have probably occupied Óbidos without loss. In a private letter to Castlereagh, he wrote: 'The affair of the advanced posts of yesterday evening was unpleasant, because it was quite useless, and was occasioned contrary to orders, solely by the impatience of the officers, and the dash and eagerness of the men. They behaved remarkably well, and did some execution with their rifles.'[24] In a letter to the Duke of Richmond, he adopted a similar tone: 'We had yesterday evening a little affair of advanced posts, foolishly brought on by the over-eagerness of the riflemen in the pursuit of an enemy's piquet, in which we lost Lieutenant Bunbury of the 95th, killed, and Pakenham, slightly wounded, and some men of the 95th and 60th. The troops behaved remarkably well, but not with great prudence.'[25] Sadly, Óbidos was not the last occasion during the campaign that inexperienced officers would cause excess casualties.

In a letter to Lieutenant Colonel Gordon in October, Wellesley lobbied to get Pakenham a promotion to major, describing him as 'really one of the best officers of rifle men that I have seen.'

18   TNA: WO 1/228: Return of killed, wounded and missing, 16 August 1808.
19   TNA: WO 12/7073: 5/60th Muster book; Griffith, *Riflemen*, pp.151–152.
20   Caldwell & Cooper, *Rifle Green*, vol.I, p.28.
21   Verner, *History And Campaigns*, vol.I, Kindle Location 2605.
22   J.P. Campos and A.G. de Blas, *Officiers de Napoléon tués ou blessés pendant la Guerre d'Espagne* (1808-1814) (Madrid: Foro para el Estudio de la Historia Militar de España, 2020), vol.1, p.455.
23   Griffon de Pleineville, *Invasion*, p.178.
24   Vane (ed.), *Correspondence*, vol.VI, p.401.
25   Wellington (ed.), *Supplementary Despatches*, vol.VI, p.115.

He ended the letter by mentioning Pakenham's political ties to the government: 'Having said so much of his military character, it is scarcely fair to him, or to you, to mention that he is the member for the county of Westmeath, and a steady friend; but the Secretary in Ireland must take care of a claim even on this ground.'[26] Wellesley's lobbying was unsuccessful as Pakenham had to purchase a majority in the 7th West India Regiment in 1810.

The Light Brigade occupied Óbidos, but the bulk of the army remained at Caldas on the 16th to allow the commissariat to catch up and for the supplies to arrive from Nazaré.[27] The 2nd Brigade was also still on the road from Alcobaça at the village of Salir de Matos, three miles northeast of Caldas, with the artillery park, and was ordered to march on to Caldas on the 16th.[28]

26   BL: Add. MS 49481: Wellesley to Gordon, 15 October 1808.
27   TNA: WO 1/415: Wellesley's Narrative, p.71.
28   NLS: Adv.Ms.46.3.6: General order 15 August 1808.

12

Roliça

During 16 August, Wellesley remained at Caldas, and Delaborde maintained his position at Roliça. Delaborde needed to delay Wellesley to allow Loison to arrive from the east and Junot to gather troops from Lisbon and march north. The village of Roliça lies in a valley approximately three miles wide and surrounded by steep and forested hills on three sides. The valley's floor is mostly gently rolling cultivated land, but there are several raised and wooded outcrops. Delaborde's main position was on a gentle rise just in front of the village, with one end anchored on the village and the adjacent hills and the other on a small wooded hill. French pickets occupied positions to the front and along the forested slopes on the French right. A mile behind the main position was a long and rugged escarpment at the head of the valley above the village of Columbeira. Wellesley described Delaborde's first position as 'posted on the heights in front of Roliça, its right resting upon the hills, its left upon an eminence on which was a windmill, and the whole covering four or five passes into the mountains on his rear.'[1] His use of the word 'heights', though perhaps technically correct, perhaps conjures an image of a more impressive hill than is the case.

The strength of Delaborde's force is a matter of contention. British accounts tend to have higher figures so that their victory seems more impressive, and the French tend to have lower estimates to enhance Delaborde's achievement in delaying the British so long. For example, Wellesley stated in his dispatch, 'I have reason to believe that his force consisted of at least 6000 men, of which about 500 were cavalry, with five pieces of cannon.'[2] Whereas Thiébault claimed that Delaborde 'had no more than 1,900 combatants.'[3] Historian Charles Oman comes up with a figure somewhere in the middle by looking at the strengths of the units from July, deducting the grenadier companies that had been formed into battalions in Lisbon, allowing for the centre companies of the 4e Suisse being at Peniche, and making some compensation for the absent sick. He estimated Delaborde's troops at around 4,000 infantry, 250 cavalry and 100 gunners.[4] Whatever the numbers, as Foy wrote in his history of the campaign: 'The strength of this corps consisted wholly in the talents of its leaders, and especially in the coolness and energy of the General, an old warrior, beloved of the soldiers, and quick in inspiring them with his own vigour and confidence.'[5] Wellesley's force,

---

1 TNA: WO 1/228: Wellesley to Castlereagh, 17 August 1808.
2 TNA: WO 1/228: Wellesley to Castlereagh, 17 August 1808.
3 Thiébault, *l'Expédition*, p.179.
4 Oman, *History*, vol.I, p.235.
5 Foy, *Invasion*, p.155.

The view along the valley towards Óbidos from the centre of Delaborde's first position. (Author's photo)

with the Portuguese, now numbered just over 15,000.[6] So, no matter which figure is correct for the strength of French, the allies had an overwhelming advantage. Delaborde would have to use all his skills to fulfil his mission and impede Wellesley without sacrificing his command.

Delaborde had detached three companies of the 70e Ligne (300–400 men) on his right flank to ensure his communications with Loison, whom he expected imminently. One company was at Bombarral, five miles southeast of Roliça, and two were at Cadaval, five miles further in the same direction. The companies at Cadaval had a detachment at a village Thiébault called Segura.[7]

Loison had arrived at Santarém with around 4,000 men on 13 August. His troops were exhausted after repeated forced marches, so he rested his men until the 16th when he marched for Torres Vedras, leaving the Légion Hanovrienne behind as it was in no state to continue. Loison's route would have taken him to within a mile of Cadaval. Delaborde had expected Loison to be at Alcoentre, about halfway between Santarém and Torres Vedras on the 13th, so he was well behind schedule. Wellesley's intelligence placed Loison at Rio Maior on the 16th, about a 25-mile march from Roliça.[8] A forced march could have brought Loison to Roliça within a day. It was this junction that Wellesley had to guard against whilst tackling Delaborde.

6   Oman, *History*, vol.I, pp.230, 234.
7   Thiébault, *l'Expédition*, p.178.
8   TNA: WO 1/228: Wellesley to Castlereagh 17 August 1808.

Order of Battle, Roliça 17 August 1808

French – *Général de division* Henri Delaborde

Général de brigade Brenier
   1/70e and 2/70e Ligne
Général de brigade Thomières
   3/2e Légère, 3/4e Légère, & 1/4e Suisse (elite companies only)
4/26e Chasseurs à Cheval
1 company of artillery – 5 guns

British & Portuguese – Lieutenant General Sir Arthur Wellesley

Right Column
   Lieutenant Colonel Trant
   Regimento de Infantaria n.º 12, one battalion
   Regimento de Infantaria n.º 21, one battalion
   Regimento de Infantaria n.º 24, half battalion
   Regimento de artilharia n.º 4
   50 Portuguese Cavalry

Centre Column
1st Brigade – Major General Hill
   Light companies[9]
   1/5th, 1/9th and 1/38th Foot
   Capt. Raynsford – 2 x 6-pdrs, 1 x 5½-inch Howitzer
3rd Brigade – Brigadier General Nightingall
   Light companies
   29th and 1/82nd Foot
   Lt. Graham – 3 x 6-pdrs
5th Brigade – Brigadier General Craufurd
   Light companies
   1/45th, 1/50th and 1/91st Foot
   Capt. Morrison – 2 x 6-pdrs, 1 x 5½-inch Howitzer
6th (Light) Brigade – Brigadier General Fane
   7 companies 5/60th Rifles and 4 companies 2/95th
   Capt. Geary – 2 x 6-pdrs, 1 x 5½-inch Howitzer

---

9   As per Wellesley's general order of 3 August the composite light battalions will appear on orders of battle, as they were a separate unit at the disposal of the brigade commander. However, they will only appear on maps when there is sufficient information in the sources to place them accurately.

Batalhão de Caçadores do Porto
20th Light Dragoons
Remaining Portuguese cavalry
Artillery Reserve – Major Viney
  Capt. Gardiner – 3 x 9-pdrs
  2nd Captain Eliot – 2 x 9-pdrs, 1 x heavy 5½-inch Howitzer

Left Column
2nd Brigade – Major General Fergusson
  Light Companies
  1/36th, 1/40th and 1/71st Foot
  Lt. Locke – 2 x 6-pdrs, 1 x 5½-inch Howitzer
4th Brigade – Brigadier General Bowes
  Light Companies
  1/6th and 1/32nd Foot
  Lt. Festing – 3 x 6-pdrs
3 companies 5/60th Rifles
20 20th Light Dragoons
20 Portuguese Cavalry

The Plan

On 16 August, Wellesley issued a general order from Caldas for the troops to assemble the following day:

> The Army will move off from their present ground at half past 4 tomorrow morning, and assemble in Contiguous Columns of Brigades, Right in front, in the Plain on this side [of] the Castle of Obidos. The Brigades of Artillery, the Park and the spare Ammunition; will be on the high Road to Obidos, and the Baggage and Commissariat Depot in the Rear; an Officer of the Quarter Master General's Department will attend each Brigade.[10]

Wellesley planned to assemble his troops just north of Óbidos and then march in three columns toward Roliça, about eight miles distant. The right column was to consist of the Portuguese line infantry (Wellesley put their number at 1,200) plus 50 Portuguese cavalry, all under the command of Trant. They were to turn Delaborde's left flank and move into the hills at his rear. The left column was to be made up of the 2nd and 4th Brigades, three companies of the 5/60th, a brigade of 6-pounders and 20 each of the British and Portuguese cavalry, all led by Ferguson. This column was to turn Delaborde's right flank by marching behind the hills on the left of the valley to the village of Bombarral, watching for Loison's appearance from the east. The centre column, consisting of the 1st, 3rd, 5th and Light Brigades, the Portuguese caçadores, the remaining cavalry, and a brigade each of 6- and 9-pounders, was to march up the centre of the valley to fix Delaborde's front.[11] The

10 NLS: Adv Ms 46.3.6: Additional General Order, 16 August 1808.
11 TNA: WO 1/228: Wellesley to Castlereagh, 17 August 1808.

The view from the tower at the southern end of Óbidos towards Roliça. There would have been far fewer buildings in 1808. (Author's photo)

The view of Delaborde's first position from the tower in Óbidos using a 300mm lens. A good field telescope could have given Wellesley a closer view. (Author's photo)

commander of the centre column is not mentioned explicitly in the sources. Wellesley may have retained direct command himself, but several sources mention Spencer taking an active role in the battle. Ferguson's column took a road to the left just south of Óbidos, and Trant turned right at the village of Dagorda.

In his diary, Captain Montague Wynyard, one of the deputy assistant adjutant generals, noted that Wellesley 'went on to the castle to reconnoitre'.[12] George Landmann of the engineers also remembers Wellesley examining the ground his troops were to advance over from the tower at the southern angle of Óbidos's walls. Landmann also takes credit for suggesting that Ferguson flank the French on the left but does not mention Trant's similar move. Landmann had scouted forwards on the left the previous day, so Wellesley ordered him to proceed with Ferguson's column.[13]

The allied troops marched at about 7:00 a.m., soon after sunrise. The four companies of the 2/95th and the seven of the 5/60th with Fane were sent onto the slopes of the hills on the left of the valley to maintain contact between the left and centre columns. With the 36th Foot was 16-year-old Ensign Roderick Murchison. It was his first action. A veteran captain saw him looking pale, so he gave him 'a good draught of Hollands gin out of his canteen', patted him on the back and reassured him that the fear would soon pass.[14]

The First Position

As the centre column advanced, the light companies in the valley and the riflemen on the slopes on the left drove in the French outposts. James Hale of the 9th Foot's light company later wrote:

> …they had several skirmishing parties formed in the olive orchards, in order to check our advance; but the light companies of the different regiments soon scoured them out. Between Obidos and Rolea, is a plain fruitful bit of land, mostly gardens and orchards for several miles, some vineyards, and almost surrounded with hills. While driving the enemy's skirmishers, our company passed through one garden, in particular, that was all onions, (at least, I could see nothing else), which I considered to be nearly two acres, and several other smaller gardens that were filled with pumpkins and melons, with some fruit trees, besides olive orchards. The weather being so warm, and water not convenient, a little fruit would have been very acceptable; but as we advanced so rapidly, we could only snatch an apple or a bunch of grapes as we passed along.[15]

Accounts from, or even mentions of, the Portuguese troops that took part in the Battle of Roliça are scarce, but Captain Fletcher Wilkie of the 38th Foot later wrote of the Caçadores:

> Before leaving Caldas we had been joined by the promised Portuguese, who were posted on the right. What they did there I never exactly heard, but I can speak for a small detachment we had on the left of the centre, about 300, who were called light troops, but were

---

12   Anon. 'From Vimeiro to Corunna', p.35.
13   Landmann, *Recollections*, vol.II, pp.133–136.
14   Geikie, *Life*, vol.I, p.35. The captain is named as Hubbard, but no such officer was with the 36th, so it was probably Captain Paul Minchin Hobart.
15   Hale, *Journal*, pp.18–19.

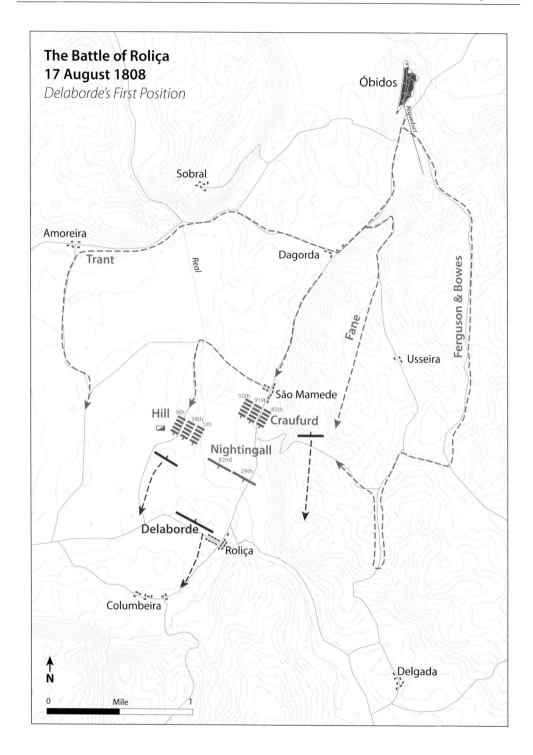

The Battle of Roliça
17 August 1808
Delaborde's First Position

Óbidos

Aqueduct

Sobral

Amoreira

Trant

Real

Dagorda

Ferguson & Bowes

Fane

Usseira

50th 91st São Mamede

Hill 9th 38th 45th
      5th Craufurd

Nightingall
82nd
29th

Delaborde

Roliça

Columbeira

N

0   Mile   1

Delgada

The area where Nightingall formed line. The French position was on a hill behind the slope pictured. (Author's photo)

chiefly formed of the students of Coimbra whom the fire of patriotism had started from their academical benches: they were armed with fowling-pieces, escopetar [hunting rifles], carbines, and other such deadly engines. The centre had halted to give time for the operations on the flanks, but our Portuguese friends seemed anxious for the fray, as they passed on in front without any orders, and the moment they got sight of the French on the lower plateau, began blazing away with great vigour; while thus employed, and before the enemy had deigned to reply by a single shot, one of these heroes came limping to the place where I stood; he was deadly pale; he could talk little English, and said he was badly wounded, although there was no appearance of anything of that kind. Serjeant Bowdler of my company, who was standing close by, said, 'Yes, my good fellow, I see you are badly wounded, and it is in the worst place, in your heart.' This sally produced a grand explosion of laughter among our men, under which the Coimbrese continued his retreat with anything but flying colours.[16]

Hill's, Nightingall's, and Craufurd's brigades moved with the guns along the main road. Before entering the small village of Sao Mamede, the troops halted, perhaps as Wilkie suggests, to allow time for the flanking columns to get into the rear of the French, and the men were then ordered to prime and load. Once through the village, Nightingall's brigade crossed a bridge over the Rio Real and formed line supported by the light companies of his and Craufurd's brigades and the 45th Foot. The 50th and the 91st of Craufurd's brigade, with half of the 9-pounders, formed a reserve to the rear just outside of Sao Mamede. The French position was about 500 metres to their front. Hill marched to the right after leaving Sao Mamede and deployed his brigade on the French left in three battalion columns supported by the cavalry. Both Hill and Nightingall advanced, expecting to be engaged, but when they reached the top of the small rise the French were already retreating, covered by their skirmishers. Delaborde had realised his flanks were being turned and

16   Wilkie, 'Recollections from the Peninsula', pp.424–425.

The French second position as seen from their first. (Author's photo)

retired in plenty of time. The two battalions of the 70e marched first, followed by the main bodies of the two light infantry battalions, then the cavalry and artillery. With Wellesley being so weak in cavalry, Delaborde knew he could safely manoeuvre.[17] The French marched through the village of Columbeira and onto the heights behind. The British artillery took up a position near a windmill on a hill and began to fire on the new French position.[18]

Wellesley described this first stage of the battle in his dispatch:

> Major General Hill and Brig. General Nightingall advanced upon the enemy's position, and at the same moment Brig. General Fane's riflemen were in the hills on his right, the Portuguese in a village upon his left, and Major General Ferguson's column was descending from the heights into the plain. From this situation the enemy retired by the passes into the mountains with the utmost regularity and the greatest celerity; and notwithstanding the rapid advance of the British infantry, the want of a sufficient body of cavalry was the cause of his suffering but little loss on the plain.[19]

Historian John Fortescue assumes that Wellesley's flanking columns of Trant and Ferguson were designed to dislodge Delaborde from his first position and that on the French retreating from there in such an orderly manner before the trap could be set 'the whole of the morning's work had been thrown away'.[20] However, it seems probable that the flanking moves were designed to be longer reaching and that for a commander with such a good eye for ground as Wellesley to have seen the heights behind Roliça and not to have assumed that the French were going to make their stand there rather than at the much weaker position on the valley floor seems unlikely. Delaborde

---

17   Griffon de Pleineville, *Invasion*, p.184.
18   Leslie, *Journal*, pp.40–41.
19   TNA: WO 1/228: Wellesley to Castlereagh, 17 August 1808.
20   Fortescue, *British Army*, vol.VI, p.211.

had occupied the forward position purely to cost Wellesley more time. However, the unexpected appearance of Ferguson descending into the valley rather than deep in Delaborde's rear now posed a problem for the allied commander as he would need to devise a new plan to force the French from the heights.

Ferguson on the Flank

Staff officer Captain Montague Wynyard, who was with Ferguson's column, wrote in his diary:

> The 2nd & 4th Brigades under General Ferguson were ordered to take a circuitory [*sic*] route to the left by Bombarral, which was effected with great difficulty. On approaching the village, a signal was made by the advance parties of an enemy discovered. The Line was immediately formed with the 40th in column on the left leading to form in line or *en potence* as might be required. The Brigades advanced and in a quarter of an hour, the enemy was discovered in front of our right flank retreating before Sir Arthur Wellesley in very good order, frequently and regularly forming to the front. At this time, Colonel Tucker, Adjutant-General, came to us from the Commander-in-Chief with an order to post the troops in the rear of the rising ground on our front, and expressing an opinion at the same time that the enemy's flank would be completely turned by our movement. This unfortunately however, was not the case for a message from Sir A. Wellesley obliged General Ferguson to take a direction more to the right, and the right flank of the enemy remained during the retreat unmolested except by the Light Corps, and after passing the heights completely so.[21]

This sequence of events would seem to agree with Wellesley's narrative: Ferguson was still descending onto the plain while the French fell back. Wynyard is not entirely clear which village they were approaching when the enemy was discovered to their front. Still, the implication is clearly that it was Bombarral, which would make the enemy one of the detached companies of the 70e. The arrival of Tucker would seem to be as the French began their retreat from their first position. For the turn 'more to the right' to have led them to a position where they did not cut into Delaborde's rear but instead arrived in front of the heights on the plain, they must have turned when still about two miles from their original objective. Wynyard clearly states that the messages came from Wellesley.

Captain Landmann of the engineers has his own version of events:

> We thus continued to advance about four miles by the road, which was sufficiently retired from the edge of the hills to conceal our line of march, no one daring to go to the right on the crest of the range of hills we were on, lest the enemy should see us. On one occasion, with the General's permission, I reconnoitred on foot to the distance of half a mile; with one pistol in my hand and the other in my sash, I crept along amongst the bushes,

---

21   Anon. 'From Vimeiro to Corunna', p.35. *En potence* – any part of the right or left wing formed at a projecting angle with the line.

and looked over into the valley, where I saw our main body considerably in the rear of us, which I hastened back to report to Ferguson.[22]

Four miles from Óbidos through the hills of the left could well have put them close to Bombarral, possibly near the village of Delgada, two miles from Bombarral, which would have meant that the main body on the plain could have been behind them at that stage. So, Wynyard's and Landmann's accounts seem to tally thus far. Landmann then continues:

> Just as I had communicated my information, I observed an aide de camp with two epaulettes, the distinction worn by those attached to His Royal Highness the Duke of York only. This officer came up at a hard gallop, with a fine white sheep-skin covering to his saddle, and extending much beyond it, and ordered General Ferguson to descend from the heights, and join the main body in a front attack; adding, that he had ascertained the road we were following would not lead us to turn the right flank of the enemy, as had been misrepresented, but lead away to our left. I was never more vexed in my life, as I was on hearing Colonel Brown's order. Down we all went, by a winding, steep, and almost impassable road for artillery, and so with much unnecessary fatigue joined the central column of attack, near the four windmills, on a sandy plain partly covered with pine and olive trees.[23]

So, if Landmann's account is correct, the bearer of the second message from Wellesley mentioned by Wynyard was Lieutenant Colonel Samuel Browne. Landmann does not mention Browne relaying an order from Wellesley but makes it sound more like Browne was acting on his own initiative. Landmann also later went back to the road that the column was on and ascertained that it would have led to the rear flank of the second French position.

Captain William Warre, one of Ferguson's aides de camp, does not mention much detail of the column's movements except: 'Our Brigade having been sent to turn the right, arrived rather late, and were scarcely engaged.'[24] Lord Burghersh, who was present, wrote in his book on Wellesley's early campaigns:

> The attack on the enemy's left was led on by the brigade under Major General Hill, while the 45th and 29th Regiments under Major General Nightingale were ordered to advance upon the centre; Major General Ferguson's brigade was brought from the heights on the left into the plain, to support this movement; by continuing however its original direction, that corps might have rendered more essential service, since it would have fallen upon the French right, and in conjunction with Brigadier General Fane's corps, would have decided the fate of the action sooner: but some mistake having arisen in an order delivered to it, this advantage was not obtained.[25]

---

22   Landmann, *Recollections*, vol.II, pp.138–139.
23   Landmann, *Recollections*, vol.II, p.139.
24   Warre, *Letters*, p.24.
25   J. Fane, M*emoir of the Early Campaigns of the Duke of Wellington in Portugal and Spain* (London: Murray, 1820), p.15.

So, Burghersh also suggests that Ferguson had been ordered to descend to the plain but that the order had somehow been in error. It may have been ambiguously written or misinterpreted.

Ensign Murchison (36th Foot) wrote that Ferguson's Brigade had been ordered into the hills on the left to cut off the French's retreat; he then continued:

> We were proceeding in this direction when the French appeared upon our flank, in consequence of which we formed line, and changing direction advanced, as the fog cleared, towards the enemy. We marched over about two leagues of hilly ground, and when within about one mile and a half of the pass we unexpectedly perceived the whole of the enemy in direct march to it, and immediately afterwards our riflemen opened their fire from the top of a hill upon one of the enemy's columns, who returned a volley and retreated a short distance.[26]

This is the only mention of fog in accounts of the battle and may refer to an early morning mist. The riflemen he refers to may well be the three companies of the 5/60th with the column. Two leagues equals just over six miles. The distance between Óbidos and Bombarral is just over seven miles. So, Murchison's account also puts the column close to their objective when they turned. One anonymous highlander of the 71st also implies that it was encountering the French that caused the change of direction: 'Half an hour after sunrise, we observed the enemy in a wood. We received orders to retreat. Having fallen back about two miles, we struck to the right, in order to come upon their flank'.[27]

The Second Position

The frontage of Delaborde's second position on the heights above Columbeira was only 800 meters long. The French occupied three promontories separated by two large defiles extending over 300 meters into the escarpment. The passes were up to 150 meters wide but narrowed sharply at the bottom. The slopes were often steep, rocky, and covered with thickets and brushwood. The left of the French position, the highest point, was protected by a steep-sided and deep river gorge. The road from Columbeira now runs up this gorge, but no road was there in 1808. The right of the position was on a lower height, around which a road snaked towards the village of Azambujeira, and there was a smaller defile on the left of this position also. The centre of the position was on a rocky outcrop that has since been identified as the site of a Bronze Age fort named the Castro da Columbeira. The defiles effectively separated the position into sections, so Delaborde placed his infantry in companies and smaller outposts on the promontories, along with his guns, with more troops on the sides of the defiles. His cavalry and a reserve were probably placed further back.

Wellesley had to redeploy his troops to tackle this more formidable second position. Many of the British troops were somewhat sheltered from the French fire on the heights as they approached by groves of holm and cork oaks. In his dispatch after the battle, Wellesley wrote:

---

26   Geikie, *Life*, vol.I, p.29.
27   Anon., *Journal of a Soldier*, p.54.

Looking along the second French position from the left. (Author's photo)

Looking along the axis of the main allied advance from the centre of the French position at Castro da Columbeira. Trant and the Portuguese marched on the far left of the image. The centre column advanced in the centre-left, through the first French position and then approached the village of Columbeira below the heights. Fane's riflemen kept to the wooded slopes on the right, and Ferguson's column marched on the high ground on the horizon to the right. (Author's photo)

Brig. General Fane's riflemen were already in the mountains on his [Delaborde's] right; and no time was lost in attacking the different passes, as well to support the riflemen as to defeat the enemy completely.

The Portuguese infantry were ordered to move up a pass on the right of the whole. The light companies of Major General Hill's brigade, and the 5th regiment, moved up a pass next on the right; and the 29th regiment, supported by the 9th regiment, under Brig. General Nightingall, a third pass; and the 45th and 82d regiments, passes on the left.[28]

Napier, Oman and Fortescue all say that Ferguson's column was ordered back into the hills on the left to complete their original flanking manoeuvre.[29] However, there is no evidence of this in Wellesley's dispatch, or in other first-hand accounts of the battle.

Brigadier General Fane and the riflemen of the 5/60th and 2/95th had been moving through the wooded hills on the left of the valley all morning. Now, they had to advance and attack the French on their right flank. Captain Jonathan Leach of the 95th wrote his account of the action in a letter soon after the campaign:

The 60th [Foot] and ourselves attacked the enemy's right and threw in so destructive a fire on their columns, such as we could get within shot of, as to make them retreat in great disorder. You cannot conceive nor can anyone who was not present on that day the situation of ourselves and the 60th. We had to ascend first one mountain so covered with brushwood that our legs were ready to sink under us, the enemy on the top of it lying down in the heath keeping up a hot and constant fire in our face and the men dropping all round us. Before we could gain the summit, the French had retreated to the next hill when they again lay concealed and kept up a running galling fire on us as we ascended. Having beaten them off the second hill and taken possession of it the enemy retreated to a wood, there being a valley between us and it and recommenced a most tremendous fire, having received a reinforcement. The action now became very severe. About this time I had a most providential escape. I was almost faint with anxiety to get the men properly placed and with the immense heat and fatigue. In short, I was like most of the others, completely fagged and would have given a guinea for one mouthful of water, when one of our officers asked me if I would take a mouthful of wine. He held his canteen to my mouth and it was not there a second when a shot went through his hand and the canteen which was in my mouth and covered my face with wine. The poor fellow dropped immediately. I left a soldier with him and proceeded with my company, pitying the officer who was wounded, but fully convinced that the ball was better through his hand than my head, which has proved the case as he is quite recovered.[30]

According to Lieutenant William Cox, the injured officer was Lieutenant Thomas Cochrane.[31] Benjamin Harris witnessed a similar but more deadly incident:

28   TNA: WO 1/228: Wellesley to Castlereagh, 17 August 1808.
29   Napier, *History*, vol.I, p.129; Oman, *History*, vol.1, p.237; Fortescue, *British Army*, vol.VI, p.211.
30   Glover & Burnham, *Riflemen of Wellington's Light Division*, pp.55–56.
31   Glover & Burnham, *Riflemen of Wellington's Light Division*, p.70.

Looking down from the French left into the river gorge where the light companies of Hill's Brigade and the 5th Foot advanced. The road was not there at the time. The Portuguese marched up another pass where the line of wind turbines now are. (Author's photo)

Joseph Cochan was by my side loading and firing very industriously about this period of the day. Thirsting with heat and action, he lifted his canteen to his mouth; 'Here's to you, old boy,' he said, as he took a pull at its contents. As he did so a bullet went through the canteen, and perforating his brain, killed him in a moment.[32]

Harris also witnessed one of the sergeants of his regiment being hit in the groin:

A man near me uttered a scream of agony; and, looking from the 29th, who were on my right, to the left, whence the screech had come, I saw one of our sergeants, named Frazer, sitting in a doubled-up position, and swaying backwards and forwards, as though he had got a terrible pain in his bowels. He continued to make so much complaint, that I arose and went to him, for he was rather a crony of mine.

'Oh ! Harris !' said he, as I took him in my arms, 'I shall die! I shall die! The agony is so great that I cannot bear it.'

It was, indeed, dreadful to look upon him; the froth came from his mouth, and the perspiration poured from his face. Thank Heaven! he was soon out of pain; and, laying

---

32   Curling (ed.), *Recollections*, p.42.

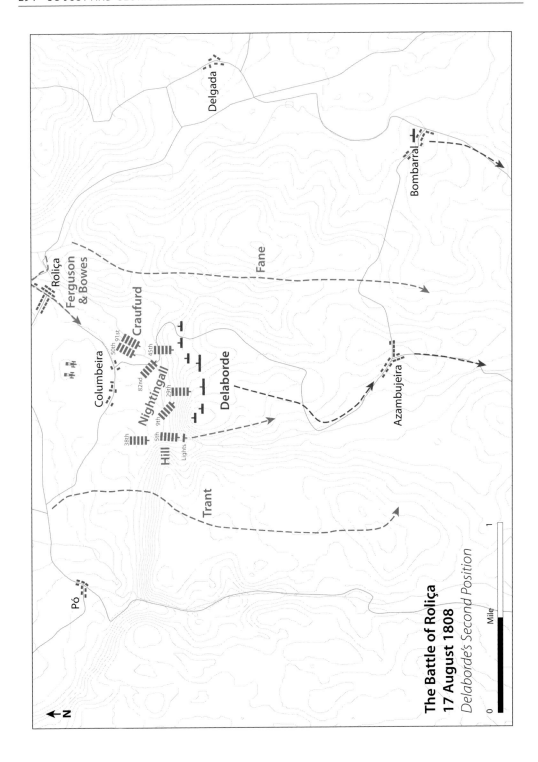

**The Battle of Roliça
17 August 1808**
Delaborde's Second Position

him down, I returned to my place. Poor fellow! he suffered more for the short time that he was dying, than any man I think I ever saw in the same circumstances.[33]

Harris later used the corpse of another rifleman as cover, stating that he 'revenged his death by the assistance of his carcase. At any rate, I tried my best to hit his enemies hard.'[34] At one point, some of the 95th Rifles were pinned down by French voltigeurs who had occupied two small buildings. They had to fix their sword bayonets and charge to drive the enemy from them. One of the buildings was full of French and British wounded.

The Brave 29th!

The most famous assault on the second French position was that of the 29th Foot. Lieutenant Charles Leslie gives the most complete account of their advance up the heights.

> The 82nd Regiment being ordered to another point of the attack, the 29th broke into open column, and advanced in column of sections through the village of Columbeira, led by the gallant Colonel Lake. They were now much galled by the enemy's sharpshooters from the heights, particularly from a high pinnacle commanding the village, and by a cannonade of round shot on the left. It being observed that the regiment was so much exposed, the left wing was ordered not to follow the right through the village, but to move round it to the left, and hence it did not reach the entrance of the pass until a considerable time after the right wing. The light company of the 29th was also detached with those of the 5th and 82nd Regiments to make a demonstration on a pass farther to the right. On leaving the village the right wing turned to the left through some vineyards, and advanced along the foot of the heights in order to gain the pass, exposed to a flank fire the whole way, from which we suffered considerably.[35]

Lieutenant Colonel Robe ordered Captain Geary's artillery brigade to fire two shrapnel shells on a French gun position on the heights, which put the French pieces out of action and helped to reduce the fire from above.[36] Private George Weale of the 29th recalled the climb up the heights in his memoir:

> The road by which we had to ascend was a narrow ravine, up which not more than two or three men could go abreast; and so difficult of access, that we found it necessary to assist ourselves in ascending by laying hold of the small brushwood, with which the hill was over grown: however, we did not confine ourselves to the road, but ascended, as well as we could, on all sides of it…[37]

---

33 Curling (ed.), *Recollections*, pp.33–34.
34 Curling (ed.), *Recollections*, p.36.
35 Leslie, *Journal*, p.41.
36 Lipscombe, *Guns*, p.40.
37 Weale, *Memoir*, p.21.

Looking down from Castro da Columbeira on the entrance to the defile up which the 29th Foot advanced.
(Author's photo)

Looking from Castro da Columbeira up the defile that the 29th ascended. The vegetation was different then, and
the current trees obscure the topography. (Author's photo)

Looking down from the end of the first section of the route up the heights taken by the 29th Foot. The tree cover hides much of the topography, but the defile rapidly narrows to two or three meters, with rocky outcrops on either side. (Author's photo)

Leslie remembers the French firing down from both sides of the gully while the 29th struggled upwards, so perhaps Weale followed later. About halfway up, at a small olive grove, the men halted and were ordered to take off their haversacks and greatcoats (which presumably would have been rolled up and slung over their backs) whilst under fire and then carried on up the hill. Leslie continues:

> Colonel Lake's horse was shot about this time, upon which Major Way dismounted, and gave up his horse to the Colonel. After clearing the narrow defile, we entered some open ground, thinly wooded, under shelter of which the officers lost no time in forming the men; the whole then pushed forward, and at last gained the wished-for heights; but we were now obliged, under a heavy fire, to take ground to the right, previous to forming in line, in order to give room for the rear to form as they came up, there not being at this time above three or four companies in line, and these much reduced from casualties. When the enemy, who appeared to have been lying down behind a broken earthen fence, which ran rather in an oblique direction along our front, suddenly rose up and opened their fire, their officers seemed to endeavour to restrain them, and apparently urged them on to the charge, as we observed them knocking down the men's firelocks with their swords, but they did not advance.

Colonel Lake called out, 'Don't fire, men; don't fire; wait a little, we shall soon charge' (meaning when more companies should come up), adding, 'the bayonet is the true weapon for a British soldier,' which were his dying words, for, as he moved towards the left to superintend the line being prolonged, he was marked and killed by a skirmisher … and his horse galloped into the French lines.

The right (in consequence of his death), not receiving, any orders to advance, opened their fire, and a desperate engagement ensued.[38]

The horse Major Way gave Lake was one of the lieutenant colonel's own, Black Jack. Lake would have been very prominent on horseback and a natural target for the French. One shot grazed his neck, and the fatal one passed from his upper left chest through to the right side and killed him instantly. Sergeant Major Richards stood over his commanding officer's body and received 13 musket ball, sword, and bayonet wounds. The 29th's surgeon, George Guthrie, treated Richards, and, apparently, his last words were, 'I should have died happy, if our gallant colonel had been spared'.[39]

Private Weale also recalled the events at the top of the heights:

> … after a most perilous struggle, six companies out of ten succeeded in gaining the summit, where we had not time to form in any compact order, before we were opposed to an overwhelming superiority of force. We long contended against this unequal odds; the firing had nearly ceased and the work of the bayonet, in the use of which the British troops so greatly excel, began; when the arrival of the 9th regiment, by the regular road, at the back of the height, relieved us from our desperate situation: their well-directed fire threw the enemy into confusion, which afforded us time to form our line, when we, in our turn, became the assailants.[40]

Weale places the advance of the 9th Foot not up the same gully that the 29th had used but possibly the larger one to the left. Leslie maintained that the 9th Foot followed the 29th up the same gully.

In his memoir, Leslie wrote that some of the soldiers of the 4e Suisse on the 29th's extreme right, probably from the grenadier company, then surrendered. At this point, the French, who had been posted along the sides of the gully, fearing being cut off, retreated through part of the 29th, capturing Major Gregory Way, five other officers and about 25 privates. Major Way wrote that 'the French in considerable force charged us and myself and two more officers may thank the French General of Brigade – Brennier – for our lives who rescued us from the Bayonets and fury of the soldiers. At the moment we were captured I had the point of one entering my Sash at the time the French General averted the blow.'[41] The French troops escorting the captured officers included two brothers named Bellegarde who, according to Leslie's reporting what one of the captured officers told him, argued as to which of them had brought down Lieutenant Colonel Lake.[42] However, in his report, Brenier credits *sous-lieutenant* François Lemaire of the 2/70e Ligne with the fatal musket

38   Leslie, *Journal*, pp.42–43.
39   M. Crumplin, *Guthrie's War* (Barnsley: Pen & Sword, 2010), p.22.
40   Weale, *Memoir*, pp.21–22.
41   D. Buttery, *Wellington against Junot* (Barnsley: Pen & Sword, 2011), p.97.
42   Leslie, *Journal*, p.44.

shot.[43] Lemaire was then himself wounded. Lake's horse, Black Jack, was returned to the regiment by Delaborde after the end of the campaign.

Leslie stated that Brevet Major Egerton ordered the 29th to fall back on the left wing, which was in the rear. He then continued:

> On observing this the enemy set up a shout, and then, but not till then, advanced upon us, as if with a view to charge; some individuals on both sides got mixed, and had personal encounters with the bayonet; they, however, did not venture to press us, nor to follow us into the woody ground, where we formed on the left wing, which had now come up, being also joined by the 9th Regiment (which was sent to support the 29th when it was found that they were so seriously engaged). The whole now rapidly pushed forward and cleared the front of the enemy, who, after an ineffectual resistance, were driven from their position.[44]

A common theme between Weale and Leslie is the 'overwhelming' number of French they faced once they reached the top of the heights. Brenier's report to Delaborde, written three days after the battle, states that he led two companies of the 70e to attack the 29th but also that other companies and some of the Swiss came to their support:

> No sooner had the 70e regiment been in position than the enemy came out in great force on our left and threatened to cut off the entire division's retreat by moving on the village of Asambougeira (sic); the moment was decisive for our salvation; the 8th company of the 2nd battalion was alone at the height of the outlet; I gave the order to the 7th company to march by its left flank to support it; I sent the order to a company of the 1st which was behind, but closer to the position, to support this company again, and I went there myself, to supervise the execution of this movement. The 29th Regiment of British Infantry was in battle opposite the two companies. In spite of the inferiority of numbers, and although a very strong column riddled them on their left flank, these companies charged the enemy with French bravery, and the enemy, attacked in their rear by M. l'Adjutant-Commandant Arnauld with other companies of the 70e and the Swiss, withdrew in disorder, leaving the battlefield covered with their dead, and eight officers, among whom were the regimental major and several captains. The flag of this regiment was already in the hands of my aide de camp, Captain Barré, who was obliged to go at the same moment to carry an order from me, leaving the flag and the flag-bearer in the hands of several soldiers of the 70e regiment, and I cannot conceive how this flag is not in our hands.[45]

One of the 29th's colours must have been retaken by the British. In September 1829, Brenier wrote on the subject of infantry manoeuvres in *Le Spectateur Militaire,* and the *United Service Journal* later quoted some of the passages on the topic of Roliça, including the fact that the 29th was initially charged by only two companies of the 70e before Arnauld brought up further troops from the right. In a footnote, Brenier then added:

43   Griffon de Pleineville, *Invasion*, p.187.
44   Leslie, *Journal*, p.43.
45   Griffon de Pleineville, *Invasion*, p.189.

Gen. Foy, and afterwards Colonel Napier, in giving an account of the affair at Rorica, have said that the enemy was charged by a battalion, but I was upon the ground and these gentlemen were not; and I am certain that all the old officers of the brave 70th will testify that the English regiment which attacked our left was only charged by two companies; I will also aver that we were not more than 2000 men in the field of battle at Azambugeira.[46]

In reply to Brenier's comments, Leslie wrote in his memoir:

With regard to General Brennier's assertion, that he, with only two companies, broke the 29th Regiment, I have to observe that it may no doubt be true that he sent two companies from his own left, but it ought at the same time to have been stated that those companies could only have come in support of troops already defending the debouch of the pass, and that neither they nor others broke through the centre of the regiment; because, at the time stated, it is sufficiently proved that there were not formed more than the remains of three or four weak companies, reduced by the dreadful fire they had been exposed to, so that he would have had no great achievement to boast of, even if correct.[47]

Another account by Captain Andrew Patisson of the 29th relates another slightly different sequence of events:

I commanded the right centre company, the fifth from the right; each scrambled up the best way he could; and, on gaining the summit, I found several officers, and about 60 privates of the 29th, who were in front of me; only one of my own company reached the top with me, the rest following fast. Here we lost that distinguished ornament of his profession, my good friend Colonel Lake, and many other gallant officers, long my companions in the regiment. My poor private, the moment he stepped up, was also knocked down by my side; in the agonies of death, he asked leave to shake hands with me; he was a good soldier, and few knew their duty better. Upon advancing, we were immediately attacked by a French platoon of ninety men, whom we repeatedly repulsed; these were, however, joined by another of the same number, who charged us with the bayonet, with whom we sustained the unequal conflict; but our little band being now considerably advanced in front, and reduced to 25, Major Wray, Captain Todd, and myself, and our brave companions, were under the painful necessity of surrendering. Even this, however, did not satisfy the sanguinary enemy, who seemed bent on bayonetting us all. After many narrow escapes, General Brennier at last came up, and with difficulty put an end to the carnage, and to the distressing scene around the dead and dying.[48]

The two platoons of 90 men each would make them slightly smaller than the establishment of French companies, but they still seemed to have outnumbered the few 29th that had reached the top of the gully by then. Multiple accounts of an action rarely agree as each participant has their point of view, and every individual's memory will be different.

---

46 'Foreign Miscellany', *United Service Journal*, 1830, part 1, p.87.
47 Leslie, *Journal*, p.45.
48 Anon. (ed.), *The Soldier's Companion, or Martial Recorder* (London: Cock, 1824), vol.I, p.441.

Private James Hale was with the 9th Foot's light company. His account is slightly confused as the distance he quotes would place him and his company with the rest of Hill's light companies, but then other sections of his narrative make it sound as if he was with the main body of the 9th Foot:

> The 29th regiment being about a quarter of a mile [400m] on our left, and having some little better road than our regiment, they ascended the heights a few minutes before us; upon which, the enemy immediately attacked them with a much superior force, and caused them to fall back with the loss of their colours, and about three hundred men: but as soon as we made our appearance on the top of the heights, it was a great relief to them: and the first thing our colonel thought most proper to do, was to show them the point of the bayonet, which we immediately did; and much to their shame and disgrace, we drove them off the heights in a few minutes; at the same time the remains of the 29th regiment gave them another grand charge, by which they retook their colours and some prisoners. But unfortunately, in this attack Lieut. Colonel Stewart, who commanded the 9th regiment, was killed; and also, the colonel of the 29th. The enemy fell back, a little distance, and then turned and attacked us again; but was received most gallantly, and soon repulsed. They afterwards made several attacks upon our regiment and the 29th, before any other regiment came up to our assistance, but without effect, as they found true Englishmen every time; and it is certain, that the 9th and 29th regiments were exposed to nearly all the French army for some time: but when some other regiments came up we obliged them to retreat; and soon after they began to feel the effects of a few cannon shot, and some shells, they retreated – very rapidly.[49]

Hale confirms the loss and recapture of the 29th's colours. A newspaper account of Lieutenant Colonel Stewart's wounding states:

> In the moment Lieut.-Col. Stuart's [sic] cheering his men to the attack, and just after Colonel Lake was wounded, he was struck by a musket ball in the groin. Some of the 9th immediately turned back, and would have assisted him, but he cried out 'I shall be taken care of, my lads – don't mind me; but push on, and support the brave 29th! On an officer of the General's staff coming up immediately after, who expressed deep sorry at Col. Stuart's situation, and his fear that they could not procure him immediate assistance, this gallant Soldier exclaimed, 'It is all over with me – I am as well as I can be – but don't lose sight of the brave 29th, for God's sake; keep up the 9th with them and all will be well!'[50]

Surgeon Guthrie of the 29th and Surgeon Andrew Brown of the 9th together pronounced Stewart's wound mortal.[51] As the 9th Foot came up in support of the 29th, the terrain and fog of war meant that they were not fully aware of how close the 29th was. When they saw some troops ahead they opened fire, perhaps thinking them red-coated Swiss, causing some serious casualties on top of those caused by the French.[52]

---

49   Hale, *Journal*, pp.19–20.
50   *General Evening Post*, 15 September 1808.
51   Crumplin, *Guthrie's War*, p.23.
52   Leslie, *Journal*, p.45.

The 45th Foot advanced on the left of the 29th. A letter from their adjutant, James Campbell, to one of his friends was published in *The Star* newspaper:

> In the action of 17 August we attacked the strongest part of the enemy, headed by the gallant General Spencer, but, from the 29th Regiment having advanced too quick, they having the road on our right, and we being obliged to climb a precipice, they suffered, as you have seen by the Gazette, very severely. Whereas we that were exposed to the whole cannon of the French, while advancing, lost only one Ensign killed, one lieutenant wounded, and nine rank and file. The 29th completely saved us from being cut to pieces, for our regiment was so entirely done up, that scarcely a man could stand when we got to the top of the precipice, some places of which only two men could get up at a time … They retired in astonishment when they saw the 29th and us formed in perfect order on the hill. We never fired a shot, and consequently were not mentioned in orders; but all the army agree that we deserve to have been noticed in the strongest terms.[53]

The 45th's colour party were amongst the first up, despite the difficulty of carrying the large and heavy colours. When they reached the top, French artillery fired on them. Ensign Robert Dawson, son of Derbyshire innkeeper, who was carrying the King's Colour, was hit by canister-shot and killed, and the staff of the Regimental Colour was broken.[54] Campbell mentioned that the 29th had advanced too quickly. In his dispatch, Wellesley also hinted at this and that the 9th did follow the 29th up the same gully: 'These passes were all difficult of access, and some of them were well defended by the enemy, particularly that which was attacked by the 29th and 9th regiments. These regiments attacked with the utmost impetuosity, and reached the enemy before those whose attacks were to be made on their flanks.'[55] Lieutenant Leslie stated in his memoir:

> We afterwards understood that it was not intended the 29th should have so soon attacked the strong pass, nor penetrate so far as we did, but were merely in the first instance to have occupied the village of Columbeira, and make a demonstration on the enemy's centre, whilst General Ferguson on the left, and General Hill on the right, should attack and turn his flanks. By some mistake, however, the order was misunderstood, and our gallant Colonel pushed on.[56]

The 5th Foot of Hill's 1st Brigade moved up the river gorge further to the right of the 29th and 9th. Their commanding officer, Lieutenant Colonel John Mackenzie, sensibly dismounted and left his horse behind before leading his battalion up the rocky slopes, sword in hand. The 5th received fire as they climbed and then charged the French as they reached the crest.[57] Captain Wilkie of the 38th Foot, also in Hill's brigade, described the hill his battalion climbed up as being 'as steep as that at Malvern, and covered with loose pebbles, having only a few stunted shrubs here and there to give security to the footing'.[58]

---

53   *The Star*, 1 November 1808.
54   Brown, *Redjackets*, p.47.
55   TNA: WO 1/228: Wellesley to Castlereagh, 17 August 1808.
56   Leslie, *Journal*, pp.44–45.
57   Morley, *Memoirs*, pp.45–46.
58   Wilkie, 'Recollections from the Peninsula', p.425.

The slope on the French left up which Hill's light companies and the 5th Foot climbed. (Author's photo)

Salomon Bleuler, *adjutant major* of the 1/4e Régiment Suisse, was with his voltigeurs and other French light infantry defending the road from Columbeira up to the heights on the French right, where Fane's riflemen were advancing. The Swiss were taking heavy casualties from the British artillery and were being cut to pieces by the thorny bushes they were in. *Lieutenant* Ignazio Chicherio took a shot in the chest, and Bleuler carried him to the rear. *Major* Jean Meslier, of the 4e Légère and commanding the light infantry to the left of the Swiss, was coming to talk to Bleuler about withdrawing when he was hit in the right arm and the left thigh. *Capitaine* Melchior Neuschler, commanding the Swiss voltigeur company, was then also shot, and Bleuler received a spent ball on his left side, which did not injure him. The grenadiers of the 4e Suisse were at one point mistaken by some of the 70e Ligne for British troops because of their redcoats and fired upon, causing several casualties.[59]

The 82nd Foot, the other battalion in the Nightingall's 3rd Brigade, proceeded up a gully to the left of the one Lake led his regiment up. Lieutenant George Wood of the 82nd recalled in his memoir:

> We now began to advance over those who had fallen: among them was my brother Sub, who had been out skirmishing; and we came under what I then thought a pretty hot fire, both of field-pieces and musketry, not having witnessed the like before: but this I found was a mere joke to what I was hereafter to experience. However, it gave me a seasoning as I was soon after knocked down by a musket-ball striking me on the left groin; and I only

59   Maag, *Schweizertruppen*, vol.I, pp.461–462.

attribute escaping a severe wound to having some papers in the pocket of my pantaloons, which prevented its penetrating the flesh; but it caused a great contusion: I was, however, in a few minutes able to proceed with the regiment, and soon had the pleasure of seeing the French flying before us.[60]

The other subaltern that had fallen was Lieutenant Richard Read, who is described as dangerously wounded on the casualty return but who survived.

In his dispatch, Wellesley wrote of the assaults up the defiles:

The enemy here made three most gallant attacks upon the 29th and 9th regiments, supported as I have above stated, with a view to cover the retreat of his defeated army, in all of which he was, however, repulsed; but he succeeded in effecting his retreat in good order, owing principally to my want of cavalry, and, secondly, to the difficulty of bringing up the passes of the mountains, with celerity, a sufficient number of troops and of cannon to support those which had first ascended.[61]

Eventually, more battalions did gain the heights and support the shattered ranks of the 29th and the 9th. Captain Geary's brigade of guns was first to the top. The guns were deployed, ready for action as French infantry counter-attacked and approached to well within musket shot. Geary fired one gun, loaded with canister, and was aiming the second when he was shot in the forehead and killed instantly.[62]

Dead on All Sides

The 2nd and 4th Brigades under Ferguson should have played a decisive role in the battle, cutting off the French retreat and ensuring the complete defeat of one of Junot's ablest subordinates and many of his best units. Instead, they played only a very limited part in the action. Ensign Murchison (36th Foot) wrote that the 2nd Brigade's artillery fired on the retreating French, that three companies of his regiment supported the brigade light companies, and that the 40th were detached to guard the baggage. The 36th marched up to the heights after the firing had ceased, and 'Swiss and French men were lying dead on all sides.'[63] Captain Wynyard, who was with Ferguson's column, wrote that the light companies of the 2nd and 4th Brigades, and presumably the three companies of the 5/60th, were ordered to support Fane's Light Brigade on the left.[64]

Lieutenant William Cowper Coles of the 40th Foot's light company, who would have been amongst the lead troops of the left column, noted that the assaults up the hill started before they reached the base of the heights: 'myself being in the Light Infantry had the opportunity of seeing much, tho not foremost, as the action commenc'd before our brigade could reach the ground.'[65] Likewise, an anonymous highlander of the 71st noted that the light company was the only portion

60   G. Wood, *The Subaltern Officer* (London: Prowett, 1825), pp.52–53.
61   TNA: WO 1/228: Wellesley to Castlereagh, 17 August 1808.
62   Lipscombe, *Guns*, pp.40–41.
63   Geikie, *Life*, vol.I, p.30.
64   Anon. 'From Vimeiro to Corunna', pp.35–36.
65   NAM: 1968-07-419-15: Coles to his father, 19 August 1808.

of his regiment to be engaged and that 'we could only see at a distance the "tug of war." The incessant discharge of musketry, and the smoke and loud roar of artillery, completed the effect: occasionally, however, a stray cannon-ball from the French would whistle over our heads, and sink with a heavy sound into the earth.'[66] Private John Macfarlane of the 71st Highlanders, 17 years old and from Glasgow, recalled the scene as they marched up the road to the heights:

> As we went on, we came to a narrow road. There was a French soldier lying shot. He appeared to be of the Grenadiers. There was a Portuguese dragging him off the road to strip him naked, for this is what they did. This gave us something to think about. After we were out of this narrow road, we saw others lying wounded, crying for water to drink, and looking to us for protection, for they were afraid of the Portuguese. We formed into line, but the French were retreating.[67]

Another soldier of the 71st had a very similar experience:

> While marching up a road, I passed over the dead body of a young Swiss soldier, his red clothing enabling us to know his nation. He had received a ball in the middle of the forehead. This was the first victim to the deity of war I had yet seen, but, as we advanced, many more met our sight. The road and contiguous fields were literally covered with dead and dying, both British and French. The horror of the scene was much increased in consequence of the hedges and long grass taking fire. We had to endure the appalling view of the impotent efforts of several poor wounded wretches endeavouring to drag themselves from the devouring flames: there was no time to render them assistance; besides, self-preservation warned us that danger was to be apprehended from the fire communicating with our cartridge-boxes. After reaching the summit of the heights, there was nothing to do but to look at the French filing off in columns.[68]

With no memoirists amongst their ranks, much of the services of the riflemen of the 5/60th at Roliça remain unrecorded, but a letter that Wellesley wrote to the Patriotic Fund in 1809 on behalf of Captain Keating James Bradford's mother sheds some light on their activities:

> This officer, who was Assistant- Adjutant-General to the army lately under my command in Portugal, and aide de camp to General Spencer, was killed at a most interesting and critical moment of the battle of the 17th of August, in the performance of a most important service on which he had been employed by me. He was sent to ascertain the exact situation of a detachment of riflemen [of the 5/60th], who, I imagined, had pushed themselves into the enemy's rear, and to form a judgment in what manner they could be supported. When he reached them they were about to give way, pressed by superior numbers, and he succeeded in rallying them before he received the wound of which he died.[69]

---

66   Anon., *Vicissitudes*, pp.10–11.
67   Eric Robson, 'Peninsular Private', p.5.
68   Anon., *Vicissitudes*, pp.11–12.
69   Wellington (ed.), *Supplementary Despatches*, vol.VI, p.201. In an earlier letter to the Duke of York, p.130, Wellesley makes it clear the riflemen were from the 60th.

Captain Landmann claims he found Bradford, wounded:

> Bradford was naturally of a high florid complexion, his hair inclining to red, young, hand-some, always well dressed, highly accomplished, and ever the gentleman. He was now pale as death, suffering excruciating pain; and, holding out his hand to me, said, 'For God's sake! do not laugh at me for showing so much suffering at a slight wound in my arm, yet I feel as if I were dying.'
>
>   I was much surprised at this declaration, for I could easily perceive that a shot had passed through his thigh, and had broken the bone, whence some blood was already oozing out; and immediately below his heart I observed in his coat a round hole, and from under his waistcoat blood was beginning to make its way, over his elastic drab-coloured pantaloons. I afterwards understood that this shot had broken his back-bone. From his manner it was evident he was totally ignorant of the two principal wounds just mentioned, and attributed his sufferings to a third wound in his arm, which, as he had truly stated, was but slight.[70]

Landmann then says some of the 71st took Bradford to the rear.

The Most Scientific and Beautiful Retreat

The battle was far from over despite the French being dislodged from the top of the heights. George Murray, who was later Wellesley's quartermaster general and arrived in Portugal later in the month, pointed out in a review of Napier's history in the *London Quarterly Review* that the advantage of Delabdorde's position did not end with the steep slopes above Columbeira. The topography beyond was also favourable to the French as 'the front to be defended became also more narrow as they fell back; and the village of Zambugeira [*sic*] presented a favourable post for checking their pursuers. Of these advantages, General Laborde, who was an able officer, did not omit to profit to the utmost in making his retreat.'[71]

Private Stephen Morley of the 5th Foot remembered that after driving the French from the top of the slopes:

> We then proceeded towards another hill, where the enemy had formed again: but as [our] route lay through vineyards, we were annoyed by a destructive fire. Our Colonel, whom no impediment could intimidate, said 'charge;' we did so, but I could go no further, having received a wound in my leg. It turned out to be only a flesh-wound, but it bled so profusely that I felt faint: a surgeon of the regiment tied it up, and I then followed and arrived in time to see the enemy in full rout, after one of our regiments had received and repulsed a charge in the most gallant style by a reserved fire, when every shot seemed to tell.[72]

---

70   Landmann, *Recollections*, vol.II, pp.147–148.
71   G. Murray, 'Review of History of the War in the Peninsula and the South of France, by W. Napier', *London Quarterly Review*, vol.LVI, April 1836, p.189.
72   Morley, *Memoirs*, p.46.

The rear of the second French position over which Delaborde retreated. Azambujeira is just visible on the right of the image. (Author's photo)

Brenier wrote in his report to Delaborde after the action that initially the retreat was in some confusion but that he placed the 1/70e behind Azambujeira and he rallied the 2/70e, which gave the other units time reform, then:

> … once the line was re-established, the retreat was made in echelons, from position to position, with the utmost order, facing three sides under the most intense artillery and musketry fire, and it was at this time that the 1st Battalion of the 70th Regiment made such a sustained and fierce fight against an English regiment coming up from the front (and which must have lost a great many men) that we were obliged to repeat the order to withdraw several times.

To help stop a potential rout, the *tambour-major* of the 70e Ligne, 'mounted a horse which he found without a rider, stood across the road and threatened to break his staff on those who wanted to pass to save themselves.'[73]

Bleuler had retreated with his Swiss troops to the top of the hill, but Delaborde galloped up and ordered them back to the fray:

> I had gone too far under the general's eye in leading the voltigeurs and tirailleurs through the bushes, and found myself almost surrounded by English chasseurs. I threw myself to the left, but there the bullets rained down. Lieutenant Rüpplin was shot in the arm; we retreated again; Laborde came again and asked us to fight an honourable retreat for him, for they were giving way to superior force on all points. I now had the grenadiers again, advanced once more, and not far away Laborde was slightly wounded in the neck, waved his hat and called out: 'Vive l'empereur!' The sergeant of the grenadiers was shot, one of

---

73   Griffon de Pleineville, *Invasion*, pp.190–191.

the Voltigeurs fell just behind me, badly wounded. I had him carried away, I always liked him. At last we could not stand it any longer. Our chasseurs à cheval lost many men; the major who commanded them was mortally wounded, and the general [Delaborde] who ordered the retreat on the plain, on foot and with a bandaged neck, told me many flattering things … General Thomieres, who was standing next to Laborde, claimed that I was blessed, and when I asserted the opposite … he took me by the shoulders and shook me, claiming that I must have bullets in my clothes. We retreated by echelons across a field, and the enemy was content to send cannonballs after us.[74]

At another point, Delaborde drove back the riflemen of the Light Brigade, leading the 2e Légère.[75]

The moment an enemy began to retreat was usually when the cavalry was ordered forward to run down and harass the retreating enemy. Sergeant Norbertus Landsheit of the 20th Light Dragoons recalled in his memoir the moment that the British cavalry was called upon:

We had watched the progress of the battle for some time, without sustaining any injury, except from a single shell, which, bursting over our column, sent a fragment through the backbone of a troop-horse, and killed him on the spot – when a cry arose, 'The cavalry to the front!' and we pushed up a sort of hollowed road towards the top of the ridge before us. Though driven from their first position, the enemy, it appeared, had rallied, and showing a line both of horse and foot, were preparing to renew the fight. Now, our cavalry were altogether incapable of coping with that of the French; and the fact became abundantly manifest, so soon as our leading files gained the brow of the hill – for the slope of a rising ground opposite was covered with them in such numbers, as to render any attempt to charge, on our parts, utterly ridiculous. Accordingly, we were directed to form up, file by file, as each emerged from the road – not in two ranks, as is usually done both on parade and in action –but in rank entire. Moreover, we were so placed, that the French officers could not possibly tell what was behind us; and thus made a show which appeared to startle them; for they soon began to change their dispositions, the infantry moving off first, the cavalry following: upon which we likewise broke again into column of threes, and rode slowly after them. But we had no desire to overtake them.[76]

The 26e Chasseurs à Cheval present would have had numbers not dissimilar to that of the 20th Light Dragoons, so it is possible that Landsheit was with a small detachment or that his impression of the French numbers, either on the day or on recollection, was mistaken. One anonymous staff officer wrote: 'Owing to our want of cavalry, the enemy … were enabled to make the most scientific and beautiful retreat that has, perhaps, ever been witnessed.'[77] The French 26e Chasseurs performed their very job well, conducting multiple small charges, forcing the British infantry to pause and slowing down the pursuit. However, they did take many casualties, including their commanding officer, *major* Weiss. Weiss's wound was not, as Bleuler stated, mortal, but it also was not to be his last of the campaign.

---

74   Maag, *Schweizertruppen*, vol.I, p.463.
75   Foy, *Invasion*, p.156.
76   Gleig, *Hussar*, vol.I, pp.252–253.
77   Neale, *Letters*, p.50.

During the pursuit, Ensign Samuel Laing of the Royal Staff Corps encountered Major General Spencer:

> General Spencer was not a very clever man, but he was certainly goodhearted and brave. The weather was hot, and the road dusty and close from the smoke of the gunpowder and, having my pocket full of apples, I was munching one now and then to moisten my throat. I observed the old General eye my apple although he was then in the advance of the men pushing up the road and the enemy retiring step by step and keeping up a sure fire at a short distance from us. I presented him with an apple, and his coolness in sitting on his horse eating his apple in front of the men, and within a few paces of the enemy, seemed to inspire the advance with the same steadiness and coolness. There was no sense or feeling of danger there. It was one joyous burst of animated activity.[78]

The French continued to fall back in good order, using the ground well and making the British fight for every successive rise. Spencer led the charge to drive the French from Azambujeira, effectively ending the action.[79] Captain Wilkie of the 38th Foot recalled of Azambujeira: 'Whether from the fire of artillery, or that it was done purposely to check the pursuit, the village was burnt to the ground, offering one of the common spectacles of war, the inhabitants standing in the street with every mark of grief and despair, as they looked at the blazing rafters of their dwellings.'[80]

The consensus of the various accounts is that the fighting ended between 4:00 and 5:00 p.m. It had been a long and hot day for the troops, but it was not over for the French. They had to put a suitable distance between themselves and the allies. Leaving three guns and many wounded in the hands of the British, Delaborde withdrew to Quinta de Maravigliata and then marched to Runa, 20 miles south of Azambujeira. *Capitaine* Desjardins, aide de camp to Brenier, rode through the British lines with two chasseurs to retrieve the three detached companies of the 70e. Delaborde then continued to Cabeça de Montachique the next day, another 14 miles closer to Lisbon.[81]

Sacred to the Memory

The official casualty return of British losses is shown in Table 19. Unsurprisingly, the 29th suffered the lion's share of the casualties at nearly half of the total men killed and a third of those wounded. Twenty percent of the regiment's rank and file and 36 percent of their officers were casualties. The 5th and 9th Foot, units that quickly followed the 29th up the slopes behind Columbeira, were the next worse hit from the line regiments. The riflemen of Fane's brigade, in action most of the day, also lost many dead and wounded, as well as some missing, with the 2/95th suffering proportionately heavier losses than the 5/60th. Many of the other regiments had few men killed or wounded, and those probably came from their light companies who had often seen action while their parent

---

78   R.P. Fereday (ed.), *The Autobiography of Samuel Laing of Papdale 1780-1868* (Kirkwall: Bellavista, 2000), p.114.
79   Fane, *Early Campaigns*, pp.16–17.
80   Wilkie, 'Recollections from the Peninsula', p.425.
81   Foy, *Invasion*, p.157; Griffon de Pleineville, *Invasion*, p.191.

battalions had not. Portuguese losses were one killed and eight wounded.[82] These probably came from the caçadores with the central column.

Table 19. British casualties at Roliça

Unit	Killed							Wounded								Missing								Total
	Lt Col	Maj	Capt	Lt	Ens	Sgt	R&F	Lt Col	Maj	Capt	Lt	Ens	Staff	Sgt	R&F	Lt Col	Maj	Capt	Lt	Ens	Sgt	Drmr	R&F	
Staff			1																					1
Royal Artillery			1												1									2
Royal Engineers										1														1
1st Brigade																								0
1/5th							3		1	1				2	39									46
1/9th							4	1	1	1		1		3	49								12	72
1/38th															4									4
2nd Brigade																								0
1/36th																								0
1/40th							1								2									3
1/71st							1								1									2
3rd Brigade																								0
29th	1					2	31		1	3	3			6	105			1	3		1	1	32	190
1/82nd							6				1			1	17									25
4th Brigade																								0
1/6th											1				2								1	4
1/32nd							1								3									4
5th Brigade																								0
1/45th						1					1				9									11
1/50th							2								1									3
1/91st																								0
Light Brigade																								0
5/60th							8				2		1	5	34								16	66
2/95th				1			6							3	25								7	42
																								0
20th LD															3									3
Total	1		2	1		3	63	1	3	6	8	1	1	20	295			1	3		1	1	68	479

Source: BL: Add MS 49481: Return of the killed, wounded and missing on 17 August 1808, dated the 18th at Lourinhã.

The figures for the casualties that are entered in the return for a battle were usually sent to the adjutant general's department by the regiments the evening or morning after the action. As one can imagine, there was often considerable confusion and fatigue in the aftermath of a battle, and any close examination of a regiment's muster books or returns usually shows some variance from

---

82   Gil, *A Infantaria Portuguesa*, vol.I, p.285.

the post-action return. For example, the records of the 5/60th list seven men killed rather than eight, with one man marked as 'died by accident on the 16th', which perhaps explains the difference. The records also only list six men as missing rather than 16, so 10 men may have returned or been found wounded after the casualty return was submitted.[83] The battle had ranged over a considerable area, parts of which were thick with undergrowth, so wounded or killed men may have lain on the field for hours, even overnight, before they were discovered. The walking wounded may also have stumbled in much later. Some of the missing might also have been temporarily absent, looting the dead and injured.

According to Thiébault, the French suffered nearly 600 casualties.[84] In his report to Junot written the day after the battle, Delaborde estimated his losses in killed and wounded at 400 men. On 27 August, he revised this to 121 killed and 451 wounded, a total of 572, but neither report mentions the number of prisoners or missing.[85] The day after the battle, Delaborde wrote to Junot, 'I am suffering only a little, my wound is not serious, it only requires some care, and I hope to be able to continue my to serve with my division.'[86]

The two battalions of the 70e Ligne had one officer killed and 17 wounded. The fatality was *sous-lieutenant* François Bocquet, 35 years old and from Neuville. Most of the wounded received gunshot wounds, several more than one, and they included *colonel* Jean Victor Rouyer and both *chefs de bataillon*, Louis Labadie and Pierre Nagonne. *Lieutenant* Jean Louis Hippolyte Paris was shot in the head and left for dead on the battlefield, but was taken prisoner and survived. *Sous-lieutenant* Louis Victor Roques, a former cadet of Fontainebleau and velite of the Grenadiers de la Garde, died of his wounds in October. An examination of the records of the 70e Ligne by historian Antonio Grajal de Blas shows they lost 62 sergeants and rank and file dead and had 64 wounded, with only two being taken prisoner.[87] The 2e Légère lost *capitaine* Claude Joseph Chevallier, 43 years old and from the Marne, killed, and three other officers wounded. The 4e Légère had three officers wounded, including *major* Jean Meslier. The 4e Suisse lost *lieutenant* Ignazio Chicherio, killed by a shot to the chest, and two other officers were wounded. *Major* Jean Baptiste Weiss, who was wounded, was the 26e Chasseurs à Cheval's only officer casualty. *Sous-lieutenant* Nicolas Joseph Perilleux of the 3e Dragons must have been on detached duty as his regiment was not present, but he is recorded as being wounded at Roliça.[88] Bleuler stated the casualties of his two companies of the 4e Suisse to be 37 killed and 27 wounded.[89]

The graves of almost all those killed remained unmarked, but a monument, paid for by the officers and men of the 29th Foot, was later erected where Lieutenant Colonel Lake was buried at the head of the gully. The inscription reads:

> Sacred to the Memory of Lieut.-Col. Lake of the 29th Reg who fell at the head of his Corps in driving the Enemy from the heights of Columbeira, on the 17th August, 1808.

---

83   Griffith, *Riflemen*, p.156.
84   Thiébault, *l'Expédition*, p.181.
85   Griffon de Pleineville, *Invasion*, p.191.
86   Griffon de Pleineville, *Invasion*, p.193.
87   '70e régiment d'infanterie de ligne, 30 frimaire an XIV [21 décembre 1805]-15 décembre 1807 (matricules 3 013 à 4 812).SHD/GR 21 YC 583', Memoire des Hommes, <https://www.memoiredeshommes.sga.defense.gouv.fr/fr/ark:/40699/e0052abc36ce2565/52abc36ce4bdf>, accessed April 2023.
88   Campos and de Blas, *Officiers de Napoléon tués ou blessés*.
89   Maag, *Schweizertruppen*, vol.I, p.464.

The memorial to Lieutenant Colonel George Lake. (Author's photo)

This Monument is Erected by his Brother Officers as a Testimony of their Regard and Esteem.

The subscription also paid for a memorial tablet in Westminster Abbey. An account of Lake's death in the *General Evening Post* stated that:

It is a singular circumstance, that, after the battle, when the body of Colonel Lake came to be sought for, it was found in the recess of the mountain to which he was carried when wounded, and there were some soldiers in decent attendance upon it, yet it was found without epaulettes, sword, or sash; and his watch, money and the other contents of his pockets, were missing.[90]

Rather charitably, the paper then assumes that some well-meaning soldier must have taken them for self-keeping and then been killed or taken prisoner. Wellesley offered a reward of 50 guineas for the return of the items, but to no avail. He also wrote to Lake's brother-in-law:

I do not recollect the occasion upon which I have written with more pain to myself than I do at present, to communicate to you the death of your gallant brother-in-law. He fell in the attack of a pass in the mountains, at the head of his regiment, the admiration of the whole army; and there is nothing to be regretted in his death, excepting the untimely moment at which it has afflicted his family, and has deprived the public of the services of an Officer who would have been an ornament to his profession, and an honor to his country.

It may at the moment increase the regret of those who lose a near and dear relation, to learn that he deserved and enjoyed the respect and affection of the world at large, and particularly of the profession to which he belonged; but I am convinced, that however acute may be the sensations which it may at first occasion, it must in the end be satisfactory to the family of such a man as Colonel Lake, to know that he was respected and loved by the whole army, and that he fell, alas! with many others, in the achievement of one of the most heroic actions that have been performed by the British army.[91]

There was no official system of informing relatives of a soldier's death. Officers' names were listed in *The Gazette*, but relatives of the rank and file may have waited years before they realised their loved one was not coming home.

Surgeon George Guthrie of the 29th treated the many wounded of his regiment and others, and he later mentioned some of the cases in medical treatises:

… the 29th regiment, to which I was attached, had 200 men wounded in storming the heights above the village of Roliça, and most of these men were lying in a line of two hundred yards extent; they were all known to me by name as well as by person: the conflict was soon over, and the difference of expression in begging for assistance, or expressing their sense of suffering, will never be obliterated from my memory; and it would have

---

90   *General Evening Post*, 15 September 1808.
91   Gurwood (ed.), *Wellington's Dispatches*, vol.IV, p.104.

been a lesson to those who deny that pain and constitutional alarm are attendant on gun shot wounds, which they would never have forgotten. From a mistaken sense of duty I marched with the regiment towards the enemy, who reserved their fire until the troops actually met, and I saw and heard the first gun-shot wound received from an enemy, that I ever dressed. It was on the shoulder, and the soldier described it as a severe numbing blow, depriving him momentarily of the use of his arm, and followed by a severer pain.[92]

Corporal Carter, of the pioneers of the 29th Regiment, was wounded ... by a musket-ball, which passed through the anterior and upper part of the forearm, fracturing the ulna. Shortly afterward a profuse hemorrhage [sic] took place, and the staff-surgeon in charge tied the brachial artery. In the night the hemorrhage recurred, and the man nearly bled to death. The arm was then amputated, when the ulnar artery was found in an open and sloughing slate.[93]

... in the act of leaving the village of Colombeira to ascend the heights of Roliça, a soldier was shot in the leg; he jumped up three or four feet, and made a considerable outcry. A second was struck at the same time by a ball on the shoulder, which did not penetrate, but gave him great pain. A third received a ball on his buff-leather belt, on the right brest [sic]. The noise made by these two blows was unmistakable. I saw this man fall, and supposed he was killed: the ball, however, had only gone through his belt, and made a mark on his chest, over the cartilage of the fourth rib, the hardness and elasticity of which had prevented further mischief. He recovered in a short time, spat a little blood in the night, and after a large bleeding was enabled to accompany me on the 20th to Vimiera, ready for the fight next morning.[94]

A soldier of the 9th Regiment was wounded ... by the point of a sword in the left side; it penetrated the chest, making a wound somewhat more than an inch long, through which air passed readily, accompanied by a very little frothy blood, which was also spit up on any effort being made to cough, leaving no doubt of the lung having been injured, that viscus appearing to be retained against the wall of the chest. As the edges of the wound could not be accurately kept in apposition by adhesive plaster, two sutures were applied through the skin, and the man was desired to lie on the injured side, with the hope that adhesion might take place, as there appeared to be no effusion of blood into the cavity, He was freely bled on each of the two days following the receipt of the wound, and gradually recovered.[95]

Another soldier of the 29th received a wound that will probably make any male reader wince:

A married soldier, of the 29th Regiment, was wounded ... by a small musket-ball, which went through both corpora cavernosa [the spongy tissue in the penis] from side to side. The man suffered very little inconvenience, and the wounds healed very well. He seemed to consider the injury as of no importance to himself, but had some idea there might be a difference of opinion in another party. There is usually a deficiency of substance at the part after such wounds, and sometimes an inconvenient curve or twist, such as often takes

92   G.J. Guthrie, *A Treatise on Gun-Shot Wounds* (London: Burgess & Hill, 1827), p.4.
93   G.J. Guthrie, *Commentaries on the Surgery of the War* (Philadelphia: Lippincott, 1862), p.197.
94   Guthrie, *Commentaries*, p.364.
95   Guthrie, *Commentaries*, pp.418–419.

place when the corpora cavernosa and the corpus spongiosum are injured or ruptured from other causes.[96]

Guthrie and his assistants set up an aid post and brigade hospital in Columbeira, and then later, he set up a small field hospital in Azambujeira. Some of the wounded were sent to the coast to be embarked on the hospital ship *Enterprise*, some to a temporary hospital in Óbidos, and some all the way to Oporto.[97]

Lieutenant Robert Birmingham was one of the officers of the 29th Foot wounded, and he eventually died on 10 September. His brother Walter, also in the 29th and taken prisoner on the 17th, wrote to the Duke of York to request permission to sell his brother's ensigncy to clear Robert's debts. Commissions of dead officers could not usually be sold, and Robert's lieutenancy had been granted for raising men, so his ensigncy was the only option.[98]

Lieutenant Colonel John Stewart of the 9th Foot is listed on the casualty return of 18 August as severely wounded, and he subsequently died. Wellesley wrote to Gordon, the Duke of York's secretary, on 20 August:

> I avail myself of the delay which has taken place in the departure of the ship which will take my dispatches to England, to acquaint you, for the information of the Commander in Chief, of the death of that gallant officer, Lieut. Colonel Stewart, of the 9th regiment, in consequence of the wounds he received in the action of the 17th; and I request that you will, at the same time, represent to his Royal Highness that the conduct of Major Molle, who was also wounded upon this occasion, was such during the action as to merit my warmest approbation; and I therefore beg leave to submit his name to the favorable consideration of his Royal Highness, to succeed to the lieutenant colonelcy unfortunately vacated by the decease of Lieut. Colonel Stewart.
>
> Should Major Molle be promoted upon this occasion, I request you will be pleased to submit to his Royal Highness, that the succession should go in the regiment in favor of Captain Aylmer, Lieut. Finlay, and Ensign Curzon.[99]

All the mentioned officers were promoted. Other recommendations for officers to fill dead men's shoes included in the 29th Foot, Major White to be promoted vice Lake. Wellesley then recommended Captain Thomas Egerton to be major, vice White, Lieutenant Walter Birmingham to be captain vice Egerton, Ensign Coker to be lieutenant vice Birmingham and volunteer James Evans to be ensign vice Coker. So, one man's misfortune led to promotion for five others. Another gentleman volunteer serving with the ranks until a vacancy appeared, Hans Stevenson Marsh of the 32nd, benefited from the death of Ensign Dawson of the 45th.[100]

The senior Royal Engineer, Captain Howard Elphinstone, was severely wounded during the battle. Captain George Landmann, in a letter written at the time to the headquarters of the Royal Engineers, wrote:

---

96   Guthrie, *Commentaries*, p.540.
97   Crumplin, *Guthrie's War*, pp.20, 23.
98   BL: Add MS 49485: Memorial of Walter Birmingham to Duke of York, undated.
99   Gurwood (ed.), *Wellington's Dispatches*, vol.IV, pp.106–107.
100 Wellington (ed.), *Supplementary Despatches*, vol.IV, p.117.

It is with the deepest regret I have to say that Captain Elphinstone was severely wounded by a musket ball in the jaw, the Surgeon's report is very favourable, and I hope he will be again able to take the command, although I fear it may be some time. I was unfortunately not able to see him myself, as we had advanced too far before I heard of the accident. Lieutenant Mulcaster was with Captain Elphinstone at the time and has seen him last night, who says he was in good spirits, and well taken care of in a small village about three miles in the rear of our present situation.[101]

Landmann took over as the expedition's Commander Royal Engineers, and Elphinstone recovered. Landmann also mentioned that one artilleryman who had been wounded had been 'burnt by the bursting of a cartridge'. The one fatality for the Royal Artillery was Captain Henry Geary. Lieutenant Colonel Robe mentioned him in his letter to Royal Artillery headquarters:

Our own loss, though small in number is irreparable, our friend Geary being the only sufferer. He was by his own desire, and as Senior Captain, in charge of Guns with the Light Brigade, and was killed while pointing his gun, within one or two hundred yards of the enemy. I regret him as an officer, for he was invaluable, and as a friend and old fellow campaigner, by no means less. His loss to his family cannot be appreciated, but it will always be a comfort, that he died as he had lived, in the very act of doing his duty to his country, and a true Christian.[102]

Geary, son of a Royal Navy captain from the Isle of Wight, left a wife and four children.[103]

Vice Admiral Cotton's papers included a list of British prisoners of war who arrived in Lisbon on 19 August. From the 29th Foot, there were Major Gregory Way, Captains George Todd and Andrew Patisson, Lieutenants Walter Birmingham, St. John Wells Lucas, Robert Stannus, Thomas Langton, Ambrose Newbold, and 25 other ranks. There were also two men of the 2/95th and 14 of the 5/60th, some of whom may have been taken on the 15th at Óbidos.[104] The prisoners were held on the *Vasco de Gama* in the Tagus.

Captain George Jarvis, deputy assistant adjutant general in charge of French prisoners, did not mention the number of prisoners taken at Roliça in his letter to his wife after the battle, but wrote, 'This will probably increase my charge as I make no doubt but many more will come over to us in consequence of the usage we gave them at their strong post.' Like most parents away from their children, many of his thoughts were of them, and he ends his letter with 'Kiss my darling children. Tell George papa is very well and Charles and Mary and that there is plenty of fruit here, he wishes he could send them some.' He then added in capital letters, presumably so his eldest son could read it. 'MY DEAR BOY I AM VERY WELL.'[105]

For the wives with the expedition, the period after a battle was naturally one of deep anxiety if they could not quickly find their husbands in the ranks. Harris of the 95th had witnessed one of his comrades fall and after the action:

---

101 TNA: WO 55/977: Landmann to Morse, 18 August 1808.
102 TNA: WO 55/1193: Robe to Macleod, 18 August 1808.
103 *General Evening Post*, 15 September 1808.
104 TNA: ADM 1/340: List of Officers etc. Stated to have actually arrived at Lisbon as Prisoners on the 19th Instant.
105 Lincolnshire Archives (LA): JARVIS/5/A/2/6: G.R.P. Jarvis to Philadelphia Jarvis, 19 August 1808.

When the roll was called after the battle, the females who missed their husbands came along the front of the line to inquire of the survivors whether they knew anything about them. Amongst other names I heard that of Cochan called in a female voice, without being replied to.

The name struck me, and I observed the poor woman who had called it, as she stood sobbing before us, and apparently afraid to make further inquiries about her husband. No man had answered to his name, or had any account to give of his fate. I myself had observed him fall, as related before, whilst drinking from his canteen; but as I looked at the poor sobbing creature before me, I felt unable to tell her of his death. At length Captain Leech observed her, and called out to the company, 'Does any man here know what has happened to Cochan? If so, let him speak out at once. 'Upon this order I immediately related what I had seen, and told the manner of his death. After awhile Mrs. Cochan appeared anxious to seek the spot where her husband fell, and in the hope of still finding him alive, asked me to accompany her over the field. She trusted, notwithstanding what I had told her, to find him yet alive. 'Do you think you could find it?' said Captain Leech, upon being referred to. I told him I was sure I could, as I had remarked many objects whilst looking for cover during the skirmishing. 'Go then,' said the captain, 'and shew the poor woman the spot, as she seems so desirous of finding the body.' I accordingly took my way over the ground we had fought upon, she following and sobbing after me, and, quickly reaching the spot where her husband's body lay, pointed it out to her. She now soon discovered all her hopes were in vain; she embraced a stiffened corpse, and after rising and contemplating his disfigured face for some minutes, with hands clasped, and tears streaming down her cheeks she took a prayer-book from her pocket, and kneeling down, repeated the service for the dead over the body. When she had finished she appeared a good deal comforted, and I took the opportunity of beckoning to a pioneer I saw near with some other men, and together we dug a hole, and quickly buried the body. Mrs. Cochan then returned with me to the company to which her husband had been attached, and laid herself down upon the heath near us. She lay amongst some other females, who were in the same distressing circumstances with herself, with the sky for her canopy, and a turf for her pillow...[106]

Harris later offered to marry the widow, but she declined, having had enough of the life of a soldier's wife, and returned to England.

I Never Saw Such Desperate Fighting

For many of Wellesley's men, Roliça was their first experience of battle. Private Joseph Cooley (38th Foot), 19 years old and from Hartshill in Warwickshire, captured the emotions of the day very well:

As soon as the enemy appeared in sight I began with myself in this may hem I prepared to dye for this day many will be huried out of time into Eternity and I perhaps may be one of them. My sins stood in aray before me and put me in far greater dread than the French that stood armed with their Weapons of War. I then began to pray that the Lord would

---

106 Curling (ed.), *Recollections*, pp.43–45.

spare me and if he did I thought I would strive to be different for the future. The scene of slaughter that day wass dreadfully terefick one might think enough to soften the most obdurate heart but alas such is the depravity of the human heart that it is not the scenes of human whoes that we behold, tho in their Nature are so dreadful and affecting, that is sufficient to change the heart for when we had caused our enemy to retreat and the action had subsided I considered myself safe and went on in my mad career of sin.[107]

The 38th was not heavily engaged during the battle. Young John Macfarlane (71st Foot) recalled that after the battle, 'A few of us sat down to talk of what we had seen that day for our conversation was more serious than it had been before. The French soldier that we saw shot through the head was above all, but we were soon to see more than what we had seen.'[108]

Wellesley praised the performance of his troops in his dispatch:

> I cannot sufficiently applaud the conduct of the troops throughout this action. The enemy's positions were formidable, and he took them up with his usual ability and celerity, and defended them most gallantly. But I must observe, that although we had such a superiority of numbers employed in the operations of this day, the troops actually engaged in the heat of the action were, from unavoidable circumstances, only the 5th, 9th, 29th, the riflemen of the 95th and 60th, and the flank companies of Major General Hill's brigade; being a number by no means equal to that of the enemy. Their conduct therefore deserves the highest commendation.[109]

In a private letter to Castlereagh, he also said:

> I never saw such desperate fighting as in the attack of the pass by Lake, and in the three attacks by the French on our troops in the mountains. These attacks were made in their best style, and our troops defended themselves capitally; and if the difficulties of the ground had not prevented me from bringing up a sufficient number of the troops and of cannon we should have taken the whole army.[110]

Lieutenant Colonel Robe, the senior officer of the Royal Artillery, though more than satisfied with the performance of his men and his guns, still could not write to his headquarters in Woolwich without some criticism:

> I do not know how this will go, and we are again on the march after the enemy. I shall – therefore defer saying, what I have to say, about our equipment, and only desire, that the spherical case, some time ago demanded may be sent forthwith. I never will leave England again provided in the manner I have been nor with less than half my whole stock in that ammunition.[111]

---

107 NAM: 1979-12-21-1: Memoirs of an unidentified soldier of 38th. Some punctuation has been added.
108 Robson, 'Peninsular Private', p.6.
109 TNA: WO 1/228: Wellesley to Castlereagh, 17 August 1808.
110 Gurwood (ed.), *Wellington's Dispatches*, vol.IV, p.103.
111 TNA: WO 55/1193: Robe to Macleod, 18 August 1808.

Spherical case shot 'consisted originally of a thin iron shell, filled with musket or carbine balls, sufficient powder being inserted with the balls to cause the bursting of the shell when ignited by the fuze.' If the fuse was adjusted correctly then the shell would burst in the air above the target and spray the area with musket balls and fragments of the shell casing. It did not replace canister shot but enabled both cannon and howitzers to fire with similar effect at longer range. It was invented in 1785 by Henry Shrapnel, an officer in the Royal Artillery, and first used in combat at Surinam in 1804 and then at Maida, the Cape, Monte Video, and Copenhagen – the Portugal campaign was not its first use, as is sometimes stated. It later became known by its inventor's name.[112] The ammunition had been particularly effective in enabling Robe's cannon to fire up onto the heights and inflict heavy casualties on the French.

In his dispatch Delaborde singled out his aides de camp – *chef de bataillon* Georges Beuret and *capitaine* Bardinet – *général de brigade* Brenier, *adjudant commandant* Arnauld, and *major* Weiss of the 26e Chasseurs. Also praised was *capitaine* Viard, another aide, 'whom I had charged with directing the flankers on my right … He killed two Englishmen with his own hand and sabred a third.' Delaborde also mentioned *chirurgien-major* Pommier, who treated the wounded under fire and found several bullets in his clothes that evening.[113] In his history of the campaign, Thiébault wrote, 'As for General de Laborde, I must add that what contributed infinitely to the animation of the troops was that, wounded by a shot in the neck at the beginning of the affair, he left neither the battlefield nor his command, and continued to give the example of the greatest devotion.'[114]

Captain Fletcher Wilkie (38th Foot) was also complimentary of the French troops:

> It was said that Laborde's Division was chiefly composed of conscripts; if so, they deserved much credit for quickly learning their business. I saw them retreat across the plain, after they abandoned the village, and their movements were made with as much precision as on a parade, retiring by files from the right of companies, wheeling up occasionally round their pivot, giving their volley to the light troops in pursuit, and then resuming their former order of march.[115]

Performing an orderly retreat under fire is a tricky manoeuvre for any body of troops and requires a high level of training and discipline. Wilkie's comments and others may reflect the fact that the 70e Ligne, which did most of the fighting, was the most experienced regiment in Junot's army (see Chapter 6), and the grenadiers and voltigeurs of the 4e Suisse would have been the best troops in their regiment. However, the 2e and 4e Légère did contain substantial numbers of recent recruits and the 26e Chasseurs were mostly Italians of questionable loyalty, but both seem to have performed well at Roliça. The French had had many months in Portugal to begin to hone their raw recruits into well-trained soldiers.

---

112 Oskar Teichman, 'Shrapnel Shell', *Journal of the Society for Army Historical Research*, vol.26, no.105 (Spring 1948), p.36.
113 Griffon de Pleineville, *Invasion*, p.193.
114 Thiébault, *l'Expédition*, pp.182–183.
115 Wilkie, 'Recollections from the Peninsula', p.425.

Abrantes

While the Portuguese troops at Roliça, like many of the British regiments, may have only had a limited role in the battle, they elsewhere took advantage of the French forces gathering near Torres Vedras and leaving behind isolated garrisons.

Once Friere learned that Loison had left Tomar, he ordered *Brigadeiro* Manuel Pinto Bacelar to capture Abrantes with the help of some Spanish troops arriving at Castelo Branco. *Capitão* Manoel de Castro Correa de Lacerda was sent forward to reconnoitre and found the garrison vulnerable. Together with three soldier-priests that Southey describes as 'Captain-Father P. Manoel Domingos Crespo, Lieutenant-Father Lourenco Pires, and Ensign-Father Jose Nicolao Beja', he decided to take the town without waiting for the Spanish. They collected 300 men, armed with hunting spears, a few muskets, and other makeshift weapons, at Vila de Rei, 20 miles north of Abrantes, and then marched south, gathering some ordenanças on the way. On the morning of 17 August, they advanced on the town, leaving 'Ensign-Father Beja' with a party to ambush the French should they retreat. When they saw the Portuguese force approaching, the small French garrison fell back to the castle and fired from the windows. Father Crespo positioned sharpshooters on the roof of a nearby church to fire on the castle. The French, with limited supplies, realised their situation was untenable and decided to break out and head for four boats on the river, laden with stores for Lisbon. As they fought through the streets towards the riverbank, they lost so many men to the Portuguese surrounding them that they eventually surrendered. Many French on the boats jumped overboard and tried swimming for the opposite shore. The Portuguese killed 52 of the French garrison and captured 117 more. Those who had managed to escape were hunted down.[116]

Three Mistakes

Speaking decades later, Wellesley said of the battle: 'Roliça was one of our most important affairs; it was terrible hard work to drive off the French. When we had got possession of the heights, they attacked us, and I had only three battalions to stand firm against them. Our men fought monstrous well … the French were commanded by Laborde, a very good officer.'[117] Historian John Fortescue claimed that Wellesley thought Roliça an important action,

> …possibly because it was one with which he was himself little satisfied. Its chief historic interest lies in the curious fact that he, who showed such surpassing skill in hiding his troops in a defensive position, should in his first action against the French have had to deal with an enemy concealed with a dexterity that he himself might have envied.[118]

Sir John Moore, who seldom had a good word to say about anybody and who was not present, was not complimentary about the British performance at Roliça and wrote in his diary in October that Roliça was,

---

116 Southey, *History*, vol.II, pp.191–192.
117 Henry, *Conversations*, p.40.
118 Fortescue, *British Army*, vol.VI, p.214.

…the repulse of a small corps, from two to three thousand men, sent to occupy a strong pass with a view to impede our march. The attack on this post was certainly misman-aged; for though by dint of great superiority of numbers we gained the pass, yet we lost a great number of men, above 500, with some valuable officers. The French said truly on this occasion that our soldiers were brave, but that our Generals showed little conduct or experience.[119]

Wellesley himself was also critical of how the battle unfolded. In a letter to his brother William, he wrote:

You will see the account of our Action on the 17th of which you will form your own judge-ment. Three mistakes prevented it from producing the entire destruction of La Borde's Corps. The first that General Ferguson was ordered to descend the heights instead of continuing his march to turn the Enemy's left in the Mountains. This was not committed by me. The second was that Lake went up the wrong pass; he ought to have gone up that on his right; he hurried his Men, did not clear the pass of the Enemy by his Light Infantry before he entered with his column; & he hurried his attack before the 5th regt. or any of the other troops ascended the other passes to support him.

This I did all I could to prevent; & if I had succeeded we should still have taken or destroyed the whole of La Borde's Corps. The third was a misfortune rather than a fault. We could not find the road by which to bring up our Artillery & a body of regularly formed Infantry. If we had had them early La Borde could not have retreated & in fact he ceased his attacks as soon as he saw our Guns & fresh Infantry advance. But it was then too late to do any thing; the day was worn out; & he had got a start of three miles which I should never have recovered. As it is the French have lost 1500 Men; & I understand that they say they never were so attacked before; & I never saw troops behave so well as they did.

We shall have another brush with them in a day or two; & if we should be successful we shall get hold of Lisbon.[120]

Most British accounts overestimate the French casualties at around 1,500. As a postscript Wellesley wrote: 'I beg that you will not communicate to any body the remarks which I have made upon the action of the 17th. because as all did their duty I do not wish to hint that there was blame any where.' But if mistakes were made, somebody made them. The allies had won the field, but Delaborde's plan had been executed as he had intended. The French had delayed the enemy's march towards Lisbon and inflicted heavy casualties on the British. Wellesley's plan had not unfolded as he had wished, and the British had suffered needless losses.

It is impossible to say who is to blame for Ferguson abandoning his march on Bombarral, only that it involved some error with an order. If Lieutenant Colonel Browne was the messenger, as Landmann claims, then it could have been his interpretation of what he had been told that was at fault if the order was verbal. If it was written, and if Wellesley did not write it, then it was the fault of whoever did. Wellesley is clear that he did not consider himself at fault.

---

119 Maurice (ed.), *Diary*, vol.II, p.267.
120 Webster, 'Some Letters', pp.4–5.

Lieutenant Colonel Torrens thought that the action had been 'a gallant affair' but then wrote: 'Nothing is to be regretted but the imputation of poor Lake who led his corps up a strong defile, different from the one on which he was directed to march without clearing his flanks before he led his column up it. He was a most gallant fellow.'[121]

Of the three mistakes, Lake's error is the easiest to attribute to an individual, but in the immediate aftermath of the battle, few were willing to speak ill of the dead. Wellesley's claim that the 29th should have advanced up the defile to the right places them in the river gorge where Hill's light companies and the 5th Foot advanced. However, in his dispatch, he made it clear that the assault of the 29th and 9th was meant to be separate. It would make a little more sense if the intended defile were to the left, not the right of where they advanced, as there is a broader pass. Lake should clearly take some blame for his peremptory attack up the wrong gully before the French had been forced to consider retreating by the attacks on the flanks, and for instead charging up without due care for his men's lives. As discussed in Chapter 8, he had taken part in many battles but not as a commanding officer; perhaps this inexperience contributed to the errors.

The third mistake, not finding a good road up to the heights, is more challenging to substantiate in any of the accounts of the battle. On the map drawn soon after the action, there is a road marked on the left of the French position, as viewed from below, where the Light Brigade advanced, but not one on the right where there is one today.[122] On the map, the road went from Columbeira along the base of the heights and then around their left through a defile, which is quite evident today. Still, the area was more heavily wooded than it is currently, and the problem may have been the quality of the road for a large body of troops and artillery rather than finding it.

With the battle not having gone as he would have wished and the heavy butcher's bill, Wellesley was clearly in a melancholic mood as his letter to his brother also includes this passage:

> I don't know what Govt. propose to do with me. I shall be the Junior of all the Lt. Generals; & of all the awkward situations in the world that which is most so is, to serve in a subordinate capacity in an Army which one has commanded. However I will do whatever they please. I think they had better order me home.[123]

Wellesley's army spent the night of the 17th in the front of and on the right of Azambujeira, while Wellesley established his headquarters in nearby Casas de Serrano. At dusk, a small French patrol appeared on the allies' left, and Wellesley heard that the first elements of Loison's force were arriving in Bombarral.[124]

On 18 August, Wellesley made some adjustments to his brigading of the army:

> The following new distribution of brigades to take place on leaving this ground: The 6th, or light brigade, to consist of the 50th Regiment, four companies of the 95th, and five

---

121 BL: Add MS 49485: Torrens to Gordon, 19 August 1808.
122 TNA: WO 78/5947: Plan of the Action of Obidos on the 17th August 1808. The map was drawn by Captain William Willerman of the Royal Staff Corps. It is not dated, but Willerman was present in Portugal in August 1808, and the fact that the title of the map mentions Óbidos rather than Roliça suggests it was created before the battle received the name it became known by.
123 Webster, 'Some Letters', p.5.
124 TNA: WO 1/415: Wellesley's narrative.

The entrance to the defile on the left of the one that Lake led the 29th Foot up. No track is marked on contemporary maps, but it is a gentler incline and broader. (Author's photo)

companies of the 60th. One company of the 60th to be attached to each of the following brigades: the 1st, 2nd, 3rd, 4th, and 5th; and to join them as soon as possible.[125]

The 5/60th was to be split into detached companies for almost all of the rest of the peninsular campaign. With the order coming just after Roliça, where both the light companies of the line regiments and the riflemen of Fane's brigade had been extensively engaged in driving in the French pickets and countering the French skirmishers, the order must have been an effort to both strengthen the light companies in terms of numbers and to distribute specialist rifle-armed troops more broadly across the brigades to counter the voltigeurs.

Wellesley had intended to follow the French south on the 18th, but after receiving news of reinforcements arriving off the coast, he instead marched to Lourinhã, 10 miles west of Azambujeira, from where he informed Castlereagh:

---

125   Wellington (ed.), *Supplementary Despatches*, vol.XIII, p.294.

Since I wrote to you last night I have heard from Brig. General Anstruther that he is on the coast, off Peniche, with the fleet of victuallers and store ships, in charge of Captain Bligh, of the Alfred, with a part of the force detached from England under Brig. General Acland, in consequence of the receipt of orders which I had left at Mondego Bay for General Acland, which he had opened.

I have ordered Brig. General Anstruther to land immediately, and I have moved to this place in order to protect his landing and facilitate his junction.

General Loison joined General Laborde in the course of last night at Torres Vedras, and I understand that both begin their march towards Lisbon this morning; I also hear that General Junot has arrived this day at Torres Vedras, with a small corps from Lisbon; and I conclude that the whole of the French army will be assembled between Torres Vedras and the capital in the course of a few days.[126]

In his private letter to Castlereagh, he wrote prophetically: 'As soon as Anstruther shall be landed I shall give you a good account of the remainder of the French army; but I am afraid I shall not gain a complete victory; that is, I shall not entirely destroy them for want of cavalry.'[127]

---

126 TNA: WO 1/228: Wellesley to Castlereagh, 17 August 1808.
127 Gurwood (ed.), *Wellington's Dispatches*, vol.IV, p.103.

13

Reinforcements

Table 20 shows the numbers of men and horses on their way from Britain and the make-up of the convoys. The reinforcements would double the number of British troops in Portugal and, at last, provide a good number of cavalry; the 3rd KGL Light Dragoons were coming with Moore and the 18th Light Dragoons with Brigadier General Charles Stewart. Also on their way were 943 rank and file of the 42nd Foot from Gibraltar and 925 rank and file of the 3rd Foot from Madeira. Detachments of the Royal Artillery accompanied both. Artillery had been allocated to Anstruther and Acland's brigades. They embarked at Portsmouth, amounting to 379 gunners and drivers plus 300 horses, but contrary winds delayed them, and they sailed with Moore's corps instead.[1]

In addition, drafts from the second battalions of the 36th and 45th Foot had also embarked.[2] Their first battalions had been allocated to Wellesley's expedition at the last minute and were seriously understrength. A captain, four lieutenants, four sergeants, and 203 rank and file of the 45th had left Nottingham on 11 July and had arrived at Hilsea near Portsmouth on the 26th. They landed at Figueira and then marched south, arriving on the morning of 21 August when they were quickly distributed between the 10 companies.[3] The drafts seem to have been gathered in a hurry as Lieutenant General Sir Hew Dalrymple was to write later, 'A considerable inconvenience has been felt from the circumstance of sending out recruits to the 45th Regiment neither armed or accoutred, which renders the regiment nearly unfit for service.'[4] A transport carrying men of the 36th Foot had to turn back due to being damaged in high winds, but all the drafts had reached the battalion by September.

Wellesley had recommended to Burrard that Moore's troops land at Figueira da Foz and march to Santarém to stop French reinforcements from Spain and prevent Junot from retreating there.[5] His initial intentions for Acland's and Antruther's troops had been to invest the fortress at Peniche, but this had changed, and he now intended them to join his main force.

1   TNA: WO 17/2464: Return of Troops embarked for Spain and Portugal in 1808; WO 72/29: Return of officers, NCOs and men embarked for Portugal. Transport Office 16 November 1808; Aspinall (ed.), *Later Correspondence*, p.182.
2   TNA: WO 17/2464: Troops embarked from Cork.
3   Brown, *Redjackets*, p.50.
4   BL: Add. MS 49484: Dalrymple to Gordon, 10 September 1808.
5   Gurwood (ed.), *Wellington's Dispatches*, vol.IV, pp.70, 78.

Table 20. Reinforcements on their way to Portugal, August 1808

	Infantry	Cavalry		Artillery		Staff		Total		Troop Ships		Cavalry Ships		Army Victuallers		Forage Ships		Camp Stores		Ordnance Stores		Total	
		Men	Horses	Men	Horses	Men	Horses	Men	Horses	No.	Tons	No.	Tons	No.	Tons	No.	Tons	No.	Tons	No.	Tons	No.	Tons
Acland/Anstruther	4,771					46	40	4871	40	28	5,784											33	6,728
Moore	11,774	646	642	1,557	678	241	199	14,218	1,519	90	19,616	57	13,243	18	4,711	2	285	4	876	10	2,122	181	40,853
18th Light Dragoons		775	773					775	773			29	6,411			3	642					32	7,053
Totals	16,545	1,421	1,415	1,557	678	287	239	19,864	2,332	118	25,400	88	20,164	21	5,145	5	927	4	876	10	2,122	246	54,634

Source: TNA: WO 72/29: Return of officers, NCOs and men embarked for Portugal. Transport Office 16 November 1808.

Table 21. Acland's and Anstruther's Brigades

Regiment	R&F	Embarked
Anstruther		
2/9th Foot	647	19 July
2/43rd Foot	749	18 July
2/52nd Foot	680	16 July
97th	699	19 July
Total	**2,775**	
Acland		
2nd	771	18 July
20th	579	18 July
1/95th (2 coys)	198	19 July
Total	**1,548**	

Source: TNA: WO 17/2464: Return of forces embarked, under the command of Sir A. Wellesley.

The brigades of Brigadier Generals Robert Anstruther and Wroth Palmer Acland had embarked at Ramsgate and Harwich in mid-July. Oman claims that these two brigades had been allocated and gathered for a raid on the French port of Boulogne.[6] However, Castlereagh's correspondence would suggest such an operation was still at a very early stage of planning and had not yet reached the point of allocating units.[7] The number of troops committed to Portugal was stretching the available manpower. Castlereagh wrote to the Duke of York on 24 July, after Acland and Anstruther had sailed, requesting that a further 5,000 men be assembled at Cork under Sir David Baird but also that 12–15,000 be readied in England for the raid on Boulogne which, with troops withdrawn from the French coast for service in the Peninsula, was now vulnerable and still held a potential invasion flotilla. York replied that he could move the 2/23rd, 2/31st and 2/81st to Cork but that assembling the troops for the raid was more problematic. He wrote that the 2/4th, 2/7th, 1/43rd, 2/59th, 2/87th, 1/88th and 11 companies of the 95th were the only battalions with over 500 men available but that the 43rd, 87th and 88th, the strongest units, were all affected by outbreaks of ophthalmia. If the Guards in London were reduced to a single battalion, he could possibly gather 10,000 men, but a single battalion of Guards was not sufficient for all the duties required in the capital. He also passed on to Castlereagh a letter from the Earl of Harrington, Commander-in-Chief in Ireland, dated 18 July, outlining his concerns at the denuding of forces in Ireland and 'the danger of leaving its internal, no less than external, defence in the hands of the militia of the country.'[8]

Acland's Brigade

Brigadier General Wroth Palmer Acland was born in 1770 and joined the 17th Foot in 1787 as an ensign. The 1790s saw him serving as a marine in the channel fleet, spending two years on half-pay, serving in the West Indies, in Flanders, back to the West Indies, and then in India and Ceylon. During that time, he moved from the 17th to the 3rd and then to the 19th Foot, rising to lieutenant colonel through a mix of purchases, exchanges and promotions. He returned to England in 1799 due to ill health and was plagued by the same unspecified complaint for the next 10 years. In 1800, he exchanged into the Coldstream Guards as a captain and lieutenant colonel. In 1805, he was appointed a brigadier general and commanded a brigade at Maida with distinction. He was assigned the command of a brigade in South America but arrived after the British had been defeated. He had been appointed to command a brigade in England in February 1808.[9]

2nd (The Queen's Royal) Regiment of Foot
The 2nd Foot was a single-battalion regiment. It had served at Den Helder in 1799, had been engaged in raids on the French coast in 1800, was with Abercromby in Egypt in 1801, had been part of the Gibraltar garrison from 1802–1805, and then had returned to Britain.[10] The 2nd had been inspected on Guernsey in May 1808 and did not impress the inspecting officer. The regiment only had a strength of 243 at the time of the previous inspection in January 1807 but had managed

---

6   Oman, *History*, vol.I, p.224.
7   Vane (ed.), *Correspondence*, vol.VI, p.384.
8   Vane (ed.), *Correspondence*, vol.VIII, pp.177–179.
9   Burnham & McGuigan, *Brigade Commanders*, pp.1–2.
10   Anon., *Historical Records of the Second Regiment of Foot* (London: Adjutant General's Office, undated), pp.54–55.

Officer of the 2nd Foot, 1807, by Reginald Augustus Wymer. (Anne S.K. Brown Military Collection)

to recruit up to a strength of 767. However, this meant that 232 men had only one full year of service behind them and 279 less than a year. Eight sergeants and 15 corporals also fell into those two brackets, so the regiment probably struggled to find good men of long service to promote. Of the new intake, 330 had come from the Army Depot on the Isle of Wight and 150 from the Militia. The confidential report noted the short height of the recruits, and while still young, they did 'not appear likely to grow.' Punishments were 'Rather frequent but not severe', the interior arrangements were 'tolerable', and the conduct of officers and NCOs 'very attentive, but there seems much of the old system remaining in this regiment.'[11]

Lieutenant Colonel William Iremonger commanded the regiment. Born in 1776, Iremonger was first commissioned in the 18th Foot in 1792 and served at the Siege of Toulon. He rose to lieutenant in 1794 and then became a captain in the 44th Foot in 1796. He fought with the 44th in Egypt in 1801, moved to the 88th Foot in 1804 as a major, served in South America in 1807, and then took command of the 2nd Foot as a lieutenant colonel in March 1808.

Private William Billows recorded the regiment's march from Ipswich to Harwich to embark in his journal:

> We marched off about one o'clock under a scorching sun, and the road in some places is confined and sandy. We marched at a rapid rate and Colonel Ironmonger would not allow us to break our sections to get some more air, so that a vast number of men fainted with a giddiness in the head. As we passed through two villages the inhabitants brought water to their doors for us to drink and sent doctors to some of the men near the town that were dying, and some of the women crying like children to see the state we marched in. The men reeled round and round and then fell. I did so myself, but some motherly women got round me and did the best they could for me. By that means I proceeded and embarked with the regiments. But two men died on the roadside, and were buried at Languard Fort.[12]

Captain Charles Steevens of the 20th Foot later wrote, 'There were at that time a great many young men in the 'Queen's' who were not able to go through as much fatigue as the old soldiers of the XX [20th] could bear, which accounted for the casualties.'[13]

20th (East Devonshire) Regiment of Foot

The 20th Foot was also a single-battalion regiment and had been in the Mediterranean for eight years, arriving in Britain at the beginning of 1808. The regiment had seen action in the later stages of the 1801 Egyptian campaign and had distinguished itself at the Battle of Maida in 1806. While in Sicily, the regiment had recruited a company from the local inhabitants. When the regiment returned to Britain, most local recruits were transferred to join the Sicilian Regiment on Malta but some opted to stay with the 20th.[14]

The regiment was inspected at the camp at Brabourne Lees in May 1808. Major General Coote Manningham reported that they were in the 'highest order' but also said that despite not

---

11   TNA: WO 27/92: Inspection 2nd Foot, May 1808.
12   W. Billows, *Nothing Pertickler Happened* (Unknown: Privately published, 2011), p.25. Published as a verbatim transcript of a hand-written journal in the possession of the family. The spelling and punctuation have been corrected to improve comprehension.
13   N. Steevens (ed.), *Reminiscences of My Military Life* (Winchester: Warren, 1878), p.51.
14   B. Smyth, *A History of the Lancashire Fusiliers* (Dublin: Sackville Press, 1903), p.221.

having commanded them for long, he was 'convinced – that as from their length of service in the Mediterranean, and their age, & worn out condition of a number of their men, they could scarcely produce for field service more than from 500 to 600 men.' Manningham thought that if the Commander-in-Chief would let them get 300–400 men from the militia, then 'they would speedily become one of the finest corps in the British Service – but from not possessing the advantage of a second battalion, they have no means beyond the common mode of recruiting in which they have hitherto been very unsuccessful of getting men.' Of the 628 privates, 589 were English and 564 had eight or more years' service. The one sergeant and 11 privates who were foreigners were probably the Sicilians.[15]

The 20th was commanded by Lieutenant Colonel Robert Ross, an Irishman born in 1766. He attended Trinity College in Dublin, purchased an ensigncy in the 25th Foot in 1789, and sailed to join them at Gibraltar. He became friends with Prince Edward Augustus, the fourth son of the King, and when the Prince requested a transfer to Quebec Ross went with him. The Prince secured Ross first a lieutenancy and then a captaincy in the 7th Foot, of which he was colonel. Ross's father died in 1795, and he returned to Britain and used his inheritance to purchase a majority in the 90th Foot, and then moved to the 20th in 1799 after a brief period on half pay and then as a brigade major. He fought with the 20th at Den Helder and was seriously wounded at the Battle of Krabbendam. The regiment then went to the Mediterranean, and he was made a brevet lieutenant colonel. He was with the 20th in Egypt and, in 1803, assumed command of the regiment on Malta. During the regiment's stay on the island, Ross would take the regiment out for long field days. Captain Charles Steevens wrote, 'we were repeatedly out for eight hours during the hot weather; frequently crossing the country, scouring the fields over the stone walls, the whole of the regiment acting as light infantry … *no other corps in the island was similarly indulged*.'[16] Ross led the 20th at Maida and was mentioned in Major General John Stuart's dispatch, who gave Ross and another officer much of the credit for the victory. He was promoted to full lieutenant colonel in January 1808.[17]

1st Battalion 95th Regiment of Foot
Captains Alexander Cameron and Smith Ramadge commanded the two companies of the 1/95th under Lieutenant Colonel Thomas Sidney Beckwith.[18] Beckwith, born in 1772, had joined the 65th Foot as an ensign in 1790 and then moved to the 71st as a lieutenant the next year and joined his regiment in India. He served at the siege of Seringapatam in 1792, the capture of Pondicherry in 1793, and on Ceylon in 1795. He was promoted captain-lieutenant in 1797 and returned to England with the headquarters of his regiment in 1798. He volunteered for the new rifle corps in 1800 and became a captain, leading his company at Copenhagen in 1801. The corps soon became the 95th Rifles, and he rose to major in 1802 and lieutenant colonel in 1803. He then led his battalion in the expeditions to Hannover and Copenhagen (1807).

---

15   TNA: WO 27/92: Inspection 20th Foot, May 1808.
16   Steevens (ed.), *Reminiscences*, p.39.
17   Burnham & McGuigan, *Brigade Commanders*, pp.251–253.
18   Caldwell & Cooper, *Rifle Green*, p.17.

Anstruther's Brigade

Brigadier General Robert Anstruther, a Scot, was born in 1768, the son of an MP and grandson of an earl. His family purchased him an ensigncy in the 3rd Foot Guards in 1785 and then purchased the step up to lieutenant and captain in 1792. He was granted a brevet majority in 1797 and then moved to the 66th Foot with that rank without purchase the same year. He then quickly purchased a lieutenant colonelcy in the 68th. In 1799, he exchanged back to the 3rd Foot Guards and, in 1805, was promoted to colonel and appointed one of the King's aides de camp. Much of his career had been as a staff officer. After serving with the Guards in Flanders in 1793–1795, he was appointed an observer to the Austrian army headquarters in 1796. At Den Helder in 1799, he was a deputy quartermaster general and received praise for his staff work. He was then Abercromby's quartermaster general in Egypt, where he again performed very well. On his return to Britain, he was appointed deputy quartermaster general to the army but was quickly moved to Ireland, where he became adjutant general. He was appointed a brigadier general on the Irish staff early in 1808.[19]

When Wellesley heard that Anstruther was asking to be employed on the expedition, he wrote, 'Nothing could give me so much satisfaction as to have Anstruther', and that he would be happy to have him either as the adjutant or quartermaster general.[20] However, Anstruther did not want a role on the staff; he wanted to command a brigade. He met with the Duke of York on 14 July at Horse Guards and was told he would have his wish and that his brigade would consist of the 2/43rd and 2/52nd Light Infantry plus two companies of the 95th Rifles (the units he would command were subsequently changed). He was also told of Acland's brigade being readied in Harwich but that he must sail for Portugal as soon as his brigade was ready and embarked. Anstruther received his final orders on the 17th, and on the 18th, he met with Charles Stewart and Edward Cooke, military undersecretary and undersecretary at the War Office. He was again pressed to take the role of quartermaster general, but he told them that George Murray would do the job better than he. He also met with Canning, saw Lord Chatham, and then dined with Castlereagh.[21]

2nd Battalion, 9th (East Norfolk) Regiment of Foot
A second battalion of the 9th Foot had been authorised in 1804 and was initially based in Sherbourne in Dorset, where it began recruiting. In 1806, it moved to Tamworth and then Burton-upon-Trent and had recruiting parties in Norfolk and Lancashire. In 1807, the battalion moved to Chelmsford, receiving 474 volunteers from the Leicestershire, West Kent, Somerset, and East and West Norfolk Militias. In September, it marched to Shorncliffe barracks, where it were inspected in May 1808 by Major General Manningham. The report noted, 'This is a fine corps – the men lately received from the Militia are universally good – tho' in their rear rank they have a certain number of boys, and low men.' The report then continued:

> Lt Col Cameron, an excellent officer, who commands them has taken uncommon pains with the Regiment, and in a few months they will no doubt be in great order, but they have much to learn – as with the exception of their field officers, and captains, they have little aid, the subalterns, & sergeants of the 2nd Battn. of the 9th being extremely young.

19 Burnham & McGuigan, *Brigade Commanders*, pp.23–24.
20 BL: Add. MS 49481: Wellesley to Gordon, 5 July 1808.
21 StAUL: msdep121/8/2/3/4/4: Anstruther's journal, pp.4–5.

Half of the sergeants and three-quarters of the corporals had less than a year's service, as did 550 of the 740 privates, but they may have been NCOs in the Militia. The vast majority of the men were English. The report also said that the battalion had 'been directed to attend particularly to their target practice' and were 'in as great a state of progressive improvement as could be expected, considering the short time they had been together.'[22] However, there seemed to be room for improvement even after arriving in Portugal. On 10 September, Dalrymple wrote that the 2/9th were 'in bad order and does not improve,' blaming poor officers.[23]

The 2/9th's commanding officer, John Cameron, was an Eton-educated Scot born in 1773. He had been commissioned as an ensign in the 43rd Foot in 1787. In 1790, he rose to lieutenant and in 1793, he accompanied his regiment on Sir Charles Grey's West Indies expedition, which captured Martinique. Cameron distinguished himself at the storming of Fort Fleur d'Épée and was promoted to captain. The 43rd was so stricken by disease that he was in command during the attempt on Guadeloupe. He was severely wounded and captured and then spent two years as a prisoner of war. He was exchanged in 1797 and returned to the 43rd in the West Indies. He was appointed major in 1800 and brought the skeleton of the regiment back to Britain. In 1807, he was promoted to lieutenant colonel in the 7th West India Regiment but quickly exchanged into the 9th Foot later the same year.

2nd Battalion, 43rd (Monmouthshire) Regiment of Foot

The 43rd Foot was one of the first regiments to be converted to light infantry under Sir John Moore in 1803. The second battalion was raised at Bromsgrove in 1804, and its numbers rose slowly towards its establishment strength over the next two years. Manningham also inspected the 2/43rd in May 1808 at Hythe in Kent. He reported that:

> This corps is in high order, and has been extremely well recruited owing to the unrelenting and meritorious exertions of their officers and NC Officers so employed. The men are of the species for a Light Infantry Regiment that could be wished, & from their youth, size, & appearance will in time become an exceeding fine body of men – much remains to be done with them, tho' in the course of a few months great progress it is to be hoped will be made.

He also noted, 'the Officers, tho' young, are fine lads and there seems to be an abundance of spirit amongst them', but also that the battalion needed a lieutenant colonel; of the two in the regiment, one was on the staff and one commanding the 1st battalion. Manningham recommended Major Hull, who had 'been more than 20 years in the army' for the vacant lieutenant colonelcy. Of the 803 privates, 408 had less than one year's service, and 260 were Irish. The battalion had received 102 volunteers from militia regiments throughout the British Isles during the six months to the end of June 1808.[24] Ensign John Patterson of the 50th Foot, who would fight alongside the 43rd at Vimeiro, wrote in his memoir, 'the 43rd, in particular, were a most shewy set of fellows, a healthy collection of John Bulls, hot from their own country, and equally hot for a slap at the Frenchmen.'[25]

---

22   TNA: WO 27/92: Inspection 2/9th Foot, May 1808.
23   BL: Add MS 49484: Dalrymple to Calvert, 10 September 1808.
24   TNA: WO 12/5633: 2/43rd Paylist.
25   Patterson, *Adventures*, p.39.

Major Edward Hull, a native of Southampton, commanded the 2/43rd. Hull had first been commissioned as an ensign in the 3rd Foot in 1787 but then spent some time on half-pay before being made a lieutenant in an independent company and then going on half-pay again. In 1792, he joined the 43rd and would stay in the regiment for the rest of his career. He was promoted to captain-lieutenant in 1795, to captain in 1796, and then major in 1804. He served alongside John Cameron in the West Indies and commanded the 1/43rd briefly during the Copenhagen expedition. On 29 August 1808, Anstruther passed on a letter from Major Hull to Sir Hew Dalrymple, 'respecting the inadequacy of the present establishment of subalterns and non-commissioned officers to carrying on the duties of the 2d battalion of that corps in the field', and Anstruther also recommended that Hull be promoted to lieutenant colonel, which he was in September.[26]

2nd Battalion, 52nd (Oxfordshire) Regiment of Foot
The 52nd Foot was also converted to light infantry in 1803 under Moore, the regiment's colonel. The second battalion was raised in 1804 at Newbury. The 2/52nd was inspected in April 1807 at Hythe. The report noted that the men were 'mostly of the same description' as 2/43rd but had not had use of the drill instructors from their 1st battalion, so their drill was not as good. The interior economy of the battalion was 'well conducted' and the 'cleanliness in their barracks and hospital remarkable.' Of the 724 privates, 253 were English and 466 were Irish. Over 500 men had two years' service or less.[27] Despite this mediocre report, the 2/52nd was ordered to be part of the Copenhagen expedition in the Reserve that Wellesley commanded.

Lieutenant Colonel John Ross commanded the 2/52nd. Commissioned as an ensign in the 36th Foot in 1793, he joined the 52nd as a lieutenant three years later and then rose steadily to captain in 1800, major in 1804 and lieutenant colonel in 1808. He saw action with the 52nd in India and at the raid on Ferrol.

97th (Queen's Own) Regiment of Foot
The 97th had only been renamed the Queen's Own from the Queen's Germans in June 1808. The regiment had been created mainly from former Austrian troops captured on the island of Minorca in 1798 – it was at first called the Minorca Regiment. The Austrians had been captured in Italy, sold to Spain by the French, and placed in Swiss regiments in Spanish service. The regiment had fought well in Egypt in 1801, with Private Antoine Lutz helping to capture a French colour. Over the subsequent years, recruiting in Britain and Ireland had slowly reduced the proportion of foreigners in its ranks. In November 1807, the regiment had lost 194 officers and men, 44 women, and 29 children when the *Rochdale* transport was wrecked on rocks near Dublin.[28]

Manningham also inspected the regiment at Brabourne Lees in May 1808. His report stated, 'This is a very fine regiment, and the appearance both of officers, and men [is] greatly in their favor', and that, 'They seem in every respect in high order.' He recommended they get 150–200 Militia men, 'which, owing to their unfortunate loss off the coast of Ireland they much want, having no 2nd battalion to give them aid in this way.' Of the 744 privates, 309 were foreign, 394 Irish and only 41 English. A third of the officers were also foreign. The regiment had 281 recent recruits, but 244

26 Gurwood (ed.), *Wellington's Dispatches*, vol.IV, p.126.
27 TNA: WO 27/91: Inspection 2/52nd Foot, April 1807.
28 'Wreck Prince of Wales and Rochdale 1807', <https://www.liverpool.ac.uk/~cmi/books/miscWr/PoW-Roch.html> accessed April 2023.

men had eight years' service, with only a few more experienced. On average, the men were slightly older and taller than in many other regiments.[29]

Lieutenant Colonel James Frederick Lyon commanded the regiment. Lyon's father, a captain in the 35th Foot, was killed at the Battle of Bunker Hill in 1775 and James was born on the transport carrying his mother back to England. He was commissioned in the 25th Foot as an ensign in 1791 and was a lieutenant two years later. The 25th Foot served as marines in the fleet, and Lyon commanded the detachment on the *Marlborough* at the Glorious First of June in 1794. Promoted to captain in 1795, he served on Grenada during the insurrection there in 1796 and then on the staff in England. He became Sir Charles Stuart's aide de camp and was with him at the capture of Minorca. When the Minorca Regiment was formed, he was given a majority and served with them in Egypt. He had been a lieutenant colonel since 1802.

Contrary Winds, Again

Anstruther set out for Deal and Ramsgate on the 19th and arrived on the 20th. HMS *St Albans* (64) was waiting for him, commanded by Captain Francis Austen, brother of the novelist. The 2/9th, 2/43rd, 2/52nd and 97th were embarked on their transports, and Anstruther ordered the senior medical officer to inspect the vessels and asked the regiments for their embarkation returns and most recent inspection returns. The two extra battalions over and above the ones he had been told he would lead were probably embarked under his command because they were closer to the Kent ports. The same is probably true of the two companies of the 1/95th, which arrived on 21 July.[30] Captain James Ferguson (43rd Foot) also mentions them embarking from Kent rather than Harwich as is usually stated.[31] The two rifle companies seemed to have been attached to Acland's brigade as soon as it landed, probably as it was a weak two-battalion brigade. The 97th Foot was similarly placed under Acland's command on 22 August.

On the 20th, 20 severe cases of ophthalmia amongst the 52nd were landed, and 63 others were put on their own transport. The convoy of 23 transports and the *St Albans* sailed at 4:00 p.m. on the 22nd, but the winds in the Channel fluctuated between strong and contrary to very light. By the 26th, the convoy was off Weymouth. Ophthalmia continued to spread amongst the 52nd, and more cases landed when the convoy reached Cawsand Bay on the 29th. Anstruther contemplated leaving the whole battalion behind. The convoy continued to battle contrary winds until 2 August, when a northwesterly wind finally allowed them to sail out into the channel and across the Bay of Biscay. On the 12th, they met the *Defiance* off Corunna and received news of Wellesley landing at Mondego Bay. Anstruther asked Captain Austen if the convoy could call into Mondego Bay and Austen agreed, even though it went against the wording of his orders. They arrived there on the 16th, and Anstruther met with Captain Malcolm of the *Donegal*, who handed over Wellesley's orders to proceed down the coast to rendezvous with Captain Bligh in the *Alfred*.[32]

---

29 TNA: WO 27/92: Inspection 97th Foot, May 1808.
30 StAUL: msdep121/8/2/3/4/4: Anstruther's journal, p.5.
31 G. Glover (ed.), *The Men of Wellington's Light Division, Unpublished Memoirs of the 43rd (Monmouthshire) Regiment in the Peninsular War* (Barnsley: Frontline, 2022), p.54; Oman, *History*, vol.I, p.248.
32 StAUL: msdep121/8/2/3/4/4: Anstruther's journal, pp.4–18; J.H. Hubback and E.C Hubback, *Jane Austen's Sailor Brothers* (London: Lane, 1906), p.201.

On 17 August, the convoy heard the cannon fire at Roliça, and Anstruther sent his aide de camp, Captain George St Leger Gordon of the 52nd Foot, ashore at São Martinho do Porto to make contact with Wellesley, which he did on the 18th. Meanwhile, the convoy lay at anchor off the Burling Islands. While he waited for news, Anstruther sent Lieutenant Hipolyte Michel of the 97th ashore to gain intelligence. In the early hours of the 19th, Anstruther received instructions from Wellesley to land near Maceira. The convoy sailed past the fortress of Peniche towards Paimogo Bay, five miles further south. A Swiss sentry fired his musket at one transport that sailed too close.[33] Captain Austen recorded in the log of the *St Albans*:

> August 19 – At anchor off the Burlings, Light airs and cloudy weather. At three o'clock a Portuguese boat came alongside with a messenger having despatches for Brigadier-General Anstruther from Sir Arthur Wellesley. At daylight a very thick fog. At eleven the fog cleared away, weighed and made sail to the southward. At three, anchored off Panago [*sic*] in company, hoisted out all the boats and sent them to disembark the troops. At six, the General and his staff quitted the ship. Light airs and fine weather. All the boats of the fleet employed landing the troops.[34]

In a letter to the Admiralty, Austen also reported that: 'One of my convoy, having a detachment of the 2nd battalion of the 52nd Regiment on board, parted company on the night of the 12th instant, and has, I suppose, in compliance with the secret rendezvous I issued on the 23rd of July, proceeded off the Tagus.'[35] It would seem possible then that a portion of the 2/52nd might have landed with Acland's brigade when it was sent from the Tagus to Maceira Bay by Vice Admiral Cotton.
Anstruther also noted the details of the landing in his diary:

> The morning was so foggy that no communication whether by signal or otherwise could be had with the transports until about 9 when it cleared up for a few minutes and the signal was made to weigh and prepare to land. It was 12 O'Clock however before the transports were under way. And the winds being very light it was near 3 before they reached the bay called Pyamago which had been chosen for landing. The place very bad; ships anchored too far out. Landing difficult and a cliff almost perpendicular to be scrambled over afterwards. Horses could not be got up that aught. All the troops assembled by midnight and arranged as well as we could for next day's march. Received notice from Sir Arthur that he had detached Spencer to cover my march which was about 7 miles. Gave orders for the 52nd to occupy the landing place to collect stragglers and bring up the rear.
>
> 20th
> Marched exactly at daylight: troops could not be collected sooner owing to the confused manner of the debarkation and the intoxication of many of the soldiers.[36]

---

33   Neale, *Letters*, p.7.
34   Hubback &Hubback, *Sailor Brothers*, pp.199–200.
35   Hubback & Hubback, *Sailor Brothers*, p.201.
36   StAUL: msdep121/8/2/3/4/4: Anstruther's journal, pp.22–24.

Paimogo Bay, where Anstruther's brigade landed, taken from just beneath the seventeenth-century fort.
(Author's photo)

An explanation for the intoxication of the troops can be found in an account of the later landing of the 2nd Foot. Private William Billows recalled that his regiment had been given a canteen of rum before they landed, with those of the less trustworthy men being sealed, and all were ordered not to drink it, but the temptation may have been too much for many.[37]

Physician Adam Neale was on board the *Westmoreland* transport, which was carrying 40 officer's horses and was brought as close inshore at Paimogo as possible so the horses could swim to the beach:

> Among the first lifted from the hold and committed to the briny deep, was a very beautiful mare, the property of General Anstruther; which, owing to the awkwardness of the grooms and sailors, was some time in the water before it could be disengaged from the slings; and the distance it had to swim being considerable, it sunk before it could make the shore. A repetition of this accident was prevented by the foresight of Captain Bligh, who immediately sent a large launch, in which the remaining horses were conveyed to *terra firma* in safety.[38]

Neale also described the landing place, 'The spot where we landed is a sandy beach, at the foot of an almost perpendicular cliff. On the summit are the ruins of an old quadrangular fort, to which we

---

37   Billows, *Nothing Pertickler Happened*, pp.26–27.
38   Neale, *Letters*, pp.7–8.

were conducted by a narrow winding path, very steep and difficult of ascent.' The troops then spent the night under the stars and could see the fires of Wellesley's camp in the distance.

On 19 August, Wellesley had issued an additional general order to extend his troops in the direction of Anstruther's landing to protect them as they marched to join the army:

> The army will halt to-morrow; excepting the 6th brigade with their guns, and the 2nd brigade with their guns, the British cavalry (excepting 50 to be left in the camp), with 50 of the Portuguese cavalry, which will march to-morrow morning at 3 o'clock, without great coats or haversacks, under the command of Major-General Spencer.
>
> The rifle and light companies of the 1st, 3rd, 4th, and 5th brigades will occupy, at the same hour, the present position of the light brigade, under the orders of Major-General Hill, the General officer of the day.
>
> Brigadier-General Fane will draw out on the road leading to Lourinha precisely at 3 o'clock, left in front, and the 2nd brigade and cavalry will immediately follow him.
>
> The 3rd brigade will immediately send a captain and fifty men to the north of the village of Vimeiro, on the road by which the army entered it this morning, and the cavalry will patrole constantly from it during the night on the road to Lourinha.[39]

Ensign Charles Paget of the 52nd recorded in his diary on the 20th: 'Under arms at two o'clock in the morning. Marched over a very delightful country covered with myrtles, aloes, etc. Saw several cottages which the French had plundered. Weather excessively hot and no water, that in our canteens being excessively warm, which obliged nearly 300 men to quit the ranks.'[40] Lieutenant Colonel John Cameron (2/9th Foot) also recorded the fact that the day was very hot in his diary but remarked that 'not a man of the 9th fell out.'[41]

As Anstruther's brigade passed Lourinhã, Lieutenant Colonel Taylor met them with the British and Portuguese cavalry. French dragoons were visible on the hills on their left.[42] Anstruther recorded:

> After three hours march fell in with the officers of the staff who assured us that the enemy's patrols were hovering about, and that Genl. Spencer with all the cavalry and about 2,000 infantry was posted two miles further on to cover my march. Uneasy about the 52nd sent Gordon back to hurry them on, and a party of cavalry to flank their march. Arrived in camp near Vimeiro about 10. 52nd followed by 1 o'clock. Found the army encamped on high hills behind the village of Vimeiro.[43]

As well as reinforcements, Anstruther brought the most recent general orders from Horse Guards, including: 'The Commander in Chief directs it to be notified that in consequence of the state of the preparation of immediate service, in which the whole of the Army is at the present moment to be held, His Majesty has been graciously pleased to dispense with the use of queues until further orders.' It had long been the practice that soldiers had to grow their hair long and form it into a

---

39   Wellington (ed.), *Supplementary Despatches*, vol.XIII, pp.294–295.

40   C. Esdaile and M. Reed (eds.), *With Moore to Corunna* (Barnsley: Pen & Sword, 2018), p.63.

41   Glover (ed.), *Line Infantry*, p.72.

42   Neale, *Letters*, p.9.

43   StAUL: msdep121/8/2/3/4/4: Anstruther's journal, pp.22–24.

queue. Commanding officers were now to ensure their 'men's hair is cut close to their necks in the neatest & most uniform manner; and that their Heads are kept perfectly clean by combing, brushing, and frequently washing them; for the latter essential purpose it His Majesty's Pleasure that a small Sponge shall hereafter be added to each man's Regimental Necessaries.'[44] Ross-Lewin of the 32nd Foot noted that the queues were cropped that day.[45]

Acland's convoy also suffered from the same contrary and strong winds as Anstruther's. Private Billows remembered being tossed about for two days in the Bay of Biscay with the women and children screaming and the men cursing and swearing. Even when they anchored off the Rock of Lisbon, the swell rolled the ship so much that it caused distress among the soldiers and families.[46] HMS *Aimable* (32) and the 10 transports had been driven further south and had fallen in with Vice Admiral Cotton's squadron off the Tagus on the 19th. As Wellesley had requested, Cotton sent them north to the coast near Mafra.[47]

Acland and Anstruther were not the only reinforcements that were in the offing. Freire had written to Wellesley to say he was bringing the bulk of the Portuguese army to join him and asked where he would like him to march. Wellesley had replied on the 18th that he expected to be in the neighbourhood of Torres Vedras on the 20th and that Freire should march his troops to see the British there. However, on the 20th, Wellesley told the Portuguese that the French were still at Torres Vedras and that he should march to Lourinhã and then follow the British to Mafra.[48]

Burrard's Voyage

Castlereagh wrote Lieutenant General Sir Harry Burrard's orders on 21 July and gave him a copy of Wellesley's original instructions. He was to proceed on HMS *Audacious* (74) to the Tagus. He was warned that Sir Hew Dalrymple might not arrive immediately but that he should 'use your endeavours to carry His Majesty's commands without loss of time into effect.' The first objective was the 'reduction of the Tagus', and the second was the 'security of Cadiz and the destruction of the enemy's forces in Andalusia.'[49]

Burrard left London immediately and arrived at Portsmouth to take command of Moore's troops on the afternoon of the 24th. He wrote to Castlereagh the next day that 'Every exertion has been used by the several departments to compleat the Service and render the Fleet fit for proceeding to it's [sic] destination and I have found in Sir John Moore, the most marked attention to assist me in this desirable object.' He also commented that transports carrying Moore's force were too small and cramped for a warm climate and that the masters were only familiar with the North Sea.[50]

Unfortunately, on the 26th, Burrard had to inform Castlereagh that the winds were against them and they could not sail until they changed. The convoy eventually sailed on the 31st, but on 8 August, Burrard wrote again off Falmouth that they were 'still beating in the channel against contrary winds' and that he had to send a horse transport carrying 36 artillery horses and 27 drivers

44   TNA: WO 123/129: General Order, 20 July 1808
45   Ross-Lewin, *Life*, vol.I, p.215.
46   Billows, *Nothing Pertickler Happened*, pp.26–27.
47   TNA: ADM 7/41: Cotton to Pole, 19 August 1808.
48   Wellesley to Freire, 18 and 20 August 1808, in 'Documentos', pp.192–193, 195.
49   TNA: WO 1/235: Castlereagh to Burrard, 21 July 1808.
50   TNA: WO 1/235: Burrard to Castlereagh, 25 July 1808.

into Plymouth after the stern of the vessel had been severely damaged by a transport carrying the 55th Foot to the West Indies colliding with it. Two other transports had been damaged by the wind and sent back to Portsmouth, one carrying KGL artillery and one some of the drafts for the 36th Foot. There were also fears that the horses would run out of forage if the voyage were delayed further.[51] They were still battling unfavourable winds on the 13th and were about 90 miles southwest of Ushant in the Bay of Biscay.[52]

Burrard transferred from the *Audacious* to the *Brazen* (18) on 16 August and sailed ahead to Oporto and then Figueira, where he received Wellesley's dispatches. Burrard had with him his adjutant general, Brigadier General Henry Clinton, and his quartermaster general, Colonel George Murray, their deputies, and his aides de camp. He read Wellesley's letters of 8, 10 and 11 August but decided against his proposal to get Moore's corps to march to Santarém for several reasons. The men had been on ships for months and may not have been up to such a march without some time to recover. Wellesley had warned him that few rations could be gathered from the local area, and the 150 mules promised by the Bishop of Oporto had not appeared and did not seem likely to arrive, so it would have been difficult for Moore to keep his men supplied. Also, Burrard worried that Moore's corps would be inferior to the French if they tried to force their way to Elvas or Almeida through Santarém. Lastly, it would have taken time to prepare Moore's column to march inland, during which Wellesley and Moore would not have been able to support each other.[53] In Wellesley's opinion, stated later at the inquiry into the Convention of Cintra, the French would only have fallen back to Santarém after a defeat, and so Moore would have been strong enough to hold the town, and that Wellesley had made arrangements for Moore to be supplied from the depot at Leiria.[54]

On the evening of the 19th, the *Brazen* came across a dispatch boat with two sailors and a marine going from São Martinho do Porto to the Burlings. Burrard heard about the 'sharp action' at Roliça, that many had been killed on both sides, but that the French had retreated. So, he thought it best if Moore landed at Mondego to support Wellesley if he was forced to fall back or to later march south to join him. Burrard was unaware of any suitable landing place for a large force between the Mondego and Lisbon. He sent Colonel Ruffane Shawe Donkin in the dispatch boat north to order Moore to disembark at Figueira. He also sent Lieutenant Colonel Thomas Carey south to São Martinho do Porto in a fishing boat to contact Wellesley.[55]

Burrard sailed on down the coast and saw the *Alfred* and Anstruther's convoy but could not join with them due to calms or contrary winds, but he did eventually learn of Wellesley's location and arrived at the anchorage in Maceira Bay on the 20th.

---

51   TNA: WO 1/235: Burrard to Castlereagh, 26 July and 8 August 1808; BL: Add. MS 49503: Murray to Gordon, 2 August 1808.
52   BL: Add. MS 49503: Murray to Gordon 13 August 1808.
53   TNA: WO 1/415: Burrard's narrative, pp.195–196.
54   TNA: WO 1/415: Wellesley's response to Burrard.
55   TNA: WO 1/415: Burrard's narrative, pp.199–201.

14

Vimeiro: The Eve of Battle

Wellesley marched from Lourinhã on the 19th to the small village of Vimeiro, which was just inland of a suitable landing site for the reinforcements at Porto Novo on Maceira Bay. On the morning of the 20th, Wellesley wrote to Bligh on the *Alfred*:

> I have just been down at Maceira, where I hope that you will land the bread, ammunition, &c., and the saddles. It appears a very good landing place, and there is a good road, and it is no great distance from thence here; but if you should think that place inconvenient, I will contrive to communicate with any other place at which you may land them.
>
> I propose to march to-morrow towards Mafra; I shall be glad if you will be off Ericeira to-morrow evening. I shall contrive to communicate with you either to-morrow or next day, and to fix on the next place of rendezvous. (I apprehend no accidents; but I should like to keep the transports for a few days, in case of the occurrence of any. They might also be useful in turning any position the enemy might take in the neighbourhood of the Rock of Lisbon.[1]

He added a postscript that if Acland's convoy joined the *Alfred*, Bligh should keep it with him and inform Wellesley immediately.

Acland's brigade arrived during the afternoon, began to disembark through the evening of the 20th, and joined the army at Vimeiro at 6:00 a.m. the following morning after sleeping on the beach.[2] Only seven and a half companies of the 20th Foot landed under the command of Lieutenant Colonel Alexander Campbell. The transport carrying Lieutenant Colonel Robert Ross and the regimental headquarters drifted away from the shore and did not return until late on the 21st.[3] The men of the 2nd Foot were only landed at daylight on the 21st, with a blanket and great-coat rolled up with three days' rations and a sealed canteen of rum, leaving their knapsacks and women on board.[4]

During the 20th several French cavalry patrols were spotted close to the British camp. The 36th Foot was in the low ground behind Vimeiro near the river. Ensign Murchison recalled seeing

---

1   Gurwood (ed.), *Wellington's Dispatches*, vol.IV, p.106.
2   Gurwood (ed.), *Wellington's Dispatches*, vol.IV, p.114.
3   R. Cannon, *Historical Record of the Twentieth or East Devonshire Regiment of Foot* (London: Parker, Furnivall & Parker, 1868), p.38.
4   Billows, *Nothing Pertickler Happened*, pp.26–27.

The beach at Porto Novo. (Author's photo)

Maceira Bay from William Bradford, *Sketches of the Country, Character and Costume in Portugal and Spain.*

patrols of dragoons and wrote: 'Several officers approached us, and one coming particularly near (I suppose he was sketching), Captain Mellish (General Ferguson's A.D.C.) offered the long odds to any one that, if permitted, he would dismount him.'[5] Surgeon George Guthrie (29th Foot) was travelling back to his regiment after treating the wounded at Roliça:

> I wished the carts at the devil in the first instance, on account of the delay they occasioned; but very soon took a particular fancy to them; for we found the French cavalry patrolling between Lourina and Vimiera, to the great alarm of both the natives and ourselves. They counted on their fingers two patrols of an officer, and twenty men each, one being before the other on one side of us, and told us they would cut us to pieces if they caught us. I had some twenty old soldiers with me, all of whom I knew well, and two or three subaltern officers of other corps, who were taking advantage of the convoy, and whose duty it was to fight. I tied the heads of my second bullocks to the tail of the cart, which preceded them, and thus continued our march across the country, which was open, although hilly, and soon satisfied my old soldiers that, with their backs against the bullock-carts, they were not to be thrashed by a patrol of cavalry.[6]

Given the aggressive patrolling of the French cavalry, Anstruther believed that a French attack was imminent and told Wellesley that he thought it would occur the next day. He surmised that Junot's only chance of defeating Wellesley was to attack before all the reinforcements arrived. Wellesley was not thoroughly convinced but was confident that he had a good position and reliable troops and took the precaution of repositioning some of the artillery. Anstruther noted, 'although not concerned that he should be attacked, made every necessary preparation for such an event.'[7]

As well as gathering intelligence for Junot, the boldness of the French cavalry prevented Wellesley from having exact information on his enemy's whereabouts. He later stated:

> Their cavalry was very active throughout the days of the 19th and the 20th; they covered the whole country; patrolled frequently up to our position; and on the 20th one patrol was pushed into the rear of our right as far as the landing place at Maceira.
>
> Under these circumstances we could gain no detailed information of the enemy's position excepting that it was very strong and occupied by their whole forces.[8]

Despite this lack of certainty, Wellesley still planned to march on the 21st towards Mafra, 20 miles south. His general order for the day began: 'The army will march at half-past four o'clock to-morrow morning.'[9] He hoped to push the advanced guard as far as the high ground there and halt the main body four or five miles outside the town. He later stated:

> By this movement the enemy's position at Torres Vedras would have been turned, and I should have brought the army into a country of which I had an excellent map and topographical accounts, which had been drawn up for the use of the late Sir Charles Stewart,

---

5   Geikie, *Life*, p.31.
6   Crumplin, *Guthrie's War*, p.27.
7   StAUL: msdep121/8/2/3/4/4: Anstruther's jounal, p.26.
8   TNA: WO 1/415: Wellesley's narrative, p.75.
9   Wellington (ed.), *Supplementary Despatches*, vol.IV, p.120.

and the Battle which it was evident would be fought in a few days, would have had for its field a country of which we had a knowledge, not very distant from Lisbon, into which Town, if we have been successful, we might have entered with the retreating Enemy.[10]

The general order then went on to deal with the more mundane subjects of a request for a return of the number of billhooks and the redistribution of camp kettles to Anstruther's brigade. The order then concluded:

A piquet of twenty Portuguese and ten British cavalry, with an infantry piquet to be furnished by the 5th brigade, consisting of one captain, two subalterns, and 100 men, with non-commissioned officers in proportion, will be posted, at seven o'clock this evening, at a large house on the hill in rear of Brigadier-General C. Craufurd's brigade, which piquet will patrol the front of the ravine, as far as the sea, during the night.[11]

It is probable, since Craufurd's brigade was on the heights behind Vimeiro near Porto Novo, that this picket was meant to both help secure the landing of Acland's brigade and also to patrol towards the south, the direction that Wellesley thought that the French might approach from.

Unfortunately for Wellesley's plans, another vessel sailed into Maceira Bay that day: the sloop HMS *Brazen*, carrying Sir Harry Burrard and his staff.

Much to be Said on Both Sides

Burrard ordered a boat be made ready to take him ashore, but Wellesley arrived on board to report to his new superior before he could disembark. Burrard later stated:

In our conversation Sir Arthur told me most fully what the difficulties were that I should have to encounter, he mentioned his want of cavalry, and the inefficiency of the artillery horses, and that the enemy were strong in the former; that their cavalry had already come very near them, and had kept them close to their encampments and that it was unsafe to stir out of them; that it would not be possible to go far into the country, at a distance from the victualers for from them we must depend for our bread.[12]

Based on Wellesley's report, Burrard decided it would be better to wait for Moore before advancing. Burrard's strategy was built around reducing the risk of disaster rather than increasing the chance of success. Wellesley's plan could have resulted in a British reverse and the need to hurriedly re-embark, or a lengthy siege of Lisbon when the weather could have forced the fleet away from the coast and left the British unsupplied and vulnerable to a French sally.[13] After Wellesley made his report, the two men had essentially the same information, but they each came to very different conclusions about what should be done next. Wellesley's plan was not without risk, but, having

---

10 TNA: WO 1/415: Wellesley's narrative, p.76.
11 Wellington (ed.), *Supplementary Despatches*, vol.IV, p.120.
12 TNA: WO 1/415: Burrard's narrative, p.201.
13 TNA: WO 1/415: Burrard's narrative, pp.203–204.

engaged the French once, he was confident his corps was sufficiently strong that he could beat them again. Burrard was far more cautious; he preferred the certainty of Moore and Wellesley combined being superior in number to any estimate of Junot's strength and was at pains to avoid any chance of a disaster, as had occurred in South America. Murray and Clinton, both experienced officers, agreed with Burrard.

Wellesley stressed the advantages of moving toward Mafra and outflanking Junot's position at Torres Vedras. If Moore was brought down to Maceira, the French could retreat via Santarém. Wellesley was concerned that if the army remained static, then the French would either attack or spend time fortifying their position near Torres Vedras, and the roads were not suitable for moving the heavy guns that might then be needed. He was also worried that increasing the numbers of troops on shore would stretch the abilities of the commissariat still further.[14] In his memoir, Lord Burghersh maintained that if the army had marched to Mafra, then they would have marched on a road separated from the French route from Torres Vedras by a tract of wooded and challenging terrain, which would have prevented the French from falling upon the column and that Junot's only option would have been to reverse course and attack the allies in a strong position at Mafra.[15]

Anstruther said of the decision in his journal that there was 'Much to be said on both sides. We were 3 or 4,000 infantry stronger than the enemy and equal in number in artillery but we have no cavalry – the country is in many places open … Upon the whole I rather think the resolution taken by Sir H Burrard is the wise one.'[16] Colonel George Murray, who was present during the conversation, later wrote:

> Sir Arthur stated that he had given orders for the army to be in readiness to move forward towards Maffra on the following morning; and that it was his intention to continue advancing along the coast until he should reach the neighbourhood of Cascaes, there to place himself in communication with the fleet; but that, in the interval between Maceira and Cascaes, there was understood to be but one point where there could be any communication with the shipping, and that somewhat precarious. The question then naturally arose as to whether the order which had been given for moving forward on the following morning should be carried into effect or not. It was conceived, that the enemy being at hand with his whole force, but without any certain knowledge being possessed as to his actual situation, he had it in his power to bring on a general action whenever he might think fit to do so; that, considering the enemy's more perfect knowledge of the country, his great superiority in cavalry, the length of the march to Maffra, and the reported badness of the roads – and adverting, likewise, to the long train of bullock carts, incapable of moving at a quicker pace than two miles in an hour – all the disadvantages of sustaining an attack whilst on the march would be experienced, probably, to their fullest extent; especially as the enemy was not so inferior in numbers, if at all inferior, as to compensate for the advantages which he in other respects possessed: – that, even if the army should reach the neighbourhood of Cascaes without being attacked on the march, or without sustaining any considerable loss, the enemy would be enabled probably to bring into the field, in the immediate vicinity of the capital, for a decisive battle, two or three thousand

---

14   Anon., *Proceedings*, p.102.
15   Fane, *Early Campaigns*, pp.27–28.
16   StAUL: msdep121/8/2/3/4/4: Anstruther's journal, pp.26–27.

men more than he could venture to draw to so great a distance from Lisbon as where the British army then was. To these considerations was also added the very important one, that, having a reinforcement of ten thousand men close at hand, Sir H. Burrard not having quitted the convoy till it had arrived off Cape Finisterre on the 16th, to move forward with the present force only, and in a state of perfect uncertainty as to when, and where, and under what circumstances, an action might take place, decisive, for a time at least, of the result of the very important enterprise in hand, was a line of policy, the prudence of which might well be questioned. Upon all these grounds, therefore, Sir Harry Burrard decided against moving the army towards Maffra on the following day; deeming it better to receive the attack, unembarrassed, and in a fixed position, known to the troops, than upon the march, under embarrassments, and on unknown ground; and resolving, should the enemy delay attacking, to strengthen the position – profit by favourable weather to land provisions and stores from the shipping at Maceira – and wait the arrival of the troops under Sir John Moore.[17]

Dusk was falling when Wellesley and Burrard finished their meeting. Burrard wrote orders for Moore to disembark at Maceira and sent the *Brazen* to Figueira while he transferred to the *Alfred* for the night.[18] The next morning, Wellesley wrote to Castlereagh, still obviously irritated by Burrard's decisions:

Sir Harry Burrard will probably acquaint your Lordship with the reasons which have induced him to call Sir John Moore's corps to the assistance of our army, which consists of 20,000 men, including the Portuguese army, which was to join this morning, notwithstanding former determinations to the contrary, and is opposed by, I am convinced, not more than 12,000 or 14,000 Frenchmen, and to halt here till Sir John's corps shall join. You will readily believe, however, that this determination is not in conformity with my opinion, and I only wish that Sir Harry had landed and seen things with his own eyes before he had made it.[19]

We Shall Give Battle to the English

On 15 August, the Emperor's birthday, salutes were fired from the forts in and around Lisbon and the ships in the Tagus. Junot held a lavish ball. In attendance were government officials, senior clergy, and high-ranking army officers. After the ball, he attended the opera, and then, during the night, he prepared to march from the city to join Delaborde and Loison. Before he left, he had arranged for Lisbon's castle to be prepared for a possible siege by ordering the gathering of weapons and supplies from the various depots and arsenals, the repairing and filling of the cisterns, and provisioning it with 100,000 rations of biscuits. The engineering works on the forts were to be

---

17   Murray, 'Review of History of the War', pp.193–194.
18   TNA: WO 1/415: Burrard's narrative, p.204.
19   Gurwood (ed.), *Wellington's Dispatches*, vol.IV, p.107.

continued. However, Junot had also previously ordered that depots of food, ammunition, and shoes be formed at Villa Franca and Santarém on the route of a possible withdrawal to Spain.[20]

He took with him as many troops from Lisbon as he thought could be spared – a regiment of grenadier companies, a battalion of the 82e Ligne, the 4e and 5e Dragons, and 10 guns, plus ammunition and baggage. Junot also took with him 1,000,000 francs worth of silver from the treasury. *Maréchal des logis chef* Jean-Auguste Oyon (4e Dragons) was recovering from a wound but did not want to be left behind in the hospital and left Lisbon with the rest of his unit. They rode silently through the dark streets to not alert the city's population to their leaving. Once outside the city, the dragoons, leading the march, advanced cautiously in case of an ambush.[21] On the 16th, the columns paused at Sacavém while a temporary bridge over a river was constructed. The following day, rumours of a landing from Cotton's squadron off the Tagus caused Junot to turn about until he learned they were unfounded. *Capitaine* Jaques Hulot of the French artillery wrote that his guns were delayed on the march from Lisbon by the locals setting fire to the long, dry grass that they had to traverse.[22]

Junot left Thiébault in charge of the column and rode to meet Loison. Later on the 17th, the day of the Battle of Roliça, he was at Cercal, just 16 miles away. He wrote to Thiébault, 'I am collecting my army at Torres Vedras. We shall give battle to the English: make haste, if you wish to be at the party.'[23] On the 19th, he wrote to *général de division* Travot, left in command at Lisbon:

> … we have not yet been able to meet the enemy: the poor disposition of the inhabitants towards us makes it almost impossible to know his movements, and the difficulty of the roads is opposed to manoeuvres and to the promptitude of communications. I am waiting today for information on the position occupied by the enemy, and if he does not come looking for us, we will go to meet him.[24]

Despite having around 26,000 men in Portugal, Junot could only gather approximately 10,000 at Torres Vedras. The brutal marches of July had led to 3,000 men being sick, becoming casualties or straggling. The garrisons at Peniche, Elvas, Almeida and Santarém totalled 5,600. The city of Lisbon, the ships on the Tagus, and the forts needed 5,400. So, 14,000 men were unavailable for the field. However, realising that Wellesley badly outnumbered him, Junot sent orders to Travot to send elements of the 66e Ligne and the elite companies of the 15e Ligne, 31e and 32e Légère, and Légion du Midi to join the field army.[25] Thiébault claims in his history that Junot could have raised the disposable force to 14,000 by evacuating Santarém, letting the Russians occupy the left bank of the Tagus, and reducing the garrison of Lisbon to 1,100 with 300 convalescents.[26] In his memoir, where he was often more critical of Junot, Thiébault wrote: 'If the English troops, especially their officers, were not in 1808 worth so much as they afterwards were – as, indeed, the combat of Roriça [sic] had brilliantly shown – this was of course no excuse for not equalising the forces when the means of doing so were at hand.'[27] The regimental history of the 12e Légère illustrates how much

20 Thiébault, *l'Expédition*, pp.185.
21 Oyon, *Campagnes*, Kindle Location 3278–3308.
22 Hulot, *Souvenirs*, p.233.
23 Foy, *Invasion*, p.159.
24 Griffon de Pleineville, *Invasion*, p.198.
25 Mackay, *Tempest*, p.278.
26 Thiébault, *l'Expédition*, p.185n.
27 A.J. Butler (trans.), *The Memoirs of Baron Thiébault* (London: Smith, Elder & Co., 1896), vol.II, p.205.

the strength of some units had changed. The provisional regiment formed by the 12e and 15e had 2,614 men earlier in the year, but by 20 August, it could only field 24 officers and 1,342 men.[28] Table 22 lists the location of the French infantry and cavalry regiments.

Table 22. Location of French troops, 20 August 1808

Regiment	Location
3/2e Légère	Field Army
3/4e Légère	Field Army
3/12e Légère	Field Army
3/15e Légère	Field Army
3/31e Légère	Left bank Tagus/2 coys marching to join Junot
3/32e Légère	Left bank Tagus/2 coys marching to join Junot
3/15e Ligne	Powder magazines Sacavém/Lisbon/ 2 coys marching to join Junot
3/26e Ligne	Belém/Bon-Succes/Ericeira
3/32e Ligne	Field Army
2/47e Ligne	On ships/Fort Bugio/Trafaria
3/58e Ligne	Field Army
3/ & 4/66e Ligne	Cascais/Marching to join Junot
1/ & 2/70e Ligne	Field Army
3/82e Ligne	Field Army
1/ & 2/86e Ligne	Field Army/4 coys Elvas
2/2e Suisse	Elvas
1/4e Suisse	Peniche/ 2 coys Field Army
1/Légion Hanovrienne	Santarém
1/Legion du Midi	Forte Sao Julião/2 coys marching to join Junot
Depot Battalion	Lisbon Castle
4/26e Chasseurs à cheval	Field Army
4/1er Dragons	Field Army
4/3e Dragons	Field Army
4/4e Dragons	Field Army
4/5e Dragons	Field Army
4/9e Dragons	Field Army
4/15e Dragons	Field Army

Source: Thiébault, *l'Expédition*, p.189

The only addition to Junot's troops came from a volunteer cavalry unit of about 100 men, formed from French émigrés in Lisbon. Amongst them were many Royalists who had taken shelter in Portugal after the revolution. For example, the Comte de Bourmont had participated in several campaigns, insurrections and conspiracies against the revolutionary government. He had been

28   Malaguti, *Historique du 87e Régiment*, p.347.

arrested after being a suspect in an assassination attempt on Napoleon but then escaped and fled to Portugal. Junot gave him a position on his staff.[29]

If Junot had gathered more men from Lisbon and its environs to face Wellesley, he could have had the advantage in numbers. But, to do so would have meant effectively abandoning the city to the Portuguese. If the French had then beaten Wellesley, they would have had to retake the city, and they would have had nowhere to fall back to if they had been defeated. The population of Lisbon was indeed getting restive and would probably have risen if Junot had taken a larger proportion of the garrison. On 2 August, the *Gazeta de Lisboa*, which had been an official mouth-piece of the French regime, carried an anonymous proclamation that urged the population to rise and 'break the chains which bind you, and to avenge with blood, and with the death of your tyrant oppressors, the insults to our Nation, and to our adored Prince.'[30] On 21 August, Cotton received an emissary from the city requesting arms and troops to help them take possession of the city now that the garrison had been reduced. The emissary said that leaders of the anti-French faction were having difficulty restraining the people. Cotton replied that if the French were defeated but not overwhelmed in the field, then the rising would have to have sufficient strength to deny the French re-entry to the city. If the people rose but could not keep Junot out, then there would be another slaughter like at Evora, and it might be better to wait until Wellesley was closer to the city.[31] *Capitaine de vaisseau* Magendie was certainly aware of the risk of an uprising and reported to Junot that on all the ships of war in the Tagus, 'the slow matches are always lit so that at the first order from you the city will be struck down if it revolts.'[32]

French cavalry patrols informed Junot that Wellesley had taken up a position at Vimeiro and that Anstruther's brigade had landed, increasing the allies' strength. Given this intelligence, Junot decided to take the initiative and attack. On the evening of the 20th, he ordered *général de brigade* Pierre Margaron forward with the cavalry division through the pass above Torres Vedras. Before his troops marched, Junot made a speech to his soldiers, which harked back to the glorious days of Austerlitz, Eylau and Friedland:

> The enemy is in front of us; he wants to delay in order to be reinforced; let us march towards him; the armies of the great Napoleon are not accustomed to waiting for the enemy, they are going to seek him out. It is Englishmen that you have to fight, it is not necessary to tell you more to excite your valour[33]

The infantry divisions were to follow the cavalry, but they were delayed by the carts and artillery, which suffered several accidents on the road. It was not until 6:00 a.m. that the last troops had cleared the pass.[34]

---

29   Southey, *History*, vol.II, p.196; 'General Louis Auguste Victor de Ghaisnes de Bourmont', <https://www.frenchempire.net/biographies/bourmont/>, accessed May 2023.

30   dos Santos, *Lisboa*, p.89.

31   TNA: ADM 7/41: Cotton to Wellesley-Pole, 22 August 1808.

32   Griffon de Pleineville, *Invasion*, p.199.

33   Griffon de Pleineville, *Invasion*, p.201.

34   C.T. Beauvais de Preau, *Victoires, Conquêtes, Désastres, Revers et Guerres Civiles des Français de 1792 a 1815* (Paris: Panckoucke, 1820), vol.18, pp.105–106.

Order of Battle, Vimeiro 21 August 1808

French – *Général de division* **Junot**

Général de division **Delaborde**
Général de brigade Brenier
    3/2e Légère, 3/4e Légère
    1/70e and 2/70e Ligne
Général de brigade Thomières
    1/86e and 2/86e Ligne (minus 4 coys at Elvas)
    1/4e Suisse (elite companies only)
Colonel Prost – 8 guns

Général de division **Loison**
Général de brigade Solignac
    3/12e Légère, 3/15e Légère
    3/58e Ligne
Général de brigade Charlot
    3/32e Ligne
    3/82e Ligne
Colonel d'Aboville – 8 guns

Reserve, *Général de division* **Kellermann**
    1e and 2e régiments de grenadiers
    Colonel Foy –10 guns

Cavalry, *Général de brigade* **Margaron**
    4/26e Chasseurs à Cheval
    4/1e Dragons, 4/3e Dragons
    4/4e Dragons, 4/5e Dragons
    4/9e Dragons, 4/15e Dragons
    Émigré Volunteers

British & Portuguese – Lieutenant General Sir Arthur Wellesley

1st Brigade – Major General Hill
    Light companies & 5/60th company
    1/5th, 1/9th and 1/38th Foot
    Capt. Raynsford – 2 x 6-pdrs, 1 x 5½-inch Howitzer
2nd Brigade – Major General Fergusson
    Light companies & 5/60th company
    1/36th, 1/40th and 1/71st Foot
    Lt. Locke – 2 x 6-pdrs, 1 x 5½-inch Howitzer
3rd Brigade – Brigadier General Nightingall
    Light companies & 5/60th company

29th and 1/82nd Foot
Lt. Graham – 3 x 6-pdrs
4th Brigade – Brigadier General Bowes
Light companies & 5/60th company
1/6th and 1/32nd Foot
Lt. Festing – 3 x 6-pdrs
5th Brigade – Brigadier General Craufurd
Light companies & 5/60th company
1/45th, and 1/91st Foot
Capt. Morrison – 2 x 6-pdrs, 1 x 5½-inch Howitzer
6th (Light) Brigade – Brigadier General Fane
1/50th Foot
5 companies 5/60th Rifles
4 companies 2/95th
2nd Capt. Eliot – 2 x 6-pdrs, 1 x 5½-inch Howitzer
7th Brigade – Brigadier General Anstruther
2/9th, 2/43rd, 2/52nd and 97th Foot
Brigadier General Acland's Brigade[35]
2nd and 7½ companies 20th Foot
2 companies 1/95th Rifles
Artillery Reserve – Major Viney
Capt. Gardiner – 3 x 9-pdrs
Lt. Hawker – 2 x 9-pdrs, 1 x heavy 5½-inch Howitzer

Portuguese – Lieutenant Colonel Trant
Batalhão de Caçadores do Porto
Regimento de Infantaria n.º 12, one battalion
Regimento de Infantaria n.º 21, one battalion
Regimento de Infantaria n.º 24, half battalion
Regimento de artilharia n.º 4
Cavalry
20th Light Dragoons
Regimento de Cavalaria n.º 6
Regimento de Cavalaria n.º 11
Regimento de Cavalaria n.º 12
Guarda Real da Polícia

Estimates for how many men Junot was able to field at Vimeiro vary widely. Oman bases his figure on a return from July and then makes various compensations for losses and detachments before arriving at a figure of just over 13,000.[36] Wellesley's own estimate was 14,000. However, Junot's chief of staff, Paul Thiébault, in his history of the campaign gives a figure of 9,200 and breaks that

---

35   Acland's brigade was only numbered the 8th after the battle. Anstruther's brigade was numbered the 7th soon after it landed.

36   Oman, *History*, vol.I, pp.246–247.

down to 3,200 for Delaborde's division, 2,700 for Loison's, 2,100 for the grenadiers and 1,200 for the cavalry.[37] Foy repeats Thiébault's figures in his own history but adds in non-combatants for a total of 11,500.[38] In his report to Napoleon Junot put his strength between 9,000 and 10,000 infantry.[39] In his thesis, Charles Mackay cites a return for Delaborde's division on 20 August and gives that division a strength of 3,603, and then, citing Junot's report to Napoleon, gives a strength for Loison's division of 3,200. He then uses Thiébault's figures for the other divisions.[40] In all these discussions it is never quite clear if all the figures are actually counting the same thing. The convention is usually to count the rank and file, as they made up the actual combat strength of the units, but some of the figures might be including sergeants, drummers, regimental staff and officers as well which would add 10–15 percent.

The numbers for the British troops can be deduced from the previously given embarkation returns, minus the casualties suffered at Roliça – although some of the slightly wounded and missing may have returned to the ranks – and allowing for other losses from illness or desertion. So, it is probable that Wellesley had just under 18,000 British rank and file present, of which perhaps five to 10 percent would have been sick or on duties such as baggage guards. The 2,000 Portuguese troops can be added to this to give a grand total of around 20,000, or approximately double the numbers Junot had. However, it is likely that the French cavalry outnumbered the allied horsemen by a similar ratio.

Accounts Received at Night

Given Burrard's decision, Wellesley issued the following order: 'The army will halt to-morrow. The men to sleep accoutred to-night, in readiness to turn out, and to be under arms at three o'clock in the morning.'[41]

At some point on the evening of the 20th, Wellesley sent a note to Brigadier General Fane:

> You have done quite right; but as we have no ground to go upon excepting a report given to your patrols by a villager, you may allow the men to fall out and lie down; but they must sleep accoutred. Before I had heard of this report I had ordered two 9-pounders to your ground, and since I have received it I have desired that you may continue to send patrols to your front, and that you will do me the favour to let me know if they should report anything extraordinary … Desire that Anstruther's brigade will likewise accoutre, and be ready to turn out at a moment's notice. I am a little jealous of your left.[42]

From this, it can be surmised that Fane had received intelligence of the approach of the French from an inhabitant of one of the nearby villages.

Fane seems to have undertaken his duties diligently and competently. Sergeant Landsheit (20th Light Dragoons) recalled in his memoir that the Light Brigade's commander had placed his tent

37 Thiébault, *l'Expédition*, pp.193–194.
38 Foy, *Invasion*, p.164.
39 Griffon de Pleineville, *Invasion*, p.201n.
40 Mackay, *Tempest*, pp.279–280.
41 Wellington (ed.), *Supplementary Despatches*, vol.IV, p.121.
42 Wellington (ed.), *Supplementary Despatches*, vol.IV, pp.119–120.

just behind the outlying cavalry vedettes to be on hand if there was a sudden attack. Fane also made sure the cavalrymen knew the ground to their front, leading the men of the picket, under the command of Lieutenant George Burgoyne, in a patrol of the area in front of their posts so they became familiar with the ground. They advanced, past a red chapel, to a village empty of its inhabitants apart from an innkeeper who provided refreshments. The patrol then returned.

At 10:00 p.m., Landsheit, as the senior sergeant present, led a patrol out past the outposts to Fane's front:

> The patrol, consisting of twelve men and a corporal, besides myself, mounted and took the road as soon as I had received my instructions. These were, to move very slowly to the front, keeping every eye and ear on the alert, till we should reach the Red Chapel – not to engage an enemy's patrol, should we fall in with one – to hasten back to the piquet on the first appearance of danger – and on no account to trust ourselves beyond the limits which General Fane had marked out. Thus instructed, I ordered the men to march; and, as far as silence and an acute observation could go, we obeyed the officer's directions to the letter. Nor, indeed, would it have been easy, on such a night, and when so occupied, to indulge in idle or ribald conversation. The moon shone full and bright, millions of stars were abroad, and the silence was so profound, that the very ripple of the stream could be heard as it wound its tortuous way along the base of the hill down the slope of which we were riding. Moreover, the perfumes that hung upon the quiet night air were exquisite. Extensive groves of myrtle and orange trees, scattered here and there over the plain, loaded the atmosphere with fragrant scents, which we inhaled with a satisfaction that was certainly not diminished because of their novelty. In a word, I do not recollect having ever been abroad at a season more perfectly delicious, or of performing a duty which partook so much of the character of a pleasurable excursion; for nothing occurred even to startle us. The world seemed asleep; and we reached the Red Chapel, fully assured that no enemy was or could be within many miles of us.[43]

The patrol paused at the chapel to eat something from their haversacks and to drink from their canteens. Landsheit then decided to disobey his orders and probe towards the deserted village they had visited earlier. Sending a corporal and two troopers ahead, the patrol rode down to the village, which was still quiet. Landsheit sought out the innkeeper again, and the man told him: 'My young man came home from Lisbon an hour ago, and passed the whole of the French army on its march; and so close are they by this time, that I expect them in the village in less than half an hour.' The dragoons pulled back from the village, but Landsheit wanted to confirm the intelligence, and they waited near the red chapel, with vedettes down the slope, waiting to hear the French troops cross a wooden bridge at the entrance to the village.

> For awhile all was still. Not a breeze moved the branches; not a beast or bird uttered a cry; in deed, the only sound distinguishable was the running water, which came upon us most musically. But by and by … Wheels began to rumble; there was a dead heavy noise, like the tread of many feet over a soft soil; and then, the wooden bridge rang again with the iron hoofs of horses. Immediately the videttes fell back, according to my orders, to

---

43   Gleig (ed.), *Hussar*, vol.I, pp.257–258.

report what they had heard, and to learn from us that we had heard it also; and then, after waiting a sufficient time, to leave no doubt upon our minds as to the formidable extent of the column that was moving, we vaulted into our saddles, and returned at a brisk trot towards the piquet.[44]

Oman names the village as Vila Facaia, which is about six miles east-southeast of Vimeiro.[45]

When the patrol returned, Fane berated Landsheit for taking so long but then praised him after he had made his report and told him to ride to inform Wellesley immediately. Landsheit continues the tale:

I rode to the house where the General dwelt, and being admitted, I found him, with a large Staff, all of them seated on a long table in the hall, back to back, and swinging their legs to and fro, like men on whose minds not the shadow of anxiety rested. Moreover, the General himself not only saw no consternation in my manner, but closely examined me as to the details of my adventure, and told me that I had done my duty well. He then desired me to go below, and get something to eat and drink from his servant, which I did, though not till I had heard him give his orders, in a calm, clear, and cheerful voice. They were in substance these: 'Now, gentlemen, go to your stations; but let there be no noise made – no sounding of bugles or beating of drums. Get your men quietly under arms, and desire all the outposts to be on the alert.' This latter admonition, it is just to add, I had already conveyed to the outposts, warning each, as I passed it on my way home, of the enemy's approach; and the consequence was, that every man knew the ticklish nature of his position, and was prepared to do his duty, according as circumstances might require.[46]

In his *History of the War in the Peninsula,* Napier refers to the intelligence from 'a German officer of dragoons'.[47] Following the publication of Landsheit's memoir by George Gleig, Napier wrote a letter to the editor of the *United Service Journal* in which he stood by his assertion that it was a German officer and not a sergeant, citing Wellington as his source and saying dismissively that 'Mr. Gleig would do well to confine his Hussar's gossip to what he is really acquainted with.'[48] Gleig wrote a reply in a subsequent issue pointing out that there were no German officers with the 20th Light Dragoons, which an examination of the 1808 *Army List* confirms, and writing, 'I confess that I see no reason for doubting the word of a good and honourable old soldier.'[49] The spat ran on for another round of letters to the editor of the journal, in the last of which Gleig said he would ignore any further statements from Napier.

The confusion appears to have been caused by Wellington's faulty recollection as seven years previously, he had said in a conversation with John Croker:

I came from the frigate [*Brazen*] about nine at night, and went to my own quarters with the army, which, from the nearness of the enemy, I naturally kept on the alert. In the dead

---

44   Gleig (ed.), *Hussar*, vol.I, p.262.
45   Oman, *History*, vol.I, p.252.
46   Gleig (ed.), *Hussar*, vol.I, p.264.
47   Napier, *History*, vol.I, p.134.
48   W. Napier, 'Colonel Napier on a Statement in the "The Hussar"', *United Service Journal*, August 1838, p.544.
49   G. Gleig, 'The Author of "The Hussar" to Colonel Napier', *United Service Journal*, September 1838, p.107.

of the night a fellow came in – a German sergeant, or quartermaster – in a great fright – so great that his hair seemed actually to stand on end – who told me that the enemy was advancing rapidly, and would be soon on us. I immediately sent round to the Generals to order them to get the troops under arms, and soon after the dawn of day we were vigorously attacked.[50]

Anstruther noted in his diary: 'Accounts received at night from Torres Verdras that the enemy was in motion by his right towards Lourinha, with the probable intention of attacking our left.'[51] Wellesley's letter to the Duke of York after the battle makes it clear that he still expected an attack on his right:

During the night of 20th and 21st my patroles gave me intelligence of the movements of the Enemy; but as they were so very superior in cavalry my patroles could not go long distance, & of course the reports were very vague and not founded on very certain grounds. But I thought it probable that if I did not attack the enemy, he would attack me; & and I prepared for an attack at daylight in the morning by posting the 9 pounders, & strengthening my right where I expected the attack from the manner in which the enemy had patrolled towards that point in the line during the 19th and 20th.[52]

However, Ensign Henry Wyndham wrote a fortnight after the battle, 'Sir Arthur in riding round and on observing the ground on the evening preceding the action had expressed his opinion that, though the enemy might make a feint upon our right or centre yet that their chief attack would be on our left.'[53] It is not clear if he heard Wellesley say this himself, but if Wellesley did suspect that the French would attack the left, it is curious that he did not redistribute his forces earlier.

A line of pickets were out in front of the main allied positions. Private Benjamin Harris of the 95th was one of them:

It was on the 20th of August that I was posted in a wood in front of our army; two roads crossed each other where stood; the night was gloomy, but not very dark, and I rather think I was the very out-sentry of the British Army. As I stood thus on my post, I was aware of the approach of two persons, and challenged in a low voice; receiving answer, I bade them come forward; they were Major Napier, of the 50th Foot, and an Officer of the 5th battalion 60th Rifles. Major Napier came close up, and looked me very hard in the face, saying, as nearly as I can remember, these words— 'Sentry, be very alert here, for we expect the enemy upon us to-night, and I do not know how soon.'

The lonely situation, and the Major's impressive manner of giving his orders, had the effect of making me doubly vigilant, and I have never forgotten him. On that night I kept a pretty sharp look-out, and listened for the slightest sound of the enemy's approach: they did not, however, then venture upon us.[54]

50   Jennings, *Croker Papers*, vol.II, p.122.
51   StAUL: msdep121/8/2/3/4/4: Anstruther's journal, p.27.
52   BL: Add. MS 49481: Wellesley to Gordon, 22 August 1808.
53   BL: Add. MS 49481: Wyndham to Gordon, 8 September 1808.
54   B. Harris, 'The Veteran Rifleman at Vimiera', *United Service Journal*, September 1839, p.106.

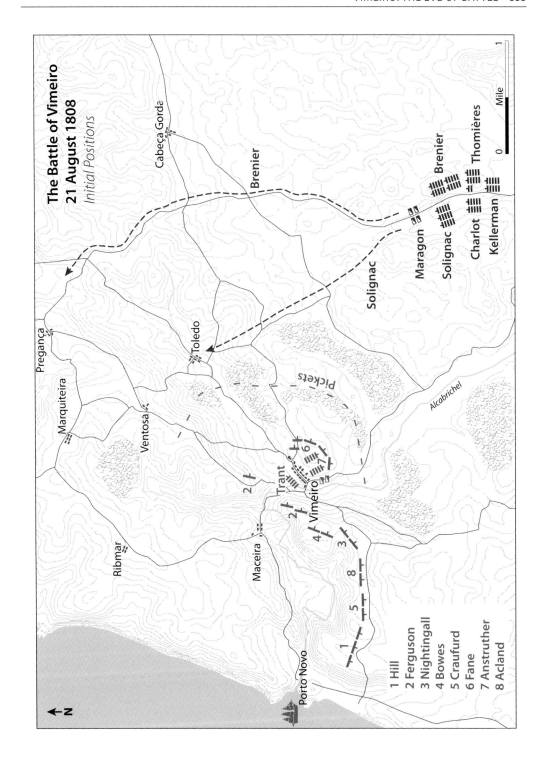

**The Battle of Vimeiro
21 August 1808**
Initial Positions

1 Hill
2 Ferguson
3 Nightingall
4 Bowes
5 Craufurd
6 Fane
7 Anstruther
8 Acland

Cabeça Gorda

Brenier

Solignac

Maragon

Solignac

Brenier

Charlot

Thomières

Kellerman

Preganca

Marquiteira

Ventosa

Toledo

Pickets

Alcobrichel

Trant

Vimeiro

Ribmar

Maceira

Porto Novo

Mile

N

Harris may have never forgotten the major, but he misremembered his name. Major Charles Napier did not join the 1st battalion of the 50th from the 2nd until after Vimeiro, replacing a wounded officer. It would have been Major Charles Hill that spoke to him.

Junot allowed his infantry and guns to rest and have breakfast after they had reached the junction of the Vimeiro and Louriñha roads. At Vimeiro, the British troops stood to at dawn, and then they were dismissed to prepare their breakfasts.

15

Vimeiro: The First Attack

The village of Vimeiro sits on the side of a river valley, two miles inland from the coast. To the southeast is a hill on which in 1808 there was only a windmill, but up which the village has now spread. To the west, towards the sea, a steeply sloped ridge dominates the surrounding countryside and extends from well northeast of the village and then curves to the south to the coast. The slopes get steeper and rockier as it gets closer to the sea. Through these hills, near the village of Maceira, is a gorge where a small river flows alongside the road to the beaches of Maceira Bay and Porto Novo. A deep ravine fronts the ridge northeast of Vimeiro below the village of Ventosa. Beyond Ventosa, the ridge fades and merges with the rolling hills towards Peniche. In 1808, many vineyards were on the gentler slopes of the hills and several large areas of woodland. These features, combined with the steeper slopes of the ridges, meant that much of the area where the battle would be fought was unsuitable for large-scale cavalry manoeuvres and limited the utility of the French superiority in that arm.

A view over Vimeiro from the ridge behind. The French advanced from the hills on the centre left of the image.
(Author's photo)

The ridge leading up to Ventosa, on the horizon, viewed from the hill above Vimeiro. (Author's photo)

Looking from the rear of the Vimeiro hill towards where the ridge curved towards the sea, where the bulk of Wellesley's troops were on the morning of the battle and where Hill's brigade remained. (Author's photo)

Wellesley had placed the bulk of his troops and eight guns at the southern end of the ridge as it curved west towards the coast, facing the direction he expected Junot to approach from. Hill's 1st Brigade was closest to the sea, then Craufurd's 5th and Nightingall's 3rd. Bowes' 4th Brigade was to the rear of Nightingall. Ferguson's 2nd had two battalions at the end of that section of the ridge directly behind Vimeiro and one across the gorge at the end of the long ridge towards Ventosa. The top of the ridge, which dominated the area, was only occupied by a picket of the 40th Foot. Wellesley wrote that it 'not been occupied, excepting by a picquet, as the camp had been taken up only for one night, and there was no water in the neighbourhood of this height.'[1]

The arrangement of the British troops corresponded generally to the line of battle defined in Wellesley's general order of 7 August, based on the seniority of the brigade commanders. Fane and Anstruther's brigades occupied the Vimeiro hill with Fane's 6-pounders and 9-pounders from the reserve that had been moved there during the night. Acland's brigade was still marching to join the army after landing. The cavalry, British and Portuguese, and reserve artillery were between the Vimeiro hill and the ridge behind. The Portuguese infantry was on the low ground near Vimeiro, and the commissariat and artillery park were also in or near the village. Forty Portuguese artillerymen were under the orders of a British artillery officer and would end up on the left during the action. The remaining 170 were part of the reserve.[2]

According to Murray, Burrard had asked Wellesley to describe the position of his force when they had met on the *Brazen*:

> Sir Arthur … stated, that it had not been taken up originally with a view to defence, so much as to convenience: that the right, however, was placed upon very commanding heights, and presented such advantageous features for defence, that the enemy, although he might try to create alarm there, would hardly venture to make it his principal point of attack: that the ground which would form the centre of the position in the event of an attack had the disadvantage of being detached, it having been necessary to occupy a plateau in advance from the rest of the position, but which covered the village of Vimeiro: that on the left, which was, however, the farthest removed from attack, the slope of the ground was unfavourable to a considerable distance; and that the plan which he had contemplated, in case any part of the enemy's force should approach on that side, was to move out and meet the attack.[3]

Capitaine Salomon Bleuler of the 4e Suisse, with his grenadiers and voltigeurs, had been tasked with a reconnaissance of the allied position. They were accompanied by a staff officer, several men of the 26e Chasseurs à cheval, and Delaborde himself. During the night, they got close enough to the British camp that at sunrise they could hear the barking of dogs and the drumming of horses' hooves on the ground. Unfortunately, one Swiss soldier accidentally fired his musket, which naturally angered Delaborde, and the approach was aborted. The two companies were then split up, with the grenadiers added to the reserve and the voltigeurs detached to Loison's division.[4]

---

1   TNA: WO 1/235: Wellesley to Burrard, 21 August 1808.
2   Gil, *A Infantaria Portuguesa*, vol.I, p.297.
3   Murray, 'Review of History of the War', p.193.
4   Maag, *Schweizertruppen*, vol.I, p.468.

At around 7:00 a.m., the French formed in columns of brigades at the junction of the roads to Vimeiro and Lourinhã, approximately three miles southeast of Vimeiro. High ground shielded them from the allied position. Delaborde's division was in front, with Brenier's brigade on the right of the road and Thomières' on the left. Loison was behind, with Solignac's brigade on the right and Charlot's on the left. Kellermann's grenadiers and the reserve artillery were at the rear. The cavalry was sent ahead and crowned the heights facing Vimeiro.

When he saw the allied position, Junot quickly realised that Wellesley's right, on the steep slopes of the ridge near the sea, was indeed too strong to assault. Junot decided his main attack would be on the village of Vimeiro itself. Delaborde was to take Thomières' brigade and attack the British position on the hill before the village, while Delaborde's other brigade, Brenier's, which had fought so well at Roliça, marched to the right past Carrasqueira and towards Pregança in the hope of turning the allied left flank. Two squadrons of dragoons were sent ahead of Brenier, past Toledo, and occupied the highest point on the Vimeiro-Lourinhã road. Loison would support the attack on Vimeiro with both of his brigades. Kellermann's grenadiers would remain in reserve. Junot would later write to Napoleon, 'the nature of the terrain dictated this disposition, forced moreover by the small number of troops that I had.'[5]

In his memoir, Thiébault is critical of Junot's decision to attack immediately, claiming that better reconnaissance should have been carried out, but, instead, Junot ordered his men forward 'without having seen anything for himself, or knowing upon what and against whom he was marching.'[6] Thiébault also, among others, disapproved of Junot's decision to split Delaborde's division, citing the advantages of keeping a division together under its commander and the units fighting alongside others they were familiar with.[7] However, the divisions and brigades at Vimeiro, while broadly based on the existing structure, had been thrown together from the available units and had spent most of their time in Portugal widely separated. It could also be argued that Delaborde's division still contained the best regiments Junot had, and so it made some sense to spearhead the attacks with them. While he had been at Napoleon's side during many of his greatest victories, Vimeiro was to be Junot's first significant battle command since Nazareth, where he only commanded 500 men.[8]

Pickets

Despite the night's events, when dawn broke over the allied camp on the 21st, there was no sign of an attack. Brigadier General Anstruther wrote in his journal: 'All quiet in the morning. Rode over the right and centre of the principal position with Sir Arthur; he thought the right flank rather thin of troops and ordered Acland's brigade (Queens, 20th, 2 Comps 95th), which had landed in the night, to be placed there in second line.' Wellesley still seems to have expected any attack to come from the south. Anstruther's journal continues:

> Returned to head-quarters about 8; towards nine report received that a patrole of the enemy had appeared on the left, and we saw them drive in the picket in front of the 40th. Other

5   Griffon de Pleineville, *Invasion*, p.209.
6   Butler (trans.), *Thiébault*, Vol.II, p.205.
7   Butler (trans.), *Thiébault*, Vol.II, p.206.
8   Mackay, *Tempest*, p.282.

patroles were soon afterwards seen along the front of the centre. Went out in front of a small wood, about 3/4 of a mile from the left of Fane's brigade, from where I saw distinctly the advance of the enemy. His force appeared to consist of a large corps of cavalry, and six or seven brigades of infantry, marching on a wide front, and advancing rapidly towards our centre. A large column seemed also pointing towards our left but being distant, and partly concealed by the heights, could not see them distinctly. Sent Gordon to report to Sir Arthur these particulars, and that there was every appearance of a General attack.[9]

The 40th Foot was the battalion of Ferguson's brigade that was across the gorge at the start of the long ridge that ran towards Ventosa. Pickets had been placed along the ridge and had been driven in by French cavalry.

At about 8:00 a.m., according to Wellesley's dispatch, the dragoons leading Brenier's column became visible on the heights towards Lourinhã, and he, by then back in his quarters, realised that the French attack would come on his left and not his right. He ordered the two battalions of Ferguson's brigade on the southern side of the gorge to Porto Novo to cross to the northern side and join the 40th and then told Nightingall, with three cannon, to follow along with Acland and Bowes. These brigades were formed across the wide top of the ridge with Ferguson's brigade in the first line, Nightingall in the second, and Acland and Bowes in column behind. They were ordered to advance to meet the French as they approached. The Portuguese infantry was moved from near Vimeiro toward Ribamar, on a height parallel to the one the other brigades marched up and near the sea to protect Porto Novo. Craufurd's brigade supported them. This move was calculated also to threaten the right flank of the French advancing from the direction of Lourinhã. This left only Hill on the section of the ridge on the right, towards the sea. His brigade moved to the centre of those heights to act as a reserve. Wellesley judged Fane and Anstruther sufficiently strong to defend the Vimeiro hill. The 20th Light Dragoons and the Portuguese cavalry remained in the rear of Fane and Anstruther.[10] In front of the left of the British position was an arc of pickets stretching from beyond the road to Toledo around to the right flank of Fane and Anstruther's position.

Captain Jonathan Leach of the 95th Rifles was in a large pine wood to the right front of Fane's position:

> On the night of the 20th [August] I was on an out-picket with a field officer and 100 men. Nothing occurred during the night but about seven in the morning the enemy began to appear on some hills in our front and shortly, some of their cavalry advanced towards the left of our army … several immense columns made their appearance towards the right and centre to take our guns which were in the first line. The pickets being only a handful of men, by way of a lookout to prevent surprise, were ordered to check the French columns by a running fire as much as possible and to retreat firing. We remained in the wood until several men were killed and the shots flew like hail, when the Field officer of the pickets ordered us to retreat precipitately as our artillery dared not fire a shot at the French columns (which were pressing hastily on) till we fell back. We retreated down a vineyard and up another hill before we could gain the British lines, the whole time exposed to the fire of a battalion of infantry. In the retreat, the Field officer of the picket received two

---

9   StAUL: msdep121/8/2/3/4/4: Anstruther's journal, pp.27–29.
10 TNA: WO 1/235: Wellesley to Burrard, 21 August 1808.

wounds of which I believe he is since dead. I received a blow, how I cannot conceive, unless a stone was knocked up by the shot against my thigh, which gave me great pain for some days and made me lame. When we reached the lines, the artillery opened with most wonderful effect.[11]

Major Charles Hill of the 50th, the field officer Leach mentions, survived his wounds. Private John Lowe of the 95th was with Leach:

We were on piquet the night preceding the battle, and Captain Leach, upon visiting rounds, about nine o'clock, came up to where I was posted, and said to me, 'Lowe, don't you hear the tattoo? We must be very much upon the alert, for, depend upon it, it is French music, and we shall be attacked tomorrow!' It was just as the Captain predicted: for I had not been long placed as advanced centinel, early in the morning, before dawn came upon us a host of French light, troops, which it was impossible for a handful of men to stand against. We consequently retired, the French light troops and column following us quickly, till we formed at last behind the 50th.[12]

Staff officer Captain Montague Wynyard recalled that the pickets of the 50th 'retired rather in confusion, but on receiving support from the rifle battalions, formed immediately, and afterwards in good order fell back upon their battalions.'[13] Ensign John Patterson later wrote in the *United Service Journal* that some centre companies of his battalion had been sent out to reinforce the pickets, including his own, but not having been trained in skirmishing, they did not perform well:

Getting bewildered among the corn-fields and olives, the young hands scarce knew which way to turn, the old ones, too, were puzzled, and when a blaze of musketry opened on them, from they knew not where, after firing at random a few shots in the air, they were literally mowed down, falling like ninepins amid the standing corn; the remnant was soon flung back upon the green-jackets, who had by this time ensconced themselves under anything they could find, but the whole were borne in on the position, leaving the scene of action mottled with their slain … Capt. Coote, of the 50th, who commanded one of the battalion companies, seeing the havoc among his helpless soldiers, sent an officer for a section of the Rifles; but before the aid could come, while endeavouring to animate his men, he was shot through the heart by a musket-ball.[14]

In his memoir, Patterson describes Coote as 'a military looking man, strong, and well built, having dark features, and sharp penetrating eyes. – He was somewhat stately in deportment, but withal, a daring soldier, steady and collected in the hour of danger.'[15] Private Benjamin Harris of the 95th came across the body of Captain Arthur Gethin Coote after the battle: 'He was quite dead, and lying on his back. He had been plundered, and his clothes were torn open. Three bullet-holes were

11   Glover & Burnham, *Riflemen of Wellington's Light Division*, pp.55–56.
12   F. Newham (ed.), *The Humble Address of John Lowe* (London: Privately published, 1827), p.30.
13   Anon. 'From Vimeiro to Corunna', p.36.
14   J. Patterson, 'On the Utility and Importance of Light Troops and Cavalry in the Field, Exemplified by Several Instances During the War in Spain', *United Service Journal*, October 1844, p.279.
15   Paterson, *Adventures*, p.42.

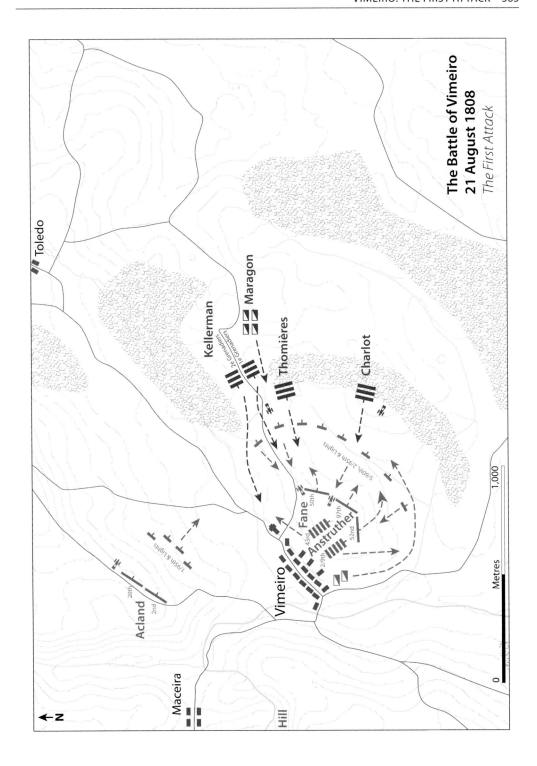

The Battle of Vimeiro
21 August 1808
The First Attack

close together in the pit of his stomach: beside him lay an empty pocket-book, and his epaulette had been pulled from his shoulder.' Harris then took Coote's shoes for himself.[16] Following Coote's death, the men of the 50th fired and retired back up the hill to the rest of the battalion.

Devilish Steady

Brigadier General Robert Anstruther returned to his brigade after visiting the forward pickets and received orders from Wellesley to march to the left, but, by then, the French were too close for him to move. The 50th Foot of Fane's brigade was on the hill's eastern side above Vimeiro, with 9-pounders to their left covering the road leading to the village. Anstruther placed the 97th Foot to the right of the 50th, facing southeast, following the curve of the hill, with the windmill marking the boundary between the brigades. Another brigade of guns was posted near the windmill. The 52nd Foot was in line to the right of the 97th but facing more to the south, following the curve of the hill. The 2/9th Foot was in open column behind and to the right of the 52nd, and the 43rd Foot was in open column behind and to the left of the 97th.[17]

Thomières' brigade, led by Delaborde, marched down the road that led into Vimeiro from the east. Delaborde was still suffering from his wound received at Roliça, and the brigade now only consisted of the two battalions of the 86e Ligne, the elite companies of the 4e Suisse having been detached. They emerged from the woods in front of Fane's position, covered by voltigeurs. They closed rapidly on Fane and Anstruther on the hill and, about 900 yards from the British, inclined to their left to bring their front parallel to the British.[18]

The British artillery opened fire as the French approached, and the pickets fired and retired. The guns would typically start firing spherical case at around 1,500 yards range. The shells would explode in the air 50 yards in front of the target, showering the enemy with carbine balls and shell casing fragments. A spherical case round for a 6-pounder would contain 50 balls. The round for a 5.5-inch howitzer would contain 208. The speed of an advancing column would allow the guns to fire several rounds before the range closed to around 650 yards, and they switched to firing round shot. The gunners would aim in front of the column so the round shot ricocheted off the ground into the ranks, wounding or killing perhaps 30 men. After a couple of rounds and with the range down to less than 350 yards, they would switch to heavy case – turning the cannon into giant shot-guns spewing musket balls. When the enemy was within 100 yards, light case would be fired for the last couple of rounds.[19] Staff officer Captain Wynyard recalled that 'The Artillery at the windmill did great execution, particularly the Brigade of Guns under the orders of Captain Hawker, the fire from which broke the enemy's column three times.'[20] Edmund Hawker was a first lieutenant at the time of the battle, and whilst it is not completely clear from Wynyard's account, the implication is that he is talking of the windmill on the Vimeiro hill rather than the others on the ridge.

The French gunners were far from idle. *Colonel* Prost, Delaborde's artillery commander, went forward with two guns to support the attack, and *colonels* d'Aboville and Foy, with Loison's artillery and the reserve, respectively, used the terrain to take up positions where they could fire on the

16   Curling (ed.), *Recollections*, p.81.
17   StAUL: msdep121/8/2/3/4/4: Anstruther's journal, p.29.
18   StAUL: msdep121/8/2/3/4/4: Anstruther's journal, p.29.
19   Franklin, *Field Artillery*, pp.34–36, 88–89, 93.
20   Anon. 'From Vimeiro to Corunna', p.36.

British position. However, most of the French pieces were of smaller calibre than the British guns, being mostly Portuguese 3- or 4-pounders.[21] Many of the artillery horses were killed, and Prost and Foy were wounded.

Fane sent out nearly all the riflemen of the five companies of the 5/60th and the four of the 2/95th that were not already with the pickets to skirmish with the voltigeurs. Benjamin Harris of the 95th was amongst them:

> The French came down upon us in a column, and the Riflemen immediately commenced a sharp fire upon them from whatever cover they could get a shelter behind, whilst our cannon played upon them from our rear. I saw regular lanes torn through their ranks as they advanced, which were immediately closed up again as they marched steadily on. Whenever we saw a round shot thus go through the mass, we raised a shout of delight.[22]

Charles Leslie (29th Foot) mentions an event that he must have heard second-hand:

> In this battle the 60th Riflemen, who were all Germans, showed great tact in taking advantage of the ground, and dexterity in the use of their arms. General Fane, who commanded the light troops, observing one of these men successfully hit one or two French officers who were gallantly exposing themselves in front leading on their men, exclaimed in the excitement of the moment, 'Well done, my fine fellow! I will give you half a doubloon for every other one you bring down' The man coolly loaded again, fired, and hit another, then looking at the General, he said gravely, 'by Got, I vill make my vortune'.[23]

As the riflemen were slowly driven back, Anstruther sent out the light company of the 97th and three companies of the 52nd to cover the retreat of the riflemen.[24] Leach and his company of the 95th fell back towards the 97th and passed around its right flank to join the other three companies. Many of the accounts mention a lot of French skirmishers, so it may have been the case that not only the voltigeur companies were deployed as skirmishers. It may also be the case that the British light and rifle troops were not forced back by the fire of their French counterparts but by the relentless advance of the column. It was not the job of skirmishers to stop a column but just to harass it and prevent the enemy light troops from harassing their own artillery and line troops and to get out of the way at the right moment so the line troops could open fire.

As Junot could see that Delaborde was suffering heavy casualties, he ordered Loison to support him with Charlot's brigade. When he had seen Wellesley moving troops onto the ridge to counter Brenier's flanking move, Junot sent Solignac's brigade to reinforce Brenier's on the flank, again splitting up a division. Thiébault wrote in his memoir:

> In this way another brigade was rendered useless on our right, while on our left another brigade was devoted to useless destruction. Yet even now, if Loison had marched with his right brigade, we should at least have had a General of division, that is, a centre of

---

21   Thiébault, *l'Expédition*, pp.196–197.
22   Curling (ed.), *Recollections*, pp.48–49.
23   Leslie, *Journal*, p.53.
24   StAUL: msdep121/8/2/3/4/4: Anstruther's journal, p.30.

command at each centre of operations; while the result of sending him to the ground occupied by Delaborde was that on one side we had, with two brigades, two Generals of division not likely to agree well, while on the other, with an equal number of troops, we had two Generals of brigade who never could agree.[25]

So, as Thomières' brigade closed with Fane's, Charlot's brigade, consisting of the 3/32e and 3/82e Ligne, emerged from a copse and approached Anstruther's brigade.

The three companies of the 50th Foot that had been skirmishing with the pickets also steadily withdrew as Thomières' brigade came on. They eventually formed up on rising ground a little to the front of the rest of the battalion. The 50th's commanding officer, Lieutenant Colonel George Walker, watched the approaching column and timed his response well:

> A massive column of the enemy composed of five regiments in close order of half battalions, supported by seven pieces of cannon, and under the command of the General of division, Loisson [sic], made a rapid march towards the hill, and though much shaken by the steady fire of the artillery, after a short pause behind a hedge to recover, it again continued to advance; till Lieutenant-Colonel Robe, R.A., no longer able to use the guns, considered them lost. Up to this time the 50th had remained at ordered arms, but as it was impossible, on the ground on which it stood, to contend against so superior a force, and Colonel Walker, having observed that the enemy's column inclined to the left, proposed to Brigadier General Fane to attempt to turn its flank by a wheel of the right wing. Permission for this having been obtained, this wing was immediately thrown into echelon of companies of about four paces to the left, advanced thus for a short distance, and then ordered to form line to the left. The rapidity, however, of the enemy's advance, and their having already opened a confused though very hot fire from the flank of their column – though only two companies of the wings were yet formed – these were so nearly in contact with end bearing on the angle of the column that Colonel Walker, thinking no time was to be lost, ordered an immediate volley and charge. The result exceeded his most sanguine expectation. The angle was instantly broken, and the drivers of the three guns advanced in front, alarmed at the fire in their rear, cutting the traces of their horses, and rushing back with them, created great confusion, which by the time the three outer companies could arrive to take part in the charge, became General. Then this immense mass, so threatening in its appearance but a few minutes before, became in an instant an ungovernable mob, carrying off its officers and flying like a flock of sheep, almost without resistance, for upwards of two miles.[26]

The 50th directly faced only two battalions, led by Delaborde, rather than five regiments led by Loison. Lieutenant Colonel Robe wrote after the battle that the French columns' 'advance was so apparently determined, that I was obliged to retire my guns to a neighbouring height, where being well supported by the 50th Regiment the matter was settled.'[27]

---

25   Butler (trans.), *Thiébault*, vol.II, p.207.
26   Orderly room records, 17 October 1812, quoted in A.E. Fyler, *The History of the 50th or (The Queen's Own) Regiment* (London: Chapman & Hall, 1895), pp.105–106.
27   TNA: WO 55/1193: Robe to Macleod, 21 August 1808.

Ensign Patterson recalled, 'When the [French], in a compact mass, arrived sufficiently up the hill, now bristled with bayonets, the black cuffs poured in a well directed volley upon the dense array. Then, cheering loudly, and led on by its gallant chief, the whole regiment rushed forward to the charge, penetrated the formidable columns, and carried all before it.'[28] Captain Wynyard wrote: 'The 50th soon after this took a more advantageous position where they were covered in some measure by a bank and in that situation gained the admiration of the whole Army by keeping the French column in check and saving two of our guns, which but for them, must have fallen into the enemy's hands.'[29] Patterson later called the 50th's charge 'one of the most decisive things of the kind that ever happened. Those alone who witnessed it can form an adequate idea of its impetuosity; affording, beyond all doubt, a most unanswerable proof of the effect which confidence will have upon the minds of men, who have before them the encouragement and example of their leader.'[30] Delaborde, impressed by the regiment, later requested that Lieutenant Colonel Walker be introduced to him.[31] Wellesley later said of the 50th at Vimeiro that they were 'not a good-looking regiment, but devilish steady, who received them admirably, and brought them to a full stop immediately, and soon drove them back...'[32] According to Landmann the fleeing French, with their white linen coats, had 'exactly the appearance of an immense flock of sheep scampering away from the much-dreaded shepherd's dog.'[33]

Private John Lowe (95th Foot) related a story that must have occurred at about this point in the battle:

> I saw the General [Fane], after having exerted his vigilant eye and voice like thunder in one direction, rush in a contrary one, and make a desperate back blow with his sword at an English Artillery-man, who, it was to be feared, through inexpertness, or faint-heartedness, or what not, was thinning the ranks of the 50th instead of the French ... his successor, as if to repair the damage done, directed the gun so accurately, that he quickly produced a gap, and a wave in the French column, which I cannot liken to any thing better than the gates of a fortified town being suddenly made to turn upon their hinges, and open...[34]

Private Benjamin Harris witnessed what was possibly the same event, but in his account, it was a red-haired fellow gunner who knocked the man down with his fist for missing the French column and does not mention a shot hitting the 50th by mistake.[35] Harris was on the flanks of the French column and witnessed the charge, as he much later related to a former officer of his acquaintance long after the wars:

> I heard the whole line (as if affronted at the Frenchmen impudence) crying out, 'D—n them – charge them, charge them.' They did indeed much outnumber us in skirmishers, and we

28 Patterson, *Adventures*, pp.45–46.
29 Anon. 'From Vimeiro to Corunna', p.36.
30 Patterson, *Camps and Quarters*, vol.I, p.215.
31 Patterson, *Camps and Quarters*, vol.I, p.216.
32 Jennings, *Croker Papers*, vol.II, p.122.
33 Landmann, *Recollections*, vol.II, p.214.
34 Newham (ed.), *Humble Address*, pp.31–32.
35 Curling (ed.), *Recollections*, p.56.

368 SO JUST AND GLORIOUS A CAUSE

were giving ground (firing and retiring), but at the same time most wickedly inclined and desirous of doing all the mischief we possibly could. I noticed General Fane to call out to the regiments in rear to restrain them, telling them he wished them to keep their ground, and not advance at that time. At last he gave the word, and down they all came, through a tremendous fire, opened upon them, of cannon and musketry, and dreadful was the slaughter as they rushed on. I think I never beheld anything more terrible than the charge of these regiments; and as they came up with us we sprung up, gave one hearty cheer, and charged along with them, treading upon our dead and wounded comrades, who lay thick in our front. The 50th were next me as we went, and I recollect the firmness with which they rushed on that charge, appearing like a wall of iron.[36]

At around 9:30 a.m., Wellesley asked Lieutenant Colonel Torrens to ride quickly to Fane and Anstruther with orders to remain in their position on the hill because he could see another French column forming in the woods nearby. Torrens later said, 'On my arrival at that position I found that General Fane had advanced a little way in front, and was engaged with some French light troops. I followed him, and delivered those orders, and he consequently retired.'[37] Wellesley must have ridden to Fane and Anstruther's position soon after as Sir Harry Burrard arrived on the Vimeiro hill at around 10:00 a.m. and met him there.

At 8:30 a.m., three horses had been brought to the beach at Porto Novo for Burrard, Clinton and Murray. As soon as the mounts were observed from the deck of the *Alfred*, the officers were rowed ashore and then rode towards Vimeiro. They soon heard the sound of guns and proceeded through vineyards to the rear of where the 50th Foot was fighting up to the top of the hill, where they met Wellesley. He explained the situation to Burrard, who, satisfied with the dispositions, told him to carry on.[38] As Burrard stated in his dispatch, 'I was fortunate enough to reach the field of action in time to witness and approve of every disposition that had been, and was afterwards made by Sir A. Wellesley; his comprehensive mind furnishing a ready resource in every emergency, and rendering it quite unnecessary to direct any alteration.'[39]

At almost the same time Thomières' brigade was routed by the 50th, Charlot's was closing within 150 yards of the British position. Anstruther recorded what happened next in his journal:

Ordered the 97th, who were concealed behind a dip of the ground, to rise and fire – after two or three rounds, they began to advance from the position and finding it impossible to stop them without great risque, ordered the 52nd to support them on their right and if possible to turn the left of the enemy. This they did very dextrously whilst the 97th made a vigorous attack in front. The enemy soon gave way and was pursued to the skirts of the wood beyond which his superiority in cavalry made it imprudent to advance; rallied the 97th and 52d and leaving strong pickets in the wood, brought them back to the position: the 9th remained in reserve and was but little engaged.[40]

36   H. Curling, 'The Bayonet', *United Service Journal*, July 1839, p.400.
37   Anon., *Proceedings*, pp.102–103.
38   TNA: WO 1/415: Burrard's narrative.
39   TNA: WO 1/235: Burrard to Castlereagh, 21 August 1808.
40   StAUL: msdep121/8/2/3/4/4: Anstruther's journal, pp.30–31.

In his dispatch, Wellesley mentions that the 52nd advanced in column to attack the French flank. At one point in the action, one of Wellesley's aides de camp rode up to Anstruther and said another unit was being sent to his assistance. Anstruther replied, 'Sir, I am not pressed, and I want no assistance. I am beating the French, and am able to beat them whenever I meet them.'[41]

Anstruther may have dismissed the 2/9th Foot's contribution as 'but little engaged', and even forgot to mention them in his report to Wellesley so that he, in turn, left them out of his dispatch, but their commander, Lieutenant Colonel John Cameron, gave a fuller account of the battalion's actions in a letter to his sister. After describing the deployment of the brigade, he wrote:

> The enemy took not a moment in occupying the pinewood and vineyards on the right. A body of cavalry threatening the right, I was ordered to form column at quarter distance, ready to form square. The cavalry went away to their right, on which the 9th formed line, each company giving its fire in succession as it came up. The fire was kept up til the enemy had abandoned the pinewood, some little time before which three companies of the 52nd were sent in pursuit.[42]

For 16-year-old Ensign Colin Campbell of the 2/9th, it was the first time he had been in action, and his company commander took him to the front of the battalion, in full view of the French guns, and walked him up and down to give the boy some confidence. Campbell, who became Field Marshal Lord Clyde and fought in the Crimea and Indian Mutiny, later said, 'It was the greatest kindness that could have been shown me at such a time, and through life I have felt grateful for it.'[43]

Ensign Charles Paget (52nd Foot) recorded his experiences of the battle in his journal:

> Brigade wheeled into line, & marched to the top of the height, formed obliquely in the rear of each other. Distinctly perceived the French columns manoeuvring on the opposite hills, & their riflemen (dressed in long white frocks) being detached from them, to the Furse and woods. – The enemy began, a kind of independent fire, on our lines. When the Gen'l sent to us to 'Remember Egypt'. Several men wounded fell out. Captain Ewart and Lt. Bell.
>
> Five men of the 97th knocked down by a Cannon Ball, one killed. Men became impatient to fire, being now in the thick of it; The infantry of the enemy gained ground on the right, when three of our companies were ordered to the valley opposite them; Reserved our fire till the Enemy drew nearer, when it was open'd with double fury; after three rounds, we observed them running in all directions, upon which three cheers were generally given; & the advance sounded; When below the companies extended & each had its separate duty.[44]

With Thomières' and Charlot's brigades driven back, Junot committed his reserve of the two regiments of grenadiers. Junot marched with *colonel* Adrien Saint Clair's first grenadier regiment towards the Vimeiro hill. *Général de division* Kellermann advanced with the second grenadier regiment around Fane's left flank and towards the village of Vimeiro via the road leading into it from the north. Thiébault characterises the state of the French at this point in the battle:

41   *The Universal Magazine*, April 1809, p.350.
42   Glover (ed.), *Line Infantry*, pp.13–14.
43   L. Shadwell, *The Life of Colin Campbell, Lord Clyde* (Edinburgh: Blackwood, 1881), vol.I, p.5.
44   NAM: 1985-04-101: Journal in Portugal and Spain 1808, 1809, entry 21 August 1808.

... as our position, became every minute more disastrous, the commander-in-chief, followed by me, went himself to this ill-starred ground. The result was that, while two out of our five brigades were 'in the air,' with no common understanding or action, and indeed were soon recalled, nearly the whole English army being free to act against them, on our left, our three remaining brigades, cut up by artillery fire, were led, besides their brigadiers, by three generals of division, a chief of the staff, and a commander-in-chief, and that in a situation where Napoleon himself could have done no more than a corporal, that is, when there was no choice save to die or to retreat.[45]

Saint Clair's grenadiers marched in a column of platoons.[46] A platoon was a tactical unit but often corresponded to the administrative company, so the columns comprised each company marching in three ranks, one behind the other. With skirmishers covering the flanks and front. *Capitiane* Bleuler (4e Suisse) was with his grenadiers:

The charge was sounded [on the drums] but the music lost itself in the shouting of 'Vive l'empereur!' We came closer and closer to the truly formidable position of the English … The cannonballs took away whole ranks and burst in the following pelotons. Junot remained at the head in his rich uniform as a senior General. One of the first cannonballs knocked down the Frenchmen who had been assigned to my platoon and the sergent de remplacement, whom I immediately replaced with one of my non-commissioned officers. Junot was now on the left wing of the column and cheered us on. Our artillery followed us on the flanks. We were about 50 yards from the English lines, still in a closed column, when the column stopped to deploy; a rolling volley like a drum roll received us as I had never heard it. The first platoons of our column fell, the gunners of our artillery fell and the horses were killed; the column was thrown back into the ravine that we had just passed at a rapid pace.[47]

The grenadiers would have faced the volleys of the 50th and 97th, re-formed on the hill, plus the riflemen of Fane's brigade. The first two platoons were wiped out, and the grenadiers were prevented from deploying into line. They instead marched obliquely to their right, to the ravine.[48]

Capitaine Jaques Louis Hulot was with the artillery of the reserve. He advanced on the flank of the grenadiers and was ordered to a position where, although sheltered from British artillery fire, a dip in the terrain meant they could fire only shells at the enemy. He was looking at where to reposition his guns for greater effect when a British column began to head towards his guns. He told his men to load with canister, but a mass of retreating French infantry got in the way. He wrote:

In vain, we wanted to stop this stampede; I took a few steps back to occupy and close the outlets of a neighbouring village, in front of which I set up my guns; they were, like me, who was on horseback, upset several times by these rushing waves. However, none of my

---

45   Butler (trans.), *Thiébault*, vol.II, p.207.
46   Foy, *Invasion*, p.171.
47   Maag, *Schweizertruppen*, vol.I, pp.470–471. Maag adds a footnote that Bleuler seems to use the description of the battle contained in Foy's history. His account does seem confused as some events he claims to have witnessed occurred at opposite ends of the battlefield.
48   Foy, *Invasion*, p.172.

artillerymen, except the wounded, thought of giving up and did not abandon the battery, and if, as I requested of the infantry, these pieces had been supported by a single battalion, we would have re-established the fight in the village and given our regiments and divisions time to rally. But at that moment I cried out to the deaf.[49]

The other section of guns with the reserve was encouraged into a poor position by infantry officers, too close to the British, and lost three-quarters of its men and horses killed or wounded before it could withdraw. A friend of Hulot's, *lieutenant* Thomas Louis Alexandre Dejort, was with those guns:

> A bullet shattered the lower jaw of Lieutenant Dejort who, nevertheless, insisted on remaining at his pieces. But his captain ordered him to go and have it bandaged; he was riding his horse when a second shot broke his thigh; this same captain had also just been wounded, and the English were arriving at his battery. Then the young student from the École Polytechnique took his pistol and blew his brains out. That is what those of the gunners who survived repeated to me on the evening of the incident.[50]

Artillery *lieutenant* Boileau, aide de camp to Junot's artillery commander *colonel* Taviel, took command of some guns that had withdrawn in disorder after their commander had been wounded. Boileau rallied the gunners, positioned the guns, and kept up a well-directed fire to cover the retreating infantry.[51] At some point after the French retreat began, Fane, his aide Lieutenant John Bringhurst, the brigade major Maclean, Captain Landmann, and Fane's orderly, Corporal Johann Schwalbach of the 5/60th, chased down a French gun that was trying to withdraw. Fane fired his pistol at one of the horses to bring it down to halt the gun's flight and capture it.[52] Whether it was for his part in the capture or other services, Schwalbach was later commissioned into the Portuguese service. Serving with the Caçadores, he fought through the rest of the Peninsular War. He remained in the Portuguese army afterwards, rose to general rank and was ennobled as a viscount.[53]

As Kellermann and the other regiment of grenadiers neared the village, Anstruther sent the 43rd Foot to support Fane. The 43rd placed two companies in the houses of the village.[54]

Ensign George Jackson of the 43rd related his part in the battle to his brother. After writing about the approach of the French columns, he stated:

> … and now we (who had been standing all this time in open column, in rear of our artillery), were ordered to advance in front of the guns, when we took up a sort of a position in rear of a small ditch (or bank), and had it not been for the unevenness of the ground, *and the enemy firing too high*, I think our loss would have been immense, for their shot rattled about us like hail, while we could not see a man of them. I think there was some bad Generalship on our side, – had we been brought forward sooner, or placed on the high

---

49   Hulot, *Souvenirs*, p.235.
50   Hulot, *Souvenirs*, p.240.
51   Beauvais de Preau, *Victoires, Conquêtes*, vol.18, p.108.
52   Landmann, *Recollections*, vol.II, p.223.
53   Griffith, *Riflemen*, p.209.
54   StAUL: msdep121/8/2/3/4/4: Anstruther's journal, p.30.

ground instead of the side of the hill, we might have repulsed them by a charge, but before we knew where they were, they had gained the hill above us, and poured a tremendous fire on us. We were now ordered to move to our left, but to effect that without disorder was impossible, – we were obliged to make the best of our way through some vineyards, and in consequence of the ground being heavy, and the vines very thick, our loss here was very great; and I thank God that while the poor fellows dropped in all directions around me, I escaped unhurt In our situation, I think any troops but light bobs, must have been totally routed, but being joined by a few riflemen, we rallied behind a bank, and meeting a column of the enemy in a narrow lane, we got above them on both sides, and drove them back, leaving the lane filled with their killed and wounded; then following them through the woods, we beat them in all directions.[55]

Jackson sent his letter to the *United Service Journal* as part of a rebuttal of John Patterson's (50th Foot) criticism of the performance of the light infantry at Vimeiro and the greater utility of rifles for light troops.[56] In his counter-argument, Jackson went on to write:

This letter was written at a time, and under circumstances, when my means of information as to numbers and many other particulars, must have been imperfect, and my judgment on some points which I touched on, immature. As, for instance, where I venture a remark on the bad Generalship in not bringing the regiment forward sooner, &c, I have since learned to believe, that all the dispositions were well and judiciously made, that the advance of the enemy's column through the valley was perceived by our commanders long before I imagined; and provided for by our move to the left, which brought us in contact with them, by throwing us across the valley and hollow road, so as completely to bar their progress in that direction. When I spoke of the shot rattling about us like hail, &c, I gave the impressions of an inexperienced youngster, and have since learned to consider that irregular fire of their advancing light skirmishers as insignificant, and as well as I recollect our chief loss was not while we stood in line, but on our moving down the side of the hill to occupy the valley; the upper part of the descent was extremely steep, so that we could keep no order in getting down, and on the more level part below we had to force our way through the vines, which are not there supported by stakes like peas, at they are generally in France, &c, but lying along the ground they trip one up at every step, and though favourable to skirmishers, they greatly impede any attempt at a regular movement. It was, I think, while getting down, and while entangled among those vines, that we suffered most, receiving just then a heavy fire from a large body of troops, part of those, as it appeared to me, who were pressing forward along the ridge to force the point near to which our line had been formed, and where they were met with so cordial a reception from the gallant old 50th. However, we rallied quickly, got our companies in order, and occupied points where we were soon enabled to repay with interest the debt we had so recently incurred; and I can vouch for it, that so far from 'firing at the clouds' nothing

---

55   G.B.J, 'Battle of Vimiera – Second Battalion, 43d – "Unus quorum,"' *United Service Journal*, March 1845, pp.445–446. Only the initials G.B.J. are used, but Jackson can be identified from the Army List.

56   J. Patterson, 'On the Utility and Importance of Light Troops and Cavalry in the Field, Exemplified by Several Instances During the War in Spain', *United Service Journal*, October 1844, pp.278–283. Patterson criticises the 43rd for being raw and not having the skills of light infantry.

could be steadier or better directed than the fire we kept up. The order to the officers was to attend particularly to it; our constant caution to the men was *fire low, aim steadily*, and *fire low*, – and well did the men obey that order, their firing was *excellent*, and it excited our admiration to observe those young soldiers, not one of whom, I believe, had ever seen a shot fired in anger before, acquit themselves so admirably; and we certainly did not consider that we should have inflicted more loss on our enemy, if the rifle had been our weapon instead of the musket, of which those furnished to us and the 52d were of rather a superior description to that in General use at the time, and *greatly superior* to those with which the French troops were armed.[57]

Anstruther relates a story that would seem to confirm the confusion of the 43rd's advance through the vineyards to the edge of the village. The sergeant major of the 2/43rd, Lawrence Steel, was at the front of his battalion's column as it moved to support Fane's left. After jumping over a hedge, he found himself amongst some French concealed behind it. One grabbed him, but he drew a pistol, shot him and then killed another with his sword. As more of the 43rd came over the hedge, the rest of the French were killed or taken prisoner.[58] Private Anthony Hamilton of the 43rd was posted close by the road that led into Vimeiro:

> It was not only a hot day but also a hot fight, and one of our men by the name of McArthur, who stood by me, having opened his mouth to catch a little fresh air, a bullet from the enemy at that moment entered his mouth obliquely, which he never perceived, until I told him his neck was covered with blood. He, however, kept the field until the battle was over.[59]

Observing from the ridge above the village, Lieutenant Leslie (29th Foot) saw:

> … a party of the 43rd Light Infantry stealing out of the village and moving behind a wall to gain the right flank of the enemy's lines, on which they opened a fire at the moment when the enemy came in contact with our troops in position. The French had been allowed to come close, then our gallant fellows, suddenly springing up, rapidly poured on them two or three volleys with great precision, and rushing on, charged with the bayonet.[60]

Part of the 2/43rd had been ordered into the churchyard of the village church and fired down on the French from the walls. The fighting in the vineyards at the edge of the village and the narrow streets became confused and close, but the 43rd managed to stop the grenadiers, who then retreated in disorder, leaving their guns and many dead and wounded behind them.

The four companies of the 2/95th were ordered to reinforce the 2/43rd but arrived after the French were already retreating and joined in the pursuit.[61]

---

57   G.B.J, 'Battle of Vimiera', pp.446–447.

58   StAUL: msdep121/8/2/3/4/4: Anstruther's journal, p.35. Anstruther does not name Steel, and his name has been taken from the 2/43rd paylist (TNA: WO 12/5633).

59   A. Hamilton, *Hamilton's Campaign with Moore and Wellington during the Peninsular War* (Troy: privately published, 1847), p.14.

60   Leslie, *Journal*, pp.49–50.

61   Lowe, *Humble Address*, p.31.

The church at Vimeiro from which part of the 2/43rd Foot fired on the French grenadiers.

As Acland's brigade moved from its original position to the long ridge behind the village, it was on the flank of the grenadiers. The British guns on the heights maintained a constant cannonade on the column. Historian Nick Lipscombe postulates that Kellermann would have seen the guns with the brigades on the ridge and calculated on suffering casualties from standard artillery rounds, but that the 'black rain' of spherical case came as a surprise.[62] The guns inflicted severe casualties on the grenadiers; they lost around 200 men in under four minutes.[63] Captain Wynyard also credits the artillery on the ridge with inflicting severe losses on the column of grenadiers.[64]

Acland sent the light companies of the 2nd and 20th Foot and his two companies of the 1/95th Rifles to clear the French from wood at the ridge's base on the column's flank. Captain Charles Steevens, commander of the 20th's light company, later wrote:

> …my company (the light company) behaved nobly on the occasion; I had only one man wounded, we knocked over several of the enemy, and took many prisoners; the French hid

62 Lipscombe, *Guns*, p.43.
63 Beauvais de Preau, *Victoires, Conquêtes*, vol.18, p.107.
64 Anon. 'From Vimeiro to Corunna', p.36.

themselves behind the trees and kept up a very heavy fire, but we advanced on them very rapidly, and drove them away in all directions, pouring in volley after volley of musketry.[65]

Steevens was ill on the day of the battle and in pain but could not bear the thought of being left on board a transport and not being at the head of his company.

The British and Portuguese cavalry had been held in reserve behind the Vimeiro hill, but Lieutenant Colonel Taylor, commander of the 20th Light Dragoons, had already had his horse wounded earlier in the day when he had reconnoitred French lines. He declared that 'he was determined for honour for himself and his regiment that day.'[66] Sergeant Landsheit described the experience of waiting with the rest of the cavalry behind the hill while the Fane and Anstruther's brigades held out against the French columns but could not see what was happening. He then wrote:

Colonel Taylor, who commanded us, repeatedly asked leave to charge, but was on each occasion held back, by the assurance that the proper moment was not yet come; till at last General Fane rode up and exclaimed, 'Now, Twentieth! now we want you. At them, my lads, and let them see what you are made of.' Then came the word, 'threes about and forward,' and with the rapidity of thought we swept round the elbow of the hill, and the battle lay before us.[67]

The Light Dragoons fielded just over 300 men at Vimeiro and the Portuguese around 260. They formed in half squadrons, with the 20th in the centre and the Portuguese on the flanks. Landsheit continued:

'Now, Twentieth! now !' shouted Sir Arthur, while his Staff clapped their hands and gave us a cheer; the sound of which was still in our ears, when we put our horses to their speed. The Portuguese likewise pushed forward, but through the dust which entirely enveloped us, the enemy threw in a fire, which seemed to have the effect of paralyzing altogether our handsome allies. Right and left they pulled up, as if by word of command, and we never saw more of them till the battle was over. But we went very differently to work. In an instant we were in the heart of the French cavalry, cutting and hacking, and upsetting men and horses in the most extraordinary manner possible, till they broke and fled in every direction, and then we fell upon the infantry. It was here that our gallant Colonel met his fate. He rode that day a horse, which was so hot that not all his exertions would suffice to control it, and he was carried headlong upon the bayonets of the French infantry, a corporal of whom shot him through the heart.[68]

Wellesley's presence and encouragement are perhaps a slight fiction, and not all the Portuguese cavalry failed to charge. Joaquim Paes de Sá, a Portuguese officer, wrote to Freire, 'I always found myself in the midst of the fire and the bullets, and one even touched my horse and another killed

65 Steevens (ed.), *Reminiscences*, pp.52–53.
66 *The Gentleman's Magazine*, November 1808, p.963.
67 Gleig (ed.), *Hussar*, vol.I, pp.268–269.
68 Gleig (ed.), *Hussar*, vol.I, pp.269–270.

a soldier near me … Our cavalry joined in the action and the Police commander and a cadet died, and others were wounded, but I must say that the most praiseworthy of all was Lieutenant Antonio Pinto.[69] Unfortunately, he does not say why Pinto deserved particular praise.

As the allied cavalry charged into the fleeing French troops, they became increasingly broken up, and the mêlée became confused as the combat devolved into small groups of horsemen surrounded by French infantry and shrouded in dust. The 26e Chasseurs à cheval led by *chef d'escadron* Prince de Salm, Junot's guard led by *colonel* de Grandsaignes – Junot's first aide de camp – and two provisional regiments of dragoons commanded by *majors* Leclerc and Thérond, charged in turn and drove back the allied cavalry. Thérond distinguished himself by saving the life of Junot, who, in an attempt to stop the French retreat, had gone too far forward with two of his other aides.[70]

The fighting became desperate, with the British dragoons disordered and increasingly enclosed by fences and vineyards. Landsheit again:

> While we were thus situated, vainly looking for an aperture through which to make a bolt, one of our men … was maintaining a most unequal combat outside the close, with four French Dragoons that beset him together. An active and powerful man himself, he was particularly fortunate in the charger which he bestrode – a noble stallion which did his part in the melée, not less effectually than his master. The animal bit, kicked, lashed out with his fore-feet, and wheeled about and about like a piece of machinery, screaming all the time; while the rider, now catching a blow, now parrying a thrust, seemed invulnerable. At last he clove one enemy to the teeth, and with a back stroke took another across the face, and sent him from his saddle. The other two hung back, and made signs to some of their comrades, but these had no time to help them, for a hearty British cheer sounded above the battle, and the 50th regiment advanced in line with fixed bayonets. The consequence was, an immediate flight by the enemy, who had calculated on making every man of the 20th prisoners.[71]

The 50th Foot had pursued the French far beyond their initial position on the hill:

> On clearing a wood, Colonel Walker, observing a party of cavalry to be drawn up on a small plain threatening his flank, deemed it necessary to put a stop to the pursuit, as a party of the 20th Dragoons, which had previously joined in it, had already (through getting entangled in a wood) suffered so seriously as to be incapable of affording any further assistance. Having from hence reported his situation and received Brigadier-General Fane's orders, Colonel Walker retired with the regiment to his former position, while the enemy continued their retreat eastward in a direction different from that of their resources.[72]

George E. Jaycock, in his book *Wellington's Command*, claims that ordering the cavalry forward was a mistake by Wellesley, given the French superiority in that arm.[73] Leaving aside that it is far from certain that Wellesley did order the charge, it could also be argued that conserving the

69   Paes to Freire, 22 August 1808, in 'Documentos', pp.197–198.
70   Griffon de Pleineville, *Invasion*, p.220.
71   Gleig (ed.), *Hussar*, vol.I, pp.271–272.
72   Fyler, *The History of the 50th*, pp.106–107.
73   Jaycock, *Command*, p.57.

cavalry for a general pursuit may have been more profitable than using them at the point they charged. But both arguments presuppose that the cavalry could not have been expected to perform a short, controlled charge to shatter the retreating infantry and then rally and return to British lines. The undisciplined nature of their charge took them far beyond the point where they should have stopped and turned the charge into the disaster it became. It cost the dragoons 20 men dead, 24 wounded, and 11 prisoners, plus 30 dead horses, 10 wounded, and one missing. Taylor was thought to have been wounded and then captured, but his body was found on the field the next day.

The action around the village of Vimeiro ended at around 10:30 a.m. However, the battle was far from over. Several accounts state that the second attack down the ridge from Ventosa only began once the attacks on Vimeiro had failed. Junot later explained to Napoleon that he had intended his two attacks to develop differently, writing that the skirmishers in front of the troops tasked with attacking the Vimeiro hill started the action before the column marching to the British left, which was meant to attack first, had reached its position.[74]

---

74   Griffon de Pleineville, *Invasion*, p.212.

16

Vimeiro: The Second Attack

Brenier had marched his brigade north to turn Wellesley's left flank and approach down the long ridge along the Lourinhã road. However, when he came to the steep, rugged valley near Toledo, he deemed it impassable for his guns and decided to take a circuitous route further north. When Solignac, sent by Junot after Brenier when he saw Wellesley reinforcing his left, arrived at the same defile, he found a point that was passable and then ascended the slopes of the ridge and arrived on the top near the settlement of Ventosa before Brenier. Well before the main body of either brigade arrived on the ridge, French dragoons encountered British pickets there.

After the allied army had stood to before daybreak, and there was no sign of a French attack, Ferguson and his aides returned to their quarters in Vimeiro. At around 8:00 a.m., Ferguson's aide de camp, William Warre, was woken by a sergeant who told him that the 40th's pickets had been driven in and that the French were advancing. Warre informed Ferguson, and they quickly rode up to the long ridge. They could see the French marching towards Fane and Anstruther's position and a strong column marching to turn the allies' left flank. Warre commented in a letter, 'but as they had to make a considerable round, we had full time to prepare.'[1] It is not clear if it was Brenier's or Solignac's columns that was spotted, or even both.

Warre was sent to tell Wellesley of the impending attack, and the British commander himself rode onto the ridge. In his dispatch, Wellesley wrote, 'The enemy first appeared about 8 o'clock in the morning, in large bodies of cavalry on our left, upon the heights on the road to Lourinha; and it was soon obvious that the attack would be made upon our advanced guard and the left of our position'.[2] Wellesley ordered the other battalions of Ferguson's brigade, followed by Nightingall's, Bowes's and Acland's brigades, onto the ridge, and the Portuguese infantry and Craufurd's brigade to a position nearer to the sea to protect Porto Novo and Maceira. Several accounts, including Warre's, mention Spencer commanding this left wing of the allied army.[3] Ferguson halted his brigade before reaching the flat top of the highest part of the ridge near Ventosa, and Nightingall's brigade arrived a little later and formed on their left. Bowes remained in reserve behind, and Acland halted overlooking Vimeiro. Ferguson's position, about a third of the way up the long incline of the ridge, seems to have been adopted intentionally as the most advantageous place to await the approach of the French. In no account is it clear how strong the forces were that had driven in the

---

1   Warre, *Letters*, pp.25, 31.
2   TNA: WO 1/235: Wellesley to Burrard, 21 August 1808.
3   Warre, *Letters*, p.26.

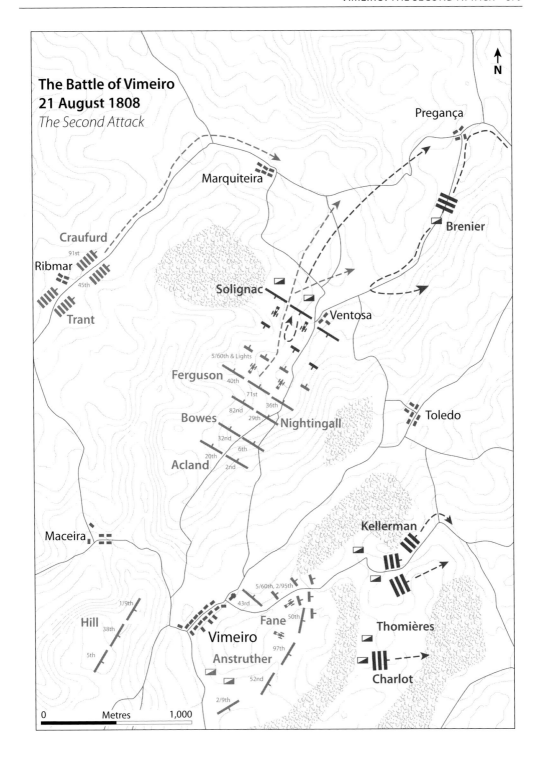

The Battle of Vimeiro
21 August 1808
The Second Attack

N

Pregança

Marquiteira

Brenier

Craufurd
91st
Ribmar
45th
Solignac
Trant

Ventosa

5/60th & Lights
Ferguson   40th
71st
82nd   36th
Bowes   29th   Nightingall

Toledo

32nd
20th   6th
Acland   2nd

Kellerman

Maceira

5/60th, 2/95th
43rd
1/9th
Hill   38th   Fane   50th
5th
Vimeiro
97th
Anstruther
52nd
2/9th

Thomières

Charlot

0   Metres   1,000

Looking down the ridge in the direction that Ferguson's, Nightingall's, Bowes's and Acland's brigades marched from. The location the photograph was taken from would have been out of sight of any French forces at Ventosa due to the slope of the hill. (Author's photo)

40th's pickets, but it does seem unlikely that French infantry had arrived in any significant force at Ventosa at this stage.

The 36th Foot, which had been camped in the valley behind Vimeiro, was marching with the rest of Ferguson's brigade up to the ridge within 10 minutes of the 40th beating to arms as the sounds of the first French attack reached them. Roderick Murchison wrote in a letter:

> We proceeded up the hill and formed line under its brow. A brigade of artillery was brought up with the greatest promptitude, and two guns, under Lieutenant Locke, being placed on the rising ground on our right, and the others on the left, three companies of the 36th were detached to the edge of the hill on our right, in order to protect the guns, which were soon annoying the advancing French close columns in the finest style with shrapnell shells, whilst our rifles and light infantry were firing in extended files as videttes.[4]

At this stage, the guns were probably firing on the columns approaching Vimeiro rather than Solignac's or Brenier's columns. The ascent up the ridge from the gorge was steep, so two companies of the 29th Foot were detailed to help haul the guns of Nightingall's brigade up onto the heights. When the brigade formed line across the ridge, behind Ferguson's, the 29th were on the right, where they had a good view of the attack on Vimeiro and the 82nd on the left. According to Charles Leslie, Wellesley and Spencer were riding near the 29th when Spencer ordered the two rightmost companies to move to allow two or three cannon to deploy and fire upon the French attacking the Vimeiro.[5]

As it was a Sunday, the 71st Highlanders had been preparing for divine service, with many of the men cleaning their uniforms and washing their shirts, when they heard the 40th's drummers

---

4   Geike, *Life*, vol.I, pp.31–32.
5   Leslie, *Journal*, p.49.

beating to arms. They marched up the ridge with the rest of Ferguson's brigade and waited to advance. The 36th were on the right, the 40th on the left, and the 71st in the centre of the brigade line, which was formed across the ridge facing northward and not along it facing east. An anonymous Highlander wrote:

> The battle had by this time commenced on the right; consequently, as at Roleia, we were obliged to stand for a while exposed to a distant cannonade. A shell also fell and burst near our company; one of the splinters wounded a man severely, who stood the third from me on the left. A party of officers went out at one time, a short distance from us, in order to obtain a closer view of the engagement; one of them, belonging to the 82d, fell dead in our sight: slain, strange to say, by the mere wind of a cannon-ball; not a scratch being on his body. The balls were now flying so thick, that we received orders to sit down: even in this position, they would ever and anon rattle through among the fixed bayonets, and descend so low as to knock the bonnets off our heads![6]

If the Highlander's account is accurate, then the 82nd Foot officer must have been Lieutenant Robert Donkin, the regiment's only officer killed during the battle.

The main body of Solignac's brigade and his guns had probably reached the hamlet of Ventosa by this stage of the battle, at the highest point of the long ridge. He had only three battalions with him, the third battalions of the 12e Légère, 15e Légère and 58e Ligne. Several British accounts say that the skirmishing between the light and 5/60th rifle companies and the French light troops continued for an extended time. The men lay down to avoid the fire of the French artillery while the skirmishing took place. It would seem that Solignac took his time and did not immediately send forward the bulk of his troops. He was probably either letting his men catch their breath after the steep ascent up the ridge or, more likely, waiting for Brenier to arrive. Solignac's three battalions were facing five, with more British troops close by in reserve. With the British being mostly out of sight, he may also have been waiting to get a clear idea of what he was facing.

Private William Lawrence of the 40th Foot's light company was with the skirmishers. His day had commenced with a breakfast of honey from a beehive he and two comrades had scavenged the day before, but his meal was interrupted by the call to arms. In his autobiography, Lawrence wrote that the British and French skirmished on the left for two hours before the main attack started there. He exchanged shots with a French light infantryman for half an hour without either of them being injured. In Lawrence's case, he was saved by the cork oak he was sheltering behind, but, eventually, a comrade arrived and hit Lawrence's French opponent with his first shot.[7] Lieutenant William Cowper Coles wrote to his father the next day:

> The attack by the Enemy, tho not making the impression that was expected, was well regulated and most skilful, their rifle men coverd the operations of the main body so well that many individuals who were in the advance had not a conception that the French intended to make the engagement general, however as their light troops extended, the more we had occasion to be prepar'd, and the whole army excepting one brigade was assembled on the

6   Anon., *Vicissitudes*, pp.14–15.
7   E. Hathaway (ed.), *A Dorset Soldier; The Autobiography of Sgt William Lawrence, 1790–1869* (Staplehurst: Spellmount, 1993), p.34.

rising of an hill, and their appearance cover'd by a constant fire from the advanc'd light infantry and our rifles. However it, became soon necessary to withdraw them, in order to give scope for action, and likewise ground for our army – the light infantry retir'd by degrees under a most desperate fire and no sooner had they attain'd the flanks of their respective brigades than the action became general.[8]

Coles uses the phrase 'rifle men' to mean skirmishers rather than troops armed with rifled weapons; such usage was common at the time.

It was not until Junot's attacks on Fane and Anstruther were petering out that Solignac launched his attack. Murchison of the 36th again:

… the fire of the enemy soon became very hot, and even though the 36th were lying on their breasts under the brow, our men were getting pretty much hit, whilst the regiment in our rear, the 82d, which at that time could not fire a shot, suffered more than we did. General Spencer, who commanded the division, when moving about to regulate the General movements, was hit by a ball in the hand, and I saw him wrap his handkerchief round it and heard him say, 'It is only a scratch!' Soon after, the light infantry in our front closed files and fell in; our guns were pulled back and then came the struggle. General Ferguson waving his hat, up we rose, old Burne (our Colonel) crying out, as he shook his yellow cane, that 'he would knock down any man who fired a shot.'

This made some merriment among the men, as tumbling over was the fashion without the application of their Colonel's cane. 'Charge!' was the word, and at once we went over the brow with a steady line of glittering steel, and with a hearty hurrah, against six regiments in close column, with six pieces of artillery, just in front of the 36th. But not an instant did the enemy stand against this most unexpected sally within pistol-shot.[9]

Murchison exaggerates the number of French regiments they faced. As he had already mentioned the edge of the hill being on their right, it is clear that the brow he refers to is a rise in the ground along the ridge's length and not the ridge's reverse slope. From this and other accounts, it seems that, as soon as Solignac began his advance, Ferguson ordered his brigade to stand and advance to meet them. An anonymous officer of the 36th later also wrote that as his regiment advanced towards the French they were told to reserve their fire, but, as men dropped in the ranks from the heavy fire of the French, one Irish recruit from Dublin could bear it no longer and raised his musket and fired. At the head of the battalion, Colonel Robert Burne turned and shook his cane and said, 'Tell that Paddy O'Rafferty, if I was near him, I'd knock him down.'[10]

One Highlander of the 71st wrote:

I had now an opportunity to see them face to face; they differed widely from us in dress in this instance, being all clothed in long white smock-frocks and trowsers, and having hairy knapsacks hanging loosely on their backs. But little time was left for observation, on account of General Ferguson riding up to the —th, which lay close beside us,

8   NAM: 1968-07-419-1: Coles to father, 22 August 1808.
9   Geicke, *Life*, vol.I, p.33.
10   Anon., 'Reminiscences of General Burne', *United Service Journal*, 1829, part two, pp.577–578.

and ordering that regiment to charge; but, for what cause I never could learn, the whole regiment remained motionless. Colonel Pack, on seeing this, went to the General, and requested permission for us to advance in their stead: and this being granted at once, we, along with the 36th and 82d regiments, instantly rushed forward, and fired a tremendous volley, which we saw did great execution. The astonished enemy, on getting such a warm reception, fell into confusion, and began to retrograde; this encouraging us, we gave three hearty cheers, and pressed on: our grenadier company, and the 36th light company, charged with the bayonet, and took six pieces of cannon. We still advanced, and two other pieces of cannon fell into our hands, the enemy not having time to hurry them across a ravine which lay in the way: meanwhile, the enemy continued his retreat, and soon disappeared over an eminence.[11]

This account is the only one that mentions a British battalion refusing to advance. By process of elimination, the regiment the Highlander is referring to but not naming can only be the 29th or 40th but accounts from each suggest that they did participate, so it is probable that the Highlander misconstrued or misremembered what occurred.

Ferguson's brigade charged the French and drove them back. Some French rallied, but the 36th and 71st charged them again, led by Ferguson, and took several guns, plus tumbrils. The French attempted to retake the guns, but the 71st again dispersed them.[12] Lawrence of the 40th wrote:

We had been skirmishing for some time, a large body of French made their appearance in our front. Our artillery greeted them pretty sharply, by ploughing furrows through them with ball, which threw them into a confused state. Our column, under General Spencer, then advanced with our cannon still playing over our heads. When we got within a short distance of the enemy, we fired and charged them. The fighting was severe and kept up for some time, but we drove them from the position they had occupied capturing about seven pieces of cannon, and some ammunition waggons.[13]

Captain Warre wrote:

A part of them rallied, but Genl. Ferguson hurraed the 36th, a very weak though fine Regt. to charge, which was done in great style three successive times, till, as they were very much thinned, and in some disorder from the rapid advance, I was sent back to hasten the support which was far behind, the gallant little Regiment forming to rally again under cover of a hedge of American aloes though much pressed. I just returned in time to join the 71st, who were charging 6 pieces of the enemy's cannon that were retiring, and the fire at this time from the enemy was really tremendous.[14]

The regimental history of the 12e Légère mentions several officers who distinguished themselves during the action, including *capitaine* Antoine Turquais, who saved the battalion's eagle after the

---

11   Anon., *Vicissitudes*, pp.15–17.
12   Warre, *Letters*, p.27.
13   Hathaway (ed.), *A Dorset Soldier*, p.34.
14   Warre, *Letters*, pp.32–33.

porte-aigle had been wounded and it was about to be captured.[15] Turquais was shot in the neck but survived.

Highlander John Macfarlane wrote of the charge of the 71st:

> Our Colonel called out not to fire till we were closer. The French fired on us. A man not far from me was shot through the head. Some of us turned our heads to him, for he was crying. The Colonel cried 'Take him away. Do not be looking round, men.' This man died. One of the balls struck my firelock or bayonet. When we got nearer, we fired on them, and they on us. At last, they turned and made off. We cheered, and went on. They turned round and fired on us. We returned the fire they made of it turned into a race.[16]

The battalions of Ferguson's and Nightingall's brigades pushed Solignac out of Ventosa and north-eastwards, where the long ridge evolved into a series of rolling hills towards Peniche. Leslie recalled the 29th advancing down a slope, and, as they approached the French, the enemy wavered and abandoned their guns.[17] Lieutenant George Wood of the 82nd wrote in his memoir that his regiment formed up alongside the 71st, 'which had been engaged some time previously, we came in for our share of the conflict of that day, by being opposed to a strong French regiment, which advanced to within half pistol-shot of us, when a most tremendous point blank fire ensued.'[18] The 82nd and 71st then charged down into a shallow valley and passed either side of a section of French guns, which were captured.

Ensign Murchison (36th Foot) wrote that the French 'rallied, it is true, once or twice, particularly behind some thick prickly-pear hedges and a hut or two on the flat table-land; but although their brave General Solignac was always cantering to their front and animating them against us, they at last fled precipitately, until they reached a small hamlet, where, however, they did make a tolerable stand.'[19] Considering his later fame, mentions of Wellesley in memoirs need to be read with caution, but Murchison's account was written on 23 August in a long letter to his uncle and then published much later. It continues:

> Here it was that Sir Arthur Wellesley overtook us after a smart gallop. He had witnessed from a distance our steady and successful charge, and our capture of the guns, and he now saw how we were thrusting the French out of this hamlet. Through the sound of the musketry, and in the midst of much confusion, I heard a shrill voice calling out, 'Where are the colours of the 36th?' and I turned round (my brother ensign, poor Peter Bone, having just been knocked down), and looking up in Sir Arthur's bright and confident face, said, 'Here they are, sir! Then he shouted, 'Very well done, my boys! Halt, halt – quite enough!'[20]

---

15   Malaguti, *Historique du 87e Régiment*, p.349.
16   Robson, 'Peninsular Private', p.6.
17   Leslie, *Journal*, p.50.
18   Wood, *Subaltern*, p.54.
19   Geicke, *Life*, vol.I, p.33.
20   Geicke, *Life*, vol.I, pp.33–34.

Staff officer Captain George Jarvis, who was with Wellesley for some of the battle, mentions him personally commanding the left wing of the army.[21] John Macfarlane of the 71st mentions Wellesley riding up to the regiment after their second charge.[22] The only mention of Wellesley being on the Vimeiro hill seems to be when he met Sir Harry Burrard there, so he likely spent most of the battle up on the ridge, where he could get a better overview of the action.

Solignac's troops fell back to the village of Pregança on a small hill. George Wood later wrote, 'The French, however, having now gained possession of the village on the heights, which had been strongly barricaded, remained there for the present, and we received orders to halt in the ravine. Indeed, a little breathing-time had become very necessary, as we had for the last two hours been firing, shouting, running, swearing, sweating, and huzzaing.'[23] The 71st also halted, one Highlander writing:

> The day being oppressively hot, we had piled arms, erroneously concluding that our labours were over, at least for the day; we were accordingly refreshing ourselves, by drinking water, and making frequent attacks on the grapes in a vineyard, when the advance of the French a second time was announced, by the clang of trumpets and beating of drums, which latter action, as it appeared, was much easier performed than the beating of us. We soon caught up our arms, and retired to a short distance. By this time the enemy were within ken; but immediately on our giving them another astounding and destructive volley, they put about, and ran up the hill with surprising speed. We ascended the hill in pursuit of them; but on arriving at the top, we found that victory had declared decidedly for the British.[24]

The French troops that attacked were not from Solignac's brigade but Brenier's, who had finally arrived on the scene and immediately advanced and surprised the resting redcoats. Brenier had four battalions of infantry – 3/2e and 3/4e Légère, 1/70e and 2/70e Ligne – plus artillery and two squadrons of dragoons.

A note on a map of the battle, showing an angle in the 36th Foot's line, drawn by Ensign Samuel Laing of the Royal Staff Corps soon after the battle, reads: 'two companies of the 36th Regt thrown back to oppose a French column of the enemy advancing on our right flank. The fire took effect and turned the enemy while forming line on his centre companies. The column of French cavalry on the left near Margaserra turned by the two guns on our left.'[25] From this description and details on the map, it would seem that Brenier's infantry advanced from Pregança, while at least some of his cavalry was on the British left near Mariquiteira. At this stage, the 71st and 82nd were halted with the captured French guns, with the 29th nearby. Ferguson had taken the 36th and 40th in pursuit of Solignac's men a little further to the northwest.

The 29th had also been allowed to stand at ease, but when Brenier's column approached, Leslie says that French cavalry appeared on their right flank, not their left, but Laing's map also shows French cavalry on that flank. The 29th was ordered to form up in four ranks, in which formation they still offered sufficient frontage to face the French infantry while being strong enough to resist cavalry. As

21   LA: JARVIS/5/A/2/8: Letter from G.R.P. Jarvis to Philadelphia Jarvis, 22 August 1808.
22   Robson, 'Peninsular Private', p.6.
23   Wood, *Subaltern*, p.55.
24   Anon., *Vicissitudes*, pp.24–25.
25   TNA: WO 78/5949: Battle of Vimiero, 21 August 1808.

the French column approached, the 71st opened fire upon them, as did the light companies of Nightingall's brigade, which had been concealed in the willows and bushes of the low ground.[26] The British seem to have been driven back by the French infantry and cavalry, losing possession of the captured guns, but then rallied and charged, driving the French back in turn. George Wood claims the 71st and 82nd fell back as a ruse de guerre to entice the French to come forward. He then says the two battalions advanced again, and the French retreated to the village and were driven out of it by 'gallant riflemen', presumably the 5/60th and the light companies.[27] Craufurd's brigade was by this time advancing towards Mariquiteira from Ribamar on Brenier's flank. His light companies and 5/60th company may have arrived in time to open fire as the French retreated.[28] The French dragoons covered their infantry's retreat, preventing it from becoming a rout but taking casu-

Piper George Clark. (Anne S.K. Brown Military Collection)

alties. During this final charge, one of the 71st's pipers, Private George Clark, received a musket ball in his leg. Unable to continue, he sat down and continued to play to encourage his comrades.[29] The Highland Society presented Clark with an inscribed set of bagpipes.[30]

The 71st halted as the French fled, piled arms again, and many began to search the discarded French knapsacks for anything of worth. Some of the highlanders went looking for water and instead found a French general.[31] Brenier was lying wounded under his horse, which had been shot under him. An aide de camp and an orderly dragoon were trying to extricate him from his mount. The aide had been wounded in the mouth and was bleeding profusely. All three were taken prisoner by the 71st, one of whom, who seems to have been a witness, wrote, 'An Irish lad, named Gaven, was the

26   Leslie, *Journal*, p.51.
27   Wood, *Subaltern*, p.56
28   Foy, *Invasion*, p.173.
29   G. Glover (ed.), *Line Infantry*, p.161.
30   *The Universal Magazine*, January 1809, p.92.
31   Robson, 'Peninsular Private', p.6.

first that espied the General, and without hesitation he made him prisoner, exclaiming, at the same time, "By Jasus! I have taken the sarjant-major of the French." Just at that time Mackay came up, and took him out of Gaven's hands'.[32] Brenier offered Corporal John McKay his watch and purse to escort him safely to the rear. McKay refused them. While this was happening, the orderly dragoon took the opportunity to ride off, pursued by numerous musket balls. Another account has the Irish soldier being offered the money and McKay preventing him from taking it. McKay took Brenier to the battalion's commander, Lieutenant Colonel Pack, and the general commented on McKay's good behaviour. Pack reportedly replied that 'British soldiers fought for honour and not for money.'[33]

John McKay was promoted to sergeant for his good behaviour, and Wellesley appointed him an assistant provost.[34] The Highland Society voted to present him with a gold medal.[35] In March 1809, McKay was commissioned as an ensign in the 4th West India Regiment, and he then moved to the 3/60th as a lieutenant in 1812 but died soon afterwards, probably of one of the diseases endemic to the West Indies.

Hearing that Brenier had been taken prisoner and Solignac had been seriously wounded, Junot's chief of staff, Thiébault, hastened to take command of the broken brigades and bring some order to the retreat, which he did. Ferguson sent his aide de camp, Captain Mellish, to inform Wellesley of the advantages of pursuing the French further.[36]

An officer of the 36th Foot wrote his account of the battle in a letter that he sent to a friend in Belfast, and that was subsequently published in a newspaper:

I have the pleasure to acquaint you that I am full to the good, and worth two dead men, though I yesterday received a clink in the General attack that the French made on us. Our brave regiment, though but a handful, charged them repeatedly, and drove them from height to height. Our loss has been very trifling, considering the incessant showers of balls under which we advanced for two hours at least. I received my memento, which thank God is but trifling, in the calf of the leg, in the first charge, but continued with my company all day. I am now a little stiff and sore, but the devil an inch will I go into hospital. I have got a mule on which I will jog, and alight when there is anything to be done. We have had some long marching, and our privations are great: no officer has any thing but the clothes on him, a second shirt, and a boat cloak. We are in General Ferguson's brigade. A braver man never entered the field. While on our charge yesterday, he repeatedly rode in front of our colours, waving his hat. Adieu, my friend: I hope soon to write to you. Excuse this scrawl—it is on the ground it is written, as we are no much burthened with tables.[37]

John Patterson (50th Foot) much later noted that after the battle, he had heard of the 'extraordinary fearless conduct' of Lieutenant Walter Ewart of the 36th's grenadier company but gave no details.[38] Warre describes Ewart as 'little Ewart, shot through the leg' but again gives no details.[39]

---

32   Anon., *Vicissitudes*, p.20.
33   Balfour Kermack, 'A Short Sketch of the Campaigns of Balfour Kermack', *Highland Light Infantry Chronicle*, October 1914, p.159.
34   Wellington (ed.), *Supplementary Despatches*, vol.VI, p.201.
35   *The Universal Magazine*, January 1809, p.92.
36   Anon., *Proceedings*, pp.94–96.
37   *General Evening Post*, 15 September 1808.
38   Patterson, *Camp and Quarters*, vol.II, p.99. Patterson goes on to say that Ewart was killed in action at Vimeiro, when in fact he died of wounds sustained at Salamanca in 1812.
39   Warre, *Letters*, p.27.

The action on the left finished at around noon. Ferguson's and Nightingall's five battalions had defeated the attacks of seven French battalions, with cavalry support, and captured six cannon and many prisoners. Ferguson's aide, William Warre, wrote, 'all I could say would not be half what he deserved in praise. His gallantry and judgement decided the day on the left. My only astonishment and that of everybody else is how he escaped. He was always in advance in the hottest fire animating everybody by his noble example.'[40] The general's orderly, a trooper of the 20th Light Dragoons, was severely wounded. Ensign Henry Wyndham wrote, 'that bravest of men General Ferguson, with his hat off, cheering the soldiers, who (by the bye) wanted checking rather than encouraging.'[41] As at Roliça, Nightingall does not seem to be mentioned in any of the surviving accounts. Warre summed up the action on the left: 'To speak of the conduct of any body would in me seem presumptuous. Every soldier seemed a hero. The fire for some time was tremendous, and the field strewed with our brave fellows in charging the guns.'[42] Bowes' brigade remained in reserve and does not seem to have fired a shot, and Acland remained closer to Vimeiro with only his light companies and the 1/95th moving forward during the attack on the village there.

A Great Deal Has Been Done

Seeing the battle was lost, Junot, according to Thiébault, got into a carriage with Madame Foy, his mistress, whose husband had been wounded, and rode through his shattered and retreating army without issuing any orders. Margaron, Delaborde and Thiébault were left to manage the retreat.[43] However, Junot told Napoleon that he stayed on the field until 6:00 p.m.[44] As the French withdrew, elements of the 66e Ligne and the elite companies of some of the Lisbon garrison arrived too late to affect the battle's outcome.[45]

Captain James Douglas of the 45th Foot, serving as a deputy assistant quartermaster general, was riding next to Wellesley when he rode up to Burrard:

> He rode up saying, 'Sir Harry, the enemy is beaten at all points, our men are fresh, having been attacked on their own ground; not half of them have been engaged; we can be in Lisbon before the enemy.'
>
> A pause of about ten seconds ensued. Burrard had his Adjutant-General on one side, and his Quartermaster-General on the other. The Adjutant-General first said, 'A great deal has been done, Sir Arthur'; the Quartermaster-General then said, 'A great deal has been done, Sir Arthur'; and Burrard then said, 'A great deal has been done, Sir Arthur.' It was decided that nothing more should be done, and the most glorious of triumphs was wrested out of the hand of the conqueror.[46]

---

40   Warre, *Letters*, p.33.
41   BL: Add. MS 49503: Wyndham to Gordon, 8 September 1808.
42   Warre, *Letters*, p.27.
43   Butler (trans.), *Thiébault*, vol.II, p.209.
44   Griffon de Pleineville, *La Première Invasion*, p.234.
45   Foy, *Invasion*, p.174.
46   Brown, *Redcoats*, p.53.

Wellesley wanted to march Hill's, Fane's, and Anstruther's brigades southeast by the most direct road to Torres Vedras (a distance of about nine miles) and to follow the defeated French troops with the other five British brigades and the Portuguese.[47] He hoped to cut off Junot's route to Lisbon and place the defeated and disordered French troops between two bodies of allied troops. He told Burrard they had 12 days' provisions and sufficient ammunition for another action. Hill's brigade had been held in reserve all day: while a few officers had contrived to get closer to the action, the brigade had not fired a shot, and the men were eager to pursue the French.[48]

When asked to justify his decision not to advance at the inquiry into the Convention of Cintra, Burrard stated: 'I answered that I saw no reason for altering my former resolution of not advancing, and as far as my recollection goes, I added that the same reasoning which before determined me to wait for the reinforcements had still its full force in my judgement and opinion.'[49] His senior staff officers, Clinton and Murray, agreed.

Burrard had witnessed the poor performance of the artillery horses during the action and had received a report from an officer of the 20th Light Dragoons that their casualties had been heavy and few were fit for further duty. He had also observed considerable numbers of enemy cavalry to the rear of the French centre and 'had also seen a corps of infantry in the rear and towards their right which was not stationary but appeared to be moving to its left, and the retreating corps retired in the same direction.'[50]

When Ferguson's aide de camp, Captain Mellish, arrived with news of the French collapse on the left, Wellesley took him to Burrard to ask permission to pursue the French again. Burrard again refused on the basis that the country there was more open and the British infantry, if they became spread out during the chase, would be vulnerable to French cavalry.[51] The timing of the two separate attacks on the British positions may have made them easier to counter, but Burrard said:

> ...these circumstances, as far as they relate to our pursuit of then, made against us, for the corps that attacked first had time to retire upon its cavalry, and had the means of getting into good order again before the left was defeated, and their left for the same purpose; that is, as soon as it was thought right to prevent our men following then into rather an open country, where they would have been exposed to cavalry.[52]

Burrard also felt that a considerable portion of the British troops would have to have been left to secure the prisoners of war, guard the landing place, and get the wounded onto the hospital ships. Acland's brigade had had little or no sleep, and many of the other brigades, even if not engaged, had been active for much of a long, hot day. At the end of the battle, the distance from one end of the British line was, Burrard estimated, four miles. Others of the generals said two or three miles, and these estimates were closer to the truth. Burrard thought that gathering sufficient troops for the pursuit would have taken some time. He also pointed out that Wellesley had said that a lack of cavalry had prevented a more effective pursuit after Roliça. With no useful quantity of cavalry, the army would have been marching blind, and the commissariat would have been vulnerable to the enemy dragoons.

---

47   Anon. (ed.), *Proceedings*, p.92.
48   Morley, *Memoirs*, pp.49-50.
49   TNA: WO 1/415: Burrard's narrative.
50   TNA: WO 1/415: Burrard's narrative.
51   Anon. (ed.), *Proceedings*, pp.92–93.
52   TNA: WO 1/415: Burrard's narrative.

Speaking in the House of Commons in February 1809, Wellesley addressed the inconsistency in his statements after Roliça, when he said lack of cavalry hindered a pursuit, and after Vimeiro, when he advocated for one:

> … the good order of the retreat in the one case, and the disorder in the other made all the difference. Although it might not be proper without an adequate force of cavalry to pursue the enemy closely, when they retired in good order on the 17th, it by no means followed, that they ought not to be pursued on the 21st, when they had been completely beaten, and had retreated in great disorder.[53]

Any arguments about the tiredness of the British troops also applied to the French, who would have been seriously fatigued after marching most of the previous day and with almost all of them being heavily engaged during the battle.

Another factor weighing on Burrard's mind was that he had formed the opinion that the Portuguese troops could render little assistance. Lieutenant Colonel Thomas Carey of his staff, whom he had sent ashore on the 19th, had ridden through the Portuguese on his way to Vimeiro and 'gave such an account of them and their proceedings, as quite precluded any hope of rendering them useful.'[54]

At the inquiry, Spencer stated that soon after the action on the left ceased, he saw some of the troops that had attacked Vimeiro re-formed about three miles away. But he also said that the artillery horses had managed to get from the Mondego to Vimeiro, so any difficulties on the way to Torres Vedras would have been overcome.[55] When Ferguson was questioned about his request to be allowed to pursue the enemy to his front, he responded that a column of 1,500 to 2,000 men, completely broken, had fled into a hollow and could have been easily cut off from the rest of the French if he had been allowed to advance.[56] Ferguson also later wrote that Wellesley's plan to march to Torres Vedras with the brigades on the right would have succeeded in cutting off the French retreat.[57]

In a letter to Horse Guards, Anstruther regretted the lack of pursuit and also felt that the British could have beaten the French to Torres Vedras and annihilated the enemy's infantry.[58] In his journal, he wrote that the decision not to pursue was, 'A measure for which it seems very difficult to account by any principal of war or of common sense.'[59]

Captain Henry Cooke, a deputy assistant adjutant general, wrote:

> Unfortunately for the glory of my country, and the reputation of our army their prayers were rejected, and altho' four brigades provisioned, fresh, eager to advance & who had not

---

53   'Convention of Cintra', House of Commons Debate, 21 February 1809, <https://api.parliament.uk/historic-hansard/commons/1809/feb/21/convention-of-cintra>, accessed May 2023.

54   TNA: WO 1/415: Burrard's narrative.

55   Anon. (ed.), *Proceedings*, p.95. Wellesley later implied that Spencer pitched his testimony to help lessen the criticism of Burrard, see Jennings, *Croker Papers*, vol.II, p.123. He also called Spencer 'Exceedingly Puzzle-headed'.

56   Anon. (ed.), *Proceedings*, pp.95–96.

57   National Records of Scotland (NRS): GD364/1/1178: Ferguson to Hope, 8 September 1808.

58   BL: Add. MS 49503: Anstruther to Gordon, 22 August 1808.

59   StAUL: msdep121/8/2/3/4/4: Anstruther's journal, pp.33–34.

fired a shot, were on the *direct* road to Tores Vedras – altho' a Brigade were close enough to worry & destroy without opposition, not an effort was made, the army regained their ground & the moment for deciding the fate of that army unfortunately lost.[60]

Burrard's quartermaster general, George Murray, writing long after the Peninsular War, summed the arguments up in a review of Napier's history:

> The victory just achieved by the repulse of all General Junot's attacks seemed to warrant the forward movement proposed, but there were other points to be considered. First, whether the proposed mode of advance was the most proper one; for the two wings of the British army were at this time about three miles asunder, whilst the enemy, although weakened and discouraged by his defeat, had, however, re-united his forces upon the high grounds which formed the left of the valley of Toledo: – to move forward, therefore, from two distant points was to fall into an error similar to that which General Junot had committed, in making two separate and distant attacks, in doing which there is always the risk of a failure of exact combination. Secondly, whether the victory obtained rendered it wise to depart from the two principles previously laid down: first, that of advancing always by the line of march nearest to the coast, keeping up a connexion with the shipping; and secondly, that of not precipitating the issue of the enterprise with a part only of the British force, the remaining part being so near, and having been the night before ordered forward for the purpose of uniting the whole. We shall content ourselves with stating these questions, without entering into any discussion upon them, observing only that a movement to Torres Vedras would have been but the commencement of a new plan of operations, for there was reason to suppose that the enemy would not attach any importance to that point, but that he would fall back upon the position of Cabeça de Montachique, which is one of the strongest in the second line in that chain of posts since rendered so famous by the effectual barrier they opposed to Massena's march upon Lisbon in the year 1810.[61]

Ensign Samuel Laing of the Royal Staff Corps returned to the battlefield the day after the action to investigate whether, if Hill's brigade had marched from the right, they could have cut off the French retreat from Torres Vedras. He concluded they could have done it; the road was good, and they had sufficient time.[62] Captain Eliot of the Royal Artillery refuted the argument that the artillery horses would have been incapable of taking part in an effective pursuit, stating, 'In all situations, except where the nature of the ground was such as to prevent it, the guns were fully adequate to keep pace with the infantry, and on a plain road – to outstrip them considerably.'[63]

Burrard, however, remained steadfast in his decision not to pursue, but it did not sit completely easy with him. He said during the inquiry:

> At the time Sir Arthur Wellesley came up to me, and publickly proposed to advance I felt the situation it placed me in, and that it was not likely my determinations should please a

---

60   BL: Add. MS 49503: Cooke to Gordon, 6 September 1808.
61   Murray, 'Review of History of the War', p.200.
62   Fereday (ed.), *Samuel Laing*, p.115.
63   Eliot, *Defence of Portugal*, p.210.

British army, who had so much signalized itself; *that* will I believe be sufficient proof that I acted according to the best of my judgement, and those who know me will be convinced very much against my feelings.[64]

He also admitted that he did not realise how desperate a situation Solignac's brigade was in when Ferguson asked for permission to pursue.

Historian Rory Muir is very critical of Burrard in his biography of Wellesley: 'It is true that he had only just landed and was unfamiliar with the terrain and the army, but few generals can ever have been presented with such an easy chance to strike a telling blow and gain lasting fame, and his refusal showed that he was unworthy of the rank he held.'[65] Muir goes on to say that a lack of confidence and fear of turning Wellesley's victory into a defeat were probably the reasons for his decision.

John Fortescue wrote that 'The movement, in Wellesley's hands, would doubtless have been successful', but is then more sympathetic to Burrard: 'His reasons for forbidding Wellesley's advance on the previous day – difficulty of supplies and want of cavalry – now seemed to him to be doubly serious, and not wholly without cause. The British cavalry after its losses in the action was weaker than ever, and the transport had suffered hardly less seriously.' Some of the carters had deserted, and many carts would become involved in transporting the wounded. He then continued:

Then also the British artillery-horses were hardly able to crawl, and Burrard was not to be persuaded that Junot had not still a reserve of troops in hand. And here, in a sense, he was right; for, though Wellesley was correct in believing that Junot had not another man to throw into the fight that day, he had always underrated the total number of the French soldiers in Portugal.[66]

Oman refers to Burrard as 'That leisurely person', 'obdurate' and 'slow and cautious'. He argues that Wellesley's right could have cut the route to Lisbon for Junot, and the left would have pushed his army reeling into the hills towards Santarém.[67] Napier, on the other hand, is perhaps uncharacteristically generous towards Burrard while not doubting that Wellesley's plan would have worked:

The project of seizing Torres Vedras and Mafra at the close of the battle, was one of those conceptions which distinguish great Generals, and it is harsh to blame sir Harry Burrard for not adopting it. Men are not gifted alike, and had he not been confirmed in his view by the advice of his staff, there was in the actual situation of affairs ample scope for doubt: the facility of executing sir Arthur's plan was not so apparent on the field of battle as it may be in the closet. The French cavalry was numerous, unharmed, full of spirit; upon the distant heights behind Junot, a fresh body of infantry had been discovered by Spencer, and the nature of the country prevented any accurate judgment of its strength being formed, the English gun-carriages were much shaken, and so badly and scantily horsed, that it was doubtful if they could keep up with the infantry in a long march; the commissariat was in

64   TNA: WO 1/415: Burrard's narrative.
65   Muir, *Wellington*, vol.I, p256.
66   Fortescue, *British Army*, vol.VI, p.232.
67   Oman, *History*, vol.I, pp.260–261.

great confusion, the native drivers were flying with the country transport; the Portuguese troops gave no promise of utility, and the English cavalry was destroyed. To overcome obstacles in the pursuit of a great object is the proof of a lofty genius: but Murray's and Clinton's objections to the attempt, exonerates sir Harry and places the vigour of sir Arthur Wellesley in a strong light. It was doubtless ill-judged of Burrard, considering the ephemeral nature of his command, to interfere at all with the dispositions of a General who was in the full career of victory, and whose superior talents and experience were well known. But it excites indignation to find a brave and honourable veteran borne to the earth as a criminal, and assailed by the most puerile, shallow writers, merely because his mind was not of the highest class.[68]

Wellesley was also more understanding of Burrard's decision and did not doubt his motives despite venting his frustration at the time. At the inquiry, he took the trouble to say:

Although I did differ, and do still differ in opinion with Lieutenant General Sir Harry Burrard respecting the measures adopted immediately after the Battle of the 21st of August, I hope it will not be deemed to presumptuous of me as an inferior officer to declare to the court and to the Publick the opinion I have always entertained that Sir Harry Burrard decided upon that occasion upon fair military grounds in the manner which appeared to him to be most conducive to the interests of the country and that he had no motive for his decision which could be supposed personal to me, or which as an officer he could not avow.[69]

In a letter to George Burrard, a close relative of Sir Harry, Wellesley was also adamant that 'There existed fair military grounds for the opinions entertained by each of us, and I don't conceive that either of us can be blamed for entertaining these opinions, or the honour or character of either attacked for acting according to opinions really entertained upon such grounds.'[70] He was deeply concerned about the calumny heaped upon Burrard, but of course, some of that public criticism may have had its roots in private letters Wellesley had sent after the battle, as George Burrard intimated in his original letter to Wellesley.

When asked at the inquiry if he thought a pursuit would have been successful, Wellesley answered:

The enemy's left, which was engaged with our right, retired by a road which leads along the heights towards Lourinha on a different side of the valley from that on which our left stood, and it began to retire at much about the same time that the attack began upon the left, consequently the left could not have been immediately employed in pursuit of those troops which had been engaged on our right. Those troops l believe continued in confusion in the woods which were on that side of the valley during a considerable part of the day, and this confusion was considerably increased, and its duration lengthened, by the attack made by our cavalry. I certainly think that if the left wing of the army had

68   Napier, *History*, vol.I, p.164.
69   TNA: WO 1/415: Wellesley's response to Burrard.
70   Wellington (ed.), *Supplementary Despatches*, vol.VI, p.155.

followed up its advantages as I proposed, not only many prisoners would have been taken belonging to the left wing of the French army, but likewise: belonging to the right, and that the whole of them were in such confusion, that, giving them full credit for great facility and discipline in forming after having been broken, it would have been very difficult, if not impossible, to form them again.[71]

Wellesley wrote to the Duke of York on the 22nd:

I think if General Hill's brigade and the advanced guard [Fane and Anstruther] had moved upon Torres Vedras, as soon as it was certain that the enemy's right had been defeated by our left, and our left had pursued their advantage, the enemy would have been cut off from Torres Vedras, and we should have been at Lisbon before him; if, indeed, any French army had remained in Portugal. But Sir Harry Burrard, who was at this time upon the ground, still thought it advisable not to move from Vimeiro; and the enemy made good their retreat to Torres Vedras.[72]

Wellesley was even more forthright in his letter to the Duke of Richmond; after claiming that Burrard had not arrived until the action was almost over, which was not true, he wrote:

Although we had, when Acland joined, not less than 17,000 men, and between 6000 and 7000 Portuguese in our neighbourhood, Sir Harry did not think these sufficient to defeat 12,000 or 14,000 Frenchmen, but determined to wait for Moore's corps, notwithstanding all that I could urge upon the subject … If he would have allowed me to move that part of the army yesterday evening, which had not been engaged in the morning, the French would not have stopped till they reached Lisbon.[73]

Referring to both Burrard and Dalrymple, Wellesley later said, 'that from the first hour these officers landed, nay even before they had landed, he perceived that he was not in possession of their confidence.'[74]

Many of the subsequent commentaries that criticise Burrard's decision are influenced by the achievements that Wellesley and his army went on to have rather than the information available at the time: Lord Burghersh is a good example, commenting on the lack of British cavalry compared to the French he wrote, in 1820:

But Sir Arthur Wellesley relied upon his own genius to provide a remedy to this objection; our infantry was in the best order, and it has too often since been tried in presence of a superior cavalry, to leave doubt in the mind of any British officer, that (if judiciously managed and supported with artillery), it is competent to advance in the face of cavalry.[75]

---

71   Anon. (ed.), *Proceedings*, p.93.
72   Gurwood (ed.), *Wellington's Dispatches*, vol.IV, pp.114–115.
73   Wellington (ed.), *Supplementary Despatches*, vol.VI, p.122.
74   'Convention of Cintra', House of Commons Debate, 21 February 1809, <https://api.parliament.uk/historic-hansard/commons/1809/feb/21/convention-of-cintra>, accessed May 2023.
75   Fane, *Early Campaigns*, p.30.

French sources tend to credit the lack of pursuit to Kellermann and the grenadiers halting the pursuit from the British centre, along with Margaron and the charges of the French cavalry.[76] The roads towards Mafra and Torres Vedras did pass through broken country, with narrow passes suitable for defence and some areas suitable for cavalry, so the French cavalry may have been able to harass and slow any pursuit.

The allied army remained in the field until 3:00 p.m. when they retired to their former positions, except for Bowes' brigade, which was posted in the rear of the village with pickets in front to secure wounded and keep watch for any return by the French.[77]

Junot wrote to Napoleon: 'I remained in the presence of the enemy (who did not dare to leave their positions to pursue us) until 6 o'clock in the evening, and I returned to take the position in front of the defile, which we passed, partly during the night, and partly the next day. On the 22nd we returned to Torres Vedras.'[78] This contradicts Thiébault's claim that he fled with Madame Foy at the end of the battle.

The first French troops neared Torres Vedras at around midnight. *Capitaine* Bleuler wrote that on the night after the battle, his Swiss soldiers 'slept, one under the other, like a flock of tired sheep'.[79] *Maréchal des logis chef* Oyon (4e Dragons) summed up the morale of the French army at that time: 'Spirits were downcast; our position became more hopeless every day. We were marching on Lisbon. What could we hope for there? Of course, the English would follow us there; the news of our defeat would have preceded us; would we even be able to go there? What were we going to become?'[80]

---

76 Beauvais de Preau, *Victoires, Conquêtes*, p.109.
77 Anon. 'From Vimeiro to Corunna', p.37.
78 Griffon de Pleineville, *Invasion*, p.234.
79 Maag, *Schweizertruppen*, vol.I, p.474.
80 Oyon, *Campagnes*, Kindle Location 3324–3334.

17

Vimeiro: Aftermath

Table 23 shows the British casualties sustained in the battle. Unsurprisingly, Fane's, Anstruther's, and Ferguson's brigades suffered the most, with Hill's, Bowes' and Craufurd's brigades having no casualties at all. The total killed was 135, and the total wounded was 534, with 51 missing.

Portuguese casualties were two soldiers killed and seven wounded, plus seven horses killed and one wounded, most, if not all, probably from the cavalry.[1] There were also some casualties and panic amongst the Portuguese carters hired by the Commissariat. James Pipon told the inquiry: 'Some disorder ensued in the Park during the battle of 21st as one of the carters was killed and three wounded. Several escaped with their oxen, others by themselves, and many were prevented.'[2]

An officer of the 50th noted that his regiment's casualties came mainly from the fire of the French voltigeurs who covered both the advance and retreat of the French columns, and he also noted that the 43rd suffered badly while skirmishing. He saw 'at least a subdivision of their men lying killed in a deep gulley or trench, as they fell over each other, from a raking discharge of round or grape shot.'[3]

Sergeant Landsheit, searching for Lieutenant Colonel Taylor's body on the battlefield immediately after the action, 'found the declivity of the hill and the plain below covered with the killed and wounded. There they lay, English and French thrown promiscuously together, while hordes of peasants, together with women from our own army, were already in full occupation as plunderers.'[4] Benjamin Harris found a soldier of the 43rd and a French grenadier who had apparently simultaneously killed each other with bayonet thrusts.[5] An officer of HMS *Alfred*, who watched the battle from the masthead of his ship, went ashore after the action:

> It is now two o'clock in the morning, and I am fatigued and sleepy, having just returned from contemplating the field of battle. It was a shocking sight – ditches actually filled with dead bodies, and every step we took the wounded French would implore us for a drop of water. Before arriving at the field we passed through a thick wood, and the distant echo of the groans made us shudder.[6]

---

1   Gil, *A Infantaria Portuguesa*, vol.I, p.302.
2   TNA: WO 72/29: Questions for the commissariat from the enquiry. Reply from James Pipon, Lisbon, 4 October 1808.
3   Patterson, *Adventures*, p.48.
4   Gleig (ed.), *Hussar*, vol.I, p.274.
5   Curling, 'The Bayonet', p.400.
6   *The Sun*, 15 September 1808.

Table 23. British casualties at Vimeiro

Brigade	Unit	Killed									Wounded									Missing									Horses		
		Lt Col	Maj	Capt	Lt	Ens	Staff	Sgt	Drm	R&F	Lt Col	Maj	Capt	Lt	Ens	Staff	Sgt	Drm	R&F	Lt Col	Maj	Capt	Lt	Ens	Staff	Sgt	Drm	R&F	K	W	M
	General Staff												1																		
	Royal Artillery																		2											2	
	Royal Engineers																						1								
	20th Light Dragoons	1								19							2		22			1							30	10	1
1st	5th Foot																														
	9th Foot																														
	38th Foot																														
2nd	36th Foot									7			1	3	1	1	1	1	34												
	40th Foot									6			1	1			2		28												
	71st Foot									12			2	4	1	1	6		86												
3rd	29th Foot									2			1				1		10												
	82nd Foot				1					7							2		51												
4th	6th Foot																														
	32nd Foot																														
5th	45th Foot																														
	91st Foot																														
Light	50th Foot			1				1		18		1		3			1	1	61												
	5/60th Foot									14				2			1		21												
	2/95th Foot							1		5				1	1				13												
7th	2/9th Foot									3							1		14												
	2/43rd Foot							1		26		1	3	2			5	2	68												
	2/52nd Foot									3			1	1			2		31												
	97th Foot									4		1		1			2		14												
Acland	2nd Foot																1		6												
	20th Foot				1									1					5												
	Royal Staff Corps																														
Total		**1**		**1**	**2**			**3**		**128**		**3**	**10**	**19**	**3**	**2**	**27**	**4**	**466**			**1**	**1**						**30**	**12**	**1**

Source: TNA: WO 1/235: Casualty Return, Vimeiro, 21 August 1808.

Some of the *Alfred*'s crew helped with burying the dead. Several Royal Navy captains and other officers made their way to the battlefield while the action was taking place and spectated, apparently having to scatter twice to avoid French cavalry. They were shocked by the level of carnage.

A newspaper published a touching story of the aftermath of the battle:

> At the close of the Battle of the 21st, a British Officer seeing an old soldier sitting on the ground, resting his head on his hand in a most disconsolate posture, approached him and said 'What's the matter, brother soldier, are you wounded?' 'No, Sir,' replied the man. 'I am well enough – too well; but I remain here to see the remains of my poor son decently taken care of.' He then pointed to a heap at a little distance, which was the body, over whose yet scarcely cold and bleeding trunk he had spread his cloak! The officer shocked at the sight, yet unwilling to leave this trying scene without endeavouring to alleviate the old man's griefs, once more addressed him, saying, 'You must not let this business sink too deep into your mind. You are too old a soldier not to know it is the fortune of war.' 'Ah!, no, Sir, rejoined the veteran; 'it is not the common fortune of war to have two sons killed before my eyes in the field of battle. This is the second of my boys I have lost in this way; and this is the second time I have watched the corpse of my child in the field of battle!'[7]

The officer reportedly made sure the old soldier was looked after. Ensign Patterson noted that many of the abandoned French knapsacks 'contained various articles of plunder, including plate in many shapes and forms, which they had robbed from the unfortunate Portuguese. Books of songs, romances, and other commodities of a similar kind, were scattered about in all directions; and many a tender billet-doux lay open to the profane gaze and the laughing comments of the vulgar multitude.'[8] He also wrote that the grapes and watermelons in the fields provided the thirsty and wounded men with much-needed refreshment that helped to sustain them until the surgeons arrived.[9] Many of the British soldiers also removed the long white linen coats from the French dead and wore them around the camp.[10]

For deputy assistant quartermaster general Captain Henry Hardinge, his wound was to be the first of several in a career that would see him rise to the rank of field marshal and governor-general of India. Lieutenant Colonel Benjamin D'Urban wrote of Hardinge in a letter:

> I grieve to tell you that our inestimable friend, Captain Hardinge, was wounded in the hottest point of attack. It is his custom to be foremost in every attack, where an unaffected gallantry of spirit irresistibly carries him. Here he was conspicuous where all were brave, and it is a consolation to know that there is not a man in this army who does not regret this misfortune. The wound is in the bottom of the left side, under the lowest rib. The ball passed through, and the surgeons are of opinion that nothing is injured which can warrant any apprehension of a bad result. At the same time, it would be deceiving you to say that he is not severely wounded, or that a perfect recovery may not be tedious because

---

7   *Daily Advertiser, Oracle and True Briton*, 16 September 1808.
8   Patterson, *Adventures*, p.47.
9   Patterson, *Camps and Quarters*, vol.I, pp.221–222.
10   Leslie, *Journal*, p.52.

of the sinews which the ball has passed through. I will not attempt to tell you how I lament this accident.[11]

Royal Engineer First Lieutenant John Wells was missing, and Captain Landmann reported this to his corps' headquarters, writing, 'I have no doubt of his being a Prisoner, for had he been killed or wounded we should have found him, as the field of Battle has remained in our hands.'[12] During the battle Brigadier General Acland had observed the Portuguese cavalry moving a little too far forward and asked Wells to tell them to fall back. Wells, whose eyesight was poor, asked where he could find the Portuguese cavalry, and Acland told him they were just beyond some rising ground. Wells rode off but went too far himself. He spotted some cavalry, who, as he could see enough to tell that they were not wearing the blue of the light dragoons, he decided must be Portuguese. He spurred his horse forward and rode up to the officer at their front and, not speaking Portuguese, delivered the order in French, which heartily amused the French dragoon he was talking to. He was taken prisoner and sent to Junot, who allowed him to give his parole so he could watch the end of the battle. He was returned after the signing of the convention.[13]

The British officers killed were Lieutenant Colonel Taylor (20th Light Dragoons), Captain Arthur Coote (50th Foot), and Lieutenants Robert Donkin (82nd Foot) and George Brooke (20th Foot).

Taylor left a widow and three young children. Kellermann said of Taylor, 'None but a very brave man would have advanced as he did.' Kellermann was close to Taylor when he died and generously returned Taylor's horse to the regiment.[14] An obituary stated:

> With an understanding of more apparent vivacity than steadiness, with all the generous spirit, and some of the foibles of a soldier (in its best sense), he rather attracted the love of the liberal, the warm-hearted, and those whose natural disinterestedness of disposition is enlarged by education, unmercenary pursuits, and an expanse of mind, than of cold calculators, and men of selfish and narrow judgments. Often imprudent, quick, and variable in his feelings, he was one of whom a slight and partial view would have been very unjust and erroneous. There were moments when in the bosom of his family he would have been willing to have forgo all the laurels, with all the toils of a soldier but the covering was slight, the flame could never long be hid; and of the profession he had embraced by choice, he would never have been content to discharge the duties without glory.[15]

Major Andrew Creagh (29th Foot), wounded whilst commanding the light companies of Nightingall's brigade, must have been quite seriously injured as he received a pension of £200 per year plus a full year's extra pay. But he continued to serve until 1829. Captain Charles Hervey Smith (40th Foot) had already received a nasty head wound at Montevideo and three wounds, two of them severe, at Buenos Aires. Listed as slightly wounded in the return, he characterised it as severe in a later statement of his army service. He eventually received a pension of £70 per year for his wounds. Captain Saumarez Brock (43rd Foot) was shot through the ankle bone and received £100 per year but continued to serve into the 1830s. The wonderfully named Lieutenant Monsoon Molesworth

11   Quoted in C. Hardinge, *Rulers of India: Viscount Hardinge* (Oxford: Clarendon Press, 1891), p.14.
12   TNA: WO 55/977: Landmann to Morse, 21 August 1808.
13   Landmann, *Recollections*, vol.II, pp.311–314.
14   *The Gentleman's Magazine*, November 1808, p.963.
15   *The Gentleman's Magazine*, November 1808, p.964.

Madden, also of the 43rd, only claimed his pension of £70 per year in 1824, perhaps when his wound began to affect his ability to serve, as he then went on half-pay in 1826. Captain John Ewart (52nd Foot) was wounded through the right arm and later received a year's pay for that injury and another sustained in 1812 at Badajoz. Amongst the 71st Highlanders, Lieutenant Ralph Dudgeon was only listed as slightly wounded but still received a year's pay for being injured in the hand and leg. Robert McAlpin had been the sergeant major of the 71st but had been promoted to ensign in the 4th Royal Veteran Battalion. However, he was still serving with his old regiment as acting adjutant. He received a pension of £70 per year in 1811 for losing the use of his arm at Vimeiro. He disappears from the *Army List* in the same year. First Lieutenant William Cox (95th Rifles) is listed on the return as wounded, but it was his brother, 2nd Lieutenant John Cox, who received a musket ball in his right shoulder, for which he was granted £20 from Lloyd's Patriotic Fund.[16]

French casualties amounted to almost 1,800 men killed, wounded, or taken prisoner. Junot told Napoleon that 900 had been killed or taken prisoner. Many of the prisoners were also wounded. *Général de division* Delaborde was injured again, and all four of Junot's infantry brigade commanders were wounded: Brenier, Charlot, Solignac and Thomières, with Brenier also becoming a prisoner. *Colonel* Foy of the artillery was wounded in the thigh, and his horse was wounded several times. Margaron, at the head of the cavalry, had two horses killed under him. The casualties amongst the French officers were particularly severe. The 3/12e Légère had only three present and fit for duty after the battle.[17] Thiébault claims that 800 French wounded were treated on the field at Vimeiro by the French surgeons.[18]

Colonel Étienne Hippolyte Grandsaignes, aide de camp to Junot, was wounded. Another aide, 46-year-old *capitaine* Jean Baptiste Lalou, was wounded twice; his thigh was fractured, and he lost an arm. Six other staff officers were also wounded, one of whom was taken prisoner. Multiple British accounts, including Wellesley's dispatch, mention that Junot's chief of staff, *général de brigade* Paul Thiébault, was found dead on the battlefield, and newspapers published copies of the French order of battle supposedly found in his pocket, but he was not even wounded and retreated with the rest of the French.[19]

Corsican *sous-lieutenant* Ambroise Antoine Baptiste Arrighi, a student of the academy at Fontainebleau and officer of the 1er Dragons, whom Foy describes as 'allied by blood to the Bonaparte family', died in one of the cavalry charges covering the retreat of Brenier's and Solignac's brigades.[20] *Major* Jean Baptiste Weiss (26e Chasseurs à Cheval), wounded at Roliça, was injured again, as was one of his lieutenants, Italian Benoît Camille Bonaventure Barziza, shot in his left foot. *Major* Hector Therond (4e Dragons) was wounded, and *sous-lieutenant* Lemoyne (3e Dragons) was shot in the right leg and the left hip.

The French artillery lost *lieutenant* Thomas Louis Alexandre Dejort, killed, two *colonels* wounded, Foy and Prost, and four other officers wounded.

In Brenier's brigade, the 2e Légère had only two officers wounded, but the 4e Légère lost *capitaine adjudant major* Étienne Allier, killed, and five other officers wounded. The 70e Ligne lost *capitaines* Étienne Gravier and Robert Pierre Radiguet, killed, and four officers wounded.[21]

---

16   Relevant entries in Hall, *Biographical Dictionary,* and *Army List* for various years.
17   Griffon de Pleineville, *Invasion*, p.229.
18   Thiébault, *l'Expédition*, p.202.
19   *The Sun*, 8 September 1808.
20   Foy, *Invasion*, p.173.
21   Details of the French officer casualties are from Campos and de Blas, *Officiers de Napoléon*.

In Thomieres' brigade the 86e Ligne lost *capitaine* Jacques Joseph Paschali, *lieutenant* Philippe Joseph Barberet and *sous-lieutenant* Jean Chappe, killed, and six officers wounded, two of whom later died of their wounds. The 4e Suisse had two officers wounded.

In Solignac's brigade, the 12e Légère lost 52-year-old *lieutenant* Jean Baptiste Palenchon and *sous-lieutenant* Jean Pierre Garay, killed, and six officers wounded, two of whom were taken prisoner and one of which died soon after the battle. The 15e Légère had *sous-lieutenant* Jean Brondes killed and one officer wounded. The commander of the 3/58e Ligne, *chef de bataillon* Jean Baptiste Raymond Bayle Dugay, was wounded. He took two sabre cuts to the head from British cavalry, was left for dead on the battlefield, and was trampled by horses. As his battalion fought on the British left, whereas the 20th Light Dragoons charged in the centre, he was perhaps serving with the grenadier regiments of the reserve. His battalion lost *capitaines* Toussaint Faure and Pierre Nicolas François Lecat, killed, and five other officers wounded, one of whom died in November.

The only officer casualty from infantry regiments not in the order of battle, and so probably serving with the grenadier regiments, seems to have been *lieutenant* François Richard (15e Ligne), who was wounded.

In Charlot's brigade, the 32e Ligne had three officers wounded, one of whom, *capitaine* Simon Cailliot, was shot in the chest and left for dead on the battlefield. The 82e Ligne lost its commander, *chef de bataillon* Paul Peytavy, *lieutenant* Charles François Fauchereau, and *sous-lieutenant* Barthelemy Serres, killed and eight officers wounded. The battalion's *chirurgien major*, Joseph Sembres, suffered a shot to the right leg, four sabre cuts to the left thigh, one sabre cut to the face (as a result of which he lost part of his lower jaw and nine teeth), and five sabre cuts to the left forearm, wrist and hand. He survived.

Royal Engineer Major Richard Fletcher, who arrived with Moore after the battle, rode over the battleground on 25 August and noted the effects of the spherical case rounds used by the British artillery, 'Many of the French were found with five wounds in the same limb, and the explosion of one shell killed and wounded twenty-three men.'[22]

The results of an analysis of the surviving records of four of the French infantry regiments present by historian Antonio Grajal de Blas are shown in Table 24. The regimental history of the 82e states that the regiment lost 100 men killed at Vimeiro and had 197 men taken prisoner. The number of wounded is not given, but five soldiers who died of wounds on the *Minerva* transport on the way to France are listed, as are 36 who were injured and taken prisoner.[23]

Table 24. Sample of French casualties

Regiment	Killed	Wounded	Died of Wounds	POW
32e Ligne	1	32	4	12
58e Ligne	16	4	2	274
70e Ligne	35	80	3	8
86e Ligne	55	99		99

Source: Data from Antonio Grajal de Blas, based on data from <www.memoiredeshommes.sga.defense.gouv.fr.>.

---

22   TNA: WO 55/977: Fletcher to Morse, 26 August 1808.
23   Arvers, *Historique du 82e Régiment*, p.102.

After the battle, Brigadier General Anstruther talked with a French artillery captain he calls 'Scheffar' from Strasbourg. The officer in question must have been *capitaine* Jean Georges Schaffer of the 6e Régiment d'Artillerie à Pied, from Marlenheim in the Bas-Rhin area of the Alsace, who had been wounded. Schaffer told Anstruther that the French had bought Portuguese guns with them as they were lighter than the 30 French pieces they had left in Lisbon.[24]

Staff officer Captain George Jarvis had 66 men under his command to deal with the French prisoners after the battle and hoped to get more staff.[25] Lieutenant Leslie wrote in his memoir, 'Two genteel-looking young men who were among the prisoners told me that they were conscripts torn from their homes, and that when their regiment gave way they threw themselves down, pretending to be wounded, in order that they might fall into our hands.'[26] Lieutenant Henry Booth (43rd Foot) called the French prisoners 'very intelligent sharp eyed fellows, all life, their wits about them'. He then also wrote that the French officers also 'appeared very intelligent and gentlemanly men, but cruel to a degree, the French very seldom give quarter.'[27] Approximately 600 prisoners taken during the campaign were placed on four transports and sent to Britain.[28]

The French wounded lying on the battlefield were in danger of not only dying from their wounds or expiring from the heat but also of being murdered by the vengeful hands of the Portuguese peasants. William Warre, who came from a wine merchant family in Oporto, wrote the day after the battle:

> I am very much fatigued, having been yesterday till past 5 P.M. collecting the wounded English and French, and conducting them to a place of safety from the Portuguese cowards, who won't fight a 1/10 of a Frenchman with arms, but plunder and murder the wounded, poor wretches. Had I time I could tell you such things of these countrymen of mine, that you would not wonder at my despising them and having unpleasantly changed my opinion of their character.[29]

The British surgeons treated the French wounded as well as their own. Surgeon George Guthrie later wrote:

> A French soldier was brought into the village after the battle of Vimiera, wounded by a sword in the right side of the chest. He said he had lost a good deal of blood; was very pale; pulse small; extremities cold; breathing hurried and oppressed; had spit up some blood. On removing the handkerchief, a gaping wound presented itself, an inch and a half long, through which the cavity of the chest could be seen, the lung having receded. The wound did not bleed. As adhesive plasters would not keep the edges of the skin in perfect contact if he attempted to move, they were sewn together, and after the application of a compress he was much relieved. The next day all the symptoms were alleviated, and after the supervention of some serious inflammatory symptoms, he was forwarded to Lisbon, for embarkation for France, in a fair state of recovery.[30]

---

24   StAUL: msdep121/8/2/3/4/4: Anstruther's journal, pp.36–37.
25   LA: JARVIS/5/A/2/8: Jarvis to Philadelphia Jarvis, 22 August 1808.
26   Leslie, *Journal*, p.52.
27   Glover (ed.), *Unpublished Memoirs of the 43rd*, p.32.
28   Krajeski, *Shadow*, p.112.
29   Warre, *Letters*, p.28.
30   Guthrie, *Commentaries*, p.419.

Guthrie also treated a French artillery driver who had been shot in the head, the ball,

> … struck him on the anterior and inferior portion of the right parietal bone … I took him under my care, thinking from his freedom from bad symptoms and the slightness of the fracture that he would probably do well. The next morning I found him apparently dying. A portion of bone being removed, a thick coagulum of blood appeared beneath, apparently extending in every direction. Three more pieces of bone were taken away and the coagulum, which appeared to be an inch in thickness, was removed with difficulty with the help of a feather. The brain did not, however, regain its level, and the man shortly after died. The middle meningeal artery was torn across on the outside of the dura mater; the wound did not pass through to the inside, and there was no blood beneath the dura matter.[31]

Guthrie was himself wounded while he was attending to one of the two injured officers of the 40th Foot on the field. The officer had been shot in the thigh, and there was no exit wound. The ball was three inches deep in the leg. Guthrie extracted it, along with a piece of the officer's shirt. While he was doing so, he was hit on the legs by a spent ball, after which he and the casualty took cover in a watercourse. His wounds were slight, and he had them quickly dressed and returned to duty.[32]

Physician Adam Neale had been in Vimeiro trying to buy a mule when the first sounds of gunfire from the pickets had been heard. He had subsequently climbed the ridge behind the village, watched the whole battle unfold, and then moved along the ridge to the rear of the 40th Foot. After the action had finished, he helped treat the wounded:

> Close to the spot where Major-General Ferguson's brigade received the attack of the French, stood a small farm house, into which, it had been determined to carry the wounded. Thither I repaired, and witnessed a scene the most distressing. Around the building, whose interior was crowded with the wounded, lay a number of poor fellows in the greatest agony, not only from the anguish of their wounds (many of which were deplorable), but from the intense heat of the sun, which increased the parching fever induced by pain and loss of blood. Two fig-trees afforded the scanty blessing of a sort of shade to the few who were huddled together beneath their almost leafless branches. Over the surrounding field lay scattered the fragments of arms, and military equipments of every description – caps, muskets, swords, bayonets, belts, and cartouch-boxes covered the ground; on which were also stretched, in many an awful group, the friend and foe, the dying and the dead.[33]

For many of the wounded, he could do little but offer kind words or a little opium, although he records bleeding an officer of his acquaintance who had had a musket ball extracted. To get some of the wounded out of the hot sun, he got the pioneers, who had been burying the dead of both armies in a mass grave, to break down the doors of a winery outbuilding and clear it. The damp floor was covered with vegetation, and as many wounded as possible moved inside. A subaltern's guard had to be provided to protect the wounded prisoners from the local population, who had

---

31   Guthrie, *Commentaries*, p.315.
32   Crumplin, *Guthrie's War*, pp.29–30.
33   Neale, *Letters*, pp.15–16.

been dispatching the French left on the field. The wife of a wounded 71st Highlander helped Neale search the house for food and made a broth of corn, tallow and hemp for the wounded.[34] That evening, Neale left the wounded in the care of a hospital mate and walked the two miles to Vimeiro:

> On crossing the fields to get into the Lourinha road, I shuddered as we involuntarily stumbled over many an unburied corpse of man and horse. We found the road almost impassable from the number of tumbrils and artillery waggons of the enemy, which were broken down in every direction. Our ears were saluted on passing the church-yard by the heavy moaning and exclamations of the wounded French, with whom the church and the cemetery were crowded — Ah, mon Dieu, mon Dieu, le sang coule je meurs, je meurs.[35] At length, with a good deal of difficulty, we reached Vimeira. The streets of the village were choked up by the long line of oxen-wains, bearing in from the fields the wounded, whose haggard countenances appeared more wretched from the glare of the torches which blazed around them, and increased the horrors of the impressive scene.[36]

Captain Harry Ross-Lewin (32nd Foot) also witnessed the scene at the church in Vimeiro:

> Upon entering the church-yard of the village of Vimeira, my attention was arrested by very unpleasant objects – one, a large wooden dish filled with hands, that had just been amputated – another, a heap of legs placed opposite. On one side of the entrance to the church lay a French surgeon who had received a six-pound shot in the body. The men who had undergone amputation, were ranged round the interior of the building. In the morning they had rushed to the combat, full of ardour and enthusiasm, and now they were stretched, pale, bloody and mangled, on the cold flags, some writhing in agony, others fainting with loss of blood, and the spirits of many poor fellows among them making a last struggle to depart from their mutilated tenements.[37]

The Commissariat had 40 empty carts that were quickly tasked with carrying the wounded to the hospitals and the beach. Another 120 of the 360 loaded carts were unloaded so that they could also be used.[38] Adam Neale helped transfer the wounded men he had looked after from the cottage to the coast:

> On reaching the shore, we found a number of our sailors, with lanthorns in their hands, busily employed in removing into the boats the wounded from Vimeira. It was highly gratifying to me to witness the very attentive and humane manner in which this service was performed by these kind honest-hearted tars; who, during the whole of a very cold night, were wading nearly up to the middle in the wash of the sea.[39]

---

34   Neale, *Letters*, pp.17–20.
35   My God, my God, the blood is flowing I am dying, I am dying.
36   Neale, *Letters*, pp.20–21.
37   Ross-Lewin, *Life*, vol.I, p.223.
38   TNA: WO 72/29: Questions for the commissariat from enquiry. Reply from James Pipon, Lisbon, 4 October 1808.
39   Neale, *Letters*, p.25.

The expedition had at least one hospital ship, the *Enterprise*. The ship would have had cradles laid out below decks for the wounded and a staff of a physician, a surgeon and four mates, six assistants, a servant to the surgeon, a baker and four washermen.[40]

Captain Francis Austen of the *St Albans* recorded in his log for 22 August, 'Sent all the boats on shore to assist in taking off the wounded of our army to the hospital ships. Boats also employed embarking French prisoners on board some of the transports.' The *St Albans* then sailed on the 24th to Oporto with a convoy of 29 transports to offload the wounded. They arrived on the 27th, and it took 24 hours to ferry all the wounded ashore. The convoy then continued to Spithead, arriving on 2 September, where the prisoners were transferred to the hulks in the harbour.[41] The French prisoners would be held until the war's end. One was Laurent Maquet of the 58e Ligne, a bricklayer from near Liege, who was confined in a prison at Portsmouth for over two years before being transferred to one in Scotland. He was released in 1814.[42] Brigadier General John Sontag at Oporto reported to Castlereagh: 'It is not possible to express to your Lordship the gratitude and zeal, expressed by all ranks of people here towards Great Britain. The wounded British soldiers were carried by Priests, Portuguese Officers and Gentlemen, from the landing place to the Hospital, carriages sent for those who could not bear that conveyance.'[43]

Private William Billows (2nd Foot) wrote that his battalion was halfway up the hill on the right of the British position when the French attacked, and they were ordered to counter march back down and onto the start of the ridge on the left where they had a good view of the battle. The morning after the action, Acland's brigade crossed the bridge into Vimeiro:

> I saw no inhabitants, but most of the houses were full of wounded men. One house I took particular notice of as I passed it. It looked like a butcher's shop, for there came out of it two doctors to look at us, with once white aprons and sleeves on their arms, but now they were covered with human blood, scarce a white place to be seen on them, and two or three wounded men laying at the door covered in blood, waiting their turn to be dressed. Oh what sites are to be seen after an action.[44]

The Reverend James Wilmot Ormsby, a chaplain on the staff, arrived on 27 August with Moore's convoy and visited the hospitals that were treating around 400 French wounded:

> A novice in such scenes, the sight affected me deeply. They were principally young men, and delicate; rendered still more so, doubtless, by their sufferings. They wore their long, white, linen coats and trousers, which serve the double purpose of cool clothing on such occasions, and saving their regimentals on march and in action. Many operations had been performed, and the surgeons said that few of them could survive. To one I addressed myself, and lamented the horrors of war; commiserating his pain, though an enemy … He replied, with a mixture of pride and indignation, that he gloried in his wounds, and that war was the greatest happiness of life. To such a disputant I had nothing to rejoin, but to wish his recovery, and that he might be doomed to bear the miseries of peace, and

---

40   D. Steel, *The Shipmaster's Assistant and Owner's Manual* (London: Steel, 1801), p.43.
41   Hubback & Hubback, *Sailor Brothers*, pp.200, 202.
42   B. Wilkin & R. Wilkin, *Fighting for Napoleon* (Barnsley: Pen & Sword, 2015), p.165.
43   TNA: WO 1/213: Sontag to Castlereagh, 2 September 1808.
44   Billows, *Nothing Pertickler Happened*, p.31.

the inconveniences of two legs, two arms, and the natural features of his face, for the remainder of his life.[45]

An Unmerciful Beating

In a general order issued after the battle, Wellesley was effusive in his praise for his troops:

> Lieutenant-General Sir A. Wellesley congratulates the army on the signal victory they have this day obtained over the enemy, and returns them his warmest thanks for their resolute and heroic conduct. He experienced the sincerest pleasure in witnessing various instances of the gallantry of the corps, and has, in particular, to notice the distinguished behaviour of the Royal Artillery, 20th light dragoons, the 36th, 40th, 43rd, 50th, 52nd, 60th, 71st, 82nd, 95th, and 97th regiments. It will afford the Lieutenant-General the greatest pleasure to report to the Commander-in-Chief the bravery displayed by all the troops, and the high sense he entertains of their meritorious and excellent conduct throughout the day.[46]

The order then went on to denominate Acland's brigade as the 8th, transfer the two companies of the 1/95th to the Light Brigade, and move a company of the 5/60th from the Light Brigade to both the 7th and 8th brigades.

Wellesley singled out the men and commanders of the same regiments in his official dispatch. He added, 'In mentioning Colonel Burne and the 36th regiment upon this occasion, I cannot avoid adding that the regular and orderly conduct of this corps throughout the service, and their gallantry and discipline in action, have been conspicuous.'[47] Burne was also singled out in Wellesley's letter to Castlereagh: 'You will see in it that I have mentioned Colonel Burne, of the 36th regiment, in a very particular manner; and I assure you that there is nothing that will give me so much satisfaction as to learn that something has been done for this old and meritorious soldier. The 36th regiment are an example to this army.' Colonel Burne seems to owe his prominence in Wellesley's letters to Anstruther. In his journal for the 22nd, Anstruther wrote, 'Sir Arthur read out his dispatches – not very elegant but clear enough, very satisfactory in as far as I am concerned. Begged him to mention Burne of the 36th particularly which is done.'[48] Burne was made governor of Carlisle Castle in September.[49]

Wellesley also gave due credit to Spencer and his brigade commanders:

> I was much indebted to Major General Spencer's judgment and experience in the decision which I formed in respect to the number of troops allotted to each point of defence, and for his advice and assistance throughout the action. In the position taken up by Major General Ferguson's brigade, and in its advances upon the enemy, that officer showed equal bravery and judgment; and much praise is due to Brig. General Fane and Brig. General

45 J.W. Ormsby, *An Account of the Operations of the British Army and of the state and sentiments of the People of Portugal and Spain* (London: Carpenter, 1809), vol.I, pp.31–32.
46 Wellington (ed.), *Supplementary Despatches*, vol.VI, p.121.
47 TNA: WO 1/235: Wellesley to Burrard, 21 August 1808.
48 StAUL: msdep121/8/2/3/4/4: Anstruther's journal, p.38.
49 Burghm & McGuigan, *Brigade Commanders*, p.72.

Anstruther for their gallant defence of their position in front of Vimeiro, and to Brig. General Nightingall, for the manner in which he supported the attack upon the enemy made by Major General Ferguson.[50]

Spencer was made a Knight Companion of the Order of the Bath for his part in the campaign, and Wellesley unsuccessfully lobbied for similar honours for Hill and Ferguson.[51] In his letter to the Duke of York the day after the battle, Wellesley stated, 'that this is the only action that I have ever been in, in which everything passed as it was directed, and no mistake was made by any of the Officers charged with its conduct.'[52] When passing on Castlereagh's reply and praise for the action to Wellesley, Burrard wrote: 'I shall ever consider it as one of the most fortunate circumstances that an opportunity was afforded me of witnessing what an able General can accomplish with a well-disciplined British army.'[53] In another letter, he wrote, 'I was near Sir Arthur the greatest part of the action, saw everything that passed, and never found a moment in which I could wish an alteration to the dispositions he made, and the longer I studied the mountainous ground we acted upon, the more I had to approve of them.'[54]

Anstruther's opinion of the battle was, 'The most satisfactory part of the whole, is the manifest and decided superiority of our infantry over that of the enemy. In fact they never had for a moment a chance of penetrating, and whenever we advanced we drove them before us without difficulty.'[55] Nightingall, ignoring the admittedly small Portuguese contribution to the victory, wrote:

> In all my various services in different parts of the world I never saw any thing so fine as the action of the 21st, and we proved that when left alone, without allies, British troops will always beat French when they meet on anything like equal terms. We had hardly more than half our force actually engaged on that day & I fancy the French had at least 12000 men.[56]

Wellesley's military secretary, Henry Torrens, wrote, 'The troops behaved with a degree of coolness and steadiness which would have reflected credit upon them on a common parade.'[57]

Staff officer Captain Henry Cooke pointed out several errors that the French made in his post-battle analysis: 'The bravery displayed by the enemy was totally characteristic of the nation; impetuous, rapid and severe; the errors committed by their commanders numerous for example – the centre column which was totally destroyed, advanced within range of grape before they deployed, altho' from the nature of the ground, 200 paces in the rear they could not have been seen.' He then said that the French retreat quickly became a scramble and that cavalry were not brought forward to cover their infantry as they fell back. Cooke felt it was 'pleasing to a British officer to observe their errors, because he then learns that the good people of England are apt to overvalue an enemy, whom tho' respected, should never be feared with such troops as we possessed.' He continued:

---

50   TNA: WO 1/235: Wellesley to Burrard, 21 August 1808.
51   Wellington (ed.), *Supplementary Despatches*, vol.VI, pp.182–183.
52   Gurwood (ed.), *Wellington's Dispatches*, vol.IV, p.114.
53   Wellington (ed.), *Supplementary Despatches*, vol.VI, p.137.
54   BL: Add MS 49485: Burrard to York, 21 August 1808.
55   BL: Add MS 49503: Anstruther to Gordon, 22 August 1808.
56   BL: Add MS 49503: Nightingall to Gordon, 25 August 1808.
57   BL: Add MS 49485: Torrens to Gordon, 22 August 1808.

Their artillery were served in a most contemptible manner, & from want of science in their officers finally lost – from the manner in which they left us, we were convinced that no efforts upon the part of their officers could avail – fatigued, beaten at every point with the loss of their whole artillery & tumbrils; minus we since learn 3500 men, it was to be hoped that some advantage might have been taken of their state, and that we should not have contented ourselves with a single victory, when the total destruction of the enemy seemed only to require that we should move.[58]

Staff officer Captain Henry Hardinge wrote, 'the courage of British troops in the field admits of no doubt, but it is a source of peculiar satisfaction to have discovered that in skill and manoeuvring light troops we are in no way inferior to the French.'[59]

Thiébault thought that Junot's decision to split Delaborde's division and send the two brigades in separate directions was where it had all started to go wrong for the French:

Some explanation of this amazing action was needed; and some thought that during the breakfast on the grass of which we had just been partaking, at which the General had drunk various wines and liqueurs, he had taken too much, or, at any rate, too much considering the heat of the day, if not in actual quantity. Others maintained that the sight of the enemy or the smell of powder excited him till he lost the use of his faculties. For my own part, ever since recalling these incidents two years later at the time of the affair at Astorga, where he sent a storming-party to destruction, I have been unable to avoid the thought that the reasons alleged – fumes of wine or dizziness from powder smoke – must have been complicated by the beginnings of mental derangement.[60]

Junot's behaviour did become increasingly erratic over the next few years, possibly the result of his several head injuries and what today would be termed traumatic brain injury and perhaps post-traumatic stress. His mental health almost completely broke down, and he was removed from his command. He died in 1813 from an infection after breaking his leg during an attempt to fly like a bird and then trying to amputate it himself.[61]

However, Thiébault's suggestion that the French should have spent the 21st resting after the night march, spending the day reconnoitring and demonstrating to gauge Wellesley's strength, and then during the night sending all but the reserve to Lourinhã to turn the allied left is also flawed.[62] It presupposes that Burrard, even if he did not advance, would not have addressed the weakness of the allied left and not have been able to respond to any attack by shifting troops, as Wellesley did.

Junot, severely outnumbered and attacking a strong defensive position with troops of questionable quality, was never very likely to triumph at Vimeiro. His decision to attack the village of Vimeiro was sound because if he had managed to push Fane and Anstruther off the hill, the commissariat and artillery park could have been taken, severely hampering any further British moves towards Lisbon. Sending Brenier to make his attack on the British left was also sensible but

58   BL: Add MS 49503: Cooke to Gordon, 6 September 1808.
59   Quoted in Hardinge, *Rulers of India*, p.16.
60   Butler (trans.), *Thiébault*, Vol.II, p.208.
61   MacKay, *Tempest*, pp.452–453.
62   Butler (trans.), *Thiébault*, Vol.II, pp.209–210.

never likely to amount to much given the numbers that Wellesley could move to that flank. Junot did not expect Brenier to have to march so far, and sending Solignac to strengthen the attack on the left weakened the main attack on the village. The French ended up conducting a series of uncoordinated actions that each had very little chance of success and that Wellesley could defeat in turn. However, writing after the battle, Junot put as positive a spin on the result as he could, stating, 'if we did not win, we were not beaten; we remained five hours in the presence of each other, without the enemy daring to leave his positions'.[63]

Junot could have taken up an entrenched defensive position closer to Lisbon instead of marching to meet Wellesley, but with Moore due to arrive any day, the population of Lisbon on the brink of revolt, the dire supply situation of his army, and the equally dire news from Spain, he felt that his position was already untenable and his only hope was to try and gain more favourable terms by giving battle, even if the chance of victory was slight.[64]

After the battle, Junot had gathered Delaborde, Loison, Kellermann and Thiébault for a council of war and asked them if they should fight again, how and where, and if not, what they should do. The council quickly concluded they were in no state to give or receive battle and should retreat to Lisbon. Morale was low, as were ammunition stocks, and the troops were exhausted. The allied troops were superior in quantity and quality and were buoyed by their victory. As Thiébault wrote in his history, 'we had nothing more to hope for from a victory, and the slightest setback put us at the discretion of the English and the Portuguese.'[65]

In his letter to Castlereagh, Wellesley wrote that he had gained a 'complete victory', that the troops had performed excellently and that 'we only wanted a few hundred more cavalry to annihilate the French army.'[66] In his letter to the Duke of Richmond, he also stated that he had 'completely defeated' the French.[67] Wellesley used similar language in a letter to his brother William:

> We gave the French an unmerciful beating yesterday. Sir Harry Burrard arrived on the evening of the 20th., & I did everything in my power to induce him to march on; which he resisted till he should be reinforced by Moore; a decision with which I was not pleased any more than I was with the manner in which it was made. Sir Harry did not come on shore that night; & as I am the 'Child of Fortune', & Sir Harry did not chuse to march towards the Enemy, the Enemy came to us with his whole force & attacked is in our position; & we gained a most compleat Victory; Sir Harry not being in the field till one of the attacks was completely beaten off, & the other begun & all the dispositions made for defeating it. The French have lost not less 3000 men I should think.

Wellesley's characterisation of the battle as a complete victory when the French, although thoroughly defeated, did retreat with much of their army intact would cause problems in the coming weeks. Still, it would have been a very modest general who wrote up such a victory in anything but such glowing terms, and generals are not, on the whole, known for their modesty. However, Wellesley also wrote, 'I have desired Campbell who is going home to tell you that I am by no means

---

63 Griffon de Pleineville, *Invasion*, p.305.
64 Griffon de Pleineville, *Invasion*, pp.307–308.
65 Thiébault, *l'Expédition*, p.205.
66 Gurwood (ed.), *Wellington's Dispatches*, vol.IV, p.115.
67 Wellington (ed.), *Supplementary Despatches*, vol.VI, p.122.

satisfied with the way in which I see things will go on here; & I should be glad to be called home to my Office [in Ireland], or any thing else in which I could be useful.'[68]

In his response to the Vimeiro dispatch, Castlereagh asked Burrard to 'signify to Lt. Gen. Sir Arthur Wellesley that the dispositions made by him to receive the Enemy and the skill and valour displayed by him effecting their total defeat have afforded His Majesty the highest satisfaction.' Castlereagh also wrote, 'The delicacy and honourable forbearance which determined you though present in the action not to interfere with the arrangements previously made by Lieut. Gen. Sir Arthur Wellesley and then in progress of execution has been observed by His Majesty with approbation.'[69] The Duke of Richmond wrote to Wellesley, 'You must have bribed him [Junot] to attack you when he did. You are certainly a lucky fellow in having the whole of the honour, which you well deserve, but which a few hours would have robbed you of. We are lucky, too, that you did command, for nobody could have done better.'[70]

At least one French general was also impressed with the performance of the British soldiers. An officer of HMS *Alfred* reported that 'One of our Lieutenants said to General Breniere, [sic] last night (who is on board us), "Now, Sir, tell me candidly what do you think of an English Soldier?" His answer was, "I never had an opinion of them until to-day – they are devils indeed."' Captain Bligh mentioned that Junot was supposed to still have 20,000 men after the battle, which perhaps shows that the prisoners had imparted the true numbers of the French in Portugal, and the lower estimates that Wellesley preferred had been discounted. Bligh wrote, 'What false accounts we must have received!'

Lieutenant Colonel Robe was again effusive in his praise of his gunners and unreserved in his criticism of the shortages he had faced when he wrote to his headquarters:

> And never was a man better supported by his officers and soldiers than I have been; I would not change one of them from the major to the youngest subaltern for any thing in the world, and only regret my son was not with me: My men are staunch and the admiration of the army, and had they been properly supplied with horses and with stores, as they should have embarked from England and Europe, would not have produced a more efficient artillery. I shall have occasion to write to you, and to the board on the latter subjects, as soon as I have time; but give me leave to say, that never more will I leave England taking my provisions of artillery on trust, and coming upon an army burthened with cast horses or no horses at all, or with brigades unsupplied with any stores to make repairs or scarce a shoe to put on horses, when I could beg them; – this may be strong, but I have reason to use the expressions, after suffering the inconveniences occasions by the want of those supplied.
>
> Nothing but the unexampled assistance and attention, of Sir A. Wellesley, and the General Officers could have brought this artillery into the field, in an efficient manner, and I am proud to say, they have never yet stopped an hour for us.
>
> I have now from experience, a right to speak of what the whole army have witnessed, the good effects of in more than one instance, I mean Shrapnell's Spherical Case: - the man must be blind, who does not allow its superiority, and I mean to demand, if left with me,

---

68   Webster, 'Some Letters', pp.5–6.
69   TNA: WO 1/235: Castlereagh to Burrard, 4 September 1808.
70   Wellington (ed.), *Supplementary Despatches*, vol.V, p.476.

on any future occasion, half of my whole stock in that sort of ammunition for my guns: This, with some other points, will be the subject of a future letter, mean time I am happy to say my loss today has only been two drivers, two horses killed, one gunner, two horses wounded.[71]

The artillery was using a mix of the Irish Commissariat horses, Portuguese mares, French prize horses and oxen. On 1 September, Robe wrote that the artillery of Wellesley's division of the army needed 250 horses to take to the field again as many of the Commissariat horses were 'blind; they now fall off very fast', and the Portuguese mares, 'tho' good of their kind, are much too weak for the service.'[72]

Wellesley was also much impressed by Shrapnel's invention and wrote in October 1808:

I shall have great pleasure in testifying at any time the great benefit which the army lately under my command derived from the spherical case shot in two actions with the enemy, a benefit which I am convinced will be enjoyed whenever they shall be judiciously and skilfully used.

I consider it, however, to be very desirable that this invention, and the use which the British army have made of it, should not be made public. Our enemies are not aware of the cause of the effect of our artillery, of which they have complained; and we may depend upon it that any public mention, or notice, of the benefit which we have derived from this description of shot, would induce them immediately to adopt it.[73]

In his memoir, Captain Landmann of the Royal Engineers mentions that Captain Eliot's 9-pounders firing on a column of cavalry at a range of 2,000 yards were 'so perfectly directed, and the fuzes cut with so much accuracy, that the cavalry turned round and effected a hasty retreat.'[74] Henry Hardinge also commented on the artillery, saying that the French 'confess ours to be superior to any of theirs. They fired much, and we have scarcely a man wounded by artillery fire. The French cavalry simply disgraced themselves.'[75]

Robe's return of the French ordnance taken listed, 'One 6 pounder, four 4 pounders, three 2 pounders, six 5½ inch howitzers, two ammunition wagons, twenty one Portuguese ammunition cars, forty horses, four mules.'[76] The carts contained powder, shells, stores and 20,000 musket rounds. The small calibre of some of the French guns is notable and must have put them at a disadvantage versus the heavier guns of the British. By the evening of the 21st, 12 captured guns had already been sent to the ships.[77] No imperial eagles were taken, but the regimental history of the 50th Foot states that the regiment 'captured a standard, pole, and box, which were borne by a sergeant between the colours during succeeding campaigns.'[78]

71   TNA: WO 55/1193: Robe to Macleod, 21 August 1808.
72   TNA: WO 55/1193: Robe to Macleod, 1 September 1808.
73   Wellington (ed.), *Supplementary Despatches*, vol.VI, p.166.
74   Landmann, *Recollections*, vol.II, p.209.
75   Quoted in Hardinge, *Rulers of India*, p.16.
76   TNA: WO 1/235: Return of Ordnance and Ammunition taken in the Action of the 21st August, 1808.
77   TNA: WO 55/1193: Robe to Macleod, 21 August 1808.
78   Fyler, *History of the 50th*, p.108.

For many of the troops, the campaign had been their first. Ensign Henry Wyndham wrote, 'I deem myself most fortunate in having been present at the actions of the 17th and 21st, as a person might have been all his life in the service without having seen a campaign which may prove as beneficial to a young military man as this.'[79] Ensign Samuel Laing of the Royal Staff Corps recorded his impressions of Roliça and Vimeiro:

> In these two actions, the first I had ever been in, the impression or feeling on my mind, and as I conceive on the minds of all who like myself were new to the business, was that joyous exhilarated state of spirits which occurs when one is engaged in a fox chase or other exhilarating pursuit which engrosses the mind. The dropping of men and the sight of the dead makes no impression, and I am convinced such was the state of mind of all to whom actual battle was a new thing, and who were so far engaged in the reality of the scene, that imagination had no room to work. I made an observation also in those two actions that the soldiers naturally I suppose leave their muskets somewhat too high. The consequence is that the bullets fall in a kind of zone of a few yards in breadth, and in the breadth of this zone they fall very thick and keep pattering the dust like hail in a dusty road but within this zone scarcely a bullet tells so that in fact the nearer to the enemy the less danger, as the bullets pass overhead and fall among those behind.[80]

Much is often made of Wellesley positioning his men on the reverse slope of a hill so that they were out of sight of the enemy and sheltered from artillery fire. As the enemy crested the hill, they would be surprised by the sudden appearance of the lines of redcoats, who would then deliver a shattering volley. There was nothing innovative about this, and examples of the practice can be found as far back as the Seven Years War.[81] Vimeiro is often cited as a case of him using the reverse slope tactic.[82] However, on the hill at Vimeiro Fane's and Anstruther's defence of their position seems to match the tactics recommended in an article entitled 'On the Attack and Defence of Unfortified Heights' and specifically a section for light infantry, in *The British Military Library* – a work written to educate young officers. The article advised that light troops be positioned on the slope towards the enemy and on the flanks. As the enemy approached, they would harass them but fall steadily back up the hill. On the crown of the hill, the enemy would be met by a formed reserve – in Fane's case, the 50th Foot – which would then force the enemy back.[83] Accounts of the battle do not mention the 50th, 97th or 52nd as being on the reverse slope. Ensign Patterson of the 50th describes their position as being:

> ... posted on an eminence, to the right of the village; the 50th, being the junior corps, was stationed in the centre, and consequently on the highest part of the hill. From hence,

---

79   BL: Add. MS 49481: Wyndham to Gordon, 8 September 1808.
80   Fereday (ed.), *Samuel Laing*, pp.114–115.
81   Jaycock, *Wellington's Command*, p.59, cites *Principes de la stratégie développés par la relation de la campagne de 1796 en Allemagne*, by Charles, Archduke of Austria, as an example of the tactic being noted much earlier.
82   Chatrand, *Vimeiro*, p.77; Jaycock, *Wellington's Command*, p.59.
83   Brent Nosworthy, 'Sir Charles Oman on Line versus Column', in P. Griffith (ed.), Modern Studies of the War in Spain and Portugal, 1808-1814 (London: Greenhill, 1999), pp.251–252; Anon., 'On the Attack and Defence of Unfortified Heights', Anon. (ed.), *The British Military Library* (London: Carpenter, 1804), vol.I, p.346.

as the day was fine, and the atmosphere quite clear, we had a distinct view of all that was going forward in the front, also a tolerably good prospect in every other direction.[84]

Patterson's and Lieutenant Colonel Walker's accounts also make it clear that the French column was still advancing up the hill when the 50th fired a volley and charged. Anstruther refers to the position of the 97th as 'concealed behind a dip of the ground'[85], which is very different to being on the reverse slope. The top of Vimeiro hill is, in places, over 50 metres wide and positioning troops slightly back from the edge of the forward slope rather than on the reverse would probably have been sufficient to offer some concealment from the French as they approached.

It is on the left, on the long ridge, that many historians claim that the reverse slope tactic was used. Oman wrote of Solignac: 'On the hill above he could see only the thin line of British skirmishers, but hidden behind the crest was the main body of Wellesley's right wing'.[86] Fortescue claims that Ferguson's and Nightingall's brigades were drawn up along the ridge facing east and that the British skirmishers engaged Solignac's brigade as they came up the slope of the ridge and then were met by the lines of redcoats at the top.[87] However, Wellesley's dispatch clearly says that the brigades on the ridge were formed 'with their right upon the valley which leads into Vimeiro, and their left upon the other ravine, which separates these heights from the range which terminates at the landing place at Maceira.'[88] So, across the ridge and not along it.

Oman's scenario also does not match the accounts of the extended skirmishing and French cannonade from those with Ferguson and Nightingall. Foy makes it clear that Solignac was already on the large flat area on top of the ridge before he made contact with Ferguson, and the contemporary maps all show the French advancing down the length of the ridge, not up its slope.[89] Napier also has Solignac advancing towards Ferguson down from the highest point of ridge.[90] According to a description of the battle that accompanied a map sent to Horse Guards, Wellesley ordered the troops on the left to 'move out of their original position to meet the enemy, they were engaged when they had advanced 1/3 of the way down the summit of the long sloping heights … [and] continued to drive them to the top of it and down from hence into the grounds beyond.'[91]

The reverse slope tactic and discussions about French columns versus British lines became popular topics for military historians in the twentieth century, and they seem to have been looking for occasions when it might have been used and imposed it inappropriately on the action at Vimeiro.

The debate about the use of the reverse slope at Vimeiro is significant in the evaluation of Wellesley's dispositions. If the reverse slope tactic was used, then Wellesley reacted quickly to Junot's attempt at outflanking him and had troops in place, ready to counter it. However, if Ferguson's and the other brigades were not on the reverse slope waiting, but marched up along the ridge to where Solignac had already occupied the highest ground, Wellesley was more seriously wrong-footed. Anyone visiting the battlefield can see how dominating the ridge is, and it does

---

84   Patterson, *Adventures*, p.40.
85   StAUL: msdep121/8/2/3/4/4: Anstruther's journal, pp.30–31.
86   Oman, *History*, vol.I, pp.257–258.
87   Fortescue, *British Army*, vol.VI, p.230.
88   TNA: WO 1/235: Wellesley to Burrard, 21 August 1808.
89   Foy, *Invasion*, p.173; TNA: WO 78/5949; WO 78/5950; MPF 1/220.
90   Napier, *History*, vol.I, p.138.
91   BL: Add. MS 49503: Explanation relating to the Battle of the 21st August between the British under Sir A Wellesley and the French forces under General Junot.

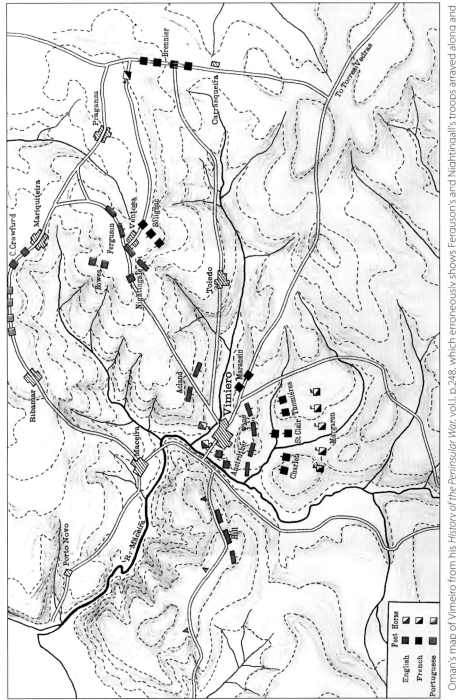

Oman's map of Vimeiro from his *History of the Peninsular War*, vol.I, p.248, which erroneously shows Ferguson's and Nightingall's troops arrayed along and not across the ridge.

seem remiss of Wellesley not to have placed more troops there, even if there was no good water source and the troops were only meant to be on the ground one night.

It was Sir Charles Oman who first seems to have claimed that reverse slopes were a central part of Wellesley's tactical repertoire. While writing his *History of the Peninsular War,* Oman tried to come up with a reason why the British so often beat the French in the battle. He decided that it was the tactical superiority of the defensive line over the attacking column. He postulated that steady troops, deployed in line, would always be able to bring sufficient fire upon an enemy advancing in column to defeat them. The whole of a battalion in line could fire whereas only the front ranks of a column could. Oman wrote extensively on column vs line in a chapter of his book *Wellington's Army*, and he also had a very similar chapter in *Studies in the Napoleonic Wars*.[92]

According to Oman, Wellesley thought that for a line to beat a column the three conditions had to be met: '(1) that the line must not be exposed before the moment of actual conflict; (2) that till the critical moment it must be screened by a line of skirmishers impenetrable to the enemy's *tirailleurs*; (3) that it must be properly covered on its flanks, either by the nature of the ground, or by cavalry and artillery.'[93] For Oman, a reverse slope position was Wellington's most commonly used method of fulfilling his first condition.[94]

Brent Nosworthy examined Oman's ideas on line versus column in a chapter of *Modern Studies of the War in Spain and Portugal, 1808–1814* and notes how influential they were, with historians such as Michael Glover and Jac Weller repeating and developing them. However, Nosworthy then looked at how well the hypothesis can be applied to battles, including the most often-quoted example of Buçaco, thereby demonstrating that the actions were more complex than simply line versus column and that many other factors help explain the allied victory. He pointed to the use of artillery and bayonet charges as elements Oman and others ignored, and concludes: 'The debate as to which possessed superior capabilities, line or column, is largely spurious, created by the naïveté of turn-of-the-century historians who were ignorant of, or eschewed, a more detailed understanding of Napoleonic era fighting methods.'[95] One side-effect of Oman's ideas and the subsequent influence of them is that the concentration on Wellington's defensive tactics has unfairly characterised him as a defensive general, when in the majority of his greatest victories – Assaye, Salamanca, Vittoria and many others – he was the attacker.

While line versus column was a factor in the allied victory at Vimeiro, there were many others of more significance, including: Wellesley's qualitative and quantitative advantage in troops, the handling of those troops by his brigade and battalion commanders, the use of spherical-case rounds, and Junot's poor coordination of his attacks.

---

92   C. Oman, *Wellington's Army* (London: Arnold, 1913), C. Oman, *Studies in the Napoleonic Wars* (Elstree: Greenhill, 1987).

93   Oman, *Studies*, p.99.

94   Oman, *Studies*, p.100.

95   B. Nosworthy, 'Sir Charles Oman on Line versus Column', in P. Griffith (ed.), *Modern Studies of the War in Spain and Portugal, 1808–1814* (London: Greenhill, 1999), p.259.

18

Negotiations

The Suspension of Arms

On the day after the battle, two significant arrivals occurred at the British camp at Vimeiro. The first was Lieutenant General Sir Hew Dalrymple. He had embarked on HMS *Phoebe* at Gibraltar on the 13th, met with Cotton off the Tagus on the 19th, and then sailed for the Mondego to meet the reinforcements from Britain. On the 21st, the ships off Porto Novo were spotted, and the *Phoebe*'s first lieutenant and one of Dalrymple's aides de camp were sent ashore for news. They came back at 1:00 a.m. with accounts of Wellesley's victory.[1] The *Phoebe* then anchored in Maceira Bay.

In the morning, Burrard heard a salute being fired in the bay and guessed that it marked Dalrymple's arrival. He sent Clinton and Murray to greet him. On their way, the two officers discussed the rapid changes of command and the effect it might have on the army, 'and a suggestion was thrown out that the only way to avert every evil consequence likely to result from it would be by Sir Hew Dalrymple allotting the whole of the force then at Vimeiro to Sir Arthur Wellesley as his corps d'armee; and the whole of that which was expected, in like manner, to Sir John Moore', until Lisbon had been taken. The idea was Murray's; he felt it would do justice to Wellesley's prior successes. It was also broadly what Castlereagh had envisaged, but neither officer would have been aware of that. Clinton suspected Dalrymple and Burrard would not be keen on the idea as it would take most command functions away from them, but agreed to the idea being floated to Dalrymple. Clinton and Murray suggested the concept to Dalrymple as they escorted him back from the beach, and he seemed amenable to the scheme.[2]

The party reached Burrard's headquarters in Maceira. Dalrymple was updated on the situation and took command. Wellesley arrived soon afterwards and urged that the army advance towards Lisbon the next day. He thought that the army had to move, writing to Castlereagh, 'we shall be poisoned here by the stench of the dead and wounded; or we shall starve, everything in the neighbourhood being already eaten up.'[3] Dalrymple initially disagreed, but Murray intervened and changed his mind. Dalrymple then asked Wellesley to get the army ready to march.[4]

---

1   Dalrymple, *Memoir*, pp.58–59.
2   Murray, 'Review of History of the War', p.201.
3   Gurwood (ed.), *Wellington's Dispatches*, vol.IV, p.115.
4   J. Harding-Edgar, *Next to Wellington: General Sir George Murray* (Warwick: Helion & Co, 2018), p.105.

The change of command from Wellesley to Burrard and then Dalrymple does not seem to have gone smoothly. Writing on the 23rd about Dalrymple, Wellesley told Castlereagh, 'it is not a very easy task to advise any man on the first day one meets with him. He must at least be prepared to receive advice.'[5] He later said that he quickly believed Dalrymple was prejudiced against him.[6] Anstruther wrote that the change of command had been 'very ill received by the army', and, 'Wellesley is in the highest degree popular indeed there is an enthusiasm respecting him which can hardly be described. Under him there is nothing this army would not attempt and few things they would not perform.'[7] Nightingall held similar views: 'The army have such entire confidence in Wellesley that they view the change of chiefs, with great regret, the more so as Sir H. Dalrymple is not popular, and has never been employed on service in command nor I understand ever served any where, except a very short period indeed on the continent in Flanders.'[8]

Anstruther caught Wellesley's 'family', his aides de camp and other personal staff 'talking very outrageously' on the 25th, and then the next day, he wrote in his journal:

> Saw Moore and Hope both holding the most proper language; pointing out the necessity of supporting Sir Hew, & protesting that no feeling of any kind but that of joy at his success and admiration of his talents existed in their minds towards Wellesley. Moore said he would speak to him respecting the improper language of the young men of his family – Burgesh, Pole etc.[9]

This implies that the young aides were speaking disrespectfully of Dalrymple. Thomas Graham, serving on Moore's staff, also noted the tone of the conversation amongst those close to Wellesley, writing 'the example of language of the greatest insubordination has been set, and which I am sorry to say has spread through the whole army to an alarming degree'.[10] Anstruther also reports a conversation Moore had with Dalrymple when he was told 'He might either land his corps or not as he liked best', and that this spread around the camp and was laughed at, but that Moore then said Dalrymple was 'very collected and decided in every thing he said and entered fully into the state of matters.'[11] Later, in October, Anstruther wrote, 'Personally I have every reason to be pleased with his [Dalyrmple's] conduct, but must confess I regret his ever having accepted the command. He had not been early enough in command – he has not in consequence the talent of acquiring the confidence of the troops.'[12] Wellesley's secretary, Henry Torrens, went so far as to inform Gordon at Horse Guards of his concerns:

> You may rest assured that the person now at our head is perfectly at a loss in the management of the machine which is placed in his hands! In saying this to you in confidence I

---

5   Wellington (ed.), *Supplementary Despatches*, vol.VI, p.123.
6   Anon., *Proceedings*, p.56.
7   BL: Add. MS 49503: Anstruther to Gordon, 22 August 1808.
8   BL: Add. MS 49503: Nightingall to Gordon, 25 August 1808.
9   StAUL: msdep121/8/2/3/4/4: Anstruther's journal, pp.39, 41.
10 Quoted in 'Commentary for Volume 1, Chapter 15: Vimeiro and Cintra (July–September 1808)', *Life of Wellington*, <https://lifeofwellington.co.uk/commentary/chapter-fifteen-vimeiro-and-cintra-july-september-1808/>, accessed July 2023.
11 StAUL: msdep121/8/2/3/4/4: Anstruther's journal, p.42.
12 BL: Add MS 49503: Anstruther to Gordon, 7 October 1808.

hope I am not going beyond the bounds of propriety; but I cannot conceal from you what makes so deep an impression on my mind.[13]

Burrard, though, was pleased to see Dalrymple:

> … I was far from sorry, when I took my old friend by the hand the next morning on his landing. There is far too much diplomacy and civil government here for my management at present, and Sir Hew will have his hands full and I have no doubt aquit himself with every advantage to his country, and honor to himself. I shall always be contented to fight under the orders of Sir H, or others, but I own that a great command would be the source of very anxious moments to me.[14]

He added, 'I am getting old and certainly not so active in mind or body as I have been or should be, and therefore wish for rest and what I am more fit for...'

The second arrival in the British camp on the 22nd, at around 1:30 p.m., was *général de division* Kellermann with a flag of truce and a cavalry escort of two squadrons. His approach caused an alarm as a Portuguese officer, on his way from Lourinhã, thought the French were attacking. Wellesley and Murray rode to the high ground on the left of the army's position and were told of Kellermann's approach. They then rode down to Vimeiro, where they met Dalrymple and Burrard. Wellesley offered to go and meet Kellermann, who had asked to speak to him, supposing he was still in command. According to Murray's account, 'Sir Hew, thanking Sir Arthur with an appearance of coldness and reserve, said he should not trouble him, but would send a staff-officer.' To some of the officers, Dalrymple appeared to have adopted a colder attitude towards Wellesley than he had at their first meeting.[15]

On the morning of the 22nd, Junot had held another council of war. Present were Delaborde, Loison, Kellermann, Thiébault, Taviel, and Vincent. The council considered the difficulties of holding Lisbon, with a hostile population at their backs and fresh British reinforcements at their front. A retreat to Spain was unlikely to succeed due to a lack of provisions and transport. Thiébault, in his history, concluded that 'it was necessary to give in to necessity, and so it was, by the force of circumstances, that we arrived at the idea of attempting a negotiation, fully resolved to obtain an honourable treaty, or to bury themselves under the ruins of Lisbon.'[16] Junot then dictated the terms for a suspension of arms to Kellermann, who was selected to go to the British camp. As he rode out *capitaine* Hulot overheard him say that 'he was going to find the English to help us get out of the mousetrap.'[17]

At around 2:00 p.m. Kellermann, with *adjudant-commandant* de Cambis and another officer, were escorted to Wellesley's headquarters in Vimeiro.[18] He presented the proposals to Dalrymple, Burrard and Wellesley. The discussions lasted for a long time, and then the British generals went to another room and discussed the terms with Clinton and Murray. Wellesley said

---

13   BL: Add MS 49485: Torrens to Gordon, 1 September 1808.
14   BL: Add MS 49485: Burrard to Gordon, 9 September 1808.
15   Anon., *Proceedings*, p.57; Murray, 'Review of History of the War', pp.201–202.
16   Thiébault, *l'Expédition*, pp.207–208.
17   Hulot, *Souvenirs*, p.236.
18   BL: Add. MS 49484: Timeline of negotiations written by Dalrymple.

he favoured granting the French a 48-hour truce to negotiate an evacuation by sea.[19] There was some discussion about referring to Napoleon as emperor, something the British government had avoided to that date, and that the French would not be prisoners of war. However, the issue the officers were most concerned about was letting the French negotiate on behalf of the Russians, as the fate of Senyavin's squadron had been included in Junot's proposed terms. It was decided that Kellermann be pressed on that point.[20] Foy claimed that Kellermann overheard the British generals having doubts over how soon Moore would arrive, the lack of food in the area, and the lack of assistance from the Portuguese. It became clear to him that Dalrymple preferred the idea of a convention over continued fighting. Kellermann then talked up the strength of the French position and the possibility of aid from the Russian squadron.[21] The negotiations paused while the generals dined.

Deputy Assistant Quartermaster General Captain James Dawes Douglas (45th Foot) had been sent to one of the ships off the coast to see if word had been received of Moore's convoy. He was told they had not yet been sighted and returned to make his report. He was led into the room where the generals were eating dinner and relayed his news. He later wrote:

> I was struck with the remarkable sensation this message appeared to cause, and was followed by a couple of A.D.C.s out of the room, who exclaimed, 'How could you give such a message before the French General Kellerman?' to which I replied 'How could you allow me to go into the room to make a report without informing me there was a French General there?'

Douglas was not blamed for the error and, in his own defence, stated, 'Kellerman was a little man with a broad Alsatian face, and in a blue great-coat, whom one might see fifty times without suspecting him to be a General.'[22] Kellermann later said that Douglas's news had enabled him to strengthen his demands.[23]

Various historians have claimed, or hinted, that Kellermann, who had spent time in the United States and could speak English well, withheld his knowledge so that he could follow the discussions between the British generals.[24] The claim seems to originate from Thiébault, who wrote, 'knowing English perfectly, he had followed the most confidential part of their conversations,' and who gave the concerns over the arrival of Moore and the good relations between the French and Russians as examples of what Kellermann overheard.[25] However, the phrasing Thiébault uses does not explicitly say that Kellermann concealed his knowledge of English; it could be interpreted as simply eavesdropping when the British generals withdrew but were still in earshot. While Dalrymple mentioned in his testimony to the inquiry that the negotiations were undertaken in French, if the British did not know Kellermann could speak English then the reaction over Douglas' faux pas seems odd.

19   Anon., *Proceedings*, p.57.
20   Murray, 'Review of History of the War', p.202.
21   Foy, *Invasion*, p.178.
22   Brown, *Redcoats*, p.54.
23   G.C. Moore-Smith, *The Life of John Colbourne, Field-Marshal Lord Seaton* (London: Murray, 1903), p.85.
24   Mackay, *The Tempest*, p.292; Glover, *Sickens*, p.135.
25   Thiébault, *Relation*, pp.209–210.

The negotiations with Kellermann continued after dinner. The main areas of contention were the demarcation line with the Portuguese troops, French baggage and property, and the fate of the Russians.

In his memoir, Dalrymple wrote that Wellesley recommended he agree to the terms and that he thought Wellesley was 'the most competent judge of the relative situations of the two armies at this point of time, I should have thought it my duty to follow, even if his judgement had not been so particularly recommended to my attention by the Secretary of State.'[26] In his evidence to the later inquiry, he stated, 'With me rested the responsibility and with Sir Arthur Wellesley much of that information by which the exercise of that responsibility could alone be justified.'[27]

Dalrymple felt considerable time pressure to reach an agreement: 'It was perfectly obvious that the anchorage of the Tagus must soon be obtained, as our fleets must be dashed to pieces, or forced to leave the coast; and upon the shipping the existence of the army might be said to depend'.[28] He was also worried that if hostilities recommenced, the French superiority in cavalry would enable them to harass any advance on Lisbon and that the poor quality of the British artillery horses would continue to limit the mobility of the guns.[29]

A suspension of arms was agreed upon but could be terminated on 48 hours' notice by either party. Kellermann suggested that Wellesley, rather than Dalrymple, sign as it was inappropriate for a Commander-in-Chief to sign a document with a more junior officer. Dalrymple asked Wellesley, and he agreed to sign.[30]

Wellesley told Torrens afterwards that he signed even though 'he totally disapproved of many points in it, and of the tone of the language in which it was drawn up.' Specifically, he objected to the clause granting neutrality to the Russian fleet and the 48-hour notice for the resumption of hostilities. He also told Torrens that he felt he did not have Dalrymple's confidence as he only agreed to the army's advance after Wellesley had lobbied Murray, and then Murray had persuaded Dalrymple.[31] However, in a letter written in October, Murray related a discussion he had with Wellesley after the meeting and stated:

> Sir Arthur said that he did not feel altogether satisfied about the business but that upon the whole he thought it is an important object to get the French out of the country, and above all, to get hold of the fortresses, which might otherwise cost us a winters campaign and a great deal of difficulty; and on these grounds that he thought the views of government would be fulfilled by such an arrangement as was proposed.[32]

Writing to Castlereagh the day after signing, Wellesley wrote, 'I beg that you will not believe that I negotiated it, that I approve of it, or that I had any hand in wording it. It was negotiated by the General himself in my presence and that of Sir Harry Burrard; and after it had been drawn out by

---

26   Dalrymple, *Memoir*, p.64.
27   TNA: WO 1/415: Dalrymple's narrative.
28   BL: Add MS 49484: Dalrymple to Gordon, 3 September 1808.
29   TNA: WO 1/415: Dalrymple's narrative.
30   Anon., *Proceedings*, p.57.
31   Anon., *Proceedings*, p.64.
32   Harding-Edgar, *Next to Wellington*, pp.106–107.

Kellermann himself, Sir Hew Dalrymple desired me to sign it.'[33] He continued that he objected to the indefinite suspension and the 48-hour notice but approved of evacuating the French.

The articles of the suspension of arms were:

1. There shall be, from this date, a Suspension of Arms between the armies of his Britannic Majesty, and his Imperial and Royal Majesty, Napoleon I for the purpose of negociating a Convention for the evacuation of Portugal by the French army.
2. The General-in-Chief of the two armies, and the Commander-in-Chief of the British fleet at the entrance of the Tagus, will appoint a day to assemble, on such part of the coast as shall be judged convenient, to negociate and conclude the said Convention.
3. The river of Sirandre shall form the line of demarkation to be established between the two armies; Torres Vedras shall not be occupied by either.
4. The General-in-Chief of the English army undertakes to include the Portuguese armies in this suspension of arms: and for them the line of demarkation shall be established from Leyria to Thomar.
5. It is agreed provisionally that the French army shall not, in any case, be considered as prisoners of war; that all the individuals who compose it shall be transported to France with their arms and baggage, and the whole of their private property, from which nothing shall be exempted.
6. No individual, whether Portuguese, or of a nation allied to France, or French, shall be called to account for his political conduct; their respective property shall be protected; and they shall be at liberty to withdraw from Portugal, within a limited time, with their property.
7. The neutrality of the port of Lisbon shall be recognised for the Russian fleet: that is to say, that, when the English army or fleet shall be in possession of the city and port, the said Russian fleet shall not be disturbed during its stay; nor stopped when it wishes to sail; nor pursued, when it shall sail, until after the time fixed by the maritime law.
8. All the artillery of French calibre, and also the horses of the cavalry, shall be transported to France.
9. This suspension of arms shall not be broken without forty-eight hours previous notice.[34]

There was also an additional article: 'The garrisons of the places occupied by the French army shall be included in the present Convention, if they have not capitulated before the 25th instant.'

Murray set off early on the 23rd to find out if the terms were agreeable to Junot, to show the provisional terms to Cotton, and to arrange a conference between Junot, Cotton and Dalrymple so that a full convention could be agreed. Murray joined Kellermann at Torres Vedras and then met Junot that evening. He got to Cotton the next morning.

After the signing of the armistice the previous day, an aide de camp from the Portuguese commander, Friere, had arrived asking for orders from Dalrymple. In his memoir, Dalrymple states that the Portuguese had not been mentioned during the discussions, 'or spoken of as having

33   Wellington (ed.), *Supplementary Despatches*, vol.VI, p.122.
34   TNA: WO 1/234: Suspension of Arms.

had any share in the battle of the 21st' and so was surprised to find out they were so close.[35] He agreed to meet Friere at Ramalhal, five miles southwest of Vimeiro on the Lisbon road.

Early in the morning of the 23rd, the bulk of the British army marched from the camp around Vimeiro to within three miles of Torres Vedras, with headquarters established at Ramalhal. Craufurd's brigade remained behind to protect the landing site.

At the meeting with Dalrymple, Friere was unhappy that he and the Junta in Oporto had not been consulted during the negotiations. Dalrymple replied that he could not view the Junta as the legitimate government of Portugal but gave him a copy of the armistice so that he could give his comments, which would then be considered during the treaty negotiations.[36]

Friere sent *Major* Ayres Pinto de Souza back with his response the next day. Pinto was told to remonstrate again that the Portuguese had not been consulted and protested that the demarcation line left substantial territory at the mercy of French vengeance and further looting. He was also to say that Dalrymple, as commander of an auxiliary army, had no right to agree to amnesty for the Portuguese who had worked with the French. As to the article on baggage and property, Friere wrote that the French 'will not only take with them the fruit of the immense robberies and conspiracies that the Generals and other individuals of this Army have done: but also the properties and public funds accumulated in Lisbon.'[37]

Pinto reported back to Freire that 'it seems to me that the business is not as ugly as it was painted' and that Dalrymple had agreed with many of the observations on the terms of the suspension and that he would try to take them into account.[38] He was also given reassurances that the baggage and property of the French would be allowed to embark would not include plunder and public funds.

Dalrymple's defence for not including the Junta in Oporto in the negotiations was that he could not expect Junot to treat with a government that the French did not recognise.[39] However, Portuguese commentaries on the suspension of arms are primarily, and perhaps justifiably, negative. Sepulveda argues, for example, that while Freire's main force took little active part in the campaign, the Portuguese commander was always prepared to support Wellesley after the meeting at Lourinhã and brought his forces forward when and where requested. So, the Portuguese were entitled to a seat at the table.[40]

When Wellesley got to Ramalhal, he gave Dalrymple a note containing the suggestion that Cotton and Senyavin agree that the Russian ships would 'not be molested, if they conducted themselves as they ought in a neutral port' rather than granting Lisbon the status of a neutral port. If that satisfied Junot, he should be pressed to allow British access to the Tagus, follow a schedule to give up the fortresses, settle some points regarding the sailing home of the French troops, get his generals to give up their booty, and organise a prisoner exchange. Wellesley, at the inquiry, stated that it was a matter of indifference to him what happened to the Russian ships and that his priority was the separation of the Russians and the French.[41] However, the fate of Senyavin's squadron was not a matter of indifference to the Admiralty or Cotton, whose orders precluded allowing the

35   Dalrymple, *Memoir*, p.65.
36   Dalrymple, *Memoir*, p.66.
37   Pinto's instructions, 24 August, in 'Documentos', pp.203–204.
38   Souza to Freire, 24 August 1808, in Sepulveda, *Historia*, vol.XI, p.153.
39   Pinto to Freire, undated, in 'Documentos', p.209.
40   Sepulveda, *Historia*, vol.XI, p.141.
41   Anon., *Proceedings*, pp.59–60.

Russians the benefit of a neutral port. Dalrymple was convinced that acting as though Lisbon was a neutral port for the Russians was out of the question.

Murray met with Cotton and Captain Halstead on the *Hibernia*. The admiral stated that he could not agree to the article covering the Russian fleet, as Dalrymple had suspected, but that he would negotiate directly with Senyavin based on the instructions he had previously had from the Admiralty. In December 1807, Canning wrote to Castlereagh that Senyavin might agree to the Russian ships being held in British ports and the crews repatriated. In April 1808, the Admiralty repeated these suggested terms for a convention with Senyavin to Cotton to remove the Russian squadron and enable the partial lifting of the Lisbon blockade.[42] So, when Murray brought the suspension of arms that offered the Russians the protection of a neutral port, Cotton had reason to believe that the article did not conform to the government's wishes.

Moore's convoy began arriving in Maceira Bay on the morning of the 24th, and he heard for the first time of the victory at Vimeiro. Moore wrote to congratulate Wellesley, who replied that he wished Moore had arrived sooner so he could have persuaded Burrard and Dalrymple to complete the victory. He also expressed concerns over the supply situation as the army's numbers increased, that in two weeks it would be impossible for the ships to remain off the coast, and that rains would make the roads impassable. Wellesley lamented the lack of progress since the 21st and hoped Moore would use his influence 'for the purpose of setting us right.'[43]

At 10:30 p.m., Murray arrived back at Dalrymple's headquarters from visiting Cotton with the news that the admiral could not accede to the terms relating to the Russian squadron, placing the continuation of the armistice in doubt.

The Convention

At daylight on 25 August, Wellesley, with Captain Malcolm, pressed Dalrymple to call an end to the armistice on the grounds of Cotton's refusal to agree to the terms covering the Russians. Dalrymple wanted to wait until Murray had rested and made his report before deciding. Later that morning, he sent for Burrard and Wellesley, and the three held a lengthy discussion. It was agreed to send Murray to Junot to explain Cotton's refusal and to give the required 48 hours' notice to end the armistice, but Murray was also authorised to continue to negotiate a definitive convention if Junot was willing to do so without the clause covering the Russians, based on the paper that Wellesley had given Dalrymple on the 23rd. The idea of a conference between the commanders was abandoned. Dalrymple wrote to Junot explaining that Cotton had instructions that precluded his agreeing to the article but that he and Senyavin would negotiate separately.[44]

At the meeting, Captain Malcolm had informed Dalrymple that Moore's troops could not land because of a heavy swell. At 5:00 p.m., Moore and Lieutenant General John Hope arrived at Ramalhal. They met with Dalrymple and agreed that, given the difficulties, Moore's troops would land gradually and that every unit landed would have the required provisions, ammunition and ordnance.[45] In his diary, Moore wrote, 'I was sorry to find everything in the greatest confusion,

---

42   Anon., *Papers presented to Parliament in 1809*, pp.225–226, 232–241, Castlereagh to Admiralty and Wellesley-Pole to Cotton, 16 April 1808.

43   Maurice (ed.), *Diary*, vol.II, p.257.

44   Anon., *Proceedings*, pp.60–61; TNA: WO 1/416: Dalrymple to Murray, and to Junot 25, August 1808.

45   Anon., *History of the Campaigns*, vol.II, p.208.

and a very general discontent. Sir Hew, though announced to the army, had not as yet taken the direction of it; much was still done by Sir Arthur Wellesley, and what was not done by him was not done at all.[46] He also wrote:

> It is evident that if any operation is to be carried on it will be miserably conducted, and that seniority in the Army List is a bad guide in the choice of a military commander. Sir Arthur Wellesley seems to have conducted his operations with ability, and they have been crowned with success. It is a pity, when so much has been thrown into his hands, that he has not been allowed to complete it, and the conduct of Government on this occasion has been absurd to a degree. I have told both Sir Hew and Sir Arthur that I wished not to interfere; that if the hostilities commenced, Sir Arthur had already done so much, that I thought it but fair he should have the command of whatever was brilliant in the finishing, I waived all pretensions as senior. I considered this as his expedition. He ought to have the command of whatever was detached. For my part I wished I could withdraw myself altogether; but I should aid as far as I could for the good of the service, and, without interference with Sir Arthur, I should take any part that was allotted to me.[47]

Cotton had suggested to Dalrymple that half of Moore's force be landed on the left bank of the Tagus at Setúbal, which the French had abandoned and which a Portuguese force was soon to occupy. The admiral thought that this would cut off Junot's retreat, stating, 'I suggest this on the presumption that the preliminary articles I read yesterday can never be acceded to so as to form a definitive treaty so much in favor of the French army twice beaten, and 30,000 British troops in Portugal – without great alteration of those articles. I can never accede to such a treaty.'[48]

Murray was reluctant to act as a negotiator, but Dalrymple and Wellesley persuaded him to accept the task.[49] At 3:00 p.m., Captain Adolphus Dalrymple set off for the French outposts, and Murray followed half an hour later with a letter to Junot giving the required 48 hours' notice but with the authority to carry on negotiations and continue the armistice, should Junot want to carry on without the articles covering the Russians.[50] The two officers arrived in Lisbon at 7:00 a.m. on 26 August.

According to Murray, when he met with Junot, the French general 'blustered a little at first about French honour, and his determination on no account to separate himself from the Russians', but Kellermann suggested that Senyavin be consulted. A staff officer was sent and returned with the news that Senyavin was happy to treat with Cotton directly. Junot protested a little more but agreed to continue negotiations.[51]

Murray wrote to Dalrymple from Lisbon that he 'went to work with General Kellerman this morning, & got on tolerably well; By twelve o'clock tomorrow I hope we shall be finished.'[52] He also said that it had been mentioned in his instructions that the French should be required to cross the Tagus. Murray thought if he pushed on that, he would have to yield on more important

46   Maurice (ed.), *Diary*, vol.II, p.257.
47   Maurice (ed.), *Diary*, vol.II, pp.258–259.
48   TNA: ADM 1/340: Cotton to Dalrymple, 25 August 1808.
49   Harding-Edgar, *Next to Wellington*, pp.108–109.
50   TNA: ADM 1/340: Dalrymple to Murray, 25 August 1808.
51   Murray, 'Review of History of the War', p.204.
52   TNA: WO 1/416: Murray to Dalrymple , 26 August 1808

articles, and it would delay them embarking. The French also wanted to take some of the captured Portuguese ships, but Murray refused them on that point and also to them holding onto some of Tagus forts until all the French had embarked. Kellermann also wanted to exchange the Spanish prisoners, but Murray thought they should just be released.

Another sticking point was the wording of the article covering the French baggage and officers' property. Dalrymple had wanted the language clarified to include the definition that baggage 'is understood to apply to the baggage usually possessed by military officers and persons attached to the Army as explained by General Kellerman in the negotiation for the agreement for the suspension of hostilities, property belonging to churches, monasteries, and galleries of painting etc cannot be carried away.'[53] However, Junot felt that such wording besmirched the honour of the French army and gave his word that it would not happen. As Murray's biographer, John Harding Edgar, says, 'In a modern context this seems naïve and weak; against the military traditions of the day, less so.'[54]

During the 26th, Moore's troops began to land, taking up the position occupied by Craufurd's brigade, which then marched to join the army near Torres Vedras. That evening, the 30,000 troops paraded for a review by Dalrymple. One witness wrote, 'The weather was delightful, and the coup-d'oeil truly magnificent. Our gaily dressed troops, extending two miles in open column, wheeled in an instant into line, the various bands struck up the favourite national air of "God save the King," and the echoes of the pine-clad hills returned the clang of presented arms.'[55] The weather, though, began to turn for the worse, and the camp would soon be battered by rain and the fleet at anchor buffeted by rising seas, leading to discomfort for the troops and increased urgency to the negotiations.

Soon after midnight, one of Junot's aides arrived at the British headquarters with the letter from Murray and one from Junot, informing Dalrymple that negotiations were continuing. Dalrymple sent for Wellesley and either Moore or Burrard, depending on either Wellesley's or Dalrymple's account. Junot had stated that an agreement with the French relied on an agreement being reached with the Russians and wrote that he was taking the armistice as indefinite until the British presented terms he agreed to.[56] Dalrymple wrote to Murray with instructions to break off negotiations if Junot continued to link the naval and military conventions but to offer to continue the talks if Junot backed down.[57] At 8:00 a.m. on the 27th, Junot's aide set off with Fitzroy Somerset carrying the letter for Murray.

Anstruther's journal entry for the 27th reads:

> Aide de Camp arrived with a letter from Murray and from Junot. Murray says every thing respecting the Russians is settled in so far that the French leave them to make their own terms, Junot's letter although not contradicting this is far from being explicit and may be construed as to any thing; at least so Sir Hew said, did not see the letter. Wellesley shewed me his project of instructions for Murray; short and plain. Church plate and property to be given up. Prisoners exchanged. Rochefort or Brest the best place to send the prisoners to. Bounty to be requested for return of ships. He also shewed me his project

53 Harding-Edgar, *Next to Wellington*, p.112.
54 Harding-Edgar, *Next to Wellington*, p.113.
55 Neale, *Letters*, p.32.
56 Anon., *Proceedings*, pp.60–61, 177–178.
57 TNA: WO 1/416: Dalrymple to Murray, 27 August 1808.

for turning the right of the Enemy's position of Cabeza de Monchique – well done, but the force with him, everything of the first six brigades, 12,000 men, two corps, hardly anything will remain in the corps, which is to attack in front, especially if Hope goes to St Ubes as is determined.[58]

However, Wellesley's plan would not be required. Junot did back down, and Murray and Kellermann began to draw up the terms of a definitive convention. According to Thiébault, at one point in the negotiations, Junot told Murray:

> Do not think, sir, that by signing the treaty you are doing me a favour: as such, I would accept nothing, neither from you, nor from anyone in the world. You are far from being less interested than I am in signing it. So say a word, and my decision is made. I tear up the treaty, I burn the fleet, I burn the navy, the arsenals, the customs houses and all the shops: I blow up the forts and all the works. I destroy the artillery. I defend Lisbon step by step. I burn everything I have to give up. I make you pay for each street by streams of blood, and I still make my way through your army; or, understanding that in this destruction all that is, or could be, in my power, I bury myself, with the debris of my army, under the ruins of the last quarter of the city, and we will then see what you and your ally will have gained by reducing me to this extremity...[59]

With a draft of the convention complete, Murray informed Dalrymple on the 28th that he was taking a copy of the convention to Cotton and sending another back to him with Dalrymple's son. Meanwhile, Moore's troops continued to land, and Wellesley moved his division closer to Torres Vedras. During the day, Major General William Carr Beresford arrived at headquarters from Madeira with news that the 3rd and 42nd Foot were off the Tagus.

The convention had 23 articles. The first 14 dealt with the embarkation of the French troops, their equipment, and private property. They were to be transported by ship to France and not considered prisoners of war. Article 15 said that if there was any dispute over the meaning of an article, it 'will be explained favourably to the French', which was standard language for the time and was typically applied to the defeated party. Article 16 stated that the French would cease raising all requisitions and contributions. The following two articles ensured that all French citizens in Portugal and all Portuguese who had assisted the occupation would be protected. Article 19 dealt with the release of the Spanish prisoners. Article 20 set up an immediate exchange of prisoners of war, 21 mandated an exchange of hostages, 22 allowed Junot to send an officer to France with the convention, and 23 said that Cotton would accommodate Junot and other senior officers on his ships – presumably to get them out of reach of a vengeful population. An additional five articles dealt with minor points of subsistence and the use of Danish vessels to transport the French.[60]

At 6:00 a.m. on the 29th, Adolphus Dalrymple and a French officer brought back the draft treaty. Sir Hew immediately thought some of the terms were problematic and assembled his lieutenant generals to discuss them. Present were Burrard, Moore, Hope, Fraser and Wellesley. The articles were read, and Wellesley minuted the objections and proposed amendments. Article 5, dealing with

---

58   StAUL: msdep121/8/2/3/4/4: Anstruther's journal, pp.42–44.
59   Thiébault, *l'Expédition*, p.217.
60   TNA: WO 1/416: Convention, 28 August 1808.

the property of the French troops, was to refer to only the usual baggage of an army and any church plate or artwork was excluded. Amendments were proposed to change the timing of the embarkation and the French giving up the forts. The wording of articles 17 and 18 on protection for foreigners in Portugal and the Portuguese who helped the French was to be clarified, and there were other minor amendments.[61] Moore thought that the change to which forts were given up when was the most important.[62] Having all the lower forts in British hands would enable the fleet to enter the harbour.

Wellesley wanted to go further and get the French to immediately give up the fortresses and cross the Tagus so the British fleet could enter the river. Wellesley wrote to Malcom that day that the original convention was 'objectionable in many parts' and that he thought the alterations insufficient, 'although the treaty will answer in its amended form.' He then said that while he supported the idea of evacuating the French, the convention 'ought to be settled in the most honorable manner to the army by which they have been beaten; and we ought not to be kept for ten days on our field of battle before the enemy (who sued on the day after the action) is brought to terms.'[63] Anstruther wrote to Gordon that as far as the convention was concerned, 'Some difference of opinion appears to prevail here and more may perhaps in England as to the propriety of what has been done in that respect', but then also went on to say that evacuating the French was the best solution.[64]

On 28 August, Cotton, after seeing what Murray and Kellermann had drafted, had written to Dalrymple and proposed amendments that he thought the French would accept and that he could agree to. He told Dalrymple that his contacts in Lisbon had told him 'that the French expected nothing less than unconditional surrender and to return as prisoners of war to France.' He also told the general that threatening weather was forcing him to weigh anchor, but he would return as soon as possible. Cotton suggested changes to the 12th article regarding which forts were given up when, to the 16th, saying that all debts to the French be cancelled, that the 17th exclude shipping and that all property confiscated by the French be returned, to the 19th that baggage and property of the Spanish prisoners be returned to them, that the 5th additional article concerning Danish shipping be deleted, and another added that all French ships of war be delivered to the British with all their stores.[65]

Dalrymple replied to Cotton the same day, '… the moment I understood your objection to the article of the basis for a treaty of convention signed by Sir Arthur Wellesley and General Kellerman, which had for its object the disposal of the Russian fleet, that article was expunged, and I was preparing to advance under the idea that hostilities would recommence.' However, Murray had been able to carry on negotiations on the rest of the treaty with the French. Dalrymple then added, 'With respect to the Articles inclosed in your letter, I have to observe in the first place that whatever regards the Russian fleet is to be negotiated between you and Admiral Siniavin consequently does not enter into the treaty with General Junot at all.' As for some of Cotton's proposed amendments he said that the French ships were not mentioned by Junot, and anyway, had been Portuguese and that they 'seem no more French property than the church plate which certainly cannot be included in the article of the basis, which provides for the officers of the army retaining their property which was distinctly explained not to include merchandise of any sort.' Dalrymple wrote that the article

61   TNA: WO 1/416: Observations on 28 August Convention.
62   Maurice (ed.), *Diary*, vol.II, p.259.
63   Gurwood (ed.), *Wellington's Dispatches*, vol.IV, pp.126–127.
64   BL: Add MS 49503: Anstruther to Gordon, 29 August 1808.
65   TNA: ADM 1/340: Cotton to Dalrymple, 28 August 1808.

on baggage 'may require great circumspection in its final arrangement' and that Murray's instructions on it were clear. Regarding objections to other articles in the suspension of arms, he stated, 'I think it is now too late to object to any part of the Basis itself which was at first acquiesced in.'[66] Many of Cotton's changes aligned with those of the lieutenant generals' meeting.

Dalrymple's covering note to Murray that accompanied the changes agreed by the lieutenant generals said that while some of the comments were 'of more or less consequence', possessing the Tagus forts was crucial.[67] This was because of the threatening season for the ships and the fact that the navy would not use anchorage if the defences were not in British hands. The fear of vessels being driven ashore was not just theoretical. In April 1804, a convoy of two frigates and 67 merchantmen bound for the West Indies were blown off course by gales in the Atlantic. HMS *Apollo* and 27 merchantmen were wrecked just north of Cape Mondego.[68] Dalrymple also pointed out that some articles, such as that about French prisoners of the Spanish, were not under his power, so it should be phrased that he would make every effort rather than offer guarantees. Another of Dalrymple's aides, Second Captain Edward Fanshawe (Royal Engineers), returned with the French officer to Lisbon with the proposed amendments.

During the 29th, Major General the Honourable Edward Paget's advance guard took up a position before Torres Vedras, and Dalrymple moved his headquarters into the town. Wellesley moved his troops to Runa the next day, and Moore's corps occupied their ground near Torres Vedras.

At 7:30 a.m. on the 31st, Murray and one of Kellermann's aides, plus Somerset and Fanshawe, arrived at Dalrymple's headquarters in Torres Vedras with the definitive convention, signed by Junot, 'in which some of the articles of the treaty of the 28th, which had been objected to, were altered, and some other good alterations inserted, not before suggested.'[69]

Of the 23 articles in the draft treaty, 14 remained unchanged in the definitive version, and one had been dropped due to changes being made to another article that made it unnecessary. Two of the original five additional articles were dropped entirely, one was slightly amended, and two were unchanged. All of the changes made to the articles were broadly to the benefit of the British. Cotton's changes to the 12th and 16th articles were made, some changes were made to the 17th, the 19th was not changed, and the 5th additional was deleted, but the extra additional article the Admiral wanted was not added. Of the nine amendments agreed at the conference of lieutenant generals, four were made in their entirety, and one was part of an article that was dropped. Two were partially amended, including mandating that some, but not all, of the forts on the Tagus could be occupied on the convention's ratification. Changes were not made to the article covering Portuguese who had collaborated with the French, and, most importantly for how the convention was going to be perceived, Murray had not been able to get the French to agree to tighter stipulations in writing as to what baggage and private property included. To imply that the French army had plundered was, apparently, an affront to their honour. Such honour would soon be found to be sorely lacking.

Sir Harry Burrard set out his thoughts on the honour of the French in a letter to Gordon:

Our Commander in Chief has his hands quite full; what with the French and their plunder, and the Portuguese, their government and jealousies, he has enough to fill all his time and

66   TNA: ADM 1/340: Dalrymple to Cotton, 28 August 1808.
67   TNA: WO 1/416: Dalrymple to Murray, 29 August 1808.
68   Knight, *Convoys*, pp.1–3.
69   Dalrymple, *Memoir*, pp.69–70.

faculties – but I doubt not he will get through it all with much credit and honor to himself and benefit to the nation. The French Generals seem sad rogues. Or rather jolly rogues, all but Kellerman, who is the go between, has feeling and is therefore awkwardly situated. With the army they have in this Kingdom, the excellence of its equipment, and the nature of the country we can find no solution to the paltry defence Junot has made, but to his desire to secure his plunder. He talked finely of the noble opportunity he had of being celebrated in history to the end of time, by giving up Lisbon, and himself with it. 'That the year 55 should be a joke to it, if his terms were not acceded to.' – but his actions, talk and bombast have all been to realize his ill acquired booty.[70]

The 'year 55' he refers to is 1755, when large parts of Lisbon were destroyed in an earthquake.

The Convention's articles were:

1. All the places and forts in the kingdom of Portugal, occupied by the French troops, shall be delivered up to the British army in the state in which they are at the period of the signature of the present Convention.
2. The French troops shall evacuate Portugal with their arms and baggage; they shall not be considered as prisoners of war; and, on their arrival in France, they shall be at liberty to serve.
3. The English Government shall furnish the means of conveyance for the French army; which shall be disembarked in any of the ports of France between Rochefort and L'Orient, inclusively.
4. The French army shall carry with it all its artillery, of French calibre, with the horses belonging to it, and the tumbrils supplied with sixty rounds per gun. All other artillery, arms, and ammunition, as also the military and naval arsenals, shall be given up to the British army and navy in the state in which they may be at the period of the ratification of the Convention.
5. The French army shall carry with it all its equipments, and all that is comprehended under the name of property of the army; that is to say, its military chest, and carriages attached to the Field Commissariat and Field Hospitals; or shall be allowed to dispose of such part of the same, on its account, as the Commander-in-Chief may judge it unnecessary to embark, In like manner, all individuals of the army shall be at liberty to dispose of their private property of every description; with full security hereafter for the purchasers.
6. The cavalry are to embark their horses; as also the Generals and other officers of all ranks. It is, however, fully understood, that the means of conveyance for horses, at the disposal of the British Commanders, are very limited; some additional conveyance may be procured in the port of Lisbon: the number of horses to be embarked by the troops shall not exceed six hundred; and the number embarked by the Staff shall not exceed two hundred. At all events every facility will be given to the French army to dispose of the horses, belonging to it, which cannot be embarked.
7. In order to facilitate the embarkation, it shall take place in three divisions; the last of which will be principally composed of the garrisons of the places, of the cavalry,

70 BL: Add MS 49485: Burrard to Gordon, 11 September 1808.

the artillery, the sick, and the equipment of the army. The first division shall embark within seven days of the date of the ratification; or sooner, if possible.

8.   The garrison of Elvas and its forts, and of Peniche and Palmela, will be embarked at Lisbon; that of Almaida at Oporto, or the nearest harbour. They will be accompanied on their march by British Commissaries, charged with providing for their subsistence and accommodation.

9.   All the sick and wounded, who cannot be embarked with the troops, are entrusted to the British army. They are to be taken care of, whilst they remain in this country, at the expence of the British Government; under the condition of the same being reimbursed by France when the final evacuation is effected. The English government will provide for their return to France; which shall take place by detachments of about one hundred and fifty (or two hundred) men at a time. A sufficient number of French medical officers shall be left behind to attend them.

10.   As soon as the vessels employed to carry the army to France shall have disembarked it in the harbours specified, or in any other of the ports of France to which stress of weather may force them, every facility shall be given them to return to England without delay; and security against capture until their arrival in a friendly port.

11.   The French army shall be concentrated in Lisbon, and within a distance of about two leagues from it. The English army will approach within three leagues of the capital; and will be so placed as to leave about one league between the two armies.

12.   The forts of St Julien, the Bugio, and Cascais, shall be occupied by the British troops on the ratification of the Convention. Lisbon and its citadel, together with the forts and batteries, as far as the Lazaretto or Tarfuria on one side, and fort St. Joseph on the other, inclusively, shall be given up on the embarkation of the second division; as shall also the harbour; and all armed vessels in it of every description, with their rigging, sails, stores, and ammunition. The fortresses of Elvas, Almaida, Peniche, and Palmela, shall be given up as soon as the British troops can arrive to occupy them. In the mean time, the General-in-Chief of the British army will give notice of the present Convention to the garrisons of those places, as also to the troops before them, in order to put a stop to all further hostilities.

13.   Commissioners shall be named, on both sides, to regulate and accelerate the execution of the arrangements agreed upon.

14.   Should there arise doubts as to the meaning of any article, it will be explained favourably to the French army.

15.   From the date of the ratification of the present Convention, all arrears of contributions, requisitions, or claims whatever, of the French Government, against the subjects of Portugal, or any other individuals residing in this country, founded on the occupation of Portugal by the French troops in the month of December 1807, which may not have been paid up, are cancelled; and all sequestrations laid upon their property, moveable or immoveable, are removed; and the free disposal of the same is restored to the proper owner.

16.   All subjects of France, or of powers in friendship or alliance with France, domiciliated in Portugal, or accidentally in this country, shall be protected: their property of every kind, moveable and immoveable, shall be respected: and they shall be at liberty either to accompany the French army, or to remain in Portugal. In either case their property is guaranteed to them; with the liberty of retaining or of disposing of it, and passing

the produce of the sale thereof into France, or any other country where they may fix their residence; the space of one year being allowed them for that purpose. It is fully understood, that the shipping is excepted from this arrangement; only, however, in so far as regards leaving the port; and that none of the stipulations above-mentioned can be made the pretext of any commercial speculation.

17.   No native of Portugal shall be rendered accountable for his political conduct during the period of the occupation of this country by the French army; and all those who have continued in the exercise of their employments, or who have accepted situations under the French Government, are placed under the protection of the British Commanders: they shall sustain no injury in their persons or property; it not having been at their option to be obedient, or not, to the French Government: they are also at liberty to avail themselves of the stipulations of the 16th Article.

18.   The Spanish troops detained on board ship in the port of Lisbon shall be given up to the Commander-in-Chief of the British army; who engages to obtain of the Spaniards to restore such French subjects, either military or civil, as may have been detained in Spain, without being taken in battle, or in consequence of military operations, but on occasion of the occurrences of the 29th of last May, and the days immediately following.

19.   There shall be an immediate exchange established for all ranks of prisoners made in Portugal since the commencement of the present hostilities.

20.   Hostages of the rank of field-officers shall be mutually furnished on the part of the British army and navy, and on that of the French army, for the reciprocal guarantee of the present Convention. The officer of the British army shall be restored on the completion of the articles which concern the army; and the officer of the navy on the disembarkation of the French troops in their own country. The like is to take place on the part of the French army.

21.   It shall be allowed to the General-in-Chief of the French army to send an officer to France with intelligence of the present Convention. A vessel will be furnished by the British Admiral to convey him to Bourdeaux or Rochefort.

22.   The British Admiral will be invited to accommodate His Excellency the Commander-in-Chief, and the other principal officers of the French army, on board of ships of war.

The three additional articles were:

1.   The individuals in the civil employment of the army made prisoners, either by the British troops, or by the Portuguese, in any part of Portugal, will be restored, as is customary, without exchange.

2.   The French army shall be subsisted from its own magazines up to the day of embarkation; the garrisons up to the day of the evacuation of the fortresses. The remainder of the magazines shall be delivered over, in the usual form, to the British Government; which charges itself with the subsistence of the men and horses of the army from the above-mentioned periods till they arrive in France; under the condition of their being reimbursed by the French Government for the excess of the expense beyond the estimates, to be made by both parties, of the value of the magazines delivered up to the British army. The provisions on board the ships of war, in possession of the French army, will be taken in account by the British Government in like manner with the magazines in the fortresses.

3.   The General commanding the British troops will take the necessary measures for re-establishing the free circulation of the means of subsistence between the country and the capital.[71]

Dalrymple gathered the available lieutenant generals and ratified the treaty. Wellesley was at Sobral de Monte Agraço, 10 miles from Torres Vedras, when he received a message from Dalrymple that the convention had been signed and he wanted to see him, but, as he said at the inquiry, 'I was so far from Torres Vedras, that I conceived I should not be able to arrive there in time, and I did not go.'[72] His literal distance from the final version of the treaty would enable him to distance himself from it figuratively as well. Lieutenant Colonel Lord Proby (1st Foot Guards), an assistant quarter master general, was sent to Junot with the signed French copy of the Convention.

On the 31st, the weather forced most of the fleet to leave the coast, stopping the flow of supplies to the army and preventing the siege train from landing, so resuming hostilities would have been problematic. Gaining the immediate use of the Tagus seemed to Dalrymple to be a priority for the safety of the fleet and the army and would be one of his main justifications for the convention.[73]

On the 30th, with the terms of the convention agreed Murray, while preparing to return to the British headquarters, wrote to a friend:

I suppose it will be thought in England that after a victory we should have imposed harder conditions. Such is generally the view of the public in the like cases and it is only those who are acquainted with all the circumstances who can support the contrary argument.

The original proposal was made on the 22nd, upon the part of the French, and the Basis of the Negotiation was signed that evening by Sir Arthur Wellesley and Gen Kellerman. During the time which has since lapsed we have had the advantage of moving reinforcements but as we were fully aware of the approach of these reinforcements when the Basis was established I leave it to you to judge whether in strict honour, we should have been justified in changing our ground on that account.

The following argument may be used in favour of the suspension of hostilities and subsequent Convention.

We were still forty miles from Lisbon having before us difficult country with the worst possible roads, and some strong passes.

Our communications with our shipping was extremely precarious, being sometimes entirely cut off by the surf. Our means of conveyance limited as well as for our supplies as for our Artillery and ammunition. Our cavalry in comparison to that of the enemy, nothing. Our infantry excellent in a fixed position but not yet much in the habit of acting in the field in considerable corps, in fighting in individual situations in which this enemy might have been sent on a march. The command fluctuating from the arrival of different Generals. The arrival of Reinforcements uncertain as to days at least if not more. On the other hand there was also the prospect getting the French out of the country at once without further risk or loss to ourselves and without further injury to Portugal. There was the advantage of putting an end to Military Operations here, and being at liberty to

71   TNA: WO 1/234: Definitive Convention.
72   Anon., *Proceedings*, p.63.
73   TNA: WO 1/415: Dalrymple's narrative.

act elsewhere with certainty in a definite time. The chance of the Enemy embarrassing us by holding out the Fortresses was guarded against as also that of his attempting a Retreat towards Spain, in which we could not have followed him, and by which it might have happened that his March would have embarrassed the operations of the Spaniards.

I don't know whether it ought to enter at all into consideration that from the nature of the Wars and Expeditions we carry on, we are exposed more than any other nation to have occasion to look towards such arrangements for ourselves. Perhaps it would be refining too much to say it may be politic to spare the honour of the French Army, and prefer sending them back without personal animosity, to tell we have beat them, than to press matters to the utmost in the risk of making them prisoners of war.[74]

On 1 September, Junot informed Dalrymple that his troops would begin the withdrawal mandated in the convention and that the forts on the Tagus would be handed over at 10:00 a.m the following day, 'and from then on nothing will be able to delay the embarkation.'[75] Colonel Rufane Donkin went to Lisbon to be a British Hostage, and British troops began moving towards Lisbon. Sir John Moore's corps marched toward Mafra, but the French had not yet vacated it, so they halted three or four miles away. Dalrymple moved headquarters to Bandalhoeira, about halfway between Torres Vedras and Mafra. On the 2nd, troops moved into Mafra, and Paget reached Sintra, a picturesque town that the British at the time spelt Cintra. Dalrymple established his headquarters there. Captain Algernon Langton wrote of Sintra, 'I was one day at Cintra, and felt at the time that I would have been contented to live there all may life; for a more beautiful romantick spot it is hardly possible to conceive.' He then waxed lyrically about the town before mentioning, 'Sir Hew took up his abode in a magnificent palace, and old Buzzard had another.'[76]

At some point, after the ratification of the treaty, Captain Andrew Patisson (29th Foot) marched into the British camp at the head of 90 prisoners of war who were 'joyfully received', and his own company 'drew up, and gave us three times three cheers.'[77] The total number of British troops recorded missing in the three actions – Óbidos, Roliça and Vimeiro – was 146, so this might not have represented all the prisoners that the French held. Then again, many men reported missing were later found wounded or dead, had taken an opportunity to desert, or arrived back with their units after the casualty return was taken.

On 3 September, the forts of São Julião da Barra, Bugio, and Cascais were occupied by the 3rd and 42nd Foot, and the Union Flag was raised over the Tagus. The Portuguese were outraged that the flag that flew was not theirs, but, as will be seen below, the Union Flag being raised was an essential part of Cotton's negotiations with Senyavin.

Dalrymple had written to the Bishop of Oporto on the 1st to tell him that the convention had been signed and that it was time to reorganise the regency council.[78] It was not until the 3rd, after he had received confirmation that Cotton had ratified the treaty that he finally got around to writing his dispatches to London. He put his location and the date at the head of the letter, so the treaty forever became known as the Convention of Cintra, even though it had not been negotiated or ratified there. He sent his son, Adolphus, to London with the dispatches.

74   Harding-Edgar, *Next to Wellington*, pp.116–117.
75   Anon., *Proceedings*, p.184.
76   LA: MG/4/5/15/40-85: Langton to Massingbird, 5 September 1808.
77   Anon. (ed.), *The Soldier's Companion*, vol.I, p.442.
78   TNA: WO 1/418: Dalrymple to Bishop, 1 September 1808.

Sintra, from William Bradford, *Sketches of the Country, Character and Costume in Portugal and Spain.*

Dalrymple outlined to Castlereagh the events that had occurred since he landed, including the negotiations and the agreements with the French. Amongst the enclosures, he said, were 'the several Articles at first agreed upon and signed by Sir Arthur Wellesley and General Kellerman'. He told Castlereagh that:

> As I landed in Portugal entirely unacquainted with the actual state of the French Army, and many circumstances of a local and incidental nature which doubtless had a great weight in deciding the question, my own opinion in favor of the expediency of expelling the French Army from Portugal by means of the convention the late defeat had induced the French General to solicit, instead of doing so by a continuation of hostilities was principally founded on the great importance of time which the season of the year rendered peculiarly vulnerable and which the Enemy could easily have consumed in the protracted defence of the strong places they occupied, had terms of convention been refused them.[79]

At some point during his time at Sintra, Dalrymple received a long letter from Castlereagh about how the British could aid the Spanish in removing the French from their country.[80] At the end of the letter, the minister wrote:

---

79   TNA: WO 1/234: Dalrymple to Castlereagh, 3 September 1808.
80   Dalrymple, *Memoir*, p.99.

I trust you will not hesitate to use the full discretion with which you have been inserted, in such a manner as your excellent judgment may point out to you to be for the advantage of His Majesty's Service, without deeming it necessary for wait for authority, or instructions from home, and I can safely assure you that you will find not only in me, but in my colleagues, the most sincere and cordial disposition to support you in the exercise of a responsibility, which I am persuaded you will not shrink from in any instance, where the good of the service may be promoted by your acting without reference home.[81]

Dalrymple would find such unqualified support sadly lacking once the news of the convention he had just negotiated landed on ministers' desks.

Wellesley's Role

One of the most contested points of debate regarding the suspension of arms and the convention is the part that Wellesley played in their negotiation and drafting. On 19 September, Dalrymple wrote to his wife:

Burrard came just in time for the Battle of Vimeiro, and I came just in time for the suspension of arms; he disclaims all honor from the first; and I did disclaim any great portion of honor for the second. I approved it of course, because I knew nothing about the state of affairs in Portugal, because Sir Arthur Wellesley did know that state; and because he was perfectly acquainted with the views of H.M. Government but certainly those articles signed by Sir Arthur were not disapproved by him indeed I do not think it likely he would wish to shrink from the degree of responsibility which must naturally attach to him.[82]

However, Wellesley did shrink from the responsibility that Dalrymple placed on him for the suspension of arms and rapidly distanced himself from the initial agreement with the French and the subsequent definitive convention.

On 23 August, Wellesley wrote to Malcolm and, when mentioning the suspension of arms, said, 'Although I signed these conditions, I beg that you will not believe that I entirely approve of the manner in which the instrument is worded.'[83] However, he seems to have consistently been in favour of seeking the evacuation of the French via a treaty. On the 25th, he wrote to Charles Stewart that if this did not happen, the French would 'secure themselves in Elvas and Almeida, and we shall have the pleasure of attacking those places regularly, or of blockading them in the autumn. If we should be able to get them away by sea, it will be possible to push our troops into Spain at an early period.'[84] On 1 September, he had told the Duke of Richmond that getting the French out of Portugal was necessary, 'and it is not of much importance in what manner that is carried into execution.'[85]

---

81   TNA: WO 6/185: Castlereagh to Dalrymple, 20 August 1808.
82   NAM: 1994-03-129-79: Dalrymple to Dalrymple, 19 September 1808.
83   Gurwood (ed.), *Wellington's Dispatches*, vol.IV, pp.117–118.
84   Gurwood (ed.), *Wellington's Dispatches*, vol.IV, pp.120.
85   Wellington (ed.), *Supplementary Despatches*, vol.VI, p.128.

Wellesley was consistent in his claims that he disagreed with some of the terms of the suspension of arms and argued against many of its articles and their wording. On 16 September, he wrote to his brother William:

> I sacrificed my own opinion & probably my reputation to a Man in whom Govt. had confided the Command of the Army; who neither deserved their confidence, or such a sacrifice on my part. My refusal to sign the Agreement could not have prevented it; & would have placed me at the Head of a party against the Comr. in Chief who was but just arrived; & created a breach between us … I did every thing I could to prevail upon him not to agree to the objectionable parts of the agreement, but in vain…[86]

After arriving back in London in October, he told Castlereagh the suspension 'was negotiated and settled by his Excellency in person, with General Kellermann, in the presence of Lieut. General Sir Harry Burrard and myself, and that I signed it by his Excellency's desire. But I could not consider myself responsible in any degree for the terms in which it was framed, or for any of its provisions'.[87]

On 14 October, Wellesley wrote to Earl Temple:

> I did not protest against any part of that instrument. I stated to the Commander of the Forces the objections which I felt to the form which was adopted, to allowing the French to treat for the Russians, to the time which was given for the suspension of hostilities, and to the verbiage … The objections which occurred to me, and which I stated, were over ruled by the Commander of the Forces; and I signed the Armistice by his desire, which he made at the suggestion of General Kellermann. I don't think that the expression of this desire could be considered tantamount to an order. I certainly think that it was so put that I could have declined to comply with it; and here is the great difficulty of my situation. Such is the temper of the times and the violence of the prejudices excited against me upon this subject, that my motives will never be understood, and I shall never have credit for those which really actuated me. I signed it, notwithstanding my objections to it, because I would not, in the face of the whole army, set myself up in opposition to the Commander of the Forces on the very day he joined his army. His task was sufficiently difficult without adding to it that further difficulty. I agreed with him upon the main point, viz. the evacuation by the French troops. My refusal to sign would not have prevented the execution of the instrument, and would only have tended to raise my character at the expense of others, and probably at that of not a little outrage and want of discipline in the army.[88]

However, Murray took the trouble to write up a note which directly contradicts Wellesley's version of events:

> When General Kellerman came into British Headquarters to make proposals for a suspension of hostilities, Sir Hew Dalrymple, Sir Harry Burrard and Sir Arthur Wellesley were

---

86   Webster, 'Some Letters', p.11.
87   Gurwood (ed.), *Wellington's Dispatches*, vol.IV, p.161.
88   Wellington (ed.), *Supplementary Despatches*, vol.VI, pp157–158.

the persons with whom the discussion of the terms took place, and amongst these people Sir Arthur took the greatest share if not the entire lead in the conversation, which his having had the command till two days before, gave him some right to do, and which is natural to the eagerness of his temper… If the Preliminaries were an improper Basis the real responsibility rests not with Sir Hew Dalrymple, but the blame is equally with Sir Harry Burrard, and Sir Arthur Wellesley.[89]

Moore thought that continuing the campaign after Vimeiro would have been fraught with difficulties, and writing of Wellesley claims that, 'The proof that what remained to be done did not appear to him so easy is that he approved, recommended, and signed the preliminary articles, which I never thought justifiable, for they were far more unfavourable to us than the final convention.' He even suggests that Wellesley wanted 'everything settled' before Moore's corps landed, implying, uncharitably perhaps, that Wellesley did not want to share the glory.[90]

Wellesley was equally vociferous in distancing himself from the definitive convention. As has been seen, he was not directly involved with the negotiations but did make suggestions and offer his opinions during discussions of the terms. Dalrymple also felt bound by the principles established in the suspension of arms and did not see how he could deviate too far from them in the final convention, so the one was built upon the foundations of the other.

On 12 September, Wellesley wrote to Castlereagh that '… I have not seen the Convention, and am not accurately acquainted with its contents.'[91] This was highly disingenuous as he had seen every version but the last because he had decided he was too far from Dalrymple's headquarters to conform to a request to attend a meeting. On the 1st, he had written to Charles Stewart outlining the major points of the final version of the convention while making it clear the information was second-hand. He then continued, 'As far as I have any knowledge of them, I have many objections both to the agreement for suspending hostilities and to the Convention for the evacuation of Portugal by the French.'[92] By the 5th, he was denying his involvement more forcefully and told Malcolm, 'I had nothing to do with the Convention as it now stands; and I have never seen it to this moment.' He probably meant that he still had not seen it rather than that he had just seen it. He then continued, 'I have only to regret that I put my name to an agreement of which I did not approve, and which I did not negotiate. If I had not done it, I really believe that they would not have dared to make such a Convention as they have made.'[93] On the 6th, in a letter to the Bishop of Oporto, he also denied negotiating the suspension of arms and seeing the convention.[94] The letter's tone is curious and could be read as undermining Dalrymple's authority with the Bishop.

Writing to Calvert at Horse Guards about the convention on the 4th, before news of its poor reception had reached him, Dalrymple stated, 'the Lieutenant Generals here from first to last have approved – even Sir A Wellesley has been the principal director of that measure which perhaps of all others I saw the most prudence in allowing him to direct. His talents are great, and when

---

89   Harding-Edgar, *Next to Wellington*, p.120. The note is undated, and may have been written much later, but in Murray's papers it is enclosed in a letter to Hope dated 14 September 1808.

90   Maurice (ed.), *Diary*, vol.II, pp.268–269.

91   TNA: WO 1/228: Wellesley to Castlereagh, 12 September 1808.

92   Gurwood (ed.), *Wellington's Dispatches*, vol.IV, p.135.

93   Gurwood (ed.), *Wellington's Dispatches*, vol.IV, p.139.

94   Gurwood (ed.), *Wellington's Dispatches*, vol.IV, p.148.

exerted on the side of caution may be relied on.'[95] In a later letter, he was unequivocal that Wellesley was actively involved in the armistice and the convention, even drafting parts of them.[96]

The debate about Wellesley's involvement continued in London after the text of the suspension of arms and convention reached ministers and was published. Writing to Horse Guards about coverage in the Morning Post on 19 and 20 September, Dalrymple wrote:

> It is only necessary for the present to assure the His Royal Highness, that although there is enough truth in the composition of the paragraphs in question to shew that more accurate information was within the reach of the person who composed them; that I am possessed of incontrovertible evidence; that Sir Arthur Wellesley not only approved of the articles he signed; but that he took a prominent part in the whole of the transaction (excepting the act of ratification, when he from accidental circumstance was not one of the lieutenant generals present) which the extent of his talents, the distinguished situation in which he was placed from his recent victory, and I may perhaps be permitted to say the energy of his manner might all be supposed to produce.[97]

The *Morning Post* had published a vigorous defence of Wellesley on 19 September, stating that he had been overruled about the pursuit, that he played no part in the negotiations and had been ordered to sign the suspension by Dalrymple. It then continued:

> Had he persisted furthering opposing the plans of his successors in command, or preserved a sullen and silent indifference to their success, what interpretations might have been put on his conduct? Had he not to fear that it would be imputed to exultation and arrogance from his own good fortune, or to a revengeful reluctance to concur in extricating the army from the difficulties into which they were thrown by the neglect of his advice. Such are likely to be the motives that would influence such a mind as that of Sir Arthur's in such an emergency. We sincerely regret he should have yielded to them. By doing so he seems to have forgotten for a moment, his country and himself:– to have missed an opportunity of gloriously offending; and instead of exhibiting a signal and salutary example of seasonable disobedience, to have suffered the patriotism of the hero to sink into submission of the mere soldier, and with one stroke of his pen, to blur the large and luminous characters of glory, still fresh from the point of his victorious sword. But it would appear, that every other sentiment was lost for a moment in a sense of duty, and he obeyed.[98]

The next day, the *Post* opened with an appeal that the public should judge calmly and fairly and not be partisan and that forcing the French to unconditional surrender would have been lengthy and costly. However, it then continued that allowing the French to return with their plunder was 'disgraceful and degrading', as was the amnesty for those Portuguese who worked with the French. The paper placed the blame squarely on Dalrymple, 'Both the Conventions, though one signed by Sir Arthur Wellesley, and the other by Colonel Murray, are to be considered as the work of Sir Hew

95   BL: Add MS 49484: Dalrymple to Calvert, 4 September 1808.
96   BL: Add MS 49484: Dalrymple to Gordon, 29 September 1808.
97   BL: Add MS 49484: Dalrymple to Gordon, 30 September 1808.
98   *Morning Post*, 19 September 1808.

Dalrymple, and of Sir Hew Dalrymple alone.' The paper points out that he was the Commander-in-Chief, and, 'It is clear, then, that as to the Convention, whether he approved or disapproved of it, whether he negotiated every line or never read a word of it, he is in no sense whatsoever responsible.' Wellesley *privately protested the armistice in the strongest terms* and 'tried all in his power to prevent [Dalrymple] from granting the terms he did to the enemy'. The *Post* does, however, say that if Wellesley objected to the suspension of arms, he should not have signed it, but also that he was just following an order. The *Post* continued that the only reason a convention was needed was that Wellesley was prevented from advancing after Vimeiro, that from the letters of officers in Portugal, it appeared that he was 'perfectly adored by the army', and that attacks on him were purely political.[99]

Within political circles, the source of the defence of Wellesley in the press was widely known. Lord Auckland wrote to Lord Grenville:

> I am told that Sir Arthur Wellesley's family and friends are loud in their protestations that he utterly disapproved it, and merely gave his signature in obedience to his Commander in Chief.
>
> It will not, however, be easy to persuade even the weakest and most credulous minds, that either the articles of war, or the principles of military subordination require an officer to sign a convention dictated by a beaten enemy because his superior officer orders him to sign it; nor indeed is there common sense in the supposition that Sir Hew Dalrymple would give such an order, and such powers, to an unwilling and resisting plenipotentiary. This line of defence, however, is to be taken; and it remains to be seen how far the Ministers, from a desire to manage the feelings of the family and connection, will countenance this explanation. In the meantime I sincerely lament the circumstance, abstractedly from its political importance, and with a view only to its effects on the feeling and character of the individual, whom I believe to possess great military talents, and powers of mind very considerable, though I cannot account for the step which he has taken.[100]

Thomas Grenville wrote to his brother, the former Prime Minister, that he had been told of how Wellesley had justified signing the suspension of arms. Thomas Grenville had:

> … some opportunity of hearing what was supposed to be his language, and these expressions are of so very flabby a quality that they have in them nothing that resembles any firmness of character, or confidence in his cause. The words quoted to me as having been used by him to Ministers are these, 'he had done his duty, had no *complaint* to make, but would not be *punished*'.[101]

General the Earl of Moira, who would be a member of the board of inquiry into the convention, wrote:

99   *Morning Post*, 20 September 1808.
100 Auckland to Grenville, 29 September 1808 in, Anon., *Report on the Manuscripts of J.B. Fortesque Esq. Preserved at Dropmore* (London: HMSO, 1912), vol.IX, p.220.
101 T. Grenville to Grenville, 19 October 1808 in, Anon., *Dropmore*, vol.VIII, pp.229–230.

It is clear that Wellesley, to have a claim to the exclusive merit of finishing the business in Portugal, overbore his commander and in fact dictated the procedure. The plea that in military obedience he merely signed a Convention which he disapproved, is so unsubstantial as at once to expose the hollowness of his defence. No notion of discipline ever yet required such an acquiescence from any officer: but it is totally out of the question when it is recollected that Sir Arthur was himself the negotiator with full powers, and that no one of the conditions of the preliminary articles could have been presented for his signature he had not previously admitted them. The truth is that he is a very gallant and gentlemanlike fellow, but very limited in talents.[102]

The fact that Wellesley's friends in London seemed to be seeking to distance Wellesley from the suspension of arms that he had signed clearly rankled Dalrymple. On 5 October, Burrard wrote a confidential letter to Gordon at Horse Guards enclosing a statement that he had been asked to write outlining that Wellesley had played significant parts in both the suspension and convention. He wrote:

I have no hesitation in stating that Sir Arthur Wellesley did not make any objection to the Articles which he signed except to the granting of forty eight hours notice &c And that he gave his opinion and assisted (at the meeting of the Lt. Generals) in the alterations made in the several articles at the ratification of them at Ramalia.[103]

However, Burrard also said he was reluctant to be brought into the controversy.

Determining the extent of Wellesley's involvement in the suspension of arms is difficult, given the contradictory statements of the witnesses and those involved. The rapidity with which Wellesley distanced himself from the suspension suggests he did not fully agree with it. Once the reaction in London became known, it was politically expedient for him and his allies to disassociate him from it, especially given his close links to the government. That closeness may have meant that Dalrymple saw a benefit in emphasising Wellesley's part in the negotiations to limit the scope of any criticism from ministers. But equally, Dalrymple felt that the end of expelling the French from Portugal justified the means of the convention. Of course, because Dalrymple commanded the responsibility for both the suspension and convention ultimately rested with him, but, given the strength of Wellesley's personality, it is difficult to believe that he was quite as passive a participant as his denials claim and some of his more disingenuous statements do not place his character in a favourable light.

The Naval Convention

While Cotton had been surprised and dismayed by the terms of the military convention, he could only view the negotiations as something of a spectator. Wellesley had welcomed Cotton's refusal to

---

102 Quoted on 'Commentary for Chapter 16: The Cintra Inquiry (September–December 1808)', *Life of Wellington*, <https://lifeofwellington.co.uk/commentary/chapter-sixteen-the-cintra-inquiry-september-december-1808/>, accessed August 2023.

103 BL: Add MS 49485: Burrard to Gordon, 5 October 1808.

agree to the article in the suspension of arms on the Russians and had hoped it would lead to the convention being radically revised, but he was disappointed.[104] For Cotton's talks with Senyavin, the admiral thought he was on much firmer ground than Dalrymple because he felt he had some indication of the government's wishes due to his orders from April. However, negotiations between Cotton and Senyavin were delayed by the British fleet having to stand off the mouth of the Tagus as the weather turned.

After Vimeiro, Senyavin had called a council of captains to discuss the squadron's situation. The captains agreed to do whatever Senyavin ordered. The admiral replied, 'I will offer to negotiate with the English admiral, but with the situation being how it is, it's unlikely that any agreement besides an unconditional surrender could be accepted. In that case, I see no other choice but to fight to the best of our ability'.[105]

Negotiations opened between Senyavin and Cotton when the Russian admiral sent a Mr Sass to Cotton with a letter that asked if Britain would consider Lisbon a neutral port, or would it become British with the Union Flag being raised in the forts when the French surrendered them.[106] Cotton sent Captain Lawrence Halstead, his captain of the fleet, to Senyavin aboard the *Tverdoi* on 1 September with his answer. Lisbon could not be considered a neutral port because it had been declared part of France and the government left by Prince João abolished. In line with his April instructions, Cotton proposed that the Russian squadron be held in British ports until after Russia and Britain signed a peace and that Senyavin and his crews would be returned to Russia. He drafted a short convention to that effect. Senyavin was naturally disappointed that his squadron would not be granted the neutrality of the port, under which condition they had entered the previous year, but had little option but to agree. He replied:

> I see with great grief and not without astonishment, that you cannot consider the Port of Lisbon in its proper situation now, nor after the French troops have evacuated & as a neutral port, but at the same time I see with satisfaction the consideration you declare, that make me equally hope that the relations of peace and amity between my nation and yours may soon be reestablished...

He then continued, 'I consent to accede to your proposals by a formal convention, with one condition, nevertheless that this convention cannot & shall not be valid without the English flag is hoisted on the forts, and that the Port of Lisbon is acknowledged as a port belonging to his Britannic Majesty.'[107]

The hoisting of British colours rather than Portuguese in the forts was problematic as Dalrymple's instructions from Castlereagh had stated that he was to act in alliance with the Portuguese. Raising the Union Flag would, understandably, cause problems with the Portuguese, so Dalrymple had to ask that Cotton agree to the Portuguese flag being raised, not the British. Cotton replied that the British flag had to remain raised until Senyavin had signed the convention.[108] During their

---

104 Wellington (ed.), *Supplementary Despatches*, vol.VI, p.126.
105 Vladimir Bogdanovich Bronevskiy, Darrin Boland (trans.), *Northern Tars in Southern Waters: The Russian Fleet in the Mediterranean, 1806-1810* (Warwick: Helion, 2019), p.624.
106 TNA: ADM 1/340: Senyavin to Cotton, 17/29 August 1808. The letters from Senyavin are dated with both the Julian and Gregorian dates. Henceforward only the Gregorian date will be used.
107 TNA: ADM 1/340: Senyavin to Cotton, 2 September 1808.
108 Krajeski, *Shadow*, p.120.

meeting, Halstead had also assured Senyavin that the ships would not have to strike their colours before the crews had left the ships.

On 3 September, Cotton sent his secretary, James Kennedy, to meet with Sass on the *Tverdoi* with a copy of the convention. However, Senyavin still had concerns surrounding the form of surrender, the neutrality of the port, and the British flag flying from the forts. He wanted answers in writing on those issues before he signed.[109]

For Senyavin, the form that the surrender of his squadron took remained a matter of both personal and national honour. Cotton had to insist on some form of surrender, but from Senyavin's point of view the Russian squadron had not been defeated. Cotton and Senyavin met on 6 September and resolved their differences. Sensitive to the Russian's pride, Cotton sent Rear Admiral Charles Tyler, his second in command, rather than a lieutenant or his secretary, with the final draft of the convention for Senyavin to sign. In a letter, he also pointed out that the British colours were still flying from the forts.[110]

The naval convention was brief and to the point. The first article stated that the Russian ships would be delivered to Cotton, immediately sent to Britain, and held there until six months after a peace between Britain and Russia. The second article stated that the Russian officers and crews would be returned to Russia without any conditions for their future service.[111]

Cotton sent Halstead back with the dispatches to London in the *Blossom*, including the naval convention. After he had sailed, Cotton received word that Senyavin wanted to alter the convention. He proposed two further articles. Firstly, that the Russian colours not be struck until the crews had left the ships in British ports, and secondly, that the ships be returned in the same state that they had been surrendered. Cotton agreed and, when he sent the additional articles to the Admiralty, wrote that they were of 'so unimportant a nature … I have acceded to without hesitation'.[112]

The Russian ships finally prepared to sail after 11 months in port. The *Jarolslav* and *Raphael* were found unseaworthy and left behind with skeleton crews, with the rest of the men being distributed to the other ships. Tyler was placed in charge of the convoy escorting the Russians, matching the seven ships of the line and frigate ship-for-ship with the *Barfleur*, *Hercule*, *Conqueror*, *Elizabeth*, *Donegal*, *Alfred*, *Ruby* and *Crocodile*. His orders made it clear he was to maintain contact with the Russians and, if necessary, use force to compel them to abide by the convention. The convoy sailed on 12 September and arrived at Spithead on 7 October. Tyler was informed that the British government could not agree to the two additional articles, and the Russian colours had to be struck. The King could not allow the colours of a hostile power to be flown in a British port. The Russian colours were taken down, but the Admiralty sensitively ruled that no other colours would be flown until the Russians had left. Senyavin and his crews left for Russia, and the ships remained. After Napoleon invaded Russia in 1812, Britain and Russia became allies again, but only two of Senyavin's ships returned home in 1813; the others had deteriorated and been sold for scrap, the proceeds being given to the Russians.[113]

Having had what he considered clear guidance from the government as acceptable terms for the surrender of the Russian squadron, Cotton may have hoped to escape the approbation that the British generals were to face. However, there was some criticism in the press regarding Russian

109 TNA: ADM 1/340: Senyavin to Cotton, 4 September 1808.
110 TNA: ADM 1/340: Cotton to Senyavin, 4 September 1808.
111 TNA: ADM 1/340: Naval Convention.
112 TNA: ADM 1/340: Cotton to Wellesley Pole, 7 September 1808.
113 Krajeski, *Shadow*, pp.123–124.

crews being free to wage war on Britain's allies, and the Admiralty objected to 'the adoption of a new principle of Maritime surrender, by the qualified detention and eventual restoration of the ships of war of the enemy.' They also made it clear that Cotton was mistaken in his belief that the April orders applied to the situation in September. However, Cotton did have the support of his friend Mulgrave, the First Lord of the Admiralty, and Canning, while not wholly approving, recognised that the terms were far better than the original article of the suspension of arms.[114] When Lord Mulgrave informed the King of the naval treaty, he replied: 'H.M. rejoyces that Sir Charles Cotton has, under all the circumstances which have occurred in Portugal, and the difficulties which attended them, so properly supported the honor of this country and of the service, by refusing to accede to any terms short of the removal of the Russian ships of war to British ports.'[115]

The mild disapproval in London of the naval convention was nothing compared to the furore that was to surround the military one.

---

114 Krajeski, *Shadow*, p.127.
115 Aspinal (ed.), *Later Correspondence*, vol.V, p.124.

19

Implementation

The reaction to the convention from within the British army in Portugal was mostly negative. The inconclusive way that the battle of the 21st had been allowed to end had already spread despondency through the army.[1] To many, their hard-won victories had been squandered by the perceived leniency of the terms. Staff officer Captain Henry Cooke wrote, 'A treaty the most astonishing has since been signed – it conveys away the whole honor of the campaign, containing terms that a victorious army in many instances might accept without discredit to themselves. I declare to you the army are disgusted, & that this disgust has the greater weight since it originated with those in high situations.'[2]

Henry Torrens, wrote on 10 September:

> … we are all in ignorance here of what is going on; and Sir Arthur Wellesley himself has never yet seen the articles of the Convention! But I am told that the detail of it, is in many points highly advantageous to the French, and such as *our* success could not give them a right to demand! I fear this business will cause great disappointment in England; and I have reason to apprehend the discontent contained in the private letters from the Army and Navy will add considerably to that feeling.[3]

Captain William Warre wrote to his father at the end of September, 'The indignation expressed in all the English Papers at the Capitulation made subsequent to that is scarce equal to what has been felt by every individual of the Army, whose glory and the gratitude of their countrymen (their best reward) has been so completely frittered away.'[4] Doctor Adam Neale compared the convention to the treaty after the Egyptian campaign of 1801 and wrote, 'Should it be so, it is no difficult task to foretel how it will be received in England, after the public expectation shall have been so highly raised by the brilliant victories of Roleia and Vimiera.'[5]

In a letter to his sister, Captain Algernon Langton refers to Burrard as a 'great fat hog' who arrived during the battle, preventing them from pursuing and destroying the French. He then writes:

---

1   BL: Add MS 49503: Wyndham to Gordon, 8 September 1808.
2   BL: Add MS 49503: Cooke to Gordon, 6 September 1808.
3   BL: Add MS 49485: Torrens to Gordon, 10 September 1808.
4   Warre, *Letters, p.36.*
5   Neale, *Letters,* p.36.

… had we done so, we should have left no opportunity for making the disgraceful Treaty which has I am afraid been concluded between us and the French. I am not acquainted exactly with the terms, but I fear they will be permitted to carry off all the plunder; and that we shall be fools enough to buy from them, the horses which they have stolen from the inhabitants.[6]

Reaction to the convention amongst the letters and memoirs of the rank and file is harder to find. In his memoir, Private William Billows (2nd Foot) wrote that he was aggrieved to see the French leave with honours when they could have been prisoners of war.[7]

Brigadier General Charles Stewart, Castlereagh's brother, had arrived in the British camp on 24 August after being sent by Moore from the convoy. In his history of the Peninsular War, he claims that the army was split between those who condemned the convention as too lenient and felt that the military advantage over Junot should have been pressed to a more favourable conclusion and those in the minority, who saw the necessity of getting the French out of Portugal as quickly as possible to avoid lengthy sieges and before the winter made maintaining the supply route from Britain difficult.[8]

Murray, in his review of William Napier's history, defends the convention on the basis that the rapid evacuation of the French was desirable, given the lateness of the season and the lack of a siege train, but also admits that had the negotiations commenced after Moore had landed then more favourable terms may have been achieved and that leaving the Portuguese out of the discussions was a mistake.[9]

Paul Thiébault, Junot's chief of staff, summed up the French attitude to the treaty by writing in his history that Junot had:

… succeeded in concluding a treaty which, in our position, it was no longer possible to hope for; a treaty, by means of which he seemed to yield, that which it was no longer in the power of men to retain; a treaty, which in England, Spain and Portugal, has been the object of a disapproval which makes it as glorious for the Duke as honourable for France, and by which the army, having also done its duty during the conquest, occupation and evacuation of Portugal, kept its weapons, its ammunition, its baggage; returned entirely to Spain one month after disembarking at Quiberon and La Rochelle; was the first to help expel from Galicia the same English army, which two months before it had fought in Portugal, and ended by making it in its turn re-embark from Corunna.[10]

Many of the French were just glad to be going home. Artillery officer *capitaine* Jaques Hulot wrote, 'We were pleasantly surprised to learn of the Cintra convention and our forthcoming return to France, happy results that we would not have dared to hope for, even after a victory.'[11]

6   LA: MG/4/5/15/40-85: Langton to Massingbird, 5 September 1808.
7   Billows, *Nothing Pertickler*, p.33.
8   C.W. Vane, *Story of the Peninsular War* (New York: Harper Bros. 1854), pp.102–103. Stewart changed his name to Vane in 1819.
9   Murray, 'Review of History of the War', p.205.
10   Thiébault, *l'Expédition*, p.227.
11   Hulot, *Souvenirs*, pp.236–237.

The Most Shameful Disregard to Honor and Probity

To oversee the implementation of the convention in Lisbon and the embarkation of the French, Dalrymple sent Lieutenant Colonel Lord Proby into the city. On 3 September, Proby reported that he was working with Kellermann to implement the treaty and that the first division of French troops was ready to embark. He also stated that he had refused a request from Junot to use five Danish ships in the harbour to transport his personal effects.[12] As reports reached British headquarters of the French embarking property plundered from the Portuguese, Major General Beresford was sent to help Proby ensure this did not happen.[13] Kellermann's assurances about the honour of the French army had quickly been proved worthless. Murray had offered Anstruther the job, but he thought it 'very unpleasant and loathsome' and switched with Beresford, who had been set to go to Almeida.[14]

On 8 September, Charles Stewart wrote to his brother Castlereagh that he 'found Proby and Beresford hard at work endeavouring to make these robbers disgorge their plunder' and then continued:

> … It is impossible things can have been worse managed on our side than they have been. When Proby was first sent in to see the articles of the Treaty executed, he was not even furnished with a copy of it and owned to Sir Hew his complete incompetence to manage so intricate an affair especially as there were parts of the convention he did not understand – many points unsettled. Sir Hew however persevered in sending him in with plein pouvoirs [full powers] & no treaty. The French endeavoured to impose a spurious one and this he detected. Beresford at last came in and since his arrival things have gone on better.[15]

Stewart added that Junot was 'the greatest robber of the whole and set the example by seizing everything in every shop and house without payment.'

Beresford and Proby soon reported that the French thought they could take everything they had in their possession when the convention was signed, no matter where it came from:

> There is no species whatever of public property that the French commander appears to have the least inclination to relinquish; & we must particularly remark that all the valuables of his Royal Highness the Prince Regent, & the plunder collected from the Church, much of which we have reason to think is still here; & much of the property of individuals is intended to be carried off; or sold.[16]

Beresford and Proby also reported that the contents of the Royal Library and Museum of Natural History had been packed up, and £22,000 held in deposit – belonging to individuals – was also set to be taken. They requested Dalrymple's assurance that they could object to such blatant looting. Dalrymple replied that the phrase 'baggage of the army' in the convention could not be construed to include the contents of museums or libraries and that:

---

12 TNA: WO 1/416: Proby to A.J. Dalrymple, 3 September 1808.
13 TNA: WO 1/416: A.J. Dalrymple to Proby, 4 September 1808.
14 StAUL: msdep121/8/2/3/4/4: Anstruther's journal, p.48.
15 Beresford, *Beresford*, p.39.
16 TNA: WO 1/416: Proby & Beresford to Dalrymple, 4 September 1808.

The article specifying, that where doubts arise, the matter will be explained favourably to the French army, must be considered as having reference to whatever regards its interest or its honour as an army, but can never be allowed to become a cloak to a system of plunder, to gratify either the avarice of individuals, or even that of the French Government.[17]

Beresford wrote to Wellesley on the 5th:

> I arrived yesterday about 10 o'clock, and commenced on my mission, which is neither agreeable, nor do I think it can be very useful, as, after reading the Convention, I could scarcely find out any occasion for appointing Commissioners for seeing carried into effect the full execution of the treaty. The speedy execution a la bonne heure, but full, is only to insist on the French doing and carrying off whatever they wish. I had been much surprised at what I had heard of the terms, yet I had not a conception, till I read them, that they could by words have been so unfavourable to our cause and to the General cause as they now appear to me. The people here of every class are enraged to the highest degree, and this treaty has lowered us much in their estimation, which, however little we may think of the people, it was not worth our while to lose.
>
> I breakfasted yesterday with Junot, but he does not appear to have taken any great liking to me, at which you will believe I am not breaking my heart. I only wish I had had the framing of the Convention; it should have been better, or you would have been left to break his head.[18]

Dalrymple, though, did stand firm on his interpretation of the property article. When Kellermann came to complain about how the commissioners were implementing it, Dalrymple told him that if any member of the French army breached the terms of the treaty, then they would forfeit its protection and be taken as a prisoner of war.[19]

The Lisboetas were getting very resentful of the blatant plundering and, under pressure, on 6 September, Junot ordered: 'In execution of article 15 of the definitive convention the General-in-Chief orders any individual belonging to the army or the French administration who has removed any effects belonging to public or private establishments to return them to the place of origin within 24 hours'.[20] To further ease tensions, a proclamation was issued jointly by the French and British commissioners that began:

> For the fulfilment of the Stipulations made in the Convention agreed upon for the evacuation of Portugal by the French army: That property of every kind confiscated or seized from subjects or other persons residing in Portugal whether from the Royal Palaces, Royal and Public Libraries and Museums, or from Individuals, which is still existing and in Portugal should be restored.[21]

A committee of three men, including Lieutenant Colonel Trant, was formed to hear and adjudicate claims for restitution.

---

17   Dalrymple to Proby & Beresford, 5 September, in Anon., *Proceedings*, p.199.
18   Wellington (ed.), *Supplementary Despatches*, vol.VI, pp.129–130.
19   TNA: WO 1/415: Dalrymple's narrative.
20   TNA: WO 1/416: Order General de l'armée No.66.
21   TNA: WO 1/416: Proclamation, 10 September 1808.

In his memoirs, Thiébault records that he took a framed mosaic from the Palácio de Queluz that Junot had given him to Beresford so that the committee could decide if he could keep it. They judged that, at the time, Junot had the right to give it to him. But Thiébault also stated that the commissioners and the committee were generally effective at preventing plunder from being embarked, including Delaborde's collection of jewels. However, the officer tasked with taking a copy of the convention to France also took with him the magnificent multi-volume fifteenth-century Belem Bible. Louis XVIII eventually bought it from Junot's widow for 80,000 Francs and returned it to Portugal.[22]

Junot was undoubtedly one of the worst offenders. On 11 September, Beresford and Proby reported that 10 chestnut horses he had taken from the Royal stables had already been embarked. Under the terms, any horses in the Royal stables on 30 June should have remained. However, according to Kellermann, Junot had appropriated these many months before, and they were usually kept in his own stables, so he was allowed to keep them. Captain Halkett, the naval officer supervising the embarkation, reported that 53 boxes of indigo worth £5,000 had been discovered and seized on one of the ships taking Junot's baggage. The French general denied all knowledge of them.[23]

Adjudant-commandant Cambis, the officer who had embarked the Prince Regent's horses, also loaded a carriage belonging to Prince Augustus Frederick, Duke of Sussex, who had lived in Lisbon before the occupation. Beresford sent an aide de camp to remonstrate with the *colonel,* but while the two officers argued, the French loaded a second carriage belonging to the Duke. The carriages were unloaded, and Cambis was threatened with being made a prisoner of war if he continued to try to embark plunder. In another case, the bayonets of Royal Marines were required to persuade one of Junot's household to disgorge looted paintings.[24]

On the 18th, Beresford and Proby sent a lengthy report to Dalrymple. It stated that when they arrived in Lisbon, the French were 'selling and preparing for embarkation, property to a large amount, which had been plundered in the most singular manner'. Money had been transferred from the treasury to the military chest, and items were taken from the magazines. The general orders to prevent plundering from Junot 'produced no effect whatsoever', and communications with Kellermann on the subject were 'marked by subterfuge'. However, the committee that had been formed managed to secure the restitution of public and private property 'to a very great amount' and that Trant's efforts and zeal, particularly, were 'most meritorious'. The sailing of the second division and Junot had to be delayed until an issue regarding money from the military chest was settled. The report concluded by stating 'that the conduct of the French has been marked by the most shameful disregard to honor and probity'.[25]

Doctor Adam Neale commented on the Portuguese outcry about plunder in a letter of 21 September, saying that the complaints were groundless:

> They certainly did attempt to smuggle many valuable articles of plunder on board; but so great has been the vigilance of General Beresford and Lord Proby, that they have in a great measure been foiled in their attempts, and forced to relinquish their booty, which has been placed in the public stores, till claimed by the individuals from whom it was cruelly wrested.[26]

22   Thiébault, *Mémoires*, vol.IV, pp.198–199.
23   TNA: WO 1/416: Proby & Beresford to Dalrymple, 11 and 12 September 1808.
24   Fane, *Early Campaigns*, pp.41-43.
25   TNA: WO 1/416: Proby & Beresford to Dalrymple, 18 September 1808.
26   Neale, *Letters*, p.72.

But he admitted that the French had melted down large quantities of church plate and minted it into coins, which, under the terms, they were permitted to keep. The coins were supposed to pay the French army's debts.[27] On 19 September, Dalrymple wrote to his wife, 'The French have not yet entirely embarked & to make them disgorge their spoils has been no small labour; they have been obliged however to do so, if not completely, at least to a great amount.'[28]

The French had form when it came to appropriating property and pushing the boundaries of conventions as far as they thought they could get away with. After the capture of Malta, when the French were allowed to return to France but gave up their arms, they left without paying their debts. The convention that saw the French leave Egypt also led to disputes over property, particularly the ancient Egyptian artefacts, and only searches of French ships and warehouses meant that the Rosetta Stone and other items ended up in the British Museum rather than the Louvre.[29]

One of the main criticisms of the Convention of Cintra was at the time, and since, that it allowed the French to retain their plunder and take it back to France. The wording of the article did not expressly deal with the issue of plunder, and the verbal agreements and assurances of Kellermann and Junot turned out to be worthless, but Dalrymple did enforce those agreements, and the efforts of Beresford and Proby, amongst others, did severely limit the kleptocratic tendencies of Junot and the rest of the French army in Portugal.

The Sooner I Go the Better

While the Convention began to be implemented, there continued to be tension within the British command, and Wellesley's lack of seniority became a problem. Despite their strained relationship, Dalrymple did plan to give him command of a column of the army if hostilities resumed, even though more senior officers were present, because of the victories he had obtained and his successful handling of the campaign.[30] Wellesley kept the command of much of his original force, but this led to an imbalance as many more senior officers in Moore's corps were not given commands commensurate with their seniority.[31]

Wellesley's victories had enhanced his reputation. After the Roliça and Vimeiro dispatches had reached London, but before the text of the convention did, the Duke of York wrote to Wellesley:

> It is impossible for me to peruse these papers, and to examine into the various operations so clearly explained in them, without feeling a strong impression of the zeal and ability with which your whole conduct was governed, and a very high sense of the spirit and exertions which actuated every individual under your command throughout this short but decisive and brilliant campaign in Portugal.[32]

27   TNA: WO 1/416: Proby & Beresford to Dalrymple, 7 September 1808.
28   NAM: 1994-03-129-79: Dalrymple to Dalrymple, 19 September.
29   Beresford, *Beresford*, pp.281–282, endnote 110.
30   TNA: WO 1/415: Dalrymple's narrative.
31   Marquess of Anglesey, *One-Leg, The Life and Times of Henry William Paget, First Marquess of Anglesey, K.G., 1768-1854* (London: Cape, 1961), p.68.
32   Wellington (ed.), Supplementary Despatches, vol.VI, p.117.

Castlereagh wrote in that same period, a long letter full of praise, stating, 'You have received the reward of the principles which have governed your conduct in an important accession of military reputation, and you have laid the foundation, I trust, of a succession of triumphs as often as we can bring British troops, on fair terms, in contact with the enemy.'[33]

Wellesley's stock could scarcely be higher, but his position within the expanded force in Portugal and his subordination after an independent command was frustrating, and he had little respect for those who had superseded him. He wrote to his brother William on 24 August, 'there is not one of them capable of commanding the Army, & at this moment it rests with me; the Departments look to me alone, & I give what orders I please not only referring to matters of discipline, but to those of General regulation; & the people of the Country will communicate with nobody else.'[34] He does not say if he was ordering those department heads who came to see him to go to Dalrymple instead. In another letter to William on the 26th, he gave vent to his frustrations more forcefully. After commenting on the progress of negotiations, he wrote:

> In the mean time we are going to Hell by another road … The General has no plan, or even an idea of a plan, nor do. I believe he knows the meaning of the Word Plan … These people are really more stupid & incapable than any I have yet met with; & if things go in this disgraceful manner I must quit them.[35]

On the 27th, Wellesley told the Duke of Richmond that he was 'not very well pleased … with the way in which things in this country are likely to go on', and that he would be happy to go home but was concerned that it then might look as though he was not prepared to serve unless he was in command.[36] On the 29th, he told Malcolm:

> I am afraid that I am so much connected with the credit of this army, that I cannot remain with it without falling as it will fall. If I could be of any use to men who have served me so well, I would stay with them for ever; but as matters are situated, I am sure that I can be of no use to them; I am convinced they cannot render any service, and I have determined to go home immediately.[37]

To Castlereagh the next day, he wrote, 'matters are not prospering here; and I feel an earnest desire to quit the army. I have been too successful with this army ever to serve with it in a subordinate situation, with satisfaction to the person who shall command it, and of course not to myself.'[38] Castlereagh had suggested that Wellesley go the Asturias to reconnoitre the country, but he had declined the role because he was a poor draftsman and a 'bad hand at description.'[39] On 5 September, Anstruther met Wellesley at headquarters and 'found him in exceeding bad humour

---

33   Wellington (ed.), *Supplementary Despatches*, vol.VI, p.125.
34   Webster, 'Some Letters', p.6.
35   Webster, 'Some Letters', p.7.
36   Wellington (ed.), *Supplementary Despatches*, vol.VI, p.126.
37   Gurwood (ed.), *Wellington's Dispatches*, vol.IV, p.127.
38   Gurwood (ed.), *Wellington's Dispatches*, vol.IV, p.132.
39   Gurwood (ed.), *Wellington's Dispatches*, vol.IV, p.146.

with Sir Hew who he said had treated him with great coldness and want of confidence.[40] Wellesley penned a letter to Castlereagh the same day and stated:

> It is quite impossible for me to continue any longer with this army; and I wish, therefore, that you would allow me to return home and resume the duties of my office … or if not, that I should remain upon the Staff in England; or, if that should not be practicable, that I should remain without employment. You will hear from others of the various causes which I must have for being dissatisfied, not only with the military and other public measures of the Commander in Chief, but with his treatment of myself. I am convinced it is better for him, for the army, and for me, that I should go away; and the sooner I go the better.[41]

A staff officer noted additional tensions between Burrard and Dalrymple and that if Wellesley left, Spencer would too, as he hated Dalrymple.[42]

On the 9th, Wellesley wrote to Richmond, very despondently, 'I am sick of all that is going on here, and I heartily wish I had never come away from Ireland, and that I was back again with you.'[43] On the 16th, he wrote another long letter to William detailing his unhappiness with the situation. The army had been re-organised, and he now had only four battalions under his command, while major generals had six and a brigadier general four as well. He claimed that everyone from Burrard down was dissatisfied, and that Dalrymple was a laughing stock. Slighted, ignored and frustrated by the idiocy of those placed above him, he felt he had no alternative but to quit.[44] The next day, he wrote to Moore in confidence, 'It appears to me to be quite impossible that we can go on as we are now constituted; the Commander in Chief must be changed, and the country and the army naturally turn their eyes to you as their commander.'[45] He then assured Moore that he could smooth things over with the government and urged him to accept the post if it was offered. On the same day, he wrote to Dalrymple to request permission to return to Ireland to take up his duties as Chief Secretary. The death of his deputy in Ireland, James Trail, on 16 August had given Wellesley the perfect excuse to leave. He sailed from Lisbon on 20 September.[46]

The Embarkation of the French

While Wellesley contemplated leaving for home, the French troops also felt they could not leave soon enough. Lisbon was a powder keg waiting for a spark. Mobs roamed the streets at night looking for Frenchmen or collaborators, and many were killed. On the river, boats full of agitators intercepted those trying to board ships.[47] William Warre wrote that:

---

40   StAUL: msdep121/8/2/3/4/4: Anstruther's journal, p.51.
41   Gurwood (ed.), *Wellington's Dispatches*, vol.IV, p.147.
42   BL: Add MS 49503: Cooke to Gordon, 6 September 1808.
43   Wellington (ed.), *Supplementary Despatches*, vol.VI, p.132.
44   Webster, 'Some Letters', pp.9–10.
45   Gurwood (ed.), *Wellington's Dispatches*, vol.IV, p.156.
46   Muir, *Wellington*, vol.I, p.262.
47   Griffon de Pleineville, *Invasion*, p.270.

In the town, but for the strong English Guards and Picquets, the mob would have murdered, and destroyed the houses of everybody connected with the French, and even now, if a French deserter, or spy (for I am informed many have been detected) is found, the cry of 'Hè Francez' is enough, unless some English are near, to have him murdered without mercy...[48]

On 11 September, the embarkation of the first French division began, which included a third of the sick from the hospitals, the administrators and the Portuguese who had worked with the occupiers and wanted to leave. British troops had to protect the operation from the vengeful Portuguese, but still, some of the French were stoned as they waited to board. The next day, the officers of the general staff embarked, and on the 13th, Junot boarded HMS *Nymphe*.[49] The baggage, artillery and the sick embarked on the 14th. Thiébault, who sailed on HMS *Fylla*, wrote in his memoir:

It was with melancholy feelings that I bade farewell to the fair sky of Lusitania. On the banks of the Tagus we left power, glory, honour, and wealth. But we were escaping from a foreign country, and going to retemper our spirits on our native soil; while for my part I was about to see my wife again, and delight her with the rich presents I was bringing back, and to realise some, at least, of my dreams of happiness.[50]

The second and third French divisions had embarked by the month's end. The British and French soldiers got along well. *Maréchal des logis chef* Oyon of the 4e Dragons claimed: 'A soldier did not move from one camp to the other until he came back showered with courtesies and brandy.'[51]

Between Vimeiro and the entry of the British into the city, Lisbon had descended into chaos. Southey writes:

Those wretches who, to the reproach of Christian states and civilized society, are bred in the corruption of all great cities, took advantage of the temporary dissolution of government as they would have done of a conflagration or an earthquake. The soldiers of the police, being Portugueze, had almost all gone to join their countrymen in arms; and the French while they went the rounds, suffered robberies to be committed in their hearing and in their sight, either not understanding the cries for help, or not choosing to interfere, now that their reign was at an end. They indeed themselves were in such danger, that they soon gave over patrolling the streets, and fired upon those who approached their quarters in the night. In this manner several Portugueze were shot; the French venturing upon this, not so much in the confidence of their own strength, as in full reliance upon the interference of the English to protect them.[52]

Certain French officers, guilty of atrocities, were particular targets for the Portuguese, such as *colonel* Jean Pierre Maransin for the sack of Beja, who wrote to his father about his narrow escape:

48   Warre, *Letters*, pp.39–40.
49   Thiébault, *l'Expédition*, p.224.
50   Butler (trans.), *Thiébault*, vol.II, p.216.
51   Oyon, *Campagnes*, Kindle Location 3468.
52   Southey, *History*, vol.II, p.239.

The embarkation of Junot. (Bibliothèque Nationale de France)

I was assaulted in my lodgings by a frenzied population. The twelve carabiniers who formed my guard had been repulsed and I withdrew to the staircase to defend myself, when my adjutant-major followed by a detachment of grenadiers came to rescue me from the difficult position in which I found myself. A detachment sent to me by the English General Spencer saved me, but I could not bring my effects or my horses; I lost everything. My soul was in a state difficult to conceive, and rage seized all my senses when, in the midst of the English detachment, I had to suffer the insults lavished on me from the rue du trésor to the naval arsenal where I was to embark. I knew that there was a price on my head, but I had always disdained the attempts of cowards who would seek the reward of a perfidious action. As soon as I entered the boat which was to carry me aboard my ship, I was assailed by a hail of bullets; my happy star still served as an aegis, none of which reached me, but the desire and the impossibility of taking revenge pressed and tormented me. It was in this desolate state that I reached my ship.[53]

Kellermann was attacked on a quay as he was returning from dining ashore with a British officer and was only saved by Royal Navy sailors, but not before he had been badly bruised. Four battalions with four cannon had to be bivouacked near Loison's quarters, and an attempt was made to kill Junot.[54]

---

53   Griffon de Pleineville, *Invasion*, p.273.
54   Southey, *History*, vol.II, p.251; Mackay, *Tempest*, p.302.

One of the French battalions moving to the arsenal left five or six men behind who were torn to pieces by a Portuguese mob. The mob then gathered around the entry to the arsenal and threatened to attack some smaller parties of the French. Only the presence of British troops stopped them. The French sick being transferred to a hospital also had to be protected by the bayonets of the redcoats. Several small French detachments were rescued from the mob, badly wounded. Captain Henry Cooke reported that French officers and their wives had to be given escorts from their houses, 'and during that day I constantly witnessed a French soldier holding by the arm of an English one as his only chance.' He then continued, 'Thus I am of opinion, that altho' we only discharged our duty, it does infinite honor to the national character. The contempt in which our men hold the Portuguese exceeds description, for they have also seen them in action.'[55] Captain William Gomm thought the French soldiers 'very amiable; they are civil, obliging, and gallant to a degree, and I don't believe half the stories that are told of them.' Conversely, he had a much lower opinion of the Portuguese: after remarking that they were insufficiently grateful to the British for their liberation, he wrote, 'that they have shown so little activity in the cause which should rouse all their energies, that they give by this means the strongest proof of their being a weak and degenerate people.'[56] His remark, of course, ignores the fact that the Portuguese had liberated most of the country themselves before Wellesley had arrived.

Captain Fletcher Wilkie (38th Foot) saved the lives of three Frenchmen – a merchant, a barber and a waiter:

> The evening after our arrival I was sent with the outlying piquet to strengthen the main-guard. I had hardly arrived there when a Frenchman came running to the guard-room to claim protection, and presently two more appeared, followed up by a large mob. I had the guard and piquet turned out, left room for the fugitives to pass, and stopped the pursuers; who calling out Vivan los Ingliles, said that the runaways were French men, and expected they would be given up directly to their vengeance. It was in vain to argue with such persons; they kept pressing on the men, so that I feared they would get within our bayo-nets' points. I ordered three men to load with ball-cartridge, and told the mob that I would shoot any one who endeavoured to force his way. This had the desired effect: they drew off, broke into groups, and kept moving about, in the hope of catching their prey; but I expected their patience would tire out before morning.[57]

An anonymous British captain wrote in his journal:

> As their numbers decreased the mob became more sanguinary; at last an almost General attack was made on all those whose imprudence had detained them from the body of the troops. Numbers were murdered in this manner, and had not the timely arrival of some parties of our troops put a stop to these assassinations, probably the streets of Lisbon would have become a scene disgraceful to the most uncivilised savages. Some of our officers had in their power to save many from the grave, and were under the necessity of

---

55   BL: Add MS 49503: Cooke to Gordon, 19 September 1808.
56   Carr-Gomm, *Letters*, p.105.
57   Wilkie, 'Recollections', pp.427–428.

acting offensively on the mob to save these devoted wretches, and often the protection of a British officer was barely sufficient to protect them from the stiletto.

The conduct of our soldiers was admirable, parties were seen protecting the French at the risk of their own lives (many British being dangerously wounded in the affray) and with their bayonets charged conveying their proteges to the quay.[58]

On 12 September, the 29th, 40th, 50th and 79th Foot had marched into the northern suburbs of Lisbon and bivouacked on the Campo Sant'Anna. The locals warmly greeted them and brought out chairs and sofas for the officers since the British troops had strict orders not to enter Portuguese homes. The French camped in squares in the lower town with cannon pointing along the approaching streets.[59]

On the 14th, British troops marched to occupy the citadel. The units involved were some of the 20th Light Dragoons, half a brigade of artillery, the grenadier companies of the 29th, 40th, 50th and 79th, plus the colours and band of the 29th, a company of the 95th, and the remainder of 50th Foot. Captain Henry Cooke was sent to the citadel to let the French *colonel* know they would be relieved. The four grenadier companies marched in and formed up in front of the French. The keys were handed over, and the magazines were inspected. The French then marched out to the naval arsenal, where the 50th was ready to protect them. A 21-gun salute was fired at noon, and the Portuguese flag was raised over the citadel. Lord Burghersh recalled:

> The joy of the inhabitants, when the national flag was hoisted, is beyond any description; an universal shout re-echoed through the town innumerable banners, emblems of a new life of liberty, were displayed from every corner of the capital. The ships in the river, decorated with the proud symbols of national independence, proclaimed the triumph of the day, by repeated discharges of artillery; and for nine nights the town was universally illuminated, in token of the joy of the inhabitants at their deliverance, and of hatred to the oppressors, who still witnessed from their transports the detestation which was manifested of them.[60]

The day after the British took possession of the city, the 4,000 Spanish prisoners were released and their arms restored in a ceremony overseen by Beresford on the Campo de Ourique. The Spanish were drawn up in a hollow square with crowds of onlookers around them. Beresford made a speech:

> … and requested that the latter would again accept their arms from the King of England, never to lay them down till the cause of Ferdinand VII, of Europe, and of humanity had triumphed. This address, which was forcibly and well delivered, had not yet come to a close, when it was drowned in the reiterated vivas of soldiers and inhabitants; while the roar of cannon, and the braying of trumpets, echoed from one end of Lisbon to another.

---

58   NAM: 1975-11-31-1: Manuscript journal of a captain in Wellington's Division in Portugal, 24 August to 16 September 1808.

59   Patterson, *Adventures*, pp.52–53; Leslie, *Journal*, p.69.

60   Fane, *Memoir*, pp.43–44.

After the troops had marched past, the officers had a grand *déjeune à la fourchette*,[61] and the Spanish officers 'became so intoxicated with wine and joy, as to dance waltzes, fandangos, &c., in their boots, swords, and complete field-equipment.' The Spanish troops were provided with equipment and cash, and when deputies from Catalonia arrived they were embarked for that province.[62]

Private William Billows (2nd Foot) recorded his impressions of Lisbon:

> We arrived at length in sight of Lisbon and its beautiful harbour with the Russian fleet riding in it. Beautiful sight to look at the shipping and the fine buildings all along the side of the Tagus. We encamped on a hill that commanded and overlooked the town. We got tents and when pitched they were comfortable to us and looked quite noble. I could stand at my tent door and count betwixt 20 or 30 windmills on the little hills surrounding us.[63]

Captain Henry Mellish, waiting to return to Britain with Ferguson, was far less complimentary:

> This is the nastiest & most miserable place I was in in my life. There are some fine buildings but the beauty of every thing is destroyed by the excessive filth, which may be truly said to reign here in all its glory. It is far beyond what you can form any idea of. In the streets you are up to ancles in it. They have no idea of sweeping, washing or any other method of cleaning even their most splendid houses. You may conceive we shall be glad to escape from this. The General (who is perhaps the cleanest man in the world) exists in misery, so that you may depend on his not delaying longer than is absolutely necessary. I am in a state very little short of the lepers we read of in scripture, as I am bitten by fleas, bugs & mosquitoes that my skin is totally changed. As I sail home I trust I shall wash & be clean.[64]

From mid-September, British troops moved further into Portugal, closer to the Spanish frontier. Two squadrons of the 18th Light Dragoons and five companies of the 95th went to Villa Viçosa, a brigade of artillery to Estremoz and another to Santarém along with the 36th Foot, five companies of the 5/60th went to Galegos, the 71st and 91st to Abrantes, the 2nd to Campo Maior, the 20th and 52nd to Elvas, and the two KGL light battalions to Evora and Montemor-o-Novo.[65]

The French garrison at Elvas did not immediately learn of the armistice or the convention. From the start of September, the 1,400 French and Swiss soldiers were besieged by a force of around 7,000 Spaniards who began to bombard the forts. It was not until the 17th that a British officer arrived with news of the convention, but the French commander, *colonel* Girod, refused to believe it, and it was not until 22 September that an officer arrived from Junot with orders to abandon the fortress and prepare for departure that the French gave up Elvas. The garrison marched out with drums beating and eagles to the fore. *Capitaine* Louis Begos, *adjudant major* of the second battalion of 2e Régiment Suisse, who was part of the garrison, claims that persistent attempts were made to entice his men to enter British service and that their departure was delayed to allow time for recruiters to persuade them. His battalion eventually sailed at the start of December and, after 12 days, came

---

61   French: lunch with a fork, a light meal.
62   Vane, *Story*, p.108.
63   Billows, *Nothing Pertickler*, p.33.
64   NU: Me4C2/1/13: Mellish to sister, 13 September 1808.
65   Anon., *Proceedings*, p.243.

within sight of France before a storm forced them back to Lisbon. They sailed again on 14 January, but not before, he claims, recruiters came aboard the transports armed with pistols, locked the officers in their cabins and then intimidated the men into volunteering.[66]

Lieutenant David Bremi (4e Suisse) wrote that while the Swiss piled arms and waited their turn to board at Belém, sergeants from British regiments arrived to persuade them to enlist. According to Bremi, some did, but the loss of the individuals who succumbed was 'more desirable than regrettable', and others who had previously served the British mentioned the harsh discipline and persuaded many to stay.[67]

When the 2e Suisse came from Elvas to embark, a Swiss officer of the 2nd Line Battalion, King's German Legion, Captain Charles Philip de Bosset, asked Burrard for permission to recruit men from the Swiss. The delays to embarkation and the bad weather meant that Bosset and his recruiters had plenty of time to work on the Swiss. The Swiss officers complained that the tactics of the recruiters were brutal and that many were taken by force. Eventually, over 900 foreign recruits sailed for Britain, with the northern Europeans being allocated to the KGL and 60th Foot, the French and Italians to the Chasseurs Britanniques, and the Swiss to the Regiment de Roll.[68]

Bosset was not the only officer recruiting. Major Davy of the 5/60th Rifles asked Dalrymple for permission to recruit German and Swiss deserters from the French army on 1 September, but the reply, via Wellesley, stated that Dalrymple did 'not approve of deserters from the enemy being enlisted in a corps destined to do the duty of advanced posts', and that orders had been received for Hanoverians to be recruited into the KGL. However, Davy was later able to recruit 200 Swiss soldiers at Oporto but was disappointed when they were allocated to a different battalion of the 60th.[69] It was not just the Foreign Corps recruiting either. After Vimeiro, 15 men from the 70e Ligne – Germans, Swiss and French – joined the 50th Foot, and the band then wore their long red plumes as trophies. John Patterson wrote, 'I never beheld a finer looking set of fellows, every man of them above six feet high, and well proportioned. They were all appointed to the grenadiers.'[70] A soldier of the 71st Highlanders also recorded that about 20 Swiss, German and Italian troops enlisted in his regiment but did not know why they chose the 71st 'unless the wearing of tartan was considered as a fine thing by these mercenary fellows.'[71]

The embarkation of the French garrison from Almeida at Oporto did not go any more smoothly than the embarkations at Lisbon. Lieutenant Dickens of HMS *Eclipse* reported that on 10 October, when the garrison arrived at Oporto, the locals were not pleased they had their arms and suspected that church plate was concealed in their baggage. Despite a British escort of 200 troops, the mob attacked the French, searching some of the baggage and finding a few items of plunder. A Portuguese deputation searched other baggage, but nothing more was found. The rest of the garrison was embarked under the cover of night, but the population were still up in arms and demanded to search the transports.

Lieutenant Colonel Sir Robert Wilson and other officers tried to appease the mob, and the captains of the *Primrose* and *Eclipse* promised to deliver the French arms and baggage ashore, but they would not agree. Eventually, in the face of 12,000 angry Portuguese, with the transports

66   Bégos, *Souvenirs*, pp.48–61.
67   Maag, *Schweizertruppen*, vol.I, p.483.
68   A. Nichols, *A Fine Corps and Will Serve Faithfully* (Warwick: Helion, 2023), pp.152–153.
69   Griffith, *Riflemen*, p.168.
70   Fyler, *History of the 50th*, p.109; Patterson, *Camp and Quarters*, vol.I, p.219.
71   Anon., *Vicissitudes*, p.31.

being threatened with sinking by cannon, and with the British sailors being withdrawn, the French *colonel* ordered his men to lay down their arms on one side of the transports and stand on the other, 'on which the transports bearing the English colours were plundered by a lawless mob, even the provisions of the vessels and cloaths of the masters and men in some measure plundered.' The French troops were then disembarked and placed in Forte de São João for their protection.[72]

Castlereagh had been worried that the French would detain the transports when they arrived in French ports, as had happened on previous occasions, and so ordered Dalrymple not to let the third division sail from Lisbon until the news had been received that the transports of the first two had been allowed to leave.[73] Unfortunately, this order did not reach Cotton until after the division had sailed, but the admiral applied it to Kellermann and some of the French sick, who were to be the last French troops to sail. After protesting, Kellermann was allowed to leave, but the sick remained until fever spread amongst them and the bad news of the progress of Moore's campaign in Spain reached Lisbon. Cotton decided on his own recognisance to embark them on 9 December in case Lisbon needed to be evacuated.[74]

The travails of many of the French troops were far from over when they boarded the transports to return to France. All the convoys carrying the French back to France were beset by bad weather. The vessels carrying the first division took 35 to 45 days to reach France.[75] Some transports were driven back to Lisbon and sailed again in December, not reaching France until early January. The vessels were provisioned for the expected voyage duration, and the delays caused by the storm meant the men suffered greatly from hunger and thirst.

In his memoir, *maréchal des logis chef* Oyon likened the storms the French troops faced to the final tribulations of a hero in a novel who 'seldom sees his misfortunes end without a shipwreck.' Sailing on 25 September, he initially laughed at his comrades' sea sickness, but as the winds increased and a storm came, 'Everyone's stomach had shed everything foreign to them; the revolutions caused by the rolling surprised me on an empty stomach, so that my nausea was followed by convulsive efforts which, not succeeding, ended by making me vomit pure blood'. During the night, the storm worsened, and by the morning, enormous waves and furious winds threatened to overwhelm the ships. He claims he saw three ships founder and many others run aground to save themselves. One of the masts of his ship came crashing down onto the deck. 'The composure of the English captain, the skill of his manoeuvres while we repaired the mess, alone saved us from the disastrous consequences that such an accident could bring with it.' The yard repaired they sailed on, but, on the 28th, another vessel collided with theirs, and the captain again saved them with last-minute manoeuvres that limited the damage to his ship but tore a 12-foot by eight-foot hole in the other. The storm lasted for eight days, but then they were becalmed. A 10-day voyage lasted for 45. It was too crowded when they reached La Rochelle, so they had to sail on and eventually landed at Auray, further up the coast. Oyon was then discharged due to the wound he had sustained in June.[76]

One of the vessels lost in the storms was the *Three Brothers*, carrying the staff and two companies of the 86e Ligne, which foundered off Vigo. The regiment lost both *chefs de bataillon,* and only

72 BL: Add MS 49503: Extract, Dickens to Cotton, 12 October 1808.
73 TNA: WO 6/185: Castlereagh to Dalrymple, 17 September 1808.
74 Krajeski, *Shadow*, p.126.
75 Thiébault, *l'Expédition*, p.226.
76 Oyon, *Campagnes*, Kindle Location 3506–3741.

31 of the crew and the troops survived by throwing themselves into a boat and rowing to shore. A passing British privateer picked up *colonel* Lacroix.[77]

Capitaine Jacques Hulot recalled that the ship he was sailing in lost a mast and had to have 12 men operating the pumps, who had to be tied in place to prevent them being washed away. They fired a cannon as a distress signal and a frigate tried to come to their aid, but the sea was too rough. The transport was blown to the Azores before the wind changed enough for them to head for France again. However, they ran into fresh storms entering the Bay of Biscay. They got close enough to La Rochelle to see the lighthouse but were blown back across the bay towards the Spanish coast. The ship's captain refused to head for Bayonne as it was not on the list of prescribed ports, but his crew mutinied and they eventually landed there.[78]

The French army embarked on 112 transports, with 10 for the sick, three for civilian administrators, 28 horse transports and two for ordnance stores, conveying 24,735 men, 213 women, 116 children, and 759 horses.[79] Henry Torrens commented, 'This unexpected strength is the only argument which can be advanced in favour of the Convention as it stands.'[80] However, these numbers were in line with the Hanoverian deserters' intelligence that Wellesley had discounted.

Thiébault totalled up the number of men of the expedition who died or were killed:

1. Men who died of fatigue, disease, hunger, men assassinated or drowned from Bayonne to Lisbon	1,700
2. Men taken in Oporto	30
3. Men lost in the Algarves	100
4. Men killed in Beja	30
5. Men killed in the upper Beira	60
6. Men dead or taken during the great marches of Loison's division, and killed at Evora	390
7. Men killed at Roliça	200
8. Men killed or taken at Vimeiro	1,000
9. Men dead in hospitals	890
Total	4,440[81]

To this, he added 900 prisoners of war taken, plus 2,000 men lost in the storms on the journey back to France, and the men of the Swiss regiments who chose to enlist in the British Army rather than return to France. Foy quotes similar figures, writing that 25,000 men invaded Portugal, with another 4,000 coming later. Of these, 3,000 died on marches or were killed by peasants, 2,000 were killed in battle, and 2,000 were lost at sea on the return journey or opted to enter British service. Of the 22,000 who returned to France, he wrote, 'They departed from thence inexperienced conscripts; they came back well trained and warlike soldiers: and they took their place in the

77   Anon., *Historique du 86e Régiment*, p.21.
78   Hulot, *Souvenirs*, pp.245–251.
79   BL: Add MS 49503: Embarkation returns.
80   BL: Add MS 49485: Torrens to Gordon, 10 September 1808.
81   Thiébault, *l'Expédition*, p.239.

columns of the Grand Army which was traversing France on its way to the Spanish Peninsula, to retrieve the disasters of the campaign.'[82]

The return of the Armée de Portugal for September is shown in Table 25. In addition to the 25,048 total on the table, 13 men faced disciplinary proceedings. The change from the 1 November 1807 return shown in Table 2 has been added to the columns. The strength of the French in Portugal was relatively static, with a drop of only 98, but, once one factors in the 4,000 or so men who arrived over the winter, the casualty figures that Thiébault and Foy quote are largely confirmed. Some units show a net gain from replacements, but many show significant losses. The number of sick in hospitals also varies, with the 70e and 86e Ligne having almost a quarter of their men sick and the 2e Division being particularly severely affected.

Table 25. The Army of Portugal, September 1808 Embarkation Return

Battalions/ Squadrons	Regiment	Present		Detached		Hospital		POW		Totals		
		Officers	Troops	Officers	Troops	Officers	Troops	Officers	Troops	November '07	September '08	Change
1er Division												
3e	15e Ligne	20	968				63	1	13	1,037	1,045	8
1er & 2e	70e Ligne	41	1,677			16	560		17	2,483	2,270	-213
1er	4e Suisse	31	694	8	222	1	35			1,303	960	-343
2e	47e Ligne	29	1,272				1	49		1,272	1,322	50
1er & 2e	86e Ligne	40	1,401	8	316	4	512			2,483	2,241	-242
										8,578	7,838	
2e Division												
3e	2e Légère	23	501	1	268		310		10	1,163	1,090	-73
3e	4e Légère	15	764	1	118	2	245		56	870	1,186	316
3e	12e Légère	10	952			5	225	4	44	1,002	1,230	228
3e	15e Légère	17	1,016			3	206		45	1,155	1,270	115
3e	32e Ligne	15	641	4	427		203		39	1,121	1,314	193
3e	58e Ligne	12	902			2	193			1,197	1,097	-100
2e	2e Suisse	3	78	30	727	2	75	1	10	1,240	923	-317
										7,748	8,110	
3e Division												
3e	31e Légère	20	799				25			601	824	223
3e	32e Légère	25	1,024				33	1	16	1,161	1,074	-87
3e	26e Ligne	13	312				50	2	92	618	456	-162
1er	Légion du Midi	14	593			2	50	2	179	902	826	-76
3e & 4e	66e Ligne	30	1,009			1	224			1,109	1,234	125
3e	82e Ligne	17	602			7	121	5	208	816	943	127
1er	Légion Hanovrienne	18	655				102			833	757	-76
										6,040	6,114	

---

82 Foy, *Invasion*, p.188.

Battalions/ Squadrons	Regiment	Present		Detached		Hospital		POW		Totals		
		Officers	Troops	Officers	Troops	Officers	Troops	Officers	Troops	November '07	September '08	Change
Division de Cavalrie												
4e	26e Chasseurs à cheval	7	236				20			*241*	*256*	15
4e	1er Dragons	8	269				29		27	*298*	*325*	27
4e	3e Dragons	7	252				25	1	20	*297*	*298*	1
4e	4e Dragons	7	238				8			*268*	*246*	-22
4e	5e Dragons	6	238				7		8	*274*	*253*	-21
4e	9e Dragons	8	236				21		11	*304*	*268*	-36
4e	15e Dragons	4	217				26			*297*	*243*	-54
	Gendarmerie impériale	1	36							*40*	*37*	-3
										2,019	**1,889**	
Artillerie												
	1er Regiment à Pied	3	104				5			*59*	*109*	50
	3e Regiment à Pied	7	304				12		6	*225*	*322*	97
	6e Regiment à Pied	5	191				20		14	*207*	*225*	18
	9 comp. d'ouvriers	1	29							*4*	*29*	25
	12 comp. de Train	5	387				22			*295*	*409*	114
Genie		14						3		*8*	*3*	-5
										798	**1,097**	
		476	18,597	52	2,078	46	3,476	20	815	**25,183**	**25,048**	-98

Source: Anon., *Proceedings*, p.243.

When the troops eventually reached French ports, surgeons examined the sick and wounded, finding that many of the wounds had become infected. Dysentery and scurvy had broken out on the transports, and the hospitals quickly filled up. Even those free of disease were emaciated and weak. Many horses had also died or were too weak for further service. With the military infrastructure and logistics of the ports overwhelmed by the arrival of so many troops, Junot's infantry divisions were dispersed to Angoulême, Saintes, and La Rochelle, and the cavalry to Niort and Saint-Jean-d'Angély.[83]

On 2 October, Napoleon wrote to Clarke, the minister of war:

As soon as the duc d'Abrantès or other officers of his army are disembarked, you will write to them that I have learned of the convention; that I do not know if I should approve it, but that while awaiting the report which I must receive I see nothing in this act which is contrary to honour, since the troops have not laid down their arms, they are returning with their flags, they are not prisoners, and they are arriving, not by a capitulation, but by

---

83   Griffon de Pleineville, *Invasion*, pp.288–289.

a convention which is more political than military. I am waiting for the duc d'Abrantès to give me a report of all the events, so that I can find out why, seeing that he had six weeks to prepare, he had not set up an entrenched camp at the mouth of the Tagus, or in any other position, with sufficient supplies to wait until he was rescued. This was what the art of war required him to do in such a situation.[84]

As was often the case, Napoleon seems to have been out of touch with the situation on the ground. No French force could have realistically come to Junot's aid. On 19 October, Napoleon wrote a little more warmly to Junot, 'You have done nothing dishonourable; you are bringing back my troops, my eagles and my cannons. I had hoped, however, that you would do better.' He then mentioned, at length, that he had told Junot to form an entrenched camp and to take a firmer hand with the Portuguese. He also berated him for surrendering Elvas. As for the convention, he said, 'You won this agreement by your courage, but not by your dispositions; and it is with good reason that the English complain that their general signed it. You would have deserved it if you had signed it in an entrenched camp, six weeks later.' He then told Junot that his troops were to be formed into the VIII Corps of the army in Spain. Napoleon then wrote, 'Before the end of the year, I want to return you to Lisbon myself. Keep close to you the officers who know the country best. Send me the best map you have; have the roads traced, and attach to it all the information on how to get back to Lisbon without making any siege.'[85]

---

84   Plon & Dumaine (eds), *Correspondance*, vol.17, 14355, p.531.
85   Plon & Dumaine (eds), *Correspondance*, vol.18, 14384, pp.2–4.

20

Controversy

The Portuguese Reaction

After a positive meeting with Dalrymple on 24 August, *Major* Pinto had hoped the Portuguese objections to some of the terms of the suspension of arms would be taken account of, but on the 31st, after seeing the final version of the convention, he wrote to Freire that, 'finally the intrigue of the French overcame the English sincerity, and our nominal protectors obtained little less than the preliminary stipulations, except for some small explanations of the article, which concerns the baggage'.[1] Dalrymple claims that Pinto was 'not sparing' in his observations on the proposed articles. The general asked for any comments to be put in writing, but this was only done after the treaty was ratified. Dalrymple felt the complaints were not really directed at him but 'to the passions and the prejudices of the people.'[2]

On 4 September, Freire wrote a letter of protest to Dalrymple. He began by saying that, in general, the treaty showed a 'want of contemplation' of the interests of the government and the people of Portugal. In particular, he objected to the clauses regarding the occupation of the forts not making it clear that such an occupation was to be temporary and that they were to be handed back to the Portuguese. He also objected to the 16th and 17th articles protecting French citizens remaining in Portugal and those who worked for the occupation. Letting those who had been disloyal leave or not be investigated was not acceptable, and the 1st additional article regarding the release of civilians employed by the French army and taken prisoner should not have been agreed to without a reciprocal clause. He also wrote that there should have been a security guarantee for the population of Lisbon while the French embarked.[3] Dalrymple replied that 'it did not appear to me as likely to produce tranquillity or happiness in Portugal, to keep alive political animosity by the infliction of punishments'. He also informed Freire that he was dealing with the rumours of French plunder being carried away and had sent Beresford to help Proby.[4] The response seemed to mollify Freire.

The Bishop of Oporto's objections to the cessation of hostilities were mainly that neither Friere nor the Junta were involved in the negotiations and that the French were allowed to take all their

---

1   Sepulveda, *Historia*, vol.XI, pp.156–158.
2   Dalrymple, *Memoir*, p.77.
3   TNA: WO 1/416: Freire to Dalrymple, 4 September 1808.
4   TNA: WO 1/416: Dalrymple to Freire, 5 September 1808.

plunder home.[5] With the convention's wording not explicitly banning the French from taking plunder home, Portuguese objections were understandable.

Dalrymple had a copy of a letter from the Bishop on re-establishing the Portuguese government in which the Bishop requested that until a new government was formed, the Junta should be treated as the country's representatives. However, Dalrymple did not think he could give a 'mere creature of a revolutionary and local Government' such legitimacy.[6] Unfortunately, in Oporto, Brigadier General von Decken, without instructions from London, had been urging the Bishop to assume the mantle of government.[7] To placate the Bishop, Dalrymple informed him that once the French left, the Prince Regent's government could be restored, but, as some of the Regency Council had co-operated with the French, he could not agree to their return to power. Instead, he planned to form a provisional council from those not tainted by collaboration with the French until the pleasure of the Prince was known and that the Bishop should be on the council and help to form it.[8] The Bishop agreed.

A Country Governed by Newspapers

The dismay at the terms of the agreements with the French in Lisbon and Oporto occurred soon after the signing of the suspension of arms and the definitive convention. The furore in London surrounding the convention began when Domingos António de Sousa Coutinho, the Portuguese ambassador, received a copy of the suspension of arms on 3 September, which Freire had sent to the Bishop of Oporto on 25 August. He sent a note, along with letters from the Bishop and Freire, to Canning at the Foreign Office asking for the comments of the British government on 'this unfortunate transaction' that was so inconsistent with the rights of Prince João and the proclamation made by Wellesley when he landed.[9]

Canning had to reply that the British government had not seen the 'supposed convention' but 'doubted its authenticity'.[10] The bulk of Canning's reply dealt with fears that the Bishop of Oporto had granted the Russian squadron the protection of a neutral port. Canning informed Castlereagh, who immediately wrote to Dalrymple, sending a copy of Coutinho's note and demanding an explanation, writing, 'the King cannot permit himself to attach any credit to such a convention having been agreed to, under the relative circumstances in which his fleet and armies were placed towards those of his enemies'.[11]

In a letter to his brother, Castlereagh listed his objections to the 'supposed convention' that Sousa had delivered. The first was that it recognised Napoleon as Emperor of France, something the government had avoided up to then. The second was that it provided the 'safe retreat of an enemy's corps destitute of all other means of escape.' The third and fourth objections related to the

5   TNA: WO 1/418: Bishop to Dalrymple, undated.
6   Dalrymple, *Memoir*, p.86.
7   Dalrymple, *Memoir*, p.87.
8   TNA: WO 1/416: Dalrymple to Bishop of Oporto, 5 September 1808. This conforms with orders Castlereagh had written but Dalrymple had probably not yet received, WO 1/418, Castlereagh to Dalrymple, 19 August 1808.
9   Sepulveda, *Historia*, vol.XI, p.182.
10   TNA: WO 1/418: Canning to Souza, 4 September 1808.
11   TNA: WO 1/418: Castlereagh to Dalrymple, 4 September 1808.

neutrality of the Russian fleet, which was cut from the final convention. The fifth was that the army was free to fight again and able to take its plunder. The sixth lamented the protection afforded to the Portuguese who had collaborated. His seventh and final objection was that after much effort, Britain was only removing Junot's army from where it had lost to a position where it could regroup and act against Spain. He also wrote, 'I should feel it an injustice by Wellesley, for which I could not forgive myself, to suppose that any power on earth could have induced him to be individually a party to such an arrangement'. He then closed the letter with, 'it is a base forgery somewhere, and nothing can induce me to believe it genuine.'[12]

The Prime Minister, the Duke of Portland, wrote to Castlereagh that the terms were 'preposterous' and that he could not believe Wellesley, or any other British officer, could have signed them.[13] Canning wrote on the morning of 17 September, just before the final version of the convention arrived in London, that Portugal 'must hate us for the Article giving up their Plunder. Instead of hailing us as deliverers, they must consider us as having interfered only to sanction and secure French Robbery.' Later that day, when he had seen the final text, he wrote, 'I confess it is even worse than my expectations. The Substance to be sure I could not expect to be different, but I did not think that I should find every sore place touched in the coarsest manner; and all the shameful parts of the transaction brought forward with such unsparing, such studious and laboured particularity.'[14]

One factor in the hostile government and press reaction was the long gap between the arrival of Burrard's Vimeiro dispatch and Dalrymple's dispatch containing the convention. Castlereagh wrote to Dalrymple on 17 September:

> I am to express the surprize felt by His Majesty, that a Convention of so important a nature as that which formed the basis of the definite arrangement should have been agreed to, so far back as the 22nd Ultimo, and no step taken till the 4th of the present month, for communicating the same to His Majesty's Minister, together with the considerations which had induced you, under the relative circumstances of the two armies, to sanction such an agreement; by which omission, His Majesty's Government has been exposed to the embarrassment of receiving the Communication in the first instance through the Channel of the Portuguese Minister to whose representations they have been obliged to reply, not only under a total ignorance but under an absolute disbelief of the facts thus brought under their notice.
>
> … My Dispatch of the 4th instant, with its enclosures will have apprized you of the impression made upon His Majesty by the Communication of the Convention in question, and must have prepared you for the Commands which I now have to convey to you from His Majesty, that you do forthwith return to England, to give explanations with respect to your Conduct transferring the command of the army, together with your Instructions, to the General Officer next to you in command.[15]

Dalrymple later admitted he should have sent word to London during the negotiations but that 'each day held out so near a prospect of final arrangement, that I was insensibly betrayed into a

---

12   Vane (ed.), *Correspondence*, vol.VI, pp.421–423.
13   Vane (ed.), *Correspondence*, vol.VI, pp.423–424.
14   Muir, 'Commentary for Chapter 16'.
15   TNA: WO 1/234: Castlereagh to Dalrymple, 17 September.

delay which I certainly cannot altogether justify.'[16] Charles Stewart foresaw the problem that the communication gap would cause, writing to Gordon, 'I fear your anxiety will be very great in England between the receipt of the dispatches of the 22nd & the next you will receive.'[17]

In the void between the Vimeiro dispatch being published on 3 September and the arrival of Dalrymple's from Sintra on the 16th, the press began to fill their column inches with rumours and fervent speculation spread through London. For example, a notice posted at Lloyd's Coffee House claimed that the French had abandoned Lisbon, had been attacked on 24 August and crushed, 5,000 French had died, 33 wagons of French plunder taken, Delaborde and Junot were prisoners, the Russian squadron had hoisted Portuguese colours, and the Royal Navy had destroyed a French squadron bringing Prince Eugène and several thousand reinforcements.[18]

Another factor in the hostile reception of the convention was the very positive press given to Wellesley's victories. Former minister Lord Auckland wrote to former Prime Minister Lord Grenville, 'In truth the necessity of such a convention is very difficult to be reconciled to Sir Arthur Wellesley's expression of "a complete victory gained by a part of his army over the whole force of the French in Portugal."'[19]

For the government, Wellesley's dispatch following Roliça and Burrard's after Vimeiro announced the first significant land victories since Egypt in 1801 and Maida in 1806. They were an opportunity to vindicate their policies on the war and give the public some positive news after the disasters in South America. So, they made sure they made the most of them in the papers, especially the part played by Wellesley who was closely linked to the government. Wellesley's family and friends also used their connections to ensure he got the credit they felt he was due for his successes and then to distance him from the suspension of arms and convention.

An undated and unsigned memorandum, ascribed to Murray and surviving in both his and Wellesley's papers, blames the government and Wellesley's friends for the reaction to the convention:

> This cry has been occasioned I think by the people of England seeing matters in a false light, and the ministers have given into it instead of endeavouring to allay it; partly because they were afraid to meet it, and partly because, misled by letters from his friends here, they thought they could separate Sir Arthur Wellesley's name from all reproach, by overwhelming Sir Hew Dalrymple.[20]

At the inquiry, Wellesley stated that he had not authorised any of his friends or relations to inform a newspaper that he was ordered to sign the cessation of hostilities.[21] However, an anonymous newspaper editor told the Duke of Buckingham that he had visited William Wellesley-Pole:

> I told him my motive for calling was to ascertain, if possible, what share Sir Arthur had in the transaction, for obvious reasons, &c. He said, that knowing the interest I took in them all, he would read for me in confidence, as much of his brother's letter to Castlereagh as he could, consistently with his duty to the secrecy he was bound to observe with respect

16   BL: Add MS 49484: Dalrymple to Castlereagh, 23 December 1808.
17   BL: Add MS 49503: Stewart to Gordon, 30 August 1808.
18   *The Star*, 3 September 1808.
19   Anon., *Dropmore*, vol.IX, p.215.
20   UoS: WP 1/212: Letter marked Murray, 1808, August. Undated, unsigned.
21   Anon., *Proceedings*, p.17.

to individuals … He then read for me, as well as I recollect, nearly as follows: 'I authorize you to make it known in any manner you think proper, that I had no share whatever in consulting upon, negotiating, or drawing up the preliminary articles of the Convention. They were done by Kellermann, in the presence of Sir Hew Dalrymple and General Burrard, and adopted by them without any alteration whatever. And I was merely ordered to sign them, which I did, conceiving it my duty so to do, without being consulted in any single instance respecting any one of these articles whatever.'[22]

The letter in question may have been one that Wellesley wrote to his brother on 24 August, stating, 'Sir Hew has agreed to a suspension of hostilities which he made me sign.'[23]

However, once he returned to London on 6 October, Wellesley wrote to Buckingham himself about the reaction to the convention, stating that 'I am accused of being the adviser of persons over whom I had no control, and who refused to follow my advice, and am made responsible for the acts of others.' After blaming Dalrymple for not making the case for a swift evacuation of the French more clearly, he wrote, 'In respect to the conduct of my case, I have determined that I will publish nothing; nor will authorize the publication of anything by others. This forbearance is particularly incumbent upon me, as the whole subject must be enquired into.' After mentioning that he did not intend to bring Sir Harry Burrard into the controversy, he said he was 'determined to stand singly. There is nothing in common between Sir Hew Dalrymple and me, or between the government and me; if the government are supposed to be involved in the question; and I shall act accordingly.'[24] In a letter to Earl Temple, Buckingham's son, he wrote that:

> I agree entirely in opinion with you, that it would be most desirable that my zealous friends should cease to defend me; but it will be very difficult to prevail upon them to do so; and, indeed, I don't know how to set about the work, for I don't know who the writers are. I can safely declare that neither I, my brother, my aides de camp, or my immediate friends have written or published one word upon the late Convention in Portugal…[25]

Castlereagh was provided ammunition for his efforts to defend his friend Wellesley by the letters from his brother, Charles Stewart, in Portugal, who was critical of Dalrymple and distanced Wellesley from responsibility for the convention.[26]

For the government, the involvement of their close ally, Wellesley, complicated their response to the crisis. His public prominence meant he drew more criticism than the unknown Dalrymple and Burrard. Public meetings began to call for an inquiry.[27]

In his memoir, Dalrymple wrote:

> Pains were, indeed, taken by the Bishop of Oporto, his partizans and adherents, to misrepresent and raise a clamour against the Convention, not only in Portugal but in England

22   Duke of Buckingham and Chandos (ed.), *Memoirs of the Court and Cabinets of George the Third* (London: Hurst and Blackett, 1855), vol.IV, p.254.
23   Webster, 'Some Letters of the Duke of Wellington', pp.6–7.
24   Buckingham (ed.), *Memoirs of the Court*, vol.IV, pp.261–262.
25   Buckingham (ed.), *Memoirs of the Court*, vol.IV, pp.266–267.
26   R. Payne, *War and Diplomacy in the Napoleonic Era* (London: Bloomsbury, 2021), pp.16–17.
27   Muir, *Wellington*, vol.I, p.271.

also. In the former their misrepresentations were soon contradicted by the evidence of facts; not so in England; they were there so powerfully seconded by the language held by ministers, and the measures they pursued, that the erroneous impression thus made upon the public mind was confirmed and perpetuated.[28]

On 28 September, Dalrymple's son, Adolphus, returned to Portugal with the dispatches from London, and amongst the mail on the same ship were newspapers and letters which told both the army and the locals how the treaty had been received. Dalrymple informed Gordon that the tenor of Castlereagh's dispatches 'was not pleasing' and that he would return to Britain as ordered.[29] He continued, 'The objections to the Convention seem to be; first, the making of any convention of the sort at all; secondly the badness of the terms for ourselves and our allies, but above all that article which it is presumed enables the French to remove plunder.'[30] To him, the advantages of a convention that had freed Portugal from occupation and left a British force of 30,000 men poised to enter Spain were clear.[31]

On the 29th, Dalrymple wrote to his wife, telling her that he would be returning to London, 'I therefore look forwards with joy to meeting my family after near these two tedious years of absence.' He then commented on the furore over the convention:

> I have this day heard of a paragraph in the morning post of the 20th which surprised me not a little, but affords a key to the hope of government as to the result of the explanation I am call'd upon to give; when Sir Arthur Wellesley himself arrives in London I think he will do wisely and I sure he will do handsomely to put this whole matter at its true grounds, make yourself quite easy and be quite sure that *I* have grounds whither in a political or a military point of view to justify myself. Whether the Convention was a wise or a foolish measure must ever remain a matter of opinion. I still assent that by it much time was gained, and that I had no reason to surmise, that that time would have been wasted or misemployed. I shall trust that will not be the case.[32]

He continued, 'Let this be a lesson to us my sweet woman to look for happiness elsewhere than in popular applause, particularly in a country governed by newspapers.' He told his wife that what grieved him most was the press coverage's effect on his friends, his family, and especially her. He was less concerned about the impact on himself:

> It so happens that my constitution and temper enable me better than many to contend with this sort of matter; I thank heaven that I have not like Sir Arthur Wellesley a friend to defend me as he has been defended, you maybe quite sure, he must himself contradict that friend before I do it or his character in the army is gone; but I feel confident he will do himself justice and support the opinion he has so openly avowed.

On 5 October, Dalrymple embarked on the *Phoebe*, the frigate that had brought him to Portugal.

---

28   Dalrymple, *Memoir*, p.76.
29   BL: Add MS 49484: Dalrymple to Calvert, 29 September 1808.
30   BL: Add MS 49484: Dalrymple to Calvert, 29 September 1808.
31   BL: Add MS 49484: Dalrymple to Calvert, 29 September 1808.
32   NAM: 1994-03-129-81: Dalrymple to Frances Dalrymple, 29 September 1808.

Sir Harry Burrard was greatly affected by the criticism in the press of his decision not to pursue the French on the 21st. On 30 September, he wrote to Gordon, 'My family, which is a large one, has very little to depend upon when I am gone, but a good name, and if I cannot leave them that benefit it will be poor indeed'. He then set out his reasons for the decision in detail and then wrote:

> Upon these grounds I trust the commander in chief will approve of my motives of conduct, whatever HRH may think of the cogency of my reasons, but I hope this can lead to no discussions with Sir Arthur W, for whom I have the highest regard, and for whose character I feel the greatest respect and therefore my earnest wish is that it may not be necessary for mine, that this should go further than the hands of HRH.[33]

On 8 October, Burrard responded to the criticism by telling Gordon that if Junot's army had been 'driven to the extremity' as Wellesley had wished after Vimeiro, 'no officer, however keen his foresight or great his experience, would have ventured to pronounce on what *day*, *week* or *month* the surrender of the French would have enabled our army to undertake the march which is now projecting into Spain.'[34] On 9 November, after receiving orders to return to Britain, he wrote to Gordon again in the depths of depression:

> I feel myself by no means equal to a great situation. My eyesight will not allow me to write at night or very long together. I feel that various and nullified business brings in a confusion which destroys my memory and I do not now possess what I did a few years back, I mean no unwillingness to responsibility. On the contrary I feel that I dread it more every day and that my anxious moments invade my rest, and weary my faculties more than I can bear.
>
> You cannot suppose that the scene that has lately past, is passing and will continue, is likely to quiet a mind thus disposed. I assure you I am truly heartsick on the occasion, and often wish a kindly bullet had gone through my temples at Vimeiro but I thank God I am resigned to what may come, and only wish to retire to a better rest for the years that are allotted me.[35]

He asked permission to retire; 'Let me find rest and oblivion'. In another letter, he commented on the press coverage; 'It is enough to make one sick to read the city politicians and their crude unmilitary jargon.' He thought that no general would want to command if they had to answer to the press in future.[36]

The British press at the time was divided broadly between those who supported the government and those who favoured the opposition. In the former camp were the *Sun*, *Daily Advertiser* and *Morning Post*. In the latter, the *Examiner*, *Morning Chronicle* and *Cobbett's Political Register*.

Dalrymple firmly placed the blame for the controversy surrounding the convention on the manipulation of the press by the government. He mentioned 'the exaggerated hopes and consequently disappointed expectations of the Nation' and the 'unworthy means used to mislead the

---

33   BL: Add MS 49485: Burrard to Gordon, 30 September 1808.
34   BL: Add MS 49485: Burrard to Gordon, 8 October 1808.
35   BL: Add MS 49485: Burrard to Gordon, 9 November 1808.
36   BL: Add MS 49485: Burrard to Gordon, 14 November 1808.

Public Opinion, and to influence the passions of the People.' He also thought that the hyperbolic coverage of the victories at Roliça and Vimeiro played a part.[37]

Even before news of Wellesley's progress reached London, the *Morning Chronicle* was speculating on Junot's options:

> It would appear to be his most sensible proceeding to capitulate, as it would be Sir Arthur Wellesley's policy to accept it, and to grant him easy terms. His position is so strong that he might hold out for a long time, and it is in the interests of the allies that our army should be speedily released from this service, that it may proceed on another.[38]

On 1 September, the *Daily Advertiser* informed its readers that 'The silence from Portugal is truly distressing'.[39] However, by 2 September, good news had reached London. The *Morning Herald* exclaimed 'Glorious News' from the army in Portugal and the 'Defeat of Junot', 'A MOST IMPORTANT AND BRILLIANT VICTORY' and 'THE TOTAL DEFEAT OF THE ENEMY'. It was claimed that Junot and the wreck of his army had been pursued to Lisbon. The paper also reported that 'On the 22d, JUNOT proposed terms of capitulation, which were rejected, and he was informed that only unconditional surrender would be accepted.'[40] The *Morning Post* declared the 'MOST GLORIOUS NEWS', the 'COMPLETE DEFEAT OF GEN. JUNOT' and printed a letter from Castlereagh to the Lord Mayor of London that stated the French had been 'COMPLETELY DEFEATED' and that Kellermann had arrived to treat for terms.[41] The opposition-supporting *Morning Chronicle* was more reserved in its coverage, and their typesetters did not have to reach for letters from the upper cases. However, the paper still trumpeted the 'Most important and glorious intelligence' and mentioned 'complete success' at Vimeiro.[42] The *Daily Advertiser* carried an account of Lieutenant Colonel Browne and Captain Campbell arriving at the Duke of York's office at 6:00 p.m. the evening before. The dispatches were said to be of a 'favourable nature'. Browne went to York's residence in Stable Yard in a chaise and four. The paper reported that Junot was said to have surrendered but thought that report premature.[43]

On Saturday, 3 September, an extraordinary edition of *The London Gazette* printed Wellesley's Roliça and Vimeiro dispatches, and the newspapers finally had some solid news to report. The *General Evening Post* included the dispatches and said, 'It is impossible to describe the joy which the news of this great victory diffused every where through the Metropolis yesterday. The Park and Tower guns were fired early in the morning, and bells in every parish were rung at intervals during the whole of the day.' The paper continued: 'It is impossible to speak of the victory obtained by Sir Arthur Wellesley in terms of applause and exultation too high'.[44]

The *Daily Advertiser* eulogised Wellesley:

---

37   NAM: 1994-03-129-83: Dalrymple's record of service, pp.50, 66.
38   *Morning Chronicle*, 16 August 1808.
39   *Daily Advertiser, Oracle and True Briton*, 1 September 1808.
40   *Morning Herald*, 2 September 1808
41   *Morning Post*, 2 September 1808.
42   *Morning Chronicle*, 2 September 1808.
43   *Daily Advertiser, Oracle and True Briton*, 2 September 1808.
44   *General Evening Post*, 3 September 1808.

The last harvest, or British threshers makeing French crops' by Charles Williams. Wellesley is pictured cutting Junot's queue off while his men are driven into the sea. (Anne S.K. Brown Military Collection)

… the whole issue of the conduct of SIR ARTHUR WELLESLEY in Portugal, ranks him amongst the highest Military Characters of his age or time –perhaps … It is scarcely possible to state the enthusiasm with which he was cheered by the whole Army as he passed the line on the close of this momentous day, and the heartfelt kindness with which his Brethren in the field ascribed to him the sole and entire honour of this Glorious Victory. In truth his conduct was most conspicuously admirable – self-possession, quickness, bravery, conduct, all combined to mark him to the whole Army, as among the very first of his profession in every natural or acquired qualification of a Soldier and a General![45]

The paper's coverage mentioned that Burrard had prevented Wellesley from pursuing Junot and predicted that Kellermann's negotiations would result in unconditional surrender or terms near that. However, another government-supporting paper, the *Sun,* published a lengthy defence of Burrard following reports of the disagreement after Vimeiro, justification for his appointment, and praise for Ferguson, Hill and Spencer.[46]

By 8 September, more details had reached the newspapers, possibly from Wellesley's friends. The *Daily Advertiser* expanded on reports that Burrard had prevented a pursuit that would have destroyed the French. The paper reminded readers that many of the regiments in Portugal had been defeated in South America and placed the credit for their redemption on Wellesley's better leadership. It also lamented the lack of cavalry in Portugal 'while so many fine-dressed regiments of Light Dragoons are in this country, and who could have followed up our victory with success.' The paper also published one of many, mostly excruciating, poems praising Wellesley that included the lines:

> Thy troops advance, thy deep-mouthed cannons roar!
> Heroic Wellesley guides the dreadful blow,
> And hurls destruction on th' insulting Foe!
> Illustrious Chief! Born armies to controul,
> In action quick, and resolute of soul,
> Warm from the field with Gallic Blood embru'd.
> Accept this meed – Thy country's gratitude![47]

On Sunday, 8 September, the *Saint James' Chronicle* published supposed details of Wellesley's life on campaign, saying that he slept on the ground with his horse beside him, that he was the first up and last down in the whole camp, and that 'wherever a corps was to be led on, from the death of its Officer, or any other cause, Sir Arthur was on the spot to head it.'[48] Anecdotes from the battles that have since become famous also emerged in the press. Both the *General Evening Post* and the *Morning Herald* carried stories of the 71st's piper, George Clark, and the capture of *général de brigade* Brennier. The *Herald* also published another tortuous poem to Wellesley that included the immortal lines:

---

45   *Daily Advertiser, Oracle and True Briton*, 3 September 1808.
46   *The Sun*, 10 September 1808.
47   *Daily Advertiser, Oracle and True Briton*, 8 September 1808.
48   *Saint James' Chronicle*, 8 September 1808.

Junot he claw'd, and curs'd and swore,
For he had no religion;
Sir Arthur all his Eagles tore,
As eagles tear a pigeon.[49]

However, not all the coverage was so favourable. The anti-government *The British Press* expressed doubts about the prudence of Wellesley advancing to engage Junot when he knew reinforcements were on their way, 'This brave and gallant officer might have been ambitious of the glory of defeating Junot single-handed.'[50]

The lack of news from Portugal after the battle dispatches also began to be news itself, *The Examiner* on 11 September stated, 'it is very strange that we have not heard from Sir Arthur Wellesley since the late battle. The wind has been fair for several days, and dispatches might have been expected, whether Junot had surrendered or not. The more we think of the battle of Vimeira, the more surprise we feel at the delay.'[51] The *Sun* tried to quash the rumours that had begun to circulate about the terms of the convention on 9 September: 'No intelligence has reached the government from Portugal when this Paper was put to Press. There are, however, several reports in circulation respecting the terms upon which the French are said to have surrendered, but they are not entitled to any credit.'[52]

The opposition *Morning Chronicle* six days later printed, 'So long as we continued without any arrivals from Portugal, the public mind was tranquil. No suspicion arose that any thing had occurred to disappoint the nation of the proper fruits of the victories which Sir Arthur Wellesley had so arduously gained.' But with the recent rumours and the lack of news 'a very serious gloom hung over the Metropolis.' The paper said that the silence from ministers was not helpful and the rumours should be addressed.[53]

On the same day, the 15th, *The Star* reported that one rumour:

> … believed to be circulated on the authority of the Portuguese Ambassador, but still not held to be official, states that a capitulation has been concluded by the British, French and Russian Commanders, which declares – that Lisbon will be a free port; that the French troops shall be permitted to return home with their arms and their *private* property, (their plunder); and that the Russian squadron shall be allowed a start of 48 hours, to enable them to withdraw unmolested to whatever place they think proper.[54]

The paper went on to say that it could not believe a British officer would sign such a document, but that reports had been circulating for a week but not believed, and that the lack of official news was causing unease. However, the same issue included:

> We stop the press to state, that this afternoon at half-past four o'clock, a son of Sir HEW DALRYMPLE, together with Captain HALSTEAD, Captain of the Fleet under Admiral

---

49 *Morning Herald*, 8 September 1808.
50 *The British Press*, 9 September 1808.
51 *The Examiner*, 11 September 1808.
52 *The Sun*, 9 September 1808.
53 *Morning Chronicle*, 15 September 1808.
54 *The Star*, 15 September 1808.

Sir CHARLES COTTON, arrived at the Admiralty, and at the Secretary of State's office, with important Information. That JUNOT and WHOLE ARMY are PRISONERS of WAR; That LISBON is OCCUPIED by the BRITISH TROOPS; and, That the RUSSIAN FLEET has SURRENDERED to Admiral SIR CHARLES COTTON.

An idea of how quickly the situation was changing can be gathered by the fact that below that stop press was: 'Since writing the above we have been informed that in the terms of the Capitulation it is stipulated that the French troops are to be sent to France! And that the Russian fleet is to be restored six months after the conclusion of a General peace!!!'

The condemnation of the convention was swift and universal. The *Evening Star* printed, 'Dispatches have at last been received from Portugal—but we are concerned to state, *not the expected dispatches!*' The paper wrote that it would have been hoped that after Wellesley's victory and reinforcement by Moore, unconditional surrender would have been demanded. 'Unconditional surrender! Our readers will exclaim, and is it not so?—No, Countrymen. On the 30th ult. Sir Hew Dalrymple signed a convention by which it is agreed:–That *the French army shall evacuate Portugal, and,* if we may credit high authority, *with their arms and baggage, and to be transported by sea to some port between L'Orient and Rochefort.*' The paper wondered what Napoleon would do to a general who signed such a convention. It also distanced, literally, Wellesley from the convention, stating that 'the brave, the meritorious Sir Arthur Wellesley' was 20 miles distant when it was signed.[55] The *Morning Chronicle* also distanced Wellesley by the same 20 miles. It claimed, 'Sir Arthur Wellesley in particular, is mentioned, as being extremely dissatisfied with the proceedings which have taken place since he was superseded in the command, and it has been said even that he was about to return home in disgust.'[56]

Another *Extraordinary* edition of the *London Gazette* was published later on the 16th with the full text of the convention. The editor of *The Examiner*, radical Leigh Hunt, wrote:

> I really feel bewildered in sitting down to comment on the very Extraordinary Gazette in this Paper: the head turns in confusion through the maze of our military politics, and the reader is dragged unwillingly from error to error, from stupidity to stupidity, till his faculties become numb, and he is converted into a mere mass of astonishment. An old Gentleman, it seems, of the name of Hugh or Hew Dalrymple, was considered a proper person by the British Government to take command of the victorious army in Portugal without knowing, as he confesses, any thing at all about the matter. An armistice in the mean time is concluded between the French and their conqueror Sir Arthur Wellesley, who, after beating them, as he says in a dreadful manner, lets them do what they please with him in the way of convention, that is, he kicks the robbers out of the drawing-room, but treats them with the utmost good nature all the way down the stairs, suffers them to keep their plunder in their pockets, and insists upon going before them to open the door.

Hunt then continued, 'Is it not monstrous, that after such a battle as that of Vimeira is *represented* to have been, the enemy should absolutely dictate his terms to us.' The emphasis is Hunt's and illustrates the problem for the government. They had spun the battle as a great and complete

55   *Evening Star*, 16 September 1808.
56   *Morning Chronicle*, 16 September 1808.

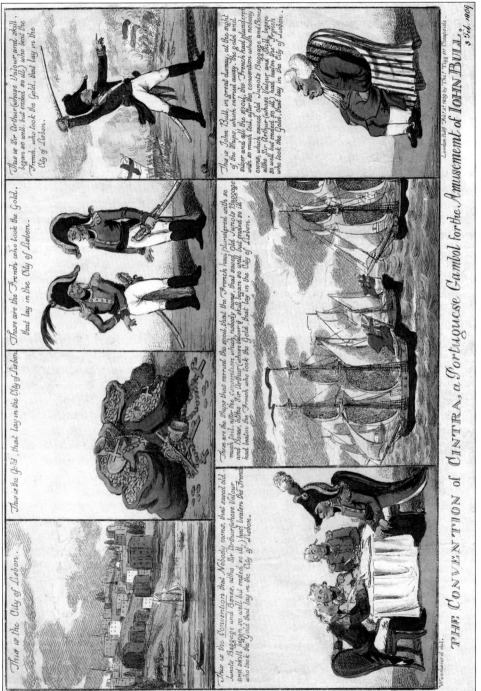

'The Convention of Cintra, a Portuguese gambol for the amusement of John Bull', by George Moutard Woodward. (Bodleian Libraries, University of Oxford)

victory, but the terms of the convention reflected the reality of a French Army still largely intact and possessing a strong defensive position. Hunt continued, 'One is not so much astonished at this Sir Hew Dalrymple, for he always might have been stupid though we did not know it; but that Sir Arthur Wellesley, the *gallant* Sir Arthur, the *glorious* Sir Arthur, the *hero* of Vimiera, should be the first to ratify the disgrace of the British arms, is a wonder apparently unaccountable.' In a presage to the discredited lions-led-by-donkeys myth of the First World War, Hunt also was at pains to point out that the generals were at fault and Britain's soldiers could be called 'excellent bull-dogs commanded by jackasses.'[57]

On 17 September, the *Morning Chronicle* wrote, 'Could we suppose the French General to have sitten down for the purpose of inventing terms of an agreement which should not only wipe off the stain which his character had received from a previous defeat, but which should transfer that stain from his own to the British character, he could not have done it more effectually than by the present Convention.' The paper then said that the excuses of worsening weather and the difficulty of getting the French out of strong positions had been offered but questioned the lack of pursuit after Vimeiro. It criticised Dalrymple and said ministers were in 'high dudgeon' over the terms.[58] The same day, the *Morning Post* was already predicting that there would be an inquiry into the Convention.[59]

As well as their opinion pieces, the papers were beginning to publish anonymously letters sent home to family and friends from army officers in Portugal, many of which supported the narrative that Wellesley would have brought things to a better conclusion if he had remained in command. The *Morning Post* published one written by an officer on 1 September:

> After thrashing the French so handsomely as we did on the 17th and 21st of August you will be a little surprised to hear that we are not yet in Lisbon. The fact is, that the arrival of *certain people* just at the moment of our success, prevented our very gallant and able chief from following it up. Had he been left to himself we should have pursued the enemy, and so great was his disorder and dismay, must have entirely dispersed or destroyed him. *Old heads*, however, popped in upon us, and instead of pushing on in a manner correspondent to the ardent wishes of both men and officers, and to the honour of British arms, we have ever since been drivelling with a negotiation, when it behoved us to bring the matter to an issue *without any conditions whatever*. I cannot paint you the feeling of disgust which actuates every one since Sir Arthur Wellesley supercession. He is indeed a very gallant fellow; and had we only been joined by a single man after the 21st, we should have been in Lisbon before this time, and that *in the most glorious and triumphant manner*.[60]

Other letters in the same edition were a little more balanced: 'You will probably not like the Convention; the army here does not like it; but we came to free Portugal, and we have done that. To starve the French we must starve 120,000 people in Lisbon, and to batter them down kill more Portuguese than French.' The letter continued that the Portuguese might have lost property, but at least they had not lost lives, and that the army hoped to march to Spain soon and could not have

---

57 *The Examiner*, 17 September 1808.
58 *Morning Chronicle*, 17 September 1808.
59 *Morning Post*, 17 September 1808.
60 *Morning Post*, 19 September 1808.

done that if they had to besiege Lisbon. The *Daily Advertiser* also defended Wellesley and said that 500 letters had arrived in London from the army, claiming that Wellesley had no part in the negotiations and would be exonerated once all the facts came out.[61] The opposition press, naturally, objected to the staunch defence of Wellesley conducted by some papers. On 30 September, the *Morning Chronicle* wrote 'of the mean and detestable arts used by the friends of Sir Arthur Wellesley, to exclude him from censure, and to throw the whole odium of the convention upon his colleague' and then gave an example of a paper declaring itself his 'authorised defender' and publishing a story that Captain Dalrymple burst into tears when questioned by ministers on the convention, 'Yet the men who write such paragraphs, talk of the illiberal personalities of Sir Arthur's opponents!'[62]

One anonymous newspaper editor wrote to the Duke of Buckingham on 17 September:

> The public indignation this day is at its height. Since the publication of the Gazette, the people seem quite wild. In the city, the discontent and murmur is not in the least restrained, and I must suppose that immediate inquiry must be made into the causes of what is universally considered a great national calamity.
>
> To do the Ministers justice, their anxiety and misery, is not second to that which the other classes of people feel. I trust your Lordship does not disapprove of what has been done on our part to put all that in a fair point of view to the world.
>
> The black edge has had a wonderful effect, and above five hundred has been sold additional. I did not think it justifiable or wise, in the first instance, to charge this calamity upon government, but confine it either to the folly, the madness, or the wickedness of those concerned immediately.[63]

A black border is traditionally used by papers announcing royal deaths. The editor then continues to report that he had received a note from Lord Sydenham, 'conveying Lord Wellesley's thanks to me for the account of the campaign in Portugal, which he said was very well done, and gave the greatest satisfaction to the friends of Sir Arthur.'[64]

It was not only newspaper editors who published polemics on the convention. The nation's greatest poet also felt the need to comment at length. William Wordsworth wrote a tome of over 200 pages condemning the convention and commenting more broadly on the situation in the Peninsula.[65]

However, not every writer who put pen to paper was critical of the Convention, and some pamphlets were supportive. An anonymous writer who wrote under the pseudonym 'a Friend of the People' published *Advantages of the Convention of Cintra, Briefly Stated in a Candid Review of that Transaction and of the Circumstances Under which it Took Place*, which claimed that the convention achieved the expedition's aims, saved lives and left the army ready to support Spain. Any continuation of hostilities would have been costly in terms of both British and Portuguese

61   *Daily Advertiser, Oracle and True Briton*, 19 September 1808. There were under 600 officers with Wellesley's force, so the 500 figure is hyperbole.
62   Morning Chronicle, 30 September 1808.
63   Buckingham (ed.), *Memoirs of the Court*, vol.IV, p.250.
64   Buckingham (ed.), *Memoirs of the Court*, vol.IV, p.251.
65   W. Wordsworth, *Concerning the Relations of Great Britain, Spain, and Portugal* (London: Longman, Hurst, Rees, and Orme, 1809).

lives: 'Had our Generals, adopting the Hotspur-like spirit with which some of the citizens of London and Westminster, drinking their wine by their fire-sides, appear to be animated, what scenes of carnage and horror must have ensued!'[66] The 'Friend of the people' also pointed out the danger of judging officers' conduct:

> The naval and military services are at best ungrateful ones; but if every pacific overture, proposed or accepted by an officer, is to be imputed to him as an act of cowardice, treachery, or imbecility, you banish fair Humanity from your camps, and make it impossible for a brave and amiable man to discharge his duty to his country with satisfaction to himself.[67]

Other pamphlets blamed the Duke of York for appointing Dalrymple in the first place, claimed Freire's objections were a forgery, and eulogised Wellesley.[68] Faced with a barrage of criticism in the press, in pamphlets, and in political circles, ministers inevitably considered how to quell or deflect that criticism elsewhere and bow to the pressure for an inquiry.

66 Anon., *Advantages of the Convention of Cintra, Briefly Stated in a Candid Review of that Transaction and of the Circumstances Under which it Took Place* (London: privately published, 1809), p.9.
67 Anon., *Advantages*, pp.25–26.
68 Review of various pamphlets, *The Monthly Review*, September to December 1808, vol.LVII, pp.324–325.

21

The Inquiry

Lady Hester Stanhope, William Pitt's niece, with many connections amongst the government and romantically linked to Moore, wrote to Gordon at Horse Guards on 26 September:

> I will only trouble you with a few lines as I suppose you must be extremely busy at this moment, and I trust preparing to hang General Dalrymple if he acted from his own judgement, if by the instructions of ministers, I'd like to see their heads upon Temple Bar, for having brought a disgrace upon the British Army. Sir Arthur Wellesley was always a great favourite of mine, but I am angry with him now, in his situation I would have burnt off my right hand in the presence of a victorious army sooner than signed such a capitulation.[1]

The construction of a gallows may not have been underway, but an inquiry into the events around the suspension of arms and the convention was becoming inevitable and being discussed by ministers. Some within opposition political circles attributed other motives to the government's desire for an inquiry. Auckland wrote to Grenville, 'I have some reason to believe that it is determined in the Cabinet to send the whole to a court of enquiry, and in that mode to suspend, to a certain degree, and for a certain period, the invectives of the country and of Parliament. In the meantime, new incidents may possibly arise to divert the General dissatisfaction.'[2] A few days later, Grenville's brother wrote to him that his, 'own expectation is that the Ministers will sacrifice Sir Hew to the public indignation, that they will pacify the enraged Wellesley who is just come home, and that Bonaparte's army will advance into Spain and render the English command there an object of less interest and ambition than it now is.'[3] Auckland had also already guessed what Dalrymple's defence would be:

> … the whole is to be thrown on Sir Hew; and he is to be defended by showing on the other hand that, in the opinions of the Generals under him, the difficulties of the country, the French possession of all the forts, the equinox, the further measures in view, the want of provisions altogether made it his duty to adopt the convention.[4]

For Wellesley, Burrard, and Dalrymple, an inquiry would be a chance to clear their reputations.

---

1   BL: Add MS 49503: Stanhope to Gordon, 26 September 1808.
2   Auckland to Grenville, 1 October 1808 in, Anon., *Dropmore*, vol.VIII, p.221.
3   T. Grenville to Grenville, 7 October 1808 in, Anon., *Dropmore*, vol.VIII, p.222.
4   Auckland to Grenville, 10 October 1808 in, Anon., *Dropmore*, vol.VIII, p.224.

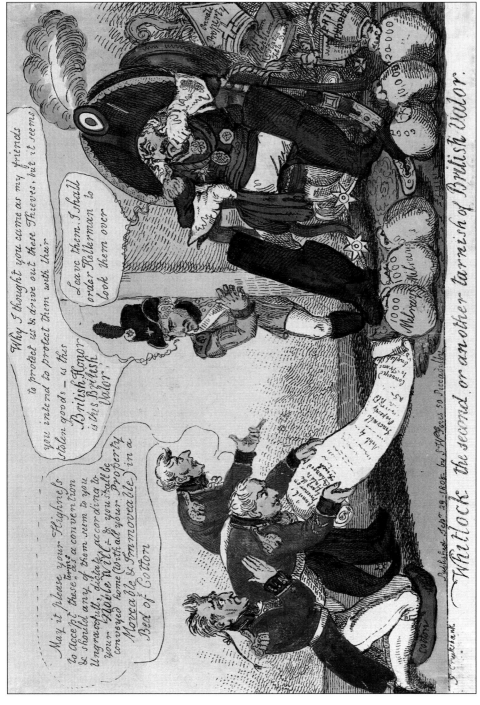

'Whitlock the second or another tarnish of British valor', by George Cruikshank. Wellesley, Burrard and Dalrymple grovel before Junot while a Portuguese figure looks on. (Public Domain)

When Dalrymple met with Castlereagh on his return to London, he was offered a choice between his conduct being investigated by a court martial or a court of inquiry. Dalrymple could not see what charges could be brought by a court martial. If charges were brought, he would have to call senior officers from Portugal as witnesses, which would lengthen the process, and he 'was impatient for an early opportunity of repelling the false and injurious imputations with which my character had been assailed.'[5]

As far as Wellesley was concerned, his allies had been exultant at his victories and their coverage in the press, but the mood swiftly changed once news of the suspension of arms and the convention broke. His brother, William, wrote to him on 30 September, 'You can have no idea of the public feeling here', and that 'it will be necessary for you to have a plain and full explanation to do yourself justice.' However, he also added that some of the public clamour was fading and that the private letters from the army had been very flattering to him.[6]

Wellesley was keen to return to the Peninsula and would have been happy to serve under Moore. He wrote to him on 8 October:

> You'll have seen by the newspapers that the late transactions in Portugal have made a stronger sensation here than it was imagined they would; and I have had what I think more than my share of the blame. I suppose that there must be an inquiry into the transactions; and till that takes place I shall leave the public to find out the truth in the best way they can, and shall not adopt any illegitimate mode of setting them right. In the mean time the abuse of the news writers of London will not deprive me of my temper or my spirits, or of the zeal with which I will forward every wish of yours.[7]

In letters to the Duke of Richmond and Marquess of Buckingham, he said he looked forward to an inquiry and offering a proper defence to the allegations.[8]

Wellesley was also at pains not to use his difference of opinion with Burrard over the pursuit of the French on 21 August as a defence for his part in the suspension of arms. He wrote to Earl Temple on 19 October:

> … the objection I have to blaming Sir Harry Burrard by way of justification of myself, I object to it on the ground that I consider it injurious to the public service, and particularly to the officers of the army, to institute public inquiries into their conduct in instances in which they have acted fairly upon their own opinions, for which opinions they had fair military grounds.[9]

He then went on to say that since he had handed over command of the army to Burrard on the 20th, any inquiry could only examine his conduct up to that date and his handling of the battle on the 21st, but that in the examination of Dalrymple's subsequent conduct, he would have the chance to explain his actions once the command had been passed to others.

---

5   Dalrymple, *Memoir*, p.129.
6   Wellington (ed.), *Supplementary Despatches*, vol.VI, p.144.
7   Wellington (ed.), *Supplementary Despatches*, vol.VI, p.150.
8   Wellington (ed.), *Supplementary Despatches*, vol.VI, pp.151–153.
9   Wellington (ed.), *Supplementary Despatches*, vol.VI, p.161.

Burrard, though not implicated in the suspension of arms or convention, was not escaping disapprobation and had also been recalled from Portugal, leaving Moore in command. He did not arrive until after the inquiry had begun. Some of the criticism was fuelled by letters from officers with the army in Portugal. Captain Algernon Langton wrote on 4 November that they had had no news from Britain for three weeks:

> … which appears so extraordinary, (considering what has been going on here) that we are quite at a loss to account for it. They surely cannot think of overlooking Sir H Burrard's conduct; & yet he is left here as commander in chief; and is feasting away in a fine palace, as if nothing has happened, but I have written more largely on this subject in a paper, which I am sending by an officer to England, and have commissioned him to get it made as publick as possible, by inserting it in one of the papers – it is dated Lisbon and signed 'by a British Officer.'[10]

Dalrymple had his own supporters, who were also looking forward to an inquiry bringing the facts out into the open. Anstruther wrote to Dalrymple in November from Almeida:

> In consequence of the remoteness of this place, and the almost incredible delays and difficulties attending all communication with it, I did not learn, till very lately, not in fact, until the arrival of Sir John Moore here, the extent and violence of the phrenzy which has seized John Bull on the subject of the Convention for the Evacuation of Portugal. It is very obvious by what persons, and by what unworthy means, the public opinion has been misled, and the passions of the multitude inflamed on this subject; and under such circumstances, I really rejoice to find that your conduct (with which that of the whole army in Portugal may be said to be identified) is about to be brought before a tribunal, capable, I trust, of judging the merit of the case, and of doing you and us that justice which a set of profligate politicians attempt to deprive us of.[11]

However, writing to Wellesley in December, Anstruther was somewhat less supportive and referred to Burrard and Dalrymple as 'two fools' and then noted that it was the tone of the convention that had the greatest effect on public opinion and that arose 'entirely from allowing the vanquished to dictate the terms in which the treaty was to be couched, a thing, I believe, never done before, nor ever will again, unless there are more Sir Hews'.[12] Vice Admiral Collingwood wrote to Cotton at the end of the year, voicing the concern that any senior officer could be similarly tried and convicted in the court of public opinion:

> I am sorry for Sir Hew Dalrymple because though I do not pretend to judge of his military ability or political sagacity, I believe him to be an honest and honorable man who has the interest of the country truly at heart and would exercise his best judgement to promote it. But it is so easy to fight battle and give law to an enemy in a coffee house, and so many

10   LA: MG/4/5/15/40-85: Langton to Massingbird, 4 November 1808.
11   NAM: 1994-03-129-83: Anstruther to Dalrymple, 21 November 1808.
12   Welington (ed.), *Supplementary Despatches*, vol.VI, p.191.

who consider themselves competent to decide, that an officer whatever his devotion may be, stands in a painful predicament if anything adverse happens.[13]

Claims and counterclaims were beginning to circulate amongst senior army officers and politicians. Wellesley's brother, William, wrote to him urgently on 19 October that Sir William Scott, judge of the High Court of Admiralty, had seen Dalrymple's papers and that the general was claiming that Wellesley played the central role in negotiations for the suspension of arms and signed it without hesitation. Dalrymple also said that 'he acted according to his instructions, which were to consult Sir Arthur in everything, and to be guided by his opinion; that Sir Arthur was stated to him to have the full confidence of Ministers, and that he did in everything submit his judgment to his, and was guided by him.' Sir William also told Wellesley-Pole that Dalrymple had documentary evidence to support his case. Wellesley-Pole wrote, 'It is now, quite clear that you and Sir Hew are at issue upon points of fact, and that he means to hold you out as responsible for everything that has passed respecting the Armistice and Convention.' He urged his brother to return to London from Dublin.[14] William wrote again to Arthur on 27 October:

> I cannot but think that excluding you from all inquiry on the plea of your not being responsible for anything that passed after the close of the battle of Vimeiro would be a fatal blow to your character with the public as a statesman, and in some degree as an officer; and I believe I speak the language of everybody who admires you, or wishes you well, when I say that a thorough investigation of your conduct, from the day you landed in Portugal to the day you left it, is indispensable for your reputation.

He said that it would be in Dalrymple's interest for the inquiry only to look at the period after he took command and for it to show that he concurred with the necessity of the suspension and convention. It would also be in Burrard's interest for the inquiry not to examine events before 22 August, as no one had accused him of participating in the negotiations. Limiting the inquiry to after Dalrymple took over would relieve Castlereagh 'from almost all his embarrassments', as it would stop any examination of the decisions over the arrangements, equipment, and command of the forces. Wellesley-Pole also thought that Horse Guards would also want a limited inquiry so that their objective, if they had one, 'must be much more to keep down the officer for whom the army has the greatest enthusiasm, and to prevent him from being called by the voice of the nation to the head of the forces upon active service, than to crush old officers of known incapacity or want of following, who never can be competitors', and he also pointed out that Dalrymple, Burrard, and Clinton were all guardsmen and 'closely united to Windsor and Whitehall'. It was clearly in Wellesley's interest for the inquiry to have broader terms of reference.[15]

However, Wellesley-Pole was mistaken about Castlereagh's wishes. He wrote again to his brother on 28 October that the minister had shown him drafts of the Duke of York's instructions regarding the inquiry and allowed him to send Wellesley copies. He wrote that Castlereagh's, 'most anxious desire was that you should have an opportunity to place your conduct in the most conspicuous

13   Krajeski, *Shadow*, p.111.
14   Wellington (ed.), *Supplementary Despatches*, vol.VI, p.164.
15   Wellington (ed.), *Supplementary Despatches*, vol.VI, pp.170-172.

point of view, and that full justice should be done to you without regard to any of the consequences that may thereby fall on him, the government, or either of the Generals.'[16]

Courts of enquiry were not authorised by the Articles of War or any act of Parliament but were based on long-established customs and precedent. One guide to the military justice system stated they were 'arbitrary, of ambiguous authority, and [had] no foundation in law.'[17] They relied purely on the powers and authority of the monarch. Courts of enquiry provided the opportunity for the actions of individuals to be examined. They resulted in reports to the monarch, which could recommend whether or not a court martial was warranted. Members and witnesses did not have to swear an oath.

On 29 October, Castlereagh wrote to the Duke of York, ordering an inquiry. As Castlereagh had promised, the inquiry would have broad terms of reference to look into the wider campaign, the suspension of arms and the convention.[18]

The president of the court would be General Sir David Dundas, with whom Wellesley had already met. Dundas had written to Gordon at Horse Guards on 15 October:

> His statement is briefly this:– *as he was prevented from following his blow on the 21st,* and *as matters stood on the 22nd* he thought it advisable to get the French out of the country upon terms not dishonourable to themselves, taking with them their arms and baggage, paying the expense of their conveyance, and retiring instantly behind the Tagus, and therefore he concurred in opinion with Sir Hew upon *a* convention.[19]

Dundas reported that Wellesley had told him that he had not negotiated the terms of the suspension of arms and only signed at Dalrymple's request, and then continued, 'You will quickly see in what a dilemma Wellesley has placed himself, and of which he is himself most fully sensible. It is impossible … not to wish him well and safe out of the scrape, but it is equally impossible not to feel that he is materially involved in one.'

Inquiry

The inquiry opened on Monday, 14 November, in the Great Hall at Chelsea Hospital. The panel comprised seven general officers picked by the Duke of York from a range of political backgrounds.[20] At about 11:00 a.m., the generals took their seats at a table, according to their seniority: Generals Sir David Dundas (President), the Earl of Moira and Lord Heathfield, and Lieutenant Generals the Earl of Pembroke, Sir George Nugent, and Oliver Nichols. They sat beneath Antonio Verrio's mural of Charles II on horseback, surrounded by allegorical figures symbolising the divine right and power of kings, including Lady Justice with her sword and balance but without the blindfold used to illustrate her impartiality. The inquiry's impartiality, or lack thereof, would become a theme in both contemporary and subsequent commentary on the hearings that followed. One

---

16   Wellington (ed.), *Supplementary Despatches*, vol.VI, pp.174-175.
17   John McArthur, *Principles and Practice of Naval and Military Courts Martial* (London: Butterworth, 1813), vol.I, p.118.
18   Anon., *Proceedings*, p.5.
19   BL: Add MS 49503: Dundas to Gordon, 15 October 1808.
20   Muir, *Wellington*, vol.I, p.276.

of the members, Moira, wrote 'that I have been made one of the members in order to impress the public (who will not know that all goes by a majority) with a fallacious belief of the earnestness and impartiality in the investigation'.[21]

Dundas was a highly respected and experienced officer, and the rest of the board had served with varying amounts of distinction during the American War but had seen little active service since, except Moira, who had served in the Low Countries in the 1790s. Historian Michael Glover refers to them as the best that could be brought together at relatively short notice.[22] Richard Ryder, the judge advocate general, sat on Dundas's right and opened proceedings by reading the King's warrant. After a preamble and the text of the suspension of arms and the convention, the warrant stated:

> We think it necessary that an Inquiry should be made by the General Officers after-named, into the conditions of the said Armistice and Convention, and into all the causes and circumstances (whether arising from the previous operations of the British army or otherwise) which led to them, and into the conduct, behaviour, and proceedings of the said Lieutenant General Sir Hew Dalrymple, and of any other Officer, or Officers, who may have held the command of our troops in Portugal, and of any other person or persons, as far as the same were connected with the said Armistice and Convention, in order that the said General Officers may report to us touching the matters aforefaid for our better information.[23]

Dundas then ordered the room to be cleared while the board deliberated what arrangements needed to be made. They ordered that Castlereagh, York and General Sir James Murray Pulteney, Secretary at War, provide copies of all relevant correspondence and that Wellesley, Burrard and Dalrymple all prepare narratives of their actions. An initial list of witnesses was drawn up of those officers available in Britain: Major Generals Spencer and Ferguson, Brigadier General Acland, Lieutenant Colonels Torrens, Browne and Tucker, and Major Campbell. The inquiry was then adjourned for three days.

On the 17th, the board convened at 11:00 a.m. but deliberated in private again until noon, when members of the public were allowed in. Dalrymple, Wellesley, and their aides de camp were present. After several procedural matters were dealt with, Dalrymple made an opening address to the court. His address sought to answer the widespread criticism of him in the press, but more particularly to counter the distancing of Wellesley from the suspension of arms that had appeared in the papers by saying that Wellesley bore the 'prominent part' of the discussions with Kellermann on 22 August.[24] According to *The Gentleman's Magazine*, Dalrymple 'spoke with firmness and precision, and appeared in good spirits.'[25]

In reply, Wellesley claimed that he had

> I never said nor never authorized any body to say, and more I can venture to say that no person connected with me, as my relations, friends or Aides de-Camp, or otherwise in the

21   Muir, 'Commentary for Chapter 16'.
22   Glover, *Sickens*, p.178.
23   Anon., *Proceedings*, p.10. A manuscript copy of the proceedings can also be found in TNA: WO 71/214.
24   Anon., *Proceedings*, p.16.
25   *The Gentleman's Magazine*, November 1808, p.1034.

service, ever gave any authority to any publisher of a newspaper or any body else to declare, that I was compelled, or even ordered to sign the paper to which my name appears.[26]

But, as has been shown, his family and friends were in touch with the press and so must have spread the story on their own initiative, based on his letters to them in which he said that Dalrymple had 'desired' – not ordered – him to sign it.[27] Wellington's biographer Rory Muir wrote of Wellesley's reply that one could 'only conclude that either Lord Wellesley and William Wellesley-Pole had concealed their part in the creation of the story of the protest from their brother (and that he naively believed them), or that he was lying.'[28]

The next day, Wellesley wrote to the Duke of Richmond and said that he had attended the inquiry and that Dalrymple 'read something from a paper complaining of the misrepresentations in the newspapers which he attributed to me and my friends, which gave me an opportunity which I wished for of explaining that I acted by his desire, and not by his order, in signing the armistice. The newspapers have, as usual, misrepresented what both of us said'.[29] The *Times* stated on the 23rd:

> We are … greatly amused at the incessant endeavours of Sir Arthur Wellesley to shake this Armistice from his shoulders. He is like the good man in Pilgrim's Progress, striving to get rid of the burthens of his sins; when up jumps the Great Irresolution, in the shape of Sir Hew, and immediately re-affixes the odious load to his back, by producing some undeniable testimony of Sir Arthur's to the propriety of that act.[30]

Wellesley read his narrative to the court on the 19th, which covered the period up to his being relieved by Burrard. The *Times* wrote that he spoke quickly 'and in so low a tone as to be scarcely audible without the bar'.[31] The inquiry met again after the weekend, on the 21st. Dalrymple was the first to speak concerning some omissions to the documents provided to the inquiry. He also addressed the court about differences in the version of his dispatch of 3 September read to the court and the one printed in the *Gazette*. The version read to the court read that the articles of the suspension of arms were 'at first agreed upon, were signed by Sir Arthur Wellesley and General Kellerman'.[32] Whereas the copy published in the *Gazette* read, 'at first agreed upon and signed by Sir Arthur Wellesley and General Kellerman.[33] The original of the dispatch held in The National Archives matches the *Gazette*.[34] Dalrymple blamed the difference on an inaccurate copy and said he never intended to imply that Wellesley solely negotiated the suspension of arms.[35]

The board then questioned Wellesley on many of the details of the campaign. Captain Pulteney Malcolm was quizzed about the landings and the state of the difficulties of the Portuguese coast.

26   Anon., *Proceedings*, p.17.
27   Welington (ed.), *Supplementary Despatches*, vol.VI, p.122.
28   Muir, 'Commentary for Chapter 16'.
29   Welington (ed.), *Supplementary Despatches*, vol.V, p.487.
30   Muir, 'Commentary for Chapter 16'.
31   Quoted in Muir, 'Commentary for Chapter 16'.
32   Anon., *Proceedings*, p.170.
33   *The London Gazette*, 16 September 1808.
34   TNA: WO 1/234: Dalrymple to Castlereagh, 3 September 1808.
35   Anon., *Proceedings*, p.29.

Then Dalrymple read his main narrative to the court, which covered the period from him receiving his orders to his recall, in which he defended the convention and its necessity, given the season and the need to progress quickly to Spain. In his memoir, Dalrymple wrote of his surprise that much of Castlereagh's correspondence, including the 20 August private letter effectively giving him carte blanche and offering the government's full support, was not included in the papers presented to the board by the government. Dalrymple had written to Castlereagh to question the omissions and been told that the minister:

> … did not consider his private letter, of the 20th of August, as in any degree material to my case, being only a repetition, in an unofficial shape, of the full powers and assurances of support conveyed, by His Majesty's commands, to Sir Arthur Wellesley. As to letters referring *to the immediate matter of my recall, they did not appear to his Lordship to contain information material to be laid before the Board.*[36]

The 20 August letter would have been quite embarrassing for Castlereagh and the government, and while Dalrymple mentioned it in his narrative, the board did not see the actual letter.

On the 22nd, Commissary General Pipon was questioned regarding what supplies were available after the Battle of Vimeiro, and then Wellesley made an address in reply to Dalrymple's narrative. He countered some inferences Dalrymple had made regarding whether he was correct to advance from the Mondego and also again countered the level of his involvement in the negotiations for the suspension of arms and claimed that from their first meeting, Dalrymple was 'prejudiced against the opinions which I should give him'.[37]

The inquiry did not meet on the 23rd, but Wellesley wrote to Richmond again and stated that the inquiry was going 'as well as I could wish' but that he had gone further in his evidence that he had planned because of the attacks that Dalrymple had made. He continued, 'If he had done what a gentleman ought to have done, and … had not attacked me when he first addressed the Court of Inquiry, and in his narrative, I should have defended for him the measure of allowing the French to evacuate Portugal, and should not have said one word about the details of the Convention.'[38]

On 24 November, Lieutenant Colonel Torrens and Captain Malcolm were questioned by Wellesley on their recollections of conversations they had with him on 22 August after the suspension had been signed. Dalrymple then read out written answers to questions he had received from the board, covering the need for and negotiation of the convention, and then the board asked him further questions. Ferguson also then read written answers to questions from the board, most of which dealt with possible scenarios after 21 August. Spencer, Acland and Nightingall were questioned on 26 November, the next day the inquiry sat. Engineer Captain Préval was asked about the strength of Lisbon's defences, and Dalrymple and Torrens were briefly questioned.

The inquiry then adjourned until 6 December as Burrard had still not arrived from Portugal, but when he did return, he asked for time to prepare his evidence, so the board did not meet again until the 13th. Burrard read his narrative, which began with receiving his orders through to Dalrymple's arrival and mainly dealt with his defence of his decision not to pursue the French, about which he was then questioned. *The Gentleman's Magazine* reported that Burrard 'was visibly affected'

36   Dalrymple, *Memoir*, p.130. Italics in original.
37   Anon., *Proceedings*, p.56.
38   Welington (ed.), *Supplementary Despatches*, vol.VI, pp.186–187.

towards the end of his testimony.[39] Wellesley, Spencer and Ferguson were also examined, at length, about the viability of a pursuit. Lord Burghersh briefly gave evidence of the discussion between Wellesley and Burrard.

On the 14th, Burrard questioned Wellesley on some details of the points of disagreement between them – where Moore was to land and the pursuit. Then Wellesley, Burrard and Dalrymple were all asked what they thought Junot's options were after the battle of the 21st and what might have happened if the suspension of arms had not been agreed. Wellesley later questioned Torrens about the conversations he was present at between Burrard and Wellesley.

Next, Wellesley gave a statement in favour of his desire to both have Moore march on Santarém and to pursue the French and was questioned on this. Burrard again defended his decision, given the facts he had at the time. Wellesley generously added: 'I have always entertained that Sir Harry Burrard decided upon that occasion upon fair military grounds, in the manner which appeared to him to be most conducive to the interests of the country; and that he had no motive for his decision which could be supposed personal to me, or which as an officer he could not avow.'[40] Burrard was asked about the negotiations, and then Dalrymple gave a final statement, clarifying some points and once more defending the necessity for a convention and closing with:

> For my own part I can most safely and solemnly afirm, that I then thought, and still continue to think, that, by the Convention, I provided in the best manner at that time possible for the interests of my country, as connected with the cause in which it was engaged; and, unless obliged to relinquish that conviction, from a deference to superior judgment, l shall cheerfully submit to the disadvantages and mortifications which it has produced to myself.[41]

The board then met privately for five days to prepare their report.

Historian Rory Muir wrote, 'it was clear to anyone who had attended the hearing that Wellesley knew how to command an army and conduct a campaign, and that Dalrymple and Burrard did not.'[42] George Tierney, a Whig MP, attended the inquiry for one of the days and:

> … came away quite disgusted with the manner in which the business was conducted. Wellesley and Burrard were placed upon the floor to examine one another! Wellesley's tone and deportment I thought very offensive. Poor Burrard made a sad figure ... I never saw so dull a man in my life. Dalrymple sat quite snug and unconcerned, much in the manner of little Jack Horner.[43]

The report to the King was ready on 22 December. It set out the events of the campaign in detail. As far as Burrard's decision not to pursue the French on 21 August was concerned, the board stated that there were numerous factors and 'fair military grounds' that could have only been decided by those on the spot and that the French superiority in cavalry would have allowed 'the enemy's infantry, without any degree of risk, to continue their retreat in the most rapid manner, till they should arrive

39   *The Gentleman's Magazine*, Supplement to 1801, p.1179.
40   Anon., *Proceedings*, p.108.
41   Anon., *Proceedings*, p.110.
42   Muir, 'Commentary for Chapter 16'.
43   Aspinal (ed.), *Later Correspondence*, vol.V, p.167n.

at any given and advantageous point of rallying and formation.[44] The report then discussed the convention and was sympathetic to Dalrymple's defence and compared the terms to those of the agreements by which the French were evacuated from Egypt in 1801. The board also pointed out that the two rapid changes of command had inevitably led to delays to the army advancing.

The board concluded that the operations of Wellesley were 'highly honourable and successful' and 'no evidence adduced can enable the Board to pronounce with confidence, whether or not a pursuit after the battle of the 21st could have been efficacious'. The summary pointed out that none of the lieutenant generals objected to the convention and that considerable advantages were gained from it. The report ended:

> On a consideration of all circumstances, as set forth in this Report, we most humbly submit our opinion, that no further military proceeding is necessary on the subject; because howsoever some of us may differ in our sentiments respecting the fitness of the Convention in the relative situation of two armies, it is our unanimous declaration that unquestionable zeal and firmness appear throughout to have been exhibited by Lieutenant Generals Sir Hew Dalrymple, Sir Harry Burrard, and Sir Arthur Wellesley as well as that the ardour and gallantry of the rest of the Officers and Soldiers on every occasion during this expedition have done honour to the troops, and reflected lustre on Your Majesty's Arms.[45]

However, the Duke of York was far from satisfied with the report and wrote to Dundas on Christmas Day and asked the board to consider

> … whether under all the circumstances which appear in evidence before you, on the relative situation of the two Armies on the 22d of August, 1808, it is your opinion that an Armistice was advisable, and if so, whether the terms of that Armistice were such as ought to have been agreed upon, and whether upon a like consideration of the relative situations of the two Armies subsequent to the Armistice, and when all the British Forces were landed, it is your opinion that a Convention was advisable, and if so, whether the Terms of that Convention were such as ought to have been agreed upon.[46]

The board then met on 27 December at the Judge Advocate General's office, and Dundas asked them whether they approved of the suspension of arms and the convention, given the relative situation of the armies at each time. Apart from the Earl of Moira, all the generals approved of the suspension of arms. Most generals approved of the convention, but Nichols and Pembroke joined Moira in disapproving of the convention. In the dissenting opinions, Nichols and Pembroke thought that the arrival of Moore should have entitled Dalrymple to press for more favourable terms. Moira believed that the British should have continued to pursue and press the French after Vimeiro and that, after Moore's arrival, it was probable that further combat would have resulted in the French acceding to harsher terms.[47]

---

44   Anon., *Proceedings*, p.117.
45   Anon., *Proceedings*, p.121.
46   Anon., *Proceedings*, p.122.
47   Anon., *Proceedings*, p.124.

Given the evidence presented, the board could do nothing else apart from recommending that there was no case for a court martial. Historian Richard Glover wrote: 'It is hard to see what other finding could have been reached by the board. Their conclusions meant, in short, that Wellesley had done well and that Dalrymple and Burrard had done their best.'[48] Glover stressed that the rapid changes of command were at the heart of the problems that beset the end of the campaign. Sir John Fortescue, historian of the British Army, was also broadly sympathetic to the difficulties Burrard and Dalrymple faced when taking command. He opined that a scapegoat was required by the government, especially Canning, to quiet the protests of the Spanish and Portuguese and that Dalrymple 'was appointed for the sacrifice; and was compelled to undergo the injustice which the common welfare in such cases so cruelly demands.'[49] Fortescue also mentions that Dalrymple was not allowed to share documents that could have bolstered his case, such as Castlereagh's 20 August letter and correspondence that detailed how some of the outcry from Oporto was specious.

Sir Charles Oman also supported the board's conclusions but was critical of Burrard and Dalrymple: 'It would be unjust to punish old and respectable generals for mere errors of judgement, and inability to rise to the height of the situation. Burrard and Dalrymple had sacrificed the most brilliant possibilities by their torpid caution, after refusing to listen to Wellesley's cogent arguments for bold action.'[50]

It could be judged that both Burrard and Dalrymple had made some questionable decisions, but, given the circumstances that they were presented with, they had each done their duty as they saw it. However, while he accepted the inquiry's report, the King felt the need to repeat his disapprobation of the terms of the convention that affected the 'interests or feelings' of the Portuguese and Spanish. In a letter to Dalrymple, sent via Castlereagh and York, he stated:

At the close of the Inquiry, the King (abstaining from any observations upon other parts of the Convention) repeats His Disapprobation of those Articles, His Majesty deeming it necessary that His sentiments should be clearly understood, as to the impropriety and danger of the unauthorized admission, into Military Conventions, of Articles of such a description, which, especially when incautiously framed, may lead to the most injurious consequences.

His Majesty cannot forbear further to observe, that Lieutenant General Sir Hew Dalrymple's delaying to transmit, for His information, the Armistice concluded on the 22d August, until the 4th September, when he at the same time transmitted the ratified Convention, was calculated to produce great public inconvenience, and that such public inconvenience did, in fact, result therefrom.[51]

Oman thought Dalrymple's censure was deserved:

It cannot be denied that these rebukes were well deserved: we have already pointed out that the three articles to which allusion is made were the only part of the Convention for which no defence is possible. It is equally clear that it was the thirteen days' gap in the

48   Glover, *Sickens*, p.190.
49   Fortescue, *British Army*, vol.VI, p.252.
50   Oman, *History*, vol.1, p.299.
51   Anon., *Proceedings*, p.265.

information sent home which gave time for the rise and development of the unreasoning popular agitation against the whole agreement made with Junot.

With a letter to Gordon dated 15 January 1809, Dalrymple enclosed his observations on the dissenting opinion of the inquiry. He pointed out again that the armistice had set the convention's broad terms: the evacuation of the French with arms and baggage. The situation of the armies did not change much during the negotiations, despite Moore's arrival, and the position of the British remained dependent on the weather and the fleet's safety, which would only worsen as the season progressed. He also pointed out that the conferences of the lieutenant generals had agreed with the terms. He went on to say, 'In the treaty as ratified by me, there were several expressions and some trifling stipulations, that I did not pretend to defend, and that even some of the amendments proposed at the meeting on the 29th were not acceded to or not very strictly enforced; therefore the dissenting Lieutenant Generals are by my own acknowledgement justified in their objections...' But he argued that he did not think 'objects so trifling' were sufficient reasons not to ratify the treaty. He felt that time had run out, '... the end proposed by myself and the other generals who sanctioned the Convention was certainly to hold the British Army in a state of preparation for the accomplishment of a further, and more important object than the dislodgement of the French from Portugal.'[52]

Wellesley, who came out best from the inquiry, was not happy with the report either. He wrote to Lord Burghersh on 11 January:

> The Report of the Court of Inquiry is indeed an extraordinary production. Opinions, like colours, are now matters of taste, and may in this view of them be inconsistent with each other. But a court of this description ought, if it touches facts, to state them correctly; and a principal member, if he observes upon the subject, ought not to pass unnoticed, or contradict, the principal fact bearing upon the question on which he observes.[53]

Moira's separate report did not impress him, and he worried it might be used against him. Moira thought that the arguments given by Wellesley and Dalrymple that the suspension and convention were necessary to get the French out of Portugal quickly were wrong. Wellesley prepared a rebuttal, which was not in the end published.[54] He was concerned about what line the government would take on the inquiry's finding in Parliament and asked Castlereagh, 'Do they mean to consider it as conclusive, and, on that ground, to justify it and all the measures of which the report approves; or do they mean to leave the whole question to be scrambled for as it may suit those who choose to mix in the scramble?'[55] Wellesley was keen to join the army in Spain and did not want any unresolved controversy left hanging over him.

---

52   BL: Add. MS 89484: 'Observations' enclosed with Dalrymple to Gordon 15 January, 1809.
53   Wellington (ed.), *Supplementary Despatches*, vol.VI, p.196.
54   Muir, 'Commentary for Chapter 16'.
55   Wellesley to Castlereagh, 9 January 1809, in Vane (ed.), *Correspondence*, vol.VII, p.25.

22

Conclusion

Michael Glover, in his introduction to *Britannia Sickens,* wrote:

> The history of the Portuguese campaign of 1808 is less important for its purely military aspects, for telling how Wellesley defeated Junot and his army, than because it is the story of how Wellesley won his first, and crucial, round with the British tradition for waging war, compounded as it was of inefficiency, ossified tradition, divided responsibility and a public clamour compound equally of ignorance and malice.[1]

Glover, while acknowledging that Wellesley benefited from an army much improved by Castlereagh's and York's reforms, calls Wellesley's victories in the Peninsula his personal triumphs. But really, the history of the Portuguese campaign of 1808 is important for telling how the British Army, after those years of reform, finally found itself ready to take on the French on the continent of Europe rather than on the colonial periphery. The history of the Portuguese campaign of 1808 is important for telling how the British government, after years of funding the armies of others in Europe, finally found a viable opportunity to intervene directly and show that Britannia, far from sickening, was ready and willing.

One of the problems of studying the campaign is the focus on Wellesley in many histories. It is difficult to distil the 1808 Wellesley from the 1815 Wellington in memoirs and accounts written after the wars against France ended. The fame and renown he won later led many to assume he was a fully formed military genius earlier in his career. He was not. In those three weeks in August 1808, he did clearly show the talent that would take him to Waterloo, but there were also what would be now termed learning experiences – missteps or problems that he faced that helped him develop as a commander.

The same is true for the army that he led. The previous campaign many of the troops had been involved with had been the disasters in South America. In Portugal, however, they had been victorious, and the officers and men were rightly flushed with their success after Vimeiro. This can be seen in their indignation at terms of the convention when they thought they had utterly defeated their foe. But every time the troops had faced the French, there had been errors caused by a lack of experience amongst their commanders, which caused needless casualties: The riflemen's reckless advance at Óbidos, the 29th Foot's attack up the wrong defile at Roliça, and the 20th Light

---

1   Glover, *Sickens*, pp.10–11.

Dragoons' imprudent charge at Vimeiro. Many of the brigade and regimental commanders in Wellesley's army had minimal combat experience, far less than their French counterparts. Still, most had performed well; especially considering the brevity of the campaign and the lack of training beforehand. Before the Egyptian campaign of 1801, Abercromby had had the time to exercise and train his force en masse. The expedition to Portugal had been thrown together at short notice. Many of the units had served together previously, and Spencer had commanded his troops for over six months, but the expedition had very little time after landing to gel into a cohesive force.

Many of the logistical problems of the campaign can, to some extent, be blamed on the late change of destination from the Americas to Iberia. However, they also illustrate Glover's 'inefficiency, ossified tradition, divided responsibility'. A more flexible and dynamic military machine could have coped with the change of destination, but the Ordnance, Transport Board, and other departments seemed incapable of rapid pivots. While Britain's island status protected it from invasion, it also limited its ability to project force abroad swiftly. The cost and availability of transports and the whims of the weather affected Britain's response to the Iberian crisis at many stages.

However, Wellesley adapted and overcame. His experience of campaigning over vast distances in India had taught him the importance of logistics. When his commissary general in Portugal, Pipon, did not rise to the challenges of lack of transport and supplies, Wellesley ensured the army was fed and could advance. It was at the operational level in Portugal that Wellesley showed his acumen. The strategy had been set, and at neither Roliça nor Vimeiro did he display any exceptional tactical brilliance or innovation. His plan for Roliça was sound, but Ferguson's column turning too soon ruined its implementation, and Delaborde's dogged defence ensured that the British paid for the mistake. However, it is doubtful that the error was Wellesley's, and it was probably caused by poor staff work and a misunderstood message. At Vimeiro, his initial disposition was premised entirely on the French approaching from the south, and he allowed a significant French force to take the high ground of the long ridge. Had the French been present in equal or superior numbers and led by a more competent general, such a mistake could have cost the British the battle.

This leads to another element of the campaign that is often overlooked in British popular histories and contemporary commentaries. Wellesley's army was not facing the veterans of La Grande Armée led by an experienced *maréchal*; Junot and his troops were not the best the French could offer. Wellesley had the advantage in both the quality and number of troops in the field. The French were never in any danger of winning either battle, and there is also plentiful evidence that Junot's preferred outcome was an early and favourable treaty rather than a prolonged and heroic defence. It can be argued that in neither action were all the troops Wellesley had at his disposal committed and that the balance of troops engaged was more equal. Still, Wellesley had the reserves should he have needed them, which, thanks to the steadiness of his troops and the skill of his brigade commanders, he did not. What the British Army required at the time was not an easy victory, and neither battle was easy, but one where the odds were in their favour and from which they could gain confidence from a hard-fought, but inevitable, win.

Wellesley's dismissal of accurate intelligence of the French numbers in favour of a lesser estimate may have helped him justify moving forward rather than waiting for reinforcements. However, his questionable assessment of intelligence that did not suit him would be an error he repeated. The fact that Junot could field less than half of his men saved Wellesley the embarrassment of being proved wrong. Lieutenant General Hope wrote on 3 September:

> Wellesley has the merit of the execution entirely, and will very deservedly reap the fruits of his talents and exertions. At the same time he has outstripped all common rules and even

the most necessary measures of prudence, and had the French general made a soldierlike and wise use of the means in his hands the other must have been easily checked and might have suffered severely.[2]

Glover's quote at the start of this chapter also states that 'Wellesley defeated Junot', but, while all victories and most defeats are placed at the feet of the commanders, the reality is often different. Histories of the actions always emphasise Wellesley's role, but when studying the campaign, it is evident that his brigade commanders, inexperienced as many of them were, had considerable agency in how they fought the battles. Fane and Anstruther seem to have managed the fighting on the hill above Vimeiro with little or no intervention from Wellesley. Similarly, Spencer and Ferguson deserve credit for driving the French back on the long ridge.

The Portuguese are also often quickly dismissed in British narratives of the campaign. They indeed played only small parts at Roliça and Vimeiro, but the rebels had already liberated most of their own country, and the threat of both the partially-rebuilt army and the danger of a rising in Lisbon limited Junot's ability to field more troops. The uneasiness of the relationship with Freire and the Portuguese also foreshadowed the problems that Wellesley would have over the coming years in his strained relationships with Spanish commanders and governments. He sometimes did not play well with others.

The events of the 1808 campaign, as well as being overshadowed by Wellesley's later career, are tainted by the controversies of the lack of pursuit after Vimeiro, the armistice, and the convention. Moore wrote in his diary at the beginning of October:

> Whether we should have been more successful had the victory on the 21st been immediately followed up, it is impossible for a person not present to decide. Every one understands that a victorious army knows no difficulties, and that against a beaten army much may be risked; but by following at that moment we removed from our ships and our supplies; the enemy had a superior cavalry unbroken, and we had a difficult country ahead, known to the enemy, unknown to us. The least check would have proved fatal to us, though the pursuit might, if unchecked, have led at once to Lisbon.[3]

Moore continued by saying that Burrard was placed in an invidious position where any credit would have gone to Wellesley and any blame to him. He even posited that had Burrard not arrived, Wellesley may not have advanced 'for people often propose when second what they would not undertake if first'. However, it seems improbable that Wellesley would not have advanced. Moore also mentions the danger of the French cavalry getting into the British rear and cutting the army off from the fleet. He concludes, 'There is no doubt that Sir Arthur was superseded at a most fortunate moment for him, after a successful action, but just as his difficulties were about to commence.' But Moore's thoughts on the subject are slightly contradictory. He also wrote:

> Had Sir Arthur Wellesley not been interfered with, had he been allowed to follow up his success on the 21st, the French army must have dispersed, and never could have reached Lisbon. After they did collect, had they been reinforced, or had any circumstance enabled

---

2   Muir, 'Commentary for Chapter 15'.
3   Maurice (ed.), *Diary*, vol.II, p.268.

them again to take the field, they would in all probability have been successful; for, unfortunately, the command of the British had been given to Sir H. Dalrymple, a man certainly not without sense, but who had never before served in the field as a General officer, who had allowed a war of sixteen years to pass without pushing for any service except in England and Guernsey, and who seemed to be completely at a loss in the situation in which he was placed.[4]

Wellesley may have been able to get to Torres Vedras before Junot. Still, it is equally possible that Junot's competent divisional commanders – Delaborde, Loison, and Kellermann – could have undertaken successful rearguard or blocking actions. Whatever might have come to pass if the British had pursued is impossible to know, but it would likely have been messy and possibly costly in casualties. Burrard was undoubtedly more cautious than Wellesley would have been, and most of the board of enquiry probably felt that they would have done the same in the same circumstances. Wellesley himself admitted that Burrard had acted in the best interests of the army as he saw it.

After the enquiry, Burrard returned to staff posts in London. All his five sons served in either the army or the navy. Two were killed in 1809 and a third at San Sebastian in 1813; Sir Harry died soon after hearing the news.

It is more apparent that Dalrymple does deserve some, but not most, of the opprobrium directed towards him. His defence of the purposes of the convention – to get the French out quickly so the army could move into Spain and to get the British shipping into safe harbours – was valid. But his failures were political and diplomatic, elements of his role that he was more experienced in than field command. He failed to consider how the suspension of arms and the convention would be perceived, and, as the King rightly censured him for, he failed to adequately take account of the feelings of the Portuguese and the Spanish.

Moore, after outlining the difficulties of advancing on Lisbon, wrote:

> Thus situated, it required an officer of decision and talents to surmount the difficulties with which we were surrounded. An officer of this description at the head of a spirited army would certainly have advanced and never would have listened to such terms; but we had no such commander. Sir Hew Dalrymple was confused and incapable beyond any man I ever saw head an army. The whole of his conduct then and since has proved him to be a very foolish man. I had always before given him credit for some degree of sense and understanding, but I see I was mistaken, so little can men be judged in ordinary intercourse or until they are placed in situations of difficulty.[5]

Moore concluded that, with Dalrymple in command, the only thing to do was 'treat on almost any terms', that the government were to blame for the convention as they had chosen to appoint a commander 'of no military experience', and that if he had arrived earlier, the French would not have been beaten in battle and Portugal would still have been occupied. However, it should be noted that, from the evidence of his diary, Moore rarely had a good word to say about anybody.

---

4   Maurice (ed.), *Diary*, vol.II, p.259.
5   Maurice (ed.), *Diary*, vol.II, pp.269–270.

Dennis Potts, in an article entitled 'Convention of Cintra, a Revisionist View', argues that, had the British forces laid siege to Lisbon, there was a chance that Junot could have held out long enough to be relieved by Napoleon over the winter, or that the advance into Spain would have been delayed long enough that the British would have met the Emperor near the border. Either event could have led to defeat for the British and a premature end to the Peninsular War. Potts concludes:

> The question of whether or not the Convention of Cintra was, on balance, worthwhile from a military point of view cannot be fully appreciated without looking at what might have happened on the Peninsula had it not taken place. The advantage of historical hindsight is that events such as the Convention of Cintra—criticized, maligned and basically thrown in the dustbin of history—can be reevaluated and fully appreciated. In this analysis, the Convention of Cintra is deserving of a new look, retrieval from the dustbin of history, and an appreciation of what it ultimately achieved for the Allied forces on the Peninsula.[6]

Of course, as has been shown, Wellesley fully supported the need to treat with the French on the 22nd. Speaking in the House of Commons in February 1809, Wellesley argued that it would have taken time to drive Junot out of his position in the hills north of Lisbon, further time to besiege Lisbon and force him across the Tagus, and then yet more time to besiege Elvas, and that the French would have likely ended up with similar terms at some point. So, the early embarkation of the French was justified.[7]

While the enquiry may not have found against either Wellesley, Burrard, or Dalrymple, none survived the controversies without some stain on their characters. In Wellesley's case, the tarnish, on the whole, did not last and was buffed out by his later success. However, his disingenuousness, bordering on dishonesty, and how he distanced himself from the suspension of arms he signed and the convention he advised on, made the episode far from his finest hour.

With the King's censure on his record, Dalrymple was never employed again. However, in May 1814, with the Peninsula War won, he wrote to Castlereagh and appealed against his reprimand, reminding him of the praise he had earned during his time at Gibraltar and the promises of support the minister had made after his appointment to command in Portugal. The two met in July, and shortly afterwards, at a levée, Castlereagh took him aside and told him matters had been settled.[8] Dalrymple received a baronetcy in May 1815 and was later appointed governor of Blackness Castle. Like Burrard, he also lost a son, Leighton, who commanded the 15th Hussars at Waterloo and died of his wounds five years after the battle. Dalrymple wrote his memoir in 1818, in which he justified his actions, but it was not published until 1830, after his death.

Lieutenant General Lord Paget summed up the campaign and gave his opinion on Wellesley in a letter to his father at the end of August:

> Wellesley's corps has certainly been superior to the French in both actions, but more particularly so in the first. Full opportunity, however, was given to prove the perfect courage and steadiness of the soldiers, and the quickness and ability of the chief. He is, I

---

6   Potts, D.W., 'Convention of Cintra, a Revisionist View', *Napoleonic Scholarship*, December 2015, p.124

7   'Convention of Cintra', <https://api.parliament.uk/historic-hansard/commons/1809/feb/21/convention-of-cintra>, accessed December 2022.

8   Dalrymple, *Memoir*, pp.135–138.

really believe, an excellent officer. Every officer speaks well of him. He is very quick, and full of resources. He has lodged me for two days, and I had during that time an opportunity of observing that he possesses much method and arrangement. He is, besides, the luckiest dog upon earth, for it is by a sort of miracle, or rather by two or three combined, to detain Moore's corps, that he has been enabled to do this by himself.[9]

Paget also pointed out that Wellesley's lack of seniority on the list of lieutenant generals would limit the future opportunities of more senior officers like himself if Wellesley were given the field commands he deserved.

Wellesley did, of course, get back to the Peninsula, but not until April 1809 after Moore had been killed at Corunna and his army evacuated – another ignominious defeat for the British Army. Wellesley retook Oporto, which had fallen again to Soult's second French invasion, and then became Viscount Wellington after his pyrrhic victory at Talavera in July. He would stay in the Peninsula until finally driving the French out and invading southwestern France in 1814.

The Portuguese Army, rebuilt under Beresford, would play a vital role in that eventual victory. However, in September 1808, after liaising with the Junta in Oporto, Brigadier General Decken wrote, 'I am afraid that whatever Great Britain will do for raising the Portuguese, they never will be fit for anything in a military point of view. The fate of Spain will decide that of Portugal, if Spain is conquered, Portugal can not be defended.'[10] Anstruther was more optimistic, writing: 'My conviction is that much resource may be drawn from this country: the people are robust, hardy, active and sober: and susceptible of strong feelings by which they may be led to do extraordinary things.'[11] Unfortunately, like so many of the men who landed in Mondego Bay, Anstruther would not live to see the eventual victory. He died in January 1809 from fatigue and exhaustion after leading his brigade to Corunna. Many more of Wellesley's men would die from fever on Walcheren and in the later Peninsula campaigns.

For Castlereagh and Canning, the drivers of British war policy, the Peninsula was the opportunity they had been waiting for. Bonaparte's heavy-handed thuggery in Spain and Portugal resulted in a rare, if brief, moment of political consensus in Britain. The Whigs and the Tories could unite behind the bravery of the Spanish and Portuguese people in their defiance against the French. There would be no more mere filching of sugar islands, and the campaign helped to forestall Napoleon's South American ambitions. Britain's contribution to the war effort would, at last, extend to the commitment of a significant number of troops on the continent rather than being based on the financial support of allies and the blockade of French ports. The Peninsula, with its long coastline and poor internal communications, was the ideal theatre for the British. However, had they known the Peninsular War would last nearly six years, they may not have been so keen to intervene.

On 8 September, Lord Grenville, a former prime minister and foreign secretary, foresaw the struggle ahead and wrote to the Duke of Buckingham:

As far as one can judge, Wellesley seems really to have done well; and the advantage of a victory in a pitched field of battle, by British troops, over a force not much inferior in numbers of French troops, is under the present circumstances extremely important. Our

9   Anglesey, *One-Leg*, p.67.
10   BL: Add MS 49503: Decken to Gordon, 21 September 1808.
11   BL: Add MS 49503: Anstruther to Gordon, 21 September 1808.

countrymen are certainly still running a great deal too fast, when they conclude that the whole struggle in Spain is over. I am afraid they will find on the contrary, that it is not yet begun. Bonaparte is evidently waiting to assemble a great and overwhelming army, with which he means again to enter Spain. The difficulties he will have to encounter are, no doubt, very great, from the nature of the country, and from the inveteracy and warlike genius of the people. But, if the war is to be carried on (as seems probable) at our cost, I am afraid we shall hear many a heavy groan in the wheels of our financial machinery, before it is concluded.[12]

The successful campaign to liberate Portugal in 1808 was the first step in a very long and very rocky road to eventual victory.

---

12   Buckingham (ed.), *Memoirs of the Court*, vol.IV, p.247.

Bibliography

Archival Sources

The National Archives, Kew (TNA)
ADM 1/19: Letters from squadron escorting Portuguese Royal Family to Brazil
ADM 1/339–340: Letters from Senior Officers, Lisbon: 1808
ADM 196/58: Royal Marine Officers
ADM 2/1365: Secret Letters
ADM 50: Admirals' Journals
ADM 7/41: Letter Book of Vice Admiral Cotton
FO 63/55–56: Viscount Strangford
MPF 1/220: Sketch plan of the Battle of Vimieiro
WO 1/213: British Army in Spain, Portugal and France Miscellaneous Correspondence
WO 1/226–237: British Army in Spain, Portugal and France (1808-1820)
WO 1/415–418: Convention of Cintra. Papers relating to the Board of General Officers
WO 1/903: Conditions of service, numbers, and miscellaneous papers
WO 12: Muster Books and Pay Lists
WO 123/129: Army Circulars, Memoranda, Orders and Regulations 1805–1808
WO 17: Monthly Returns to the Adjutant General
WO 27/91–92: Inspection Returns, 1807
WO 55/1193: Artillery Letters
WO 55/977: Engineer Papers, Miscellaneous
WO 6/156: Commissioners of Transport
WO 6/185: Secret Letters
WO 72/29: Courts Martial Correspondence, Portugal Convention
WO 78/5947: Survey and plan of the action of Obidos [Roliça], 17 August 1808
WO 78/5949–5950: Battle of Vimeiro, maps
WO 90/1: General Courts Martial Registers, abroad

The British Library (BL)
Add MS 35059: Correspondence of Lord Hill
Add Ms 46837: Sir Henry Wyn, Correspondence with Francis Drake
Add MS 49481–49485: Correspondence, Sir James Willoughby Gordon
Add Ms 49502–49503: Correspondence, Sir James Willoughby Gordon

National Library of Scotland (NLS)
Adv.MS.46.3.6: General orders relating to the Peninsular War

National Records of Scotland (NRS)
GD364/1/1178: Papers of Sir John Hope, Peninsular expedition, 1808

Royal Engineers Museum (REM)
4201-305: Peninsular Letters of Captain Landmann and Fanshawe 1808–1810
4201-274: Transcripts of letters Howard Elphinstone to his wife

National Army Museum (NAM)
1959-03-127: Correspondence of William Granville Eliot, Royal Artillery 1805-1809
1968-07-419-15: Letters of Lt. William Cowper Coles
1975-11-31-1: Manuscript journal of a captain in Wellington's Division in Portugal, 24 August to 16 September 1808
1979-12-21-1: Manuscript memoirs of an unidentified soldier of 38th (1st Staffordshire) Regiment of Foot, of his career in the Army 1808-1815
1985-04-101: Journal in Portugal and Spain 1808, 1809
1994-03-129: Papers & Correspondence relating to Sir Hew Dalrymple
1997-04-067: 91 manuscript letters of Lt Col (later Lt Gen) William Warre written during the Peninsular War, 1808-1812

Special Collections, Hartley Library, University of Southampton (UoS)
Wellington Papers
WP 1/205: Letters to the Duke, June 1808
WP 1/206: Letters from the Duke, June 1808
WP 1/212: Papers relating to the evacuation of Portugal by the French Army

St Andrew's University Library, Special Collections (StAUL)
msdep121/8/2/3/4/4: Field diary of General Robert Anstruther on campaign in Portugal

Lincolnshire Archives (LA)
MG/4/5/15: P.L. Massingberd Letter Books
JARVIS/5/A/2: Letters between George Jarvis, his wife, Philadelphia

Nottingham University, Manuscripts and Special Collections (NU)
Me4C2/1: Letters from Henry Francis Mellish, to his sister, Miss Ann Mellish; 1797-1809

Lambeth Palace Library
MS 3263: Beloe Papers

Books

Alison, A., *Lives of Lord Castlereagh and Sir Charles Stewart* (Edinburgh: Blackwood, 1861)
Amaral, M. *The Portuguese Army and the Commencement of the Peninsular War* (Lisbon: Tribuna, 2007)
Anglesey, Marquess of, *One-Leg, The Life and Letters of Henry William Paget, First Marquess of Anglesey, K.G., 1768-1854* (London: Cape, 1961)
Anon. (ed.), *Copy of The Proceedings upon the Inquiry Relative to The Armistice and Convention, &c Made and Concluded in Portugal, in August 1808, Between the Commanders of the British and French Armies* (London: House of Commons, 1809)
Anon. (ed.), *The British Military Library* (London: Carpenter, 1804)
Anon. (ed.), *The Soldier's Companion, or Martial Recorder* (London: Cock, 1824)
Anon. *Noticias Biograficas do Coronel Trant* (Lisbon: Impressão Regia, 1811)
Anon., *A History of the Campaigns of the British Forces in Spain and Portugal* (London: Goddard, 1812)
Anon., *A History of the Campaigns of the British Forces in Spain and Portugal* (London: Goddard, 1812)
Anon., *Advantages of the Convention of Cintra, Briefly Stated in a Candid Review of that Transaction and of the Circumstances Under which it Took Place* (London: privately published, 1809)
Anon., *Almanach Para o Anno de 1800* (Lisbon: Galhardo, 1800)
Anon., *Almanak Militar dos Officiaes do Exercito de Portugal* (Lisbon: Eugenio Augusto, 1825)
Anon., *Aperçu Nouveau sur les Campagnes des Français en Portugal* (Paris: Delaunay, 1818)
Anon., *Bulletin des Lois du Royaume de France* (Paris: La Imprimerie Royale, 1820)

Anon., *Historical Records of the Second Regiment of Foot* (London: Adjutant General's Office, undated)

Anon., *Historique du 86e Régiment d'Infanterie* (Paris: Charles-Lavauzelle, 1886)

Anon., *Journal of a Soldier of the Seventy-First* (Edinburgh: W. & C. Tait, 1819)

Anon., *Mappa Historico-militar-politico e Moral da Cidade de Evora ou Exacta Narraçaõ do Terrivel Assalto que á Mesma Cidade deo o General Loison com Hum Excercito de Nove Mil Homens em o Fatal dia 29 de Julho de 1808* (Lisbon: Galhardo, 1814)

Anon., *Memoria Histórica da Invasão dos Francezes em Portugal no ano de 1807* (Rio de Janeiro: Impressão Regia, 1808)

Anon., *Minutes of the Proceedings of the Court of Inquiry upon the Treaty of Armistice and Convention of Cintra* (London: Tipper & Booth, 1808)

Anon., *Papers Presented to Parliament in 1809* (London: Strahan, 1809)

Anon., *Parliamentary Reports: Accounts &c* (London: House of Commons, undated)

Anon., *Report on the Manuscripts of J.B. Fortesque Esq. Preserved at Dropmore* (London: HMSO, 1912)

Anon., *Rules and Regulations for the Formations, Field Exercises and Movements of His Majesty's Forces* (London: War Office, 1798)

Anon., *Vicissitudes in the Life of a Scottish Soldier* (London: Colburn, 1827)

Arvers, P., *Historique du 82e Régiment d'Infanterie de Ligne* (Paris: Lahure, 1876)

Aspinall, A. (ed.), *The Later Correspondence of George III* (Cambridge: Cambridge University Press, 1970)

Bankes, G.N., *The Autobiography of Sergeant William Lawrence* (London: Sampson Low, Marston, Searle, & Rivington, 1886)

Barrow, J., *The Life and Correspondence of Admiral Sir William Sidney Smith* (London: Bentley, 1848)

Beauvais de Preau, C.T., *Victoires, Conquêtes, Désastres, Revers et Guerres Civiles des Français de 1792 a 1815* (Paris: Panckoucke, 1820)

Bégos, L., *Souvenirs des Campagnes du Lieutenant-Colonel Louis Bégos* (Lausanne: Delafontaine, 1859)

Belhomme, V., *Historique de 90e Régiment d'Infanterie de Ligne, ex-15e Légère* (Paris: Tanera, 1875)

Beresford, M. De La Poer, *Marshal William Carr Beresford* (Newbridge: Irish Academic Press, 2019)

Beresford, M. De La Poer, *Peninsular and Waterloo General, Sir Denis Pack and the War Against Napoleon* (Barnsley: Pen & Sword, 2022)

Bew, J., *Castlereagh* (London: Quercus, 2011)

Billows, W., *Nothing Pertickler Happened* (Unknown: Privately published, 2011)

Blake, N., *Steering to Glory: A Day in the Life of a Ship of the Line* (London, Chatham, 2005)

Bradford, William, *Sketches of the Country, Character and Costume in Portugal and Spain: Made During the Campaign and on the Route of the British Army in 1808 and 1809* (London: Booth, 1809)

Brett-James, A., *Wellington at War* (London: St. Macmillan, 1961)

Brougham, H., *The Life and Times of Henry Lord Brougham* (New York: Harper Bros., 1871)

Brown, S., *Fit to Command* (Warwick: Helion, 2023)

Brown, S., *Wellington's Redjackets* (Barnsley: Frontline, 2015)

Buckingham and Chandos, Duke of (ed.), *Memoirs of the Court and Cabinets of George the Third* (London: Hurst and Blackett, 1855)

Burnham, R. & McGuigan, R., *The British Army Against Napoleon, Facts, Lists, and Trivia 1805-1815* (Barnsley: Frontline Books, 2010)

Burnham, R. & McGuigan, R., *Wellington's Brigade Commanders, Peninsula & Waterloo* (Barnsley: Pen & Sword, 2017)

Burnham, R., *Charging Against Wellington: Napoleon's Cavalry in the Peninsula 1807-1814* (Barnsley: Frontline, 2011)

Bury, J.P.T., and Barry, J.C. (eds), *An Englishman in Paris: 1803* (London: Bles, 1953)

Butler, A.J., (trans.), *The Memoirs of Baron Thiébault* (London: Smith, Elder & Co., 1896)

Buttery, D., *Wellington against Junot* (Barnsley: Pen & Sword, 2011)

Caldwell, G.J., and Cooper, R.B.E., *Rifle Green in the Peninsula* (Leicester: Bugle Horn, 1998)

Campos, J.P., and de Blas, A.G., *Officiers de Napoléon tués ou blessés pendant la Guerre d'Espagne (1808-1814)* (Madrid: Foro para el Estudio de la Historia Militar de España, 2020)

Cannon, R., *Historical record of the Ninth, or the East Norfolk Regiment of Foot* (London: Adjutant General's Office, 1848)

Cannon, R., *Historical Record of the Twentieth or East Devonshire Regiment of Foot* (London: Parker, Furnivall & Parker, 1868)

Carr-Gomm, F.C. (ed.), *Letters and Journals of Field-Marshal Sir William Maynard Gomm* (London: Murray, 1881)

Chartrand, R., *The Portuguese Army of the Napoleonic Wars* (Oxford: Osprey, 2001)

Clammer, D., *Ladies, Wives and Women British Army Wives in the Revolutionary and Napoleonic Wars 1793–1815* (Warwick: Helion, 2022)

Clarke, F.L., *The Life of the Most Noble Arthur, Marquis and Earl of Wellington* (London: Cundee, 1812)

Cope, W.H., *The History of the Rifle Brigade* (London: Chatto & Windus, 1877)

Crowdy, T.E., *French Light Infantry 1784–1815* (Warwick: Helion, 2021)

Crowdy, T.E., *Napoleon's Infantry Handbook* (Barnsley: Pen & Sword, 2015)

Crumplin, M., *Guthrie's War* (Barnsley: Pen & Sword, 2010)

Curling, H. (ed.), *Recollections of Rifleman Harris* (London: Hurst, 1848)

Dalrymple, H., *Memoir written by General Sir Hew Dalrymple of his Proceedings as Connected with the Affairs of Spain, and the Commencement of the Peninsular War* (London: Boone, 1830)

Daly, G., *The British Soldier in the Peninsular War* (Basingstoke: Palgrave Macmillian, 2013)

Davies, H.J., *Spying for Wellington* (Norman: University of Oklahoma Press, 2018)

Davies, H.J., *Wellington's Wars, the Making of a Military Genius* (New Haven: Yale University Press, 2012)

Dawson, P.L., *Napoleon's Peninsular War* (Barnsley: Frontline, 2020)

De Bonnières de Wierre, A., *Historique du 3e Régiment de dragons: 1649-1892,* (Nantes: Bourgeois, 1892)

De Brito, P., *An Introduction to the Anglo-Portuguese Army Logistics in the Peninsular War* (Parede: Tibuna de História, 2012)

De La Fuente, F., *Dom Miguel Pereira Forjaz* (Lisbon: Tribuna, 2011)

Deane, A., *Nelson's Favourite, HMS Agamemnon at War 1781-1809* (London: Chatham, 1996)

Delbauve, E., *Historique du 26e Régiment d'Infanterie* (Paris: Berger-Leverault, 1889)

Dempsey, G., *Napoleon's Mercenaries* (London: Greenhill, 2002)

Dos Santos, J.M.F., *Lisboa e a Invasão de Junot: população, periódicos e panfletos (1807-1808)* (MA Dissertation: Universidade Nova de Lisboa, 2014)

Du Motey, H.R., *Un Héros de la Grande-Armee* (Paris: Picard, 1911)

Duncan, F., *History of the Royal Regiment of Artillery* (London: Murray, 1873) Vol.II .

Ede-Borrett, S., *Swiss Regiments in the Service of France 1798-1815* (Warwick: Helion, 2019)

Eliot, W.G., *A Treatise on the Defence of Portugal* (London: Egerton, 1811)

Elting, J.R., *Swords Around a Throne: Napoleon's Grande Armée* (London: Weidenfield and Nicolson, 1989)

Esdaile, C. & Reed, M., (eds.), *With Moore to Corunna* (Barnsley: Pen & Sword, 2018)

Esdaile, C., *The Peninsular War* (London: Allen Lane, 2002)

Everard, H., *History of Thomas Farrington's Regiment, subsequently designated the 29th (Worcestershire) Foot* (Worcester: Littlebury, 1891)

Fane, J., *Memoir of the Early Campaigns of the Duke of Wellington in Portugal and Spain* (London: Murray, 1820)

Fereday, R.P. (ed.), *The Autobiography of Samuel Laing of Papdale 1780-1868* (Kirkwall: Bellavista, 2000)

Fieffé, E., *Histoire des Troupes Étrangères au Service de France* (Paris: Librairie Militaire, 1854)

Fletcher, I., *Galloping at Everything: The British Cavalry in the Peninsular War and at Waterloo 1808–15* (Staplehurst: Spellmount, 1999)

Fletcher, I., *Voices from the Peninsula* (Barnsley: Frontline, 2016)

Fletcher, I., *Wellington's Regiments* (Staplehurst: Spellmount, 1994)

Fortescue, J.W., *A History of the British Army* (London: Macmillan & Co, 1906)

Foy, M., *Histoire de la Guerre de la Péninsule sous Napoleon* (Paris: Baudouin, 1827)

Foy, M., *History of the War in the Peninsula under Napoleon* (London: Treuttel, 1827)

Foy, M., *Junot's Invasion of Portugal* (Felling: Worley, 2000)

Franklin, C.E., *British Napoleonic Field Artillery* (Stoud: Spellmount, 2012)

Fyler, A.E., *The History of the 50th or (The Queen's Own) Regiment* (London: Chapman & Hall, 1895)

G. Glover (ed.), *The Men of Wellington's Light Division, Unpublished Memoirs of the 43rd (Monmouthshire) Regiment in the Peninsular War* (Barnsley: Frontline, 2022)

Geikie, A., *Life of Sir Roderick I. Murchison* (London: Murray, 1875)

Gil, Ferreira, *A Infantaria Portuguesa na Guerra da Peninsula* (Lisboa: Tipografia da Cooperativa Militar, 1912)

Girod de l'Ain, M., *Vie Militaire du General Foy* (Paris: Plon, 1900)

Gleig, G., *The Hussar,* (London: Henry Colburn, 1837)

Glover, G., (ed.), *The Napoleonic Archive: Volume 1: British Line Infantry Memoirs* (Godmanchester: Trotman, 2021)

Glover, G., and R. Burnham, *Riflemen of Wellington's Light Division in the Peninsular War* (Barnsley: Frontline, 2023)

Glover, G., *The Two Battles of Copenhagen* 1801 and 1807 (Barnsley: Pen & Sword, 2018)

Glover, M., *Britannia Sickens, Sir Arthur Wellesley and the Convention of Cintra* (London: Leo Cooper, 1970)

Glover, R., *Britain at Bay* (London: Allen & Unwin, 1973)

Glover, R., *Peninsular Preparation: The Reform of the British Army 1795–1809* (Cambridge: Cambridge University Press, 1963)

Goff, G.L., *Historical Records of the 91st Argyllshire Highlanders* (London: Bentley, 1891)

Grasset, A., *La Guerre d'Espagne 1807-1813* (Paris: Berger-Leverault, 1914)

Gray, E.G., *The Trumpet of Glory* (London: Hale, 1985)

Greig, M., *Dead Men Telling Tales* (Oxford: Oxford University Press, 2021)

Griffith, P. (ed.), *Modern Studies of the War in Spain and Portugal, 1808-1814* (London: Greenhill, 1999)

Griffith, R. (ed.), *Armies and Enemies of Napoleon, 1789–1815* (Warwick: Helion, 2022)

Griffith, R., *Riflemen: The History of the 5th Battalion, 60th (Royal American) Regiment, 1797-1818* (Warwick: Helion, 2019)

Griffon de Pleineville, N., *La Première Invasion du Portugal par l'Armée Napoléonienne (1807-1808)* (Paris: Economica, 2017)

Gurwood, J. (ed.), *The Dispatches of Field Marshall the Duke of Wellington* (London: John Murray, 1837–1839)

Guthrie, G.J., *A Treatise on Gun-Shot Wounds* (London: Burgess & Hill, 1827)

Guthrie, G.J., *Commentaries on the Surgery of the War* (Philadelphia: Lippincott, 1862)

Guy, A. (ed.), *The Road to Waterloo* (London: Sutton, 1990)

Hale, J., *Journal of James Hale, late Sergeant in the Ninth Regiment of Foot* (Cirencester: Watkins, 1826)

Hall, C.D., *Wellington's Navy* (London: Chatham, 2004)

Hall, J.A., *The Biographical Dictionary of British Officers Killed & Wounded, 1808-1814* (London: Greenhill, 1998).

Halliday, A., *Observations on the Present State of the Portuguese Army* (London: Murray, 1811)

Halliday, A., *The Present State of Portugal and the Portuguese Army* (Edinburgh: Clarke, 1812)

Hamilton, A., *Hamilton's Campaign with Moore and Wellington during the Peninsular War* (Troy, privately published, 1847)

Harding-Edgar, J. *Next to Wellington: General Sir George Murray* (Warwick: Helion & Co, 2018)

Hardinge, C., *Rulers of India: Viscount Hardinge* (Oxford: Clarendon Press, 1891)

Harris, B., *The Recollections of Rifleman Harris* (London: Century, 1985)

Hathaway, E. (ed.), *A Dorset Soldier; The Autobiography of Sgt William Lawrence, 1790–1869* (Staplehurst: Spellmount, 1993)

Hayter, A., *The Backbone, Diaries of a Military Family in the Napoleonic Wars* (Durham: Pentland Press, 1993)

Henry, P., *Notes of Conversations with the Duke of Wellington 1831-1851* (London: Murray, 1889)

Holmes, R., *Wellington, The Iron Duke* (London: Harper Collins, 2002)

Howard, E., *Memoirs of Admiral Sir Sidney Smith* (London: Bentley, 1839)

Hubback, J.H, & Hubback, E.C., *Jane Austen's Sailor Brothers* (London: Lane, 1906)

Hulot, J.L., *Souvenirs Militaires du Baron Hulot* (Paris: Spectateur Militaire, 1886)

Humble, R., *Napoleon's Peninsular Marshals* (London: Macdonald, 1973)

James, C., *An Universal Military Dictionary* (London: Egerton, 1810)

James, C., *An Universal Military Dictionary* (London: Egerton, 1816)

James, W., *The Naval History of Great Britain from the Declaration of War by France in 1793 to the Accession of George IV* (London: Bentley, 1859)

Jaycock, G.E., *Wellington's Command* (Barnsley: Pen & Sword, 2019)

Jennings, L.J., *The Croker Papers* (London: Murray, 1885)

Johnson, D., *Napoleon's Cavalry and its Leaders* (London: Batsford, 1978)

Junot, L., *Memoirs of Madame Junot* (Paris: The Napoleon Society, 1895)

Ker Porter, R., *Letters from Portugal and Spain Written During the March of the British Troops under Sir John Moore* (London: Longman, 1809)

Knight, R., *Britain Against Napoleon: The Organisation of Victory 1793-1815* (London: Penguin, 2013)

Knight, R., *Convoys* (New Haven: Yale University Press, 2022)

Krajeski, P.C., *In the Shadow of Nelson, The Naval Leadership of Admiral Sir Charles Cotton 1753–1812* (Westport: Greenwood Press, 2000)

Ladimir, F. & Moreau, E., *Campagnes, Triomphes, Revers, Désastres et Guerres Civiles des Francais de 1792 a la paix de 1856* (Paris: Librairie Populaire des Villes et des Campagnes, 1856)

Landmann, G., *Recollections of My Military Life* (London: Hurst & Blackett, 1854)

Lansing, M., *Liberators and Heroes of South America* (Boston: Page, 1940)

Lavallée, T., *Physical, Historical, and Military Geography* (London: Standford, 1868)

Le Mesurier, H., *The British Commissary* (London: Egerton, 1801)

Leach, J., *Rough Sketches of the Life of an Old Soldier* (London: Longman, 1831)

Lecestre, L., *Lettres inédites de Napoléon 1er (An VIII–1815)* (Paris: Librairie Plon, 1897)

Lemaitre, L., *Historique du 4e Régiment de Dragons* (Paris: Charles-Lavauzelle, 1894)

Leslie, C., *Military Journal of Colonel Leslie, K. H, of Balquhain* (Aberdeen: Aberdeen University Press, 1887)

Leslie, J.H., *The Services of the Royal Regiment of Artillery in the Peninsular War 1808 to 1814* (London: Rees, 1908)

Light, K., *The Saving of an Empire* (Ely: Melrose, 2009)

Lipscombe, N., *Wellington's Guns* (Oxford: Osprey, 2013)

Maag, A., *Geschichte der Schweizertruppen im Kriege Napoleons I in Spanien und Portugal (1807-1814)* (Biel: Kuhn, 1892)

McArthur, John, *Principles and Practice of Naval and Military Courts Martial* (London: Butterworth, 1813)

Mackay, C.H., *The Tempest: The Life and Career of Jean-Andoche Junot, 1771–1813* (PhD thesis: Florida State University, 1995)

Malaguti, C.J.E., *Historique du 87e Régiment d'Infanterie de Ligne* (Saint-Quentin: Moureau, 1892)

Marshall, J., *Royal Naval Biography or, Memoirs of the Services of all the Flag-Officer, Superannuated Rear-Admirals, Retired Captains, Post-Captains and Commanders* (London: Longman 1823)

Martinet, M., *Historique de 9e Régiment de Dragons* (Paris: Hamel, 1888)

Martinien, A., *Tableaux, par Corps et par Batailles, des Officiers Tués et Blessés Pendant les Guerres de l'Empire (1805-1815)* (Paris, Charles-La Vauzelle, undated)

Martinien, A., *Tableaux, par Corps et par Batailles, des Officiers Tués et Blessés Pendant les Guerres de l'Empire (1805-1815) Supplement* (Paris, Fournier, 1909)

Martinovich, P., *The Sea is My Element* (Warwick: Helion, 2021)

Maurice, J.F. (ed.), *The Diary of Sir John Moore* (London: Arnold, 1904)

Mikaberidze, A., *The Napoleonic Wars, A Global History* (Oxford: Oxford University Press, 2020)

Mikaberidze, A., *The Russian Officer Corps in the Revolutionary and Napoleonic Wars* (New York: Savas Beatie, 2005)

Mollo, J., *The Prince's Dolls* (London: Leo Cooper, 1997)

Moore-Smith, G.C., *The Life of John Colborne, Field-Marshal Lord Seaton* (London: Murray, 1903)

Mooresom, W.S., *Historical Record of the Fifty-Second Regiment* (London: Bentley, 1860)

Morley, S., *Memoirs of a Serjeant of the 5th Regt. of Foot, Containing an Account of his Service in Hanover, South America, and the Peninsula* (Cambridge: Ken Trotman, 1999)

Muir, R. *Wellington: The Path to Victory 1769-1814* (New Haven: Yale, 2015)

Muir, R., *Britain and the Defeat of Napoleon 1807-1815* (New Haven: Yale, 1996)

Muir, R., Burnham, R., Muir, H., & McGuigan R., *Inside Wellington's Peninsular Army 1808-1814* (Barnsley: Pen & Sword, 2014)

Mullié, C., *Biographie des célébrités militaires des armées de terre et de mer de 1789 à 1850* (Paris: Poignavant, 1851)

Mullié, M.C., *Biographie des Célébrités Militaires des Armées de Terre et de Mer de 1789 à 1850* (Paris: Surcy, 1851)

Napier, W. *A Reply to Lord Strangford's 'Observations' on Some Passages in Lieut-Col Napier's History of the Peninsular War* (London: Murray, 1828)

Napier, W., *History of the War in the Peninsula & in the South of France* (London: Warne, 1886)

Napier, W.C.E. (ed.), *Passages in the Early Military Life of General Sir George T. Napier, K.C.B.* (London: Murray, 1884)

Neale, A., *Letters from Portugal and Spain* (London: Phillips, 1809)

Neves, J.A., *Historia Geral Invasão dos Franceses em Portugal* (Lisbon: Ferreira, 1810)

Nevill, R., *Light Come, Light Go; Gambling – Gamesters – Wagers – The Turf* (London: Macmillan, 1909)

Newham, F. (ed.), *The Humble Address of John Lowe* (London: Privately published, 1827)

Newnham Collingwood, G.L., *A Selection from the Public and Private Correspondence of Vice Admiral Lord Collingwood* (London: Ridgway, 1828)

Nichols, A., *A Fine Corps and Will Serve Faithfully* (Warwick: Helion, 2023)

O'Neil, T., *A Concise and Accurate Account of the Proceedings of the Squadron under the Command of Rear Admiral Sir Sydney Smith in Effecting the Escape of the Royal Family of Portugal to the Brazils* (London, privately published, 1810)

Oman, C., *A History of the Peninsular War* (Oxford: Clarendon Press, 1902)

Oman, C., *Wellington's Army 1809-1814* (London: Arnold, 1913)

Oman, C., *Studies in the Napoleonic Wars* (Elstree: Greenhill, 1987)

Ormsby, J.W., *An Account of the Operations of the British Army and of the state and sentiments of the People of Portugal and Spain* (London: Carpenter, 1809)

Oyon, J.A., *Campagnes et Souvenirs de Maréchal de Logis Jean-Auguste Oyon* (Wagram Press, Kindle Edition)

Patterson, J., *Camps and Quarters, or Scenes and Impressions, of Military Life* (London: Saunders & Otley, 1840)

Patterson, J., *The Adventures of Captain John Patterson* (London: T & W Boone, 1837)

Payne, R., *War and Diplomacy in the Napoleonic Era* (London: Bloomsbury, 2021)

Philippart, J. (ed.), *The Royal Military Calendar* (London: Egerton, 1820)

Picard, E., and L. Tuetey (eds), *Unpublished Correspondence of Napoleon I* (New York: Duffield, 1913)

Picard, L., *Guerres d'Espagne: Le Prologue, 1807 Expédition du Portugal* (Paris: Jouve, 1911)

Piéron, G.L.E., *Histoire d'un régiment, la 32e Demi-Brigade* (Paris: Vasseur, 1890)

Plon, H., & Dumaine, J. (eds), *Correspondance de Napoléon 1er* (Paris: Imprimeur de l'Empereur, 1865)

Pocock, T., *A Thirst for Glory, the Life of Admiral Sir Sidney Smith* (London: Aurum, 1996)

Reiter, J., *The Late Lord, The Life of John Pitt 2nd Earl of Chatham* (Barnsley: Pen & Sword, 2017)

Rigaud, G., *Celer et Audax* (Oxford: Hall & Stacy, 1879)

Robson, M., *Britain, Portugal and South America in the Napoleonic Wars* (London: Tauris, 2011)

Ross-Lewin, H., *The Life of a Soldier: A Narrative of Twenty-Seven Years' Service in Various Parts of the World* (London: Bentley, 1834)

Rottenburg, F. de, *Regulations for the Exercise of Riflemen and Light Infantry and Instructions for their Conduct in the Field* (London: War Office, 1803)

Roussel, J., *État militaire de France, pour l'année 1788* (Paris: Onfroy, 1788)

Russell, Lord, *Knight of the Sword, The Life and Letters Admiral Sir William Sidney Smith* (London: Gollancz, 1964)

Saint-Just, V. de, *Historique du 5e Régiment de Dragons* (Paris: Hachette, 1891)

Sepulveda, C., *Historia Organica e Politica do Exercito Português* (Lisbon: Imprensa Nacional, 1902-1923)

Shadwell, L., *The Life of Colin Campbell, Lord Clyde* (Edinburgh: Blackwood, 1881)

Sidney, E., *The Life of Lord Hill* (London: John Murray, 1845)

Sigler, J.L., *General Paul Thiébault His Life and His Legacy* (Florida State University: PhD Thesis, 2006)

Six, G., *Dictionnaire Biographique des Généraux et Amiraux de la Révolution et de l'Empire: 1792-1814* (Paris, Librarie Historique et Nobiliaire, 1934)

Smyth, B., *A History of the Lancashire Fusiliers* (Dublin: Sackville Press, 1903)

Smythies, R.H.R, *Historical Records of the 40th (2nd Somersetshire) Regiment* (Devonport: Swiss, 1894)

Southey, R., *History of the Peninsular War* (London: Murray, 1828)

Sparrow, E., *Secret Service, British Agents in France 1792-1815* (Woodbridge: The Boydell Press, 1999)

Steel, D., *The Shipmaster's Assistant and Owner's Manual* (London: Steel, 1801)

Steevens, N (ed.), *Reminiscences of My Military Life* (Winchester: Warren, 1878)

Stewart, D., *Sketches of the Character, Manners, and Present State of the Highlanders of Scotland* (Edinburgh: Constable, 1825)

Stockdale, J., *A Narrative of the Campaign which Preceded the Convention of Cintra in Portugal* (London: Stockdale, 1809)

Stockdale, J., *The Proceedings on the Enquiry into the Armistice and Convention of Cintra* (London: Stockdale, 1809)

Strangford, P., *Further Observations on Some Passages in Lieut-Col Napier's History of the Peninsular War* (London: Murray, 1828)

Strangford, P., *Observations on Some Passages in Lieut-Col Napier's History of the Peninsular War* (London: Murray, 1828)

Stuart, D.M., *The Daughters of George III* (Stroud: Fonthill, 2016)

Sutcliffe, R., *British Expeditionary Warfare and the Defeat of Napoleon, 1793–1815* (Woodbridge: Boydell, 2016)

Thiébault, P., *Mémoires du General Baron Thiébault* (Paris: Plon, 1895)

Thiébault, P., *Relation de l'Expédition du Portugal faite en 1807 et 1808* (Paris: Magimel, Anselin & Pochard, 1817)

Thomas, R.N.W., *No Want of Courage: The British Army in Flanders, 1793–1795* (Warwick: Helion, 2022)

Thompson, M.S., *Wellington's Engineers* (Barnsley: Pen & Sword, 2015)

Uffindell, A., *The National Army Museum Book of Wellington's Armies* (London: Sidgwick & Jackson, 2003)

Urban, M., *The Man Who Broke Napoleon's Codes* (London: Faber & Faber, 2001)

Vane, C.W. (ed.), *Correspondence, Despatches, and other Papers of Viscount Castlereagh* (London: Shoberl, 1851)

Vane, C.W., *Story of the Peninsular War* (New York: Harper Bros. 1854)

Verner, W., *History and Campaigns Of The Rifle Brigade* (Wagram Press, Kindle Edition)

Verner, W., *The First British Rifle Corps* (London: Allen & Co, 1890)

Warre, E. (ed.), *Letters from the Peninsula 1808-1812* (London: Murray, 1909)

Weale, G., *An Interesting Memoir of George Weale* (Leamington: private publication, 1838)

Wellington, 2nd Duke of (ed.), *Civil Correspondence and Memoranda of Field Marshal Arthur Duke of Wellington* (London: Murray, 1860)

Wellington, 2nd Duke of (ed.), *Supplementary Despatches, Correspondence and Memoranda of Field Marshal Arthur Duke of Wellington* (London, Murray, 1860)

Wilkin B. & Wilkin R., *Fighting for Napoleon* (Barnsley: Pen & Sword, 2015)

Wilkin B. & Wilkin R., *Fighting the British* (Barnsley: Pen & Sword, 2018)

Winfield, R., *British Warships in the Age of Sail, 1793–1817: Design, Construction, Careers and Fates* (Barnsley: Seaforth, 2014)

Wood, G., *The Subaltern Officer* (London: Prowett, 1825)

Woolgar, C.(ed.), *Wellington Studies I* (Southampton: University of Southampton, 1996)

Woolgar, C.(ed.), *Wellington Studies II* (Southampton: University of Southampton, 1999)

Woolgar, C. (ed.), *Wellington Studies V* (Southampton: University of Southampton, 2013)

Wordsworth, W. *Concerning the Relations of Great Britain, Spain, and Portugal* (London: Longman, Hurst, Rees, and Orme, 1809).

Wyld, J., *Maps and Plans Showing the Principle Movements, Battles and Sieges, in which the British Army was Engaged during the War from 1808 to 1814 in the Spanish Peninsula and South of France* (London: Wyld, 1841)

Wyld, J., *Memoir Annexed to an Atlas containing Plans of the Principal Battles, Sieges, and Affairs in which The British Troops were Engaged During the War in the Spanish Peninsula and the South of France from 1808 to 1814* (London: Wyld, 1841)

Journal Articles

Anon. 'From Vimeiro to Corunna', *Royal United Services Institution Journal*, 114:656, pp.33–42

Anon. (ed.), 'Documentos', *Boletim do Arquivo Histórico Militar*, vol.1 (1930), pp.164–262

Anon., 'Foreign Miscellany', *United Service Journal*, 1830, part 1, pp.85–92

Anon., 'Major-General Sir Nicholas Trant, K.C.T.S.', *The United Service Journal*, part 1, 1840, pp.99–100

Anon., 'Memoir of Rear Admiral Bligh, C.B.', *United Service Journal*, part 1, 1831, pp.343–345

Anon., 'Reminiscences of General Burne', *United Service Journal*, 1829, part two, pp.574–578

Anon., 'The United Services', *United Service Journal*, part 2, 1843, pp.547–555

Anon'. The Late Admiral Sir Charles Cotton, Bart.', *The Naval Chronicle*, vol.27, January–June 1812, p.213

Barada, J., 'Notes sur L'Expédition de Portugal 1807-1808,' *Carnet de la Sabretache*, No. 263 January-February 1920, pp.201–211

Curling, H, 'The Bayonet', *United Service Journal*, July 1839, pp.399–400

Ellis, J.D. 'Drummers for the Devil? The Black Soldiers of the 29th (Worcestershire) Regiment of Foot, 1759-1843', *Journal of the Society for Army Historical Research*, Vol. 80, No. 323 (Autumn2002), pp.186-202

Ellis, J.D., 'Drummers for the Devil? The Black Soldiers of the 29th (Worcestershire) Regiment of Foot, 1759-1843', *Journal of the Society for Army Historical Research,* vol.80, no.323 (Autumn 2002), pp.186–193

G.B.J, 'Battle of Vimiera – Second Battalion, 43d – "Unus quorum"', *United Service Journal*, Part 1, 1845, pp.443–450

Gleig, G., 'The Author of "The Hussar" to Colonel Napier', *United Service Journal*, Part 3, 1838, p.107

Gregory, D., 'British Occupations Of Madeira During the Wars Against Napoleon', *Journal of the Society for Army Historical Research*, Vol. 66, No. 266 (Summer1988), pp.80-96

Harris, B., 'The Veteran Rifleman at Vimiera', *United Service Journal*, September 1839, p.106

Hicks, P., 'Napoleon, Tilsit, Copenhagen, and Portugal', *Napoleonica. La Revue*, No.2, 2008, pp.87–99

Horward, D.D., 'Portugal and the Anglo-Russian Naval Crisis (1808)', *Naval War College Review*, vol.34, no.3 (May-June 1981), pp.48-74

Kermack, Balfour, 'A Short Sketch of the Campaigns of Balfour Kermack', *Highland Light Infantry Chronicle*, October 1914, pp.159-166

McGuffie, T.H., 'British Artillery in the Vimeiro Campaign', *Journal of the Society for Army Historical Research*, Vol. 23, No. 94 (Summer,1945), pp.80-81

McGuffie, T.H., 'Note on the French Artillery Captured at Vimeiro', *Journal of the Society for Army Historical Research*, Vol. 23, No. 94 (Summer,1945), p.82

Martin, J. 'Letter, 22 October 1808', *The Naval Chronicle*, vol.20, pp.443–445

Murray, G., 'Review of History of the War in the Peninsula and the South of France, by W. Napier', *London Quarterly Review*, vol. LVI, April 1836, pp.131–219

Napier, W., 'Colonel Napier on a Statement in the "The Hussar"', *United Service Journal*, Part 2, 1838, p.544

Patterson, J., 'On the Utility and Importance of Light Troops and Cavalry in the Field, Exemplified by Several Instances During the War in Spain', *United Service Journal*, Part 2, 1844, pp.278–283

Peaty, J., 'Architect of Victory: The Reforms of the Duke Of York', *Journal of the Society for Army Historical Research*, vol.84, no.340 (Winter 2006), pp. 339–348

Potts, D.W., 'Convention of Cintra, a Revisionist View', *Napoleonic Scholarship*, December 2015, pp.109–124

Raleigh, 'Naval Transactions on the Coast of Portugal', The *Naval Chronicle*, vol.XXI, Jan-Jun 1809, pp.377–397

Reiter, J., '"As Far as the Ordnance Department is Concerned": Sir Arthur Wellesley, Lord Chatham and the Politics of Military Decision-Making, 1808-1809', *Journal of the Society for Army Historical Research*, vol.101, no.402, Autumn 2022, pp.174–193

Robson, E., 'Peninsular Private', *Journal of the Society for Army Historical Research*, Vol. 32, No. 129 (Spring,1954), pp. 4-14

Schneer, R.M., 'Arthur Wellesley and the Cintra Convention: A New Look at an Old Puzzle', *Journal of British Studies*, Vol. 19, No. 2 (Spring, 1980), pp.93–119

Teichman, O., 'Shrapnel Shell', *Journal of the Society for Army Historical Research*, Vol. 26, No. 105 (Spring,1948), pp.36–37

Weatherside, T., 'Letter to the Editor', *The Naval Chronicle*, vol.20, p.304

Webster, C., 'Some Letters of the Duke of Wellington to his Brother William Wellesley-Pole', *Camden Miscellany*, vol.XVIII (1948), pp.1–38

Wilkie, F. 'Military Anecdotes', *United Service Journal*, Part 3, 1843, pp.238–247

Wilkie, F., 'Recollections from the Peninsula', *United Service Journal*, Part 3, 1843, pp.422–429

Willis, C. 'Colonel George Lake and the Battle of Roliça', *British Historical Society of Portugal Review*, 1996, pp.95–105

Wynyard, M., 'From Vimeiro to Corunna', *Royal United Services Institution Journal*, vol.114, no.656, pp.33–42

Online Sources

All Things Georgian, <https://georgianera.wordpress.com/>

Anon., 'La trágica muerte del General Solano', *Instituto Nacional Sanmartiniano*, <https://sanmartiniano.cultura.gob.ar/noticia/general-solano/>

Anon., 'The Black Drummers of the 29th', *The Worcester Regiment*, <http://www.worcestershireregiment.com/wr.php?main=inc/em_drummers>

Carvalho, Elesiário de, 'Relação da deserção de um Corpo de Cavalaria do Guarda da Polícia de Lisboa, que chegou a esta Cidade no dia 4 do corrente', *Colecção da Minerva Lusitana*, <https://www.arqnet.pt/exercito/minerva19.html>

Challis, Lionel S., 'Peninsula Roll Call', *The Napoleon Series*, <https://www.napoleon-series.org/research/biographies/GreatBritain/Challis/c_ChallisIntro.html>

Cruz, Elio da, 'Padrões da Teixeira', <http://padroesteixeira.blogspot.com/2006/05/padres-da-teixeira.html>

Dubief, S., 'Le General Junot en Egypte', *Napoleon.org*, <https://www.napoleon.org/histoire-des-2-empires/articles/le-General-junot-en-egypte/>

Ellis, J.D., 'The Visual Representation, Role and Origin of Black Soldiers in British Army Regiments During the Early Nineteenth Century', *The Black Presence in Britain*, <https://blackpresence.co.uk/the-visual-representation-role-and-origin-of-black-soldiers-in-british-army-regiments-during-the-early-nineteenth-century/>

Frenchempire.net, <https://www.frenchempire.net/biographies/>

Hansard, <https://hansard.parliament.uk/>

Memoire des Hommes, <https://www.memoiredeshommes.sga.defense.gouv.fr/>

Muir, R., *Wellington*, <https://lifeofwellington.co.uk>

Murphy, D., 'Smythe, Percy Clinton Sydney', Dictionary of Irish Biography, <https://www.dib.ie/biography/smythe-percy-clinton-sydney-a8181>

Oxford Dictionary of National Biography (ODNB), <https://www.oxforddnb.com>

Roberts, D., '"Uncle Arthur Wellesley? He's not all that!" – Wicked William goes to War', *Wicked William*, <https://www.wickedwilliam.com/uncle-arthur-wellesley-hes-wicked-william-goes-war/>

The Gazette, <https://www.thegazette.co.uk/>

Three Decks - Warships in the Age of Sail, <https://threedecks.org>

Young, A.J.N., 'James Pipon of Noirmont in the Commissariat', <https://www.theislandwiki.org/index.php/James_Pipon_of_Noirmont_in_the_Commissariat>

Index

From Reason to Revolution – Warfare 1721-1815

http://www.helion.co.uk/series/from-reason-to-revolution-1721-1815.php

The 'From Reason to Revolution' series covers the period of military history 1721–1815, an era in which fortress-based strategy and linear battles gave way to the nation-in-arms and the beginnings of total war.

This era saw the evolution and growth of light troops of all arms, and of increasingly flexible command systems to cope with the growing armies fielded by nations able to mobilise far greater proportions of their manpower than ever before. Many of these developments were fired by the great political upheavals of the era, with revolutions in America and France bringing about social change which in turn fed back into the military sphere as whole nations readied themselves for war. Only in the closing years of the period, as the reactionary powers began to regain the upper hand, did a military synthesis of the best of the old and the new become possible.

The series examines the military and naval history of the period in a greater degree of detail than has hitherto been attempted, and has a very wide brief, with the intention of covering all aspects from the battles, campaigns, logistics, and tactics, to the personalities, armies, uniforms, and equipment.

Submissions

The publishers would be pleased to receive submissions for this series. Please email reasontorevolution@helion.co.uk, or write to Helion & Company Limited, Unit 8 Amherst Business Centre, Budbrooke Road, Warwick, CV34 5WE

You may also be interested in:

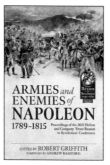

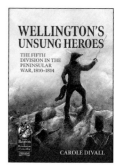

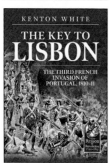

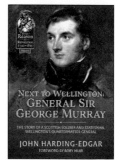